THE
ALPHABET

The Hand-Produced Book
The Illuminated Book
(assisted by Reinhold Regensburger)
The Story of the Aleph-Beth
Writing: Its Origins and Early Development
Le Iscrizioni antico-ebraiche palestinesi
L'Alfabeto nella Storia della Civiltà

THE
ALPHABET

A Key to
the History of Mankind

DAVID DIRINGER
D.Litt. *(Flor.)*, M.A. *(Cantab.)*

THIRD EDITION
completely revised with the assistance of
REINHOLD REGENSBURGER

VOLUME I

FUNK & WAGNALLS
NEW YORK

Published by Funk & Wagnalls, *A Division of*
Reader's Digest Books, Inc.

First published by Hutchinson & Co.
(Publishers) Ltd. in April 1948

Second edition, revised April 1949
Reprinted (with amendments) January 1953
Reprinted (with amendments) October 1953
Third edition (completely revised, in two volumes) 1968

Printed in Great Britain

Contents

Chapter

Chapter

PART TWO

ALPHABETIC SCRIPTS

Chapter

Chapter

Chapter

alphabet; bibliography. Adaptation of scripts to Turki dialects; other scripts; unknown scripts and forgeries. External development of letters: calligraphy. Numerical, musical, and scientific notation. Abbreviations and stenography (shorthand). Signalling and special alphabets; selected bibliography.

Acknowledgements

EVERY conscientious effort has been made to give due acknowledgement and full credit for borrowed material, but if through any unwitting oversight some trespass has been committed, by quoting from secondary sources, forgiveness is sought in advance, apology is freely offered, and correction promised in any subsequent editions.

Thanks are gratefully given to the following persons, institutions and publishers, for some of the illustrations used in this volume:

Director of Archæology, H. E. H. the Nizam's Government, Hyderabad-Deccan.
Director of the British Museum, London.
Director of the Manx Museum, Douglas.
Society of Archæology and Society for Coptic Archæology, Cairo.
École Française d'Extrême Orient, Saigon.
Wellcome-Marston Archæological Expedition to the Near East, London.
Jewish Palestine Exploration Society, Jerusalem.
Antiquity, Gloucester.
Archiv Orientální, Prague.
University of Chicago Press, Chicago.
Messrs. Schapiro, Valentine and Co., London.
Dunlop Rubber Co. Ltd., London.
Casa Editrice Barbèra and *Rinascimento del Libro*, Florence.
Prof. I. C. Ward, Dr. A. V. Kunst and Mr. A. Master, formerly of the London School of Oriental and African Studies.
Prof. J. W. Gonggryp and Mr. C. Dibelaor

Foreword

By Sir Ellis Minns, Litt.D., F.B.A.

IF IT IS SPEECH that marks man off from the beast, and the great discoveries of the use of tools, the use of fire, taming animals, tilling the ground, working metals are long strides in his progress, the invention of writing and its improvement into a practical system may fairly be taken as the step leading directly to full civilization.

It is true that one or two recent writers have cried down writing as the instrument by which cliques of priests and rulers enslaved the far more useful handworkers. But without writing these authors could not have brought this injustice to our attention, and it is no doubt by writing that they will set it straight.

Be this as it may, the history of writing makes an attractive story; I have felt the attraction ever since as a schoolboy I read Isaac Taylor's *Alphabet*, and for more than twenty years I have yearly lectured on the subject. It is difficult to exaggerate how much it has grown since his time, many new scripts have been discovered, to several of them the key had to be found, to a few it is still missing. Some ten years ago Dr. Diringer's great Italian work *L'Alfabeto nella Storia della Civiltà*, for me superseded all former sources. Now I welcome the same store of learning duly increased and recast in an English form.

The whole matter has a special interest as affording the best opportunity for studying the phenomena of diffusion and of independent invention and of the mixed process which has been called 'idea diffusion,' the stimulus to invention afforded by the knowledge that a problem has been solved, though its particular solution may not be known, or may not be acceptable. By its very nature writing keeps a record of its own development. Our author proves with a new completeness the astonishing fact that almost certainly every alphabetic writing of any importance derives from one source, and the obscure scripts were devised by men who were aware of the existence of perfected alphabets. This is a fascinating result; it is so rare in life that so sweeping a generalization is tenable.

Though he calls his book *The Alphabet*, our author deals first with non-alphabetic writings, the great systems of Egypt, Mesopotamia, China and Central America, and the various ideographic odds and ends. These are all separate inventions, great inventions no doubt, but not so great as to be unique. It is very interesting to note how close to each other were the mental processes by which the three great systems were built up.

Then he clears the syllabaries out of the way, poor half and half things derived from more complicated scripts without reaching true simplicity.

Finally he attacks the thorny problem of the real alphabet. He bids us give up our hope that the key is in the Sinaitic script, but will not say more than that alphabet-making was in the air in Syria during the first half of the second millennium B.C. We must commend his self-restraint in not leading us beyond the edge of solid ground.

The writings of Asia, either ideographic or alphabetic, amount to about a hundred, another hundred fills the Indian world and its derivatives. No one has explored this last labyrinth as deeply as our author—I am not sure that many would wish to do so.

The climax is the story of the Greek alphabet and its descendants, some fifty scripts, the part of the tale which comes nearest to us. But it has its surprises, we have to accept that our Latin alphabet would not be what it is if it had been derived directly from western Greek: to those like me who dislike the Etruscans, it is a grief that we should have got our alphabet through them; for myself I think it would have been better without their share in it. To the Etruscans also, through small neighbouring peoples, it seems that we northern Teutons owed our runic writing: for many years scholars derived it alternately from Greek and from Latin—now the strife is over and we can happily credit the Raetians or some such tribe with teaching our ancestors to write.

Here is the story duly enlightened by a great series of illustrations. We owe much to the publishers for their liberality in this respect. Taylor had to manage with some hundred pictures, they have allowed us generous measure, nearly one thousand illustrations grouped in over two hundred and fifty 'figures.' These enable us to follow the fascinating story in all its ramifications as set out so clearly and diligently by our author. At last we have in English a worthy successor to Isaac Taylor.

Preface

THE PURPOSE of this book is to provide an introduction to the fascinating subject of the history of the alphabet. In the First Part I shall try to give a historical sketch of the development of the non-alphabetic scripts, although the present book will deal more particularly with the origins and development of the alphabet, to which the Second Part is dedicated. The main problems of the primitive means of communicating ideas, of the origins and the beginnings of writing, together with a more detailed study of the non-alphabetic scripts and the development of handwriting, must be left to my next book on writing as a whole.

Even so, a book on the development of the alphabet of the narrow dimensions dictated by publishing difficulties can achieve its goal only if the reader is prepared to accept various limitations. For instance, he must not expect to find a complete bibliography: had this been attempted, the space available would have been filled with nothing but the names of authors and titles of books. Those who wish to pursue the study further are referred to the bibliographical works cited in my book *L'Alfabeto nella Storia della Civiltà*, Florence, Barbèra, 1937. Specific references have generally been omitted for the sake of brevity and clearness and in the interest of the general reader; but it must not be supposed that the debt of this book to previous scholars is ignored.

It is not possible to deal in detail with all the alphabets of all the modern nations of the world. I shall, instead, devote more space to less-known problems, to those which present more interest from the standpoint of the history of writing, to the origins of some single scripts, to the connection between the various systems, and so forth. Some chapters may, in consequence, seem disproportionate in comparison with others, since unanimity cannot be achieved on matters of treatment; questions which seem most important to one person, may appear unimportant to others. I shall do my best to simplify as far as possible the more intricate problems by presenting my conclusions and by indicating whenever practicable the basic proofs out of which my conclusions grew. If the general reader will exercise the necessary patience, he will be able to survey the main documentary evidence revealing the development of writing, particularly of the alphabetic scripts used in the past or in the present day. At the same time, the general sketch of the subject, the facts presented and much of the interpretation put upon them will, I hope, appeal to students of writing whose presuppositions differ from mine, and to all scholars who are specialists in the individual fields here examined, but not in the subject as a whole.

For obvious reasons, no attempt has been made to give an exhaustive account of all the pertinent material, and documentation has been restricted to a minimum. Doubtful material has been eliminated as far as possible, and nothing has been included which is not strictly verifiable from different sources. Speculation has been omitted except in some special cases.

On the whole, I have attempted to treat the history of writing on the same lines as other types of history, but those sections in which too little is known, are presented as a series of unembellished facts. In some instances, in view of the dearth of original documentary sources, I have not felt disposed to indulge in speculation.

A work of this kind cannot possibly be carried out without troubling many people, and I am therefore glad to acknowledge my gratitude to all those who have helped and supported me. Dr. L. D. Barnett, Dr. R. D. Barnett, Dr. E. Cerulli, Miss H. Herne, Mr. G. F. Hudson, Miss Evelyn Jamison, Mr. A. Master, Dr. M. A. Murray, Mrs. Hilda Freeman, Mrs. Beauchamp Tufnell, Miss Olga Tufnell and Mrs. K. P. K. Whitaker (Miss Lai Po Kan) have read parts of my text in typescript and have made valuable criticisms and suggestions in detail. To all these scholars I am greatly indebted.

Furthermore, I tender my sincere gratitude to the late Sir Ellis H. Minns for his interest and help, not only in reading the proofs of the book at an early stage, but also for contributing much of his vast knowledge and experience.

My thanks must also be expressed to the Society for the Protection of Science and Learning, to the Wellcome-Marston Archæological Research Expedition to the Near East, to the Institute of Archæology, University of London, and to the London School of Oriental and African Studies, who have helped me in one way or another.

Finally, in view of the special technical difficulties involved, due acknowledgment must be made of the skill and care of the printers, whose interest went beyond their usual function, and the result of their expert and patient counsel appears on every page.

As far as possible I have omitted the diacritical marks which have been devised by modern philologists for use in transcribing various alphabets into Roman script. These marks, which serve to indicate the precise value and pronunciation of certain symbols, consist of points, dashes, circumflex accents, and so forth, added for instance to the letters g, h, s, t, etc., and so forming the special signs, $ǵ$, $ḥ$, $ś$, $š$, $ṣ$, $ṭ$, and many others.

These diacritical marks are indispensable in learned and technical works, but they would only confuse the general reader, more especially since the phonetic values represented by them are not constant; for instance the value of the Semitic $ṣ$ is quite different from that of the Indian $ṣ$; and the same is true of other letters and sounds in various languages.

In the spelling and transliteration of Egyptian, Semitic, Indian, Chinese, Greek and other words, especially place-names and proper names, the practice commonly adopted has in general been followed, but here and there consistency has been abandoned in order to present to the reader familiar names in their familiar forms. Some spellings are, for purposes of economy, simplified in cases where no confusion will result. On the whole, inconsistencies in a composite work like this are unavoidable, and the general reader should understand that a quite satisfactory solution of the problem of transliteration has not been found. Indeed, I have to admit that after trying hard at an early stage to arrive at some consistency, I had to abandon the attempt as hopeless, and welter in the prevailing chaos; in some cases divergent transliterations still cause difficulties, but it is reasonable to assume that general readers are indifferent to what experts know, while experts do not always agree as to the precise spelling. Besides, some scientific transliterations are as formidable-looking as Chinese or hieroglyphs.

On the whole, the consonants are transliterated according to the English sounds, while for the vowels I use the system, generally adopted, of transliteration according to the Italian phonetic values, corresponding roughly to the following sounds: *a* as in 'father,' *e* as in bell,' *i* as in 'field,' *o* as in 'order,' *u* as in 'rude'; the letter *y* is employed with the same phonetic value as in English.

It will be found that some practices, *e.g.* 'idea-diffusion,' are not infrequently referred to in different sections of the book. Indeed, instead of any attempt to give, as it were, definite description of these practices, it has seemed better, at the cost of repetition, to give a separate description for each case, even at some sacrifice of strict uniformity.

Smaller type has been used for certain sections of the book, which contain either introductory and explanatory matter or bibliography. These are intended respectively for two different types of readers, since the manual has been planned to serve a twofold purpose. The general reader will, it is hoped, welcome the information supplied by the notes on the history of some little-known peoples and on the linguistic and ethnic problems presented by others. The student, on the contrary, who may use the book as an approach to the study of individual scripts and alphabets, will undoubtedly find in the bibliographies a valuable aid to further study. Of these, the general bibliography (in chronological order) will be found at the end of the volume, and the bibliographies (also in chronological order) dealing with particular subjects at the end of the relevant chapters or of the paragraphs in which the script in question is discussed.

London, 1947   D. D.

PREFACE TO THIRD EDITION

THE PREPARATION of this revised and enlarged edition has given me an opportunity to bring the contents up to date, to correct a number of inaccuracies, and to add the more important bibliographical notation of the advancing research in this vast field of knowledge. There has been some rearrangement of material, but the principal points remain. However, some sections have been entirely rewritten so as to cover the latest research, and the number of illustrations has been considerably increased. It is my hope that readers of the book may gain from it a fresh appreciation of the vast effort that the publishers have made towards a better understanding of the role played by writing and the alphabet as a key to the history of mankind and of its civilization. In this connection, I should like to record my gratitude to Hutchinson and Company for the care and attention they have given to the host of problems which arose in the production of this edition, and to Daniel Brostoff, for his share in the task.

In deciding to produce this edition in two volumes, the first containing the text, and the second containing the illustrations, the publisher has made it much easier for the reader to consult the work. Indeed, our central concern has been communication with the user. Finally I must express my gratitude to the Alden Press, and particularly my friend Mr. Hugh Williamson, for the special care which they gave to the printing of this work.

To scholars mentioned in the Preface to the first edition, as having kindly helped in the production of the work, I would add the names of my friend and collaborator Dr. R. Regensburger and of Mr. and Mrs. L. A. Freeman, to whom I am grateful for the generous help they have given in the production of this revised edition.

Cambridge 1968   DAVID DIRINGER

Introduction

STUDY OF HISTORY OF WRITING

How many people try to realize what writing has meant to mankind? How could there be accumulation of wisdom without its being recorded in written characters? If culture is, as many scholars think, 'a communicable intelligence,' and if writing is, as it is, one of the most important means of communication—the only one indeed which can defy time and space—it is not an exaggeration to say that writing is the main currency of man's civilization. Wherever there has been civilization there have been writing and reading, in the remote past as in the present day. Written language has become the vehicle of civilization, and so of learning and education. Writing is thus one of the main aspects of culture which clearly distinguish mankind from the animal world.

The first and perhaps the most obvious consideration is that writing gives permanence to man's knowledge. Without letters, there can be no knowledge of much importance. Evidences for studying the earlier cultural development of ancient civilization are very scanty, and always indirect, until we reach the introduction of writing and the production of written sources. The history of writing should, therefore, be considered one of the more important, perhaps the most important, of the departments of historical science, and a clue to the story of man's intellectual progress.

No wonder that in the past writing was held in much esteem. The ancient Egyptians attributed its creation either to Thoth, the god who invented nearly all the cultural elements, or to Isis. The Babylonian god of writing, Nebo, Marduk's son, was also the god of man's destiny. An ancient Jewish tradition considered Moses as the inventor of script. Greek myths attributed writing to Hermes or to other gods. The ancient Chinese, Indians and many other peoples also believed in the divine origin of script. Writing had always an enormous importance in learning and a magic power over the unlearned, in such a way that even today 'illiterate' is almost synonymous with 'ignorant.'

Nowadays, however astonishing it may sound, the history of writing is the true Cinderella with the learned and the layman alike. No such object is taught either in the universities or in the secondary or primary schools; no important museum, until recently, has thought it necessary to offer to the public a comprehensive exhibition of the story of writing. On June 8th, 1959, the present author founded in Cambridge

I

(England) the Alphabet Museum and Seminar—now partly transferred to Tel Aviv—a main object being to collect and assemble all the material relating to the history of writing.

Although thousands of articles on matters forming part of our subject have appeared in hundreds of anthropological, archæological, philological and other learned periodicals, published in every civilized country, and in the transactions of various learned societies, learned books dealing with this subject as a whole are very few and mainly out of date or incomplete.

In particular, no serious attempt has been made to collect and present within reasonable compass for popular interest the vast amount of matter relating to the history of writing. The author does not claim to have done this, and he hopes that this book will not be considered an exhibition of that type of scholarship which wishes to be regarded as omniscient and encyclopædic. There cannot, obviously, be much originality in a book of this kind unless it be the way in which things which belong together are brought together and their relationships and outside influences classified; it is an effort to put the whole matter, as far as possible, in its true light. Indeed, the limited number of books dealing with the whole subject, in contrast to the infinite number of articles treating of some detailed question within it, scattered over an infinite number of journals, can be explained, partly at least, by the difficulties involved in an investigation of this enormous field of human knowledge, the history of writing. In fact, the subject demands a new type of historian, a historian who is alike anthropologist, ethnologist, psychologist, philologist, classical scholar, archæologist, palæographer, orientalist, egyptologist, americanist, etc.

Although, as already mentioned, the history of writing does not constitute a subject of teaching in a university or any other school, it forms the main basis for two important branches of study:

(1) *Epigraphy* (with its sub-divisions, such as Greek epigraphy, Latin epigraphy, Hebrew epigraphy, and so forth), that is the science which deals mainly with ancient inscriptions, including their study, decipherment and interpretation, *i.e.*, records cut, engraved or moulded on hard material, such as stone, metal or clay.

(2) *Palæography* (with parallel sub-divisions, such as Greek palæography, Latin palæography, papyrology, etc.), which treats mainly of writing—including the study, decipherment and interpretation of the texts—that is painted or traced in ink or colour, with a stylus, brush, reed or pen, on soft materials, such as paper, parchment, papyrus, linen or wax. The study of palæography is of the greatest practical importance to textual criticism, to classical philology, to ancient and mediæval history, and to other branches of historical science, whereas the study of epigraphy has revolutionized our whole knowledge of the ancient world. Thanks to epigraphy, the last century has witnessed the rediscovery and reconstruction of entire civilizations, belonging to remote antiquity, and in some instances presenting a highly organized society.

Certain branches of the history of writing form part of other departments of learning: for instance, hieroglyphic, hieratic and demotic writing are comprehended in egyptology, cuneiform writing in assyriology; the writing of primitive peoples is dealt with by anthropologists or ethnologists, Chinese writing by sinologists, Arabic scripts by arabists; the development of Indian writing forms part of Indian epigraphy and palæography. Philologists and glottologists—students of the science of languages—deal also with the development of writing in connection with the language or languages with which they are concerned. On the other hand, graphology, 'the science of writing,' is more concerned with the psychological and biological points of view than with the history of writing. *See* A. O. Mendel, *Personality in Handwriting*, New York, 1947.

The cultured man is also sometimes interested in one or other branch of the history of writing. Egyptology and assyriology, including the study of hieroglyphic, hieratic, demotic and cuneiform writings, had a certain popularity or their 'good time' at one period or another during the last century; hittitology, that is the branch of learning concerned with the Hittites (the ancient inhabitants of Asia Minor and northern Syria) and their scripts, was popular at the end of the last century and in the first decades of the present (even in the last ten or fifteen years); alphabetology, the new department which deals with the intricate problems of the origin of the Alphabet, had a brief 'good time' recently in the U.S.A.

WRITING AND EARLY CIVILIZATION

Unquestionably, while man's creative and destructive powers have been developing for an incalculable number of years, the intellectual progress of mankind developed only at a very late stage; only yesterday, a few thousand years ago, can it be said that man's spiritual advance began. It is very important from the point of view of the history of writing, to stress the significance of this fact. It is, for instance, the best argument against certain picturesque theories about lost continents such as 'Atlantis' or 'Lemuria' since there is no doubt that during the whole history of civilization, the lay-out of the principal land-masses has not much changed. In consequence, it seems probable that the various peoples and tribes on the various continents or blocks of continents developed their early civilizations, including writing, more or less independently.

In man's spiritual advance—or more generally, the growth of civilization—the origin and the development of writing hold a place of supreme importance, second only to that of the beginnings of speech, as an essential means of communication within human society. Writing, an art peculiar to man, even more than speech, presupposes language, of which it is in some sense a refinement. From the point of view of invention, the importance of writing is paramount even in comparison with language, which is not a creation of man, as writing is, but a natural distinction of mankind. Mankind lived for an enormous period without writing, and there is no doubt that writing was preceded by articulate speech.

For many thousands of years languages have been developing, changing and disappearing throughout all the continents without leaving any trace, because the people who spoke them disappeared and there was no method of recording them for future generations.

Writing is the graphic counterpart of speech. Each element, symbol, letter, 'hieroglyph', written word, in the system of writing corresponds to a specific element, sound or group of sounds, such as syllable or spoken word, in the primary system. Writing is thus the natural method, or rather the most important of natural methods of transferring speech, that is of communicating ideas between those who are debarred by distance of time or space or by other causes, from intercourse by means of speech. Other, less important methods are, for instance, the different gesture-languages such as those of the deaf-mutes, and those used at sea or in the mountains. In other words, writing reproduces sounds, which come from the mouth, or unspoken thoughts, which come from the brain, by permanent visual symbols on paper, stone, metal, wood, leather, linen, or some other material.

Not only has the intellectual progress of man been very recent in comparison with man's material power; written records have been very recent in man's cultural history. However, prehistoric cave wall-paintings and carving on small objects can be traced in part to the Upper or late Palæolithic period; circles and other symbols, full of variety and distinction, are also found in use in prehistoric ages as property marks or for similar purposes, but we can hardly see any connection in such cases with known ancient systems of writing, although they may eventually be regarded as preliminary devices produced by the urge to record events or ideas. As a matter of fact, when one is faced with phenomena of vast significance, such as the creation of a system of writing, the inquiry into the first causes is extraordinarily difficult, just as it is in the case of a war or revolution. Even in recent cases it is very difficult, sometimes, to give an exact date to the origins of such events; in tracing them back through the past, one runs the risk of reaching back to very distant times, since cause and effect condition each other and follow each other in turn. To avoid this, a starting point must be chosen. To study the history of writing, we must take as the starting point the earliest known ancient systems of writing, and particularly the cuneiform and hieroglyphic systems. Indeed, there is no evidence to prove that any complete system of writing was employed before the middle of the fourth millennium B.C.

VARIOUS STAGES OF WRITING

The alphabet is the basis of modern civilized writing, but it has not always been so and the purpose of this book is to trace how alphabets came into being and attained their position as a fundamental in the communication of ideas and the dissemination of knowledge. Much of this history is controversial and it would be begging the question to refer to it as evolution. The struggle for life is the main condition of existence for a script as for other things. The best fitted resists and survives, although sometimes the surrounding circumstances may bear a greater influence on the survival of a script than its merits as a system of writing.

If writing be taken for the moment in its broadest possible sense to mean the conveyance of ideas or sounds by marks on a suitable medium which may range from stone and wood to clay and paper, writing may be classified according to its nature and to certain recognized terms. These terms indicate types of writing and stages of development, but they are not necessarily chronological. It is a fact that the crudest forms of writing, both ancient and modern, are non-alphabetical, but these non-alphabetic systems are not always earlier in time than alphabetic scripts. It would appear that various kinds of writing sometimes develop contemporaneously in different or even in the same parts of the world. Some of the crudest forms of writing are in use to this day and indeed have come into use long after alphabets were firmly established and widely used. The distinction of these various stages of writing is not always clear or certain.

EMBRYO-WRITING
(Figs. Introd. 1-16)

Man has used all sorts of methods and devices for transmission of thought: images, symbols or arbitrary signs. Rude systems of conveying ideas are found everywhere, in use, in survival, or in tradition; many more have totally disappeared in course of time. Combinations of material objects and conventional symbols are frequently met. The symbolical objects are carved, engraved, drawn or painted; so are the symbolical or conventional signs like marks, strokes, circles or lines. In these various primitive devices, whether ancient or modern, we have not really to do with conscious writing.

Iconography and 'Sympathetic Magic'—Rock pictures (Figs. Introd. 1-11)

Man began his writing with picture-writing, just as the child likes to begin, but the first attempts to express ideas graphically or rather pictorially, were undifferentiated; they could belong to the history of art or to the history of magic or to the history of writing. Indeed, when ancient man first essayed to scratch, draw or paint schematic figures of animals, geometric patterns, crude pictures of objects, on cave walls in the Upper Palaeolithic period—perhaps 25,000 to 20,000 B.C.—he did it probably for purposes of 'sympathetic magic' or for ritual practices, and not because of any urge to record important events or to communicate ideas. The same may perhaps be said of the markings—generally dots and lines—on numerous river pebbles of Azilian culture (middle-stone age), coloured with peroxide of iron (Fig. Introd. 1a), of the various geometric signs or conventionalized figures of men, painted or engraved on stones, termed 'petroglyphs,' of megalithic tombs (neolithic age), and the like, found in various Mediterranean or other countries (Figs. Introd. 1b and 2-11). It is extremely interesting to compare the aforementioned symbols of the Azilian pebbles (Fig. Introd. 1a) with the symbols of the Australian stone *churingas* of modern times.

However, these prehistoric symbols were almost certainly 'mainly a blend of art and magic rather than writing' (E. A. Speiser).

The Old Stone Age paintings of Spain are mainly hidden in subterranean caves; in northern Europe and in North Africa, they have survived on the surface of the ground. Rock walls in the Atlas region and in various parts of the Sahara are adorned with rock pictures, which are either engravings (mainly in the Atlas region) or paintings (mainly in the central Saharan area). The style of the latter is naturalistic, animated, whereas the former contain in part conventionalized designs, crude animal outlines, and purely geometric symbols.

Scattered all over South Africa, caves and rock-shelters have been found, in which a great number of paintings are still visible. The variety of subjects is immense, including animals of all sorts and human figures in various attitudes and actions. Most interesting are a few symbols found occasionally among paintings, which have never been explained; they occur also among the stone engravings which are numerous in the lower valleys of the Vaal and Orange Rivers. The South African paintings are probably the work of the ancestors of the present Bushmen, and are therefore called 'Bushman art.'

In Siberia, rock pictures are comparatively common; they are sometimes engravings or chippings, and sometimes paintings. Many rock pictures have been found in India; they contain figures of men and animals, or geometric designs of uncertain significance. In Australia (Fig. Introd. 11*h*), there are rock paintings belonging to various periods. 'Those in the rock shelters of the western part of North Kimberley are still the objects of religious practice among the natives' (L. Adam). In the vast area of Polynesia, Melanesia and Micronesia, 'rock drawings, engravings and paintings are a universal feature' (L. Adam). Interesting are the Papuan pictograms published in the *Journal of the Royal Anthropological Institute of Great Britain and Ireland*, 1936.

Every year new discoveries are reported. Interesting marks were discovered in Katanga (Congo): Fig. Introd. 6. A number of primitive drawings were found in caves in Uzbekistan (U.S.S.R.) in the summer months of 1945. 'In April, 1946, an expedition led by Prof. A. P. Potselugevsky, a linguist, discovered very ancient cave paintings in the Kara Kalin region of Turkmenia' (I. Borozdin). For central Asia and Siberia *see*, for instance, A. N. Tallgren, 'Inner Asiatic and Siberian Rock Pictures,' *Eurasia*, etc., 1933. *See* also Figs. Introd. 3–11.

The ideas of writing and drawing were identical in prehistoric Egypt and in early Greece, as is shown by the Egyptian word *s-sh* and by the Greek *gráphein* (etymologically connected with German *kerben*, 'to notch'), which mean both 'writing' and 'drawing.' The word *gráphein* gave us the main component of many words connected with writing, such as pictography, calligraphy, stenography, iconography, and so forth.

Iconography (the first component of this term derives—through the Latinized form—from Greek *eikón*, 'image') is the most primitive stage of representing thought.

As the French scholar Maurice Dunand points out, iconography suggests a static impression, and not definite ideas following each other. The order of the representation is not that of the words in a discourse; all the articulations giving detailed information are wanting, and the contents are generally ambiguous. Iconography is generally used for the arrangement of pictures representing familiar subjects.

Mnemonic Devices (Figs. Introd. 12-16)

One of the commonest devices to recall to mind something to be done, is to tie a knot in a handkerchief; the simplest application of knots as a mnemonic device or memory-aid, is in keeping a record of numbers; a historical example is related by Herodotus, iv, 98; the Catholic and other rosaries are similar mnemonic devices.

The knot-device is the basis of the famous Peruvian *quipus*, *quipos* or *kipus*, consisting generally of a number of threads or cords of different length, thickness and colour, generally of twisted wool, hanging from a top-band or cross-bar (Fig. Introd. 12a). They were generally employed for purposes of enumeration, but in some cases historical events or edicts could be conveyed through these means. Some other ancient peoples (in China and Tibet) and some primitive tribes of the present day, such as the Li of Hainan, the Sonthals of Bengal, some tribes of the Japanese Riukiu Islands (Fig. Introd. 12a), of the Polynesian islands, of central and western Africa, of California and southern Peru, have also employed knotted cords and similar mnemonic devices. In the Solomon Islands, in the Carolines, in the Pelew (Spanish, Palao; native Bälau) and the Marquesan islands, strings with knots and loops are still used for the exchange of news. 'The Marquesan bards (*ono-ono*) used to associate their liturgical poems with ... little bags of plaited coconut fibre from which hung knotted cords. The exact significance of these bags is not clear, but the knots are said ... to have been aids to the memories of the reciters of genealogies' (Métraux).

The Makonde people, an important tribe of former Tanganyika, also employed, or still employ, the knotted string for the reckoning of time and events. Figure Introd. 12 represents a piece of bark-cord about a foot long, with eleven knots at regular intervals; it was intended to serve as a kind of calendar. The Makonde author of this document, if we can so call it, was going on an eleven days' journey; he left this cord to his wife, saying: 'This knot'—touching the first—'is today, when I am starting; tomorrow'—touching the second knot—'I shall be on the road, and I shall be walking the whole of the second and third day, but here'—seizing the fifth knot—'I shall reach the end of my journey. I shall stay there the sixth day, and start for home on the seventh. Do not forget, wife, to undo a knot every day, and on the tenth you will have to cook food for me; for, see, this is the eleventh day when I shall come back' (Weule): Fig. Introd. 12a.

The notched stick was employed as an aid in conveying messages (Fig. Introd. 12a and b). It was notched in the presence of the messenger to whom the significance of each notch was verbally emphasized. This mnemonic device was employed not only by some primitive peoples of Australia, North America, West Africa, China, Mongolia and S.E. Asia, but also in ancient Scandinavia. Some old usages in England ('tally-sticks'), Italy and Russia were also based on similar devices. As a matter of fact tallies mainly express numbers, but in many instances they were also, and are still, used as memory-aids. The Ainus of the Far East were said to employ both notches on sticks and knotted cords. Sticks and nets were used to aid the memory in the Fiji Islands as well as among the native Pinyas of Australia. The Indo-Chinese Khas still keep their accounts or send their messages by means of small pieces of bamboo, marked with notches, which are made at closer or longer intervals, according to the signification that has been arranged. The Rev. J. H. Weeks, a missionary of the Baptist Missionary Society, referring to the Bangala of the Upper Congo River, says that they often used knots in counting and keeping accounts, and also notches cut in sticks. Sometimes a piece of twine was knotted and preserved, and sometimes only the fringe of the cloth. Notches were sometimes cut on a small stick and sometimes on the post of the house. The months that one worked would be cut on a stick, but for every elephant and hippopotamus killed a notch would be made on a house post. Very often they would put a secret mark of ownership on an article, but this was generally a simple notch in a certain place known only to the owner.

An interesting symbolic device was the *wampum* of the North American Iroquois; it was a sort of broad belt formed of strings of shells or beads arranged in patterns according to the story to be recorded (Fig. Introd. 12c). Worn sometimes as an ornament or girdle, it was also used as money.

'In the year 1852 a message reached the President of the United States in the form of a diplomatic packet, presented with the customary peace-pipe, by a delegation of the Pueblos of New Mexico, offering him friendship and negotiation, and opening symbolically a road from the Moqui country to Washington.

'The objects on the packet refresh the memory of the interpreter, who remarks: "These two figures represent the Moqui people and the President; the cord is the road which separates them; the feather tied to the cord is the meeting point; that part of the cord which is white signifies the distance between the Moqui and the place of meeting; and that part which is stained is the distance between the President and the same point. Your Excellency will perceive that the distance between the Moqui and the place of meeting is short, while the other is very long." (The group of feathers between the white and coloured cords symbolizes the geographical position of the Navajos with respect to Washington') (T. Thompson, *The A B C of our Alphabet*, London and New York, 1945).

Mention may, finally, be made of other devices for recording or identification of trade marks, used since ancient times: heraldic signs, including coat-armour, pennons and other devices of distinction, tattooing and similar distinctive marks, such as the *wusums* or cattle-marks and brands of Arab tribes east of Damascus, the *tamgas* or symbolical marks or seals of the early Turks and allied peoples, and so forth. For Eskimo pictographic ivory carvings see Fig. Introd. 13.

Marks have been found on ancient pottery or masonry in Palestine (Figs. Introd. 4 and 5a), Crete (Fig. Introd. 5a), Egypt (Fig. Introd. 5a), Cyprus, and in other Mediterranean countries; at Tordos, in Transylvania, etc. Interesting are the so-called *Bœmarken* of the inhabitants of the German-Frisian island of Föhr, in the North Sea: each house had its own symbol, which in some instances represented the trade of the owner. Property marks have been found amongst the Lapps in Sweden, the Votiaks, a Finnish people of north-eastern Russia, the Cherkassians, the Kadiuéo of South America, the Ainus of Yezo Island, on the Moresby archipelago, in Australia, amongst the Masai of eastern Africa, amongst various peoples of central Africa, and so forth.

Symbolic Means of Communication

Some other devices may be considered as preliminary stages of writing; for instance, some sorts of codes or tokens for sending messages are found among various primitive peoples. Such are the symbolical epistles *aroko*, 'to convey news,' of the Jebu or Yebu and other tribes in Nigeria, western Africa (Fig. Introd. 14); the Lu-tze, on the Tibeto-Chinese frontier, used similar means for sending messages: a piece of chicken liver, three pieces of chicken fat, and a chili, wrapped in red paper, indicated 'prepare to fight at once'.

Calumet, the reed 'peace-pipe' of some North American Indians, may also be mentioned: Calumet (from Latin *calamellus* or *calamettus*, diminutive of *calamus*) is a sacred decorated reed tobacco pipe used as symbol of peace or war; to accept it when offered is to accept friendship, to reject it is to accept war.

Also the *ndangas* and *bolongas* of the Bangala people of the Upper Congo River should be mentioned. When a message of any importance was sent, the sender would give the messenger a piece of plantain leaf having the mid-rib of the leaf about six inches long, and four flaps or wings to it, two on each side. This the messenger would carry and deliver with the message. With less important messages, tokens were sent such as the sender's knife, or pipe, or spear, but these were returned by the messenger. Ordinary messages were sent without any tokens. A token—generally of no intrinsic value—was given by a debtor to a creditor on contraction of a debt.

Mention may be made of the devices used by Samoyedes (Fig. Introd. 15a.3), or in primitive trade exchanges of North American Indians, in Sumatra, and so on; and of the magic religious mnemonic ceremonies of some primitive peoples of central and eastern Africa, Malacca (Fig. Introd. 15a.2), and elsewhere. The Kakhyens, on the south-eastern borders of Tibet, hang on strings, stretching across the pathway to their villages, small stars of split rattan and other emblems. To this category belongs also the throwing of divinatory bones, still practised by many African tribes: families of individuals appear to have sets of from four to sixteen 'bones,' on which they carve various designs; they throw the bones when in difficulty, but also in playing certain games of chance.

Dr. Métraux, in his book on *Easter Island*, has pointed out that the Maori orators and reciters added emphasis to their words by the manipulation of a finely engraved club held in the hand. 'The genealogists made use of a staff marked with notches representing the ancestors. This aid to memory was really a useless accessory, because the reciter knew his list of ancestors off by heart; but the staff enabled him to give the audience a concrete image of the generations of ancestors. The priests of Tahiti and the Tuamotus symbolized the liturgical poem by a staff or an object of plaited straw, which they deposited on the altar after finishing the chant it represented.'

Reference can also be made to such modern devices as coins and stamps, as well as dice, domino, and card games.

All these primitive devices can only be mentioned in a book such as this, chiefly devoted to the history of the Alphabet, but the author hopes, as already mentioned, to deal with them more extensively in a further work which will treat of writing as a whole with an examination also of its origins. In Prof. F. Rosenthal's opinion, 'pre-historic drawings and mnemonic devices—unless they were secondary to writing proper—can be definitely ruled out as forms of writing.'

The main classes of true writing are characterized as follows:

PICTOGRAPHY OR PICTURE-WRITING

This is the most primitive stage of true writing. A picture or sketch represents or symbolizes the thing shown; thus a circle might represent the sun, a sketch of an animal would represent the animal shown, a sketch of a man would indicate a man, and a cross would symbolize Jesus's death. Straight narrative can be thus recorded in a sequence of pictures, drawings or symbols, which yield their meaning to later decipherers with a fair degree of clarity, and can be, by the reader, expressed in speech in every language. It is possible to read, but intrinsic phonetism (the term derives from Greek *phonê*, 'voice') is still absent, that is to say, the symbols do not represent speech-sounds. In short, pictography is a semantic representation ('semantic,' from Greek *séma*, 'sign'), and not a phonetic one.

Some modern advertisements (Fig. Introd. 16) can represent true pictography.

However, picture-writing even in its more elementary stage is more than a picture. It differs from picturing, which is the beginning of pure pictorial representation or art, in the fact that it is the utilitarian beginning of written language, aiming to convey to the mind not the pure representation of an event, but a narrative of the event, each notion or idea being expressed by a little picture or sketch, which we term a *pictograph*. The distinction is important, for the change from embryo-writing to picture-writing implies an immense progress in the art of transmitting and also (quite incidentally) perpetuating thought.

Picture-writings are found everywhere. They are the work of ancient peoples (the prehistoric inhabitants of Egypt, Mesopotamia, Phoenicia, Crete, Spain, southern

France, and many other countries) in their primitive stage of culture, or of modern tribes (of central Africa, North America and Australia). The bark of trees, tables of wood, skins of animals, also bones or ivory, and the surfaces of rocks, were all, and are still, used for this purpose.

IDEOGRAPHIC WRITING

This is a highly developed picture-writing, being a pictorial representation of ideas to be conveyed from one person to another. In this system, the pictographs represent not so much the things they show as the underlying idea associated with those things. Thus, a circle might represent not only the sun, but also heat or light or a god associated with the sun, or the word 'day.' Similarly, an animal might be depicted not only by a picture of the animal, but also by a sketch of an animal's head, and the idea 'to go' by two lines representing legs. The symbols employed in ideographic writings are called *ideographs*, that is symbols representing ideas.

Simple ideographs are nearly the same in many primitive scripts. For instance, an eye with tears dropping from it, as the symbol representing sorrow, is to be seen not only in a crude rock-painting of California, but also in the more developed Maya and Aztec scripts as well as in the early hieroglyphic or Chinese writings. Other simple ideas, such as rejecting, that is 'turning one's back' on someone, fighting or wooing, can also be sketched unambiguously by this method (*see* p. 92).

Pure ideographic writings have been found among many native tribes of North America (Figs. Introd. 15*b*, 17*a* and *d*), and of central America, among some negro peoples of Africa (Fig. Introd. 17*b*), and many Polynesian and Australian indigenes, as well as among the Yukaghirs of north-eastern Siberia (Fig. Introd. 17*c*). Mention should also be made of the 'patterns' of the Gypsies—*see*, for instance, *The Journal of the Gypsy Lore Society*, N.S. vol. V, pp. 153–5.

These primitive devices generally do not constitute complete systems of writing. Some ideographic scripts, however, may constitute complete systems; they will be dealt with in part 1, chapter 9.

ANALYTIC SCRIPTS (Map I)

The scripts of the ancient Mesopotamians, Egyptians, Cretans and Hittites, which with others will be examined in the first part of the present book, are generally but improperly called 'ideographic.' They are, indeed, not purely ideographic. Some of them may have been so in origin, but even in the earliest inscriptions which have come to light, they consist of symbols (*see* below), combined in various ways. Such systems of writing may be called *transitional*, representing the transition stage between the pure ideographic writing and the pure phonetic system, and making use of the two, side by side. On the other hand, as pointed out by Dr. S. Smith, formerly of the British Museum, even the word 'transitional,' as employed for systems of writing lasting 3,000 years or more, would not seem appropriate; the term 'analytic' may perhaps be more suitable.

PHONETIC WRITING

In the picture-writings and the pure ideographic scripts, there is no connection between the depicted symbol and the spoken name for it; the symbols can be 'read' in any language. Phonetic writing is a great step forward. Writing has become the graphic counterpart of speech. Each element in this system of writing corresponds to a specific element, that is sound, in the language to be represented. The signs thus no longer represent objects or ideas, but sounds or groups of sounds; in short, the written forms become secondary forms of the spoken ones. A direct relationship has thus been established between the spoken language and the script, that is, writing has become a representation of speech. The symbols, being no longer self-interpreting pictures, must be explained through the language they represent. The single signs may be of any shape, and generally there is no connection between the external form of the symbol and the sound it represents. Phonetic writing may be syllabic or alphabetic, the former being the less advanced stage of the two.

Syllabaries or Syllabic Writing

A syllabary or syllabic system of writing is a set of phonetic symbols, the single symbols representing syllables, also vowels when these constitute syllables; so that a combination of signs representing a group of syllables would convey a spoken word. The syllabic system, indeed, developed more easily and appeared as a creation more often than did an alphabet.

The Assyrian cuneiform writing appears in later documents practically as a syllabary. Syllabaries existed in ancient Byblos (Syria) and Cyprus, the latter having probably developed from a Minoan script. Two syllabaries, evolved in ancient times from Chinese scripts, are still employed in Japan. Artificial modern syllabaries exist or existed in western Africa and in North America. All these scripts will be examined in chapter 10.

In the case of a language that for reasons of phonetic decay or otherwise, has multiplied the consonants in a single syllable, the syllabary becomes a cumbrous mode of writing, especially because it generally contains only open syllables, that is syllables in which the vowel is final, not 'closed' by a consonant. Thus, for instance, while it would be easy to represent by a syllabary a word like *fa-mi-ly*, the word 'strength' would have to be written *se-te-re-ne-ge-the* or the like, and such a representation of sounds would be far from satisfactory. Indeed, it has been rightly pointed out that 'a complete syllabic script would contain the number of consonants multiplied by the number of vowels,' and would require a much greater number of symbols than alphabetic writing.

THE ALPHABET

The alphabet is the last, the most highly developed, the most convenient and the most easily adaptable system of writing. Alphabetic writing is now universally employed by civilized peoples; its use is acquired in childhood with ease. There is an enormous advantage, obviously, in the use of letters which represent single sounds rather than ideas or syllables. No sinologist knows all the 80,000 or so Chinese symbols, but it is also far from easy to master the 9,000 or so symbols actually employed by Chinese scholars. How far simpler it is to use 22 or 24 or 26 signs only! Also, the alphabet may be passed from one language to another without great difficulty: the same alphabet is used now for English, French, Italian, German, Spanish, Portuguese, Turkish, Polish, Dutch, Czech, Croatian, Welsh, Finnish, Hungarian and others, and has derived from the alphabet once used by the ancient Hebrews, Phœnicians, Aramaeans, Greeks, Etruscans and Romans.

Thanks to the simplicity of the alphabet, writing has become very common; it is no longer a more or less exclusive domain of the priestly or other privileged classes, as it was in Egypt, or Mesopotamia, or China. Education has become largely a matter of reading and writing, and is possible for all. The fact that alphabetic writing has survived with relatively little change for three and a half millennia, notwithstanding the introduction of printing and the typewriter, and the extensive use of shorthand-writing, is the best evidence for its suitability to serve the needs of the modern world. It is this simplicity, adaptability and suitability which have secured the triumph of the alphabet over the other systems of writing.

Alphabetic writing and its origin constitute a story in themselves; they offer a new field for research which American scholars are beginning to call 'alphabetology.' Some better term should be devised. No other system of writing has had so extensive, so intricate and so interesting a history. In the second part of the present book, the author will endeavour to explain the genesis and development of this last and most important stage of writing.

The author will trace in the following pages the use and development of these various systems and others with their histories so far as is possible, and will try to ascertain just to whom we are indebted for our present ABC.

Part I

NON-ALPHABETIC
SYSTEMS OF
WRITING

The first nine chapters treat of 'analytic' systems of writing, commonly termed 'ideographic' scripts. They are: Cuneiform writing (chapter 1), Egyptian writings (chapter 2), Cretan scripts (chapter 3), Indus Valley script (chapter 4), the Hittite hieroglyphic script (chapter 5), Chinese writing (chapter 6), the scripts of ancient Central America and Mexico (chapter 7), the 'mysterious' script of Easter Island (chapter 8) and other 'ideographic' scripts (chapter 9).

The order in which these scripts are dealt with is roughly chronological, as far as the order of the appearance of these systems can be ascertained today. See also Map I.

Chapter 10 treats of syllabic systems of writing, namely of ancient Byblos, the Linear B of Crete, and the Cypriote syllabary, of the Japanese scripts, and of the syllabaries of African and North American natives. Chapter 11 deals with early Persian and Meroïtic quasi-alphabetic scripts.

CHAPTER I

Cuneiform Writing

THE NAME

CUNEIFORM is probably the most ancient system of writing. The name 'cuneiform' (from Latin *cuneus*, 'wedge,' and *forma*, 'form,' 'shape'), or 'wedge-shaped', is given to ancient scripts the characters of which are formed by a combination of strokes having the shape of a wedge, cone or nail. Thomas Hyde (1636–1703), Regius Professor of Hebrew in the University of Oxford, was the first to use the term 'cuneiform': *Istius modi enim ductuli pyramidales seu Cuneiformes . . . sunt peculiares Persepoli, nec alibi terrarum cernuntur . . . (Historia religionis veterum Persarum eorumque Magorum . . .* Oxonii, E Theatro Sheldoniano, 1709, p. 526). The German traveller Engelbert Kæmpfer in his book *Amœnitates exoticæ* (Lemgo, Westph., 1712) called them 'litterae cuneatae.' The system was also called 'arrow-headed'; but this term has now fallen out of use. The Germans call it *Keilschrift* ('wedge-script'), the Arabs *mismari* ('nail-writing').

The first man who observed and published cuneiform signs was the famous Italian traveller Pietro della Valle (1586–1652), who, in October 1621, saw some Persian cuneiforms in Persepolis.

BEGINNINGS

The exact date of the invention of this system of writing is unknown. It was, however, already in existence in the late fourth or early third millennium B.C. It seems that the great invention was due to the Sumerians, a people who spoke not a Semitic or Indo-European, but an agglutinative language. Their ethnic and linguistic affiliations still defy classification. Some scholars, however, are beginning to doubt whether we are right in crediting the Sumerians with this achievement. We are also unable to decide whether this system was invented in Mesopotamia or elsewhere, which seems more probable. The question of the origin of the early linear script of the Elamites (*see* further on), of the hieroglyphic writing (chapter 2), and of the Indus Valley script (chapter 4), which have probably some connection with the origins of cuneiform writing, makes the whole problem still more intricate. Whatever the truth, the earliest extant written 'cuneiform' documents, discovered at Uruk or Warka (the Biblical Erech), or at Kish, Lagash, Nippur, Ur, Shuruppak, Jemdet Nasr, Eridu, and other places, are couched in a crude pictographic script and probably in the Sumerian language (Fig. 1.1).

Paradoxically enough, at the beginning 'cuneiform' writing was not cuneiform at all; the characters were purely pictorial, and the picture-symbols represented the various objects, animate and inanimate (Fig. 1.2).

According to the American scholar Prof. Speiser, the property marks, the primitive prototypes of those which appear on the Mesopotamian cylinder seals, were the beginnings of the script out of which the cuneiform system arose.

At a second stage, the symbols also represented abstract ideas; signs were borrowed from others denoting words related in meaning, for instance the solar disc came to indicate also the ideas of 'day,' 'light,' and 'brightness.' Characters used in this way are called, although not quite correctly, *ideographs*: they are, to be more exact, word-signs. But the use of bare word-signs is not common; as soon as the need for the representation of continuous discourse arose, it became evident that a number of the vital elements of speech, such as inflexions, pronouns, adverbs, prepositions, or personal names, especially of foreigners, could not be represented by this means. Hence, the picture-symbols came to be used to represent not only objects or related abstract ideas, but also the phonetic value of words without any regard to their meaning as pictures. In other words, the cuneiform writing became a *rebus-writing*; many symbols were 'sound-pictures' or *phonograms*, symbolizing word-sounds as such, or phonetic complements. In this connection, the highest achievement of the cuneiform system was the production of a syllabary, that is the use of syllabic signs and vowels, but it never showed any tendency towards an alphabetic system. There are, however, two apparent exceptions to this generalization, the Early Persian cuneiform writing (part 1, chapter 11), evolved under the influence of the Aramaic alphabet, and the Ras Shamrah alphabet (part 2, chapter 1), connected only in the external form of the characters with the cuneiform system.

DEVELOPMENT OF SYSTEM (Fig. 1.3)

The range of expression of cuneiform signs was very wide; some of them were *polyphones*, having more than one phonetic value; others were *homophones* (Fig. 1.4a), having similar phonetic values, and yet representing entirely different objects. In order to remove ambiguities, there were introduced the *determinatives*: that is signs which were placed before or after the words to be determined but were not pronounced. These signs defined the meaning of a word by denoting the class (deities, countries or mountains, male proper names, birds, fishes, plural, etc.) to which it belonged (Fig. 1.4b). Thus, in general, the same cuneiform sign might stand for a simple syllable or vowel, or it might express a whole idea or word by itself, or yet again it might indicate only the class in which the particular word was being employed.

At the same time, the script evolved in its external form (Fig. 1.3). Gradually, the pictures began to be simplified and conventionalized; and ultimately became linear. There are relatively few Mesopotamian documents extant which give us early writing (Fig. 1.5). These consist of clay or stone tablets and on them the signs appear pretty clearly to be developments of earlier forms. The original signs have not survived since their makers may have employed perishable materials, such as wood or a kind of papyrus leaf. In the following centuries, some scribes found it convenient to turn the clay tablet in such a way that the pictographs appear lying on their back, while in inscriptions on stone or metal the old position of the signs persisted for a few centuries more. However, as the writing developed, the practice in the case of monumental inscriptions came into line with that followed on clay tablets, and the signs were regularly turned at an angle of 90 degrees (Fig. 1.3, col. 2).

The change from the linear script to wedge-shaped strokes (Fig. 1.3) came about in the following way.

The Sumerians found themselves in a country abounding in clay, and in using it as a writing material, they soon discovered that one could draw a character in the damp clay—the written clay tablets or bricks were then exposed to the sun or baked hard in a kiln, so that the record became durable—much better and more quickly by impressing them than by scratching. On the other hand, curves, circles and fine and long lines could not be impressed satisfactorily, so that all these lines, curves and circles were replaced by combinations of short, straight, vertical, horizontal or oblique strokes, or angles. These were impressed, line by line, with the edge of a rectangular broad-headed *stylus*, consisting of a straight piece of stick or reed, bone, hard wood or metal. Assyrian monuments represent scribes holding the stylus in their closed fist (*see* Fig. 1.6.). Naturally, the strokes impressed were thick on the top and on the left—the direction of writing being then from left to right—thus giving birth to a series of wedge-shaped characters, called by the users 'fingers'; and this peculiarity became more pronounced as time went on. The wedge-constructed characters were also cut on stone, metal, glass and other hard material, or painted. For the Assyrian writing-boards *see* p. 23.

The Assyrians simplified the whole cuneiform system (indeed, this simplification was a gradual process from earlier times down to the Assyrian period); nevertheless, they still needed a total of about 570 signs, although only about 300 of them were in frequent use. At a later stage, the Assyrian cuneiform system practically became a syllabic script (Fig. 1.4c), and the Persians, under the influence of the Aramaic alphabet, reduced it to a quasi-alphabetic system. The simplification of the single cuneiform characters was very typical of the learned Assyrian scribes; there also was a constant progress particularly in the Assyrian inscriptions, in reducing the number of wedges used in a sign (Fig. 1.3, col. 4), and in rendering the writing more square in appearance. The final result was the artistic calligraphy of the Assyrian library scribes (Fig. 1.6).

THE PEOPLES WHO EMPLOYED CUNEIFORM WRITING

SUMERIANS

We have already mentioned the Sumerians as the earliest known users of cuneiform writing. Whether they invented this system or not, there is no doubt that it was they who originally developed this writing along the lines explained above. We know very little about the origins of the Sumerians, and as yet we cannot even decide whether they were the aboriginal inhabitants of Mesopotamia or whether they came in from outside. The second hypothesis is the more probable. The Sumerians probably entered Mesopotamia in the fourth millennium B.C., and conquered the land from the Semites, who however continued the struggle for over 1,300 years, until with the help of new Semitic invaders from the Arabian peninsula (the Amurru or Amorites), they gradually pushed back the Sumerians during the first half of the third millennium B.C., into the southern part of the valley, and finally in the first centuries of the next millennium defeated them completely. The loss of independence, however, did not mean the end of Sumerian history; political decay did not prevent the continuation of Sumerian cultural supremacy. The Semitic victors not only, as we shall see, adopted the script of the Sumerians and their literary and religious language, but they borrowed also a considerable part of their literature.

The Sumerians represented the dominant cultural group of the Near East for more than 1,500 years, *i.e.*, from the late fourth millennium until the first centuries of the second millennium B.C., in which period they produced a vast and highly developed literature, consisting of myths, hymns and epics; *see* Figs. 1.7–9. *See* also Fig. 1.14*a*.

Several thousands of tablets and fragments containing literary compositions, mainly of the period around 2,000 B.C. have so far been discovered. Others, numbering tens of thousands, are of very varied scope. Some are legal records, such as court decisions, wills and so forth, others are economic memoranda (accounts, receipts, contracts, etc.), others again are of administrative, linguistic or historical import or consist of merely private correspondence. Sumerian, probably extinct as a spoken language in the eighteenth century B.C., remained as a ritual and learned language for many centuries more and formed the basic intellectual study of the Babylonians and the Assyrians; it also sought to be mastered by the Hittites and other peoples, persisting until the end of the cuneiform system.

AKKADIANS (BABYLONIANS AND ASSYRIANS)

About the middle of the third millennium B.C., the Sumerian cuneiform writing was taken over by the Semites who lived in the Tigris–Euphrates valley, and it became their national script. But this 'handing-on' was not quite easy, because Sumerian and the Semitic Akkadian (Assyrian and Babylonian) belonged to quite different linguistic families. Therefore arose—for the first time in history—the need for dictionaries. The Akkadian scribes compiled textbooks which contained (1) Sumerian cuneiforms, (2) their Akkadian equivalents, (3) translations of whole Sumerian sentences. They needed these, because they still had to use Sumerian in 'theology' and law (see Meissner, in *Akademie der Wissenschaften zu Berlin, Philologisch-Historische Classe*, 13. 2, 1941).

In the long development of the cuneiform writing of the Mesopotamian Semites, we can distinguish in particular six periods:

(1) The Early Akkadian period and Ur III, roughly from the middle of the twenty-fifth century B.C. to the middle of the nineteenth century B.C.;
(2) The Early Babylonian or Amorite period, eighteenth–sixteenth centuries B.C.;
(3) the Kassite period, from the sixteenth century to 1171 B.C.;
(4) the Assyrian period, twelfth–seventh centuries B.C.;
(5) the Neo-Babylonian period, sixth century B.C.; and
(6) the revival and end of the cuneiform writing, third century B.C. to first century A.D.

The two greatest periods of vigour in Assyro-Babylonian history, that of Hammurabi (c. 1728–1686 B.C.) in Babylonia, and the ninth to seventh centuries in Assyria, were marked by a corresponding flourishing of cuneiform writing (Fig. 1.10). Hammurabi's dynasty was the classical age of Babylonian literature and science; practically all the existing Babylonian literature was put into writing in that period (Fig. 1.12b), while the thousands of letters on clay tablets which have survived from that epoch show that commerce was thriving to an extent that argues an advanced state of society.

With the victory of Hammurabi over Larsa, Eshnunna and Mari, the ascendancy of Babylon—once an insignificant town—began. It rose to be the administrative and commercial centre of a rich empire, which lasted for over a century and a half (c. 1700–1530 B.C.). It was finally destroyed by the Hittite king Muršiliš c. 1530. From that time the city of Babylon lay in ruins for about two centuries. The union, stability and prosperity brought to Babylonia by Hammurabi made it possible for scholars to devote themselves to learned pursuits with a singlemindedness and continuity heretofore unknown. The following two centuries saw an extraordinary development of empirical scientific and scholarly interest, as is illustrated by many works on philology, lexicography, astronomy, mathematics, and numerous branches of magic and divination which were composed at that time, frequently in a form which remained canonical throughout later Mesopotamian history. While the Babylonians of the period did not equal their Egyptian contemporaries in their literary and rhetorical sophistication or in their knowledge of practical engineering and medicine, they surpassed them notably in less utilitarian, but more intellectual pursuits.

For example, they developed mathematics to the stage of being able to solve quadratic equations by the method of false position, employing a technique which was in some respects identical with that of the Greek algebraist Diophantos in the third century A.D. (F. Thureau-Dangin, *Textes mathématiques babyloniens*, Leiden, 1938, pp. XIX–XL, and his papers in *Revue d'Assyriologie*, vols. XXXIV and XXXV; Neugebauer and Sachs, *Mathematical Cuneiform Texts*, New Haven, 1945). In astronomy they produced the great canonical list of stars and constellations and interested themselves in the movements of the planets, as we know from the Venus tables and other sources (S. Langdon and J. K. Fotheringham, *The Venus Tablets of Ammizaduga*, London, 1928). They arranged cuneiform signs, Sumerian and Akkadian words, and grammatical forms, in great lists and dictionaries which remained standard works down to the latest times.

'They prepared elaborate compendia of various branches of divination and magic, such as prediction by omens of every conceivable kind (including astrology, hepatoscopy, lekanomancy, and so on), and such as exorcism of evil spirits by incantatory rites. In theology, the great list of the gods which was prepared by these early scholars remained 'canonical.' In short, they showed such taste and talent for collecting and systematizing all recognized knowledge that Mesopotamian learning nearly stagnated for a thousand years thereafter' (W. F. Albright, *From Stone Age to Christianity*, 2nd edition, 1957).

Modern Old Testament scholars were astonished when, at the beginning of this century, the famous code of Hammurabi (Fig. 1.8) was discovered, and they saw how often it anticipated and in some respects even went beyond the much later Mosaic legislation. 'The Code of Hammurabi (*c.* 1700 B.C.) was, as we now know, only the continuation of a series of Sumerian codes with the same formulation and point of view.... The tremendous effort devoted to the systematization of knowledge and especially of divination (knowledge of the future) surpasses anything found in Egypt' (Albright). Figure 1.11 shows a beautiful sculptured tablet of the Babylonian 'middle ages' (870 B.C.).

In the second millennium B.C. cuneiform writing and the Akkadian language became the international language of the ancient civilized world; this has been proved for the fifteenth and fourteenth centuries—a very difficult time from a political standpoint—by the Amarna Tablets and the tablets discovered at Boghaz-Köy and indeed all over Western Asia. The interesting Mesopotamian 'cylinder seals' (Figs. 1.14b–f) employed for sealing documents, enjoyed a vogue of over three thousand years; they have been published by the thousand; they were lengthwise perforated and probably hung by a string or a chain around the neck.

The rich library of the Assyrian kings contained thousands of tablets of religious, mythological and magical literature, numerous books of science, mathematics, law, history, magic, medicine and astronomy (Fig. 1.12a). The Assyrian so-called syllabaries, or rather dictionaries, are larger and more complete than the Babylonian, and contain very fine examples of lexicography. The Assyrian kings left complete records of their campaigns and activities, impressed on hollow cylinders or prisms (Fig. 1.10*b*), with six, seven, eight or even ten faces, each covered with as much minute writing as it could possibly hold. Many of these 'books' and cylinders may be seen in the British Museum.

In 1953 two sets of Assyrian writing-boards (one of ivory, the other of wood, probably of the walnut-tree) were discovered in a well at Nimrud. They were filled with a mass consisting of bees' wax and orpiment—the latter doubtless added to make the wax more ductile. The boards, which may be dated 707/705 B.C., were fastened to each other by hinges, not however like the Roman writing tablets, but in the 'Japanese' way, the hinges of the following tablets being always on the opposite sides. The ivory writing board is of especial interest, because it seems possible, although not fully proved, that no less than sixteen boards were fastened together in order to form a single *hekkaidekaptychon*, the biggest polyptychon so far known. (Mallowan, in *Iraq*, XVI, Pt. 1, 1954, pp. 98–107; D. J. Wiseman, in *Iraq*, XVII, Pt. 1, 1955, pp. 3–13; Margaret Howard, in *Iraq*, XVII, Pt. 1, 1955, pp. 14 ff.). It is apparently the only *polyptychon* which has more than nine leaves.

OTHER PEOPLES

In addition to the Sumerians, Babylonians and Assyrians, many other peoples, belonging to different races and speaking different languages (the Elamites, the Kassites, the Hittites, the Mitanni and Hurri, the Luwi, the Balai, the Urartu, the Persians) took over cuneiform writing.

The Hurri hail probably from the region south of the Caucasus and appear in history about 2400 B.C. in the Zagros region; later they are found in Northern Mesopotamia, especially east of the Tigris. They developed a considerable literature, and apparently were the mediators between the Sumero-Akkadian culture and that of the Hittites. From about 1950 to *c.* 1880 B.C. a dynasty of Akkadian princes of Aššur reigned in Katpatuka (Cappadocia) in Eastern Asia Minor. They used cuneiforms for their commercial documents which were found in great numbers at Kanish (today Kültepe). The Amurru (*i.e.*, Westerners, so called by the Babylonians) in the eighteenth century B.C. invaded northwestern Mesopotamia, from the frontiers of Babylonia up the Euphrates to south of Karchemish, and eastward to the Khabur basin; for some centuries they dominated these parts: they even conquered Babylon and Aššur. The Kaššu (Kassites, Cossaeans) came from the southern Zagros mountains, and conquered in the sixteenth century B.C. the whole of southern Mesopotamia, where they ruled *c.* 450 years. Before 1500 B.C., the Mitanni created a powerful kingdom in northern Mesopotamia, which held the whole country between the Mediterranean and the Zagros under its sway. The kings of the Mitanni may have been of Iranian descent; they worshipped Indo-Iranian deities Mithra, Indra, Varuna, and the Nasatyas (Albright).

Some of these peoples adapted cuneiform more or less successfully to their own languages introducing the necessary changes; others took it over without great modifications; and some preferred to adopt it together with the Akkadian language. The *Cappadocian Tablets*, couched in Assyrian, of the end of the third millennium B.C., may indicate that the local population of Cappadocia must also, at that period, have known cuneiform writing; the *Amarna Tablets*, of the fifteenth–fourteenth centuries B.C., already mentioned, show that the Canaanites also used it; there has even been found an inscription couched in the Egyptian language in cuneiform writing.

We have mentioned the various peoples who adopted the cuneiform writing of the Mesopotamian Semites. A few of these peoples, the Elamites, the Hittites and the Persians, are of special interest from the standpoint of the history of writing. The two last will be dealt with further on, but here a few words must be said about the Elamites and their scripts.

ELAMITES

Elam is the Biblical term corresponding to the Babylonian and Assyrian *Elamtu* or *Elamu*, and to the Greek *Elymais*; the Sumerian term was *Numma*; the later Greek term was *Susiane*, from the Elamite capital Susa, the Biblical *Shushan;* the indigenous term, at least in the neo-Elamite texts, was *Khapirti* or *Khatamti*, which was the name of one of the main tribes of the Elamites.

Elam is the name of the ancient country situated to the north of the Persian Gulf and to the east of the lower Tigris, which corresponds roughly with the modern Persian province of Khuzistan. Elam is frequently mentioned in the Bible and in many Babylonian and Assyrian inscriptions. For many centuries, it was one of the main important kingdoms of western Asia, but about 640 B.C. it lost its independence to Assyria. Its early history is closely interwoven with that of southern Mesopotamia. Its ancient civilization was equal to the contemporary civilization of the Sumerians and the Mesopotamian Semites. The country was inhabited by non-Semitic and non-Indo-European tribes who spoke agglutinative dialects apparently related to the Caucasian group of languages.

Early Elamite Script

The early Elamites (*c.* 2150 B.C.) possessed an indigenous script; there are nine inscriptions in stone and some hundreds of clay tablets extant (Fig. 1.15*a*). The characters are of geometric linear type; they derive probably from pictographic symbols (Fig. 1.15*b*), but their original forms are not always known. The direction of the script is generally from right to left, but sometimes from left to right or without any definite rules. This early Elamite script, which has been partly deciphered, appears to be related to the early form of cuneiform writing. It may be (1) that both the scripts have derived from another more primitive writing; or (2) that one of them was invented earlier, while the other is an artificial creation impelled by *idea-diffusion* or *stimulus-diffusion* (a term suggested by the American scholar A. L. Kroeber), the stimulus to invention being afforded by knowledge of the existence of writing while the actual symbols were not adopted; it is 'an instance of the borrowing of an *idea*,' as O. G. S. Crawford called it.

Some scholars hold that cuneiform writing derived from the original form of the early Elamite script. The problem of origins remains unsolved.

Neo-Elamite Writing

At a later period, the Elamites abandoned their indigenous script, and adopted the Babylonian cuneiform writing, introducing, however, many changes. The neo-Elamite cuneiform writing is very much simplified (Fig. 1.15c), there are only a few word-signs and determinatives, the greater part of the signs being syllabic; the number of all the characters is 113, while the number of the syllabic signs is over eighty. Prof. Wiseman has drawn my attention to the fact that the Neo-Elamite writing parallels the Old Persian cuneiform script in idea, and was only rarely used alongside Aramaic.

THE END OF CUNEIFORM WRITING

Cuneiform writing lingered on into the Christian Era, kept alive by some conservative priests, jurists and astronomers. Private and business correspondence was the first to abandon it; letters in this script, numerous before the Persian conquest, ceased at the beginning of the fifth century B.C., as the spoken Babylonian language fell into disuse. At the end of the same century, legal contracts and similar documents ceased to be written in cuneiform characters. Aramaic took their place (*see* p. 200). There was a short period of renaissance for it and for ancient science in the third–first centuries B.C., owing to the favour of the Seleucid dynasty. The latest record extant is a tablet of A.D. 75. After this, it was ignored by man, for nearly sixteen centuries, until Pietro della Valle (1586–1652), the famous Italian traveller, observed and copied some inscriptions in Persepolis in October 1621.

DECIPHERMENT

The decipherment of the cuneiform scripts was the achievement of the nineteenth century. At the end of the eighteenth century not a word could be read with certainty; at the end of the nineteenth, the contents of thousands of lengthy records of great empires were recovered for modern knowledge. The most recent of the cuneiform writings, the early Persian script (Figs. 1.16 and 17), which will be discussed later, was the first to be deciphered (Figs. 1.16a and 17); the Babylonian, a much older script, was the second; the neo-Elamite script was the third; and the earliest cuneiform script of all, the Sumerian, was the last to be deciphered. The reason for this apparently curious sequence in deciphering the various cuneiform scripts, is that whereas the early Persian writing was a semi-alphabet of about forty characters (and the language an Indo-European idiom), and the neo-Elamite system was a quasi-syllabic script, the Babylonian writing, on the other hand, was a 'transitional' system with over 640 signs, and the Sumerian script presented the additional difficulty that its language was quite unknown. In fact, even the very name Sumer was unknown, and there was no clearly recognizable trace of that people and language in the whole of ancient literature. Nevertheless, English, French, German, Danish and Irish scholars in close co-operation achieved the marvellous feat of deciphering the various scripts and their various languages. The German High-School teacher, G. F. Grotefend, in 1802 laid the basis for the decipherment, but the Englishman, Major (later Major General Sir) Henry C. Rawlinson, who copied, deciphered and published in 1846 a complete translation of the early Persian text of the tri-lingual inscription of Behistun, and a few years later tackled successfully the problem of the Babylonian writing, is the real 'father' of modern decipherment. The decipherment of the Babylonian and Assyrian scripts led finally to that of the other cuneiform writings and the languages for which they were used.

BIBLIOGRAPHY

WEISSBACH, F. H. *Zur Lösung der sumerischen Frage*, Leipsic, 1897.

THUREAU-DANGIN, F. *Recherches sur l'origine de l'écriture*, Paris, 1898; *Les Cylindres de Gudea*, etc., Paris, 1925; *Les homophones sumériens*, Paris, 1929.

MESSERSCHMIDT, L. *Die Entzifferung der Keilschrift*, Berlin, 1900.

KING, L. W., *Assyrian Language. Easy Lessons in Cuneiform Inscriptions*, London, 1901; *A History of Sumer and Akkad*, London, 1910.

WINCKLER, H. *Keilinschriftliches Textbuch zum Alten Testament*, 2nd ed., Leipsic, 1903.

FOSSEY, CH. *Manuel d'assyriologie*, Vol. I, Paris, 1904; Vol. II, Paris, 1926.

LANGDON, S. H. *Building Inscriptions of the Neo-Babylonian Empire*, Paris, 1905; *A Sumerian Grammar and Chrestomathy*, etc., Paris, 1911; *Die neubabylonischen Königsinschriften*, etc., Leipsic, 1912; *Babylonian Liturgies*, Paris, 1913; *Oxford Editions of Cuneiform Inscriptions*, Oxford, 1923; *Pictographic Inscriptions from Jemdet-Nasr*, Oxford, 1928.

WEBER, O. *Die Literatur der Babylonier und Assyrer*, Leipsic, 1907; *Altorientalische Siegelbilder*, Leipsic, 1920.

BORK, F. *Die Mitannisprache*, Berlin, 1909; *Die Strichinschriften von Susa*, Königsberg, 1924; 'Schriftprobleme aus Elam,' *Archiv für Schreib- und Buchwesen*, 1928; *Elamische Studien*, Leipsic, 1933; *Der Mitanibrief (sic!) und seine Sprache*, Königsberg, 1939.

LEHMANN-HAUPT, C. F. *Armenien einst und jetzt*, 3 vols., Berlin and Leipsic, 1910–31; *Corpus Inscriptionum Chaldicarum*, Berlin and Leipsic, 1928 onwards.

MESSERSCHMIDT, L. and SCHRÖDER, O. *Keilschrifttexte aus Assur historischen Inhalts*, Leipsic, 1911–2; O. Schröder, *Keilschrifttexte aus Assur verschiedenen Inhalts*, Leipsic, 1920.

HANDCOCK, P. S. P. *Mesopotamian Archæology*, London, 1912; *Selections from the Tell El-Amarna Letters*, London, 1920.

BARTON, G. A. *The Origin and Development of Babylonian Writing*, Baltimore, 1913; *Miscellaneous Babylonian Descriptions*, New Haven, 1918.

KNUDTZON, J. *Die El-Amarna Tafeln*, 2 vols., 1915; re-edited by S. A. B. Mercer, *The Tell el-Amarna Tablets*, 2 vols., Toronto, 1939.

Hittite Cuneiform Texts: Keilschrifttexte and *Keilschrifturkunden aus Boghazköy* (by Figulla, Forrer, Hrozný, Weber and Weidner), Leipsic, 1916–23; *Hittite Texts in the Cuneiform Character*, London, British Museum, 1920 onwards.

MEISSNER, B. *Altorientalische Texte und Untersuchungen*, Leiden, 1916 onwards; *Babylonien und Assyrien*, 2 vols., Heidelberg, 1920–5.

NEES, J. B. and KEISER, C. E. *Historical, Religious and Economic Texts and Antiquities*, New Haven, 1920.

WOOLLEY, C. L. *Dead Towns and Living Men*, etc., London, 1920; *The Sumerians*, Oxford, 1928; *Ur of the Chaldees*, London, 1929, 1935 and 1938; *Digging up the Past*, London, 1937; *Excavations at Ur*, London and New York, 1954; (*Ur Excavations*, Vols. II, IV, V, London and Philadelphia, 1924, 1939, 1954).

POEBEL, A. *Grundzuege der sumerischen Grammatik*, Rostock, 1923.

The Cambridge Ancient History, vol. I, Cambridge, 1923.

HALL, H. R. *Ancient History of the Near East*, 6th edit., London, 1924.

SMITH, S. *Babylonian Historical Texts*, London, 1924.

WALLIS BUDGE, E. A. *The Rise and Progress of Assyriology*, London, 1925.

UNGNAD, A. *Babylonisch-assyrische Grammatik*, 2nd ed., Munich, 1925; *Babylonisch-assyrisches Keilschriftlesebuch*, Munich, 1927.

KŒNIG, F. W., BORK F. and HUESING, G. *Corpus Inscriptionum Elamicarum*, I, Leipsic, 1926.

DOUGHERTY, R. 'Writing upon parchment and papyrus among the Babylonians and Assyrians', in *J. Amer. Orient. Soc.*, XLVIII (1928), 109ff.

UNGER, E. *Die Keilschrift*, Leipsic, 1929.

SPEISER, E. A. *Mesopotamian Origins*, etc., Philadelphia, 1930.

FRANKFORT, H. *Archæology and the Sumerian Problem*, Chicago, 1932; *Cylinder Seals*, London, 1939.

FRIEDRICH, J. *Einführung ins Urartäische*, Leipsic, 1933.

BURROWS, E. *Ur Excavations: Texts. Archaic Texts*, London, 1935.

Miscellanea orientalia dedicata Antonio Deimel (articles by W. Eilers, J. Schaumberger, N. Schneider and others), Rome, 1935.

ANDRAE, W. in *Handbuch der Deutschen Forschungsgemeinschaft*, Berlin, 1935; 'The Story of Uruk,' *Antiquity*, 1936, pp. 133, 145.

CAMERON, C. G. *History of Early Iran*, Chicago, 1936.

PFEIFFER, R. H. *One Hundred New Selected Nuzi Texts*, etc., New Haven, 1936; and E. R. Lacheman, *Miscellaneous Texts from Nuzi*, Cambridge, Mass., 1942.

FALKENSTEIN, A. *Archaische Texte aus Uruk*, Leipsic, 1936.

LLOYD, S. *Mesopotamia*, London, 1936; *Mesopotamian Excavations on Sumerian Sites*, London, 1936.

DHORME, E. *La Littérature babylonienne et assyrienne*, Paris, 1937.

RUTTEN, M. *Eléments d'accadien*, Paris, 1937; 'Notes de paléographie cunéiforme,' *Revue des Études Semitiques*, 1940.

STEPHENS, F. J. *Votive and Historical Texts from Babylonia and Assyria*, New Haven, 1937; *Old Assyrian Letters and Business Documents*, New Haven, 1944.

MEEK, TH. J. 'The Present State of Mesopotamian Studies,' *The Haverford Symposium on Archaeology and the Bible*, New Haven, 1938.

RYCKMANS, G. *Grammaire accadienne*, Louvain, 1938; 4th ed., revised by P. Naster, Louvain, 1960.

CLARK, C. *The Art of Early Writing*, London, 1938.

FRIEDRICH, J. *Kleine Beiträge zur churritischen Grammatik*, Leipsic, 1939; *Hethitisches Elementarbuch*, I, Heidelberg, 1940; II, 1946.

CHIERA, E. *They Wrote on Clay*, 1938; *Les Tablettes Babyloniennes*, Paris, 1940.

DEIMEL, A. *Šumerische Grammatik*, etc., 2nd ed., Rome, 1939.

POHL, A. and SKEHAN, P. W. 'Keilschriftbibliographie 1939-1945,' *Orientalia*, 1940-6; Pohl A. and Gordon, C. H., idem (I.x. 1945-I.x.1946), ibid., 1947.

D

CONTENAU, G. 'Les debuts de l'écriture cunéiforme,' etc., *Revue des Études Sémitiques*, 1940; *Everyday Life in Babylon and Assyria*, London, 1954.

CHRISTIAN, V. *Altertumskunde des Zweistromlandes*, etc., Leipsic, 1940.

HERZFELD, E. E. *Iran in the Ancient East*, London-New York, 1941.

NASTER, P. *Chrestomathie accadienne*, Louvain, 1941.

KRAMER, S. N. 'Sumerian Literature,' *Proc. Amer. Phil Soc.*, 1942; *Sumerian Mythology*, Philadelphia, 1944; *History begins at Sumer*, London, 1958; 'Sumerian Literature, A General Survey,' in *The Bible and the Ancient Near East* (ed. by G. E. Wright), London, 1961.

BOSON, G. *Quattro elenchi di segni sillabici cuneiformi*, Milan, 1942.

HUART, C. and DELAPORTE, L. *L'Iran antique*, etc., Paris, 1943.

GELB, I. J. *Hurrians and Subarians*, Chicago, 1944.

VROURYR, N. E. *Inscriptions ouartéenes et Annales des rois d'Assyrie*, Antwerp, 1944.

LABAT, R. *Manuel d'épigraphie akkadienne*, Paris, 1948.

PORADA, E. *Corpus of Ancient Near Eastern Seals in N. Amer. Collect.*, Washington, 1948.

DRIVER, G. R. *Semitic Writing from Pictograph to Alphabet* ('The Schweich Lectures of the British Academy, 1944'), London-Oxford, 1948 (Part I, *Cuneiform Scripts*, is an excellent monograph on the subject); 2nd ed., 1954.

FRANKFORT, H. *The Birth of Civilization in the Near East*, London, 1951.

JESTIN, R. *Abrégé de Grammaire sumérienne*, Paris, 1951 (bibliography).

WISEMAN, D. J. *The Alalakh Tablets*, London, 1953.

RUTTEN, M. *Les documents épigraphiques de Tchogha Zembil*, Paris, 1953.

SALONEN, A. E_2-Ku_6-nu-ku_2—*Das Haus das Fische nicht frisst*, Helsinki, 1953.

ARO, J. *Abnormal Plene Writings in Akkadian Texts*, Helsinki, 1953.

PAPER, H. H. *The Phonology and Morphology of Royal Achaemenid Elamite*, Ann Arbor, 1955.

SCHMÖKEL, H. *Das Land Sumer*, 2nd ed., Stuttgart, 1956 (bibliography).

HALLO, W. W. *Early Mesopotamian Royal Titles*, New Haven, 1957; 'Royal Inscriptions of the Early Old Babylonian Period: a Bibliography,' *Bibliotheca Orientalis*, 1961.

GURNEY, O. R. (ed.), *The Sultantepe Tablets*, London, 1957–

HACKMANN, G. G. *Sumerian and Akkadian Administrative Texts*, New Haven, 1958.

MESHCHANINOV, I. I. *Grammatical Structure of the Urartu Language* (in Russian), Leningrad, 1958.

Semitic Museum, Harvard University, *Excavations at Nuzi*, Cambridge, Mass., 1958.

IRWIN, K. G. *Man learns to write*, Toronto, 1958.

Colt Archaeological Expedition, 1936/37, *Excavations at Nessana*, London-Oxford, 1958.

PARROT, A. *Sumer*, Paris, 1960; Engl. transl. by S. Gilbert and J. Emmons, London, 1960 (brought-up-to-date bibliog.).

JONES, T. B. and SNYDER, S. W. *Sumerian Economic Texts from the Third Ur Dynasty: a Catalogue and Discussion* etc., Minneapolis and London, 1961.

POPE, M. 'The Origins of Writing in the Near East', *Antiquity*, March, 1966.

Scientific journals, Catalogues of the British Museum, of the University of Pennsylvania Museum, of the Istanbul Museum of the Ancient Orient, of Staatliche Museen, Berlin, etc.

Articles on *Assyriology*, *Cuneiform Writing*, *Mesopotamia*, etc., in *Encyclopædia Britannica* and similar works should also be consulted.

CHAPTER 2

Ancient Egyptian Scripts

HIEROGLYPHIC WRITING

THIS is one of the most important systems of writing of the ancient world. The Greeks called this writing *hieroglyphikà grámmata* (from *hierós*, 'holy,' *glýphein*, to 'carve,' and *grámma*, 'letter'), *i.e.*, sacred carved letters, because when it first came to their notice it was used and understood only by the priests and stood in contrast to demotic. The term 'hieroglyphic' appears—as commonly known—in Clement of Alexandria (*c.* A.D. 200), *Strom.* V, 4; in fact, it already was used by Diodorus Siculus (d. in or after 21 B.C.), Plutarch (A.D. *c.* 46–120), and Ptolemy (A.D. *c.* 100–178). The term was accurate enough at the time, because that system of writing was then used mainly for inscriptions carved on temple walls, in tombs, etc.; it is, however, not altogether exact, because hieroglyphic writing was employed also for inscriptions which were not carved, but painted on stone, wood, earthenware, and other material, and in earlier times also for profane writing. The style is, however, a monumental writing par excellence.

What the Egyptians themselves called this script in earlier times, is not certain. At a late period the expression *mdw-ntr* ('speech of the god') is used to denote hieroglyphics, in contrast to demotic script, but without properly distinguishing speech and script. The god Thoth was considered to have given to mankind, both the language to express their minds and the script to record it.

The terms 'hieroglyphs' and 'hieroglyphic' are applied also, although incorrectly, to the Hittite 'hieroglyphic' writing (*see* chapter 5) and to the Mayan writing (*see* chapter 7); indeed, the word 'hieroglyphs' is even used for any unintelligible characters.

ORIGINS

It is still a moot point—at least, in some scientific circles—which script, the Egyptian or the Sumerian, is the older. Both were already in existence in the early third millennium B.C. The early history of hieroglyphic writing, however, is still uncertain. It is almost universally accepted that it was parallel in many respects with that of the cuneiform, Chinese, Mayan, and other 'analytic' scripts, but that its early development went along the special ways which we shall explain below. Some cautious scholars, however, are beginning to doubt whether we are right in assuming a process of gradual evolution.

The system, they suggest, was created 'artificially' as a whole, at the time of the unification of Egypt under the first dynasty, by someone who knew already of the existence of writing. This opinion, which, as already said, has been called the theory of 'idea-diffusion' or 'stimulus-diffusion', is perhaps right, but is very difficult to prove. Prof. E. A. Speiser argues that Egypt 'seems to have borrowed the new idea but substituted native forms for foreign symbols.'

Naturally enough, the ancient Egyptians were supposed to regard writing as the brain-child of the moon-god, Thoth; for them, predynastic times were 'the time of the gods.'

It is true that the earliest known fully developed hieroglyphic inscriptions present essentially the same mode of writing as the inscriptions written some 3,000 years later. Nevertheless, the cautious scholars mentioned above regard the few ancient documents extant as pure pictorial representation, in effect, as pictures only and not as crude pictography, that is, as picture-writing or as transition from pictography to ideographic script, while the majority regard the documents as important evidence of the various initial stages in the development of hieroglyphic writing.

Figures 2.1–2 represent Egyptian scribes.

Amongst the most ancient documents extant, two deserve particular mention: the Palette of Nar-mer, c. 2900 B.C. (Fig. 2.3a) and the Plaque, or rather Label of Hor-'Aḥa, also c. 2900 B.C. (Fig. 2.3b)—both of whom, and particularly the latter, have been identified with Men(es), the traditional founder of the First Dynasty. According to some scholars, these and other similar labels would represent a fully developed Egyptian writing; but in Professor Egerton's opinion 'the name of the king and the title of the servant on the obverse of the Palette of Nar-mer were clearly "writing," as the phonetic principle is in use: whereas the hawk leading the captives in the Delta is at most a "rebus" and thus "pictorial." The bottom register of the Hor-'Aḥa and other similar labels (possibly quantities of material belonging to the coronation *tt s.t wv-t* (?), "taking the great seat" (?)) are surely "hieroglyphs" all right, but in a state where the phonetic principle has not yet evolved a stage where the syntactical elements of a sentence would be expressed.' In this sense he would hardly regard hieroglyphic writing as a 'fully developed' system before the Fourth Dynasty (2250 B.C.), though of course some of the forms on the early subjects continue the same throughout Egyptian history. However, the evidence is quite unsatisfactory as we have only tomb objects, which by the nature of their subject-matter are not likely to give us connected material. This applies even to *stelae*.

It is now commonly agreed that the rise of the first dynasty may be placed about 2900 B.C., but it must be remembered that no complete system of Egyptian chronology can as yet be formulated. The 'high' system, which placed the beginning of the first dynasty in the first half of the sixth millennium B.C. (Champollion, Bœckh, Unger, Petrie and others), and also the system which placed it in the fifth millennium

(Brugsch, Wallis Budge and others) can now be disregarded, and even the 'low' chronology (Lepsius, Bunsen, Lieblein and others, who suggested the first half of the fourth millennium B.C.) has been progressively brought down lower and lower. Eduard Meyer, in particular, after having placed the beginning of the first dynasty in *c.* 3315 B.C., later on shifted it to *c.* 3197 B.C. The date 3000 B.C. to 2900 B.C., on which there seems to be increasing agreement today (Albright, Scharff, Stier, Wilson, Schott, Stock and others), would synchronize with the beginning of the classical Sumerian age.

CHRONOLOGY OF ANCIENT EGYPT

N.B.: dates of the third and of the early second millennium B.C. are approximate

2900 B.C. onwards	1st dynasty	
2600 „	3rd dynasty, the pyramid builders	Old
2550 „	4th dynasty	Kingdom;
2450 „	5th dynasty	Capital:
2300–2200	6th dynasty	Memphis
2250 onwards	Intermediate age	
2175–2120	9th dynasty	
2040/30	re-union of Egypt	Middle Kingdom;
1991–1788	12th dynasty	Capital: Thebes
1788 onwards	2nd intermediate age	
1710–1550	'Hyksos' period	
1570–1310	18th dynasty	
1490–1435	Tuthmosis III	
1406–1370	Amenophis III	
1380–1353	Amarna period	
1370–1353	Amenophis IV: Echnaton	New Kingdom;
1310–1200	19th dynasty	various capitals
1290–1224	Ramesses II	
1200–1065	20th dynasty	
1175–1144	Ramesses III	
1065–935	21st dynasty, Tanites	
935–735	22nd dynasty	
712	Aethiopian conquest	
671–656	Assyrian conquest	
663–609	Psamtik 1: 26th dynasty	
656	Psamtik I liberates Egypt	
609–594	Necho II	
569–526	Amasis II	
525	Kambujiya (Kambyses) conquers Egypt	
332	Alexander conquers Egypt	
323–30	Ptolemies	
30 B.C.	Rome conquers Egypt	
641 A.D.	Arabs conquer Egypt	

HISTORY OF HIEROGLYPHIC WRITING

If we do not accept the theory of the 'artificial' origin of the hieroglyphic writing, we must follow the common theory that, at the beginning, this system went through the usual stages of primitive pictographs, ideographic characters, and rebus-writing, parallel to the initial stages of cuneiform writing (*see* above); moreover, as in cuneiform writing, the *determinatives* were introduced (Fig. 2.4), in order to remove the ambiguities of the *polyphones*.

These technical terms—belonging to the modern scientific apparatus—have, of course little relevance to the way the Egyptians thought about their writing, and perhaps may even confuse the issue. Indeed, it may be assumed that for the Egyptians any hieroglyph was capable of any of the customary usages, its actual practical application depending upon convention, not least scribal convention. The main point is this: physical objects could be drawn, ideas could not. Nor could minor parts of speech which indicate connected thought in writing. It was simple to use the symbol for 'eye' (Fig. 2.5a) as a determinative for 'see' or 'look' (Figs. 2.4, 5). But when it came to the problem of representing thought, the Egyptians employed two methods: (i) the same signs were used for allied concepts (the symbol 'sun' also for 'day' or 'light'; the symbol 'thorn' also for 'sharp'), and (ii) signs representing certain words were used also for *homophones*—the same words with quite different meanings (the symbol * 'star,' *sb³*, was also used for 'door,' *sb³*, and 'teach,' *sb³*). Subsequently, it became the practice to distinguish all but the most obvious words both phonetically and by determinative.

In general, it may be said that the employment of hieroglyphic characters was threefold: (1) word-signs (Fig. 2.5a); (2) phonograms and phonetic complements; (3) determinatives (Fig. 2.4). The Egyptian hieroglyphic system contained 604 symbols, apart from the numbers, and the numerous ligatures and variants. The use of bare word-signs is not very common. Phonograms consisted usually of the bare root of the words whence they were derived. Egyptian writing, like the Semitic alphabets, expressed consonants only, and as there was practically no great need for tri-consonantal phonograms—indeed, a number of signs are equally ideograms and tri-consonantal phonograms—the phonograms were mainly bi-consonantal (Fig. 2.5a) or uni-consonantal (Fig. 2.5b). There were about seventy-five bi-consonantal phonograms, of which some fifty were commonly used. The most important phonograms—from the point of view of the history of the Alphabet—were the uni-consonantal signs; these, however, were not (or at least not all of them were) the most frequent ones. The origin of some of them is still obscure; in a few cases more than one origin may be suspected; in other cases we do not know whether *acrophony*—the use of a word-sign to represent the first consonant of the name of the object—played any considerable part. In the majority of cases, single consonants came to be denoted by symbols representing certain objects whose names (some of which had already fallen into disuse in very ancient times) contained *prominently* the consonant in question or, for reasons of phonetic decay, were reduced to one syllable only. However that may be, the hieroglyphic writing contained (Fig. 2.5*b*) twenty-four uni-consonantal signs, increased later by *homophones* to about thirty, which covered the whole range of Egyptian consonantal sounds. It is therefore believed that the Egyptians were 'alphabet-conscious' (R. W. Sloley) and possessed the world's earliest alphabet.

We cannot, however, exclude a different opinion; in a true alphabet each sign generally denotes one sound only, and each sound is represented by a single, constant symbol, whereas in Egyptian there existed different signs for the same sound, which could be represented in various ways. Even if we agreed that the Egyptians had acquired an 'alphabet,' we should conclude that they did not know how to use it. As a matter of fact, in practice they rarely employed it when they could use word-signs or multi-consonantal phonograms, and they rarely employed it without determinatives, *i.e.*, signs which were not to be read, but served simply as guides to the sense of the word; thus, the 'alphabetic' signs needed 'to be guided.' In general, word-signs, tri-consonantal, bi-consonantal and uni-consonantal signs, and determinatives were combined into a cumbersome, complicated script, and this crystallized aspect of the writing was maintained during the 3,000 years and more of its history. The latest hieroglyphic inscription is dated 24.8.394 A.D. (reign of Theodosius I).

This opinion is, however, partly contradicted by facts aptly described by an authority such as Edgerton:

The Egyptians already in the Middle Kingdom used an orthography specially adapted for the transcription of foreign names which was in effect a system of groups representing consonant or consonant+vowel, by which fairly accurate transcription could be secured (see the conflicting views of Albright and Edgerton, and particularly the Middle Kingdom cursing-texts). This group-writing was more and more extensively used during the New Kingdom even for Egyptian words, and forms the basis of much demotic spelling. It was not that the Egyptians could not use an alphabetic system—they often did. But in so far as hieroglyphs were concerned, it did not suit them to do so for a number of reasons:

(I) Hieroglyphs had magical value;

(II) ideograms and determinatives were a help, not a hindrance, to understanding;

(III) hieroglyphs remained a picture-writing, extensively used for decorative purposes;

(IV) where for religious or magical reasons, cryptography was to be employed, the system lent itself admirably to adaptations making it unintelligible to the uninitiated, but clear to the temple scribes (*see* Fairman); and

(V) why abandon a system hallowed by time and divinity, which worked out in practice?

In any case, is the word 'alphabet' really apt in the case of hieroglyphs, except as a convenience to indicate uni-consonantal signs? Some, like Vergote, would even have it that the uni-consonantal signs are really syllabic and carry a vowel with them. The definition 'alphabet' is that it should be approximately a 'one-sound–one-sign' system: hieroglyphs by nature spurned this.

The direction of writing was normally from right to left, the signs facing the beginning of the line (Figs. 2.6 *a*, *b*); sometimes, however, inscriptions were written from left to right, and sometimes, for purposes of symmetry, in both directions; in the latter cases, each of the two parts usually faces towards the centre, reading from there outwards. But the direction downwards, from top to bottom is frequently used, too.

Egyptian hieroglyphic inscriptions and papyri are represented in Figs. 2.7–9.

The Egyptian scripts were essentially national (in complete contrast with cuneiform writing); they originated in Egypt, they were employed only for Egyptian speech (but at least one demotic papyrus appears to contain an Aramaic text), they developed in Egypt, and they died out in Egypt.

HIERATIC WRITING

So long as writing was used only for inscriptions, which were of a monumental character, royal, religious or funerary, intended to last for a very long time, it was natural to make use of elaborately drawn, carved or painted pictures of objects; but for business documents, private letters and literary manuscripts, where the main concern was speed, hieroglyphic writing was found to be too cumbrous. Besides, in drawing on papyrus, which was mainly used for cursive writing, the brush-pen naturally gave to the signs a bolder, more cursive form. Little by little, alongside the hieroglyphic system, which in contrast with cuneiform writing, preserved its pictorial character right to the end of its existence, a cursive form was developed, in which the signs lost more and more of their original pictorial character (Fig. 2.6c). This cursive form of hieroglyphic writing is termed *hieratic*.

'Hieratic' (in Greek, *hieratikós*, 'sacred, priestly') is the name given by Clement of Alexandria (*Strom.* v, 4) to the writing employed in his time mainly by priests for the Egyptian religious texts as opposed to the demotic writing (*see* below), which was the script of everyday life, of business documents and private letters. In earlier times, however, hieratic writing was the only Egyptian cursive script, in contrast to the monumental hieroglyphic writing, and was employed for any cursive writing of sacred and profane character. Hieratic is in fact nothing but a cursive form of writing adapted from hieroglyphic and used beside it for 3,000 years. Figures 2.10–15 represent a selection of hieratic papyri.

External changes do not necessarily involve internal changes. While the hieratic signs in their most cursive forms hardly retained any clear trace of the original hieroglyphic pictures, in fact they were only cursive transcriptions, sign by sign, of hieroglyphic symbols. In practice, however, many single signs were linked together by the sweep of the brush, and so ligatured groups were formed.

A kind of hieratic writing already existed in the period of the first dynasty. In course of time, it developed more and more till it became rather obscure. In the seventh century B.C., when, as we shall see below, the demotic writing came into being, hieratic became in practice the script of the priestly class and was used mainly for literal transcription of religious and other traditional texts; it continued to be used extensively by priests in all periods, and was employed up till the third century A.D.

The direction of hieratic was originally vertical, and later horizontal, from right to left.

DEMOTIC WRITING

This was a highly cursive derivative of hieratic. The term 'demotic,' from the Greek *demotikà grámmata* (*démos*, 'people'), that is 'popular, vulgar characters,' is taken from Herodotus (ii, 36), while Clement of Alexandria (*Strom.* v, 4), calls this script *grámmata epistolographiká*, 'epistolary characters,' a translation of the demotic word s*ḫnš*ʿ.*w*, 'writing of letters.' *Enchorial* (Greek *enchórios*, 'of the country') is another term for this system of writing.

Professor Edgerton rightly points out that the position about 'hieratic' and 'demotic' is difficult to state clearly. For the period from Ramesses III (1198–1167 B.C.) onwards we have few, if any, papyrus documents from Lower Egypt; the documents whose origin is known for certain come from Upper Egypt, which was virtually a separate state from the time of Herihor (*c.* 1090 B.C.) down to Shabaka (712–663 B.C.). During this period, in Lower Egypt hieratic must have developed differently from that of Upper Egypt; for when the country was again united under the Ethiopian (XXVth) Dynasty (712–663 B.C.) and administration once more took effect at a distance from Memphis, the contemporary Lower Egyptian style of 'demotic' began to be more generally used; and when, after the Assyrian interlude, Psamtik I (648–609 B.C.) moved the capital to Saïs, 'demotic' was naturally used by the royal scribes, and by the end of the Dynasty had completely ousted the Upper Egyptian hand, which had survived for some time in a form known as 'abnormal hieratic,' into which some demotic groups had filtered.

The earliest demotic documents date from early in the seventh century. That literary compositions do not survive from the earlier period is probably mainly chance: funerary and magical books, however, probably only started to be written in demotic in the Ptolemaic period (from 300 B.C. onwards), and were often interspersed with hieratic material, that is, the hieratic of the religious books which is really the old Middle Kingdom hieratic, and bears no relation to the business hieratic of the Theban scribes of the XXth Dynasty (1200–1065 B.C.), which is often much more cursive than literary demotic. The two systems differ rather in the type than the degree of abbreviations used.

However, the earliest extant demotic documents belong to the early seventh century B.C., the latest is dated A.D. 476. In origin, demotic was, as already mentioned, a derivative of hieratic (Fig. 2.10), and like it, as a system of writing was neither purely syllabic nor—even less so—alphabetic. Its script, therefore, consisted essentially of word-signs, phonograms and determinatives. Externally, however, the form of its signs became so cursive that its aspect was quite different from that of hieroglyphic. In addition, whole associated groups of hieratic characters were fused by ligatures into single demotic signs. Demotic emerged as a new form of writing, mainly because the hieratic business hand had deteriorated, so much that it had become obscure. Thus demotic, the new more cursive form of hieratic, having developed in lower Egypt into a proper system of writing, became gradually the 'popular' script of the whole of Egypt. It was used at first for ordinary purposes such as business and private letters but, in course of time, it was employed also for lengthy literary compositions and for copies of ancient books. In the course of time demotic gradually developed; it received its stereotyped form about 300 B.C. On the whole, demotic is very difficult to read, and the main difficulty lies not in the language, but in the script.

In the Ptolemaic period, demotic was considered to be of even greater importance than hieratic, and at least of the same importance as Greek and hieroglyphic; royal and priestly decrees were engraved on *stelae* in triplicate in hieroglyphic, demotic and Greek versions, demotic occupying, as on the Rosetta Stone (Fig. 2.18) the middle portion of the monument. Demotic continued to be used until the very end of Egyptian paganism in the fifth century A.D. Moreover, it handed on to the Coptic alphabet certain signs, for sounds which could not be expressed by Greek letters (*see* part 2, chapter 8).

Demotic was written horizontally, from right to left (Fig. 2.16).

DECIPHERMENT OF EGYPTIAN SCRIPTS

When the nineteenth century began, not a word of hieroglyphic writing could be read. For thousands of years, this ancient system of writing, one of the earliest used by civilized man, preserved in secret, beneath the splendid protective covering of the sands of Egypt, the story of mighty potentates and powerful empires for ages after they had passed away. Its decipherment is one of the romantic achievements of modern science, and a fine example also of international scholarship. No results rewarded the attempted decipherments of the *savants* of the sixteenth century, that is the Italians G. P. Valeriano (1556) and M. Mercati (1589), or of the seventeenth century with the learned Jesuit Athanasius Kircher, but in the eighteenth century Warburton guessed the existence of 'alphabetic' characters, and De Guignes guessed that some of the signs were determinatives, while the Danish scholar G. Zoëga in 1797 recognized that the oval rings or 'cartouches' contained royal names (Fig. 2.17).

With the beginning of the nineteenth century, real progress in decipherment of demotic, and later of hieroglyphic was made by the Swedish orientalist J. D. Åkerblad, by the French scholar Silvestre de Sacy, and particularly by Dr. Thomas

Young, of Emmanuel College, Cambridge. The key was provided by the famous Rosetta Stone (Fig. 2.18). It is a priestly decree drawn up in 197/6 B.C. in honour of Ptolemy (V) Epiphanes (205–181 B.C.), in two versions and three scripts: the Egyptian text was given in hieroglyphic (14 lines) and in demotic (32 lines), and the Greek text in Greek characters (54 lines). It was found in the fort of Saint Julien de Rosetta, in 1799, during Napoleon's attempted conquest of Egypt, by the French Captain M. Boussard; in 1801 it passed into British hands and is now in the British Museum (B.M. 960, No. 24).

Starting from the known, the demotic and the hieroglyphic writings were slowly made to yield up their secrets. With the help of the Greek text of the inscription and a knowledge of Coptic (which is the last stage of the Egyptian language) together with Åkerblad's decipherment of several phrases in the demotic text, and more particularly Young's identification in the hieroglyphic text of several names of gods and persons—the hieroglyphic spelling of the names was one of the bases of the whole decipherment—the French Egyptologist Jean François Champollion (1790–1832) at length published in 1822 a masterly dissertation on hieroglyphic writing. In this, and in his subsequent researches he laid the foundation of the modern science of Egyptology (Fig. 2.19). Much scientific scepticism, however, persisted until the results of the successful decipherment were confirmed by the 'Decree of Canopus,' a stele found in 1866 by the German Egyptologist R. Lepsius. Naturally, much remained to be done by future investigators, as indeed much even now remains to be done to complete our knowledge of Egyptian philology. Nevertheless, by the labours of a succession of brilliant scholars—the past thirty years have also had their dramatic triumphs—an entire civilization extending over three and a half millennia has been revealed.

BIBLIOGRAPHY

Hieratische Papyri aus den Klg. Museen zu Berlin, 5 vols., Leipsic, 1901–11.

SETHE, K. *Die altägyptischen Pyramidentexte*, 4 vols., Leipsic, 1908–22; *Das hieroglyphische Schriftsystem*, Glückstadt and Hamburg, 1935; *Vom Bilde zum Buchstaben*, etc., Leipsic, 1939.

BREASTED, J. H. *Ancient Records of Egypt*, Chicago, 1909.

MŒLLER, G. *Hieratische Paläographie*, 4 vols., Leipsic, 1909–36.

WALLIS BUDGE, E. A. *Facsimiles of Egyptian Hieratic Papyri in the British Museum*, London, 1910; 2nd series, London, 1923; *An Egyptian Hieroglyphic Dictionary*, London, 1920 (new ed., posthumous, 2 vols., New York, 1960); *The Rosetta Stone*, London, 1935.

Hieroglyphic Texts from Egyptian Stelæ, etc., *in the British Museum*, 8 parts, London, 1911–39.

GARDINER, A. H. *Literary Texts of the New Kingdom, Egyptian Hieratic Texts*, Leipsic, 1911; 'The Nature and Development of the Egyptian Hieroglyphic Writing,' *Journ. of Egypt. Archæol.*, 1915; *Egyptian Grammar*, Oxford Univ. Press, 1927; 2nd ed., 1950; *Catalogue of the Egyptian Hieroglyphic Printing Type*, etc., Oxford, 1928; *Kadesh Inscriptions of Ramesses II*, Oxford, 1960.

ERMAN, A. *Die Hieroglyphen*, Berlin and Leipsic, 1912; *Die Entzifferung der Hieroglyphen*, Berlin, 1922; *Ägyptische Grammatik*, 4th ed., Berlin, 1928; *Ägyptische Inschriften der Kgl. Museen zu Berlin*, 2 vols., Leipsic, 1913–24; *Die Welt am Nil*, Leipsic, 1936.

BONNET, H. *Ägyptisches Schrifttum*, Leipsic, 1919.

PEET, T. E. 'The Antiquity of Egyptian Civilization,' *Journ. of Egypt. Archæol.*, 1922; *A Comparative Study of the Literatures of Egypt, Palestine and Mesopotamia*, London, 1931; *Ancient Egypt* (in E. Eyre, *European Civilization*, etc.), London, 1934; *The Present Position of Egyptological Studies*, Oxford, 1934.

FLINDERS PETRIE, W. M. *Egypt and Israel*, new ed., London, 1923; *Ancient Egyptians*, London, 1925; *Egyptian Tales translated from Papyri*, 4th ed., London, 1926; *The Making of Egypt*, Oxford, 1939.

SPIEGELBERG, W. *Demotische Grammatik*, Heidelberg, 1925.

NAVILLE, E. *L'écriture égyptienne*, Paris, 1926.

RŒDER, G. 'Der Schmuckwert der ägyptischen Hieroglyphen,' *Buch und Schrift*, 1928.

FAULKNER, R. O. *The Plural and Dual in Old Egyptian*, Brussels, 1929.

ALBRIGHT, W. F. *The Vocalization of the Egyptian Syllabic Orthography*, New Haven, 1934.

CAPRILE, E. 'Il deciframento dei geroglifici,' *Sapere*, 1936.

GRAPOW, H. *Sprachliche und schriftliche Formung ägyptischer Texte*, Glueckstadt, 1936; 'Zur Erforschungsgeschichte des Demotischen,' *Orientalische Literatur Zeitung*, 1937.

ERICHSEN, W. *Demotische Lesestücke*, 3 parts, Leipsic, 1937; *Demotisches Glossar*, Copenhagen, 1954.

SEIDL, E. *Demotische Urkundenlehre nach den früehptolomäischen Texten*, Munich, 1937.

WILSON, J. A., 'The Present State of Egyptian Studies,' *The Haverford Symposium*, New Haven, 1938.

GLANVILLE, S. R. K. *Catalogue of Demotic Papyri in the British Museum*, London, 1939; *The Legacy of Egypt*, Oxford, 1942.

EDGERTON, W. F. *Egyptian Phonetic Writing, from its Invention to the Close of the Nineteenth Dynasty*, communication presented at the Fifteenth Meeting of the American Oriental Society (Baltimore, 4th December, 1939), *Journ. of the Amer. Orient. Soc.*, 1939.

LEFEBVRE, G. *Grammaire de l'égyptien classique*, Cairo, 1940 (2nd ed., 1955).

STEINDORFF G. and SEELE, K. C. *When Egypt Ruled the East*, Chicago, 1942.

SCHARFF, A. 'Archäologische Beiträge zur Frage der Entstehung der Hieroglyphenschrift,' *Sitzungsb. d. Bayer. Akad. der Wissensch.*, 1942.

VIKENTIEV, V. 'Les Monuments archaïques, II. La tablette en ivoire de Naqâda,' *Annales du Service des Antiquités de l'Egypte*, 1942.

GRDSELOFF, B. 'La tablette de Naqâda,' etc., *Annales*, etc. 1944.

DE BUCK, A. *Egyptische Grammatica*, Leyden, 1944; *Egyptian Readingbook*, I, Leyden, 1948.

Ancient Egyptian Onomasticon, 3 vols., London-Oxford, 1947.

SCHOTT, S. *Hieroglyphen. Untersuchungen zum Ursprung der Schrift*, Wiesbaden, 1951.

VAN MENSEL, P. J. D. *Hoe Ould Egypte schreef*, Averbode, 1951.

JANSSEN, J. *Hiërogliefen*, Leiden, 1952.

MALININE M. (ed.), *Choix de textes juridiques en hiératique "anormal" et en démotique (XXV-XXVII dynasties)*, Paris, 1953.

LACAU, P. *Sur le système hiéroglyphique*, Cairo, 1954.

OTTO, E. *Die biographischen Inschriften der aegyptischen Spaetzeit. Ihre geistesgeschichtliche und literarische Bedeutung*, Leiden, 1954.

BRUNNER-TRAUT, E. *Die altägyptischen Scherbenbilder (Bildostraka) der deutschen Museen und Sammlungen*, Wiesbaden, 1956.

MERCER, S. A. B. *Literary Criticism of the Pyramid Texts*, London, 1956.

CERNÝ, J. and GARDINER, A. H. *Hieratic Ostraca*, vol. I, Oxford, 1957.

LICHTHEIM, M. *Demotic Ostraca from Medinet Habu*, Chicago, 1957.

(CUMMINGS) DAVIES, N. M. *Picture Writing in Ancient Egypt*, London, 1958.

IVERSEN, E. *Papyrus Carlsberg u. VII Fragments of a Hieroglyphic Dictionary*, Copenhagen, 1958.

JUNKER, H. *Der grosse Pylon des Temples der Isis in Philä*, Vienna, 1958.

KEES, H., SCHOTT, S., BRUNNER, H., OTTO, E. and MORENZ, S. *Aegyptische Schrift und Sprache*, (in *Handbuch der Orientalistik*, I, i-1), Leiden, 1958.

CAMINOS, R. A. *The Chronicle of Prince Osorkon*, Rome, 1958.

HELCK, W. *Zur Verwaltung des Mittleren und Neuen Reiches*, Leiden, 1958.

SEELE, K. C. *Tomb of Tjanefer at Thebes*, Chicago, 1959.

POSENER, G., SAUNERON, S. and YOYOTTE, J. *Dictionnaire de la civilisation égyptienne*, Paris, 1959.

PARKER, R. A. (ed.), *Vienna Demotic Papyrus on Eclipse and Lunar Omina*, Providence, R. I., 1960.

DE RACHEWILTZ, B. *The Rock-tomb IRW-K³-PTḤ*, Leiden, 1960.

PESTMAN, P. W. *Marriage and Matrimonial Property in Ancient Egypt*, 1961.

LAMBDIN, T. O. 'Egypt: Its Language and Literature', and WILSON, J. A. 'Egyptian Culture and Religion', in *The Bible and the Ancient Near East* (ed. by G. E. Wright), London, 1961.

DAVID, M. V. *Le débat sur les écritures et l'hieroglyphe aux XVIIᵉ et XVIIIᵉ siécles etc.*, Paris, 1965 (bibl.).

POPE, M. 'The Origins of Writing in the Near East,' *Antiquity*, March 1966.

The *Journal of Egyptian Archæology*, published by the Egypt Exploration Society, London, 1914 onwards.

CHAPTER 3

Cretan Scripts

MINOAN CIVILIZATION

THE ancient culture of Crete—the only European country which had a civilization to compare with the contemporary civilizations of Egypt and Mesopotamia—has left many problems which will probably remain unsolved for all time. Serious scholars agree that the Cretan civilization presents distinctive features. It is generally known as 'Ægean,' from the Ægean Islands, whose civilization in its turn originated from Crete, or 'Minoan,' a term suggested by the late Sir Arthur Evans, from the mythical Minos, the thalassocratic king of the 'Ægean Empire.' The ancient inhabitants of Crete undoubtedly attained a very high culture. This is demonstrated not only by architectural remains, fresco-painting and ceramic art, but also by the considerable influence exercised on the civilization of the Greek mainland and the islands, and by the Greek traditions, which regarded Crete as an ancient centre of a great civilization. Finally, the indigenous Cretan scripts are eloquent of the same fact. Yet, to what race did the Cretan people or peoples belong? What language did they speak? Where did they come from? What was their history? Who were their rulers? No reply can be given to all these and many other questions. We do not even know the very name of that mysterious people (or peoples?).

Yet, archæology has made a great contribution towards the knowledge of that important culture. In the last sixty years, explorations and excavation have unearthed beautiful palaces, and have discovered many works of art. A fairly exact chronology has been established on the basis, mainly, of synchronisms between foreign products, especially pottery found in Crete, and Cretan products found in Egypt, Mesopotamia and other countries.

English excavations and explorations at Knossos, Italian excavations and explorations at Phaistos and Hagia Triada, followed by American, Greek and French excavations in various other places, have revealed that there was in Crete a long neolithic period, of perhaps 5,000 years or more, followed by a Bronze-age civilization, conventionally termed 'Minoan.' This Bronze-age epoch has been divided by Evans into three periods, termed *early, middle* and *late Minoan* and abbreviated into *E.M., M.M.* and *L.M.,* and each of them is subdivided into three phases, I, II, III. There are thus nine cultural phases, *E.M.* I, II, III; *M.M.* I, II, III; and *L.M.* I, II, III. The Cretan neolithic period is believed to have coincided in part with the Egyptian pre-dynastic age; while the beginning of *E.M.* seems to have coincided, roughly, with the later period of the First Dynasty of Egypt, and of the classical Sumerian dynasties; hence, it may be dated *c.* 2800 B.C., the phase lasting about eight hundred years. *M.M.* may be dated roughly in the first half of the second millennium B.C.; *L.M.*, in the second half of the same millennium. Minoan civilization seems to have come to an end abruptly, about 1100 B.C., owing probably to political disturbances in the eastern Mediterranean, similar to those which somewhat earlier caused the downfall of the Hittite empire (*see* below) and the decline of the Egyptian empire.

UNDECIPHERED SCRIPTS OF CRETE

Pictographic Scripts

From the beginning of *E.M.*I (*c.* 2800 B.C.), seal-engraving was practised; the seals were made mostly of steatite, later also of ivory; they were large, conical or three-sided. The engraved subjects were mainly decorative designs such as meanders, but there were also some crude picture-symbols including simplified human figures, and some seals seem to show a definite Egyptian style. It is an open question whether these pictorial devices should be considered true writing.

The first phase of *M.M.* (*c.* twentieth–nineteenth centuries B.C.) saw an elaboration of the early decorative devices and the transformation of the representational drawings into true pictograms. It was the beginning of a true system of writing. Short pictographic inscriptions were cut on hard three- or four-sided seals. Building stones with linear masons' marks, and vases with property marks are attributed to the same period (Fig. Introd. 5*a*), but it is doubtful whether the latter should be regarded as a true script.

Still, we are at the beginning of writing; the script of this period may be termed 'Pictographic Class A' (Fig. 3.1*a*). The 'Pictographic Class B' of *M.M.*II is more developed and more cursive, and is represented not only by inscriptions on seals, made of rock crystal, jasper, cornelian and so forth, in three- or four-sided, or circular form, but also by inscriptions on clay tablets, labels or bars (Fig. 3.1*b*).

The symbols—numbering, according to Evans, about 135—represent (Fig. 3.1*c*) human figures, parts of the body, arms, domestic animals, religious symbols, ships, wheat, olive sprays, and also some geometric figures. This script according to Evans is already partly ideographic and partly phonetic, and may also contain determinatives. There is already a numerical system, influenced by the Egyptian one, a stroke for the unit, a dot for ten, a longer stroke for a hundred, a lozenge for a thousand; there are even signs for fractions. The direction of writing is sometimes from left to right and sometimes *boustrophedon* (alternately from left to right and from right to left).

Linear Scripts

In the last phase of *M.M.*, roughly in the seventeenth century B.C., the pictographic writing gave place to a linear script, which Evans distinguished into two classes:

'Linear A' (Fig. 3.2) and 'Linear B' (Figs. 11.5, 9). 'A' continues in *L.M.* I, roughly in the sixteenth century B.C.; until recently the documents of Linear B were attributed to about 1400 B.C. The discovery, in 1939, of the archives at Pylos, in S.W. Peleponnesus, containing about 600 tablets written in Linear B, and dated *c.* 1200 B.C., has shown conclusively that Linear B continued to be employed at least until that date.

The inscriptions of Linear A are engraved on stone or metal, incised on clay (Fig. 3.3*a*), or written with ink on pottery (Fig. 3.3*b*). Some have been found outside Crete (Figs. 3.3*c, d*), and prove that this 'Minoan' script spread abroad. The symbols number, according to Evans, about ninety; according to Sundwall, seventy-seven or seventy-six only; about one-third or perhaps nearly half can be connected with the pictographs of the preceding class.

Direction of writing, from left to right. The signs never face the beginning of the lines. The script seems to be partly ideographic and partly phonetic, although nothing can be said with certainty, the script being undeciphered.

Linear B, appearing at Knossos and at Pylos, is found on numerous clay tablets belonging to the archives of the Palaces. The script was therefore regarded as a kind of *aulic* or official script. The tablets seemed to be mostly inventories and accounts. According to Evans, the script in question was a parallel evolution to Linear A, but Sundwall may be right in regarding Linear B as a development of Linear A. The number of the main signs in Linear B is about 80, out of which 48 can be connected with Linear A. The numeration is also partly changed; the units are represented by upright lines, the tens by horizontals, the hundreds by circles, the thousands by circles with four spurs, and the ten thousands by similar signs with a dash in the middle.

Both Linear A and B are cursive and do not appear on the beautifully cut seals of the same period, which are purely pictorial. As Linear B has signs in common with Linear A, whose documents are found mostly in Crete, it may or may not have been developed out of it. In any case, the semantic relation between the two scripts is not certain, and so it has so far not been possible to decipher Linear A with the help of the knowledge won by the decipherment of Linear B. Linear B, which was a syllabic system of writing, will be dealt with in chapter 10.

ORIGIN OF CRETAN SCRIPTS

The problem of the origin of the Cretan writing does not seem very difficult. It was probably an indigenous creation influenced strongly by the Egyptian hieroglyphic writing, but the border-line between influence and direct derivation is not clear. Indeed, some scholars hold the theory of a derivation from the Egyptian writings, not only of the Cretan pictographic scripts, but also of the linear scripts. I do not think this is the case; no more than a certain percentage of the Cretan characters are identical, and that probably externally only, with the Egyptian hieroglyphs. Many Cretan pictographs are, without any doubt, of indigenous invention, since they are strictly connected with Cretan customs and religion and the indigenous agriculture.

In short, in my opinion, Cretan writing as a whole, and particularly the linear scripts, are an indigenous creation, although the inspiration came, without doubt, from Egypt. Some scholars suggest Anatolian connections; these are evident in the case of Cretan influence on the origins of the scripts of Asia Minor, but certainly not vice versa; chronological reasons alone would preclude such possibilities.

ATTEMPTED DECIPHERMENTS

UNTIL recently, the attempted decipherments of the Cretan scripts yielded no results, although a comparison with the Cypriote syllabary, which may have been a derivation of the Cretan scripts, would help in the interpretation of the Cretan signs—so it was thought—if the Cretan language were known. Indeed, the main difficulty of the decipherment of Cretan writing was to be found in the fact that the Cretan idiom has not been identified, and there are no clues to help in its decipherment. The one thing which seems pretty certain is that the Cretan language was a non-Indo-European idiom, but nothing can be said about its affinities. It has survived in a very few words—like *thálassa*, 'sea', and *terébinthos*, 'terebinth'—, and many names, like Knossos, Corinth, with the -*ss*- and -*nth*- terminations. A relationship with the indigenous peoples of Asia Minor is suspected.

I may mention Professor Hrozný's attempt at the decipherment of the Cretan scripts and language. As to the former, he suggested affinities with the Hittite hieroglyphic writing, the Indus Valley script, and partly also with the Babylonian cuneiform and early Egyptian hieroglyphic writing, but especially with the Phœnician letters. Of the last, as many as seventeen, out of twenty-two, resemble Cretan signs. The starting point of Hrozný's decipherment was the script of the inscriptions, written in Cretan 'Linear A' and partly in 'Linear B,' which were found in Greece, and were considered by him not only written in Cretan script, but also couched in Cretan language. In Hrozný's opinion, the Cretan language was Indo-European holding a mediate position between the language of the Hittite cuneiform inscriptions and the language of the Hittite hieroglyphic writing. No scholar was influenced by him.

After the decipherment of Linear B—*see* chapt. 10—Linear A was tackled by Professor Cyrus Gordon, who suggested that the language of the Linear A inscriptions is Semitic. This theory has not found many followers.

It is still premature in a general book of the kind of the present manual to discuss in detail the far-reaching conclusions of Gordon's attempted decipherment.

It is an open question whether the 'eteo-Cretan' inscriptions from Praïsos, written in the Greek alphabet but in an unknown language, are in ancient Cretan; some scholars hold that they are composed in an Indo-European speech; in this case they cannot be connected with the ancient Cretan tongue. Racially, the ancient Cretans seem to have belonged to the Mediterranean type; they were *dolichocephalic* (long-headed), 'brunet,' of short stature.

E

THE PHAISTOS DISC

Finally, mention must be made of the Phaistos disc (Figs. 3.4–6), which is not only the most remarkable of all inscriptions found in Crete, but also the first known stamped object of its kind. It was found on July 3rd, 1908, and belongs perhaps to about 1700 B.C. It is an irregularly circular terra-cotta tablet, about 6–7 inches in diameter, with characters impressed by means of separate stamps and printed on both sides of the disc, along a spiral line dividing the face of the disc into five coils; these are sub-divided, by vertical lines, into groups of symbols which may represent words or sentences. The characters are highly pictorial but they show no relationship with Cretan pictographs, except for a few casual resemblances. The signs number 241 in all; 123 (divided into thirty-one groups) on one face of the tablet, and 118 (thirty groups) on the other. The signs include a galley, hatchet, eagle, hide, carpenter's square, rosette, vase, house; characteristic is a male head with a plumed head-dress, frequently repeated. The Italian Professor Pernier, discoverer of the disc, recognized forty-five different symbols, which he divided into seven groups, of which the more important are human figures and parts of the body; animals and parts of animals; vegetation and plants; arms and tools. The direction of writing is from right to left; it starts from the external line; the human and animal figures face towards the right.

It is thought, largely on account of the plumed head-dress, that the disc was not of indigenous origin, but belongs to the south-west coast of Asia Minor; this theory is held by Evans, Levi, Pendlebury, and many others. Some scholars (among them Meyer, Mr. and Mrs. Hawes), connect it with the Philistines, who appeared on the historical horizon some 400 years later than the supposed date of the disc. Macalister thought that the coast of North Africa might have been the home-country of the disc. It must, however, be pointed out that until the present day nothing resembling it has appeared either in Anatolia or elsewhere, nor is there any trace outside Crete of a similar script, especially at the period in question. In conclusion, in my opinion there is not sufficient evidence as yet to exclude the possibility that the disc was of Cretan origin.

For one of the numerous attempted decipherments (by Professor B. Schwartz), see Fig. 3.6a.

BIBLIOGRAPHY

LAGRANGE, M.-J. La Crête ancienne, Paris, 1908.

BURROWS, R. M. The Discoveries in Crete, etc., London, 2nd ed., 1908.

EVANS, A. J. Scripta Minoa, London, 1909; The Palace of Minos at Knossos, 5 vols., London, 1921–35.

HAWES, CH. H. and H. Crete, the Forerunner of Greece, London and New York, 1909.

DUSSAUD, R. Les civilisations préhelleniques, 2nd ed., Paris, 1914.

HALL, H. R. Ægean Archæology, London, 1915.

SUNDWALL, J. 'Die kretische Linearschrift,' Archäologisches Jahrbuch, Berlin, 1915; 'Der Ursprung der kretischen Schrift,' Acta Academiæ Aboensis. Humaniora, 1920; 'Kretische Schrift,' Reallexikon der Vorgeschichte, Vol. VII; Altkretische Urkundenstudien, Åbo, 1936; Forsch. u. Fortschr., 1939, p. 293.

BOSSERT, H. TH. *Alt-Kreta*, Berlin, 1921; 3rd ed., Berlin, 1937.

FIMMEN, D. *Die kretisch-mykenische Kultur*, Leipsic and Berlin, 1921.

WACE, A. J. 'Early Ægean Civilization,' and 'Crete and Mycene,' *The Cambridge Ancient History*, I and II, Cambridge, 1923 and 1924.

GLOTZ, G. *La civilisation égéenne*, Paris, 1923.

WEICHBERGER, K. 'Die minoischen Schriftzeichen,' *Buch und Schrift*, 1930.

CHAPOUTHIER, F. *Les écritures minoennes au palais de Mallia*, Paris, 1930.

PERSSON, A. W. 'Schrift und Sprache in Alt-Kreta,' *Uppsalas Universitets Årsskrift*, Upsala, 1930; 'Die spätmykenische Inschrift aus Asine,' *Corolla archæologica principi hereditario regni Sueciæ Gustavo Adolpho dedicata*, Lund, 1932.

STAWELL, F. M. *A Clue to the Cretan Scripts*, London, 1931.

PENDLEBURY, J. D. S. *The Archæology of Crete*, London, 1939.

Illustrated London News, No. 5224, June 3rd, 1939.

VON BISSING, F. W. *Schrift im Alten Orient, Kypros und Kreta* (Otto, W. *Handbuch der Archæologie*, Vol. I), Munich, 1939.

BLEGEN, C. *Amer. Journ. of Archæology*, 1939, pp. 557–67.

DANIEL, J. F. *Amer. Journ. of Archæology*, 1941.

MERIGGI, P. *Die Antike*, 1941, pp. 170–6.

HROZNÝ, B. 'Kretas und Vorgriechenlands Inschriften, Geschichte und Kultur. I. Ein Entzifferungsversuch,' *Archivum Orientale Pragense*, 1943; 'Les inscriptions crétoises. II. Essai de déchiffrement,' *Archiv Orientální*, 1946.

PUGLIESE CARRATELLI, G. 'Le iscrizioni preeleniche,' etc., *Monumenti Antichi*, 1944.

KOBER, A. E. *Amer. Journ. of Archæology*, 1944.

MYRES, J. L. 'The Minoan Signary,' *Journ. of Hellenic Studies*, 1948.

MYLONOS, G. E. 'Prehistoric Greek Scripts,' *Archaeology*, Winter, 1948.

PAGE, D. *History and the Homeric Iliad*. University of California Press, 1959 (Chapter V: *The Documents from Pylos and Cnossos*).

SCHWARTZ, B. *Journ. of Near East. Studies*, XVIII, 1959, pp. 105–12, 222–8.

BRICE, W. C. (ed.), *Inscriptions in the Linear Script of Class A*, Oxford, 1961.

DAVIS, S. *The Phaistos Disc and the Eteocretan Inscriptions from Psychro and Praisos*, Johannesburg, 1961; *Greece and Rome*, XI, 1964, p. 106.

REVERDIN, O. *Crete and its Treasures*, London and New York, 1961.

EPHRON, D. 'Hygieia Tharso and Iaon: The Phaistos Disk', *Harvard Studies in Class. Phil.* LXVI, 1962, pp. 1–91 (with excellent bibliogr.).

POPE, M. W. *AegeanWriting and Linear A*, Lund, 1964 (with bibliogr.); 'The Origins of Writing in the Near East,' *Antiquity*, March, 1966.

GWYNN, B. V. *Some Observations on the Phaistos Disc*, Parts I and II, in MS. (1966).

See also Bibliography to the Section on Linear B in Chapter 10.

N.B. I am indebted to the late Professor Sir John (Linton) Myres for his kind help and for having supplied me with the lists of the main symbols of Linear A and B even before his article appeared in the *Journal of Hellenic Studies*. I am also grateful to my late friend Michael Ventris who prepared the drawings of Fig. 3.2*a* and 11.5*c*.

CHAPTER 4

Indus Valley Civilization and its Undeciphered Script

GENERAL SKETCH

TWENTY-FIVE years of excavation, exploration and study have added 2,000 years to the history of India, an achievement which may be considered one of the most remarkable in archæology. The old assumption that the Indo-Aryans, about the middle of the second millennium B.C., entered a land of primitive savagery, and created all the civilization of any importance in India, has, in consequence, proved totally wrong.

Complete cities of the third millennium B.C. have been unearthed; regular and well-planned streets running from east to west and from north to south, a magnificent drainage and water-system, a great public bath (for ritual purposes?) with a swimming pool, an enormous warehouse, bear evidence to a careful system of town-planning. Spacious and well-equipped private houses built of baked bricks and supplied with wells, one or more bathrooms and other excellent sanitary arrangements; sculpture in the round in alabaster and marble, large numbers of clay and faience figurines, stone, copper and bronze tools, elaborately carved stone or ivory seals with mysterious inscriptions (*see* below), stamp seals or seal amulets of faience with animal figures in relief (generally a bull, a rhinoceros, or an elephant), finely wrought gold, silver and copper-gilt jewellery, etched cornelian beads, faience bangles and other personal ornaments, and all the other objects which were found associated with this culture, bear witness to a very high degree of civilization.

There are many other evidences of a flourishing economy based on agriculture (wheat, barley, the date palm), and on cattle-rearing and domestication of animals. The buffalo, ox, sheep, pig, dog, elephant, and camel are known, but not the cat and the horse. Commercial relations were carried on by land and sea; spinning and weaving and manufacture of cotton were practised.

EXPLORATION, EXCAVATION AND STUDIES

The prehistoric cultures of N.W. India may be divided (according to Stuart Piggott, 1946), into the urban civilization of the *Harappa Culture*, and the various peasant cultures (excavated mainly since 1931). All of them are still an enigma not only to the lay public but also to the majority of the scholars concerned, because of insufficient excavation, the scarcity of analytical studies, and inadequate publication. Future excavations and studies should throw a flood of new light on the whole prehistoric civilization of India.

As yet, however, the Harappa Culture stands unparalleled, and it is with this civilization that we are concerned here. The excavated sites are few; the two great cities of Harappa (Punjab) and Mohenjo-daro (Sind), 450-odd miles away to the south-west, and some smaller towns (e.g. Chanhu-daro, south of Mohenjo-daro) and villages in southern Sind. The mounds of Harappa were the first to be recognized by modern science, having been noted by Masson about 1820, and studied by Cunningham in 1853, while some seals were published in 1875. More recent excavations were made in January, 1921, by Rai Bahadur Daya Ram Sahni, and very important excavations from 1926 to 1934 were conducted by Madhu Sarup Vats.

The prehistoric site of Mohenjo-daro, which from the architectural point of view is much more imposing than Harappa, was first recognized in 1922; the excavations of 1922–7 were carried out by Sir John Marshall, who, in 1931, in collaboration with S. Langdon, S. Smith and C. J. Gadd, published a magnificent work on Mohenjo-daro and the Indus Civilization, while in 1937 and 1938 E. J. H. Mackay published the results of his excavations conducted between 1927 and 1931. The researches of G. R. Hunter are recommended particularly for the study of the mysterious script, while many English and American scholars have contributed important studies on the cultural and chronological relationship with Mesopotamia and Iran in the fourth and third millennia B.C.

In a lecture delivered on 16 February, 1966 to the Constitution Club, New Delhi, Shri S. R. Rao (Deputy Director General of Archæology in India) stated that whilst Harappa, Mohenjo-daro and many other sites now belong to Pakistan, as a result of the systematic exploration of the region by the Indian Government, one hundred Harappan sites have been discovered, the most important being Lothal, a city with a systematic town-planning, warehouse and dockyard. The numerous Harappan objects include seals, sealings, stone weights, copper implements, ornaments in gold and semi-precious stones, and so on.

CULTURAL AND CHRONOLOGICAL RELATIONSHIPS WITH OTHER CIVILIZATIONS

Who were the people who created this Indus Valley civilization? Sir John Marshall's opinion, based on the few skeletal remains, is that the founders of these cities were of Mediterranean type, the great dolichocephalic race of southern Asia and Europe, who came in from the west. This opinion is acceptable, but it does not solve the whole problem. We do not know the name of the people, what language they spoke, whence they came, whether their civilization was wholly imported and whether, or how much, India herself contributed to its development. It is quite possible that the Indus Valley cultures were the blending of different local cultures with the civilization imported by newcomers from the west, who, according to some scholars, were probably related to the founders of the most ancient civilizations of northern Mesopotamia and southern Iran. However, nothing definite can be said as yet. The true origins of the Harappa Culture are still unknown and the problem of its appearance in India is still unsolved.

As to its date, there is no other means of establishing it except by synchronisms, *i.e.*, through the appearance of objects, clearly of Indus Valley origin, in foreign countries, and the parallel presence of foreign objects in India. In this latter case the correspondences seem to be rather vague and the chronology inconclusive. On the other hand, it is easier to relate the Harappa Culture to the history of Sumerian Mesopotamia on the basis of objects of Indus Valley origin found in Mesopotamia. More than thirty steatite seals, including a few with inscriptions in Indus Valley script, have been found in various Mesopotamian sites. Some of them belong definitely to the Harappa Culture, others may be suspected to have had this origin, or to have been made in Mesopotamia under Indian influence.

However, there is still no general agreement regarding their date, and in consequence there is none regarding the chronology of the Harappa Culture. Nevertheless, whereas the first discoverers (Marshall) dated it, in round figures, between 3250 and 2750 B.C., the tendency of more recent research is to lower these figures considerably. Sir Mortimer Wheeler in 1953 very cautiously opined that most of the oldest Akkadian seals found in the Indus Valley were Sargonid, one perhaps, pre-Sargonid, *i.e.*, if we follow Albright's chronology, dating about 2360 B.C. Therefore an earlier date than *c.* 2500 B.C. for the beginning of the Harappa Culture is unlikely. The latest seal may be Kassite, *i.e.*, about 1600 B.C. and so we cannot be far wrong in assigning the Harappa Culture to *c.* 2500–*c.* 1500 B.C.

THE INDUS VALLEY SCRIPT

The most noteworthy characteristic of the Harappa culture is the use of an indigenous script, which appears on large numbers of finely cut seals of stone or copper from various sites. Many of these seals are apparently amulets. At times the designs are beautiful, but for the most part the inspiration of the work seems to have been utilitarian rather than æsthetic. About 800 of these seals are inscribed (Figs. 4.1, 2). The writing may be defined as one of stylized pictographs (Fig. 4.3a).

All attempts at decipherment having hitherto failed—*see*, however, further on and Fig. 4.3b—the only thing we can do at present is to attempt an external classification of the signs. Even this is not easy because to differentiate between the various symbols is not always possible, and it is difficult to decide whether certain signs are graphic variations of the same character or different characters. Thus, according to some scholars (Gadd and Smith) the number of the characters of this script is 396; according to others (Langdon) 288, or (Hunter) 253. Smith has divided all the signs into three main groups; final signs, initial signs and numerals.

With about 300 symbols, the Indus valley script cannot be either alphabetic or syllabic; on the other hand, the number of symbols would be too small for a purely ideographic script. For this and other reasons, it is probable that the script is partly ideographic and partly phonetic (probably syllabic), and that it contains also some determinative signs. A large number of signs seem, in the opinion of some scholars, to bear a kind of accent which, according to Sir Mortimer Wheeler, would indicate phonetic maturity. This, however, would presuppose a phonetic script; but is the Indus valley script phonetic? This seems unlikely. Nearly all inscriptions being seal-inscriptions, it is probable that they represent mainly proper names. As Hunter points out, the absence of inscriptions other than on seals indicates that some perishable material must have been employed.

During the whole time of its existence the script apparently did not change; all seals and even the graffiti roughly scratched on potsherds show the same exactness. This fact seems to hint at the likely existence of a caste of scribes, who jealously preserved the old forms.

The script runs from right to left; although if there is a second line—which is rare, since no Indus valley inscription contains more than seventeen signs—it is read from left to right; we would thus have here a *boustrophedon* writing (*see* p. 359).

ORIGIN

Two other problems must be mentioned; the origin of the script, and its influence on the creation of other writings. It seems obvious that the Indus Valley script, which is rather schematic and linear in the extant inscriptions, was originally pictographic, but it is impossible to decide whether it was truly indigenous or imported. A connection between this script and the common ancestor of the cuneiform writing and of the early Elamite script is probable, but it is impossible to determine what the connection was. Some solutions—none of them can be considered certain—may be suggested, for instance: (1) The Indus Valley script was perhaps derived from an, at present unknown, early script, which may have been the common ancestor also of the cuneiform and early Elamite writings. (2) All three might have been local creations, one probably the prototype of the cuneiform or of the early Elamite script, being an original invention and the other two being creations inspired by idea-diffusion, *i.e.*, the knowledge of the existence of writing.

ATTEMPTED DECIPHERMENTS

Valiant but fruitless attempts have been made to decipher it. Meriggi attempted to explain the inscriptions ideographically, *i.e.*, considering the single symbols as true ideograms; Langdon and Hunter attempted to connect this script with the *Brahmī* alphabet, the prototype of nearly all the Indian scripts, but their views are not convincing. Even less convincing is a recent (1939) attempt by B. Hrozný, the famous decipherer of Hittite, to connect this script with Hittite hieroglyphic writing. According to Hrozný, the Indus Valley people were a mixed race ruled by Indo-European conquerors, and the same as the people who invented the Hittite hieroglyphic writing.

Hunter has followed the sound method of tabulating every occurrence of each sign. He believes that he has thereby obtained the interpretation of certain symbols, such as the ordinal suffix, the ablative and dative terminations, the numeral signs, the determinatives for 'slave' and 'son,' and the word 'son.' I am still sceptical of the results of his interpretation, but I believe that his method and, in a lesser degree, Meriggi's method are perhaps preferable to that of Professor Hrozný, who by way of 'it may be,' 'it seems,' 'it is possible,' 'it is probable,' has arrived at far-reaching conclusions. Hrozný 'recognizes' nearly 110 symbols as the 'most important phonetic signs'; of these no less than eighty-six are considered to be the symbols for six sounds only: forty-five signs for the sound *si, se, sa, s*. In my view, Professor Albright is right in writing 'While acknowledging Hrozný's brilliance as a decipherer, one cannot help feeling that he has tackled too difficult a task.'

A more recent decipherment, or attempt at decipherment, by the Indian scholar Sudhansu Kumar Ray, deserves particular mention. In his three 'memoranda'—*Indus Script: Memorandum No. 1*, New Delhi, 1963; *Indus Script: Memorandum No. 2*, New Delhi, 1965; and *Indus Script: Methods of my Study*, New Delhi, 1966—S. K. Ray states that he has succeeded in deciphering the Indus Valley script, which consists of alphabetic signs, biliteral and triliteral phonograms, ideograms and determinatives. The Brahmī script is a simplification of the Indus Valley script.

It is very difficult to express an opinion on this decipherment. As Ray says, 'The analytical study of the Indus script is an interesting but huge task. Naturally, it cannot be a one-man show.'

The difficulty of expressing an opinion is increased by the lack of scientific method employed for the decipherment. Indeed, Ray writes: 'My methods, it is true, are not academic. As a matter of fact, I did not like to begin with any scholarly method, because it has deluded many of us. . . . I am a graphic artist and an experienced typographer. . . . While working on the Indus script, I have never depended on any "scholastic attire". On the contrary, my approach was always that of a humble compositor in an ancient press at Mohenjo-daro; as if I had been composing the seal-texts with different types stored in its type-cases, five thousand years ago. What I wanted was that the typographical study should be undertaken at first before the philological studies.' Does this method work? I doubt it.

Moreover, even if this 'method' worked in the case of the relationship between the Indus Valley script and the Indian writing—a jump of two thousand years or so—would it entitle the decipherer to make the Indus script the prototype of the North-Semitic and the Greek alphabets? Still, *chi vivrà vedrà*!

SUPPOSED INFLUENCES ON OTHER SCRIPTS

As to the supposed influences of the Indus Valley script on other writings, we have already mentioned the suggested connection with the *Brahmī* alphabet. The theory that the latter was a derivative from the Indus Valley script has been widely accepted (by Langdon, Hunter, Hutton and others), but there are no traces of such a script in the most ancient Indian literature. Thus, I do not think there is any demonstrable connection between the Indus Valley script and the *Brahmī*—*see* also p. 257 ff.

Still less acceptable is Hunter's suggestion that the Indus Valley script influenced the creation of the Phoenician and the Sabaean alphabets and of the Cypriote syllabary, among others. The similarity of certain signs is purely external and accidental. Finally, a suggestion has been made by G. de Hevesy, that the Indus Valley script should be connected with the mysterious Easter Island writing; apart from some external resemblances (Fig. 4.4)—which in some cases are exaggerated by de Hevesy—between the symbols, the only connection between the two scripts, distant in time by thousands of years and distant in space by thousands of miles, seems to be the fact that both of them are still mysterious; to try to connect them would make the problem still more involved without hope of achieving any results—*see* also p. 98.

BIBLIOGRAPHY

The two most important works on Indus Valley civilization and its script are: Sir John Marshall, *Mohenjo-Daro and the Indus Civilization*, 3 vols., London, 1931; and G. R. Hunter, *The Script of Harappa and Mohenjodaro and its Connection with other Scripts*, London, 1934.

The reader may also consult the following publications:

WADDELL, L. A. *The Indo-Sumerian Seals Deciphered*, London, 1925.

VATS, M. S., *Excavations at Harappa*, etc., 2 vols., Calcutta, 1930.

PRAN NATH, 'The Script on the Indus Valley Seals,' *Ind. Hist. Quart.*, 1931; *The Decipherment of the Inscriptions of Harappa and Mohenjo Daro*, Benares, 1946.

GADD, C. J. 'Seals of Ancient Indian Style found at Ur,' *Proc. Brit. Acad.*, 1932.

DE HEVESY, G. 'Sur une écriture océanienne paraissant d'origine néolitique,' *Bull. de la Soc. Préhist. Franç.*, 1933; 'Osterinselschrift und Indusschrift,' *Orient. Liter. Zeit.*, 1934.

FÀBRI, C. L. 'Latest Attempts to Read the Indus Script,' *Indian Culture*, Vol. I, Calcutta, 1934.

FRANKFORT, H. 'The Indus Civilization,' etc., *Ann. Bibl. of Ind. Archæol. 1932*, Leyden, 1934.

MERIGGI, P. 'Zur Indusschrift,' *Zeitschr. der Deutschen Morgenl. Gesellschaft*, 1934; 'Über weitere Indussiegel aus Vorderasien,' *Orientalische Literatur Zeitung*, 1937.

MACKAY, E. J. H. *The Indus Civilization*, London, 1935 (German edition *Die Induskultur*, Leipsic, 1938); *Illustr. Lond. News*, 1936 (14 and 21.11); *Bull. Mus. of Fine Arts*, Boston, Oct. 1936; *Journ. of the Amer. Orient. Soc.*, 1937; *Further Excavations at Mohenjo-Daro*, Delhi, 1937–8.

HERAS, P. H. 'Mohenjo-Daro, the People and the Land,' *Indian Culture*, Vol. III, Calcutta, 1937; 'La escritura proto-índica y su desciframento,' *Ampurias*, Barcelona, 1940.

ROSS, A. S. C. *The 'Numeral Signs' of the Mohenjo-Daro Script*, Delhi, 1938.

DIKSHIT, K. N. *Prehistoric Civilizations of the Indus Valley*, Madras, 1939.

NORMAN BROWN, W. *Journ. of the Amer. Orient. Soc.*, 1939, Suppl. No. 4.

HROZNÝ, B. *Die älteste Völkerwanderung und die proto-indische Zivilisation* (also in Czech), Prague 1939; 'Inschriften und Kultur der Proto-Inder von Mohendscho-Daro und Harappa (ca. 2400–2100 v. Chr.). Ein Entzifferungsversuch,' *Archiv Orientální*, 1941 and 1942; *Les inscriptions proto-indiennes. Essai de déchiffrement* I (Vol. XIV of the Monographs of the Archiv Orientální, Prague); *Die älteste Geschichte Vorderasiens und Indiens*, 2nd ed., Prague, 1943; *Histoire de l'Asie antérieure*, etc., Paris, 1947.

PIGGOTT, S. *Prehistoric India*, Harmondsworth, 1950.

WHEELER, R. E. M. *The Indus Civilization*, Cambridge, 1953.

POPE, M. 'The Origins of Writing in the Near East', *Antiquity*, March, 1966.

CHAPTER 5

Hittites and their Scripts

HITTITES

THE Hittites, a group of peoples of differing ethnical and linguistic affinities who inhabited Asia Minor and northern Syria from the third to the first millennia B.C., developed a high civilization, and for more than 200 years (*c.* 1400–1200 B.C.) constituted one of the chief empires of the Near East.

In using the term 'Hittites,' we must make it clear that it is far from exact. The term is taken from the Bible, where the Hittites, in Hebrew *Ḥittim* or *benê-Ḥeth* (whence the German term 'Hethiter'), are frequently mentioned as one of the pre-Israelitish peoples of Palestine. They were even regarded as ethnically related to the Canaanites, Ḥeth being considered as the second-born son of Canaan (*Gen.*, X, 15); while Ezekiel, in speaking of Jerusalem, writes: 'Thy birth and thy nativity is the land of the Canaanites; the Amorite was thy father, and thy mother was an Hittite' (*Ez.*, xvi, 3, 45). On the other hand, many Biblical passages refer to Hittite kings of Syria.

Egyptian inscriptions mention the powerful *Kheta*-empire, whose rulers from the fifteenth to the thirteenth centuries B.C. fought with the Egyptians for the supremacy of Syria, but often concluded with them treaties and marriage-alliances.

In cuneiform inscriptions, there are various references: (1) The people of *Khatti* are mentioned in the eighteenth century B.C. as overthrowing the Ḥammurabi dynasty of Babylonia. (2) The power of *Khatti* in Syria in the fourteenth century B.C. is reflected in the Amarna Tablets. (3) Assyrian inscriptions show that the people of *Khatti* fought frequently with the Assyrians from the time of Tiglath-pileser I, *c.* 1100 B.C., until the final conquest of Carchemish by Sargon II, in 717 B.C. (4) Inscriptions from Urartu of the ninth–eighth centuries B.C. contain several allusions to the expeditions against the people of *Khatti*.

Greek references are very few and very vague. It is uncertain whether the *Keteioi* of the *Odyssey* (xi, 521), were really the 'Hittites.' Herodotus (i, 76) speaks of them as 'Syrians,' while Strabo (XII, iii, 9) terms them *Leukosyroi*, 'White Syrians.'

An ancient source of confusion has been introduced by the fact that these 'Hittites' were themselves usurpers of the name, which never occurs in Hittite inscriptions except in the form *Ḥattili*, meaning 'language of Ḥattušaš.' This language is, however, not that of the Hittite dynasty, but of the indigenous non-Indo-European people with their capital Ḫattušaš, who inhabited eastern Asia Minor prior to the invasion of the Indo-Europeans. It is therefore this indigenous people whom strictly speaking we should call Ḫattic or Hittite: but in order to avoid confusion some scholars call them 'Proto-Ḫattic' or Proto-Hittite.

On the other hand, the native term for the Indo-European language of the Hittite empire has not yet been discovered. Various terms have been suggested for this language, such as Kanish, from the important Hittite city of Kanesh or Kanish. Some Hittitologists accept the term *Našili* or *Nešumnili*. It is, however, preferable, following the great majority of scholars, to use the term 'Ḫattic' for the original meaning, *i.e.*, for the indigenous inhabitants of the land Ḫatti and their non-Indo-European language, and to employ conventionally the Biblical form of the same stem, Hittite, for the rulers of the Hittite empire and their Indo-European language. The term Hittite is used also for the Hittite kingdoms of northern Syria which existed after the Hittite empire came to an end, and for the 'Hittite hieroglyphic writing' (*see* below).

THE PEOPLES. THEIR LANGUAGES AND CIVILIZATION

Racially, the Hittites—as shown both on their own and the Egyptian monuments—belonged to the so-called Armenoid or Hittite type, one of the three brunette sub-types of the broad-headed white races. They were dark, robust, thick set, prognathous, with a backward sloping forehead, outward drooping eyes, a large, prominent and aquiline nose, the upper lip protruding and the chin somewhat retreating. They had straight black hair, no beard and lively black eyes. We can assume that this Armenoid type was a predominant among the Hittites, but it is highly probable that they were of mixed stock, as may be proved by linguistic evidence.

The rich royal archives, discovered in 1906–7 at Boghaz-Köy, now Boghaz Kalé, the ancient Ḫattušaš, capital of the empire, are the main source for the study of Hittite history and civilization, and practically our only source for the study of the Hittite language. Some documents are written in the Akkadian language and Akkadian cuneiform script, the diplomatic language and script of the ancient Near East, but the bulk is in the Hittite language and Hittite cuneiform script.

This Hittite language has been recognized as an Indo-European speech since its decipherment in 1915 by the Czech scholar B. Hrozný, who has been mentioned before.

Previously, fantastic theories were not lacking, and even connections with the Peruvian Kechua or the Japanese or the Aztecs were suggested. Nowadays, most philologists are agreed that Hittite was among the first, or the first, of the Indo-European languages to separate from the parent stock. But the American scholar Sturtevant holds that Hittite and the primitive Indo-European speech descended from a still earlier stock which he calls primitive Indo-Hittite. According to Sturtevant, Hittite alone preserves certain archaic features, while the historical Indo-European languages agree in the same innovations. Sturtevant's theory, accepted by some scholars (*e.g.*, Gœtze, 1945), has been attacked by others (*e.g.*, Gelb and Bonfante, 1945). The grammar of Hittite, its noun and verb form, are clearly Indo-European; but only a part of its vocabulary is so, Hittite showing large influences of other, non-Indo-European languages, particularly of the indigenous language, Hattic. We may assume that when the Indo-Europeans arrived in their new homeland, they found themselves faced by powerful tribes more numerous than themselves, and speedily realized that if they were to survive, they must not stand aloof but mix with the native tribes.

The ritual texts of Boghaz-Köy contain many passages in three other languages. One of these, *Luili* or *Luwian*, at first mistakenly regarded as a Finno-Ugrian language, is closely related to Hittite, but it seems to show a still greater influence of the in-digenous languages of Asia Minor. *Hurrian* is another native language; it is a non-Indo-European speech, and differs but very little from the language of the Mitanni (it is perhaps the same); while the third language, the Hattic speech already referred to, was the non-Indo-European language used by the indigenous population of Asia Minor, and belonged perhaps to the Caucasian group of languages. A language called *Palaumnili*, 'the language of the country of Pala,' is mentioned in the Boghaz-Köy documents, but nothing can be said as yet about it.

In short, the ethnical and linguistic evidence suggest that: (1) eastern Asia Minor was inhabited originally by the Hattic people, speaking a non-Indo-European tongue and belonging to the Armenoid type; (2) with the invasion of the Indo-European Hittites, the indigenous inhabitants did not disappear, but accepted the foreign Indo-European rulers, intermixing with them to such an extent that their own racial type became predominant, while their language strongly influenced the speech of the newcomers, and their ethnic name continued to be used abroad to describe the whole empire.

Hittite civilization possesses certain original characteristics, although its debt is great in every respect to other contemporary cultures, especially that of Babylon. That it reached a high level is abundantly shown by its rich literature, religious, lexicographical and historical, by the advanced military, administrative and political organization of the Hittite empire, and by the mastery in diplomacy shown by its rulers in the fifteenth–thirteenth centuries B.C. Moreover, the development of com-munications between the capital and the outlying provinces; the distinct individuality of its artistic monuments; the social, economic and juridical attainment displayed in the Hittite code and other documents; and more especially the creation of an indigenous script (*see* below) with the peculiar style of carving in relief the figures and characters of the inscriptions (Fig. 5.1, *a* and *b*); all combine to demonstrate that Hittite civilization was not inferior to that of the Egyptians, the Babylonians or the Assyrians.

The Hittite Pantheon is, roughly speaking, a mixture of Mesopotamian and local elements; Hittite mythology is strongly influenced by Sumero-Babylonian myths, and the interpretation of omens, also mostly of Babylonian origin, underwent essential modifications in particular details.

MAIN HISTORICAL EVENTS

CHRONOLOGY

(based on O. R. Gurney, *The Hittites*)

c. 1900 B.C.	Ḫatti living in Asia Minor
c. 1740–c. 1460	First Kingdom of Ḫattušaš
c. 1680–c. 1650	Labarnaš I
c. 1650–c. 1620	Labarnaš II = Ḫattušiliš I
shortly after 1600	Muršiliš I conquers Babylon
c. 1460–c. 1190	Second Kingdom of Ḫattušaš
c. 1400	Rise of the Mitanni
c. 1375–c. 1335	Šuppiluliumaš
c. 1334–c. 1306	Muršiliš II
c. 1306–c. 1282	Mutawalliš
c. 1286/85	Mutawalliš triumphs over Ramesses II in the battle of Qadeš
c. 1275–c. 1250	Ḫattušiliš III
c. 1250–c. 1220	Tudhaliyaš IV
c. 1190	Downfall of the Second Kingdom of Ḫattušaš
	Small Hittite states survive in Syria until
717	Sargon II of Assyria conquers Carchemiš

About the middle of the third millennium B.C., eastern Asia Minor was divided into a number of city-states; after a long struggle, one of them, the city of Ḫatti (Khatti), gained the supremacy over the others. During the last centuries of the third millennium B.C., an Indo-European invasion, identified by some scholars with the coming of the Luwians, took place, and about 2000 B.C., the Hittites, another Indo-European people, invaded the country. The city of Ḫatti, or Ḫattušaš, became the capital of a strong kingdom, which even succeeded in overthrowing the Babylonian empire. The good fortune of this Hittite empire did not last long (from c. 1740 B.C. to c. 1460 B.C.). During the sixteenth and fifteenth centuries B.C., it was in eclipse, but with the rise of the Hittite New Empire, which lasted from the beginning of the fourteenth to the end of the thirteenth century B.C., Hittite power had no rival on its eastern borders, and was no wise inferior to the Egyptian empire. Some Hittite kings were great military leaders and excellent diplomats and administrators. However, at the beginning of the twelfth century B.C. the Hittite empire came to an end, overthrown by barbarian hordes, attacking by land and sea, and known as the Sea-Peoples, probably of Indo-European affinities. The Hittite political and cultural centre was transferred to northern Syria, where small Hittite states arose, the most important of them being Carchemish. In the eighth century B.C. all these small kingdoms were conquered by the Assyrians: Carchemish fell to Sargon II in 717 B.C.

HITTITE HIEROGLYPHIC WRITING

The so-called Hittite hieroglyphic writing appears to have been employed for a few centuries only, when its users had already adapted the early Babylonian cuneiform writing to their language to form the script known as the Hittite cuneiform writing. This continued to be used until the end of the Hittite Empire, both for official purposes and for those of daily life.

There is no direct evidence that Hittite hieroglyphic writing was employed before 1500 B.C.; an inscription published by R. D. Barnett belongs roughly to that period. However, the majority of the inscriptions in this writing belong to the period of the Syrian Hittite states, particularly to the tenth–eighth centuries B.C. The latest inscriptions may be attributed to about 600 B.C. (Fig. 5.3b). It is a peculiar fact that in the Hittite mother-country not many such inscriptions have been discovered, the greater number having been found in northern Syria, particularly in Carchemish (Figs. 5.1a and b, and perhaps Fig. 5.3a), Hamath, and Aleppo. The majority of the inscriptions are in relief (Figs. 5.3a and b, and 5.6) or engraved (Figs. 5.3a and b, and 5.6) on stone monuments or on rocks, a few are on lead, some are on seals or are impressions in clay, the famous Tarkondemos seal is in silver. Some inscriptions, particularly those discovered at Ashur, present a more cursive type of writing (Fig. 5.4a).

The first discovery of a Hittite hieroglyphic inscription was made as early as 1812 in Ḥamath (N.-Syria), but the first serious studies were those of Sayce and Wright, who recognized that the inscriptions were the work of the Hittites and tried, without success, to decipher them by the methods that had been successful with the Egyptian hieroglyphic writing. However, thanks to the researches of these two scholars and many others (Forrer, Meriggi, Gelb, Bossert), Hittite hieroglyphic writing seems to have yielded to some extent to modern science. Not all scholars accept the results obtained, but there is increasing agreement on the main points of the decipherment.

The inscriptions begin at the top right-hand side. The direction of writing is generally *boustrophedon*—alternating in direction with the successive rows, like oxen ploughing a field—but sometimes from right to left or from left to right. The characters face always towards the beginning of the line. Appropriate signs separate the individual words.

The number of the signs is about 220, but according to Meriggi, the Hittite hieroglyphic system numbered as many as 419 symbols. They are partly ideographic and partly phonetic; the greater part of the characters are ideograms (Fig. 5.5a): for instance, the symbols for 'god,' 'king,' 'prince,' 'great,' 'city,' 'sacrifice,' 'land,' 'ox,' or signs representing animals, plants, parts of the body, and so forth, employed either as word-signs or determinatives. Fifty-seven signs have according to Gelb (Fig. 5.5b) a syllabic value.

With the discovery of the Karatepe inscriptions (*see* p. 190), it was thought that the long awaited bi-lingual inscription would provide the key to the final decipherment of the Hittite hieroglyphs. Indeed, some scholars have suggested that we have here a new 'Rosetta Stone.' Professor I. J. Gelb rejects this suggestion, asserting that the basic decipherment of the Hittite hieroglyphs was achieved between 1930 and 1935, that is many years before the discovery of the Karatepe inscriptions. These 'add greatly to our knowledge of the vocabulary,' but 'add nothing to our knowledge of Hittite hieroglyph grammar, and little, if anything, to our knowledge of writing.' Be this as it may, the Karatepe inscriptions are of paramount importance for our knowledge of the Hittite hieroglyphic writing: *see* also Figs. 5, 6 and 7.

ORIGIN OF HITTITE HIEROGLYPHIC WRITING

The problem of the origin of the Hittite hieroglyphic writing has not yet been solved. Some scholars have derived it from the Egyptian hieroglyphics, others from the Cretan pictographic script. In fact, the form of Hittite hieroglyphic writing is highly pictorial, as is indeed that of the Egyptian hieroglyphics and the Cretan pictographs, but this does not mean necessarily that it must have derived from one of them.

Indeed, a comparison between Hittite hieroglyphic writing and the Egyptian hieroglyphics shows that there is no direct connection between them; and while there are some external similarities between Cretan pictographs and Hittite hieroglyphics (Fig. 5.4*b*), no connection can be proved so long as the Cretan pictographic script remains undeciphered; the chronological difficulties must also be considered.

The present author's view is this: with the expansion of the Hittite Empire, the necessity arose for a monumental script for writing on stone. Perhaps impressed by the beauties of Egyptian writing, with which they were familiar, the Hittite rulers decided on a pictorial script as most appropriate for this purpose; Kroeber's theory of 'stimulus-diffusion' or 'idea-diffusion' would here seem to fit perfectly. At a late period a simpler cursive form of Hittite hieroglyphic writing developed (Fig. 5.4*a*).

As to the date of the creation of Hittite hieroglyphic writing, nothing can be said with certainty, but we may assume that the script existed already about the middle of the second millennium B.C., discounting certain opinions that are palpably absurd. Such are the views of the Italian Ribezzo that Hittite hieroglyphic writing was invented before 3000 B.C. and for over 1,000 years was excluded from official use and employed mainly on perishable material, and the theory of the famous Czech Hittitologist Hrozný that Hittite hieroglyphic writing originated perhaps at the beginning of the third millennium B.C. and was connected with the Indus Valley script.

BIBLIOGRAPHY

MESSERSCHMIDT, L. 'Corpus Inscriptionum Hettiticarum,' *Mitteil. der Vorderasiatischen Gesellschaft*, 1900 and 1906.
THOMPSON, R. C. *A New Decipherment of the Hittite Hieroglyphs*, Oxford, 1913.
HOGARTH, D. G., LAWRENCE, T. E. and WOOLLEY, C. L. *Carchemish*, 2 vols., London, 1914 and 1921.
HROZNÝ, B. *Die Sprache der Hethiter*, etc., Leipsic, 1916–7; *Über die Völker und Sprachen des alten Chatti-Landes*, Leipsic, 1920; *Les inscriptions hittites hiéroglyphiques*, 3 vols., Prague, 1933–7.

COWLEY, A. E. *The Hittites*, London, 1920.

HOGARTH, D. G. *Hittite Seals*, Oxford, 1920; *The Hittite Monuments of S. Asia Minor* (Ramsay, *Anatolian Studies*), Manchester, 1923; 'The Hittites of Asia Minor; and 'The Hittites of Syria,' *The Cambridge Ancient History*, vols. 2–3, Cambridge, 1924–5.

FRANK, C. *Die sogenannten hettitschen Hieroglypheninschriften*, etc., Leipsic, 1923.

ANDRÄ, W. *Hettitische Inschriften auf Bleistreifen aus Assur*, Leipsic, 1924.

GÖTZE, A. *Das Hethiter-Reich*, Leipsic, 1928; *Kulturgeschichte des alten Orients: Kleinasien*, Munich, 1933; *Hethiter, Churriter und Assyrer*, Oslo, 1936; 'The Present State of Anatolian and Hittite Studies,' *The Haverford Symposium*, New Haven, 1938; 'Hittite and Anatolian Studies' in *The Bible and the Ancient Near East* (ed. by G. E. Wright), London, 1961.

GARSTANG, J. *The Hittite Empire*, London, 1929.

GELB, I. J. *Hittite Hieroglyphs*, 3 vols., Chicago, 1931–42; *Inscriptions from Alishar and Vicinity*, Chicago, 1935; *Hittite Hieroglyphic Monuments*, Chicago, 1939.

BOSSERT, H. TH. *Šantaš und Kupapa*, Leipsic, 1932.

FORRER, E. O. *Die hethitische Bilderschrift*, Chicago, 1932.

STURTEVANT, E. H. *A Comparative Grammar of the Hittite Language*, Philadelphia, 1933; *A Hittite Glossary*, 2nd ed., Philadelphia, 1936.

CONTENAU, G. *La civilisation des Hittites et des Mitanniens*, Paris, 1934.

MERIGGI, P. *Die längsten Bauinschriften in 'hethitischen' Hieroglyphen*, Leipsic, 1934.

FURLANI, G. *La religione degli Hittiti*, Bologna, 1936.

FRIEDRICH, J. *Entzifferungsgeschichte der hethitischen Hieroglyphenschrift*, Leipsic, 1939; *Entzifferung verschollener Schriften und Sprachen*, Berlin, 1954.

DELAPORTE, L. 'Les Hittites,' *Dictionnaire de la Bible*, Suppl. IV., 1941.

DUSSAUD, R. *Les religions des Hittites*, etc. (Part II of an excellent work on oriental religions, Part I being E. Dhorme's *Les religions de Babylonie et d'Assyrie*), Paris, 1945.

GURNEY, O. R. *The Hittites*, London, 1952.

LLOYD, S. *Early Anatolia*, London, 1956.

LAROCHE, E. *Dictionnaire de la Langue louvite*, Paris, 1959.

HUXLEY, G. L. *Achæans and Hittites*, Oxford, 1960.

DIAKONOFF, I. M. and TSERETELI, G. V. (ed.), *Studies on Hittite and Hurrian* (in Russian; summaries in English), Moscow, 1961.

GAMKRELIDZE, T. V. 'The Akkado-Hittite Syllabary and the Problem of the Origin of the Hittite Script,' *Archiv Orientální*, 1961.

Many important articles have been published in *Revue Hittite et Asianique*, *Orientalische Literaturzeitung*, and other journals.

LITERATURE ON KARATEPE

BOSSERT, H. TH. *Archiv Orientální*, XVIII, 3, pp. 24 f.; *Jahrbuch für kleinasiatische Forschung*, 1, p. 272.; 'Found at last: a Bi-lingual Key to the previously undecipherable Hittite Hieroglyphic Inscriptions,' *Lond. Illustr. News*, 14. 5. 1949; 'Sur quelques problèmes historiques des inscriptions de Karatepe,' *Revue Hittite et Asianique*, 1949; and *Die Ausgrabungen auf dem Karatepe*, Erster Vorbericht, Ankara, 1950.

BOSSERT, H. TH. and ÇAMBEL, H. *Karatepe*. First report, Istanbul, 1946.

BOSSERT, H. TH. and ALKIM, U. B. *Karatepe*. Second report, Istanbul, 1947.

DUPONT-SOMMER, A. 'Azitawadda, roi des Danouniens,' *Revue d'Assyriologie*, 1948, pp. 161–88.

ALKIM, U. B. 'Les résultats archéologiques des fouilles de Karatepe,' *Revue Hittite et Asianique*, 1948/49 (with full bibliogr.).

F

GORDON, C. H. 'Azitawadda's Phoenician Inscription,' *J. Near Eastern Studies*, 1949.

HONEYMAN, A. M. 'Epigraphic Discoveries at Karatepe,' *Palestine Exploration Quart.*, 1949.

MARCUS, R. and GELB, I. J. 'The Phoenician Stele Inscription from Cilicia,' *J. Near Eastern Studies*, 1949.

OBERMANN, J. *New Discoveries at Karatepe*. A complete text of the Phoenician royal inscription from Cilicia, New Haven, 1949.

O'CALLAGHAN, R. 'The Great Phœnician Portal Inscription from Karatepe,' *Orientalia*, Rome, 1949; 'An Approach to some Religious Problems of Karatepe,' *Archiv Orientální*, 1950.

BOSSERT, H. TH., ALKIM, U. B., ÇAMBEL, H., ONGUNSUN, N. and SÜZEN, J. *Die Ausgrabungen auf dem Karatepe*, Ankara, 1950.

FRIEDRICH, J. 'Phönizisch-Punische Grammatik,' *Analecta Orientalia*, 32, Rome, 1951.

GURNEY, O. R. *The Hittites*, London, 1952.

BARNETT, R. D. 'Karatepe, the Key to the Hittite Hieroglyphs,' *Anatolian Studies*, III (1953), pp. 53–95.

CHAPTER 6

Chinese Language and Writing

CHRONOLOGY OF CHINA

2697–2205 B.C. (traditional dates)	The 'Five Emperors': at least seven names of 'Emperors' are given: legendary period.
2205–1766 B.C. (traditional dates)	The 'First Dynasty' or the Hsia-Dynasty (family name: Szu): names of seventeen 'Emperors,' probably only partly historical.
1766–1122 B.C. (traditional dates)	The 'Second Dynasty' or the Shang- or Yin-Dynasty (family name: Tzu). State capitals: Po, Ao, Yin.
1122–255 B.C.	The 'Third Dynasty' or the Chou-Dynasty (family name: Chi). Capitals: Fêng (1122–771) and Loyang (770–255).
255 or 221–206 B.C.	The Ch'in- or Ts'in- Dynasty (family name: Ying). Capital: Hsien-yang.
206 B.C.–A.D. 220	Han-Dynasty (family name: Liu).
206 B.C.–A.D. 25	Early or Western Han; capital: Ch'angan.
A.D. 25–220	Late or Eastern Han; capital: Loyang.
220–280	San-Kuo or Period of the Three Kingdoms:
220–265	Wei (family name: Ts'ao; capital: Loyang);
221–264	Shu-han (family name: Liu; capital: Ch'engtu);
229–280	Wu (family name: Sun; capital: Nanking).
265–420	Chin- or Tsin-Dynasty (family name: Szuma); capitals: Ch'angan and Loyang (265–316), Nanking (317–420).
386–589	Northern and Southern dynasties:
386–581	Northern dynasties: Northern Wei (family names: T'o-pa and Yüan; capitals: Tat'ung and Loyang);
	Western Wei (T'o-pa; Ch'angan);
	Eastern Wei (T'o-pa; K'aifêng);
	Northern Ch'i (Kao; Yeh);
	Northern Chou (Yü-wen; Ch'angan).
420–589	Southern dynasties: Sung (family name: Liu); Ch'i (Hsiao); Liang (Hsiao), Ch'en (Ch'en); capitals: Nanking (420–589) and Ch'angling (502–589).
(581) 589–618	Sui-Dynasty (family name: Yang; capitals: Ch'angan and Loyang).
618–907	T'ang-Dynasty (family name: Liu; capital: Ch'angan).
907–960	Wu Tai (the Five dynasties: Late Liang, Late T'ang, Late Ts'in, Late Han, Late Chou); capitals: K'aifêng, Loyang, Wei-chou. In the north, also the Khitan or Liao.
960–1279	Sung-Dynasty (family name: Chao); capitals: K'aifêng (960–1126) and Hangchou (1127–1279).
(1206) 1227–1368	Yüan- (or Mongolian) Dynasty; family name: Ch'i-wo-wen; capitals: Holin (Karakorum) and Peking (Tatu).

1368–1644	Ming-Dynasty; family name: Chu; capitals: Nanking (1368–1420) and Peking (1421–1644).
(1583) 1644–1911	Ch'ing- (or Manchurian) Dynasty; family name: Aisin Goro (Ai-hsin-chiao-lo); capitals: Liaoyang (1621–1643) and Peking (1644–1911).
1911 onwards	Republic; capitals: Peking; Nanking; Chungking; Peking.

ORIGIN OF CHINESE CULTURE

The early history of the Chinese people and the origin of their culture is in the twilight between the legendary and the historical. The so-called 'First Dynasty' or the dynasty of the Hsia, dated by Chinese tradition in the third millennium B.C., and in the first quarter of the second, is nowadays considered by some scholars as legendary. While there is much talk of the 4,000 or more years of Chinese history, we know that it existed, and perhaps also the names of several rulers.

The 'Second Dynasty,' or the dynasty of the Shang known also as Yin, is generally dated 1766–1122 B.C., but the chronology is far from certain. We have the names of the monarchs and certain information about the culture of that period. Chinese civilization had then already assumed definite characteristics. The bronzes attributed to the period exhibit high technical skill. Writing was already well developed; there were even some local varieties. When we come to the 'Third Dynasty,' or the dynasty of the Chou, commonly dated 1122–255 B.C., we find ourselves on firmer ground, although, while 'all authorities on the chronology of ancient China are in general agreement concerning both the relative and the absolute dating of events later than 841 B.C.,' for the period earlier than this, 'there is great difference of opinion both as to relative and as to absolute chronology' (H. G. Creel).

Professor Latourette points out that Chinese culture first definitely appears in what is now North Central China. 'It is significant that this is where the trade routes across Central Asia from the West enter China, and that Chinese civilisation is probably not as old as that of the ancient centres of the Western world. One cannot help but suspect something more than a coincidence.' I do not think, however, that the theory—suggested by some scholars—that Chinese culture derived from that of the Sumerians, can hold its ground. There is another theory, attempting to find in Central Asia the common source of both the earliest Mesopotamian and the earliest Chinese civilization, but positive proof is wanting. I agree, therefore, with Scott Latourette: 'We must wait for further discoveries in China and Central Asia before we dare give a final opinion.'

CHINESE LANGUAGE

The Chinese written language kept its intelligibility because each word had its symbol, which has been preserved (though it has undergone external development), whereas the spoken language was split up into many dialects mutually unintelligible. Thus, the literary language kept its unity, and an educated Chinese can read with equal facility an old text or a modern paper. But the pronunciation will vary greatly according to dialect. In a certain way, the case of the Arabic numerals or other mathematical symbols is a parallel one: 2, 3, 5, 7, etc., are understood everywhere, but when read they sound 'two,' 'three,' 'five,' 'seven,' etc., in English; *zwei, drei, fünf, sieben*, etc., in German; *due, tre, cinque, sette*, etc., in Italian; and so on and so forth.

The three well-known divisions of human speech are the isolating, the agglutinative, and the inflecting. The Indo-European and the Semitic languages offer familiar examples of the inflecting stage. The Caucasian languages, Japanese and Korean, some native languages of Africa and America, and numerous other languages are of the agglutinative type.

Chinese belongs to the Tibeto-Chinese family of languages, which are partly agglutinative and partly isolating. No family of languages has such a great number of languages and dialects, and of speakers, and is spoken over so wide an extent, as the Tibeto-Chinese family, extending from Peking to Baltistan (N. Kashmir), and from central Asia to southern Burma. The Tibeto-Chinese family is sub-divided into the Tibeto-Burmese and the Thai-Chinese sub-families. Chinese, belonging to the latter, was probably once an agglutinative speech, but it is now monosyllabic—*i.e.*, consisting of monosyllabic words—and isolating, that is to say, it does not contain terminations or other grammatical forms. The old prefixes and suffixes having been worn away, and having lost their significance, are replaced by independent words without the possibility of a real inflexion; it is also lacking in a syntactical structure. Thus, as a rule, if it is desired to modify the sense of a word in respect of time, place or other relation, this is not done by adding a prefix or a suffix (that is by incorporation of a vowel or a syllable with the main word, as is done in the agglutinative languages), but by adding some other separate word having a meaning of its own.

Therefore, the language as spoken in its many dialects and written in various ways, consists of monosyllables, and compounds made from monosyllables (Fig. 6.00), exactly as 'house-maid' is made from 'house' and 'maid.' To express the distinction between a 'cow,' an 'ox,' and a 'calf,' the compounds 'mama-cow,' 'papa-cow,' and 'little cow' are used. There is an extreme paucity of grammatical structure in Chinese; strictly speaking, there is no Chinese grammar, and hardly any syntax. Each word is a stem word; it never changes; the same word can be a verb, a noun, an adjective; the meaning is determined only by the place of the word in the sentence: for instance *ta* ('greatness') and *jên* ('man') in this order (*ta jên*) means 'great man,' whereas *jên ta* means 'man is great.' There is no distinction between 'am,' 'are,' 'is,' 'was,' 'were,' 'have been,' 'has been,' 'will be,' and so on; all these forms are expressed by the invariable form 'be.' The characteristic 'tone' in Chinese speech, which appears so difficult to a foreigner, is of great help in mastering the language.

A tone is an acoustic pitch or musical stress, or change of pitch, and pitch only. The tones are of utmost importance; they are just as important as the vowel itself. Without the tone, the word has some other meaning or no meaning at all. A word pronounced on a low pitch means one thing, on a rising pitch another, on a high pitch another. The Chinese tones have, thus, nothing to do with stress or length or abruptness of the Indo-European languages. So characteristic are the tones in the Tibeto-Chinese languages, that some scholars have suggested terming them 'polytonic.' The number of tones varies from language to language, from dialect to dialect; for instance, Thai and Cantonese each have six, Burmese has but two tones. In Professor Nienmin Sun's opinion, the four Peking tones are pronounced as follows:

(1) the upper-level tone, with an even, flat voice and an indifferent intonation, like the word 'thing';

(2) the lower-level tone, with a considerable raising of the voice, as in the case of English 'what?';

(3) the rising tone, with a falling and rising voice, as in the case of 'well!';

(4) the vanishing tone, with a brief and resolute lowering of the voice in the case of English 'now!'.

The possible combinations of the 450 or so Chinese syllables amount, thanks to the tones, to about 1,200. Some dialects consist of a greater number of different syllables; the Peking dialect is said to consist of about 1,380; the Canton dialect of 1,868; and the Amoy dialect of about 2,500. Even so, the number of words would still be insufficient for the speech of a highly civilized people, if it did not include very many *homonyms*, that is, words with the same sound but different meaning. If these homonyms were to be written in alphabetic script, the ambiguity would certainly be much greater than it is in the present writing, in which, for example, for the sound *shih* there are 239 characters (54, 40, 79 and 66 respectively for the different tones). According to Professor Karlgren, in the Mandarin dialect (*see* below) there are 69 words which are pronounced *i*, 59 *shih*, 29 *ku*, and so forth, and the average number of words for each syllable is ten. However, thanks to the means of variation (that is, the tones), each word is pronounced in a different musical note, and the Chinese language has been able to retain its power of expression. Another device which helps one to understand the exact meaning is the employment of 'synonym-compounds' (Karlgren), that is to say, pairs of words of similar meaning, which make each other recognizable; cf. also 'pidgin English' *look-see* (E. H. Minns).

Professor B. Karlgren has classified the development of the Chinese language as follows:

(1) *Archaic Chinese*, from the earliest time to the Early Han dynasty;

(2) *Old Chinese*: later documents, and particularly those of the Sui and the T'ang dynasties, present new linguistic developments. The transliteration of foreign words which, in ancient times, were adopted in Chinese, throw some light on the old pronunciation. More valuable still, and more numerous, are the Chinese words lent to Annamite or Vietnamese (end of T'ang-Dynasty), to Korea and Japan (*see* further on);

(3) *Middle Chinese* is preserved in works belonging to 1050 onwards;

(4) *Old Mandarin*, already fully developed in the dictionary *Hung-wu-cheng-yün*, of 1375; and

(5) *New Mandarin*: this is the official language as it is spoken in the northern and western provinces of China.

The linguistic problem of China is still further complicated by the existence of a great number of local dialects. The principal dialects may be mentioned:

I, the Mandarin (*kuan'-hua*), divided into Northern (Peking), Southern (Nanking), and Western (Yün-nan and Szŭ-Ch'uan);

II, the dialects of the region Wu (the Shanghai or Sungkiang dialect; the Wen-chou; and the Ningpuo dialect);

III, the dialects of the region Min or Fuchien province (the Fuchou dialect; the Amoy dialect; and the Swatow dialect);

IV, the dialects of the region Yüeh or Kuang'tung province (the Cantonese and the Hakka dialects).

The Sino-Japanese dialect originating from a Wu dialect of the fifth and sixth centuries A.D. is called *Go-on*, whereas the later Sino-Japanese pronunciation, known as *Kan-on*, springs from a Northern dialect of China. The Sino-Korean derives from a Northern dialect of about A.D. 600.

In recent times, thanks to the modern educational system, the so-called Mandarin dialect has become a kind of standard spoken dialect and has even been accepted for the new literature. It has thus become the *Kuoyu* (the 'National Language'), the standard language in China, as distinct from the various dialects. (The Mandarin, originally a Northern Chinese dialect, has three main variations, *see* above; but the Peking one predominates; it is much distorted, with its great changes.)

CHINESE WRITING

Chinese writing is the only ancient 'ideographic' or rather 'analytic' system of writing which is not only still used, but is employed by a nation comprising nearly a quarter of the population of the world, and in a country larger than the whole European continent. Indeed, the number of Chinese speakers is estimated at 700,000,000 (24 per cent of mankind). Notwithstanding its extensive use by a people of high and ancient culture, with a history of almost 4,000 years, the internal development of Chinese writing has been practically imperceptible. The main evolution of the Chinese characters was, indeed, technical, external—'calligraphic' as we may call it. Chinese writing has never passed beyond the analytic stage and, thus, has never reached even the syllabic stage. The reason for this lies in the character of the Chinese language, as just expounded.

ORIGIN OF CHINESE WRITING

The problem of the origin of Chinese writing is still open. A dependence on the cuneiform writing has been suggested, but this does not seem probable, considering that Chinese signs are pictograms. There is, however, no doubt that there exist certain internal similarities between the Chinese and the early cuneiform and Egyptian writings, as indeed between all the ideographic-analytical scripts. The already mentioned theory, emphasized by the American scholar A. L. Kroeber, of 'idea-diffusion' or 'stimulus-diffusion' gives us perhaps the right solution. On this basis it is urged that the generic idea of the existence of writing (after it had developed in Mesopotamia, in Iran, in the Indus Valley, and perhaps in some other nearer places, still unknown to us), when it reached China, might have induced some great Chinese personality to 'invent' or 'create' a particular script for the Chinese speech.

Local traditions connect the origins of Chinese writing with the eight mystic trigrams much used in divinations, *pa kua* (Fig. 6.1*a*) meaning 'eight divination-diagrams,' and the hexagrams, derived from the trigrams, or with a knot-device similar to the ancient Peruvian *quipus* (*see* p. 7).

On the other hand, the use of tally-sticks, the typical Chinese gestures (Fig. 6.1*b*), ornamentation, ritual symbolism and so forth, certainly played a more or less considerable part in the creation of the Chinese characters.

(*See* B. Chang Chêng-ming, *L'écriture chinoise et le geste humain*, etc., Shanghai and Paris, 1937.)

Professor W. Perceval Yetts, the great authority on Chinese writing, rightly points out that in the earliest Chinese documents extant—which may belong to the Shang-Yin dynasty (perhaps from 1766 to 1122 B.C.)—'the principles of script construction were the same as when Hsü Shên defined them in the *Shuo wên* Preface (second century A.D., D.D.); and they have not changed since.' Professor Yetts, therefore, comes to the conclusion that 'structural evolution came to an end at some distant date unknown to us.'

Indeed, unless we admit—as Professor Yetts argues—that this structural evolution of Chinese writing was in progress for several centuries before the second millennium B.C., we may suggest that the Chinese system was created artificially, as a whole, by someone who knew already of the existence of writing. On the other hand, it should be borne in mind that as far as China's remote past is concerned, 'All is vague and uncertain prior to the beginning of the historical period about 800 B.C.; and much that has been written is mere conjecture concerning the Shang-Yin dynasty, which is supposed to have reigned for six centuries and a half, till overthrown by the Chou in 1122 B.C. Still more misty is the Hsia dynasty, reputed forerunner of the Shang-Yin, and very little is known of the conditions in China during the third and second millennia B.C.' (W. P. Yetts).

The attempt of some scholars to prove the Sumerian origin of the primeval writing of China, implies at least great exaggerations. The general conception of writing might perhaps have been borrowed, directly or indirectly, from the Sumerians, but not a single sign taken from the Sumerian system can be found. A dependence on the Egyptian hieroglyphics is still more unlikely. Chinese writing bears a thoroughly Chinese stamp, no less than Chinese art and customs. As Professor Creel points out, at present, the issue is a dead one. 'New evidence may appear, but as matters stand there is no proof that Chinese writing originated or was developed anywhere save within the limits of what we know as China.'

According to L. C. Hopkins, followed by other scholars, the earliest development of Chinese writing came from the hands of the professional diviners, while according to others it was due to the progressive complexity of governmental machinery.

The date of the invention or creation of Chinese writing is also unknown; we may assume, however, that it was already in existence in the early second millennium B.C. On the other hand, the prehistoric, or even legendary, emperors Fu-hsi, Shên-nung, and Huang-ti, or the secretaries of the latter, Ts'ang Chieh and Chü Sung (the *tzu shen*, 'gods of writing'), to whom the invention and systematization of the Chinese characters is attributed, are placed in most chronologies in the first half or about the middle of the third millennium B.C., discounting a traditional attribution to 4477–4363 B.C.

Chinese tradition, according to the *Shuo wên* (*see* below), attributes to the first of the aforementioned 'gods of writing,' the invention of the *pa kua*; to the second, the invention of a knot-device memory aid; whereas, on the initiative of Huang-ti, Ts'ang Chieh created the *ku wên*, or 'ancient figures.' The *ta chuan*, or 'great seal' characters, according to the *Shuo wên* appeared the first time in the *Shih Chou p'ien*, a book written by Chou about the ninth century B.C. About 213 B.C., the *hsiao chuan*, or 'small seal' characters are said to have been introduced by Li Szŭ and two other ministers of the first Ch'in emperor, whereas a simpler script, called *li shu*, 'was adopted to facilitate the drafting of documents relating to the multitude of prisoners at that time' (W. P. Yetts).

This Chinese tradition was until recently believed to correspond more or less to historical facts. Nowadays, serious sinologists not only consider the first of the mentioned 'inventors' of Chinese writing as legendary culture-heroes, but also deny the existence of Chou, the reformer of writing. *Chou* according to L. C. Hopkins means 'deduction from omens observed,' or 'an oracular response,' and the *chou wên* characters would, therefore, probably indicate the writing employed for instance in the 'Honan bones' (*see* below). Li Szŭ is certainly a historical person; however, he is now considered not as an inventor of a system of writing but as an ancient 'standardizer' of Chinese script.

On the other hand, as Professor Creel has pointed out, excavations in Chinese neolithic sites have so far produced nothing which appears to be writing, although 'Chinese archæologists are searching with special attention for traces of primitive Chinese writing.' On the whole, there is no evidence to show that Chinese writing existed before the second millennium B.C.; the earliest extant Chinese inscriptions, on bones, belong (*see* below) to the fourteenth century B.C.; whereas the earliest extant Sumerian inscribed documents are attributed to the late centuries of the fourth millennium B.C., and the Egyptian to the early centuries of the next millennium.

EARLIEST INSCRIPTIONS

Epigraphy has constituted an important branch of Chinese scholarship from the time of Ou-yang Hsiu, who in the middle of the eleventh century A.D. published the book *Chi ku lo po wei*, Notes on over 400 inscriptions dating from earliest times to 'Five Dynasties.' A bibliography published over forty years ago (*Chin shih wên*, 'inscriptions on metal and stone,' Peking, 1926) contains some 800 works on epigraphy.

Until the end of the last century there were very few inscriptions extant, other than those on bronzes, which could be attributed with certainty to a period anterior to the last quarter of the third century B.C. (Ch'in dynasty). According to H. G. Creel, 'most of the things used by these people, which might have come down to us as evidence of their culture, were very perishable. ... Their books were written on tablets of wood or bamboo. In the wet climate of China such materials decay quickly.' The inscriptions on pottery vessels (with characters usually single) and jade—one of them being inscribed with eleven characters—are rare. Probably no stone inscriptions are extant; the 'Yü Tablet' (Fig. 6.2), the supposed copy of a prehistoric Chinese inscription of the eighteenth century B.C., is according to Professor W. Perceval Yetts 'an undoubted forgery.'

The famous inscribed 'Stone Drums' (Fig. 6.2)—now in the gateway of the Confucian Temple of Peking—(ten roughly chiselled mountain boulders or truncated pillars, one and a half to nearly three feet high, with an average circumference of seven feet) are commonly attributed to the reign of Hsüan (827–782 B.C.) or even to the last century of the second millennium B.C. According to Professor Yetts and other scholars, they belong to the third century B.C. It is generally accepted that they are inscribed in *ta chuan*.

A great many of the Chinese bronzes are inscribed (Fig. 6.2), but till the end of the Shang-Yin dynasty (1122 B.C.?) such inscriptions were usually very short, some containing only one or two characters indicating a name, or suggesting a sacrificial function, dedications or invocations to ancestors—for instance, the inscription 'For Father Ting,' and so forth. On the other hand, some of the bronze inscriptions, especially those of later times, are quite lengthy. Many of them are very accurately dated, to the year, month, and day, but the dates recorded are of little help: some are of merely local importance; others add the specification 'of the king' (which obviously was sufficient at the time), but omit the name of the king.

An epoch-making discovery was made in 1899. In the village Hsiao-t'un (perhaps the ancient town of Ho Tan Chia), near An-yang, in northern Honan, there were excavated, in circumstances imperfectly known, several thousand fragments of oracle bones and tortoiseshell engraved in ancient Chinese characters (Figs. 6.2–4). They are in a surprisingly good state of preservation, and this is probably due to the protective properties of loess in which they were buried. Some of the fragments show an uncommon smoothness and finish. 'The surfaces of some were polished until they gleamed like glass. Most of them had queer oval notches on their backs, and T-shaped cracks' (H. G. Creel).

The exact date of these inscriptions is uncertain; some scholars attribute them to the latter part of the Shang-Yin dynasty, others think that the writing recorded was already obsolete in the period to which these bones are attributed. According to Professor Creel, 'we have a great many bones which unquestionably date from the reign of Wu Ting (1324–1266 B.C.). Whether some of our inscriptions go back to the time of Pan Kêng (1401–1374 B.C.) is a question which is still being debated.'

The inscriptions are generally believed to be remains of archives left by royal diviners; they are responses given to private individuals who came to seek the aid of divination in the affairs of daily life. 'It is not to be supposed that once these bits of bone reached the hands of scholars they were deciphered easily. At first, even Chinese palæographers could make out no more than a word here and there, while the very nature of the inscriptions remained a mystery.' However, 'it is now possible to read most of the characters in almost any inscription and to understand quite adequately the meaning of most inscriptions. This adventure in scholarship has been as thrilling and in many ways as notable an achievement as the decipherment of the Egyptian hieroglyphics.' 'Most of this work has been by Chinese scholars' (H. G. Creel).

Although these inscriptions are very short—most of them containing not more than ten to twelve characters, and the longest hardly exceeding sixty—their importance from the point of view of the history of writing is paramount; there appear to be some 3,000 different characters, of which however not more than some 600 have been identified. Amongst the various difficulties offered by the script of the 'Honan bones,' there is that of the uncertain discrimination between different characters and mere variants of a character.

STORY OF CHINESE CHARACTERS

In the long history of Chinese writing, there are two fields of development: (1) the external form of the Chinese symbols, and (2) the systematization of the Chinese characters according to form, sound and meaning.

External Form of Chinese Symbols

The main changes in the shapes of the single symbols, from the original pictograms (Fig. 6.6) to the classical Chinese writing, were due to the changes in the materials used for writing; thus, when the narrow bamboo stylus was used and writing was done on silk and slips of bamboo or wood, lines and curves could be easily traced, and they were all equally thick; these peculiarities are shown in the *ta chuan*, 'greater seal' characters (Figs. 6.2 and 5), and the *hsiao chuan*, 'lesser seal' characters (Fig. 6.2). Bronze tools, shaped like the 'burin' or knives were employed for the engraved script.

The invention of *pi*, the writing-brush made of elastic hair, enormously influenced the formal evolution of the script; curves became straight or nearly so, and the likeness to the original pictures was in most cases destroyed (the transformation of the early cuneiform writing presents a good parallel case). This invention is traditionally attributed to General Mêng T'ien, the builder of the Great Wall (during his campaigns against the Hsiung-nu of Mongolia), who died about 210 B.C., but must precede him. The fluid was generally a dark varnish. A further development of the external forms of the character came with the invention of paper in A.D. 105.

MAIN VARIETIES OF CHINESE WRITING

On the whole, the main varieties of early Chinese writing are the *ku wên*, or 'ancient figures,' the *ta chuan*, or 'greater seal,' the *hsiao chuan*, or 'lesser seal' and *li shu* or 'official script' (Figs. 6.2 and 5). 'These four figured in the original *Shuo wên*, where most of the leading or 'entry' characters were in 'lesser seal,' the text was in *li shu*, and examples of *ku wên* and *chou wên* (synonymous with *ta chuan*) were cited in order to explain steps in evolution' (W. P. Yetts). *See* also Fig. 6.5.

These varieties are traditionally regarded as belonging to the following periods of development:

(1) Period of origin (Shang-Yin-Dynasty and beginning of Chou-Dynasty): *ku wên*; apparently there are 1,098 preserved characters, in 4,200 forms.

(2) Period of first reformation (Chou-Dynasty): according to tradition, about 800 B.C. the imperial historian Chou made up a list of all the existing characters and determined the form which henceforth should be employed in official documents; this 'reformed' writing is known as *Chou-wên* (Chou-script) or *ta chuan* ('greater seal' script).

(3) After some time, decadence again set in; the scribes did not take too much care; the characters were still too intricate and often were changed at will, the more so as the political division of China called forth new centres of writers. Moreover, Emperor Shih-huang-ti (246–209 B.C.) of the Ch'in-Dynasty ordered all books to be burnt, because of a grudge against the literary men, who indulged in too much disapproval of his politics. This vandalism and the vandalism with which all wars were waged (especially when the aim was to extirpate a decaying dynasty) have resulted in the present deplorable lack of ancient Chinese documents: large libraries went up in flames, and even bronze works of art bearing old characters were dashed to pieces or melted. This chaos was followed by the Period of the second reformation. About 213 B.C. Li Szŭ, Minister of the 'imperial book-burner,' drew up a new list (*San ts'ang*) of 3,300 characters, now known as the *hsiao chuan* ('lesser seal').

(4) The Period of the invention of *pi*, the writing-brush (*see* above). This change of writing implement produced a new form of script, the calligraphic *li shu* or *li tzŭ*. The curved strokes became rectangular, the round lines became square, the right angles thicker; the horizontal lines abbreviated and thinner, and when descending, the brush

painted coarser strokes; indeed, the pressing down of the point produced a spurt. The first Han-Dynasty (206 B.C.–25 A.D.) made good the loss of the books, and although few works had escaped destruction, an extensive literature came into being, of which many copies (in later editions) are extant; also the little that had remained from antiquity was collected and re-edited, partly in the ancient Chinese characters.

The *Shuo wên* mentions five other varieties of Chinese writing employed under the Ch'in-Dynasty (221–206 B.C.), the *k'o fu*, inscribed on tallies; the *ch'ung shu*, fanciful characters shaped like birds or insects; the *mu yin*, used for stamps or seals; and two varieties of the *shu shu*, one employed for official notices, and the other used for inscriptions. Another style of writing, the *pa fên* lies midway between the *hsiao chuan* and the *li shu*.

There are no documents extant written uniformly in any of the most ancient scripts. On the earliest bronzes extant and on the 'Honan bones,' the *ku wên* predominate, some of which are already in an evolved form, but there are also some simple pictograms, as well as some symbols which may be regarded as *ta chuan*. According to L. C. Hopkins, both the *ta chuan* (traditionally, as already said, attributed to *c.* ninth century B.C.) and the *hsiao chuan* (attributed to *c.* 220 B.C.) have been created under the Shang-Yin dynasty, whereas Li Szŭ, as already mentioned, was only a standardizer of the *hsiao chuan*. Concerning the *li shu*, it is generally accepted that this style was created under the Ch'in dynasty, but whereas the tradition attributes its invention to Ch'êng Miao, according to Prof. Yetts 'more likely it resulted from the administrative needs of the centralized government recently set up.' Abbreviation and simplification are the main characteristics of the *li shu*, which became the prototype of the various Chinese scripts employed for nearly 2,000 years till the present day.

Out of the *li shu*, many forms of writing developed. Mention may be made of the following (*see* Fig. 6.5):

(1) The actual classical script *k'ai shu* (called also 'clerkly hand'), which was invented by Wang Hsi Chih (A.D. 321–379).

(2) The very cursive *ts'ao shu*, or 'grass character' which 'so curtails the usual strokes as to be comparable to a species of shorthand, requiring special study. It seems to have been in use as early as 200 B.C.' (Latourette).

(3) The *lien pi tzŭ*, also known as *hsing shu* or "running hand", used in ordinary correspondence, developed at a much later period.

(4) Various, less important, cursive scripts, such as *Sung tzŭ* (the cursive script of the Sung dynasty, A.D. 960–1279), the *lien tzŭ*, and other forms of writing.

Figures 6.11–13 give a selection of Chinese calligraphy in cursive script. Figures 6.14–17 represent Chinese printed books or manuscripts.

Among the great number of various scripts used in the past or today, we have mentioned only the most important, but Chinese calligraphy knows of many other forms of writing. There are, or were in the past, more than a hundred ornamental scripts with fancy names (Fig. 6.00), such as the script of the precious stones, the script of the stars, of the clouds, of the dragons, of the birds, of the bells and vases, of the tadpoles (*k'o tou tzŭ*; Fig. 6.2—probably a forgery, see p. 68), and many magic scripts. The tadpole script was an archaic form: certain characters are very like tadpoles, for instance the character 'son,' etc.

Systematization of Chinese Characters

The systematization of the Chinese characters is the second important field in the history of Chinese writing. The natural development of an ideographic-'transitional' script and its many different varieties; the spreading of the knowledge of writing all over the immense territory of China, and various other obvious factors, were the causes of the excessive multiplication of symbols, including numerous useless doubles, abbreviations, cursive varieties, faulty forms due to the ignorance of many scribes, and so forth.

In order to reduce this mass of written symbols, Chinese scholars from fairly early times devoted considerable effort as well as ingenuity to introduce some method in the intricate system of writing. The earliest classification, *Erh ya*, seems to have been compiled about the eleventh century B.C. It is a collection of terms and phrases arranged under nineteen categories. According to tradition, about the ninth century B.C., Chou compiled a catalogue of the standard symbols (*ku wên* or *chou wên*, now considered synonymous with *ta chuan*); this tradition, however, is doubtful (*see* above). At the end of the third century B.C., Li Szŭ published the official catalogue *San ts'ang*, containing 3,300 characters (*see* above).

Four centuries later, in the second century A.D., Hsü Shên published the lexicon *Shuo wên* (or *Shuo-wên-chieh-tzŭ*, meaning 'An Explanation of Ancient Figures and an Analysis of Compound Characters'), amending and commending Li Szŭ's catalogue and classifying the Chinese characters. He reproduced 10,516 symbols (of which 9,353 were simples and 1,163 doubles), under 540 rational *keys* or *radicals* (classifiers). Hsü Shên 'was chiefly concerned with the form of characters and their origins, though he added brief explanations of the meanings. His sources were the surviving classics, the writings of his predecessors, and inscriptions on bronze and stone' (W. P. Yetts). The *Shuo wên* may still be regarded as the main source for the study of ancient Chinese writing.

Phonetic Dictionaries

In its beginnings, Chinese writing perhaps represented the spoken language: even this problem is still *sub judice*; while according to B. Karlgren, the writing of the early period 'was the natural reproduction of the spoken language', in H. G. Creel's opinion, it 'was couched in an idiom quite different from the spoken tongue.' However, at the time there was no need to reproduce in writing the many bisyllabic compounds used as words in the modern common speech.

On the whole, nowadays Chinese writing represents the forgotten speech of several thousand years ago. It appeals, therefore, to the eye rather than to the ear. The Chinese written language, notable for its richness of expression and flexibility, is in its rules of composition, its style and its vocabulary, far removed from the vernacular, which, besides, developed dialects so different that they are mutually almost unintelligible. Scholars who cannot understand each other's speech, can read the same books and communicate by writing.

Tradition assigns the invention or the development of Chinese 'phonetics' or spelling, to Buddhist missionaries from India; in translating their sacred books into Chinese, they were anxious to introduce some system in order to read and explain their holy scriptures correctly. However, the most important system of Chinese spelling is the syllabic method *fan ch'ieh*, which gives the sound of a character by writing two other characters, the first to represent the initial and the palatalization, the second to represent the final—including the vowel—, the labialization and the tone.

About A.D. 500, Chinese scholars started the publication of the phonetic dictionaries, *yün fu*, classified according to the sound and the tone of the words.

Of the original *Yü p'ien*, published in A.D. 543, which was the earliest dictionary to employ the *fan ch'ieh* system, only a fragment, found in Japan, is extant. In A.D. 601 the *Ch'ieh yün* was published; it was a phonetic dictionary of northern China. It was enlarged in 751 under the title *T'ang yün*, which was included in the *Shuo-wên-chieh-tzŭ*, compiled in 986 by an imperial commission presided over by Hsü Hsüan. It was revised again, in 1011, by an imperial commission and republished as *Kuang yün*, arranged according to 206 finals, classed under the four tones. This was followed by various revisions and editions until K'ang-hsi (1662–1722) published his famous dictionary containing as many as 44,449 (subsequently increased to at least 50,000) Chinese characters, classified under 214 keys only, the greater part of the symbols, more than 30,000, being either out of date or doubles or faulty signs.

CLASSIFICATION OF CHINESE CHARACTERS

The Chinese lexicographers divide the Chinese characters—each one being a more or less stylized picture or ideograph—into six categories, *liu shu*, or 'six scripts' (Fig. 6.7, 8). They are, to be exact, 'modes of expressing spoken words in writing' (W. P. Yetts).

(1) The symbols *hsiang* or *hsiang hsing*, 'likeness of shape,' *i.e.*, pictorial—consisting of the simple drawings of objects, of animals and human beings, and so forth—form the basis of Chinese writing, as of any ideographic 'transitional' script.

The *hsiang* may be called pictograms; they are *wên*, crude 'figures,' attempts to picture natural objects; in other words, rude pictorial symbols representing the human figure, certain parts of the body, various animals, fishes, stars, plants, objects of daily life, and so forth. A circle (often oblate or flattened on one side) with a dot or stroke inside it, represented the 'sun'; the sketch of the crescent or the waning moon, represented the 'moon.' A range of rugged peaks stood for 'mountain.' The rugged sketch of an infant stood for 'child.' A round hole indicated 'mouth.' A 'tree' was represented by a sketch of the branches and the roots. Lines representing the swiftly running waters of a stream stood for 'river' or 'water.' At the same time, the picture-symbol *jih*, 'sun,' stood also for 'day,' the picture-symbol *yüeh*, 'moon' stood also for 'month,' and so forth. The *Shuo wên* contains 364 examples of *hsiang*.

(2) The *chih shih*, 'indicative' or self-explanatory characters: abstract ideas are represented by signs borrowed from other words related to them in meaning, or by the representation of the gesture usually accompanying the abstract idea in question; a handicraft for instance is represented by the tool commonly employed in the trade in question.

Not many characters belong to this class. It contains the simplest numerals, such as 'one,' 'two,' 'three,' represented by one, two or three lines; the words *shang*, 'above,' and *hsia*, 'below,' represented by a dot or a short line drawn *above* or *below* a longer line. 'To speak,' *yên*, is represented by the sketch of a 'mouth' with a 'tongue' in it; *tan*, 'dawn,' but also 'day,' is represented by the 'sun' above the 'horizon,' and *hsi*, 'evening,' by a pale moon, that is by the 'moon' without its internal line. Similar devices were employed for writing 'half' or 'middle,' 'square' or 'zone,' 'limit' or 'border' or 'frontier' (Fig. 6.00). A 'sprout' proceeding out of the 'ground' stood for 'to be born,' 'to bear' or 'to begin,' and so forth.

(3) *Hui i*, or suggestive, *i.e.*, logical aggregates or suggestive compounds which 'assemble ideas' (*hui i*); they are based on a natural association of ideas, their significance being indicated by their component parts. The characters belonging to this class, by their composition convey the required meaning; they thus may be called 'ideographic combinations' (W. P. Yetts), or simply 'ideograms.' On the whole, abstract ideas are here represented by characters consisting of two or more simple figures put together.

These simple figures may be identical (for instance, two figures 'woman' indicate 'quarrel'; three such figures, 'intrigue'; two figures 'east' indicate 'everywhere'; two symbols 'tree' indicate 'forest'); or different (*e.g.*, 'to hear' and 'door' indicate 'to listen'; 'man' and 'word' = 'sincere,' 'true,' 'trust'; the symbol for 'brightness' is composed of 'sun' and 'moon'). This is a very interesting class, and the *Shuo wên* contains 1,167 such characters. China being an overwhelmingly agricultural country, the characters connected with agriculture are numerous; for instance, 'field' + 'strength' = 'young'; 'tree' + 'hand' = 'to collect'; 'wheat' + 'knife' = 'profit.'

(4) *Chuan chu*, 'Deflections and Inversions'; the meaning of certain words is indicated, by generalization or analogy, by characters representing other words, or by turning the sign upwards, downwards or sidewards; for instance, the character 'prince' written in a different way, gives the meaning 'officer' or 'clerk'; the character 'corpse' is a derivation from the symbol 'man'; the word 'old' is deflected to form the word 'ancestor.' The character for *tzu*, 'child,' turned upside-down, is used in ancient inscriptions to represent *t'u*, 'childbirth'; the symbol *shan*, 'mountain,' rotated through a right angle, indicates *fou*, 'tableland,' 'huge' (Yetts). See Fig. 6.0.

The exact meaning of *chuan chu* is uncertain. Professor Yetts suggests 'shifted axes.' 'Sometimes the entire character is reversed, while the pivotal axis remains constant.' Professor Latourette suggests 'turned round' or characters related in sense. However, as Latourette points out, this class is concerned only with peculiarities in the use of characters.

(5) *Chia chieh*, 'borrow-help' or adoptive, that is characters borrowed, for words hitherto unwritten, which resemble in sound but not in sense. 'Accidental and intentional interchange of characters representing homophones' (Yetts). Also 'false borrowing' and arbitrary symbols as well as 'misused' characters, that is, 'borrowed because of close resemblance in aspect, despite unlikeness either in sense or sound' (Yetts).

On the whole, certain *homophones* (Fig. 6.6), that is, words having the same sound but a different meaning, or conventional symbols or local homophones, or even erroneous characters once adopted for words for which there were no other signs, continued to be employed as regular Chinese characters; for instance, one of the symbols for 'scorpion,' *wan*, has been borrowed from *wan*, '10,000'; the symbol for 'bear' which indicates 'a large mammal with long, shaggy hair, rudimentary tail and plantigrade feet', may also be used for 'bear' = 'to support,' 'to endure'; *tsu*, 'foot,' is used to express *tsu*, 'to be sufficient'; *kò*, 'to sing,' indicates also 'elder brother,' the latter being pronounced *ko* in popular speech only; the character *shih*, 'arrow,' represents also *shih*, 'dung'; the symbol for *ti* or *t'i*, 'a stalk bearing a flower or fruit,' in early times represented also the word *ti*, 'emperor': later an extra stroke was added on the top, indicating that the *ti* in question was the one 'above the heads of men', that is the 'sovereign ruler' (Fig. 6.00). This class includes also names of certain animals and plants.

(6) *Hsing shêng*, meaning 'formulate' or 'harmonize sound,' generally known as phonetic compounds, number 7,697 in the *Shuo wên* and constitute the most important class; nowadays, it comprises over seventy-five per cent of the Chinese characters. It is this class—the cuneiform and the Egyptian writings presenting similar but not identical devices—which made it possible to increase, even to excess, the number of Chinese symbols, and at the same time to eliminate the obvious ambiguities.

Indeed, the characters belonging to this class consist of two parts: (*a*) the phonetic element (Fig. 6.8), which, in analogy with the characters of the preceding class, gives the rough pronunciation, the sound of the symbol; and (*b*) the radical or determinative, the element (represented above or below, inside or around, to the right or the left, of the other element) which indicates the meaning of the word or, rather, to which category of things or ideas the concept denoted by the character belongs. For instance, the phonetic element *kò*, 'fruit' (a picture of a cluster of fruit on a tree; 'radical' tree), together with the determinative *shui*, 'water,' indicates *k'o*, 'river'; together with the determinative 'words,' it expresses *k'ó*, 'to inquire, to examine,' and so forth. Analogously, *kûng* (meaning 'handiwork'), added to the 'radical' or 'determinative' *shui*, 'water,' indicates the word *kung*, now pronounced *chiang* or *kiâng* in

Peking and *kong* in some southern dialects, meaning 'river'; added to the determinative *hsin*, 'heart,' it means *k'ŭng*, 'impatience'; with *yên*, 'words' = 'quarrel.' Similarly, the character *fâng*, 'square,' employed as a phonetic, and added to the character 'earth,' used as a determinative, indicates the word *fâng*, 'place'; *fu*, 'no' or 'not' (used as a phonetic) + 'mouth' = *fu*, 'to oppose'; + 'grass' = *fu*, 'luxuriant'; + 'heart' = 'sorry,' + 'hand' = 'to shake off' or 'to wave to and fro' (Latourette). So the words 'drink,' 'eat,' 'inquire,' 'throat' belong to the radical 'mouth'; the words 'way,' 'transport,' 'far,' 'near' belong to the radical 'foot.'

The first two classes are also called *wên*, or 'figures,' whereas the classes (3) to (6) are also known as *tzŭ*, or 'derivatives.'

Modern Chinese Writing (*see* also Figs. 6.18–21.)

Lastly, we must mention the classification employed in modern Chinese dictionaries, which may be of three kinds: (*a*) according to the meaning of the words; (*b*) phonetic, according to the sound and the 'tones'; and (*c*) graphic, according to the external form of the symbols.

(*a*) Chinese compound characters can be decomposed into primary elements; Chinese ancient authors recognized some 500–600 elements, but modern scholars estimate the number at 300 (Fig. 6.9).

(*b*) We have already mentioned that the phonetic elements used in Chinese, including the 'tones,' cannot be very numerous; according to some Chinese scholars there are 'one thousand mothers of sound,' which is roughly right.

(*c*) From the external, graphic or calligraphic, point of view, the Chinese characters can be reduced to nine strokes; some of them, however, having two or even four variants, so that some symbols contain as many as seventeen strokes (Fig. 6.8).

On the whole, the Chinese characters are classified in 214 categories, distinguished by certain radicals or 'keys,' according to the number of strokes they contain; for instance, 'keys' 1st–6th contain one stroke; 7th–29th, two strokes; 30th–60th, three strokes, and so forth; the keys 212th–213th, sixteen strokes; the 214th 'key,' seventeen strokes. The single 'keys'—some of which contain over 1,000 characters, for instance, the 140th 'key,' *ts'ao*, 'grass,' 1,431 symbols; the 85th 'key,' *shui*, 'water,' 1,354 characters—are classified internally according to the number of strokes of the phonetic element. See also Fig. 6.0.

The direction of writing Chinese is vertical, from top to bottom; the columns begin on the right-hand side of the page.

Chinese writing being too complicated, not many peoples adopted it or adapted it to their language; but the Japanese (pp. 123 ff.), the Vietnamese and some non-Chinese peoples of China did so. It has, however, influenced externally many other scripts, particularly the Mongolian scripts (pp. 249) and the Korean alphabet (pp. 353 ff.).

The Vietnamese, belonging to the same linguistic family as the Chinese, formerly used two types of script based on Chinese characters, (1) *chũ' nho* ('the script of the learned language'), consisting of Chinese ideograms as employed in Chinese, and (2) *chũ' nôm* ('the script of the spoken language'), *i.e.*, Chinese characters adapted to Vietnamese. Nowadays, they employ the *quôc ngũ* or *chũ quôc ngũ* ('the script of the language of the country'), which is an adaptation of the Latin alphabet to Vietnamese; it consists of twenty-four letters and a series of accents and other diacritical marks to express the six tones of the Vietnamese tongue.

REPRESENTATION OF CHINESE BY LATIN ALPHABET

The difficulties in representing Chinese by the Roman script are very great. As long ago as 1859, Sir Thomas Wade devised a system of Romanization for Chinese words. It is still the most widely accepted among English speakers, and I have used it here. A new system, called *Gwoyeu Romatzyh* (or G.W.), meaning 'National Language Latin Script,' was promulgated by the Chinese Ministry of Education in 1928. In this new system, aspirates and tones are indicated not by auxiliary signs or figures, as in the old systems, but by slight variations in the spelling. *See* W. Simon, *The New Official Chinese-Latin Script*, London, Probsthain, 1942.

BIBLIOGRAPHY

EDKINS, J. *Introduction to the Study of the Chinese Characters*, London and Hertford, 1876.

COUVREUR, S. *Dictionnaire classique de la langue chinoise*, Ho-kien-fu, 1904.

CHALFANT, F. H. 'Early Chinese Writing,' *Memoirs of the Carnegie Museum*, Pittsburgh, 1906; 2nd edition, 1911.

FORKE, A. 'Neuere Versuche mit chinesischer Buchstabenschrift,' *Mitteil. des Seminars für Orientalische Sprachen*, Berlin, 1906; *Der Ursprung der Chinesen auf Grund ihrer alten Bilderschrift*, Hamburg, 1925.

LAUFER, B. 'A Theory of the Origin of Chinese Writing,' *American Anthropologist*, 1907; *Archaic Chinese Bronzes of the Shang, Chou and Han Periods*, New York, 1922; *Paper and Printing in Ancient China*, Chicago, 1931.

HOPKINS, L. C. *The Development of Chinese Writing*, London, 1910; 'The Chinese Numerals and their Notational System,' *J. Roy. Asiat. Soc.*, 1916; 'Pictographic Reconnaissances', the same journal, 1916-28; 'L'écriture dans l'ancienne Chine,' *Scientia*, 1920; 'On Chinese Characters' (in T. L. Bullock, *Chinese Written Language*, 3rd ed.), Shanghai, 1923.

OWEN, G. *The Evolution of Chinese Writing*, Oxford, 1911.

CHALMERS, J. *An Account of the Structure of Chinese Characters*, 2nd ed., Shanghai, 1911.

CHAVANNES, E. *Les Documents Chinois découverts par Aurel Stein*, Oxford, 1913.

FRANKE, O. and LAUFER, B. *Epigraphische Denkmäler aus China*, Berlin, 1914.

VISSIÈRE, A. *Premières leçons de chinois*, 2nd ed., Leyden, 1914.

COURANT, M. *La langue chinoise parlée*, Paris and Lyon, 1914.

SCHINDLER, B. 'Die Prinzipien der chinesischen Schriftbildung,' *Ostasiatische Zeitschrift*, Berlin, 1915-6, 'Die äussere Gestalt der chinesischen Schrift,' the same journal, 1916-8, etc.

KARLGREN, B. 'Contributions à l'analyse des caractères chinois,' *Hirth Anniversary Volume*, London, 1922; *Sound and Symbol in Chinese*, London, 1923; *Analytic Dictionary of Chinese and Sino-Japanese*, Paris-Vienna, 1923; *Philology and Ancient China*, Oslo, 1926; *The Romanization of Chinese*, London, 1928; *Yin and Chou in Chinese Bronzes. On the Script of the Chou Dynasty*, Stockholm, 1936; *Grammata Serica, Script and Phonetics in Chinese and Sino-Japanese*, Stockholm, 1940.

BULLOCK, T. L. and GILES, H. A. *Progressive Exercises in the Chinese Written Language*, London and Shanghai, 1924.

CH'U TÊ-I, *Bronzes antiques de la Chine*, Paris and Brussels, 1924.

KOOP, A. J. *Early Chinese Bronzes*, London, 1924.

TADAHIRO TAKATA, *Kochu hen*. Encyclopædia of Archaic and Seal Characters, Tokyo, 1925.

BLAKNEY, R. B. *A Course in the Analysis of Chinese Characters*, Shanghai, 1926.

MASPERO, H. *La Chine antique*, Paris, 1927; *La langue chinoise*, Paris, 1934.

WIEGER, L. *Chinese Characters*, Hsien-hsien, 1927, and Peking, 1940; *China throughout the Ages*, Hsien-hsien, 1928.

WICHNER, F. 'Über den chinesischen Kalender,' *Archiv für Schreib- und Buchwesen*, 1927; 'Lateinschrift in China', the same journal, 1930.

HACKMANN, H. *Der Zusammenhang zwischen Schrift und Kultur in China*, Munich, 1928; and in *Archiv für Schreib- und Buchwesen*, 1930.

KÜMMEL, O. *Chinesische Bronzen*, Berlin, 1928.

SIRÉN, O. *Les peintures chinoises dans les collections americaines*, Paris, 1928.

PERCEVAL YETTS, W. *The George Eumoforpoulos Collection. Catalogue of the Chinese and Corean Bronzes*, etc., 3 vols., London, 1929–32; *The Cull Chinese Bronzes*, London, 1939.

SCHUBERT, J. 'Etwas über die Versuche zur Vereinfachung der chinesischen Schrift', and 'Lateinschrift oder Nationalschrift in China,' *Archiv für Schreib- und Buchwesen*, 1930.

MO-JO KUO, *Studies of Inscriptions on Bronzes of the Yin and Chou Dynasties*, Peking, 1931.

BRITTON, R. S. *The Couling-Chalfant Collection of Inscribed Oracle Bone*, Shanghai, 1935.

COOLE, A. B. *Coins in China's History*, Tientsin, 1936.

CREEL, H. G. *The Birth of China*, etc., London, 1936; *Studies in Early Chinese Culture*, Washington, 1938.

KIM, CH. 'Die Lesung einiger alter Bronze-Inschriften,' *Ostasiatische Zeitschrift*, Berlin, 1937.

CHÊN-YÜ LO, *San tai chi chin wên ts'un*, Corpus of nearly 5,000 ancient Chinese bronze inscriptions, n.p., 1937.

MULLIE, J. *The Structural Principles of the Chinese Language*, Peking, 1937.

SCHULER, P. B. *Altes Erbe des neuen China*, Paderborn, 1937.

YANG YÜ-HSUN, *La Calligraphie chinoise depuis les Han*, Paris, 1937.

CHIANG, Y. *Chinese Calligraphy*, etc., London, 1938.

VAN GULIK, R. H. *Mi Fu on Ink-Stones*, Peking, 1938.

KÊNG JUNG, *Chin wên pien. Inscriptions on Bronzes*, 2nd ed., Ch'ang-sha, 1939; *Shang chou i ch'i t'ung k'ao. The Bronzes of Shang and Chou*, 2 vols., Peking, 1941.

HUANG CHÜAN-SHÊNG, *Origine et évolution de l'écriture*, etc., Paris, 1939.

KENNEDY, G. A. *Serial Arrangement of Chinese Characters*, Yale University Press, 1941.

VON ROSTHORN, A. 'Zur Geschichte der chinesischen Schrift,' *Wiener Zeitschrift für die Kunde des Morgenlandes*, 1941.

MARGOULIES, G. *La langue et l'écriture chinoises*, Paris, 1943.

SIMON, W. *How to Study and Write Chinese Characters*, London, 1944; *1,200 Chinese Basic Characters*, London, 1944; 3rd rev. ed., Hollywood-by-the-Sea, 1957.

SKALICKA, V. 'Sur la typologie de la langue chinoise parlée,' *Archiv Orientální*, Prague, 1946.

SCOTT LATOURETTE, K. *The Development of China*, 6th ed., Boston and New York, 1946.

LODGE, J. E., WENLEY, A. G. and POPE, J. A. *A Description and Illustrative Catalogue of Chinese Bronzes*, Washington, 1946.

BACHHOFER, L. *A Short History of Chinese Art*, New York, 1946.

HEDON, H. H. 'Das neue Schrift-Chinesisch', *Universitas*, II, 6 (June 1947) [on James Yen's Simplified Script].

CORTA, F. *De Latinizatione Linguae Sinensis* (Dossiers de la Commission Synodale), Shanghai, 1948.

NIEN-MIN SUN, 'Art and Language Meet,' *The Christian Science Monitor*, 12.3.1949.

CHIANG YEE, *Chinese Calligraphy*, 2nd ed., London, 1954.

HSIA, T. T. *China's Language Reforms*, Yale, 1956.

WAN, J. F. and HSIA, T. T. *Most commonly used Chinese Characters*, Yale, 1957.

FENOLLOSA, E. F. *Chinese Written Character as a Medium for Poetry*, Washington, 1957.

TS'UN-HSUIN CH'IEN, *The pre-printing Records of China; a Study of the Development of Early Chinese Inscriptions and Books*, Chicago, 1957.

LO TCHANG-PEI and LIU CHOU-SHIANG, 'Vers l'unification de la langue chinois'; and WOU JU-TCHANG, 'La réforme de l'écriture chinoise,' *Recherches Internationales à la Lumière du Marxisme*, Paris, 1958.

DOBSON, W. A. C. H. *Late Archaic Chinese*, Toronto, 1959; *Early Archaic Chinese*, Toronto, 1961.

CHAPTER 7

Pre-Columbian Scripts of America

GENERAL SKETCH

To understand the particular importance of the existence of writing in ancient Mexico and Central America, one must view it in relation to the general problem of ancient culture-building. It has been shown that there is a striking similarity in place, time and culture underlying the great civilizations of antiquity. These have originated and developed, roughly speaking, simultaneously, mainly in great river valleys situated in one continuous land-area, within the northern sub-tropical belt, and nowhere else. They appeared successively later in time the farther we travel, east or west, from western Asia. Their culture was based on the knowledge of writing, the employment of metals, the cultivation of wheat, the domestication of certain animals, the use of the wheel, and town-building. No other area presents this homogeneity in fundamentals. The indigenous civilization of Mexico and Central America seems— but it is far from being certain—to form in some respects an exception; it would be perhaps the only exception. It is because of this problem, which is the main reason to our dedicating a whole chapter to that region, that we must deal briefly with the other problems concerning the cultures of ancient Mexico and Central America.

For the American pre-Columbian mnemonic devices (and particularly for the Peruvian *quipus*) *see* p. 7; for the recent ideographic scripts of Amerindians *see* p. 110 f., and for the Cherokee syllabary *see* p. 128 ff.

'MYSTERY' OF ANCIENT MEXICO

The first European conquest in the West Indies, during the last years of the fifteenth, and the first years of the sixteenth centuries, had proved to be a failure to the Spanish adventurers in search of riches. Then a rumour began to spread that beyond the mountains of the adjacent mainland there lived the emperor of a people called the Aztecs who dwelt in golden castles and slept in golden beds and ate from golden plates. Ferdinand (Hernan) Cortés (1485-1547) and his 900 adventurers landed in Tabasco on 12th March, 1519. In two years and five months, with the help of fifteen horsemen and fourteen cannon he conquered the capital and annihilated the 'Aztec empire.'

Nearly 2,000 ruins, some of them with carved, sculptured walls and doorways, and figures in stucco, the remnants of ancient cities—which, strangely enough, were not used as residential centres, but almost certainly as religious centres, and perhaps as markets and courts of justice—and the remains of villages, are scattered over nearly all of the present Republic of Mexico, and the neighbouring countries to the south. Sculptures, great monoliths, small terra-cotta masks and idols, constantly ploughed up in some parts of the country, arms, jewels, and many other objects there discovered are proofs of a certain degree of culture attained by the native peoples. The Mexicans played various ball games with that strange thing which we now call an indiarubber ball. The 'devilish scrolls,' as the Spanish fanatical priests described the Mexican manuscripts (which were diligently destroyed by the archbishop Zumárraga), and the tablets, slabs and monoliths carved with 'hieroglyphics' showed that the natives were acquainted with writing.

The conquerors were obviously puzzled by the many strange, mainly truncated, pyramids—the great pyramid of Cholula measures 1,440 feet upon its base, its height is 200 feet, the area on its summit measures more than an acre—and the mysterious courts and quadrangles, with carved stone halls about them ('mansions in skies,' as some explorer called them), found on the high slopes and table lands of Mexico. The sculptured façades of 'palaces' and pyramid-temples, ruined and abandoned in the dense, tropical forests of Yucatán, and particularly the sculptured *stelae* of great beauty and individuality protruding strangely from the jungle, have excited the imagination of romantic travellers and explorers.

The accounts of the conquerors show that the Spaniards were vastly impressed with the evidences of the wealth of the native rulers and the advanced culture of the priestly classes; we know now, however, how highly coloured those accounts were, and that the exaggeration was due partly to the wish of the adventurers to impress their monarch and their people at home, and partly to their great ignorance. Indeed, the native peoples who showed a certain development in some respects, were barbaric in others; their temples were the scenes of cruelties and human sacrifices; no animal had been domesticated; only stone tools were used, although metal abounds in America; their weapons were those of savages; they did not employ the wheel either in pottery-making or for vehicles; they were still in the stone age.

However, the study and pseudo-study of those civilizations, or rather semi-civilizations, the problems connected with the origins of those peoples, their languages, and their 'possible affinities' with the various European and Asiatic races, have agitated European scholars and wealthy amateurs for centuries. No part of the world has formed the subject of so many wild theories, and few present so many riddles to solve. Theories and analogies have been adduced pointing to every other continent, even to those which have never existed, as the long sought place of origin. Thus, the most fantastic theories have been suggested; the legendary continent of Atlantis, and the supposed vigorous and cultured race who were reputed to inhabit it, is the most popular among them. Some explorer tried hard to prove that not only were the Mexican and the Egyptian civilizations connected, but that the Mexican was the original of the Egyptian. Lord Kingsborough expended a fortune to prove, in eight volumes, the supposition of the Spanish historian Garcia that the natives of America are no less than the descendants of the Ten Tribes of Israel. Many other peoples (Carthaginians, Libyans, Assyrians, Persians, Japanese, Australasians, Hindus, Eskimos, Mongolians, Tatars, Irish, Welsh and others) have been successively considered as candidates for the paternity of the Mexican races. Unscientific writing on the subject has continued until the present day.

STUDY OF ANCIENT MEXICO AND CENTRAL AMERICA

The time is not within sight when a complete and generally agreed elucidation of all the problems connected with this fascinating subject can be put forward; the chronological questions, for example, are certainly not to be explained with ease. Nevertheless, it must not be supposed that Mexican archæology has been neglected. Famous Americanists (British, North- and Central-American, German, French, Italian, Russian, and others) have devoted thereto years of hard study and research, and many splendid results have been achieved. The labours of painstaking investigators (explorers, archæologists, ethnologists, linguists) and the results obtained by archæological expeditions sent out to work on the spot, are constantly affording evidence that a great mass of potential information still exists waiting to be uncovered.

In order to solve the intricate problems of history, ethnology and linguistics, much research work has still to be done. Investigation on the spot is not easy; it is rendered still more difficult by the inaccessibility of some parts of the region and the malarial infection of others. Havoc and destruction have been wrought upon many famous sites, both by man and nature; the natural levers of root and branch in the tropical jungle of Yucatán were efficient agents in throwing down pyramids and walls which the ignorant inhabitants only spared because of their inaccessibility. From the ethnological point of view, not only were the pre-Columbian cultures and idioms most heterogeneous, but there now exist few native peoples whose culture has not been much changed by European civilization. Many dialects are still unintelligible. Although much systematic work has already been done, no comprehensive linguistic study has been published.

Of particular importance for the study of the Mayan language is the *Motul Dictionary* (MS. preserved in the John Carter Brown Library, at Providence, Rhode Island, U.S.A.), which Thompson regards as the finest Maya-Spanish dictionary ever made.

Modern research work on Maya writing and language can be said to have begun about 1850 with the activity of the Yucatecan scholar Juan Pio Perez (d. 1859), and particularly in 1864 with Abbé Brasseur de Bourbourg's publication of Diego de Landa's book. Dr. Ernst Foerstemann's publication of the reproduction of *Codex Dresden*, in 1880, is a milestone in Maya research. Between 1889 and 1902, A. P. Maudslay published (in four volumes of beautiful plates and one of text) the results of his seven expeditions to Central America. Also of great importance are Daniel Garrison Brinton's researches into the Maya calendar (1893 and 1895). In 1897, J. Thompson Goodman published *The Archaic Maya Inscriptions*. For the present century it would be sufficient to mention the great names of Eduard Seler, William E. Gates, Sylvanus Griswold Morley, Herbert Joseph Spinden, Richard C. E. Long, John Edgar Teeple, Hermann Beyer, Thomas A. Joyce, and particularly J. Eric Thompson. For the recent research-work of Soviet scholars, *see* further on.

CULTURES OF ANCIENT MEXICO AND CENTRAL AMERICA

Space does not allow me to give a comprehensive summary of what is known on this subject; and it would be useless to present any decisive judgment on the many controversial problems or to suggest tentative solutions without giving the necessary evidence, which would take me far outside the purpose of this book. I shall try, however, to present very briefly the results which are more or less generally accepted by the experts in those studies which are connected with the subject of this book.

Concerning the main problem whether there is any relation in culture between pre-Conquest Mexico and the ancient Old World, it is probable that if there be any connection, it is of infinite remoteness and could have had no influence whatever on the origin of the ancient Mexican scripts. Professor Arthur Posnansky (in *Tiahuanaco, the Cradle of American Man*, New York, 1945) gives a quite new solution of the whole problem: Tiahuanaco, situated on the shore of Lake Titicaca (Bolivia) in the high Andes of South America, is according to Posnansky the enchanted spot where Indian legend as well as archæological proof place the primacy of human settlement and culture, not only of the western hemisphere but of our planet. It is outside the purpose of this book to go into details.

There is a fairly general agreement, nowadays, concerning the part played by the Mayas, the Toltecs and the Aztecs in the cultural development of ancient Mexico. Until the early nineteenth century, the whole civilization of ancient Mexico was attributed to the Aztecs; then, the Toltecs received that great honour; now, the scholars of the twentieth century regard the Mayas of ancient Central America as the originators of the highest pre-Columbian civilization of America, although all the old Central-American cultures influenced each other. The Zapotecs are regarded as the intermediaries between the Mayas and the Nahua civilization of Mexico; both the Aztecs and the Toltecs belonged to the same linguistic group as the Nahuas. We shall deal briefly with these peoples.

MAIN PEOPLES WHO DEVELOPED ANCIENT MEXICAN AND CENTRAL AMERICAN CULTURES

Mayas

The Mayas, one of the most important peoples of native America, and the most highly civilized of pre-Columbian America, still form the bulk of the population of Yucatán. They may be divided into three main groups:

(1) the Mayas proper, numbering about 300,000, in Yucatán and the neighbouring states of Mexico and Guatemala, are subdivided into many tribes;

(2) the Quiché, numbering some 500,000 natives between Lake Atitlan and the Pacific, southern Guatemala; and

(3) the Huaxtec (numbering about 50,000; in Vera Cruz, Hidalgo, Tamaulipas, San Luis Potosi), already separated from the main stock in ancient times.

On the basis of the dates of the Mayan inscriptions, it is considered certain that there existed a Maya Old Empire, which flourished at least between A.D. 320 and 889 in southern Yucatán; the origin of its culture and the reasons of its end are at present buried in mystery. J. E. S. Thompson distinguishes the following main periods in Mayan history: (1) Formative period, B.C. 500–320 A.D.; (2) Classical period, A.D. 320–889; and (3) Mexican period in Yucatán, A.D. 987–1452 (overthrow of Mayapan) or to 1539/41 (Spanish conquest).

Main dates: A.D. 320 is the earliest certain Maya date (inscribed on the Leyden jade-plate); 328—the earliest known *stele* (found at Uaxactun); 475—earliest known date in Yucatán (on a stone lintel in Oxkintok); 573—earliest known date on east coast (*Stele* I, Tuluum); 633—end of early phase of classical period; 711—traditional date of founding of Chichen Itzá; 790—apex of custom of marking passage of time (this date is commemorated on *stelae*, altars or lintels in nineteen Maya cities); 889— last date recorded on a *stele;* and Mayas abandon Chichen Itzá.

At the time of their first appearance, the Maya script and astronomical and mathematical knowledge are fully developed, and this presupposes a previous evolution of long duration (of which nothing is known), unless there was some cultural importation, which is hardly thinkable. As the correlation of Maya dates with our calendar is still not agreed upon—there are at least three different opinions on this matter, some differing by as much as 260 years—the date of the beginning of Maya Old Empire civilization is still uncertain, the most probable date being the last centuries of the pre-Christian Era. Concerning the reason, or reasons, for the decline of Maya Old Empire (Mitchell's article on this subject in *Antiquity*, September, 1930, is very instructive), many theories have been suggested. One may assume that there may have been more than one reason, and it is to be hoped that future investigation will find the real solution of this and the other problems. Mitchell writes: 'Rome and Copán, the dominant cities of the dominant empires of two continents, may have fallen on the same day,' *i.e.*, Rome in 1527 and Copán in 1530. I should like to add: 'and perhaps for similar, rather complex, reasons.'

The Classical or Old Empire period was the golden age of Mayan art and culture; it was the period of the great cities of Palenque (north Chiapas), Copán (west Honduras), and many others, Copán being the main religious and cultural centre, Palenque perhaps the seat of art. The mathematical and astronomical science seem to have been far ahead of the contemporary knowledge of any other people. The Mayas had already a sign for zero; their calendar was even more accurate than the Gregorian calendar still in use, and is capable of dealing with periods of time of over 90,000,000 years (Fig. 7.1). Their writing presents the same stage of advancement in the most ancient as in the most recent inscriptions. Their art is highly developed.

The later history of the Mayas, which has no bearing on our subject, may be divided into three periods: (1) the 'transitional epoch,' (2) the 'New Empire epoch' (or 'Mexican period in Yucatán'), which continued, in a rather degenerate manner, Maya tradition and culture in northern Yucatán, for some further centuries; and (3) the 'period of decadence' which lasted until the arrival of the Spaniards. The sites of the once flourishing Maya Old Empire were then long forgotten.

Zapotecs

The great State of Oaxaca in southern Mexico offers nowadays the most complex linguistic situation existing in Mexico; there live a large number of tribal and linguistic groups which differ greatly in culture; these differences reflect partly the heterogeneity of the pre-Columbian cultures. The most important tribes are, now as then, those of the Zapotecs and Mixtecs, who in ancient times probably played the part of cultural intermediaries between the Maya Old Empire of the east, and the Toltec 'Empire' of the west. Nothing, however, is known about their history. Zapotec is now spoken by several thousand Indians in the southern part of Oaxaca. A Zapotec dialect, called the Villa Alta dialect, is spoken in the Villa Alta district of north-eastern Oaxaca.

Toltecs

The term Toltec ('Skilled Worker') was used by the Aztecs to describe their predecessors, the 'Master-Builders,' who, however, called themselves *Aculhuaque* ('Strong' or 'Tall Men'). They were the supposed originators of Mexico's golden age. They were excellent architects; at their traditional capital Tollan, they built pyramids, temples, palaces and storeyed buildings. They were the first authenticated immigrants to the valley of Mexico who spoke a dialect belonging to the Nahuan group, or *Nahuatl-tolli*, which was a *polysynthetic* or *incorporative* speech; that is, the single words embody the conception of a whole sentence; for instance, the name of the famous last Azteca 'emperor' Montezuma or Montecuzoma (really, *Montecuzomai thuicamina*) means 'when-the-chief-is-angry-he-shoots-to-heaven.'

Very little is known about the Toltec history. About the middle of the first millennium A.D., they seem to have entered Mexico, and about A.D. 770, they arrived at the site of their future capital, Tollan. Their culture which reached its apogee about the end of the ninth century was probably related in some respects to the Mayan. Quetzalcoatl or Quetzalcohuatl, regarded by various authorities as 'Air-god,' 'Sun-god,' 'Culture-hero,' was the traditional originator of their culture, 'the Father of the Toltecs.'

At the end of the tenth century, the less civilized Chichimeca invaded the country. They, like their predecessors, spoke Nahuatl, but are considered by some experts as of Otomi origin. The Toltecs disappeared from the historical horizon, but the prominence of the Chichimeca did not last long. There followed a period of warfare between the various tribes; for some time the Otomi or Hia-hiu (an industrious non-Nahuatl-speaking race) had pre-eminence. About the twelfth century the Aztecs settled in the country.

The Toltecs apparently used script, numerals, and a calendar, related to those of the Maya. The extant codices (*Vindobonensis, Bodleianus, Annals of Cuauhtitlan, Ixtlilxototitl*) are post-Conquest; but on the various buildings which can, with more or less certainty, be attributed to Toltec workmanship (mostly pyramids and temples), glyphs are to be seen which may be regarded as writing. The ruins of Teotihuacan show some glyphs; but far more important are those of Xocicalco and the calendrical glyphs of the monuments near Santa Lucia Cotumahualpa (after G. C. Vaillant, *The Aztecs of Mexico*, Pelican Books, 1950, and a lecture by G. A. Burland).

Aztecs

The Aztecs or Azteca (the 'Crane People') received their name from the Tecpanecs, by whom they were enslaved at the beginning of the fourteenth century; according to their own tradition, they started their migration (in 1168?) from the mythical Island of Aztlan (Aztlan means only 'Aztec-place)', situated in the north; they came indeed from the north. The Aztecs spoke a Nahuatl language. Aztec is now spoken by 650,000 people in northern and central Mexico. In their manuscripts they are depicted as heroic fighters who made victorious marches through many places; as a matter of fact, they were a semi-barbarous tribe who for about two centuries played no part at all, or a very insignificant one, in Mexican history.

It was obviously for mere reasons of defence that they settled (in A.D. 1325, according to the Mendoza Codex) on the salt marshes on the west edge of the Lake Tezcuco or Texcoco, the original settlement consisting probably of crude pile-buildings standing in the water; and thus founded a kind of Venice, the town Tenochtitlan, which became the modern Mexico City. The glyph *Tenochtitlan* in Mexican manuscripts consists of a rock (*tetl*), from which a cactus plant (*nochtli*) is growing; the termination *tlan* indicates 'the place of.'

Another century passed by, before the Aztecs became one of the most important peoples of the *Anahuac* ('Near-the-water'), that is, the Mexican plateau. About 1430 they founded, under their ruler Itzcoatl, a league with two neighbouring city-states, and they became the leading member of this Aztec confederacy. Under a series of warrior-rulers, the Aztecs were now embarked on a period of 'imperialistic' expansion, which only the Spanish conquest stopped. In less than ninety years they succeeded in subduing some thirty city-states, but it would be erroneous to make comparisons with Asiatic or European empires; the main purpose of the Aztecs was to loot, to exact tribute and to obtain prisoners for their sacrifices. Some Mexican tribes and city-states remained independent and continued to wage war against the Aztecs until the arrival of the Spaniards, whose conquest was much facilitated by the savage hatred and feuds between the native tribes.

The Aztec civilization, or semi-civilization, was a mosaic of elements borrowed from other cultures, mainly Maya and Toltec, and barbarism. The Aztecs developed considerable skill in the art of metal working and architecture, but even in these respects they do not seem to have shown much originality. Their mathematical and astronomical knowledge was probably of Maya origin. Their writing, which is also probably of Maya origin, shows a certain evolution, from the point of view of history of writing, but from the aesthetic point of view it is degenerate.

INDIGENOUS SCRIPTS OF PRE-COLUMBIAN AMERICA

As the result of the Spanish intolerance and inquisition, very few documents written by American pre-Columbian natives are known to have survived. Of the truly pre-conquest Aztec codices only fourteen main manuscripts are extant: five are in England, four in Italy, two in France, one each in the U.S.A., Mexico, and Austria. Only three Maya manuscripts have survived (Figs. 7.1–3): the beautiful Dresden Codex (an eleventh- or twelfth-century copy of an original assigned to the Mayan classical period, *i.e.*, fifth to ninth century A.D.), the Tro-Cortesianus or Madrid Codex (a fifteenth-century, rather crude workmanship), and the Peresianus or Paris Codex (also crude; slightly earlier than the Madrid Codex, but much later than the Dresden Codex). Codex Dresden deals with astronomy and divination; Codex Madrid with divination and ritual, and other ceremonies; whilst Codex Paris on its *verso* side deals with divination, its *obverse* illustrates ceremonies and perhaps also historical 'prophecies.'

There is extant a great number of Aztec manuscripts written under Spanish domination.

Masses of pre-Columbian manuscripts are known to have been burned by the fanatical Spanish priests.

Of paramount importance for the study of Maya literature are the *Books of Chilam Balam*, written in Yucatec language and Latin character; they contain many oral traditions and songs of ancient times; they are chronicles of native history, prophecies, mythology, ritual, almanacs, astrology, medical lore, and so on. The most important books are those of Chumayel, Tizimin and Mani. Quiché legends and traditions have been preserved in the *Popel Vuh* (or 'Community Book'), written in Quiché language and Latin script. The first part deals with cosmogony; the second and a great part of the third are purely mythological.

MAYA SCRIPT

The Aztec writing is—see further on—probably nothing but a degenerate derivative of the Maya script; indeed, from the æsthetic point of view, there cannot even be a comparison between the beautiful cartouches or 'glyphs' of the Maya inscriptions and the crude, barbaric picture-writing of the Aztec manuscripts; there is no likeness even in the external form of the symbols of the two scripts. Nevertheless, while a simple adoption by the Aztecs of the Maya script is not probable, there can hardly be any doubt that the Mexican peoples received at least the idea of writing from the Mayas. How and when the Mayas invented writing we do not know, and we shall probably never be able to solve this problem.

The three manuscripts (Figs. 7.1–3) already mentioned are not the only Maya written material extant; more than 1,000 beautiful and mainly well-preserved *stelae* (huge, vertical monolithic pillars), carved—or, more rarely, incised—all over in low relief with glyphs and figures (Figs. 7.4*a*, *b*), and also large oval stones or altars, similarly carved (Fig. 7.4*c*), have been discovered in many places; Maya 'hieroglyphs' were also sculptured or incised on ball-court markers and rings, steps, panels, walls of buildings, lintels of stone or wood (Fig. 7.5), and wooden ceilings; some were modelled in stucco; some were incised on personal ornaments (such as jade and shell). Some polychrome clay pottery painted with glyphs and figures, as well as carvings and engravings on metal and bone have also been found.

The dates of the manuscripts are still uncertain; they seem, however, to belong to the later Maya period, whereas the *stelae* seem to belong to an earlier period. As a matter of fact, these monolithic pillars are dated, most of the dates being of the ninth and tenth cycles of Maya chronology (that is probably the second half of the third and the first half of the fourth century A.D.). The *stelae* served as time-markers, being apparently erected at 5-, 10-, or 20-year intervals, and recorded the principal events of the town in the period concerned.

The cartouches or glyphs are highly conventionalized, containing sometimes many picture-signs gathered into a single frame, and they have some external but undoubtedly casual resemblance to the Egyptian cartouches.

The script is still mainly undeciphered, except the calendrical symbols and some notation signs. This fact is the more sad as the knowledge of the Maya writing has been lost in the last two and a half centuries only. It is known that a large number of Maya manuscripts were in existence at the time of the conquest, and according to Spanish sources records in Maya 'hieroglyphic' writing continued to be made as late as at the end of the seventeenth century, when some Spaniards seem still to have understood it. It is, however, not certain that the script of that period was identical with that of the earlier period. As J. E. S. Thompson points out, in some inscriptions (principally composed of dates and counts) most of the glyphs can be read; in others (apparently mainly concerned with ritual) the percentage of deciphered glyphs is quite low; in still others, not a glyph has been deciphered.

Maya System of Writing

It is one of the ironies of history that the man who seems to have been responsible for the wholesale destruction of Maya manuscripts, is the main source for our knowledge of Maya history and civilization, including what we know of their writing. That man was Diego de Landa (1524–79), the second bishop of Yucatán. Unfortunately, a part only of his *Relación de las cosas de Yucatán*, written about 1566, is extant; its eighth edition was published in English translation in 1941 by the well-known Americanist Alfred M. Tozzer; the numerous notes, the full bibliography on the Mayas, the translations of four other well-chosen early Spanish documents, containing information about the ancient Mayas, make this publication an important handbook on the ancient Mayas in general.

We cannot say much about the Maya system of writing: *see*, however, last paragraph of this section. According to Landa, it was composed of 'letters,' 'characters,' 'figures' and 'signs.' Landa himself gives us the names and the representations of the 'letters' of the Maya 'alphabet' (Fig. 7.6*a*). It is not difficult to trace the origin of some of the 'letters,' but the modern scholars who tried to make use of this alphabet in deciphering Maya written documents met with failure. With some exceptions, it is now held that Landa's alphabet is more or less artificial, leaving open the question whether it was a Spanish fabrication, or an indigenous trick, or else a misunderstood explanation of the actual intricate character of the Maya script. It was perhaps the outcome of Landa's insistent inquiries; he may himself *a priori* have supposed the existence of such an alphabet.

The whole problem is still debatable. However, Maya writing was certainly neither an alphabet nor a syllabary (except insofar as most Maya words are monosyllables); it was partly pictorial and partly conventionalized, partly ideographic and in all probability partly phonetic. In J. E. S. Thompson's opinion, the Maya simple phonetic writing might be described as an advanced form of *rebus*-writing in that the picture has become so conventionalized that the original object is no longer recognizable.

Still, thanks to Landa, we can read the symbols of the days and the months (Figs. 7.6*b*, *c*). There are usually at least two forms for the same symbol, one (the 'head variant') being usually the profile of a deity or animal, the other (the 'symbolic' or 'normal form') being connected with the face form.

The day was called *kin*, 'the sun.' The calendar was more complicated than the Aztec calendar, which derived from it, and the names were different. There were two kinds of months, *u*, 'moon,' of 30 days, and *uinal*, of 20 days, which was the basis of the solar year, *tun*. This had 18 *uinals*, and five supplementary days, called *xma kaba kin*, 'without-name-days,' also *uayab* or *uayeb haab*, 'the bed of the year,' or *u yail kin* or *u yail haab*, 'the unfortunate days.' The Mayas had no leap year, but the length of the tropical year was very accurately determined: 20 *tun* formed a *katun* or *edad* of (20 × 360) 7,200 days, and 20 *katun* a *bactun* of 144,000 days. J. E. S. Thompson points out that the Mayas thought in vast expanses of time—they calculated a date over 500 million years in the past without error. Although there is no direct evidence for the Mayane us of higher epochs, scholars generally agree that the Mayas distinguished the following higher periods: 1 *pictun* = 20 *bactun*; 1 *calabtun* = 20 *pictun*; 1 *kinchiltun* = 20 *calabtun*; 1 *alautun* = 20 *kinchiltun* (= 64,000,000 *tun*, or solar years): *see*, for instance, Fig. 7.6*d*.

The days were defined by their names and numbered consecutively from 1 to 13; the arbitrary period of 260 days, *tzolkin*, combined with the *tun*, gave the Maya cycle of 52 years.

The numeration was vigesimal. The character for zero—the importance of which was recognized by the Mayas many centuries before any other people in the world—was similar to a shell, the numerals (Fig. 7.6*d*) 1–4 were represented by dots, the numerals 5, 10, 15 by sticks, lines or bars, 20 perhaps by the moon; the symbols for the multiples of 20 (400, 8,000, 160,000, etc.) are still uncertain; it may be, however, that they had the 'place-value' notation.

According to Landa, and also to other Spanish contemporary writers, the Maya script 'was a possession only of the priests, the sons of the priests, some of the principal lords . . .', and furthermore 'not all the priests knew how to describe it.' Writing was so highly esteemed that its invention and that of books were attributed to the most important deity of the Mayas, Itzamna, the son of the creator-god, Hunab Ku, who was the god of heaven and of the sun. Paul Schellhas—the German scholar, who has identified in the Maya codices a number of gods and has given them letters of the alphabet—identifies Itzamna in the *Dresden Codex* as god D.

RECENT DECIPHERMENT OF MAYA SCRIPT

The study of the Maya script was a new development in Russia after the second world war, and particularly during the last fifteen years. In an article published in the Russian magazine *Soviet Ethnography*, 1952/No. 3, and in a book published in 1955 (*The Script of the Ancient Mayas*, in Russian and Spanish, Academy of Sciences of the USSR, Moscow, 1955), J. J. Knorozov distinguishes the following groups of the Mayan glyphs:

(1) Ideograms, not many in number, the majority of the Maya symbols being phonetic;

(2) vowels, such as *a, o, e, i, u*, used mainly to represent the initial or final vocalic sound and rarely the middle vocalic sound of a word;

(3) syllabic symbols representing a vowel followed by a consonant (such as *ah, ak, et*);

(4) alphabetic-syllabic signs, which are sometimes employed as consonants only (at the end of a word, such as *pak, kutz, kuk*) and sometimes as syllables (at the beginning of a word, such as *kam, tzul, kuch*);

(5) syllabic symbols, representing consonant-vowel-consonant (such as *bal, nal, thul*).

His conclusions, however, have not yet been accepted by the main authorities on the subject. More recently, the scientist S. Sobolev reported in the magazine *Soviet Union* the achievement of three young scholars (Yevreinov, Kosarev and Ustinov), who, working under the aegis of the Siberian department of the Soviet Academy of Sciences, with the help of electronic computer techniques, have succeeded in deciphering about 40 per cent of the Dresden and Madrid codices, or approximately 600 sentences. This research work takes place in Novosibirsk; the computer accomplished about one milliard operations in two full days of work, but apparently for the three MSS extant, 10 to 11 milliard operations will be required. We learned from *Atlantis*, April 1961, that Soviet scholars had stated that these MSS. would be deciphered and edited within 3-4 months.

AZTEC CHARACTER

Aztec Codices (Figs. 7.7-9)

The 'Aztec' codices—as these manuscripts are called—are painted in colours, on coarse cloth made from the fibre of the *agave americana* or on a long sheet of *amatl* paper, of an average width of six or seven inches, but of different lengths. The sheet was folded up screen fashion to form the leaves. The surface of the sheet was covered with a very thin coating of white varnish to receive the text, which was generally painted on both sides in a wide range of colours: red, yellow, blue, green, purple, brown, orange, black, white; some of them in more than one shade. The colours are outlined in black, but they are crude, and the pictures are without artistic merit; they were obviously merely utilitarian. The sheet was fastened to what may be called the binding of the codex, which was of fine, thin wood covered with brilliant varnish; each cover measured nearly the same as the leaves; the binding had no back. For 'modern' production of similar paper see Fig. 7.11*a*.

The 'Aztec' manuscripts have been divided by some scholars into four groups: (1) Aztec proper; (2) Xicalanca (northern Oaxaca); (3) Mixtec (central Oaxaca); and (4) Zapotec, Cuitateco, Mazateco, Mixe and Chinanteco (Oaxaca and Chiapas). A clear distinction, however, cannot be made as yet.

The greater part of the codices is devoted to divinations, rituals and astrology; a few are concerned primarily with genealogies and sequences of political events, being in fact a kind of history.

The pre-Columbian codices have been written mainly by the native priests, amongst whose duties was that of keeping written records of the ceremonies appropriate for the various religious festivals, of tributes due to the king and the temples, of legal trials, of historical events, and so forth. The post-Conquest manuscripts deal with historical and religious matters, for instance, with religious catechism (Figs. 7.10*b, c*).

H

The manuscripts have been partly deciphered; many of the dieties have been identified, the personal and place names can be read, some of the ceremonies are understood, but we are still far from complete victory; in many cases the decipherment is a more or less acceptable guess which cannot be either proved or disproved.

Aztec Script

The 'Aztec' writing is highly pictographic; indeed, it is the most highly pictographic of all the analytic scripts. Practically all the symbols are crude pictures. There are numerous instances of pure ideographic writing (Fig. 7.10*f*); the effort of the scribes is directed rather to the idea than to the sound. In this regard, the script is more in the nature of mnemonic aids, to be supplemented by oral description, than of a true writing.

The migrations of the Aztecs, for example, were represented by footsteps (Fig. 7.10*c*), from place to place; in the tribute-lists, the objects such as shields, garments, mosaic, or strings of beads, were depicted, accompanied by the pictographs of numbers.

In some respects, however, the writing may already be considered as analytic; many conventional signs have phonetic value; these are word-signs or syllables. Abstract ideas are represented by signs borrowed from *homophones* (words having the same sound but a different meaning), even when such homophones give only the rough pronunciation of the word in question. On the other hand the word 'widow,' was expressed by a weeping eye accompanied by the name of a woman. A syllable could be expressed by an object whose name began with it. In other words, it was partly on the same principle as *rebus*-writing (the other analytic scripts, cuneiform, hieroglyphic, Chinese writing, had similar devices), and it was employed mainly to write personal names, place names (Fig. 7.10*e*) or names of deities. *Rebus*-writing, however, appears to have been extremely rare before the arrival of the Spaniards. Generally speaking, Aztec glyphs consist almost entirely of calendar signs (Fig. 7.10*d*) and glyphs for names of persons and towns.

The transcription of such names was facilitated by the use of the *ikonomatic* system, as it is called, in names: in men's names, such as 'Smoking Star,' 'Eagle Star,' 'Stoned Jaguar,' 'Blue Dog,' 'Blood-drinking Eagle,' 'Jaguar Claw,' 'Bloody Face'; in women's names, as for instance, 'Plumed Serpent,' 'Jewelled Parrot,' 'Sun Fan,' and so forth. Historical events were depicted with considerable ingenuity by pictographs which were accompanied by symbols showing the place and the year.

As numbers and dates played a very important part in Aztec writing, I must say a few words about this subject. The numeral system was vigesimal; numbers from 1 to 19 were represented by dots or circles, 20 by a religious banner, 400 (20 × 20) by a pine tree, 8,000 (20 × 20 × 20) by an incense-pouch.

The Aztec calendar was probably derived from the Maya calendar (*see* above), but it was much simpler than the latter. It was two-fold, and comprised the ritual year (*tonalamatl*) of 260 days, employed for divination, ceremonial computations and movable feasts, and the solar year of 365 days, consisting of 18 months of 20 days each, each day having its name and being represented by a pictorial symbol (Fig. 7.11*b*), followed by a period of 5 days called *nemontini* or 'useless days,' which were of very bad omen. In dating, the day-symbols were preceded by the numbers 1–13; and the two sequences run concurrently in unchanging order. The *tonalamatl* was divided into twenty 13-day periods, or weeks. The year was always distinguished by the sign of the day on which it began; there were, however, only four year-signs, and these also were accompanied by the series of numbers 1–13. The period 13 × 4 (52) years constituted the shorter cycle, and 104 years the longer cycle.

BIBLIOGRAPHY

FÖRSTEMANN, E. 'Zur Entzifferung der Maya Handschriften' (a series of articles), *Zeitschrift für Ethnologie*, Berlin, 1887–95; commentaries to the Maya MSS. (1) of Dresden, Dresden, 1901; (2) of the Madrid *Tro-Cortesianus*, Danzig, 1902; (3) of the Paris *Codex Peresianus*, Danzig, 1903.

GOODMAN, J. T. *The Archaic Maya Inscriptions*, London, 1897.

SELLER, E. *Gesammelte Abhandlungen*, etc., 5 vols, Berlin, 1902–23.

LUMHOLZ, C. *Unknown Mexico*, New York, 1902.

BOWDITCH, C. P. *Mexican and Central American Antiquities*, etc., Washington, 1904; *The Numeration, Calendar Systems and Astronomical Knowledge of the Mayas*, Cambridge, Mass., 1910.

LEHMANN, W. *Methods and Results in Mexican Research*, Paris, 1909; *L'art ancient du Mexique*, Paris, 1922.

GATES, W. E. *Perez Codex*, Point Loma, Cal., 1910; *An Outline Dictionary of Maya Glyphs*, etc., Baltimore, 1931.

BEUCHAT, H. *Manuel d'archéologie américaine*, Paris, 1912; *Manual de arqueología americana*, Madrid, 1918.

SPENCE, L. *The Civilization of Ancient Mexico*, Cambridge, 1912; *The Gods of Mexico*, London, 1923.

JOYCE, T. A. *Mexican Archæology*, London, 1914 and 1920 (2nd impression); *Maya and Mexican Art*, London, 1927.

MORLEY, S. G. *An Introduction to the Study of the Maya Hieroglyphs*, Washington, 1915; *The Inscriptions at Copán*, Washington, 1920; *The Inscriptions of Peten*, 5 vols., Washington, 1938; *The Ancient Maya*, Stanford University, 1947.

GANN, T. W. F. *The Maya Indians of Southern Yucatán and Northern British Honduras*, Washington, 1918; *In an Unknown Land*, London, 1924; *Mystery Cities*, New York, 1925; *Ancient Cities and Modern Tribes*, New York, 1926; *Glories of the Maya*, New York, 1931; *Mexico*, London, 1936.

TOZZER, A. M. *A Maya Grammar*, Cambridge, Mass., 1921; *Maya Research*, New York–Orleans, 1934; *Landa's Relación de las cosas de Yucatán*, Cambridge, Mass., 1941.

CALLEGARI, G. V. 'Dell'arte della scrittura nell'antico Messico. I Nahoa,' *Scienza per Tutti*, Milan, 1922; *Introduzione allo studio delle antichità americane*, Milan, 1930; 'L'enigma Maya,' *Atti dell'Accademia Roveretana*, etc., 1932 (bibliogr.); *Dei sistemi grafici degli Aztechi*, Milan, 1934; 'Dei toponimi grafici degli Aztechi,' *Boll. dell'Accademia Italiana di Stenografia*, 1936.

SPINDEN, H. J. *The Reduction of Maya Dates*, Cambridge, Mass., 1924; *Ancient Civilizations of Mexico and Central America*, 3rd ed., New York, 1928; *Indian Manuscripts of Southern Mexico*, Washington, 1935.

RIVET, P. 'Les Origines de l'homme américain,' *Anthropologie*, 1926; 'Les Malayo-Polynésiens en Amérique, *J. d'Amer. de Paris*, 1926.

DANZEL, T. W. *Handbuch der präkolumbischen Kulturen in Latein-America*, Hamburg and Berlin, 1927.

PREUSS, K. T. 'Mexikanische Religion' (in H. Haas, *Bilderatlas zur Religionsgeschichte*), Leipsic, 1930;

'Die mexikanische Bilderhandschrift Historia Tolteca-Chichimeca,' *Bässler Archiv*, Berlin, 1937.

BEYER, H. *The Analysis of the Maya Hieroglyphs*, Leyden, 1930; 'Mayan Hieroglyphs,' etc., *Anthropos*, Vol. XXVI, 1931.

WHORF, B. L. *The Phonetic Value of Certain Characters in Maya Writing*, Cambridge, Mass., 1933; 'Maya Writing and its Decipherment,' *Maya Research*, New York–Orleans, 1935; *Decipherment of the Linguistic Portion of the Maya Hieroglyphs*, Washington, 1941 and 1942.

THOMPSON, J. E. *Mexico before Cortez*, New York–London, 1933; *A New Method of Deciphering Yucatán Dates, etc.*, Washington, 1936; *Maya Hieroglyphic Writing*, Washington, 1950; 2nd ed., Toronto, 1960; *The Rise and Fall of Maya Civilization*, London, 1956.

VILLACORTA, C., ANTONIO, J., and VILLACORTA, C. A. *Codices Mayas Dresdensis, Peresianus, Tro-Cortesianus*, Guatemala, 1933.

GIACALONE, B. *Gli Aztechi*, Genoa, 1934; *I Maja*, Genoa, 1935.

MITCHELL, J. L. *The Conquest of the Maya*, London, 1934.

KUNIKE, H. 'Die Tageszeichen der Mexikaner und der Maya,' *Intern. Archiv für Ethnographie*, 1935.

WEITZEL, R. B. 'Maya Correlation Problem,' *Maya Research*, 1936.

SCHELLHAS, P. 'Fifty Years of Maya Research,' *Maya Research*, 1936.

Handbook of Latin American Studies, 6 vols., Cambridge, Mass., 1936–41.

LONG, R. C. E. 'Maya Writing and Its Decipherment,' *Maya Research*, 1937.

The Maya and their Neighbors (volume dedicated to A. M. Tozzer), New York, 1940.

Los Mayos Antiguos (by various authors), Mexico, 1941.

LINCOLN, J. ST. *The Maya Calendar of the Ixil of Guatemala*, Washington, 1942.

KELEMAN, P. *Medieval American Art*, 2 vols., New York, 1943.

MAKEMSON, A. W. *The Astronomical Tables of the Maya*, Washington, 1943.

VAILLANT, G. C. *The Aztecs of Mexico*, Garden City, New York, 1944 (Pelican Books, 1950, 1951, 1953, 1955).

TOSCANO, S. *Arte precolomb. de México y de la América Central*, Mexico, 1944.

JÁKEMAN, M. W. *The Origins and History of the Mayas*, Los Angeles, 1945.

DIFFIE, B. W. *Latin-American Civilization*, Harrisburg, Pa., 1945.

Codice Selden A. Pictografía antigua mexicana procedente de la mixteca, Mexico, 1946.

ALCALÁ, E. S. *Códice Pérez. Traducción libre del maya al castellano*, Mérida (Yucatán), 1949.

KNOROZOV, J. J., *Soviet Ethnography*, 1952/3; *The Script of the ancient Mayas* (in Russian and Spanish), Moscow, 1955.

PÉRET, B. *Livre de Chilám Balám de Chumayol; trad. de l'espagnol et presenté*, Paris, 1955.

BURLAND, C. E. *Selden Roll*, Berlin, 1955.

Codice de Calkini (facsimile), Campeche, 1957.

DARK, P. J. C. *Mixtec Ethnohistory; a method of analysis of the Codical art*, London, 1958.

ROBERTSON, D. *Manuscript-painting of the Early Colonial Period*, New Haven, 1959 (Oxford, 1960).

ROBERTSON, D. and McAFEE, B. 'The Techialogan Codex of Tepotzotlán: Codex X' (Rylands Mexican MS. 1), *Bull. of the John Rylands Library*, 1960.

SOUSTELLE, J. *Chez les Aztèques*, Paris, 1960/61.

GALLEN KAMP, C. *Maya: the Riddle and Rediscovery of a Lost Civilization*, London, 1960.

CHAPTER 8

Mysterious Script of Easter Island

'MYSTERIOUS' PROBLEM

A quiet and remote islet, 70 square miles in area, lost in the Pacific Ocean, about 2,500 miles west of the coast of Chile, to whom it belongs, and about 1,750 miles east of the Gambier islands, presents many mysteries to the romantic imagination. Various peculiar 'prehistoric' remains have been discovered there, among them about 200 colossal stone images; two typical specimens are in the British Museum. Some of the images are over 30 feet high: they are carved out of a reddish brown trachitic lava, quarried in the island at some distance from their present position, where they stand in rows facing the sea.

There are also immense walls of large, flat stones, likewise facing the sea, upon slopes and headlands, while some 250 huge stone pedestals, burial-places, known as *ahu*, are placed on the land side of the walls on a broad terrace, upon which the images were standing. Remains of stone houses nearly 100 feet long by 20 feet wide are also to be seen and like all these monuments are now in ruins.

These 'prehistoric' remains, in striking contrast with the smallness of the number of the present population—about 700 (1953)—give sufficient food to the mystery-mongers for fancy stories of relics of antediluvian days, of a race of giants who once inhabited the island, of the 'Lemuria,' the vast continent of the Pacific Ocean lost in remote ages.

On this very island, some wooden tablets covered with pictographic writing, unique in Polynesia, have been noted since the late sixties of the last century.

FACTS

Easter Island, christened so by the Dutch admiral J. Roggeveen who discovered it on Easter Day, 1722, is not its only name; the Spaniards called it San Carlos, the natives Te Pito ('navel')-te-Henua ('earth') or Rapa-nui ('Great Rapa'); it is also termed Waihu or 'Land's End.' (The confusion between Davis Land and Easter Island persists to this day in the minds of many writers.) It lies in 27° 8′ S. lat., 109° 28′ W. long.; is entirely volcanic, triangular in shape and curiously symmetrical.

The main problems which the fancy stories try to solve are the following: When and whence came the aboriginal inhabitants of the island? did they emigrate from South America or from the Polynesian Islands? were the stone-images made by the ancestors of the present natives or by a previous people? when, where and how was the script created and what was its actual character?

The serious scholars who dealt with this matter are more or less in agreement in regard to the general problems; the natives seem to be of Polynesian origin with a considerable Melanesian, negroid, admixture; there is no evidence of a culture previous to that of the ancestors of the present natives; according to some local traditions, corroborated by other evidence, the immigration of the earliest inhabitants should be assigned to the twelfth or thirteenth century A.D. The problem of the origin of the script, however, is still a moot point.

THE SCRIPT

The script seems to have been noted for the first time in 1770 (Fig. 8.1a).

In the late sixties of the last century the attention of Father Roussel of the Catholic Mission (founded in 1864) was drawn to the wooden tablets carved with figures. Either then or sometime previously, many tablets seem to have been destroyed, but a few were sent to Bishop Jaussen of Tahiti. Indeed, Brother Eyraud of the Catholic Mission mentioned in his first letter having seen 'tablets and staves covered with strange signs in all the houses.' There are at present about twenty-one tablets, a staff and three or four *rei-miro* (or breast-plates) extant. The tablets (Figs. 8.1b, c and 8.2) are known as *kohau rongo-rongo* (*kohau* = staves; *rongo-rongo* = the Easter Island bards); they are mainly fragments of all sizes up to 6 feet. According to Métraux, the term *kohau rongo-rongo*—to be translated 'reciting staff' or 'chanters' staff,' and not (as commonly translated) 'talking wood' or 'intelligent wood'—suggests that the 'staves were the original form of these accessories employed by the chanters.' Five tablets are preserved in the collection of the missionaries of the Picputian Society at Braine-le-Comte (Belgium); three specimens are in the Bishop Museum at Honolulu (Hawai); two in the Smithsonian Inst. at Washington (D.C.); several other tablets are in the British Museum, and in the museums of Santiago (Chile), Berlin, Vienna and Leningrad. 'Whatever the shape and size of these pieces of wood, they are invariably covered with signs on both sides, without the slightest space being wasted' (Métraux). 'When the symbols are incised on a cylindrical staff, they run all round the circumference without anything to show where the inscription begins or ends. It is as if the scribe had been determined to engrave as many signs on the wood as possible' (Métraux).

The symbols were incised with a shark's tooth; the direction of writing is *boustrophedon*, that is, alternate lines from left to right and from right to left; the alternate rows are in inverted positions, so that the reader is obliged to turn the tablet upside down at the end of each line. A mere glance at Figs. 8.1 and 2 is sufficient to show that the script is highly pictographic, although some characters are already stylized, and all the symbols of the same height. Human figures, birds, fishes, crabs, turtles, fish-hooks, wooden pendants, stylized adzes—these can easily be recognized. Moreover, some of the signs which nowadays appear as geometric, originally may have depicted objects we can no longer identify.

The script is still undeciphered; various attempts have been made to decipher it with the help of the natives, but without definite results. However, thanks to the stories told by the natives, we know the contents of some tablets. Certain of them seem to deal with ceremonies, some may be lists of wars, others are like prayers, and so forth. The characters seem to be mainly memory-aid symbols, to be supplemented by oral explanation.

Of particular interest is Dr. Métraux' attempt to classify the Easter Island symbols. One of the main tablets, the *Aruku-kurenga*, contains 960 symbols; nearly a fifth of this number is taken up by one symbol—the image of the sooty tern, symbolizing the god Make-make—which is repeated 183 times. 'An individual with a lozenge for a head is reproduced ninety-four times. Depictions of human beings and birds represent about one-third of the symbols. This proportion does not seem to favour the hypothesis of a syllabic or alphabetic script.'

The script *rongo-rongo* was the monopoly of organized teachers; every clan had its own 'writing-professors,' that is, experts in the art, who were known as *tangata-rongo-rongo*, 'rongo-rongo-men.'

A less elaborate kind of rongo-rongo was called *tau* or *ta'u*, which was still known at the end of the last century; a specimen of this script, written by an old and invalid native, has been published by Mrs. K. Scoresby Routledge; *see* also D. Diringer, *L'Alfabeto nella Storia della Civiltà* (Florence, 1937, Fig. 103, 4). Also Dr. Métraux was informed that 'these tablets contained a list of exploits accomplished by an individual whose memory was celebrated by his son in a solemn feast.'

Origin

Among the many difficult problems presented by the *rongo-rongo* script, the most important concerns the origin of this writing. Was it invented on the island, or imported from outside? The latter suggestion seems the more probable. Were the tablets written on the island or imported from outside? When was this script created? No answers can be given with certainty; some can be guessed, but no proof or evidence can be produced. As Dr. Métraux has pointed out, the efforts to extract an explanation of the tablets from the Easter Islanders were fruitless. 'Placed in front of a tablet, they intoned chants without even trying to spell out the characters.' More-over, even at the first attempt at decipherment—undertaken by Father Zumbohm— 'differences of opinion between the chanters were so great that the discouraged missionary abandoned all hope of learning anything from them' (Métraux).

According to local traditions, Hotu-matua, an ancestor of the Pascuans, accompanied by 300 warriors and their families, came to the island with two big boats, and brought with him sixty-seven inscribed wooden tablets (a number like this is not conventional, and can easily correspond to the truth). The date of this event (twelfth-thirteenth century A.D.) is worked out upon the traditional list of the local 'kings.' However, even this tradition does not explain the origin of the script.

Connections with other Scripts

An astonishing thesis has been suggested by G. de Hevesy; according to this Hungarian scholar, the Easter Island script appears to be connected with the Indus Valley script, and both seem to have derived from an unknown system of writing, of an intermediate country, such as New Zealand. Even if we admit that there is some likeness between Easter Island symbols and Indus Valley signs, evidence would still be lacking of the relationship of the two scripts, unless the similarities of the signs correspond with the identity of their phonetic values. Besides, as A. Métraux points out, 'These similarities are the result of small adjustments (changing of proportion, obliteration of small details, misrepresentations and so forth). Of course they are small details but they impair perhaps the value of the analogies and make the resemblances more close than they actually should be.'

There may be some external likeness between the Easter Island writing and the Indus Valley script (*see* Fig. 4.4, and p. 51), but the distance of time, 3,000 to 3,500 years, if not more, and of space, 13,000 miles, and the lack of any evidence of intermediate scripts belonging to the remote age of the Indus Valley script, seem to exclude any possibility of connection between the two. The fact that Munda speech (*see* p. 317) stretches from India across the Pacific—which may be the chief thing in favour of de Hevesy's theory—makes the problem still more complicated.

Similar objections may be made to von Heine-Geldern's theory. This scholar compares the Indus Valley and Easter Island symbols with those of the Chinese Honan bones and shells. In his opinion the Easter Island script derived from a southern Chinese script related to a contemporary script used in China proper. Furthermore, all these scripts and that of Indus Valley may go back to a very early system of writing in use in Central Asia or Iran—but nothing is known of such a script.

And, once more, the same objections go against Professor Imbelloni's theory. He sees a close analogy between some Easter Island symbols and the Sinhalese Brahmī script of the third century B.C. He also sees a resemblance between the Easter Island symbols and some Lolo characters (see p. 102 f.), as well as some Caroline characters (see p. 134 ff.), and concludes with the suggestion of the existence of a basic 'Indo-Pacific graphic system'—a theory which has no 'leg to stand on.'

Professor von Koenigswald comparing Easter Island symbols with those of a series of patterns embroidered on cloth from the Island of Sumatra, and with symbols from other places, has propounded a theory suggesting a Polynesian migration from Indonesia (starting from Sumatra and passing through Java) both to the Hawaian islands and to Easter Island.

RECENT ATTEMPTS AT DECIPHERMENT

The Russian Professors Kudriatseff, Olderogge, Butinoff and Knorozoff have done excellent work on the Easter Island script. They have pointed out that several rows of signs in different tablets were identical, and have suggested that certain combinations of two or more symbols may correspond to words or sentences. In Olderogge's opinion, some Easter Island symbols seem to be ideograms and others to have a phonetic value—both ideograms and phonetic symbols being accompanied by determinatives. On the whole, argues Olderogge, the Easter Island script had already reached a stage of development comparable to the early Egyptian.

It is perhaps easier to agree with Dr. Métraux' theory; he proposes the following 'provisional interpretation' of the tablets: The *rongo-rongo* used staves to augment the effect of their recitations. On these staves they engraved sacred symbols; these may originally have been aids to memory, but 'later the decorative or mystic aspect of the symbols gained over their pictographic significance.' 'We may suppose that the signs were arbitrarily associated with the chants, each symbol representing a significant word, a phrase, a sentence, or even a verse.' Dr. Métraux further points out that the custom of chanting a poem while looking at a figure has not entirely disappeared from Easter Island, and he quotes the remark of one informant: 'Our ancestors recited poems from tablets covered with images; we in our ignorance, recite them from the string-figures.'

The most recent attempt at decipherment is that by Dr. Thomas Barthel (1958). His conclusions (pp. 314–7) are as follows: The Easter Island script is more evolved than mere pictography; its symbols are mostly stylized and it may be regarded as a 'Konturschrift.' It uses a limited fund (about 120) of graphic elements, which can be increased to about 1,500–2,000 combinations following strict rules. The majority of the symbols are ideograms with fixed meanings, but some ideograms could have variable though allied meanings. The majority of characters have also constant phonetic values, and this fact makes it impossible to write names and—in view of the richness of the Polynesian language in homonyms—to construct *rebus*-fashion new symbols. It was not possible to render speech completely with all grammatical particles; the main ideas were expressed—in a sort of telegraphic style—by 'catch-words.' By this 'test-condensation' and 'partial phonetic indication,' understanding of the contents was difficult, but not impossible. On the whole, Dr. Barthel defines the Easter Island script as 'a conventional system of recording with a limited number of symbols.'

However, the problem of the origin of this script is still wrapped in mystery.

BIBLIOGRAPHY

GEISLER, KAP. LT. *Die Osterinsel, eine Stätte prehistorischer Kultur in der Süedsee*, Berlin, 1883.
HABERLAND, M. 'Über Schrifttafeln von der Osterinsel,' *Mitteil. der Anthropol. Geselsch. zu Wien*, 1886.

THOMSON, W. J. *Te Pito te Henua, or Easter Island*, Washington, 1891.

DE HARLEZ, C. 'L'Ile de Pâques et ses monuments graphiques,' *Le Muséon*, 1895–6.

CHURCHILL, W. *Easter Island*, etc., Washington, 1912.

SANDBERG, H. O. 'Easter Island, the Mystery of the Pacific,' *Pan-American Union Bulletin*, Washington, 1912.

SCORESBY ROUTLEDGE, K. *Easter Island*, London, 1917; *The Mystery of Easter Island*, London, 1919.

MACMILLAN BROWN, J. *The Riddle of the Pacific*, London, 1924.

IMBELLONI, J. *La Esfinge Indiana*, etc., Buenos Aires, Córdoba, 1926; 'Estado actual del problema que plantean las tabletas de la Isla de Pascua,' *Revista Geografica Americana*, 1933; *Los ultimos descubrimentos sobre la escritura indecifrabile de la Isla de Pascua*, Buenos Aires, 1935; 'Las "Tabletas Parlantes" de Pascua' etc., *Runa*, Buenos Aires, 1951.

CASEY, R. J. *Easter Island*, Indianapolis, 1931; London, 1932.

DE HEVESY, G. 'Écriture de l'Ile de Pâques,' *Bull. de la Soc. des Amér. de Belgique*, 1932; 'Sur une écriture océanienne paraissant d'origine néolitique, *Bull. de la Soc. Préhist. Franç.*, 1933; 'Osterinselschrift und Indusschrift, '*Orientalische Literatur Zeitung*, 1934; 'The Easter Island and the Indus Valley Scripts,' *Anthropos*, 1938.

RAY, S. H. 'Note on Inscribed Tablets from Easter Island,' *Man*, 1932.

AHNNE, E. 'Les hiéroglyphes de l'Ile de Pâques,' *Bull. de la Soc. des Études Océaniennes*, 1933.

LAVACHERY, H. 'Les bois employés dans l'Ile de Pâques,' *Bull. de la Soc. des Américanistes de Belgique*, 1934; *Ile de Pâques*, Paris, 1935; 'Easter Island, Polynesia,' *Antiquity*, No. 37, 1936; 'Les pétroglyphes de l'Ile de Pâques,' *Outre-Mer*, Paris, 1937; Stèles et pierres-levées à l'Ile de Pâques', *Süedseestudien* etc., Bâle, 1951.

MÉTRAUX, A. 'The Proto-Indian Script and the Easter Island Tablets,' *Anthropos*, 1938; *Ethnology of Easter Island*, Honolulu, 1940; *Easter Island*, London, 1957.

VON HEINE-GELDERN, R. 'Die Osterinselschrift,' *Anthropos*, 1938; 'Heyerdahl's Hypothesis of Polynesian Origins: a Criticism,' *The Geograph. Journ.*, London, 1950.

VIVANTE, A. and IMBELLONI, J. *Libro de las Atlántidas*, Buenos Aires, 1939.

VAYSON DE PRADENNE, A. *Prehistory*, etc., London, 1940.

CRAIGHILL HANDY, E. S. 'Two Unique Petroglyphs in the Marquesas,' etc., *Studies in the Anthropology of Oceania and Asia*, Cambridge, Mass., 1943.

OLDEROGGE, D. A. 'Parallel Texts of some Easter Island Tablets (in Russian), *Sovjetskaya Etnogr.*, 1947; 'Parallel Texts of Easter Island Tablets' (in Russian), *Sborn. Mus. Antrop. i Etnogr.*, 1949.

KUDRIATSEFF, B. G. *Easter Island Script* (in Russian), *ibid*.

VON KOENIGSWALD, G. H. R. 'Über sumatranische Schiffstücher und ihre Beziehungen zur Kunst Oceaniens,' *Süedseestudien*, Bâle, 1951.

BUTINOV, N. A. and KNOROZOV, Y. V. *Preliminary Report on the Study of the Written Language of Easter Island* (in Russian). Paper read to the All-Union Conference of Ethnologists, Leningrad, May, 1956.

BARTHEL, T. *Grundlagen zur Entzifferung der Osterinselschrift*, Hamburg, 1958.

See also the publications of Professor Hrozný cited in the bibliography of Chapter 4.

CHAPTER 9

Other Ideographic Scripts

GENERAL SKETCH

THERE existed in the past and there exist even nowadays various scripts which we may call ideographic or 'transitional.' Some are known, others are still unknown, while some have disappeared without leaving any trace. They are all more or less interesting from the standpoint of the history of writing, of cultural inter-relations, of idea diffusion and as evidence of the originality and capacity of single individuals of all races. Space does not allow me to deal fully with these scripts in the present book, mainly because they usually have no direct connection with alphabetic scripts and also because their influence has been rather limited. Their origins are generally unknown, but it is obvious that their creation was influenced by the existence of writing amongst neighbouring peoples. Some of these scripts might be a late invention, some might be ancient ones; some might be transformations or survivals of ancient scripts. Nobody knows. Mention may here be made of a few of these still more or less unknown writings.

'IDEOGRAPHIC' SCRIPTS OF NON-CHINESE PEOPLES
OF CHINA

At one time there were immense regions inside what we call China that were non-Chinese, and the Chinese had barely the power necessary to keep a check on these internal and inveterate foes, always ready to break the net which from time to time was spread over them. The indigenous chiefs were recognized as Chinese officials by the addition of Chinese office names to their own native appellations. Such native states, entirely enclosed in Chinese territory, lasted for many centuries, and the broken tribes still in existence within and without the borders of China are fragments of these non-Chinese peoples. Nowadays, these aboriginal tribes remain in bulk, unabsorbed by the Chinese, only in the south-western provinces of China. Some of these—for instance, Yün-nan—can be considered as 'anthropological museums' because of their great variety of peoples.

LO-LO NA-KHI GROUP

The languages of the Lo-lo Na-khi Group belong to the Tibeto-Burmese sub-family of the Tibeto-Chinese family of languages. This group has received much study at the hands of French missionaries. Lolo is itself a sub-group of various languages, spoken by about 1,800,000 people in the south-western provinces of China, mainly in Yün-nan and Sze-chwan. The region between these two provinces known as Ta Liang-shan or Mt. Liang is not an easily accessible place. The inhabitants are termed the Independent Lolo. The very few Chinese families who live there are under Lolo protection. The Lolo live also in northern Vietnam.

The Lolo are termed Lo-lo or Lu-lu or Lo-man or else Ts'wan. The name Lo-lo appears in Chinese sources since A.D. 1275; the indigenous term, however, is Ne-su, meaning 'We' (*ne*)—'men' (*su*).

The proper home of the Na-khi or Mo-s(s)o or Musu is the valley of the Mekong immediately to the east of Upper Burma and the valley of the Yang-tse round Li-kiang (north-western Yün-nan); they are also scattered throughout other provinces of south-western China. The term Mo-so is Chinese; the indigenous name is Na-khi or Na-shi; the Tibetan term is Djong, which has an insulting meaning, as has also (according to Sir Ellis Minns) the Chinese term Mo-so, 'miserable.'

The Na-khi are mentioned several times in Chinese historical sources; first at the end of the eighth century A.D. In the second half of the thirteenth century they became a vassal state of Qubilay Khan, and later they recognized the shadowy authority of China. They finally lost their independence to China about 1725, but some tribes until recent times lived under the rule of their own chiefs.

Lo-lo Script

The existence of the Lo-lo script was noted by Europeans in the seventies of the last century. In 1886, Mr. F. S. A. Bourne obtained from a Lolo-man a list of all the characters he could remember, and their total did not go beyond 376. According to some scholars, however, the Lo-lo script contains some 3,000 symbols. There are many Lo-lo manuscripts extant, and some of them are finely illustrated.

On the whole, symbols are apparently ideographic, and are said to be mainly adaptations, contractions and combinations of Chinese signs, but many of them seem to be phonetic. There are a few local varieties (Fig. 9.2*a*), of which there are two main groups, according to the direction of writing; the independent tribes of Ta Liang-shan (in Sze-chwan) still employ a horizontal script, from right to left (Fig. 9.1*b*); while the other tribes use mainly the vertical script in columns running from left to right (Fig. 9.1*a*). Very little is known of the early development of this script. An inscription of Tsan-tsin-gay, near the Lu-ch'üan-hsien, is attributed to A.D. 1533.

Professor de Lacouperie considered the Lo-lo script as a link connecting the various systems of India, Indonesia and Indo-China with those of Korea and Japan, but there are no proofs corroborating such theory. Figure 9.1*c* gives a specimen of a Lo-lo printed book, edited by Prince Len.

Na-khi Script (Fig. 9.3)

The Na-khi script also offers many open problems. Nobody knows when and how the script originated. According to Père Desgodins, the discoverer of the script in the middle of the last century, the writing does not seem a survival of former times, and it was apparently made up for the purpose by the *tombas* or medicine-men. De Lacouperie, however, rightly pointed out the possibility that 'this sacred writing embodies survivals of the pictorial stage of notation independent of synchronical dates and progresses elsewhere." Nowadays, the southern Na-khi employ the Chinese character, while the Na-khi of the north use the Tibetan alphabet. The illustrated Na-khi manuscripts, of which the John Rylands Library of Manchester has a small collection, consist mostly of little books, oblong in shape, measuring about three inches in height by ten inches in width; the leaves are of thick, rough paper of uneven texture. Figure 9.3*a* shows the first page of a Na-khi manuscript from the John Rylands Library. Figures 9.3*b*, *c* reproduce a Na-khi manuscript from the Author's collection.

The largest collection, known to us, of Na-khi books, is preserved in the Library of Congress, Washington, D.C., where there are some 600 volumes, which have been acquired by Dr. Joseph F. Rock, the authority on Na-khi manuscripts. In Rock's opinion, most of the Na-khi MSS. contain chants sung from memory by the priests, or *tombas*, at funeral ceremonies. The MSS. serve as 'prompt books,' suggesting by vivid pictographs each stanza of a rhymed chant memorized by the *tomba*, who uses the written text only to recall to memory the stanzas in proper order. Proper names can be and often are written in full, but if the entire text of these 'dramas' were given completely, the MSS. would be many times as bulky as they now are and the text probably too lengthy to be read rapidly enough to chant to the proper time and rhythm.

Moreover, according to Rock, historical books or semi-legendary ones are included in all ceremonies, for example the *Pbö-pa-go-sho* (the legend of the trip of the bat, the *yi-dzu-leu-par*, to heaven to obtain a set of Na-khi books) is chanted at all ceremonies.

MAN GROUP

The languages classed under the name of 'Man' are mainly spoken in China and Vietnam, partly also in Burma. The term 'Man' is Chinese, and means a 'Southern Barbarian.' It is applied by the Chinese to certain wild tribes, of which the Miao or Miao-tzu and Yao are the main representatives.

These languages are imperfectly known; they are regarded by some scholars as an independent group, by others, as belonging to the Tibeto-Burmese linguistic sub-family. In a recent article, G. B. Downer has pointed out that 'no affiliation of the

Miao-Yao languages with any of the neighbouring groups—Tibeto-Burmese, Chinese, Thai-Sui or Mon-Khmer—has as yet been convincingly demonstrated.' According to some scholars, they are 'aboriginal' languages of eastern Asia.

The Miao-tzu are nowadays a mountainous people of south-western China, but at one time they occupied a portion of central China. They live also, widely scattered in villages far up among the mountains, in northern Burma and in 'Indo-China', to the north-west of Vietnam and to the north of Laos. They number about 2,000,000 in China and over 500,000 in Vietnam and Laos and are sub-divided into about seventy tribes, some of which enjoy a certain autonomy. The main Chinese classification of these tribes, speaking different dialects, is according to the colour of the women's attire: Ho Miao ('Black Miao'), Pai Miao ('White Miao'), Hung Miao ('Red Miao'), Hwa Miao ('Floral Miao'), and so forth.

The Yao (called also Yao-ming, Yao-tze, Yao-tse, Yau or Yiu), numbering about 50,000, live mainly in the south-western portions of the Chinese provinces of Kwantung and Kwang-si, but also in Upper Burma, Vietnam, Laos, and northern Thailand. G. B. Downer has pointed out that the Yao dialects constitute a clearly differentiated branch of the Miao-Yao language family, both in vocabulary and phonology. Indeed, unlike the Miao, the Yao have a wide range of vowels and final consonants. In China, the Yao are generally found to the east and south of the Miao, but in the other regions (where they seem to have immigrated in a recent period), the Yao and the Miao are geographically mixed. They are also subdivided into various tribes, distinguished by differences in dress, customs and language.

Figure 11.2*f* illustrates several signs of the cryptic ideographic script of the Miao-tzu, while Fig. 9.2*e* shows some symbols of the script, also cryptic and ideographic, of the Yao. For the Pu-shui, a Shan tribe, *see* p. 331.

For the Miao Pollard syllabic system of writing *see* next chapter.

CENTRAL AND NORTHERN CHINA

A few 'systems' of non-Chinese writing are known to have existed in central and northern China. We may mention here the script of the K'itans or Khitans, of which only five symbols are known (Fig. 9.2*b*), and which was for two centuries the official script of the Liao-dynasty of that people. More important are the two scripts of the Tatar people, the Niu-chih, successors to the Khitans; the more ancient of the two was adopted in A.D. 1119 as the national script (Fig. 9.2*d*). This was revised in 1138 and called the 'little' script (Fig. 9.2*c*).

Tangut (or Si-Hia or Hsi-hsia) Script

From A.D. 982 to 1227, between China and Tibet on the latter's northern border, there stood a powerful kingdom which was swept away by the Mongols. Its name was Tangut or Si-Hia ('western Hia') or Hsi-hsia. The language spoken by that population, and preserved for us by a Chinese philologist, is the only ancient Tibeto-

Burmese language with which we are acquainted. The Si-Hia form of speech is now many centuries dead.

The Tangut king Chao Yüan-hao, otherwise Wei-i, who had married a Khitan princess, is reputed to have invented the Si-Hia character in 1037. It was written like the Chinese from top to bottom, and in columns from right to left.

The character was a highly evolved ideographic-syllabic system of writing. There are extant a few inscriptions (the earliest belonging to the eleventh century A.D.) and some manuscripts. The script was widely employed for over two centuries. Figure 9.4 shows the syllabic signs of the writing, whereas Fig. 9.5, 6 is a specimen of a Chinese–Si-Hia glossary.

BIBLIOGRAPHY

WYLIE, M. A. 'On an Ancient Buddhist Inscription,' etc., *J. Roy. Asiat. Soc.*, 1871.

COLBOURNE BARKER, J. in *The Journal of the Roy. Geogr. Society*, 1882.

DE LACOUPERIE, T. 'On a Lolo-Manuscript Written on Satin,' *J. Roy. Asiat. Soc.*, 1882; 'Beginning of Writing in and around Tibet,' the same journal, 1885.

DEVÉRIA, G. 'La stèle de Yen-t'ai,' *Revue de l'Extreme Orient*, 1883; 'Les Lolos et les Miao-tze,' *Journal Asiatique*, 1891; *L'écriture du Royaume de Si-Hia ou Tangout*, Paris, 1898.

VIAL, P. *De la langue et de l'Écriture indigènes au Yûn-Nân*, Paris, 1890; *Les Lolos*, etc., Shanghai, 1898; *Dictionnaire français-lolo, dialecte Gni*, Hongkong, 1909.

BUSHELL, S. W. 'The Hsi-Hsia Dynasty of Tangut, their Money and Peculiar Script,' *China Branch of the Roy. Asiat. Soc.*, 1895–6.

PARKER, E. H. 'The Lolo Written Character,' *The Indian Antiquary*, 1895.

MORISSE, M. G. 'Contribution préliminaire a l'étude de l'écriture et de la langue Si-hia,' *Académie des Inscriptions et Belles Lettres. Mémoires*, Paris, 1904.

IVANOV, A. 'Zur Kenntnis der Hsi-hsia-Sprache,' *Bull. of the Imperial Russian Academy of Science*, 1909; 'Documents from Khara-kho' (= the ancient Hsi-Hsia capital), in Russian, *Bull. of the Imperial Russian Geographical Society*, 1913.

LEGENDRE, A.-F. 'Les Lo-lo,' *T'oung Pao*, 1909.

D'OLLONE, H. M. G. *Mission d'Ollone*, 1906–9, etc., *Écritures des peuples non chinois de la Chine*, etc., Paris, 1912; *In Forbidden China*, etc., London, 1912.

BACOT, J. *Les Mo-So*, etc., Leyden, 1913.

STÜBE, R. 'Die Schriftdenkmäler der Hsi-Hsia,' *Archiv für Schriftkunde*, 1914.

HESTERMANN, F. 'Die nichtchinesische Schrift der Lolo in Yuennan (Südwest-China),' *Wiener Zeitschr. für die Kunde des Morgenlandes*, 1915.

LAUFER, B. *The Si-Hia Language. A Study in Indo-Chinese Philology*, Leyden, 1916; 'The Nichols Mo-so Manuscript,' *The Geographical Review*, 1916.

SABINA, F. M. *Histoire des Miao*, Hongkong, 1924.

VON ZACH, E. 'Eine merkwürdige Schrift,' *Deutsche Wacht*, 1927.

YOUNG, CHING-CHI, 'L'écriture et les manuscripts lolos,' *Orient et Occident*, 1935.

CHIN, CH.-K. *Die Kultur der Miao-Tse*, Hamburg, 1937.

SIGURET, J. *Territories et populations des confins du Yûnnan*, Peking and Leipsic, 1937.

TELFORD, J. H. *Handbook of the Lahu (Muhso) Language*, etc., Rangoon, 1938.

EBERHARD, W. *Kultur und Siedlung der Randvölker Chinas*, Leyden, 1942.

ROCK, J. F. in *Ann. Rep. of Library of Congress*, 1930, 1934, 1936; personal correspondence to the present writer; *Dictionary of the Na-khi Pictographic Characters* (in preparation).

WEST AFRICAN 'IDEOGRAPHIC' SCRIPTS

NSIBIDI

I have already mentioned various West African devices for transmission of thought (p. 7 f. and 11). *Nsibidi* or *Nchibiddi* or *Nchibiddy* seems to be the only true 'ideographic' script of the West African natives (Fig. 9.7).

The Name

The meaning of the term is uncertain. According to Mr. Goldie, the word Nsibidi is connected with the Efik verb *sibi*, 'to cut,' but the Rev. J. K. Macgregor pointed out that *sibi* actually means 'to slice,' and not to make cuts as referred to in the verb 'to engrave.' In Macgregor's opinion, the term Nsibidi is derived from an Ibo word *sibidi*, meaning to 'play,' 'for they had learned these things through the playing of the *idiok*.' Finally, P. A. Talbot points out that the Ekoi explanation of the name is derived from the verb *nchibbi*, 'to turn,' and 'this has taken to itself the meaning of agility of mind, and, therefore, of cunning or double meaning.'

Until 1904, the existence of Nsibidi was unknown to Europeans. Its first discovery was made by T. D. Maxwell, at the time District Commissioner in Calabar, and, independently, a year later, that is, in 1905, J. K. Macgregor discovered its existence. Twenty-four signs were published in the Government Civil List of July, 1905.

Origin

The origin of Nsibidi is uncertain. According to a local tradition, the script originated among the Uguakima (or Ebe or Uyanga), sub-tribe of the Ibo tribe, living between Ikorana on the Cross River and Uwet on the Calabar River, and there is a charming story about how the Uyanga learned this script from the baboons called *idiok*, who crowded round their camp-fires. On the other hand, P. A. Talbot could not find any trace of the existence among the Ibo of any system of writing, whereas the Ekoi claim to have invented the whole system.

However, both the story about the monkeys and the Ekoi tradition only show that Nsibidi must be so old that even the local tradition lost any trace of its true origin. Also Talbot considers it 'of considerable antiquity.' Some scholars have even detected certain resemblances between the Nsibidi and the Egyptian hieroglyphic writing, one of the most remarkable being the fact that the Nsibidi sign for 'house' is rectangular in shape (Fig. 9.7*d*[6]), whereas all dwellings of the natives who use Nsibidi are round. However, I do not think there can be any reasonable direct connection between the two scripts.

Nsibidi is, or was, employed in the Calabar District of southern Nigeria, and up the Cross River and inland from it on both banks.

The Script

The script is purely ideographic, that is, each sign represents an idea or even more than one. It is to a large extent pictographic, but in the course of years many signs have become highly conventionalized. Some Nsibidi signs are known to many people, but the majority of the symbols are known only to those belonging to the Nsibidi secret society, into which men were or still are regularly initiated after undergoing a period of preparation. To the uninitiated the signs are mysterious and therefore magical, capable of doing harm because of the 'medicine' that may have been used in making them. According to E. Dayrell, there are several kinds of Nsibidi which strangers belonging to another society would not understand, whereas the signs common to all the societies are most often tattooed on the face, arms and legs, etc., of the people. On the whole, the natives have a strange desire to hide the knowledge of the script, as much as they can, from the eyes of the Europeans. On the other hand, Nsibidi is used mainly to express love, and many a self-respecting native would disclaim all knowledge of how to write some of the words that this term covers.

Nsibidi, however, can be used for any kind of communication. Figure 9.7c[1] represents the record of a court case from a town on the Enion Creek. Figure 9.7c[2] shows the record of a trial by the Nsibidi Club, drawn on a small calabash.

Nsibidi was also employed to give public notice or private warning of anything, to forbid people to go on a certain road, to warn a friend that he is to be seized, to convey the wishes of a chief, and for other communications. For a long time messages have been sent in Nsibidi script cut or painted on split palm stems.

BIBLIOGRAPHY

MACGREGOR, J. K. 'Some Notes on Nsibidi,' *J. Roy. Anthrop. Institute of Great Britain and Ireland*, 1909.
DAYRELL, E. 'Further Notes on 'Nsibidi Signs,' the same journal, 1911.
TALBOT, P. A. *In Shadow of the Bush*, London, 1912.

BAMUN (OR BAMUM) SCRIPT

IN the grasslands of the Cameroons (5°–6° north, 11° east of Greenwich) live the Bamum (or Bamom, Bamoun, Banun), numbering about 75,000; their capital is Fumban. They are a branch of the Tikar tribe and speak a Bantu language, although with very many admixtures from other languages. Most words are monosyllabic; the language is tonic, *i.e.*, the same word may have quite different meanings according to the tone in which it is pronounced. Until the end of the last century, the Bamum had no script of their own, nor did they use any foreign script.

In the 1870's, Sultan Nsangu governed them; when in, or shortly before, 1880 he fell in a battle, his son Njoya, still a boy (born *c.* 1867), succeeded him. Shortly afterwards, Germany acquired the Cameroons as a colony.

The young Njoya was acquainted with the Arabic script as well as with German or English words in the Latin script. Whatever his reasons—either as Delafosse suggests, to evade the Germans, or, according to Labouret, to develop the culture of the Bamum—about 1896–7 he invented a script. 'One night he dreamt: he saw a man

I

who said to him: "King, take a wooden tablet and design on it the hand of a man; then wash the tablet and drink the water." So the Sultan designed the hand on the tablet and gave it to the man; he in turn wrote something on it and returned it. The Sultan saw many people seated around; these were all schoolboys who had paper in their hands; they wrote on it and handed it on, each to his neighbour.' The next morning the Sultan did as he was directed and asked his courtiers to help him to invent a script; but he did not find very much sympathy. Nevertheless he did not tire, and with the help of two Muslim mullahs, Moma and Isaiah, he succeeded in inventing a script; he then proceeded to teach it.

Over a period of many years Njoya invented seven scripts; although the main authority, Dugast and Jeffreys, call these scripts 'alphabets,' this term is far from accurate; the first five scripts were, indeed, pictographic and ideographic (Fig. 9.8a). Njoya has certainly to be admired, first because he did not copy any other script, and secondly, because in the course of time he developed great phonetic understanding.

THE SEVEN SCRIPTS

First script called *lewa* ('book'), invented about 1896–7. It had 465—or, according to some sources—511 symbols and the numerals (one to ten). The direction of the script was either from top to bottom or from left to right, or even from bottom to top; only the direction from right to left was to be avoided, because the neighbouring Haussa wrote in this direction, and it ought not to be thought that the script was borrowed from them. The Sultan invented a most interesting sign 𝄢 (changed later into ℺), called nʒəmli, which had two purposes: (1) it was placed before proper names of persons or peoples; (2) it differentiated between two *homonyms* according to their degree of nobility (man is nobler than a homonymous animal, plant, or thing; an animal or a plant is nobler than a homonymous thing). The sign even differentiated between homonymous things, one of which was regarded as nobler than the other.

Second script, called *mbima* ('mixed'), was invented about 1899–1900. It had 427 symbols and ten numerals. It was a simplification of the first script; Njoya omitted seventy-two symbols, but added forty-five new ones. This script, too, was pictographic in character.

Third script, called *nyi nyi nʃa mfw'* (the names of the first four symbols), invented about 1902. This script was a further simplification; Njoya dropped fifty-six more symbols, leaving 371 symbols and ten numerals. He used this script to write his *History of the Bamum* and for his correspondence with his mother.

Fourth script, called *rii nyi nʃa mfw'* (the names of the first four symbols), invented about 1907–8. It had 285 symbols and ten numerals, and was again a simplification of its predecessor. In the order of the script, two symbols were always grouped together, each group followed by the *dirimens* o, *kum*; but this arrangement was

merely for mnemonic purposes; the pupils learning it by heart had just to pronounce: *rii nyi* 'stop,' etc.

Fifth script, rii nyi mfw' mɛn, also invented about 1907–8; it had 195 symbols and
ten numerals. In this script a translation of the Bible was written.

These five scripts are not only functionally related—all five were pictographic,
and each following script was only a simplification—but at least the third, the fourth
and the fifth, were used simultaneously. Whoever, with great pain, had mastered
the third script, did not abandon it, when the fourth and fifth were invented; he
just continued with it.

It was the *sixth script* which meant a real step forward. It was called *a ka u ku* (names
of the first four symbols), and was invented after 1910. It was monosyllabic and
phonetic; it had only eighty-two symbols and ten numerals. The eighty-two
symbols included: fifty-six symbols representing either monosyllabic words or
single phonemes; one symbol representing *m*; six symbols, representing the vowels:
a, u, e, ə, i, and *wü* or *ü*; fifteen symbols were syllabic phonemes without a precise
meaning; one symbol standing for the affix *pa*; one symbol for the affix *kət*, indicating
a 'superlative'; one symbol for the *nʒəmli* (*see* above under *First Script*); one symbol
for the *kə'ndɔn*, a superimposed accent which changed the sound phonetically; with
its aid Njoya was able to express 160 phonemes. The sixth script was used to write
the *Code of Marriage*, the registers of births, deaths and marriages, and the judg-
ments. A calligraphic refinement of the sixth script was called *lerəwa niet*.

About 1913 Njoya set out to create a printing press. The preparations took seven
years, and the press was finished by 1920. But about this time Njoya was so annoyed
by the French administration that, in a fit of rage, he destroyed all the machinery.

Seventh script, called *mfɛmfɛ* ('new') or *a ka u ku mfɛmfɛ* ('new or little *a ka u ku*'),
was invented in 1918: see Fig. 9.8*b*. It had only seventy-two symbols (seventy
ordinary symbols, one *nʒəmli* and one *kə'ndɔn*) and the ten symbols for the figures
one to ten. In 1921 Njoya introduced the symbol S ('zero'), which displaced the symbol for 'ten.' Dugast and Jeffreys praise Njoya's phonetic achievements, especially because he invented a symbol for the 'coup de glotte'—it seems that they mean a kind
of *'alef* or *'ayin*.

Njoya made very comprehensive use of his invention. He wrote a *History of the
Bamum and their Customs*, a book on *Religion*, a book on *Medicine and Local Pharma-
cology;* he started a topographical survey of his country and let a map be drawn. The
History of the Bamum survives, fortunately, in two copies; one complete and one incomplete; Professor Jeffreys had a copy of the latter made by scribes who had
originally served Njoya; he presented it to the Pitt-Rivers Museum in Oxford.

When, after the First World War, the French obtained the Cameroons, the strong
personality of the Sultan clashed with the French administration. So the French
exiled him to Yaunde in 1931, where he died in 1933. His scripts survived, but are
slowly dying out.

The sixth and seventh scripts, in particular, are very remarkable.

BIBLIOGRAPHY

GÖHRING, PASTOR (of the mission of Bâle), 'Der König von Bamum und seine Schrift,' *Der Evangelische Heidenbote*, 1907, 84 f., and 1908; *Sämtliche Zeichen der vom König Njoya von Bamum erfundenen Schrift*, Bâle, 1907.

VAN GENNEP, A. 'Une nouvelle écriture nègre,' *Revue des Études ethnographiques et sociologiques*, vol. 1, pp. 129–139, Paris, 1908.

STRUCK, B. 'König Ndschoya von Bamum als Topograph,' *Globus* 94 (1908), pp. 206–9.

MEINHOF, C. 'Zur Entstehung der Schrift,' *Zeitschrift für Ägyptische Sprache und Altertumskunde*, 1911, pp. 49 ff.

HERTZ, A. 'Ein Beitrag zur Entwicklung der Schrift,' *Archiv für die gesamte Psychologie*, 1917; 'Les débuts de l'écriture,' *Revue archéologique*, 1934.

DELAFOSSE, M. 'Naissance et évolution d'un système d'écriture de création contemporaire,' *Revue d'ethnographie et traditions populaires*, 1922.

RHEIN-WUHRMANN, A. *Mein Bamumvolk*, Stuttgart-Bâle, 1925.

SCHRAMM, A. 'Die Bamumschrift,' *Archiv für Schreib- und Buchwesen*, 1927.

BOXBERGER, 'Das Opfer; aus meiner Residentenzeit in Bamum,' *Atlantis*, 1930.

OLDENBURG, R. 'Bamum,' *Atlantis*, 1930, p. 161.

CRAWFORD, O. G. S. *Antiquity*, December 1935.

DUGAST, I. and JEFFREYS, M. D. W. *L'écriture des Bamum*, Paris, 1950 (with bibliography).

JEFFREYS, M. D. W. 'The Alphabet of Njoya,' *West African Review*, 23 (1952).

See now, particularly, SCHMITT, A. *Die Bamum-Schrift*, 3 vols., Wiesbaden, 1963.

RECENT IDEOGRAPHIC SCRIPTS OF AMERINDIANS
(*See also pp. 80 ff. and 128 ff.*)

(1) In some parts of the Paucartambo Valley, in Peru, fragments painted in red and blue on old Dutch paper, or in light red on dark brown woven material, have been found. These contain in pictographic symbols stories connected with the New Testament. Nothing is known of the origin of this script, of its connection with the Catholic missionaries, or of its diffusion; Fig. 9.9*a* shows some examples of this writing.

(2) Much more is known of a local script of another South American native tribe, the Aymarà, who live mainly in the region around Lake Titicaca (Bolivia-Peru). We are informed of the existence of this script by the German ethnologist Tschudi (*Rüsen in Südamerika*, V, 1869, p. 282 *ff.*). The script was invented by an old native of Sampaya, who was a zealous Catholic, in order to teach his tribesmen the Catholic cathechism. The writing was purely ideographic and highly pictographic. The drawing of the signs was very crude. After the death of the inventor, his pupil, Juan de Dios Apasa, continued the teaching of this writing, but after the latter's death, the script fell into disuse. Fig. 9.9*b* shows a specimen of this Aymarà script.

(3) The native Central American tribe Cuna (*Tule*, 'person,' is the native name), who live mainly in Panama near Darien, numbering about 25,000 people and speaking a language belonging to the linguistic family of the Chibcha, have their own ideographic, highly pictorial system. Nothing is known about the origin of

this script. Some scholars suggest that it was already in use in pre-Columbian times and that it is connected with the pre-Conquest scripts of Central America and Mexico. It is, however, preferable to consider this writing as a more recent creation.

The script is *boustrophedon*, *i.e.*, in alternate lines from right to left and from left to right. The texts begin with the bottom line on the right-hand side. This writing is mainly used for magic and ritual purposes. *See* Fig. 9.9*c*.

(4) The North American Indians have not, as far as can be established, developed any complete system which can properly be considered as true writing; their pictographic mnemonic devices have already been mentioned (*see* p. 7 ff.). The missionary Chr. Kauder succeeded, however, in reducing into an ideographic system of writing the crude pictographs employed by the Micmac or Megum, a tribe belonging to the great linguistic family of the Algonkians. The Micmacs live in Canada, on the shores of the Gulf of St. Lawrence and on the islands, chiefly in Nova Scotia. Kauder even succeeded in printing (at Vienna in 1866) a religious work in three volumes for which he used 5,701 symbols (Fig. 9.9*d*).

BIBLIOGRAPHY

MALLERY, G. *Picture Writing of the American Indians*, Washington, 1893.
NORDENSKIŒLD, E. *Picture-Writings and other Documents*, Gœteborg, 1928 and 1930.

MINAHASSA SCRIPT

'Minahassa,' from Nimahasa, means 'confederation,' or rather a 'country that has been formed by binding a number of territories into one.' It is the north-eastern extremity of Celebes, now constituting a district of the Residency of Menado; 4,786 square kilometres, inhabited by 250,000 people living in about 300 villages. The Minahassas are divided into eight tribes.

Unlike the other peoples of Celebes, professing mainly (as far as they are not pagans) the Muslim faith, nearly the whole population of Minahassa is Christian. Very few are illiterates, although the Minahassas are also called 'Alfuros,' meaning 'wild, half-savage.' They speak Malay dialects, but physically they are different from the other tribes of the island; some authorities even suggested Japanese characteristics. According to their tradition, they immigrated from the north into the island.

The Minahassas seem to have had an ideographic script, of which very little is now known. Only two pages of a Minahassa manuscript (partly reproduced in Fig. 9.9*b*) have been published.

CHUKCHA SCRIPT

Mention should also be made of some undeveloped ideographic scripts used by nomadic tribes of the U.S.S.R. in north-eastern Europe and Asia, particularly in the Chukcha or Chukotsky peninsula; some tribes have spread to Kamtchatka.

They belong to the aboriginal or Palæo-Siberian group, and are mainly nomad reindeer breeders and hunters, as well as seal and whale hunters.

This section terminates with the ideographic script which is probably the most recently invented. The Chukcha, or Tschuktchis, Chanktus ('Men'), or Tuski ('Brothers, confederates'), are a Luoravetian, Palæo-Asiatic, Mongoloid people inhabiting the shores of the Arctic Ocean and Behring Sea in north-eastern Siberia.

The Chukcha had no written language before about 1930. About that time, a Chukcha shepherd named Tenevil', who lived in the region of the upper Anadyr, invented a peculiar script. The Leningrad Arctic Institute possesses a collection of fourteen wooden tablets written by Tenevil', and brought there in 1933 by the Chukcha expedition of that Institute. The script is a quite primitive ideography; the characters, however, are stylized. Figure 9.10*a* shows a specimen of this script, and Fig. 9.10*b* reproduces some symbols.

BIBLIOGRAPHY

BOGORAZ, V. G. in KREJNOVICH, E. A. *Languages and Literatures of the Palæo-Asiatic Peoples* (constituting Part III of *Languages and Literatures of the Northern Peoples*, edited as Vol. III of the Linguistic Section of the Russian Institute for the 'Study of the Peoples of the North'), in Russian, Leningrad, 1934.

BOUDA, K. in *Zeitschr. deutscher morgenl. Gesellschaft*, 1937.

FRIEDRICH, J. 'Die Wortschrift des Tschuktschen Tenevil' (Zu einigen Schrifterfindungen der neuesten Zeit), the same journal, 1938.

CHAPTER 10

Syllabic Systems of Writing

SYLLABARIES

THE history of writing does not present many pure syllabaries. The most important syllabaries are: (1) The pseudo-hieroglyphic script of Byblos (Syria) and the syllabary of ancient Cyprus; (2) the two Japanese syllabaries still in use; and (3) syllabaries recently compiled by, or for, certain indigenous peoples of western Africa and northern America. We shall deal here briefly with each of these groups.

PSEUDO-HIEROGLYPHIC SCRIPT OF BYBLOS

Inscriptions

There are now ten inscriptions or fragments extant (Figs. 10.1–4), on stone or bronze, written in a pseudo-hieroglyphic script, presumably bearing some resemblance to Egyptian hieroglyphics. The whole material has been edited in a splendid publication by the discoverer himself (M. Dunand, *Byblia Grammata. Documents et recherches sur le developpement de l'écriture en Phénicie*. République Libanaise. Ministère de l'Education Nationale et des Beaux-Arts. Direction des Antiquités. Études et Documents d'Archéologie. Tome II, Beyrouth, Imprimérie Catholique, 1945). As M. Dunand points out, two of the documents seem to be fragments of one and the same inscription; the number of the inscriptions would thus be nine. Of these, six are bronze tablets, and M. Dunand rightly emphasizes that this proportion is unique in Near Eastern epigraphy. The most remarkable is a rectangular bronze tablet (Fig. 10.1a) containing 41 lines (19 of which are on the *verso*) and consisting of 461 symbols, of which 64 are different. Another rectangular bronze tablet (Fig. 10.1c) contains 15 lines, of which two are on the reverse side, consisting of 217 symbols, of which 53 are different.

The other bronze inscriptions are *spatulae* (Figs. 10.1d and 2), containing respectively 41, 12, 29 and 33 symbols. The three or four stone inscriptions (Figs. 10.1b, 3 and 4c) consist of one stele and three fragments, two of which, as mentioned, may be parts of the same inscription. On these stone inscriptions there are extant respectively 119, 17, 6 and 13 symbols. All the inscriptions contain a total of 1038 signs.

The Script

In all, the documents contain 114 different signs, which Dunand distinguishes into symbols representing: (1) animals (13 signs), (2) vegetation (also represented by 13 signs), (3) the sky and the earth, (4) tools (as many as 26 signs), (5) objects connected with the cult (6 signs), (6) 10 symbols connected with navigation, (7) 17 signs representing objects which cannot be determined, (8) 8 geometric figures, and (9) 12 signs of uncertain meaning or incomplete ones. The smaller bronze-tablet contains on its *verso* a sign in the shape of the numeral 1, repeated seven times, and one *spatula* contains a similar sign repeated five times. Groups of two signs are very frequent. About 50 symbols are, more or less, similar to Egyptian hieroglyphics; others may find parallels in the scripts of Crete, Cyprus, Indus Valley, Sinai or Canaan.

Dunand believes that the 114 symbols do not constitute the totality of the system, which according to him was probably neither an alphabet nor a syllabary, nor an ideographic script, but a semi-ideographic and semi-phonetic writing, perhaps also including determinatives, or a syllabic polyphonic system like the later cuneiform script, in which the scribe could represent the same sounds by various signs.

M. Dunand argues that this pseudo-hieroglyphic script originated under Egyptian influence, at the end of the First Period of the Bronze Age, that is about the twenty-second century B.C.; but according to other authorities, we cannot go beyond the second millennium. Twenty-five symbols seem to have been directly borrowed from the Egyptian hieroglyphic script, and the shapes of about the same number of signs seem to have been suggested by Egyptian hieroglyphs. The consonantal principle and the selected symbols to represent mono-consonantal words were used by the Egyptians at the beginning of the third millennium B.C., but the Phœnicians developed these advantages about 1,000 years later, and have thus accomplished a new invention in the 'career' of consonantal representation. Until the end of Bronze I, Byblos had no writing of its own; the pseudo-hieroglyphic script was a contribution of the early Phœnician civilization after the ruin of the civilization of the third millennium B.C. From the cultural and economic points of view, Phœnicia was then in a very favourable position to invent a proper script. Finally, according to M. Dunand, the documents extant do not allow us to determine the chronology of the development of this script, but a *spatula* (Fig. 10.1,2), containing a Phœnician inscription and some scratching in pseudo-hieroglyphic writing, proves that the latter was still employed at the time when the alphabet was already used.

Decipherment

Professor Edouard Dhorme, the well-known orientalist and one of the decipherers of the Ugarit alphabet, may have succeeded in deciphering the pseudo-hieroglyphic inscriptions, showing that they are in Phœnician syllabic script: *see* Fig. 10.4*b*. He delivered two communications on the subject to the Paris Académie des Inscriptions on 2nd August and 27th September, 1946, and I am in the fortunate position of publishing the following notes which I received from Paris through the kindness of Miss Hilda Herne.

Académie des Inscriptions et Belles Lettres. Le 2 Août, 1946.

M. Edouard Dhorme, Professeur au Collège de France, fait une communication sur les textes pseudo-hiéroglyphiques de Byblos en Phénicie.

'These texts, discovered and published by M. M. Dunand, are couched in an unknown script, of more than 140 symbols of hieroglyphic appearance. Without the help of a bilingual and without even the help of a stroke indicating the separation of the words, M. Dhorme has succeeded in determining the syllabary of this unknown script, and in defining the language which it represents. This language is pure Phœnician; there is no connection between the objects represented by the signs and their phonetic values. M. Dhorme translates one of the bronze tablets of Byblos. . . .

'This discovery is of outstanding interest for the history of writing, of the alphabet, and of the civilization of the Near East in the middle of the second millennium B.C. It is a milestone in the annals of epigraphy and linguistics.'

Académie des Inscriptions et Belles Lettres. Le 27 Septembre, 1946. Seconde communication de M. Edouard Dhorme, Professeur au Collège de France, sur le 'déchiffrement des inscriptions pseudo-hiéroglyphiques de Byblos.'

'In continuation of his communication of 2nd August, in which he announced that he had achieved the decipherment of the pseudo-hieroglyphic inscriptions of Byblos, couched in a hitherto unknown script and language.' According to Professor Dhorme, this Phœnician system of writing of the middle of the second millennium B.C. made use of over a hundred signs based on foreign syllabaries to represent their Semitic tongue. Professor Dhorme then translated a text of forty lines engraved on a bronze tablet, made by the smelters and engravers of the temple of Byblos. Egyptian influence on Byblos, attested by the ancient legends of Osiris and by the archæological discoveries, can now, according to Professor Dhorme, be confirmed by this inscription and by the other one, translated and explained in the previous communication'.

Finally, I am extremely glad to be able to publish the following note which the decipherer himself kindly sent me, and for which I express to him my deepest gratitude:

(1) I think (writes Professor Dhorme) that the pseudo-hieroglyphic texts of Byblos date from the period of Amenophis IV (that is to say, c. 1375 B.C.—D. D.).

(2) I am in disagreement with Dunand on the problem of the origin of the Alphabet.

(3) I have completely deciphered the tablets c and d (Figs. 10.1a and c—D. D.). I will publish these texts and the others in *Syria* with a nearly complete syllabary. (*See,* now, E. Dhorme, 'Déchiffrem. d. inscript. pseudo-hiérogl. de Byblos,' *Syria,* 1946–8, pp. 1–35, and our Fig. 10.1c).

(4) The syllabary is 'plethoric,' that is to say, as in Akkadian, there are sometimes many different signs to represent the same syllable. The tablet d (here, Fig. 10.1a) uses numerous *matres lectionis.*

(5) The number of signs is about one hundred (Dunand has classified some identical signs as distinct symbols).

(6) With some rare exceptions, in the script of Byblos there is no connection between the shapes of the signs and their consonantic or syllabic value. For instance, the eye does not represent the *'ayin*, but a *shin*; the pupil of the eye is a *sin* or *samekh*, and so forth.

(7) The engravers or scribes of Byblos gave to the hieroglyphic signs meanings proper to their tongue, without taking into consideration their origin. The texts are in pure Phœnician.

(8) My starting-point was the last line of the tablet *c* (here, Fig. 10.1*c*), in which the last sign written seven times is a numeral (3+40 or 3+4), preceded by the word *b sh n t*, 'in the years.' Hence, *nkh°sh*, 'bronze,' in the first line; *mzbḥ*, 'altar,' in the 6th line; *btmz*, 'in Tammuz,' in the 14th line, etc., etc.

The whole problem has been re-examined by H. Sobelman in 'The Proto-Byblian Inscriptions,' *The Journal of Semitic Studies*, 1961. Sobelman points out that Dhorme's decipherment has been rejected by leading Semitists including Albright, Rowley and De Langhe.

MINOAN 'LINEAR B'
(for the nomenclature *see* p. 42)

Before the Dorians invaded the Peloponnese, it was inhabited by other Greek tribes, who may or may not be identical with the Achaeans, *i.e.*, the *Achaioi* mentioned by Homer and the *Akhiyavash* mentioned in the Hittite inscriptions. They were apparently the bearers of the civilization described in the *Iliad* and *Odyssey*. At the time of the Dorian immigration—probably *c.* 1200–1100 B.C.—these tribes were partially subjugated to form the Helots of Sparta, partially squeezed into the barren highlands of Arcadia and Achaia. That we now know more about the early history is due to one of the most amazing decipherments in the history of writing, the decipherment of 'Linear B,' by Ventris, in 1952.

Sir Arthur Evans, as mentioned on pp. 41 f., had found a great number of inscribed seals and clay tablets in Crete and had divided the scripts into several classes. Some are clearly pictographic; but two classes consist of signs similar to letters; he called them 'Linear Class A' and 'Linear Class B' (Figs. 10.5 and 6*a*). In 1939 Blegen started excavations at Ano Englianos in Messenia, probably the ancient Pylos, the seat of Nestor; his first experimental trench cut a room containing archives, with *c.* 600 clay tablets inscribed with 'Linear B.' When Sir Arthur Evans died in 1941, he had not yet finished the publication of the 'Linear B' inscriptions from Crete; this was done after his death by Sir John Myres (*Scripta Minoa*, vol. 11, Oxford, 1952), and by a lucky chance this almost coincided with Bennett's publication of the Pylos tablets (Princeton, 1951). Apart from the inscriptions discussed in chapter 3 and the Pylos tablets just mentioned, some tablets were found by the late Professor A. J. B.

Wace, at Mycenae, and also some inscribed jars at Thebes and other places on the Greek mainland.

When, in 1936, Sir Arthur Evans gave a lecture on his discoveries, it happened that a schoolboy of 14 years attended: Michael Ventris (1922-1956; he died in a motor accident at the age of only 34 years). This lecture set his mind working. At school he studied classics, but at University he gave it up and read architecture, becoming an architect. His works published in 1951-2 opened the last stage of decipherment. Ventris found a true helpmate in John Chadwick, an exellent classical philologist at the University of Cambridge.

Preparatory Work

A certain amount of preparatory work had already begun; but the way was barred by Sir Arthur Evans's conviction that the language written in 'Linear B' must be Cretan, and by the almost incredible fact that in the years preceding the publication of *Scripta Minoa II*, Ventris was denied access to the Knossos material which was under Sir John Myres's supervision. The most important discovery was announced in the observation made by Alice Kober in the *American Journal of Archæology*, lii, 1948, p. 101, that 'Linear B' had masculine and feminine endings; an early death prevented her from going on.

The Decipherment

Ventris started from the conventional belief that the language expressed by 'Linear B' was unknown, but was certainly not Greek; this belief, however, did not hinder him. Although there was no bilingual inscription extant, as in Champollion's or Grotefend's cases, the world had learned a lot about cryptography in the last two wars and apparently it was by such methods that he approached the texts. That meant that at one and the same time several (sometimes a great many) possible solutions are present in the mind of the decipherer, but that all of a sudden, one of them makes sense, and not only for one or two words; indeed—as with a click—for almost the whole material.

During the time of decipherment, Ventris was in constant touch with about two dozen scholars on the basis of 'work notes' which illuminate the progress of his thought. If these could be collected and printed, they would doubtless show a master-mind at work through trial and error till a solution was reached. For example, he wrote on June 7th, 1952:

'Dear Diringer,

I expect you have seen the recent publication of Myres's *Scripta Minoa* Vol. II. The last diagram[1] of the Minoan Linear Script B which you included in the *Alphabet* was largely based on the signary which Myres had published there. Dr. Bennett of Yale has lately used what I consider to be a very much better arrangement

---

[1] The drawing was prepared by Michael Ventris himself. D.D.

of the signary in his publication of the *Pylos Tablets*, and is preparing a revised index to the Knossos material and corrections to the texts, using this signary to arrange the material. I have just completed a diagram showing this signary, after discussion with Bennett, and you may care to have a copy of it for your file. The agreement between the scripts of Knossos *c.* 1400 B.C. and Pylos *c.* 1200 (?) is very close indeed. The signs 18, 19, 47, 49, 63, 71, 82, 87 and 88 are either very rare, or doubtful variants of other signs, and can almost be omitted from any diagram intended to show only the "working syllabary," which amounts to about seventy-eight signs common to both series. I suspect that about a dozen of the less common signs are, in addition, homophones for other signs, and the effective syllabic range may have been about sixty-five syllables, or less.

We have made a good deal of progress in analysing the material, and I have a feeling that decipherment is now just around the corner. I hope we may be able to supply some phonetic values to go with these signs before long.

Yours,
Michael Ventris'

Ventris's Grid (Fig. 10.6*b*)

Ventris observed that 'Linear B' had—besides some fifty ideograms—about eighty-eight signs which looked very much like what was in the finds at Knossos, as well as at Pylos, Mycenae, Thebes (*see* Figs. 10.7, 8) and in other mainland pottery inscriptions. The number of signs excluded the possibility of an alphabet, but made it likely that they formed a syllabary, consisting of 'open' syllables (*i.e.*, consonant followed by vowel). And so it was. In various stages of his work Ventris arranged the signs in grids, the horizontal lines of which corresponded with the commencing consonant of the open syllable, the vertical ones with the vowel which followed the consonant. In his second pre-decipherment grid he arranged fifty-five of the commonest signs out of the eighty-eight (seven of them in two alternative positions; those which only seldom occurred were omitted) in a grid of sixteen horizontal and five vertical lines. The horizontal lines indicated either syllables consisting of a vowel only, or open syllables beginning with the semi-consonants *j* or *w*, or with the consonants *d, k, m, n, p, qw, r, s* or *t*; the five vertical columns indicated the vocalic values of these open syllables according to the five vowels *a, e, i, o,* and *u*. By combining the consonants or semi-consonants—or the lack of consonants in the first horizontal lines—with the vowels, he was able to fill the grid in fifty-five places by open syllables: *a, e, i, o, u; da* (twice), *di, do, du* (*du* was at first not discovered, because he looked upon the two signs for *du* and *da* as identical in effect; later he found that one of them meant *du*); *ka, ke, ki, ko, ku,* etc. This pre-decipherment grid (Fig. 10.6*b*) was a statement of the internal relationship of the signs, based upon evidence of one sign replacing another in various ways. Values obtained for a few of these signs allowed him to read off other values by extrapolation. These values were then checked by identification of fresh words, and so on.

Tentatively he inserted the phonetical values obtained in this way into texts of 'Linear B,' and bits of it made sense. And not only was it clear that the type of the language was Indo-European; it was, indeed, Greek. It was Greek of an early archaic type, written under some queer orthographic rules which made the words look very unfamiliar. Since this archaic Greek dialect is separated from Plato's Attic Greek by nearly one thousand years and therefore necessarily must be different, any criticism from the standpoint of Classical Greek grammar or vocabulary is inadmissible.

The material which Ventris had at his disposal was meagre. No religious or literary texts, no historical or legal texts, only more or less dry lists of commodities. The Pylos tablets are just enumerations of commodities, carefully described, so that they could be easily identified and 'Nestor' could not be deceived. (Some examples of Ventris's first readings are reproduced on Fig. 10.5).

Nevertheless, from this scanty material Ventris succeeded in identifying not only Greek words and personal names, but also verbs and elements of accidence which could hardly be explained except as Greek. Since there was no bilingual inscription for checking, Ventris could proffer at the beginning only the internal evidence that, if scholars would accept his decipherment, words and combinations of words would make sense and would not contradict the solution of other parts of the texts. But very soon new documents were found, and when deciphered according to the results obtained by Ventris, they made sense, too. Most convincing of all: when Ventris showed a slide of a tablet, discovered some time later, at a Congress at Copenhagen in 1954, 'the whole of the large audience broke into applause before he had said a word.'

Although some scholars asserted that Ventris and Chadwick deceived themselves and did not really decipher 'Linear B,' this opposition may now be regarded as superseded.

The result seems to be that 'Linear B' (Fig. 10.9) was the script of the Achaeans both in Crete and on the mainland—at least between the destruction of Knossos (*c.* 1400 B.C. [?])—and *c.* 1200 B.C. (time of the Pylos tablets).

BIBLIOGRAPHY

BENNETT, E. L., JR. *The Pylos Tablets*, Princeton, 1951; *A Minoan Linear B Index*, Newhaven, 1953; *The Pylos Tablets; Texts of the Inscriptions found 1939–1954*, Princeton, 1955; *The Mycenaean Tablets, II*, Philadelphia, 1958.

EVANS, A. J. (Sir John Myres, ed.). *Scripta Minoa*, vol. II, Oxford, 1952.

VENTRIS, M. and CHADWICK, J. 'Evidence for Greek Dialect in the Mycenaean Archives,' *J. Hellenic Studies*, 1953; *Documents in Mycenaean Greek*, Cambridge, 1956; BENNETT, E. L. JR., CHADWICK, J. and VENTRIS, M. 'The Knossos Tablets. A Revised Transliteration of all the Texts in Mycenaean Greek recoverable from Evans' excavation of 1900–04, based on independent examination,' *Bulletin of the Institute of Classical Studies*, Supplementary Papers, 2, London, 1956 (Second edition, with corrections; Suppl. No. 7, 1959).

CHADWICK, J. 'Greek Records in the Minoan Script,' *Antiquity*, 1953; *The Decipherment of Linear B*, Cambridge, 1958 (Pelican Book, 1961); 'Mycenaean Greek,' *Proceedings of the VIII International Congress of Linguists*, 1958; 'New Fragments of Linear B Tablets from Knossos,' *Annual of the British School at Athens*, 1958; 'A Linear B Inscription from Thebes,' *Živa Antika*, 1958; 'Inscribed Sealings from Mycenae,' *Eranos*, 1959; 'Minoan Linear A,' *Antiquity*, 1959; *The Decipherment of Linear B*, repr. with a *Postscript*, July, 1959, New York, 1960.

GEORGIEV, V. *Problems of the Minoan Language* (in Bulgarian), Sofia, 1950; *Interpretation of the Creto-Mycenaean Inscriptions*, Sofia, 1954.

KTISTOPOULOS, K. D. *Peri ten anagnosin tês Minoikês graphês*, Athens, 1955 (A Survey of the Literature on the Decipherment).

BEATTIE, A. J. 'Mr. Ventris' Decipherment of the Minoan Linear B Script,' *J.Hellenic Studies*, 1956 (CHADWICK, J. 'Minoan Linear B: A Reply,' *ibid.* 1957).

CASSOLA, F. *La Ionia nel mondo miceneo*, Naples, 1957.

STUBBINGS, F. H. 'Mycenaean Deciphered,' *Greece and Rome*, 1957.

WEBSTER, T. B. L. *From Mycenae to Homer*, London, 1958 (repr., 1960).

LEJEUNE, M. *Mémoires de philologie mycénienne*, Paris, 1958; 'Études de philologie mycénienne,' *Revue des Études Anciennes*, 1959; 'Observations sur la langue des tablettes de Pylos,' *Actas del Primer Congress Español de Estudios Clasicos*, 1959.

Minutes of the Minoan Linear B Seminar of the London University Institute of Classical Studies; *Atti del Primo Colloquio Internazionale di Studi Minoico-Micenei*, 1956, and *Atti del Secondo Colloquio Internazionale*, 1958, etc., and so on.

GRUMACH, E. *Minoica. Festschrift zum 80. Geburtstag von J. Sundwall*, Berlin, 1958.

GALIANO, M. S. *Diecisiete Tablillas micenicas*, Madrid, 1959.

PERUZZI, E. *Le iscrizioni minoiche*, Florence, 1960.

Nestor, 1st July 1960: 'discovery of a few pieces of Linear B inscriptions' 'in the 1960 excavations at Pylos.'

SEVERYNS, A. *Grèce et Proche-Orient avant Homère*, Brussels, 1960.

GALLAVOTTI, C. and SACCONI, A. (ed.) *Inscriptiones ad Mycenaeam aetatem pertinentes* etc., Rome, 1961.

MOON, B. E. *Mycenaean Civilization, Publications 1956–1960.* (A second Bibliography), London, 1961.

BOARDMAN, J. *The Cretan Collection in Oxford*, Oxford, 1961.

ROSÉN, H. B. 'The "Mycenaean" Documents' (in Hebrew), *Eškolot*, 1962.

Nestor (1st January), 1962, 'Syllabarii Mycenaei transcriptio'.

GRUMACH, E. *Bibliographie der kretisch-mykenischen Epigraphik*, Berlin, 1962.

Various authors, *A Companion to Homer*, Cambridge, 1962.

CYPRIOTE SYLLABARY

Ancient Cyprus and her Script

The island of Cyprus was a great metallurgical centre of the ancient world; it was the coveted outpost in the Mediterranean of Asia Minor, the nearest point of which is forty-four miles distant, and of Syria, about seventy miles away, and it was situated within a few days' sail of Egypt and the island of Crete. Cyprus was the country which can be said to have had the only pure syllabic writing of the Old World, apart perhaps from the pseudo-hieroglyphic script of Byblos and Linear B.

The classical Cypriote script was mainly deciphered in the last thirty-five years of the nineteenth century, thanks to the fact that the majority of the Cypriote inscriptions extant, numbering about 185, are couched in Greek. On the whole, the Cypriote syllabary seems to have been employed from the sixth to the third century B.C., and even later. The inscriptions belong mainly to the fifth and fourth centuries B.C. The rarity of Cypriote inscriptions in the earlier periods is not easy to explain, unless perishable writing-material was used.

The Cypriote signs are purely linear and are composed of combinations of strokes which are straight or only slightly curved. Some have an external resemblance to North Semitic or Greek letters, but their phonetic value is quite different. The deciphered Cypriote syllabary, which is still fragmentary, consists (Fig. 10.10a) of about fifty-five symbols, each representing an open syllable (such as *pa, ko, ne, se*) or a vowel. The script had been created for a non-Greek speech and the representation of the Greek sounds is rather imperfect.

We do not know whether the Cypriote script was better suited to the speech for which it had been created, as the indigenous language is not yet deciphered. Anatolian affinities, especially Phrygian and Carian, have been suggested; anthropological deductions indicate that the Bronze Age population of Cyprus belonged to the 'Armenoid,' brachycephalous ('short-headed') racial group, which also included the Hittites and other western Asiatic peoples.

The main inconveniences in the transcription of Greek words were as follows: (1) There was no distinction between long and short vowels. (2) There was no distinction between the sounds *t, d, th*; *p, b, ph*; *g, k, kh*. (3) Closed syllables and syllables containing two consonants, such as *pt, st, dr,* had to be represented by two or more open syllables, but the reduplication of the same consonant, as in *ll*, and the nasal sounds (*m,n*) preceding other consonants, were omitted. Thus, *ka-re* was written for 'gar,' *a-ti-ri-a-se* for 'andrias,' *pa-si-le-ve-o-se* for 'basileus,' *po-to-li-ne* for 'ptolin,' *a-po-lo-ni* for 'Apolloni,' *a-po-ro-ti-ta-i* for 'Aphrodite,' *pe-pa-me-ro-ne* for 'pemphameron,' *o-ka-to-se* for 'Onkantos,' *sa-ta-si-ka-ra-te-se* for 'Stasikrates', etc.

The direction of writing is generally from right to left, but sometimes from left to right or *boustrophedon* (alternate lines, from right to left and from left to right).

Origin of Cypriote Syllabary

The origin of the Cypriote script has aroused much controversy; some students have suggested the cuneiform writing, and particularly the late Assyrian script, as the progenitor of the Cypriote syllabary; others have suggested as such the Hittite hieroglyphic writing. In fact, some Cypriote signs do resemble Hittite hieroglyphs. However, both these theories, and other opinions, such as the possibility of the derivation of the Cypriote syllabary from a prehistoric linear script of the eastern Mediterranean, are now considered out of date. A pitcher in the Cyprus Museum (Room III, Division 14, No. 61), attributed to Period III of the Early Bronze Age (*c.* 2400–2100 B.C.) contains an inscription (engraved on the handle), composed of linear signs which constitute the earliest writing discovered in Cyprus. According to Mr. Dikaios, the Curator of the Museum, 'the nature of the signs is undetermined and, although some correspondences are traced with Minoan signs, it is thought that they may belong to a script such as those which were in existence in Syria and Palestine before the middle of the second millennium B.C. It is also possible that we have in this inscription the earliest evidence of the original language of the Cypriotes before the Mycenæan penetration and the introduction of the Minoan-Mycenæan script.' There is also in the Cyprus Museum (Room III, Division 14, No. 68) a bowl with painted ornamentation 'including stags and signs probably belonging to a script in use at the end of the Early Bronze Age' (Dikaios).

Nowadays, it is generally accepted that the Cypriote script was derived from the Cretan linear scripts. The main evidence is provided by the so-called Cypro-Minoan script (Fig. 10.10b,c). The Cyprus Museum is in possession of two jugs of white plain ware from Katydhata, and a fragment of a large jar from Enkomi (Room III, Division 25, Nos. 134–6), all with engraved inscriptions in this script. 'These inscriptions, which were engraved with a sharp tool after baking, appear to have some connection with the vessels' contents or ownership' (Dikaios).

The inscriptions in the Cypro-Minoan or Cypro-Mycenæan script belong to the Bronze Age, and mainly to the period called Late Cypriote II C, which is dated by the Swedish scholar Erik Sjœqvist 1275–1200 B.C. On the other hand, according to Dikaios, the Cypro-Mycenæan or Cypro-Minoan script was in use in Cyprus from 1400 B.C. to the end of the Late Bronze Age (middle of the eleventh century B.C.). 'It coincides with the arrival of Mycenæan settlers in Cyprus and was probably introduced by them.'

The signs of the undeciphered Cypro-Mycenæan writing have been classified and analysed by various scholars, and particularly by A. W. Persson and S. Casson. This latter English scholar, after careful search, recognized in the Cypro-Minoan inscriptions found on the island of Cyprus, on the Greek mainland, on the Aegean islands and in Palestine, a total of seventy-six Cypro-Minoan characters and five numerals, out of which about ten to twelve characters are identical with the classical Cypriote and eight may possibly be identified.

Thus, on the whole, although we have not a sufficient basis for transliterations of Cypro-Minoan inscriptions using the classic Cypriote syllabary, modern scholars are agreed that the two scripts were connected. It is generally accepted that the Cypro-Minoan script formed the link between the Cretan linear scripts (see under Linear B) and the Cypriote syllabary. The problem of the identification of the single signs, however, cannot be solved so long as both the Cypriote native language and the Cypro-Minoan writing remain undeciphered. Vague comparisons are dangerous and conclusions based on such comparisons must be provisional. An attempt at the decipherment of the Cypro-Minoan script is reproduced in Fig. 10.10b.

The famous Asine inscription of the end of the Mycenæan age (about 1200 B.C.) seems to be written in a script similar to the Cypro-Minoan writing.

BIBLIOGRAPHY

DI CESNOLA, L. P. *Cyprus*, London, 1877.

MYRES, J. L. and OHNEFALSCH-RICHTER, M. *The Cyprus Museum*, Oxford, 1899.

MURRAY, A. S., SMITH, A. H. and WALTERS, H. B. *Excavations in Cyprus*, London, 1900.

OBERHUMER, E. *Die Insel Cypern*, etc., Munich, 1903.

COBHAM, C. D. *An Attempt at a Bibliography of Cyprus*, Cambridge, 1908.

MYRES, J. L. *Handbook of the Cesnola Collection of Antiquities from Cyprus*, New York, 1914.

BORK, F. *Die Sprache von Alasija*, Leipsic, 1930.

CASSON, S. *Ancient Cyprus*, London, 1937; 'The Cypriote Script of the Bronze Age,' *Iraq*, London, 1939.

HILL, G. *A History of Cyprus*, Vol. I, Cambridge, 1940.

DANIEL, J. F. 'Prolegomena to the Cypro-Minoan Script,' *Amer. J. Archaeology*, 1941. (*See* also under *Cretan Scripts*.)

DIKAIOS, P. *A Guide to the Cyprus Museum*, Nicosia, 1947.

BEATTIE, A. J. 'A Cyprian Contract Concerning the Use of Land,' *Classical Quarterly*, 1959, 169–172.

KARAGEORGHIS, V. 'Chronique des fouilles et découvertes archéologiques à Chypre en 1959,' *Bulletin de Correspondance Hellénique*, 1960 (including a Mycenæan vase from Akhera with Cypro-Minoan signs on its handles; a bronze bowl, of 'Late Cypriote III,' with Cypro-Minoan inscription; and an inscribed pitcher of 'White-Painted IV,' or 'VI' ware).

MASSON, O. *Les Inscriptions Chypriotes syllabiques*, etc., Paris, 1961.

JAPANESE SCRIPTS

Prehistoric Japanese 'Writings'

The Japanese have never had a script of indigenous creation, although such a writing is mentioned in the ancient historical work *Shoku-nihongi*, belonging to the eighth century A.D. (?) According to local traditions the Japanese used in early times a knot-device as means of communication, but (as already said in the Introduction), a knot-device cannot be considered a true writing. On the other hand, the origins of the ancient, long forgotten Japanese scripts, *ahiru*, *ijumo*, *anaichi*, *iyo* and *moritsune*, are uncertain. It is generally accepted that these *shinji* or *kami no moji* ('divine characters') termed also *jindaimoji* or *kamiyo no moji* ('characters of the divine period'), have descended from the Korean script Nitok (*see* p. 354), or constituted a secondary branch of it, but there is no evidence corroborating such theory. At any rate, there is no connection between these prehistoric Japanese scripts and modern Japanese writing.

Origin of Japanese Scripts

As regards her culture, Japan must, in a certain way, be regarded as a colony of China, but the beginnings of Chinese influence upon Japan lie in the same obscurity as the rest of early Japanese history. Most Chinese influences, according to the accepted tradition, reached Japan by way of Korea. Thus the Japanese, either directly or through Korea, were inevitably led to adopt the Chinese system of writing. The

K

earliest trade and cultural relations between China and Japan may be dated in the last centuries B.C., but the introduction of Chinese writing into Japan would seem to have taken place somewhere in the third or fourth century A.D.

According to tradition, in the third century A.D., Japan sent envoys to Korea in search of men of learning, They brought back one Onin or Wang Jên, a wise man of the imperial family of China. Onin taught the Japanese Chinese writing and instructed them in the culture of his nation. He was later deified. Another tradition attributes the introduction of Chinese writing into Japan to two Korean scholars, Ajiki and Wani, the tutors of a Japanese crown prince of the fifth century A.D. After the introduction of Buddhism many Chinese scholars and priests emigrated to Japan. Thus the study of both the Chinese language and the Chinese script increased enormously, and obviously the necessity arose for the translation of Chinese works into Japanese and for the adaptation of Chinese writing to Japanese. This adaptation was, from the very beginning, no easy matter, as can be seen from the *Kojiki* (a kind of Japanese ancient history, of A.D. 711-2), in which Chinese symbols are written with Chinese syntax but are intended to be read differently.

In order to realize the great difficulties in the adaptation of Chinese writing to Japanese speech—apart from the fact that Japanese, unlike Chinese, is not monosyllabic, but an agglutinative language—one must consider the following factors:

(1) the great number of Chinese characters which form the basis of the Japanese scripts;

(2) the fact that these characters had sometimes an ideographic, and sometimes a phonetic value;

(3) the pronunciation of Chinese characters varies in the different Chinese provinces and has changed in the various historical periods;

(4) the Japanese borrowed Chinese characters in different periods and from different regions;

(5) nearly every Japanese word can be given either the Japanese or a Chinese pronunciation and there is no absolute rule governing the choice.

It follows from a consideration of the aforementioned factors that many Japanese words have various alternative pronunciations. (*See* Harold G. Henderson, *Handbook of Japanese Grammar*, London, Allen and Unwin, 1945.)

Generally speaking, Japanese characters can be pronounced in the following ways: (1) Japanese pronunciation, *kun*, that is, Chinese ideograms are translated into Japanese; and (2) the so-called Chinese pronunciation, *on*, which has little affinity with the spoken Chinese of today and is the pronunciation of Chinese words as they sounded to Japanese ears at the time when the characters in question were first adopted. This category can be sub-divided into three classes: (*a*) *go-on*, the pronunciation derived from the Chinese dialect used in the third century A.D. in the realm *Go* (in Chinese *Wu*), in the Shanghai region; this pronunciation was mainly superseded by the pronunciation (*b*) *kan-on* (*Han*), which was derived from the dialect of northern China and was introduced into Japan by Chinese priests during the seventh, eighth and ninth centuries; (c) the pronunciation *to-in* (*T'ang*), derived from a dialect in vogue between the tenth and seventeenth centuries and introduced into Japan in 1655 by the sect Obaku; this is employed almost exclusively for Buddhist texts.

Japanese Ideograms

There are tens of thousands of Japanese ideograms. The average cultured Japanese can read and write correctly about two thousand symbols. A highly educated person, a university graduate, for instance, may know about seven to eight thousand symbols, but only specialists in the subject are able to read classical literary Japanese. Since 1900, Japanese educational reformers have tried to reduce the number of ideograms used in the elementary schools, but even there the minimum of characters used is about 1,200. An official communiqué issued by the 'Domei' Agency on 19th June, 1942, reported that special commissions of philologists, after twenty years of research work, had decided to reduce the essential ideograms to 2,028. However, the situation at present is that every word has its own character and the reader who does not happen to know the meaning of a symbol will also be unable to pronounce it.

In Japanese writing, ideograms are employed only to represent nouns, adjectives and verb-roots. But Japanese, as said above, is an agglutinative language, and has grammatical terminations (which are lacking in Chinese), prepositions and so forth. At first the Japanese used for this purpose Chinese ideograms having a similar sound, for instance the Chinese ideogram *t'ien*, 'sky,' pronounced in Japanese approximately *ten*, was used for the termination *-te*. This device proved too cumbersome; as a consequence, the syllabaries were created.

Japanese Syllabic Scripts

During the eighth and ninth centuries A.D. there came into use in Japan a special syllabic system of writing called *kana* (perhaps from *kanna*, *kari na*, 'borrowed names') in two forms (Fig. 10.11): (1) *kata kana* or *yamato* ('Japanese') *gana*, used mainly in learned works, official documents and for the transliteration of personal names, especially of Europeans; (2) *hira* ('plain, simple') *gana*, used for grammatical terminations, and similar purposes, and mainly employed in newspapers, novels, and so forth. The creation of *kata kana* is attributed to Kibi(no) Mabi or Kibi *daijin* ('minister' Kibi), who flourished in the middle of the eighth century A.D.; *hira gana* is attributed to the Buddhist abbot Kobodaishi (who is also considered to be the author of the *iroha* poem: see below), of the beginning of the ninth century. However, all the *kana* signs have developed from the Chinese characters which happened to be in most use at the time; *kata kana* from the *k'ai-shu*, *hira gana* from the *ts'ao-shu* symbols. The Chinese originals of the *kana* were adopted either in the Chinese language with the early Japanese pronunciation, or in the early Japanese speech (which was quite different from modern Japanese); for instance, the Chinese ideogram for 'woman,' *nü* has been introduced as the *kana* sign for *me*, 'woman' in Japanese, whereas the ideogram for 'three,' *san*, has been adopted for the word *san*, although it appears also for *mi*, 'three' in Japanese, and the *kana* signs for *mi* are derived from it.

As a matter of fact the *kana* signs should not be considered as true syllabic scripts, because—a comparison with the Egyptian and the cuneiform writing is instructive—as has already been stated, they are not used as independent scripts, but only as indications of the tenses of verbs, prepositional or other grammatical variations (while the Chinese characters, *kanji*, continue to be employed for nouns, verbs and adjectives), or may be used as phonetic complements, written alongside the ideographs as a clue to their pronunciation. The standard form of Japanese writing is *kana-majiri, i.e.,* Chinese characters with *hira gana* to give the Japanese pronunciation and to supply endings, etc.; whereas *shin-kata kana*, that is, *kata kana* written alongside the Chinese characters, and *kunten*, using Japanese numerals beside the Chinese characters to show the order in which they should be read, are used more seldom.

However, the Japanese syllabaries could be used independently, and for this reason they are dealt with in this chapter. The various attempts to adopt the *kana* signs as a complete script, thus discarding the ideograms, have not, as yet, succeeded. Nevertheless, various texts printed in *kana* signs only, were laid before the Congress of Orientalists in Paris, in 1888. The *Kana no kai* Society was founded, which published the magazine *Kana no tekagami*, 'The Mirror of the Kana,' and set out to purify the *kana* scripts and encourage the disuse of the ideograms.

Both *kata kana* and *hira gana* contain the traditional early Japanese forty-seven syllables. These constitute the *iroha* or *irofa* order of the characters; the term *iroha* or *irofa* is based on the acrological principle, that is, it consists of the names of the first three syllables (*see* Fig. 10.11). There are in addition a sign for *n*, which is not pronounced, and two other symbols, bringing the total to fifty. These form the *gojü-on* ('fifty sounds') order commonly used in the dictionaries; this order is based on the Sanskrit grammar. Unlike the *kata kana*, the *hira gana* signs have many variants. In all, there exist about three hundred *hira gana* symbols, out of which only about a hundred are used in printing; in everyday writing, one sign is generally employed for each syllable (Fig. 10.11). The *hira gana* script is highly cursive; frequent ligatures make it exceedingly difficult to read.

The *kana* signs represent only open syllables; in fact, Japanese contains only open syllables, viz., consonants followed by vowels, or vowels. Similar sounds are distinguished by diacritical marks; a *maru* sign (^{0}) distinguishes *p* from *f*; a *nigori* (") *b, d, g, ds, z* from *f, t, k, ts, s*. Not knowing the sound *l*, Japanese replaces it in European words by *r*. A tiny sign *tsu* indicates the reduplication of a consonant; a thick comma under a syllable represents its reduplication.

Classic Japanese writing consists of strong bold strokes made with a brush dipped in Chinese ink; it takes years of practice to make a good calligrapher. Figures 10.12 and 13 reproduce specimens of Japanese calligraphy. The original disposition of writing was, as in Chinese, in vertical columns from right to left, but the strokes of the single characters were written mainly from left to right. Nowadays, no fixed rule is observed; some books are even printed in columns to be read from left to right and, to further complicate matters, there has arisen a new custom of writing horizontally as well, sometimes from right to left and sometimes from left to right. Thus, there is often no means of telling how to read a sign. Fairly recently (about the middle of August, 1942), the Japanese News Agency 'Domei' announced a decision of the Minister for Instruction that the direction of writing from left to right should be generally introduced.

Suggested Introduction of Latin Alphabet

The many attempts to adapt the Latin alphabet to the Japanese speech have, so far, not achieved much success. In 1885, the *Romaji-kai* Society was formed and its activities included the publication of the magazine *Romaji-zasshi* which was printed exclusively in Latin characters. All these attempts have hitherto failed, mainly owing to: (1) the inherent conservatism of oriental peoples; (2) the strong inheritance of Chinese language and culture; and (3) the innumerable Chinese homophones: Sir Ellis Minns pointed out that, for instance, *to* and *tô* comprise seventy-one words in Gubbins's Dictionary.

After the defeat of Japanese militarism in the war against western democracy, an outside initiative suggested the replacing of the Japanese ideographic-syllabic script by the Latin alphabet. As the whole problem is still *sub judice*, I can quote only the report of the newspapers:

'A drastic overhauling of the Japanese educational system was recommended to General Douglas MacArthur in a report of the United States education mission to Japan, made public today. Making one of the most sweeping departures from the traditional Japanese cultural system, the commission called for the abolition of the Chinese-derived ideographs from the Japanese written language, and the substitution of the Roman alphabet as a measure to eliminate what it termed one of the hardest grades in Japanese progress. The mission of twenty-seven American educators (was) headed by Dr. George D. Stoddard. . . . General MacArthur called the report a document of ideals high in the democratic tradition, but he pointed out that many reforms, such as language reform, might take years to complete.

'The mission took issue with the Ministry of Education in recommending the abolition of Chinese characters and the substitution of the Roman alphabet. The most recent proposal from the Ministry was a curtailment of the Chinese 'kanji' and an increase in the use of phonetic characters. This the American mission apparently considered unsatisfactory. Declaring that much useful time of Japanese students was wasted in memorizing the Chinese characters, the mission proposed the "prompt establishment of a Japanese committee of scholars, educators and statesmen to formulate means of adapting the Roman alphabet to Japanese sounds, and its introduction into the schools, newspapers, magazines and books." The present system, the mission asserted, constitutes a formidable obstacle to learning.' (*New York Times*, 7th April, 1946.)

Will an outside initiative be more successful than the local ones? What will be the Chinese reaction to the western interference in a problem so strictly connected with Chinese culture, Japan being—as it has already been pointed out—culturally a Chinese colony?

At any rate, twenty years have passed, and no reform is in sight!

BIBLIOGRAPHY

LANGE, R. *Einführung in die japanische Schrift*, Berlin, 1896; *Übung- und Lesebuch zum Studium der japanischen Schrift*, Berlin, 1904; *Lehrbuch der japanischen Umgangssprache*, Berlin, 1906; *Thesaurus Japonicus* etc., 3 vols., Berlin, 1913–20.

CHAMBERLAIN, B. H. *A Practical Introduction to the Study of Japanese Writing* (*Moji no shirube*), 2nd ed., London and Tokyo, 1905; *A Simplified Grammar of the Japanese Language* (edition revised by J. G. McHroy), Chicago, 1924; *Things Japanese*, etc., 6th ed., London and Kobe, 1939.

ROSE-INNES, A. *3000 Chinese-Japanese Characters*, etc., Nagasaki, 1913 (?); *Japanese Reading for Beginners*, 5 vols, Yokohama and Tokyo, 1934.

SANSOM, G. B. *Historical Grammar of Japanese*, Oxford, 1928; *Japan, A Short Cultural History*, London, 1928.

VACCARI, O. and E. E. *Complete Course of Japanese Conversation-Grammar*, Tokyo, 1937.

BUSCHAN, G. *Kulturgeschichte Japans*, Vienna, 1938.

CARR, D. 'The New Official Romanization of Japanese,' *J. Amer. Orient. Soc.*, 1939: In 1937, the spelling in Roman letters was unified; it was called *Kokutei* ('official') *Romazi* or *Sinkokutei Romazi* ('New Official Romanization'); previously, the system *Nipponsiki no Romazi* ('Japanese style of Romanization') and the mixed English-Italian system named after Hepburn were used.

KENNEDY, G. A. *Introduction to Kana Orthography*, Yale University, 1942.

ISEMONGER, N. E. *The Elements of Japanese Writing*, 2nd ed., London, 1943.

DANIELS, O. *Dictionary of Japanese* (Sôsho = Ts'ao-shu) *Writing Forms*, London, 1944.

HENDERSON, H. G. *Handbook of Japanese Grammar*, London, 1945.

CHEROKEE SYLLABARY

The Script (*see* also pp. 7 f., 11, 87 ff., 132 f.).

The most developed script ever created by an American native is the Cherokee syllabary; the Cherokees are a North American Indian tribe speaking an Iroquois language. They lived formerly in northern Georgia and North Carolina (U.S.A.,) but were moved to Indian territory in 1838–9.

The Cherokee script was invented in 1821 by a native called Sequoya or Sikwaya, also John Gist or Guest or Guess. He seems to have been uneducated but intelligent. At any rate, he understood the advantages which writing could bring to his people. At first he created an ideographic script, but soon realized how cumbersome it was and invented the syllabary. After about ten years, this script was so widespread that nearly all the male members of the tribe could write and read and many Cherokee manuscripts are extant. Nowadays, however, the script has fallen into disuse.

The Cherokee syllabary consists of eighty-five signs (Fig. 10.14), which can be divided into four groups:

(1) symbols derived from Latin characters, either capitals or small letters, but with entirely different values;

(2) Roman letters inverted or otherwise transformed (for instance by the addition of strokes), likewise with different values;

(3) European numeral signs (used in the same way as Latin letters); and

(4) arbitrary characters.

On the whole, the system is characterized by a superabundance of consonants and consonant-clusters, combined with a great variability of vowels. It is, however, scientifically sound and proved very easy to learn.

Origin

The origin of this syllabary is one of the best historic examples of the creation of a system of writing. Some scholars suggest that Sequoya's knowledge of the English alphabet was deficient, and consider this to be the reason why the phonetic values of his signs differ from those of the Roman letters. This explanation, however, seems at fault. The fact that there is no single case of a Cherokee symbol retaining the original phonetic value, *i.e.*, that of the Latin letters, is in my opinion the clearest proof that Sequoya's intention was to create a script quite different from the English alphabet. Further, the fact that Sequoya's syllabary represents Cherokee quite satisfactorily, proves that the creator of this script knew how to deal with the problems he had to face.

It is difficult to explain why Sequoya replaced the Roman alphabetic system of writing with a syllabary. It has been suggested, perhaps rightly, that he did not grasp the principle of alphabetic writing, and was satisfied with breaking up the words into their constituent syllables. There is, however, also the possibility that Sequoya preferred the use of a syllabic system, which in itself is suitable to the Cherokee speech, though not so easily suitable for a language like English, which contains many accumulations of consonants (such as e.g., 'stretch').

However, the Cherokee script is one of the best examples of the borrowing of a form of writing without retaining the original phonetic values of the symbols concerned.

Morice's and Eubanks' Cherokee-Scripts

J. Mooney mentions two new scripts which were created about 1890; but the attempts to introduce them for the Cherokee tongue failed.

(1) Father Morice, attached to a mission station at Stuart's Lake, British Columbia, elaborated a semi-alphabet on the plan of the Déné (or Tinné) and Cree syllabaries. 'In this system all related sounds are represented by the same character in different positions or with the addition of a dot or stroke.' For instance, ∨ expressed the sound *hu*; an inverted ∧, was *hâ*; with the apex to the left, <, *ha*; to the right, >,

hûⁿ. As Mooney pointed out, the plan was very simple, and the signs easily distinguishable, 'but unfortunately not adapted to word combination in manuscript' (*see* also p. 132 f.).

(2) The other system was much more ingenious: it was invented by William Eubanks, a Cherokee half-breed, of Tahlequah, Indian Territory, and was a kind of shorthand, well adapted to rapid manuscript writing. 'By means of dots variously placed, fifteen basic characters, each made with a single stroke, either straight or curved, represent correctly every sound in the language' (Mooney).

BIBLIOGRAPHY

Missionary Herald, 1828, pp. 330–1.

TRACY, J. *A History of the American Board of Commissioners for Foreign Missions*, Worcester, 1840.

FOSTER, G. E. *Se-quo-yah*, Philadelphia, 1885.

ROYCE, C. C. *The Cherokee Nation of Indians*, Washington, 1887.

PILLING, J. C. 'Guess', *Bibliography of the Iroquoian Languages* (Bureau of American Ethnology), Washington, 1888.

MOONEY, J. 'The Sacred Formulas of the Cherokees,' *Seventh Annual Rep. of the Bur. of Ethnol.*, Washington, 1891; 'Improved Cherokee Alphabets,' *American Anthropologist*, 1892; 'Myths of the Cherokees,' *19th Report of Bureau of American Ethnology*, Washington, 1900; 'Cherokee,' *Handbook of the American Indians*, Part 1, Washington, 1907.

PARKER, T. V. *Cherokee Indians*, New York, 1909.

LUMMIS, C. F. 'Sequoya,' *Handbook of American Indians*, Part 2, Washington, 1910.

BASS, A. *Cherokee Messenger*, Oklahoma, 1936.

MOONEY, J. and OLBRECHTS, F. M. 'The Swimmer Manuscript,' etc. 'Cherokee Sacred Formulas,' etc., *Smiths Inst. Bur. of Amer. Ethnol. Bull.*, Washington, 1932.

FOREMAN, G. *Sequoyah*, Oklahoma, 1938.

KRŒBER, A. L. 'Stimulus Diffusion,' *American Anthropologist*, 1940.

GILBERT, W. H., JR. 'The Eastern Cherokees,' *Anthropological Papers*, No. 23, *Bureau of American Ethnology*, Washington, 1943.

WEST AFRICA: VAI SYLLABARY

The Vai are a western African tribe of a certain culture, speaking a Mandingo dialect and living on a small territory on the Atlantic Coast, from the river Sulima in Sierra Leone to the river Half-cape-Mount in Liberia.

Until quite recently, the script of the Vai was considered to be the only modern syllabic writing used by African natives. Today, however, other indigenous syllabaries, belonging to western Africa, are known.

The Script

The Vai script was discovered in 1848 by Commodore F. E. Forbes and reported in 1849 by the missionary S. W. Kœlle. The writing consists of 226 symbols representing vowels or open syllables (one or more consonants followed by a vowel). Many signs are very complicated. Some syllables can be expressed by more than one symbol. Many symbols have a number of variants, some being used rarely, others no longer employed. The whole script is in continuous evolution, as can be seen from Fig. 10.15. The direction of writing is from left to right.

Origin

The origin of the Vai syllabary is uncertain. A native, named Momoru Doalu Bukere or Momolu Duwalu Bukele is said to have invented this writing about 1829 or 1839. According to a native tradition, on the other hand, it was invented by eight Vai negroes; while there is another tradition that it had already been in existence for at least two centuries, having been invented by a people living in the neighbourhood of the source of the river Niger. The solution of the problem seems to be a compromise between the various suggestions; that is, it seems that the writing had been in existence for some time, but it was ideographic and was finally reduced to a syllabic writing by Momolu Duwalu Bukele.

If this theory is right, the Vai syllabary should have been dealt with in chapter 9 (before the *Bamun script*). It is, however, far from certain, and therefore I prefer to treat of it on the basis of its present, that is *syllabic*, character.

BIBLIOGRAPHY

NORRIS, E. *Despatch Communicating the Discovery of a Native Written Character at Bohmar*, etc., London, 1849.

KŒLLE, S. W. *Narrative of an Expedition into the Vy country of West Africa and the Discovery of a System of Syllabic Writing*, etc., London, 1849; *Outlines of a Grammar of the Vei Language*, etc., London, 1854.

STEINTHAL, H. *Die Mande-Neger-Sprachen*, etc., Berlin, 1867.

DELAFOSSE, M. 'Les Vai, leur Langue et leur système d'écriture,' *L'Anthropologie*, Paris, 1899.

JOHNSTON, H. *Liberia*, London, 1906.

MIGEOD, F. W. H. 'The Syllabic Writing of the Vai People,' *J. African Society*, London, 1909–10; *The Languages of West Africa*, 2 vols., London, 1911–3.

MASSAQUOI, M. 'The Vai People and their Syllabic Writing,' *J. African Society*, London, 1910–11.

MEINHOF, C. 'Zur Entstehung der Schrift,' *Zeitschrift für Ägyptische Sprache und Altertumskunde*, 1911.

KLINGENHEBEN, A. 'The Vai Script,' *Africa*, London, 1933.

MENDE SYLLABARY

The Mende, neighbours of the aforementioned Vai, speaking a related language, employ a script which seems to have been created recently by Kìsimi Kamára (or Kamála), a native Muslim tailor of Vama (Bari), who accomplished his task in three and a half months. Later, owing to the efforts of the local chief Vandi Kong of Potoru, the script (Fig. 10.16) was adopted in various other places.

It is not clear whether it is an original creation or a transformation of already existing symbols, nor how much its invention was influenced by other scripts, particularly by the Vai syllabary and the Arabic alphabet.

In August, 1945 R. Firth—who allowed me to use this information before he himself did—tried to collect some more information about this script. He inquired about it amongst the natives of Bo (a large place of about 10,000 inhabitants), and was told that only about ten people in the town knew this writing. At his dictation, one of the 'literates' wrote three phrases (Fig. 10.16, bottom line). When, later, Professor Firth tested another native, only the first two syllables of the first phrases were read correctly. He was also told that the script was very seldom employed, though it was used to write to friends and was known to others besides the Muslims. Any Mende dialect can be written in it. Some syllables are not necessarily always expressed by the same sign.

BIBLIOGRAPHY

Sumner, A. T. *Sierra Leone Studies*, 1932.
Klingenheben, A. *Africa*, 1934.
Eberl-Elber, R. *Westafricas letztes Rätsel*, Salzburg-Graz, etc., 1936.
Friedrich, J. 'Die Silbenschrift des Mende-Negers Kisimi Kamala (Zu einigen Schrifterfindungen der neuesten Zeit),' *Zeitschr. der Deutschen Morgenl. Gesellschaft*, 1938.
Personal information from Professor Raymond Firth of the London School of Economics.

NATIVE CANADIAN TRIBES

With the exception of the already mentioned Cherokee syllabary, and apart from the phonetic systems devised by linguists for purely scientific purposes, some earlier systems of writing Amerindian languages have been devised by missionaries eager to convert the natives to Christianity. John Eliot was the first of a long series of Englishmen who set themselves the task of giving a written form to a native North American language. Graduating from Jesus College Cambridge, in 1623, he arrived in Massachusetts in 1631, learned the native language, preached in it, became 'phonetician, lexicographer, grammarian all in one.' He set to work on the translation of the Bible into the native tongue, and the whole Bible was printed in 1663. However, he did not design a special system of writing, but adapted the Roman characters to the native speech.

Cree Syllabary

James Evans was the first European to devise a system of writing for an Amerindian form of speech. He invented the Plain Cree character which is partly syllabic and partly alphabetic. The script is very simple and purely geometric (Fig. 10.17). It consists of twelve symbols which are either vowels or basic consonants, the outline of which remains the same, but turns sideways, upwards or downwards according to the vowel sound with which it is accompanied. When final, the symbols are abbreviated. In 1833, a few Biblical passages were printed in this script at a fur trading post in Saskatchewan on birch bark, with ink made of soot and fish oil, from type cast in hand-cut wooden moulds with lead from tea-chest linings.

The Plain or Western Cree syllabary was adopted also for the Moose and Eastern or Swampy Cree dialects (Fig. 10.17), as well as for the Chippewa or Ojibway (Fig. 10.17) and the Slave or Tinné forms of speech (Fig. 10.17). The scripts were practically identical except for certain sounds missing in one or another language.

Similar systems were adopted for the Muskhokee or Creek and the Choctaw dialects, and for the Baffin Land dialect of the Eskimo language (Fig. 10.17). The last was reduced to written form by Edmund J. Peck, of the Church Missionary Society, before 1878; the same script was adopted for the Ungava dialect of the Eskimo language. All these systems attained a certain amount of currency for a time, although they were employed mainly for religious purposes. However, there is no doubt that as soon as the younger generations of the natives acquire a knowledge of English, these special systems of writing entirely discontinue.

Cree is a language belonging to the Algonkian group, spoken by about 15,000 people occupying a large territory in Canada on the eastern shore of Hudson Bay and James Bay, and from Hudson Bay west to Lake Winnipeg and the Saskatchewan River. The Chippewa or Ojibway are another Algonkian tribe; they number about 30,000 and occupy the territory about Lake Superior and westwards to northern Minnesota. The Algonkian Slave or Tinné dialect is spoken by natives living along the Mackenzie River, north-western Canada. The Muskhokee dialect is the principal dialect of the Muskhogean group; politically, the Muskhokee were the dominant tribe of the Creek Confederacy; therefore, their language is also called (but improperly) Creek. Choctaw is another important Muskhogean dialect; it has now about 18,000 speakers, who live in eastern Oklahoma and in Mississippi.

Eskimo dialects differ very widely, especially in their vocabularies. Beside the aforementioned Baffin Land syllabic alphabet, now scarcely used, the main characters employed with various modifications to suit the peculiarities in the pronunciation of the different Eskimo dialects are: (1) the Roman character, adapted to (a) the Greenland dialect, spoken by some 11,000 people in Greenland; (b) the Kuskokwim dialect, spoken by some 5,000 people along the Kuskokwim Bay and River, Bristol Bay, Alaska; (c) the Labrador dialect, spoken in Labrador; and (d) the Mackenzie River dialect, spoken along the Mackenzie River and Coronation Gulf, northern Canada; and (2) the Russian alphabet, adapted to the dialects spoken respectively in the Aleutian islands of Atka Aleut, Kadiak Aleut and Unalaska Aleut.

BIBLIOGRAPHY

PECK, E. J. *Portions of the Holy Scripture for the use of the Esquimaux*, London, 1878 (the first publication in Eskimo employing the syllabic character).

PILLING, J. C. 'Bibliography of the Eskimo Language,' *Smiths. Inst. Bur. of Ethnology*, Washington, D.C., 1887, 'Bibliography of the Algonquian Languages,' *Bur. of Ethnol. Miscell. Publ.*, Washington, 1891.

NORTH, E. M. *The Book of a Thousand Tongues*, New York and London, 1938.

SOUTH-WESTERN CHINA: POLLARD AND ALLIED SYSTEMS
(for the non-Chinese peoples of south-western China, *see* also pp. 101–104.)

The Miao cryptic script has already been mentioned. The missionaries who, at the end of the last century and at the beginning of the present, preached the Gospel to the illiterate Miao mountaineers, did not know of the existence of the indigenous script. At first they tried to teach them Chinese and to present them the Scriptures in Chinese translation, but the task proved to be much too hard.

Faced by this situation, Samuel Pollard and the other members of the Bible Christian Mission decided to reduce the Miao language to written form by inventing a special system of writing. They accomplished this about 1904. The new script was a syllabary, consisting of very simple, purely geometric symbols (Fig. 10.18). According to the missionaries the success of the invention 'was immediate and phenomenal. It is said that when the first copies of one of these hill-folk's Gospels reached Yünnan-fu, the provincial capital, every copy had been sold within two hours, although the consignment made up twenty-nine horse-loads.'

Pollard's system has been adopted for, and adapted to, the Hwa Miao and Chuan dialects, and to some other non-Chinese dialects, such as Kopu, spoken mainly in Luchuan and Hsintien (Yün-nan), as well as Laka, Nosu, and the eastern dialect of Lisu, also spoken in Yün-nan (*see* Fig. 10.18).

The Lisu or Li-su or Li-zu, a hill tribe of Yün-nan, living mainly in the upper valleys of the rivers Salween and Mekong, as well as in the Salween valley of northern Burma, are regarded by some scholars as the most ancient inhabitants of south-western China. Their language seems to have affinities with Lo-lo dialects. On the other hand, some customs of theirs suggest Indonesian affinities, whereas Haddon classified them as belonging to the group called by him *protomorphus*(?); according to other scholars they have Caucasian affinities.

Similar syllabic systems have been devised (*see* Fig. 10.18) for the western or Hwa dialect of Lisu as well as for its already mentioned eastern dialect spoken in Yün-nan and in northern Burma, and for Lo-lo spoken in the north-western portion of Yün-nan (*see* also p. 101 ff.). The former was invented about 1915 by American Baptist missionaries; the latter, about 1930, by missionaries of the British and Foreign Bible Society. Both systems consist of Roman capital letters with different positions for the signs, and with quite different phonetic values from those of the Roman alphabet.

CAROLINE ISLANDS: WOLEAI SYLLABARY

Woleai Island

Woleai, known also as Wolea, Uleai or Oleai, is a small reef island belonging to the western group of the Caroline islands, 'whose population (600 all told) has a struggle to live on a poor soil and in presence of the recurring havoc of cyclones.' (Macmillan Brown.)

Native Script

Professor J. Macmillan Brown, who visited this islet in July, 1913, discovered there a curious native script. In 1914 he published on this matter a brief note and 'a full list of the characters' which were written by the native chief Egilimar (Fig. 10.19*a*).

The list contains fifty-one symbols. These mainly represent syllables, which are either open (*na, ro, pu, mä, bö, rü*, etc.) or closed (*bag, warr, tüt*), or else consonants followed by diphthongs (*boa, doo, pui, moi, raa*, etc.), or two consonants followed by a vowel or diphthong (*shrö, nga, chroa, gkaa*, and so forth): *see* Fig. 10.19*b*.

It may be noted that there are two characters for the syllable *ma*, and so also for the sound *boa*. Professor Macmillan Brown has pointed out that 'two, if not three' of the characters employed by Egilimar to write his own name, 'are not given in the list.' Another curious thing is that Egilimar employs four signs to write 'Brun' (for Brown) namely, *bä, raa, uh* and *noo*, and does not use the sign *ru*, whereas the name 'Runge' is rightly represented by the signs *ru-nga*.

The script is, however, rightly regarded as syllabic (Macmillan Brown and Mason). On the other hand, unless we consider this system as imperfect, it is hardly thinkable that the fifty-one signs represent 'the entire syllabary' (Mason), as may be seen from the list of sounds, for which the symbols have been reproduced in Fig. 10.19.

Macmillan Brown has already noted that this script is unlike any other known writing. The signs are generally geometric and highly conventionalized. According to Brown, however, 'some retain a resemblance to the thing to which their name or sound corresponds.' For instance, the sign *pu* 'has manifestly originated' in a representation of a 'fish' or *pu* in the native language; similarly also *shrü*, a 'fishbone,' *lö*, a 'bottle,' *ngä*, 'bamboo,' *warr*, 'canoe,' etc. If this suggestion be right, the script would be rather a kind of rebus-writing than a pure syllabary.

Origin

The above-mentioned suggestion of Macmillan Brown is not in full agreement with another suggestion of his, which is probably right. 'The script is now known only to five men on the islet; but it is probably a relic of a wide usage in the archipelago. There is no possibility of any one of the five having invented it. . . .' On the other hand, I should not assert categorically that 'if invented by them since Europeans arrived, it would have taken the form either of the European alphabet or of the things bought or sold . . .'; the Cherokee syllabary, the Bamun writing, and other scripts prove that Macmillan Brown's statement is not exact. Indeed, there are a few Woleai signs which do resemble Latin letters, although they generally do not agree phonetically; *mä* resembles the M, *ngä* the N, *shä* is a kind of cursive S, *na* and *voa* look like an X, *goo* has the shape of a T, *ma* resembles a cursive C, so does *gä*, *moa* looks like an F, etc.

However, Brown's opinion—accepted also by Mason—is probably right. 'This Oleai script is manifestly the product of long ages for the use of the organizers of a highly organized community of considerable size. In other words, it must have belonged to the ruling class of an empire of some extent, that needed constant record of the facts of intercourse and organization.'

In this case, the origin of the Woleai script is perhaps in some way connected with the Further Indian branch of scripts, although this connection does not appear evident either from the graphic or from the phonetic points of view. There is, however, the possibility of the mixed process of invention and borrowing, called 'idea diffusion'—to which reference has been made many times in the present book—the stimulus to invention afforded by the knowledge that a problem has been solved.

Whatever the solution of the problem may be, it is not easy to find a suitable place for this script in the history of writing.

BIBLIOGRAPHY

MACMILLAN BROWN, J. 'A New Pacific Ocean Script,' *Man* (London), June, 1914.

CHAPTER 11

Quasi-Alphabetic Scripts

Two ancient systems of writing, the early Persian cuneiform writing and the Meroitic scripts, practically reached the stage of the alphabet, but the first stopped before attaining the threshold, the latter on the threshold. However, it is preferable to deal with these scripts separately, in this chapter, for the following reasons:

1. The early Persian script is nearer a syllabary than an alphabet, although its system is not much more syllabic than the Ethiopic or Deva-nagari scripts which are generally considered as alphabets.

2. Both the early Persian and the Meroitic scripts have developed from ideographic writings (the former from the cuneiform, the latter from Egyptian scripts), and have been transformed into almost purely phonetic writings by the influence of other scripts.

3. It would be difficult to find a suitable place for these systems in the following chapters, because their connection with alphabetic writing is still uncertain.

Thus, even if there were no other valid reasons, simple convenience would suggest inclusion in this place.

EARLY PERSIAN CUNEIFORM SCRIPT

The Script

This was the official script of the Achæmenid dynasty, under whose rule (from the middle of the sixth century B.C. until the victories of Alexander the Great) the Persians came to occupy the foremost place in the then-known world. French scholars also call this script *persépolitain* (from the ancient city of Persepolis).

The early Persian script consisted of forty-one symbols (Fig. 11.1), of which four were ideograms for 'king,' 'province,' 'country,' and 'Awra-Mazda,' and one a sign of division between words. The remainder were phonetic symbols which may be divided into five groups:

1. Three vowels (*a, i, u*).

2. Thirteen consonants (*kh, ch, th, p, b, f, y, l, s, z, sh, thr, h*) each of which might have the value of a pure consonant or a consonant followed by a short *a* (a long *a* was represented by an additional *a*-symbol).

3. Ten symbols for the consonants *k* (or *q*), *g, t, n, r*, each in two forms, that is, one

for the pure consonant or the consonant followed by a short *a*, the other for the consonant followed by *u*.

4. Four symbols for the consonants *dj* and *v* (*w*) in two forms, namely (*a*) for the pure consonant or the consonant followed by a short *a*; and (*b*) for the consonant followed by *i*.

5. Six symbols for the consonants *d* and *m*, *i.e.*, (*a*) pure consonant or consonant + short *a*; (*b*) consonant + *u*; (*c*) consonant + *i*.

Nasals preceding consonants were omitted. The symbols represented only vowels or open syllables beginning with a simple consonant. The direction of writing was from left to right.

Origin and End

The Persian cuneiform script was probably not a natural development from the cuneiform writing, but an artificial creation based on the neo-Babylonian cuneiforms; the creation of a *quasi*-alphabetic system of writing was obviously suggested by the already widely circulating Aramaic alphabet. It is rightly argued that the script was drawn up on official order.

Some scholars attribute the invention of the early Persian script to Cyrus the Great (about 550–529 B.C.). This theory is based mainly on three brief inscriptions of Cyrus (this is certainly not—as some scholars thought—'Cyrus the younger,' a son of Darius II), found at Mashad-i-Murghab (Pasargadæ), about thirty miles east of Persepolis. Others regard Darius the Great (521–486 B.C.) as the inventor of this script, this opinion being based mainly on a passage in the famous Behistun inscription. It must, however, also be pointed out that from the beginning of Darius' reign early Persian inscriptions have come down to us in considerable numbers.

In 1930, Professor E. E. Herzfeld published an early Persian inscription of Ariaramna, the great-grandfather of Darius the Great. The inscription was discovered in Hamadan, the ancient Hagmatana (known by its Greek name Ecbatana), capital of Media. The text, incomplete, consists of ten lines of writing, engraved on the upper part of a gold tablet. A similar inscription, of Arsames, the son of Ariaramna, apparently still unpublished, was also found in Hamadan. Herzfeld, followed by other distinguished scholars, such as the French linguist Benveniste and the British assyriologist S. Smith, considers the inscription of Ariaramna as genuine, placing the inventions of the early Persian script at least three generations before Darius the Great, whereas other scholars, such as Schäder, Brandenstein and Kent, hold that the inscription of Ariaramna was engraved at the time of Artaxerxes II. According to Professor Kent, the inscriptions of Ariaramna and Arsames were engraved 'to do honour to the royal ancestors of Ariaramna's line'—apparently as a part of anti-Cyrus activity by Artaxerxes. Kent accepts Weissbach's theory that the early Persian script was probably an invention of the time of Cyrus the Great, who, however, made but a limited use of writing, and 'had no craze for recording his exploits, as Darius did.' The problem, however, is still *sub judice*.

The early Persian script did not last long—its end coincided with the end of the Achæmenid dynasty and empire. It exercised no influence on future developments in writing.

Inscriptions

The early Persian inscriptions, which have been found mainly in Persepolis, belong to the period from the end of the sixth until the middle of the fourth century B.C. Besides the imposing monumental inscriptions, inscribed tablets of gold and silver have been found. However, the clay tablet as a vehicle for writing slowly declined in favour of the new writing materials then used by the western nations within the Persian Empire, that is, papyrus, skins or parchment, for which the cuneiform symbols were found to be unsuitable. The Persian language was thus written in the Aramaic alphabet and this developed afterwards into the script employed for middle Persian and known as Pahlavi (*see* part 2, chapter 16).

Decipherment

Although early Persian was practically the last language to which cuneiform writing had been adapted, it provided the channel, as already mentioned, for the revelation of the age-old secret of the various cuneiform scripts. Owing to the relative simplicity of the early Persian system of writing and to our knowledge of the Persian language, the Persian version of the famous Behistûn inscription became the starting point for the decipherment of the older, more complicated, cuneiform systems of writing (*see* pp. 25 f.)

BIBLIOGRAPHY

HÜSING, G. *Orientalische Literatur Zeitung*, 1900, 1908 and 1911.

MESSERSCHMIDT, L. *Die Entzifferung der Keilschrift*, Leipsic, 1903.

HOMMEL, F. *Grundriss der Geographie und Geschichte des alten Orients*, Munich, 1904.

JACKSON, A. V. W. *Persia Past and Present*, New York, 1906.

KING, L. W. and THOMPSON, R. C. *The Sculptures and Inscription of Darius the Great on the Rock of Behistûn in Persia*, London, 1907.

BANG, W. *Die altpersischen Keilinschriften*, Leipsic, 1908.

TOLMAN, H. C. *Ancient Persian Lexicon and Texts*, New York, 1908. (Still remains the best English manual.)

WEISSBACH, F. H. *Die Keilinschriften der Achæmeniden*, Leipsic, 1911: *Die Denkmäler und Inschriften an der Mündung des Nahr-el-Kelb*, Berlin and Leipsic, 1922.

FRIEDRICH, J. 'Metrische Form der altpersischen Keilschrifttexte,' *Orientalische Literatur Zeitung*, 1928.

HERZFELD, E. E. *A New Inscription of Darius from Hamadan*, Calcutta, 1928; 'Die Magna Charta von Susa,' *Archäologische Mitteilungen aus Iran*, Berlin, 1929, 1936, etc.; *Altpersische Inschriften*, Berlin, 1938.

MEILLET, A. *Grammaire du vieux-perse*, 2nd ed. (E. Benveniste), Paris, 1931.

HUDSON-WILLIAMS, T. *A Short Grammar of Old Persian*, Cardiff, 1936.

HARTMANN, H. 'Zur neuen Inschrift des Xerxes von Persepolis,' *Orientalische Literatur Zeitung*, 1937.

KÖNIG, F. W. *Relief und Inschrift des Königs Dareios I. am Felsen von Bagistan*, Leyden, 1938.

L

HINZ, W. 'Zu den altpersischen Inschriften von Susa,' *Zeitschr. der Deutschen Morgenl. Gesellschaft*, 1941; *Altpersischer Wortschatz*, Leipsic, 1942.

OLMSTEAD, A. T. *History of the Persian Empire (Achaemenid Period)*, Chicago, 1948.

See also under 'Cuneiform Writing.'

MEROITIC SCRIPTS

Meroë

These scripts are termed Meroitic from the name of the city Meroë, which was the later capital (after Napata, the earlier capital, had been destroyed) of the so-called Early Ethiopian or Nubian kingdom, situated to the south of Egypt. This kingdom was in earlier times under Egyptian political domination and cultural influence. It became independent about the ninth to eighth century B.C. but continued for many centuries to employ the Egyptian language and writing.

In the last centuries B.C., Nubian culture became more independent and started to employ its own language. It seems that at the end of the third or during the second century B.C., the indigenous script had been created. The rise of the Axum kingdom, which soon became a strong power (*see* p. 180), brought the political and cultural independence of the Meroitic kingdom to an end.

The Scripts

The Meroitic inscriptions (Figs. 11.2*c, d*) were discovered in the Nile valley between the first cataract in the north and Soba, on the Blue Nile, in the south. They belong mainly to the second to fourth centuries A.D., but may in part be attributed to the first or even to the second century B.C. The script had two types (Fig. 11.2*a*): (*a*) the monumental, hieroglyphic form of writing, and (*b*) the cursive, demotic type. Both are descended from Egyptian scripts. There are, however, fundamental differences; the Meroitic symbols are purely phonetic and, with the exception of two syllabic signs, are alphabetic. All the ballast of ideograms, bi-consonantal signs and determinatives, which rendered Egyptian scripts so intricate, has been discarded. The number of signs has thus been reduced to twenty-three. There are no ligatures and the words are separated by two or three dots placed vertically.

Origin

The monumental, hieroglyphic type has obviously descended from the Egyptian hieroglyphic writing, although the symbols agree in a few cases only (Fig. 11.2*b*). The origin of the cursive script is not quite so certain. Some scholars suggested a connection with the Ethiopic script, others a derivation from another southern Arabian alphabet, but it is now accepted by the majority of scholars that the Meroitic cursive type was evolved from the demotic script, although the signs became more simplified and stylized.

What we have said about the origin of the Meroitic scripts concerns the form of the signs only. It is quite obvious that the creation of an alphabetic writing from the complicated Egyptian scripts was such an outstanding feat that it could have been achieved only by an outstanding personality or under the influence of another alphabetic script. The latter seems to have been the case, and it is probably the Greek alphabet which influenced this invention. The fact that the Meroitic scripts possess vowels would favour such a suggestion.

Influences

The Meroitic scripts influenced the creation of the 'Nubian' alphabet which descended from the Coptic script but adopted three Meroitic signs for sounds for which Coptic writing had no symbols (*see* p. 371). It had also some influence on the Ethiopic script.

Greek influence on the Meroitic scripts, as already mentioned, is to be seen in the introduction of the vowels. It is, however, noteworthy that the Meroitic scripts did not possess signs for the vowels *o* and *u*.

BIBLIOGRAPHY

SAYCE, A. H. 'The Decipherment of Meroitic Hieroglyphs', and GRIFFITH, F. Ll. 'The Inscriptions from Meroë,' in GARSTANG, J. *Meroë. The City of the Ethiopians*, etc., Oxford, 1911.

GRIFFITH, F. Ll. *The Meroitic Inscriptions*, I., London, 1911; II, London, 1912; 'Meroitic Studies', I–VI, *J. Egyptian Archæology*, 1916, 1917, 1925 and 1929; 'Meroitic Funerary Inscriptions,' etc., *Recueil Champollion*, Paris, 1922.

ZYHLARZ, E. 'Das meroitische Sprachproblem,' *Anthropos*, 1930.

Part 2

ALPHABETIC SCRIPTS

In chapter 12 I shall deal not only with the problem of the origin of the alphabet, but also with various scripts which are partly undeciphered and had only limited use, in space and time, but, notwithstanding, are palæographically important, being considered in one way or another to be connected with the problem of the origin of the alphabet.

Chapter 13 is dedicated to the South Semitic alphabets, whose connection with the North Semitic alphabet is still uncertain. In chapters 14, 15 and 17, I shall examine the alphabetic scripts belonging respectively to the Canaanite, the Aramaic and the Indian main branches of scripts. Chapters 19–22 will deal with the Greek, the Etruscan and the Latin alphabets, and their direct or indirect offshoots. In chapters 16 and 18 there will be examined the non-Semitic offshoots of the Aramaic alphabets, and the Further-Indian offshoots of the Indian branch.

I have tried to introduce logical divisions and sub-divisions in this immense material. Two chapters, 17 and 18, may appear somewhat too long in comparison with the others. These chapters deal with matters which are commonly not taken into due consideration by the general histories of the alphabet, and are much less known than the other branches. I thought, therefore, it would be useful to allot them more space.

CHAPTER 12

Origin of Alphabet

THE PROBLEM

A learned professor said to me once: 'I have been told that you are dealing with the history of *the alphabet*. Can you tell me which alphabet you mean—the Egyptian, the Hebrew, the Latin, the Arabic, the Chinese?' I explained—as I have done in the Introduction to this book—why the Egyptian, the Chinese and other similar systems of writing should not be termed alphabets. And I added that in dealing with the history of *the alphabet*, I include all the alphabets, because all of them probably derived from one original alphabet.

Whereas the Alphabet has been a treasured possession of Europe since about 900–800 B.C., it is surprising to observe how late the word itself appeared. The word 'Alphabet' by which all western nations denote the ordered sequence of letters—the Slavonic nations use an imitation of this word—cannot be observed before the third century after Christ. During the preceding hundreds of years the Greeks used τὸ γράμμα or τὸ στοιχεῖον, generally in the plural τὰ γράμματα or τὰ στοιχεῖα, the Romans *literae* or *elementa*, which are translations of the Greek words.

The Pseudo-Tertullian work κατάλογος αἱρέσεων (chapter 5) mentions 'ex Graecorum alphabeto'—but when was this work written? Altaner, *Patrologie*, Freiburg, 1951, seems to attribute it to Hippolytos of Rome (flourished from *c.* A.D. 200, died A.D. 235); if this attribution is accepted we have here the first mention of the word 'Alphabet.'

In the fourth century Epiphanios and St. Jerome use it: Epiphanios, bishop of Constantia (the old Salamis on Cyprus) may have been born between A.D. 310 and 320 and died in 403. He uses ὁ and ἡ ἀλφάβητος. He says (t. 2, p. 161 C): κατὰ τὴν τοῦ ἀλφαβήτου παρ' Ἑβραίοις στοιχείωσιν; (t. 1 p. 629 C): Μίαν μὲν [βίβλιον] ἰσάριμον σεικοιδύο στοιχείων τῶν κατὰ τὴν τῶν Σύρων στοιχείωσιν, δι' ἀλφαβήτων συγκειμένην. To St. Jerome (*c.* 347–419/420) the word seems already familiar: 'habet et in lamentationibus Hieremias quattuor alphabeta'; 'alphabetum hebraicum discerem,' etc.

Etymologically, the word 'alphabet' does not present any difficulty; it is derived from the names of the first two letters of the Greek alphabet. These names, however, and most of the other names of the Greek letters, with the exception of the additional ones, such as *épsilon*, *ŏmikron*, *ōméga*, *phi* and *psi* are, as far as they have any meaning or a more or less known etymology, of Semitic origin, although the Semitic names (as we shall see below) are not identical.

The story of the alphabet from the end of the second millennium B.C. until today is, on the whole, not very hard to trace, though many details, and the origins of some scripts, are still uncertain. It is its pre- and proto-history that is still wrapped in obscurity. The principal problem, still unsolved, is that of its origin. I have dealt with this particular problem in an article, 'The Origins of the Alphabet,' *Antiquity*, Vol. XVII, pp. 77–90, June, 1943. (I wish to thank its Editor, for having allowed me to reproduce the illustrations here.)

Since classic times, this problem has been a matter of serious study. The Greeks and Romans held five conflicting opinions as to who were the inventors of the alphabet: the Phœnician, the Egyptian, the Assyrian, the Cretan, and the Hebrew, and in modern times, various theories, some not very different in part from those of ancient days, have been current. Each country situated in, or more or less near to, the eastern Mediterranean, has been seriously regarded as a claimant. Other theories—some influenced by political considerations including the Pan-Germanic theory of Germanic runes—need not be seriously treated. Of all the theories the Egyptian has enjoyed by far the most popular reception.

EGYPTIAN THEORY

The earliest modern view, already held by previous scholars, was that of Lenormant, published by De Rougé in 1874, that Egypt was the starting place of the Alphabet. The Egyptian theory has been subdivided into three theories; the hieroglyphic—Champollion, Lenormant, Halévy (Fig. 12.1*a*); the hieratic—Luzzatto, De Rougé, Taylor (Fig. 12.1*b*), Kyle and, more recently, Montet, Mallon, Ullman and Ronze-valle; the demotic—Bauer; the last cannot be taken seriously, because the demotic script originated later than the Alphabet. On the whole it may be said that the Egyptian symbols were so numerous (604 without the ligatures and numbers; many of them had some variants) that accidental resemblances to some of them are to be expected. In this connection I may mention that Dr. Gardiner's *Egyptian Grammar* contains 734 hieroglyphic symbols, and Lefèvre indicates 749. In later times, that is, in the periods of the Saïte and Ptolemaic kings, there were a few thousand hieroglyphic symbols.

Since earliest times Egyptian writing, in addition to the signs for words with three consonants, also used—as we have already mentioned in the chapter on Egyptian writing—signs for bi-consonantal and uni-consonantal words or parts of words. Later the uni-consonantal signs were used very seldom, at any rate much less frequently and hardly ever without ideographic symbols. Furthermore, in a true alphabet each sign generally denotes one sound only, and each sound should be represented by a single, consonant symbol, while in the Egyptian scripts there existed different signs for the same sound. Thus, the same sound could be written in different ways. Apart from many other considerations, I am unable to believe that if the Alphabet had really originated in Egypt, the Egyptians would have continued to use—for so many centuries—their old and extremely complicated writing. Furthermore, even if we make all possible allowances for the conservatism of the Egyptians, we still cannot understand why they did not use their own alphabet—if they had one—when, centuries after the introduction of the alphabet, they found it necessary to simplify the hieroglyphic and hieratic scripts. They thus preferred to create the demotic script, which therefore had no special tradition—as had the hieroglyphic and hieratic scripts.

OTHER THEORIES

The attempts made to show that the cuneiform scripts (Delitzsch), either the Sumerian (Hommel, 1904, or Waddell, 1927), or the Babylonian (Peters, Hommel, Ball, Peiser, Lidzbarski; partly also Ebeling, in 1934), or the Assyrian (Deecke), or else the syllabary of Cyprus (Prätorius, König), or the Hittite hieroglyphics (Sayce), are the true parents of the alphabet, may be regarded as even less successful. The pan-Germanists (Wartenberg, Wilke, Wilser, von Lichtenberg), and especially the Nazis (Schuchhardt, Günther) were sure, naturally, that the inventors of the alphabet belonged to the pure Aryan, nordic (fair and blue-eyed) race.

CRETAN THEORY

Sir Arthur Evans (Figs. 12.1a, b), followed by other scholars (such as Reinach and Dussaud), developed the theory that the alphabet was taken from Crete to Palestine by the Philistines, and was borrowed from them by the Phœnicians. This is obviously impossible; the Philistines conquered the coast of Palestine about 1220 B.C. when the alphabet was already some centuries old. The Cretan theory had recently many other adherents (Dayet, Sundwall, Chapouthier) and lastly Grumach (Fig. 12.2c). It is, strictly speaking, an Egyptian–Cretan–North Semitic alphabet theory, as the last illustration clearly shows. It is certainly true that many alphabetic characters have a resemblance to Cretan linear signs, but the similarity is only external (i.e., of the shape of the characters) and not internal (i.e. by phonetic value). Thus the resemblances may be accidental, especially as they concern mainly pure geometric signs which may easily be found in any primitive script. However, it is quite possible, and even probable, that the inventor of the alphabet knew something about the Cretan signs, and used some of them independently of their phonetic value.

PREHISTORIC-GEOMETRIC SIGNS THEORY

A different view has been offered by Sir W. M. Flinders Petrie, who argued that both the Phœnician and Greek alphabets, together with those of Asia Minor and the South

Semitic, as well as the Cypriote syllabary, the script of some Egyptian undeciphered inscriptions, and the early Sinaitic writing, developed from the prehistoric-geometric marks employed throughout the Mediterranean area from the earliest times. But Petrie is practically alone in supposing that these marks had any significance, and his theory of the development of various local alphabets from such marks has not found general acceptance. His theory was more recently transformed by T. H. Gaster (Fig. 12.3a). At any rate, it is just possible that the great inventor used some of these signs, with which he was evidently familiar, in the same way as he might have used the above-mentioned Cretan signs.

IDEOGRAPHIC THEORY

It has also been argued, by Sir John Evans (1823–1908) from the possible resemblance of a few early alphabetic letters to the objects denoted by their names, that the letters were once pictures used as ideograms. A similar opinion was propounded in 1914 (*Introduction à l'Ancient Testament*, Lausanne, 1914, p. 32) by Lucien Gauthier. The intrinsic probability of some Egyptian or Babylonian influence forbids the postulate of a totally unknown ideographic system of which, moreover, no trace has come to us. But it is interesting to know that this theory was suggested ninety-five years ago, when knowledge of oriental epigraphy was extremely slight (*On the Alphabet and its Origins*—lecture delivered on March, 15th, 1872). However, the recent theory of the French scholar Maurice Dunand (*see* below), if acceptable, would at least partly confirm Evans's ingenuity.

SINAITIC THEORY

The Egyptian theory was revived in 1915–7, independently by Dr. (later Sir) Alan H. Gardiner and by Professor Kurt Sethe who, dealing with the Proto-Sinaitic inscriptions, came to the conclusion that we have here to do with a stage of writing intermediate between Egyptian hieroglyphics and the Semitic alphabet. Over sixty years ago (1–18. 3. 1905) Sir W. F. Flinders Petrie excavated at Serābit el-Khâdem in the Southern Sinai the ruins of the temple of Hathor and examined other remains of the third and the second millennia B.C., including the ancient turquoise mines. He found twelve inscriptions written in a hitherto unknown script. Thanks to the additional inscriptions found in the years 1927, 1929, 1930, 1935 and the following years, there are over fifty early Sinaitic inscriptions, but the majority are badly preserved, or are more or less fragmentary.

The dates of these inscriptions are disputed: some scholars (Gardiner, Butin, and others) attribute them to the end of the twelfth dynasty, that is about 1770 B.C.; others (including Sethe and Bauer) to the Hyksos period, particularly to the seventeenth or sixteenth century B.C.; still others (Petrie and, more recently, Albright) date these inscriptions to the fifteenth century B.C.

Several attempts have been made to decipher the early Sinaitic inscriptions (Fig. 12.4), but Gardiner's classical identifications of the name of the goddess *Ba'alat* (name of the chief Canaanite goddess, who was called Hathor by the Egyptians) is the only one agreed upon by nearly all the scholars (Fig. 12.3*b*). Acceptance of the reading of one word as a probability, and recognition of the ingenuity of the method by which the reading was obtained, together with the fact that none of the sceptics has as yet proposed a plausible alternative, do not necessarily involve accepting Sir Alan Gardiner's Sinaitic theory. Gardiner's step towards decipherment—as Albright has pointed out—must remain basic to any system, but it is still only one step, and it has left the problem open. Although this theory had been accepted by many leading scholars, in M. Dunand's opinion, for instance, it has not been proved either that the acrophonic principle of the Sinaitic script is conclusive, or that the Alphabet descended from the latter script, or even that the Sinaitic script represents an alphabetic writing, or that the language of the Sinaitic inscriptions is Semitic.

In this connection it may be useful to say a few words about the decipherment of the early Sinaitic inscriptions. Although (1) these inscriptions have been known since Sir W. M. Flinders Petrie's discovery in 1905, and (2) the Sinaitic theory of the origin of the alphabet has been suggested by Gardiner and Sethe, in 1916; notwithstanding (3) that many eminent scholars have dealt with this problem and with that of the decipherment of the early Sinaitic inscriptions, and (4) that the majority of the scholars hold the opinion that these inscriptions are couched in a Semitic language and a script connected on the one hand with the Egyptian hieroglyphics and on the other hand with the North Semitic alphabet, which are both known; and finally (5) in spite of the discovery (*see* below) of, and research on the early Canaanite inscriptions and the 'missing-link' theory, we are still in almost the same situation today in regard to the decipherment of the early Sinaitic inscriptions, as that so aptly indicated by the propounder of the Sinaitic theory over fifty years ago in the following statement: 'Unfortunately, however, I have no suggestions for the reading of any other word, so that the decipherment of the name Ba'alat must remain, so far as I am concerned, an unverifiable hypothesis' (Gardiner, in *J. Egyptian Archaeology*, III/I, January, 1916, p. 15). How different has been the history of the decipherment of the Ugarit alphabet (*see* below)! The reason for this difference lies mainly in the fact that the early Sinaitic inscriptions do not provide sufficient material for their decipherment any more than they can help us to solve the problem of the origin of the alphabet or that of decipherment of the early Canaanite script.

On the other hand, in Professor T. H. Gaster's opinion, we are not required to accept the whole decipherment in order to prove the case. 'It is sufficient only to recognize—what one cannot deny—that the word *mtn* (gift) has been correctly read on the celebrated ewer from Lachish (*see* p. 156 and Fig. 12.9*a*[7]) and the word *b'lt* (goddess) in the inscriptions from Sinai.'

The whole problem has been re-examined by Professor Albright in the *B.A.S.O.R.* No. 110 (April, 1948) (*The Early Alphabetic Inscriptions from Sinai and their*

Decipherment). Albright identifies nineteen out of a total of twenty-five to twenty-seven Sinaitic signs, but he regards 'the Proto-Sinaitic script as normal alphabetical Canaanite from the early fifteenth century B.C. The language is also vulgar Canaanite. . . .'

Albright affirms that his decipherment yields results which fully agree with our present knowledge of the phonology, morphology and vocabulary of the north-west Semitic language then spoken in Palestine, Phœnicia and Lower Egypt. He then concludes, 'It follows that Gardiner's theory of the acrophonic origin of the alphabet is right.'

Be this as it may, the early Sinaitic writing cannot be regarded as the great mother-alphabet of all the alphabetic scripts, and does not represent 'the missing link' between the Egyptian hieroglyphic writing and the North Semitic alphabet.

UGARITIC CUNEIFORM ALPHABET

The accidental find in 1928 of a subterranean tunnel in the village of Râs Shamrah (to the north of Latakiya [ancient Laodicea] in north Syria) led to an epoch-making discovery during systematic excavations of the site of the ancient important city of Ugarit. C. F. A. Schaeffer, G. Chenet and Ch. Virolleaud found there in 1929 and the following years clay-tablets, belonging mainly to the fourteenth century B.C., which proved to be documents of inestimable value in many fields of research, such as epigraphy, philology, the history of religion, etc. Solitary Ugaritic tablets, perhaps in a variation of the Ugaritic alphabet, have been found in Palestine (at Beth-Shemesh and on Mount Tabor). From the point of view of the history of the Alphabet, the particularly important fact is that most of the documents are written in a hitherto unknown cuneiform alphabet of 32 letters (Figs. 12.5 and 6*a*). The system was soon deciphered independently by the late German scholar H. Bauer and by the French scholars E. Dhorme and Ch. Virolleaud; it is probably the shortest case of decipherment on record. The main Ugarit system consists of twenty-seven purely consonantal sounds and three alephs, for the sounds '*a*, '*i* and '*u*. The symbols are simple cuneiform signs; but the main connection with the other cuneiform systems is that they were impressed in a similar way with a stylus on clay-tablets; the direction of writing was the same, namely from left to right, unlike the North Semitic alphabet. Externally, about eight Ugaritic letters resemble more or less North Semitic letters having the same phonetic values (Fig. 12.3*c*).

But, in spite of this, the relation of the Ugaritic alphabet with the North Semitic is disputed. Among the theories dealing with the origin of the former, the most natural is that it was invented by a native who knew the North Semitic alphabet, but was accustomed to the use of clay and stylus which were not suitable for the writing of linear letters (or, perhaps it was invented by the priests of Ugarit in order to continue the use of cuneiform signs which may have been considered the correct ones for religious uses). The creator of the Ugaritic alphabet borrowed from the North

Semitic the idea of an alphabet for consonantal writing, and from the cuneiform scripts he imitated the wedge-shaped elements which he arranged in various simple combinations.

This opinion seems to be confirmed by the discovery in Ugarit, in 1949, of a small tablet containing the oldest known *ABC* (Fig. 12.6*d*). In this, the thirty Ugaritic letters are so placed that the twenty-two phonemes which are the same as in the North Semitic alphabet, appear in exactly the same order. Another, though fragmentary *ABC*, was previously published, but not recognized as such, by Professor C. H. Gordon (*Ugaritic Handbook*, No. 320); it confirms the order of the Ugaritic alphabet. Another was found in 1957 (*B.A.S.O.R.* No. 121 [Febr. 1951], p. 21). Three letters were later additions and were added after the *taw*, that is, at the end of the alphabet (just as was done later by the Greeks, the Romans, and other peoples, when they added new letters to the alphabet they had adopted). The remaining five letters seem to represent sounds which, in the North Semitic alphabet, were amalgamated with related sounds (some, however, are preserved in Arabic). This theory would presume the existence of a Proto-Semitic alphabet, containing twenty-seven letters. According to C. H. Gordon, the five extra letters could have dropped out of the longer version to form the shorter one. Indeed, 'If we try to make additions out of the five letters, there is no way (with reference to graphic forms or phonetic function) to explain their haphazard insertion.' Professor Albright is 'in full agreement that the new listing of letters of the alphabet reflects an early South Canaanite stage in which there were five additional phonemes.'

It has been suggested—as just mentioned—that the Early Canaanite alphabet may have represented the Proto-Semitic alphabet of twenty-seven letters, but the whole problem is still open. If we accept the theory of this Proto-Semitic alphabet, then we have to agree with the late E. A. Speiser (*B.A.S.O.R.*, No. 121, p. 21) that 'the discovery of the oldest alphabet known to us to date has solved or clarified some old problems and has also raised a number of new issues.' However, no serious scholar will oppose Speiser's conclusion: 'One thing, at least, is now clear and beyond dispute: we are still a long way from fully understanding our ABC.'

At any rate, it is probable that the cuneiform alphabet was definitely invented, not adapted from another system, as suggested by some scholars, although direct evidence is wanting. The late German scholar Bauer thought that the Ugarit alphabet was invented for a non-Semitic tongue. According to the French orientalist Dunand, the inventor of the cuneiform alphabet certainly knew the Byblos alphabetic script (*see* below), but did not adopt it probably for political reasons.

Amongst the various problems connected with the Ugarit alphabet, which cannot be explained satisfactorily, the most important is that this cuneiform alphabet contains thirty-two signs, while the North Semitic alphabet contains twenty-two symbols only; for instance, instead of the one North Semitic *aleph*, there are in the Râs Shamrah alphabet three *alephs* (symbols Nos. 1, 2, 3 in Fig. 12.6*a*), for the sounds '*a*, '*i-'e*, and '*u-'o*; there is a sign for the sound *zh*, the French *j* (No. 31), and seven other additional signs (Nos. 7, 12, 20, 22, 25, 29, 30) for sounds which in later Phœnician and Hebrew were amalgamated with related sounds, but are kept separated in Arabic. Of the additional signs, three are thought to have been added because of the fact that this script was used also for a non-Semitic speech (Hurrian); while the other surplus symbols are considered as a proof that the Ugarit alphabet was invented before the North Semitic alphabet was stabilized.

C. H. Gordon, *Ugaritic Grammar*, Rome, Pontificium Institutum Biblicum, 1940, is a handy and comprehensive manual on all the problems connected with the Ugarit script. For more recent bibliography on the Ugaritic alphabet and its relation to the North Semitic alphabet, see W. F. Albright, *B.A.S.O.R.*, No. 118 (April, 1950), pp. 12–4, and No. 119 (October, 1950), pp. 23–4, C. H. Gordon, *Orientalia*, XIX (1950) pp. 374–6, and E. A. Speiser *B.A.S.O.R.*, No. 121 (February, 1951), pp. 17–21.

THE PSEUDO–HIEROGLYPHIC SCRIPT OF BYBLOS AND THE ORIGIN OF THE ALPHABET ACCORDING TO M. DUNAND

Other very important documents (*see* p. 113 ff.) discovered by the French scholar M. Dunand in 1929, 1933, and in the following years, at Byblos, Syria, present a hitherto unknown type of writing which, according to Dunand, seems to be referred to in an ancient tradition quoted by Philo of Byblos. It has eighty or more characters and is therefore recognized as syllabic.

Maurice Dunand regards the syllabic pseudo-hieroglyphic script of Byblos as the prototype of the alphabet. According to him signs intermediate between the two systems of writing (Fig. 12.6*b*) appear on some inscriptions from Byblos (Fig. 12.6*b*: signs marked (¹)). These 'intermediate' signs are regarded by Dunand as the 'linear representation' of the pseudo-hieroglyphic symbols. If the pseudo-hieroglyphic script was the invention of a non-Semitic people, the linear script may, according to Dunand, be its simplification adapted to the Phœnician tongue.

Dunand's theory of the origin of the alphabet from the Byblos pseudo-hieroglyphic script is based on six points:

(1) both scripts were in use, in succession, in the same locality;

(2) all the Phœnician letters, with the exception of the *kheth* and the *qoph*, resemble symbols of the pseudo-hieroglyphic script or the Byblos linear writing (Fig. 12.6*b*);

(3) both the scripts are written from right to left;

(4) there are inscriptions extant on similar documents (*spatulæ*, Fig. 12.7*b* as compared with Figs. 10.1*d* and 2);

(5) the direction of writing of the Byblos hieroglyphic script is, unlike the Egyptian hieroglyphic script, similar to that of the alphabet, and the lines are always horizontal;

(6) in some pseudo-hieroglyphic inscriptions, as in some very early alphabetic texts, the words are separated by vertical strokes.

Apart from the pseudo-hieroglyphic script, Dunand points out that various signs resembling early alphabetic letters, such as *sh*, *m* and *'ayin*, are engraved on objects found in Byblos, and attributed to the period of the Egyptian Middle Kingdom (roughly 2000–1800 B.C.).

Five apparently 'alphabetiform' signs (Fig. 12.6c) are engraved on a statuette in bronze, also found in Byblos, and attributed to the end of the Egyptian twelfth dynasty or to the period of the thirteenth dynasty (that is to the early or middle eighteenth century B.C.). Dunand suggests the possibility of reading l(i) Amn, 'to (me) Ammon,' written in boustrophedon style. This inscription, according to M. Dunand, may be 'the incunabula of the alphabetic script.' Assuming that this is actually the case, we may—argues Dunand—arrive at the following conclusions:

(1) the Phœnician alphabet was already fully formed during the period of the Middle Kingdom, certainly in that of the thirteenth dynasty;

(2) it was contemporary with the pseudo-hieroglyphic script;

(3) it becomes plausible to add the aforementioned signs (appearing on objects belonging to the Middle Kingdom) to the agreed list of the known alphabetic characters so that it is just possible to date the earliest use of the alphabet in the period of the twelfth dynasty.

Having dated the origin of the alphabet in the period of the twelfth or thirteenth dynasty (c. 2000–1780 B.C.), Dunand considers that the possibility of the alphabet being derived from any other but the Egyptian or the cuneiform script should be excluded.

Maurice Dunand thus puts back the use of the alphabetic script by five or six centuries (Fig. 12.0). Three new inscriptions, also found in Byblos, according to Dunand fill the gap. They are:

(1) the 'Abdo inscription, a small fragment of pottery, which may be attributed to the eighteenth century B.C. or the early seventeenth century. It contains an inscription consisting of one horizontal line (Fig. 12.7a); Dunand reads: 'bd' b[n] klby hy [tsr], 'Abdo son of Kelubay, the potter';

(2) the Shafaṭba'al inscription (Fig. 12.8), consisting of five lines engraved on a chalk limestone block, found in the centre of the Byblos acropolis. This inscription is attributed by Dunand, both on archæological and palæographical grounds, also to the end of the eighteenth or to the early seventeenth century B.C., perhaps somewhat earlier than the previous one;

(3) the Asdrubal spatula; it is an inscription (Fig. 12.7b) engraved on a spatula, similar in shape to the spatulæ inscribed in pseudo-hieroglyphic writing (see p. 113); according to Dunand it probably belongs to the fourteenth century B.C.

For Dunand's new dating see p. 159.

Dunand's theory regarding the origin of the alphabet thus involves two problems, which may not necessarily be connected one with another:

(1) the suggestion that the Byblos pseudo-hieroglyphic script is the prototype of the alphabet may be acceptable, although no definite opinion can be expressed, as long as Dhorme's decipherment of the Byblos script is not being considered, or has been

rejected. The date of the texts is uncertain. The theory on the whole has not found adherents as yet, not having proved entirely satisfactory;

(2) the suggestion that we should date the origin of the alphabet (independently of its connection with the pseudo-hieroglyphic script), in the period of the twelfth or the thirteenth dynasty, is of such great importance that it should not be accepted unless it rests on a very sound foundation. Unfortunately, the present foundation is still very weak. Also the 'connecting link' between the suggested 'incunabula of the alphabet' (see p. 153) and the Akhiram inscription (see below) consists of far too few documents; moreover, these are of uncertain date, and cannot be regarded as sufficient material by which to trace the development of the alphabet through half a millennium. I feel that M. Dunand makes no clear distinction between conjecture and proof. In short, the problem, in my opinion, is still open. See note on p. 159.

One thing is certain, that in Byblos one or more attempts to introduce alphabetic writing were made in the early second millennium B.C.

KAHÛN AND RELATED INSCRIPTIONS

In Kahûn and other places of northern Egypt have been found inscriptions of the second millennium B.C. The script is unknown, but seems somewhat connected, externally at least, with the prehistoric geometric signs employed in Egypt and certain other countries from the third millennium onwards. This may be another attempt at alphabetical writing. Maurice Dunand mentions also a document from Karnak (near Luxor), published by Max Müller in *Egyptological Researches*, I, pp. 37 ff.

BALU'A INSCRIPTION

More important is the enigmatic inscription discovered in 1931 at Balu'a (Moab, Transjordan) which may be of the early twelfth century B.C. This inscription, engraved on a stele with a relief in Egyptian style, is badly worn and damaged, the letters being blurred and uncertain. Notwithstanding various endeavours, it remains undeciphered, and its graphic relationship is extremely obscure. Some signs seem to show affinity with Proto-Sinaitic symbols, others with South Semitic letters. These similarities, according to Professor G. R. Driver, suggest either a date before the differentiation of the various forms of these scripts, or an eclectic script based on an arbitrary choice between or an indistinct recollection of them. Professor Albright's suggestion that the text belongs to a much earlier period than the relief, and that the writing is a variant of the pseudo-hieroglyphic script of Byblos (attributed by him to the third millennium B.C.), is attractive but not very probable. Recently it has been suggested that the Balu'a script may be related to Minoan Linear A. This is very unlikely.

OTHER ATTEMPTS AT ALPHABETIC WRITING

There may have been other attempts, partly connected and partly independent, all having the same aim: to create a simpler means of communicating than those at the time in use. A seal inscription, possibly from Asia Minor and a few other documents are in this category. More important are the *Mesopotamian 'Proto-Arabic' or Chaldean* inscriptions. Two inscriptions incised on brick and a *graffito*, discovered by Sir Leonard Woolley in a temple at Ur just beneath a pavement of Nebuchadnezzar II (604–562 B.C.) and therefore very probably belonging to the seventh or the eighth century B.C., were published by the late Jesuit scholar Eric Burrows in the *J. Roy. Asiatic Society*, 1927, pp. 795–806. The script of these inscriptions seems to be allied to South-Semitic writing.

In Professor Albright's opinion, a few other inscriptions may belong to this group: a cylinder seal of 'typical Babylonian' character from the late eighth or seventh century B.C., two *graffiti* from Hamath, antedating the destruction of the city by the Assyrians in 720 B.C., and perhaps a few others. These short inscriptions present various problems still awaiting solution.

The evidence of many different attempts made with the same purpose and making use in some cases of the same 'rough material,' is probably one of the reasons why it is so difficult to determine the origins of alphabetical writing.

There are also many instances in which it is not easy to decide whether we are dealing with a new script, or with an adaptation of an existing one to another language. A fragmentary inscription consisting of twenty-five undeciphered signs in three lines in relief on terra-cotta, has been found in Babylonia. The Dutch scholar M. T. Bœhl published in the *Archiv für Orientforschung*, VIII, 4/5, 1933, pp. 169–74, two tablets (bought in 1897, in Constantinople), one with eight lines of writing on each side, and the other with six lines on each side. The script is still undeciphered. The provenance and the age of the tablets are uncertain. It seems, however, that the script is a relatively late creation, probably a transformation of an existing writing.

The solution of the problem of the origin of the Alphabet may come from Palestine, where several Middle and Late Bronze Age inscriptions (eighteenth-seventeenth, fourteenth and thirteenth centuries B.C.) have been discovered since 1929. The importance of these documents in the history of the Alphabet is paramount, but in my opinion it has been somewhat distorted by many scholars. I shall not now deal with the problem in greater detail; see my articles in *Antiquity*, 1943, and in the *J. Amer. Orient. Soc.*, 1943.

Following the discovery on Tell-ed-Duweir (the site of ancient Lachish) of the Early Canaanite inscriptions, the Sinaitic theory (*see* p. 148 ff.) was revived by A. H. Gardiner, and endorsed by other leading scholars, such as Albright, Flight and others. In the *Editio Princeps* of the Lachish Canaanite inscriptions, Dr. T. H. Gaster states that the writing of the Early Canaanite inscriptions 'constitutes an important "missing link" in the history of our own alphabet, representing the long sought intermediate

M

stage between the Sinaitic and the earliest known Phœnician forms.' This Sinaitic-Canaanite-Phœnician theory has been accepted by several scholars; and thus the problem of the origin of the Alphabet would seem to have been solved; as such it was presented to the general reader. In fact, the problem is still open.

The fourteen known Early Canaanite inscriptions can be divided into three groups according to date:

(*a*) the *Gezer Potsherd*, found in 1929 (Fig. 12.9*a*[1]); the *Shechem Stone Plaque*, found in 1934 (Fig. 12.9*a*[2]); and the *Lachish Dagger* or *Lachish IV* (Fig. 12.9) found in November 1934, with an inscription brought to light in December 1936 following the cleaning of the dagger. The objects of this group belong to the Middle Bronze Age III or 'Early Hyksos' (Albright's nomenclature) and can be dated to the eighteenth–seventeenth century B.C.;

(*b*) an *Oblong Seal*, found in Lachish early in 1935, belonging to the third quarter of the fifteenth century B.C.; this contains an inscription in characters which are somewhat allied to the Early Canaanite script. A similar inscription was recently published by Professor A. Gœtze, *A Seal with an Early Alphabetic Inscription*, *B.A.S.O.R.*, No. 129 (February, 1953), pp. 8 ff. An inscribed *Censer Lid* (Fig. 12.9*a*), from Lachish, where it was found in 1936, belongs to the second half of the fifteenth century or the first half of the fourteenth century B.C. The *Lachish Bowl No. 1* (Fig. 12.9*a*[8], *b*) belongs approximately to the second quarter of the fourteenth century B.C. The *Tell el-Ḥeṣy Potsherd* (Fig. 12.9*a*[4]), found in 1891; the *Tell el-'Ajjûl Pot* (Fig, 9*a*[5]) found in 1932; and the *Beth Shemesh Ostracon* (Fig. 12.9*a*[6]), found in 1930, may also be dated to the fourteenth century B.C.;

(*c*) the *Lachish Ewer* (Figs. 12.9*a*[7] and 10*a*), found in 1934, belongs to the third quarter of the thirteenth century B.C.; the *Lachish Bowl No. 2* (Fig. 9.9*a*[8]), also found in 1934, is of the thirteenth century B.C.; and the *Lachish Sherds No. 6* (Figs. 12.9*a*[11] and 10*b*), a few bowl-fragments with undecipherable traces of an inscription, once painted in dark-red paint, belong to the same century. We may add, finally, an inscribed golden bracelet from Megiddo, containing eight signs, attributed by the excavators to 1300–1200 B.C. (P. L. Guy, *Megiddo Tombs*, pp. 173 ff.) and the signs painted or engraved on a few stones (Fig. 12.9*a*[9]) in the foundations of the Temple of Jerusalem, which closely resemble some of the Lachish signs.

Have we really sufficient data to be able to affirm that in the Early Canaanite inscriptions we have characters which 'obviously stood midway between the much discussed semi-hieroglyphic Sinai script and the later Phœnician alphabet'? (Gardiner). If we accept the chronology of Albright, who also endorses the 'missing link' theory, though in a somewhat different form, we cannot agree that the Early Canaanite Middle Bronze Age inscriptions, which are two centuries earlier than the Proto-Sinaitic, constitute the missing link between the latter and the North Semitic alphabet.

Therefore, in Albright's opinion, endorsed also by his pupil Dr. Frank M. Cross Jr. *B.A.S.O.R.*, No. 134 (April, 1954), the Proto-Sinaitic characters were developed from the Middle Bronze Age Early Canaanite letters (see above, our group *a*) and the latter 'are definitely nearer the original hieroglyphic forms than are the corresponding letters of the Sinai script.' On the other hand, the 'Late-Bronze inscriptions (*i.e.*, our group *c*), which are all demonstrably or probably from the thirteenth century, are about half-way between the Proto-Sinaitic texts and the tenth-century texts from Byblos, to judge by the forms of characters.' In full agreement with this theory, Cross regards the Palaeo-Sinaitic inscriptions as written in 'Proto-Canaanite alphabetic symbols' and Syria/Palestine as the place of origin of the Alphabet. In collaboration with Dr. D. N. Freedman, another pupil of Professor Albright, Cross reaches the following conclusion: 'While in the past there has been some doubt, it is now certain that the alphabet was derived acrophonically, under direct or indirect Egyptian influence, with a centre of radiation somewhere in Canaan, probably in Phoenicia proper. This alphabet was the ancestor of the standard Phoenician, Aramaic and early Hebrew scripts, on one hand, and the different South Semitic scripts on the other' (*Early Hebrew Orthogr.*, p. 9). It remains to be seen, however, whether Sir Alan Gardiner—the creator of the Sinaitic theory (Egypt-Sinai-Canaan-Phœnicia)—would accept the transposition (Egypt-Canaan-Sinai-Canaan-Phœnicia).

In the opinion of the present author, neither the Sinaitic theory, nor the Canaanite-Sinaitic theory solves the mystery of the origin of the Alphabet. Our knowledge of the Sinaitic characters and, even more so, of the Early Canaanite symbols, is far from being sufficiently complete to permit of certainty: the identifications of the single signs suggested by the scholars who accept the 'missing link' theory generally disagree, while only complete agreement on the reading could provide any basis for a sound theory. The very few identifications agreed upon can be explained without accepting the 'missing link' theory; indeed, in most instances they concern signs which resemble North Semitic letters, though this external resemblance does not necessarily prove the identity of phonetic values.

In conclusion, it may be preferable to regard the Early Canaanite script as another, more or less independent effort—or indeed as representing perhaps more than one attempt—of the second millennium B.C. to introduce an alphabetic writing. Various authors have suggested 'that alphabet-making was at the time in the air' (A. C. Moorhouse); and 'the simple, but undecipherable Palestinian system suggests that during the first two-thirds of the second millennium B.C., that country was a centre of experiments,' aiming at the invention of an alphabet (Dunand).

It does not exclude, of course, the possibility of this attempt having some connection with the Egyptian, the early Sinaitic and the Cretan scripts, on the one hand, and the North Semitic alphabet on the other. Since the writing of some early Canaanite inscriptions is nearer to the North Semitic alphabet than is that of the other attempts, perhaps with the exception of that of Byblos, it is also possible that this early Canaanite script was either the prototype of our alphabet or rather a secondary branch of the prototype, but it is premature to present any such opinion as an unquestionable certainty.

For those readers who have a fondness for curious facts, I should like to point out

that, probably by a sheer coincidence, the three groups of the early Canaanite inscriptions correspond roughly, the first to the Age of the Patriarchs; the second, to
the Age of Joshua; the third, to the Age of the Judges; and that the *lacuna* of two or
three centuries between the first and the second groups corresponds roughly to the
period of oppression of the Israelites in Egypt.

In default of other evidence, it is preferable to hold the opinion that the actual
prototype was not remarkably different from the writing of the earliest North
Semitic inscriptions now extant, which are probably not later than the third group of
the early Canaanite inscriptions. The North Semitic alphabet was for many centuries
so constant that it is impossible to think of any alteration in the first centuries of
its existence being so radical as to bring about an entire change in the form of
many characters.

NORTH SEMITIC INSCRIPTIONS

Until 1923 our knowledge of the native epigraphy of Syria and Palestine was rather
unsatisfactory. The earliest datable known examples of the North Semitic alphabet
were (*a*) the Moabite stone (Fig. 14.14) or Stone of Mesha' (2 *Kings*, iii, 4–5) dating
from about the middle of the ninth century B.C.; (*b*) a Phœnician inscription (Fig.
14.18*b*), found in Cyprus, on the fragments of a bowl dedicated to Ba'al of Lebanon,
formerly assigned to the same century; (*c*) some Aramaic inscriptions (Fig. 15.2) from
Zenjirli in Syria, of the ninth and eighth centuries B.C. These inscriptions, and particularly the Mesha' Stone, constituted—and in some books still constitute—the starting point for the study of the history of the alphabet.

A new chapter was begun with the discovery, by the French scholar P. Montet, in
1923 at Byblos (Phœnicia), of the Aḥiram epitaph. About its date there has been
some disagreement. While several leading scholars prefer the tenth or eleventh
century B.C., others (and I think they are right) believe that the only evidence we
have is archæological. This was said to indicate the thirteenth century B.C., whereas
the majority of the scholars date the two Aḥiram inscriptions in question in the
twelfth or eleventh century B.C. I am now inclined to accept the latter date.

However, the epigraph on Aḥiram's sarcophagus (Figs. 12.11*a*, *b*) and the
graffito on his tomb (Fig. 12.11*c*) until recently were considered as the oldest North
Semitic inscriptions extant, followed by the Yeḥimilk inscription of the eleventh
century B.C., the Gezer calendar (Fig. 14.3*c*) of *c*. 1000 B.C., the Roueisseh spearhead
inscription (*c*. eleventh–tenth century B.C.), the Abiba'al (Fig. 12.11*d*) and Eliba'al inscriptions (tenth century B.C.). According to my opinion, until Maurice Dunand's
more recent discoveries (*see* p. 152 ff.), only these inscriptions were to be regarded as
a trustworthy starting-point for the history of the alphabet. Two of the three early
alphabetic inscriptions of Byblos (Figs. 12.7, 8), if M. Dunand's original dating were
correct, which seems to be doubtful, would have antedated the invention of the
North Semitic alphabet by about half a millennium. Figure 12.12 shows the early

development of the North Semitic alphabet according to the theory of the French excavator, Maurice Dunand; the dates, however, are not agreed upon.

Maurice Dunand in the *Post-scriptum* (dated April, 1946) to his book *Byblia Grammata*, 1945, and in his information given more recently to the present author, dated these inscriptions as follows: 'Abdo, fourteenth century B.C., Shafaṭba'al, fourteenth-thirteenth centuries; Asdrubal, twelfth century (?); Aḥiram, twelfth-eleventh centuries; Yeḥimilk, eleventh century; Roueisseh, eleventh century; Abiba'al tenth century; Eliba'al, tenth century; Meša', *c*. 842 B.C.

NORTH SEMITIC ALPHABET

There is no doubt that the North Semitic alphabet is the earliest most completely known form of the Alphabet transmitted to the west through the Greek, and to the east through the Aramaic alphabets. The main characteristics of the North Semitic alphabet are that it consisted of twenty-two letters or symbols, which correspond roughly to the first twenty-two letters of the Greek alphabet. The direction of writing was uniformly from right to left. The twenty-two letters expressed, as in modern Hebrew, consonants only, though some of them came to be used as long vowels. Both the names and the sounds of the letters rest mainly on tradition. We do not know whether the modern Hebrew names of the letters correspond exactly to those of the North Semitic alphabet, but the differences do not seem to have been important. There is little doubt that the Greek names of the letters are derived from the North Semitic. While the Greek names have no meaning in Greek, the Semitic names (at least, most of them) are words in Semitic languages. It is, therefore, reasonably certain that the Greeks, when they borrowed their alphabet from a Semitic source, took over the names with the letters; and we can assume that these names existed (in a more or less similar form) at the end of the second or the beginning of the first millennium B.C., when the Greeks adopted the North Semitic alphabet.

ORIGINAL ALPHABETIC WRITING

The incontestable facts about the original alphabetic writing may be summarized in this way: in the earliest stage (corresponding to the second half of the second millennium B.C.) of its history, the North Semitic alphabet was used by the Semitic-speaking inhabitants of Syria and Palestine, and was quite familiar to them. This script, compared with that of the Phœnician and of the Early Hebrew inscriptions of the first half of the first millennium B.C., shows, as stated, close resemblances to them even in detail. This is the best evidence that the forms of the original letters were constant, and did not differ widely from their later shapes. It may be observed, finally, that a considerable degree of caution should be exercised in coming to conclusions or forming theories on this problem, because the evidence is so fragmentary, and in that respect so much inferior to what we possess about the more ancient Egyptian and Mesopotamian scripts.

As the letters of the earliest North Semitic inscriptions extant show a certain external evolution, we can assume that the Proto-Semitic alphabet was some centuries older than, for instance, the aforementioned Aḥiram and Yeḥimilk inscriptions. This assumption is supported by the probability that, as already mentioned, the Ugarit alphabet, which apparently originated in the fifteenth century B.C., presupposes the existence of the Proto-Semitic alphabet. On the other hand, cuneiform writing was currently used by the Semites of Syria and Palestine at the date of the Tell el-'Amarna letters (fifteenth-fourteenth centuries B.C.). This may be evidence that the alphabet was still of recent origin. It is, however, more probable that side by side with the cuneiform script, used for diplomatic purposes and for international business, there existed already a common native script.

WHERE, WHEN, HOW, AND BY WHOM, WAS THE ALPHABET INVENTED?

When one is faced with a cardinal historical problem, such as the origin of the Alphabet, inquiry into first causes is extraordinarily difficult, just as in the case of a war or revolution. For, as the late Professor Chiera pointed out, there never was a man who could sit down and say: 'Now I am going to be the first man to write.' The Alphabet, that supreme achievement of man, which makes possible the very existence of the highest civilization, by transmitting to later generations the acquisitions of the earlier, was the result not of one, but of many factors. Even with recent events of any magnitude, it is difficult to determine their precise origin; in tracing back their causes, we reach a welter, where cause and effect condition and follow each other in turn. To avoid this perplexity, a starting point must be chosen, a birth certificate so to speak.

Thus, anyone wishing to study the history of the Alphabet, must take as the starting point the earliest known inscriptions written in the fully developed system, which we know as the North Semitic alphabet. In our present state of knowledge, only this can be considered the true ancestor of the Alphabet. Thus, the script of the Aḥiram epitaph—now generally attributed to the eleventh century B.C.—and of the somewhat earlier inscriptions ('Abdo, Shafaṭba'al and Asdrubal) more recently found at Byblos, and of a few tenth-century inscriptions from Byblos and Gezer, may be considered a trustworthy starting-point for the history of the Alphabet. This script, compared with that of the Phœnician, the Early Hebrew, and the Aramaic inscriptions of the first half of the first millennium B.C., shows—as said above—close resemblances, external (i.e., in shape of letters) as well as internal (in phonetic values). This is the best evidence that the forms of the original letters were more or less constant, and that they did not differ widely from the forms of the letters in their later stages.

On this assumption, and exercising all due caution—because the evidence is so nebulous and fragmentary—we may try to reconstruct a working hypothesis for the origin of the Alphabet. A few points help us:

(1) internal evidence: the letters of the A(k)hiram inscription show a certain external evolution; certain forms of 'āleph, wāw, têth, yôdh, nûn, 'ayin, pē and rêsh point to a cursive rather than to a monumental development. One gets the impression that the stone-cutter copied this inscription from a text written on papyrus. Moreover, the phonetic values of a few symbols, particularly the sāmekh and the shín, show that already in very early times some letters may have dropped out and others amalgamated with the existing ones. On the whole, therefore, the internal evidence suggests that this script originated some centuries earlier;

(2) this suggestion is strengthened by more important evidence of an external nature. The Ugaritic alphabet, which was probably created in the fifteenth century B.C., presupposes the existence of the North Semitic, or rather of its direct predecessor, an imaginary Proto-Semitic alphabet. This presupposition is confirmed by the South Semitic alphabet, which was somewhat connected with the North Semitic alphabet, but cannot have been descended from it. Indeed, for instance, the Sabæan letters b, d, h and p have a more archaic appearance and are closer to certain Sinaitic symbols than to North Semitic letters. Moreover, like the Ugaritic alphabet, the South Semitic possessed symbols for phonemes which were no longer represented in the North Semitic alphabet. We may thus conclude that this imaginary Proto-Semitic alphabet existed in the later part of the first half of the second millennium B.C.;

(3) concerning this imaginary Proto-Semitic alphabet, it is highly improbable that it is represented by the Proto-Sinaitic script, although this latter may be regarded as a sort of link between the Proto-Semitic and the South Semitic alphabets. More probable is the suggestion that the Early Canaanite script represents the Proto-Semitic alphabet. But, even in this instance, we have not sufficient evidence to supply the answer. There is, indeed, the possibility that the Early Canaanite alphabet represents a secondary parallel branch of the Proto-Semitic alphabet.

However, we reach the following conclusion.

The prototype alphabet, which we have referred to as 'Proto-Semitic,' probably originated in the second quarter of the second millennium B.C., i.e., in the Hyksos period, now commonly dated 1730–1580 B.C. The political situation in the Near East at that period favoured the creation of a 'revolutionary' writing, a script which we can perhaps term 'democratic' (or rather, a 'people's script'), as against the 'theocratic' scripts of Egypt, Mesopotamia, or China. As with other significant innovations—such as the adoption of the 'Roman' type of writing in England and Germany, the adoption of the decimal system in weights and measures, spelling reform, reform of the monetary system, and so on—alphabetic writing, to begin with, was strongly opposed by the conservative, politically stabilized states and theocratically governed societies. It took centuries till the alphabet established itself, and then only in newly founded states; it doubtless took very many centuries to establish itself in the old states.

The nationality of the inventors of the Proto-Semitic alphabet is unknown. The clue given by the significance of the traditional names (*see* below) of the letters is too slight: the eventually Aramaic form of these names in Greek is not decisive evidence, especially for such an early period. It is generally accepted that Semites (including also the Hebrews), Hurrians, Hittites and Indo-Iranians participated in the vast Hyksos movement; the Semitic elements, however, seem to have been dominant. It is hardly thinkable that the alphabet was invented by the Hyksos ruling-classes, as no evidence has come from Egypt, but there is no doubt that the upheaval brought about by the Hyksos movement might have induced some local population to create a 'non-monopolistic' means of communication.

Palestine and Syria, as everyone knows, formed a sort of bridge uniting the great civilizations of Egypt and Mesopotamia. The Syrian littoral is now known to have had a highly developed culture in the second millennium B.C. and a well-organized and active priestly literary school. Traders were constantly passing through these countries, and the lands changed hands a number of times at different periods of their history. For many years large Egyptian trading posts had been established on various Palestinian and Syrian sites. Clay tablets in cuneiform writing discovered in scattered places both in Palestine and Syria, testify to constant Mesopotamian influence. Hittites had likewise made their culture felt. Here was a country known also to have been subjected to many influences from the west; from Crete, Cyprus, and later on from Greece. 'There was always an active movement of cultural elements tending to create an almost imperceptible synthesis.' Having received various elements of culture from every surrounding region in the south-west (Egypt), in the north-east (Mesopotamia), in the north (Anatolia), and in the west (Crete, Cyprus and Greece), Syria and Palestine handed these elements on, somewhat altered as a rule, to other contiguous regions. Sir John Myres, in full agreement with the present theory, writes: '. . . it is no accident that the true alphabet originated in one of the very few regions where, by a series of historical accidents, the cuneiform, hieroglyphic, and probably also the Minoan systems, overlaid each other and set people thinking about a revolutionary change.' J. A. Montgomery also refers to this region as an 'arena of a welter of competing essays at writing.'

It is not in Sinai, the mountain desert region, that the origin of our alphabet is to be sought: the Israeli scholar Dr. Yeivin is certainly right when he points out in his criticism of my theory that many prophets were born in little towns far away from international commercial routes or in desert villages; he seems, however, to have overlooked the difference between the divine and philosophical thoughts of the prophets and the extremely practical purposes of the alphabet. At any rate, it is quite evident that Palestine and Syria offered all the required conditions for the invention and the elaboration of alphabetic writing. A. Levy (a century ago), M. Lidzbarski, E. J. Pilcher and F. Prætorius, already regarded the alphabet, partly at least, as the invention of the local population of Syria/Palestine. More recently, this theory has found staunch defendants in great authorities on the subject, such as the English Semitist Cook, the French orientalists Dussaud and Schæffer, the German Egyptologist von Bissing, the Finnish archæologist Sundwall, the Dutch theologian de Groot, the late German authority on the alphabet Hans Bauer, the American orientalist R. P. Blake, the German scholar Schott, and some others, amongst them the author of this book. Dunand, too, attributes the invention of the alphabet to a Semitic school or a person of high authority, and believes that Byblos may have been the seat of the invention. However, the exact birthplace of the alphabet is unknown; the names of two towns, Qiryat Sepher, the 'City of the Letter' (in Palestine), and Byblos, the 'Book-town' (in Syria), are significant, but no evidence is available as yet.

The same may of course be said of Professor Tur-Sinai's opinion, 'The historic alphabet of twenty-two signs, as first developed and adapted to Hebrew and Aramaic, was created in Israel, for the purpose of Israel's religious law, and forms part of Israel's religious tradition.' 'Thus the alphabet as it was taught by priests in words and sentences from its very beginning, is a religious document, proclaiming the belief in one God.' In other words, 'the Canaanitic alphabet, beginning and foundation of all learning, is a creation of Israel's genius and a witness to the ancient origin of its *Torah*.'

INFLUENCE OF OTHER SYSTEMS

The present hypothesis leaves sufficient room for the influence of the older systems, the Egyptian, the cuneiform, the Cretan, and perhaps also of the prehistoric-geometric signs. It is unlikely that the inventors were without precedent, and it is extremely improbable that an alphabet invented in Palestine or Syria in the second millennium B.C. was uninfluenced by the scripts of Egypt, Babylonia or Crete. Only in this way can the 'polygenetic' theory of the origin of the alphabet, propounded by Delitzsch some seventy years ago and by Lindblom in 1931–2, be considered as acceptable. Both the conception of consonantal writing and the acrophonic principle (if it existed in the Proto-Semitic alphabet) may have been borrowed from Egypt. The influence of the Babylonian writing may be traced in the names of some letters. The influence of the Cretan scripts and of the prehistoric-geometric signs may be purely external, affecting the form of some letters. Other alphabetic signs may have originated in conventional symbols, and it may be supposed that they were mainly arbitrary inventions.

DECISIVE ACHIEVEMENT

At any rate, it must be said that the great achievement of the invention was not the creation of the *signs*. It lies in the adoption of a purely alphabetic system, which denoted each sound by one sign only. For this achievement, simple as it *now* seems to us, the inventor, or the inventors are to be ranked among the greatest benefactors of mankind. No other people in the world had been able to develop a true alphabetic writing. The more or less civilized peoples of Egypt, Mesopotamia, Crete, Asia Minor, Indus Valley, China, Central America, reached an advanced stage in the history of writing, but could not get beyond the transitional stage. A few peoples (the Cretans, Cypriotes, Japanese and others), developed a syllabary. But only the Syro-Palestinian Semites produced a genius who created the alphabetic writing, from which have descended all past and present alphabets.

Each important civilization modifies its script and time may make its relation to some of its near relatives quite unrecognizable. Thus, the Brahmī, the great mother-script of India, the Korean alphabet, the Mongolian scripts are derived from the same source as the Greek, the Latin, the Runic, the Hebrew, the Arabic, the Russian alphabets, although it is practically impossible for a layman to see a real resemblance between them.

THE GREEK TERMS GRÁMMATA, STOICHEÎA AND SYLLABAÍ

The importance of these terms may be gauged from the interesting passages from Plato's (*c.* 429–347 B.C.) *Theaitetos* and *Kratylos*, probably the earliest extant scientific discussion of the terms 'alphabetic letters' and 'syllables.' In order to leave the reader free to judge about the meaning of these terms, we have retained here the three Greek words. *Grámmata* is derived from *gráphein*, 'to scratch, to graze, to draw lines, to write'; hence the meaning in classical times would be 'letters, characters'; but there is the possibility that Plato sometimes may mean 'sounds.' *Stoicheía* is derived from *stéichein*, 'to walk, to march, especially in line or order,' and it means 'element, simple sound.' *Syllabé*, derived from *syllambánein* 'to collect, to gather together,' means 'grip, hold, that which holds together, that which is held together, especially of several letters taken together so as to form one sound, syllable.'

Plato, *Theaitetos* 202 D–203 C [based on Harold North Fowler's translation] [Socrates and Theaitetos are discussing the term *Stoicheía*].

SOCRATES: One point, however, in what has been said is unsatisfactory to me.

THEAITETOS: Which point?

SOCRATES: Just that which seems to be the cleverest, [namely] that the
202 E   *stoicheía* are un-knowable, but the *syllabaí* are knowable.

THEAITETOS: Is that not right?

   . . . .

203 A   SOCRATES: the *stoicheía* and the *syllabaí* of the *grámmata* . . . Let us, then, take them up and examine them, or rather, let's examine ourselves and see whether we learned *grámmata* in accordance with his [Theodoros'] theory or not. Now first: The *syllabaí* have a rational explanation, but the *stoicheía* not?

THEAITETOS: Hm . . . perhaps so.

SOCRATES: Quite certainly, I think. Now if anyone should ask you about the first *syllabé* of Socrates thus: 'Theaitetos, tell me what is *sô*?' What would you reply?

THEAITETOS: I should answer: '*Sîgma* and *ô*.' ....

203 B SOCRATES: Come now, give me, too, the explanation of the *Sîgma* in the same manner.

THEAITETOS: How could one say the *stoicheîa* of the *stoicheîon*? For really, Socrates, the *Sîgma* belongs to the voiceless [things], a mere noise, as if the tongue hisses; and *Bêta* has neither a voice nor even a hiss, nor have most of the other *stoicheîa*; and so it is quite right to say that they have no rational explanation, since even the most distinct ones, the Seven [vowels] have only voice, but no rational explanation whatsoever.

SOCRATES: We have brought to a successful issue the point concerning understanding, my friend.

THEAITETOS: It seems we have.

ABSENCE OF VOWELS

The main characteristics of the North Semitic alphabet are that it consisted of twenty-two letters or symbols, which correspond to the twenty-two letters of its descendant, the modern Hebrew alphabet. The method of writing was uniformly from right to left. The twenty-two letters expressed consonants only, though some of them came to be used as vowels. This absence of vowels has not been satisfactorily explained. Maurice Dunand thinks that the Semites purposely did not mark the vowel sounds, and he rightly points out that this imperfection was one of the reasons of the diffusion of the alphabet and of its ready adaptability. Other scholars have conjectured that each letter at first did not represent a single sound but had a syllabic value. The supposition is used in support of the hypothesis of the Egyptian origin and is suggested by it. Another explanation is that the vowels were supplied locally, the sound varying with the different dialects, so that the inventors left the vowels to be supplied according to local practice. This, however, is hardly convincing.

In Driver's opinion, this omission of the vowels is explicable only on the assumption that those who were inventing and working out the North Semitic alphabet had before them none in the model on which they worked. That (Driver believes) must have been the Egyptian system, in which the absence of vowels was inherent in a method derived from pictography and which did not, till a relatively late date, advance beyond that stage. This theory of Professor Driver is to be taken into serious account, though as a whole it cannot be proved beyond doubt.

At any rate, we must take into consideration the fact that the alphabet was created for Semitic languages and is sufficiently suited to them. This is also proved by the fact that even nowadays neither the Hebrew nor the Arabic languages use the vocalic punctuation except in a few justifiable cases. In fact, the Semitic languages are based chiefly on roots, which give us the fundamental conception, and are represented by consonants, while the vowel sounds give us only the complements, the details, such as the part of speech, the voice, the mood, the tense.

Some scholars believe that, as the North Semitic script did not possess vowels, it cannot be considered a true alphabet; according to them, only the Greeks created a true alphabet. Professor I. J. Gelb (in his *Study of Writing*, London and Chicago, 1952, pp. 147 ff. and *passim*) goes so far as to regard the North Semitic alphabet (or the 'West Semitic,' as he calls it) as a syllabary. But syllabaries are based rather on vowels (with or without consonants) than on consonants. Suffice it to say that if we accept Gelb's definition of syllabic writing 'in the sense that it shows correctly the consonants and does not indicate the vowels,' then we have to correct the *Oxford English Dictionary*, which defines 'syllable' (a term employed from the fourteenth century onwards) as follows: 'A vocal sound or set of sounds uttered with a single effort of articulation and forming a word or an element of a word; each of the elements of spoken language comprising a sound of greater sonority (vowel or vowel-equivalent) with or without one or more sounds of less sonority (consonants or consonant-equivalents); also a character or set of characters forming a corresponding element of written language.' Gelb's premises that the evolution of writing is from a word-syllabic script (the Egyptian) through a syllabic writing (the 'West Semitic' syllabary) to an alphabetic writing (the Greek alphabet) may be disproved by Professor G. R. Driver's thesis: 'while a syllabic writing can be evolved from a purely consonantic alphabet, as the Ethiopic syllabary shows, syllabic writing is a blind alley from which there is no escape. Neither a purely consonantal alphabet nor one of consonants and vowels was ever evolved from the Akkadian syllabary. . . . "

The North Semitic alphabet was from the first moment of its existence a true alphabet; at least, as far as Semitic languages are concerned. It was certainly not perfect, but perfection has not yet been reached by any alphabet, although at least in theory it does not seem very difficult of achievement. Perfection in an alphabet implies the accurate rendering of phonemes, that is, each sound must be represented by a single constant symbol, and not more than one sound by the same symbol. As it is, all alphabets omit symbols for some sounds (representing these, when necessary, by combinations of symbols; as for example the English *sh* and *th*), while most of them contain redundant symbols. It is generally accepted that writing was in the first place an attempt to represent speech accurately, but even in those early stages the attempt was largely a failure. The number of the letters was too small in the beginning and they have never been sufficiently increased, while the phonetic system of any language is far too complicated to be accurately expressed in writing by any reasonably small group of symbols.

However, in the long history of the alphabet, while it is relatively easy to attach a permanent value to the various consonantal sounds, it is quite different with the vowel sounds. Today the same vowel indicates varying sounds (especially in English), and it is almost impossible for us to know what exact sound was given to it by ancient peoples. This difficulty will be appreciated more fully if we reflect that in England, for example, the same word is pronounced very differently in different parts of the country, and this is due rather to the varied methods of pronouncing the vowels than to those of pronouncing the consonants. It is the many and subtle differences between the vowels, so inadequately represented by existing symbols, which chiefly puzzle those who desire to speak English perfectly. These remarks will explain better why the North Semitic purely consonantal alphabet could remain almost unaltered for so many centuries. We do not mean to suggest that the absence of vowels in the Proto-Semitic alphabet was intentional, but we may say that in the long run this absence became a benefit rather than a disadvantage.

OTHER CHARACTERISTIC PROBLEMS

Of the other less important deficiencies, one has already been referred to: that is, the letters *sāmekh* and *shîn*, expressing the sounds *s* and *sh*. Without going into historical-phonetical disquisitions (the variety of *s* which is expressed by the letter *shîn* originally had a slightly different sound from that expressed by the letter *sāmekh*, and in the opinion of some experts it was expressed by a symbol now lost, which became amalgamated with the letter *shîn*), the fact remains that whilst the sound *s* can be expressed not only by the letter *sāmekh*, but also by the letter *shîn*, the latter represents two distinct sounds *s* and *sh*.

NAMES OF LETTERS

Both the names and the sounds of the letters of the North Semitic alphabet rest mainly on tradition.

The names of the letters of the North Semitic alphabet are preserved in the modern Hebrew alphabet. We do not know whether the modern Hebrew letter-names correspond exactly to those of the ancient Semitic script, but the differences do not seem to have been very important. The Greek names are derived from the Semitic ones. The following are the Hebrew names of the twenty-two letters of the North Semitic alphabet: *'āleph, bêth, gîmel, dāleth, hē, wāw, zayin, ḥêth, ṭêth, yôd, kaph, lāmed, mēm, nûn, sāmekh, 'ayin, pē, ṣādê, qôph, rêsh, shîn, tâw*. Thus, nearly all these names end with a consonant, while their Greek equivalents (*alpha, beta, gamma*, and so forth) end with a vowel. This difference has been explained in two ways; some scholars have suggested that the Greek forms were taken from an Aramaic source, the Aramaic language having preference for the emphatic form which ends in a vowel and drops the vowel of the preceding syllable; others consider the terminal vocalization of the Greek letters as being more in agreement with Greek speech. However, it is reasonably certain that the Greeks, when they borrowed their alphabet from Semitic sources, took over the names with the letters. Therefore, we can assume that these names existed at the end of the second millennium B.C., when the

Greeks adopted the Semitic alphabet, although the exact form of some of the names is uncertain.

The most ancient transliterations of the Semitic letters into their Greek equivalents and comparison with some Semitic languages, show that the early distinctions of the North Semitic alphabet between some letters (for example, between *sāmekh* and *sín*) were lost at a later stage. Some scholars attribute this fact to the use in later times of Aramaic, in which for example *sāmekh* displaced *sín*.

It is generally believed—this theory was already propounded by the great German Semitist W. Gesenius—that the Semitic names were derived from the form of the object 'originally represented by the signs'; so, for example, it is commonly accepted that the second letter had originally the form of a house, and because of this form it was called *bêth*, meaning 'house.' This opinion does not seem correct, although there may have been such a connection in a few cases. Generally speaking, as already suggested by the French orientalist François Lenormant in 1875, the original names of the letters seem to have been chosen independently of a supposed form; this opinion was also held by H. Bauer.

Sethe and Dunand hold that there was a connection between the names of the letters and their original shapes. According to Dunand, the purpose of the names of the letters 'was to suggest and to remind the memory of the letter in question. Although the resemblances (between the name and the object represented) were sometimes superficial, they were nevertheless real.' Thus, according to Dunand, 'no name is arbitrary (except the *hē*), all of them are simple, in common use.' On the other hand, if we accept the main principle, that is, that the alphabet was an original creation, then the names and the order of the letters could not have the great importance many scholars attach to them. A modern *ABC*-book for children teaches *A* for '*aeroplane*,' or *A* for '*apple*,' or *A* for '*acorn*,' etc.; *B* for '*bunny*,' or *B* for '*bee*,' or *B* for '*butterfly*,' etc.; *C* for '*cat*,' or *C* for '*candy*,' or *C* for '*coat*,' etc., and so on. The choice of the original names as a mnemonic device must have been similarly free. We could assume that where resemblance to an object was noted in the shape of the letter, that may, at times, have prompted the choice of a name. Otherwise, any common word, beginning with the relative letter, would do as a name sufficient to remind the memory of the letter in question.

However, the Semitic names of the letters refer mainly to everyday objects—such as house (*bêth*), door (*dāleth*), hook (*wāw*); to parts of the body, hand (*yôd* for *yad*), palm or open hand (*kaph*), eye ('*ayin*), mouth (*pē*), head (*rêsh* for *rosh*), tooth (*shín* for *shēn*); to animals, ox ('*āleph*), camel (*gīmel* for *gamal*), fish (*nûn* or *sāmekh* for *samakh*), monkey (*qôph*)—the Semitic names for which began with the very sound the letter indicated, that is *b, d, w, y, k, ', p, q, r*, and so forth. The name of the last letter was simply 'sign' or 'mark' (*tāw*). Some of the letters, such as *ḥêth* and *ṭêth*, are regarded by a few scholars as additions. It is noteworthy that while the majority of the names are very easy to explain, the names of the letters considered as additions present difficulties and have not in fact been explained satisfactorily.

There are a few other names whose meaning is still uncertain; these are *hē*, which according to Dunand was made up simply by the consonant *h* followed by the vowel *e* (as there was no Phœnician or Hebrew word beginning with that aspirate); *zayín*, which is explained by some scholars as 'weapon,' by others as a substitution for *zayit*, 'olive,' etc.; according to Dunand it was connected with the Hebrew root *'zn*, and indicated 'balance,' in Hebrew *moznayim*; *ḥêth*, according to Dunand, means 'fence' or 'barrier'; *ṭêth* is explained by Dunand as 'ball' or 'clew' (for instance, of wool or cotton); *lāmed* may indicate, according to Dunand, the rod of the teacher; *sāmekh* is generally explained, as mentioned above, as 'fish'; Dunand's explanation as 'support,' 'fulcrum,' seems to be more satisfactory; *ṣādê*, which according to some scholars means 'step, stair(s),' or 'nose,' or else, 'scythe,' 'javelin,' is explained by Dunand as being connected with the root *ṣwd*, and may indicate '(fishing-)hook,' '(fishing-)rod.'

Dunand holds that the Semitic names of the letters are very ancient; originally they were pure Phœnician, and the Greeks adopted them from the Phœnicians, as for instance is shown by the names *gamma* and *ro*, derived from the original *gamal* and *rosh*, while the Semitic names were later changed under Aramaic influence into *gīmel* and *rêsh*.

The phonetic value of each letter is, and probably was, in North Semitic, that of the first letter of its name; this device is known as the acrophonic principle. Thus the value of *bêth* is *b*, of *gīmel* is *g* (hard as in 'gang'), of *hē* is *h*, of *wāw* is *w*, and so on. The phonetic value of the North Semitic letters, in nearly all the instances, more or less corresponds with the phonetic value of the modern Hebrew letters. In a few instances, however, as we know from comparison with some ancient or modern Semitic languages (Ugaritic or Arabic) and the most ancient transliterations of the Semitic letters into their Greek equivalents, the exact sound of the North Semitic characters and the early distinction between some of them (for instance between the *s*-sounds in *sāmekh* and *sín*, which is a variety of *shín*) were lost at a later stage.

ORDER OF LETTERS

As to the order of the letters, various theories have been propounded, but here again it is highly probable that the matter has no particular significance.

The sequence of the ancient North Semitic letters seems to correspond with that of the modern Hebrew letters, as may be inferred from various passages in the Hebrew Bible, such as: *Naḥum*, i, 2–14; *Lamentations*, i–iv; *Proverbs*, xxxi, 10–31; *Psalms*, ix, x, xxv (the *qôph* is missing), xxxiv, cxi, cxii. A partial Early Hebrew sample-alphabet, discovered in 1938 in Lachish on the upper step of the staircase which led up to the Palace, and which may belong to the late ninth or early eighth century B.C. (Fig. 14.3*b*) provides secondary evidence for the early order of the Hebrew letters. The discovery, in 1949, of an Ugaritic tablet of the fourteenth century B.C., containing the thirty letters of the Ugaritic alphabet (Fig. 12.6*a*)—which is thus the oldest known *ABC*—including the symbols for the twenty-two North Semitic letters in the same order as they appear in the modern Hebrew alphabet, confirms the opinion that the letter-sequence of the North Semitic alphabet, as transmitted by Hebrew tradition and by the early Greeks and Etruscans, goes back to the fifteenth century B.C. at the latest.

There is some appearance of phonetic grouping in the order of the letters of the North Semitic alphabet, but this may be accidental.

MAIN BRANCHES OF EARLY ALPHABETS

I have already mentioned the early North Semitic inscriptions (Figs. 12.7, 8, 11 and 12), belonging to the last centuries of the second millennium B.C. At the end of this millennium, with the definite or temporary political decay of the great nations of the Bronze Age, the Egyptians, the Babylonians, the Assyrians, the Hittites, the Cretans, we enter a new historical world. In Syria and Palestine, the geographical centre of the 'fertile crescent,' three nations, Israel, Phœnicia and Aram, played an increasingly important part. To the south of the 'fertile crescent', the Sabæans, a South Arabian people, attained a position of wealth and importance as the commercial intermediaries between the east and the Mediterranean. To the west, seeds were sown amongst the eager-minded peoples which later constituted the nation of Hellas, the Greeks.

These conditions favoured the development of four branches of the alphabet; (1) the so-called Canaanite branch, subdivided into two secondary branches: (a) the Early Hebrew, and (b) the Phœnician; (2). the Aramaic branch—both, the Canaanite and Aramaic branches, constituting the North Semitic main branch; (3) the South Semitic or Sabæan branch; and (4) the Greek alphabet, which became the progenitor of the western alphabets.

BIBLIOGRAPHY

A great number of scholars in Semitics, Egyptology and allied subjects have written books or articles on the origin of the Alphabet or on problems connected with this vast field of study. American scholars (W. F. Albright, C. C. Torrey, M. Sprengling, J. Obermann, A. T. Olmstead, E. Grant, J. A. Montgomery, R. F. Butin, B. L. Ullman, Z. S. Harris, C. H. Gordon, F. M. Cross, D. N. Freedman, and many others), as well as British (A. H. Gardiner, A. E. Cowley, S. Langdon, S. H. Hooke, T. H. Gaster, E. Burrows, J. W. Jack, G. R. Driver, and others), French (E. Dhorme, R. Dussaud, P. Montet, M. Dunand, Ch. Virolleaud, R. De Vaux, J. G. Février, and others), and German (H. Bauer, H. Jensen, J. Friedrich, H. Grimme, E. Littman, E. Ebeling, A. Alt, R. Eisler, and others), Israeli scholars (H. L. Ginsberg, S. Yeivin, B. Mazar, H. Tur-Sinai, and others), Dutch, Belgian, Finnish and Scandinavian (F. M. Th. Bœhl, G. Ryckmans, R. De Langhe, J. Lindblom, N. A. van den Oudenrijn, J. Sundwall, and many others), Swiss and Italian (S. Moscati and others), as well as Egyptian, Syrian, and Iraqi; they all have written publications on matters dealt with in this chapter.

Any reader who would like to pursue the subject, will find exhaustive material written by the scholars mentioned in the many American and European journals, such as the *Bulletin of the American Schools of Oriental Research*, the *Journal of Near Eastern Studies* (Chicago), the *Palestine Exploration Quarterly* (London), the *Journal of Egyptian Archæology* (London), the *Journal of the Royal Asiatic Society*, the

Journal of the American Oriental Society, the *American Journal of Archæology*, the French *Syria* and *Revue Biblique*, the Belgian *Le Muséon*, the Dutch *Ex Oriente Lux*, the German *Archiv für Orientforschung*, *Zeitschrift der deutschen morgenländischen Gesellschaft*, the Israeli *Bulletin of the Israel Exploration Society*, the Italian *Rivista degli Studi Orientali*, the learned magazines of Egypt, Iraq, Syria and Lebanon, and a host of other journals of the Old and New World.

Following are some major studies, alphabetically arranged, of more recent date, concerned with the origin of the Alphabet, all of them containing bibliography:

ALBRIGHT, W. F. *From the Stone Age to Christianity*, Baltimore, 1940; *Archæology and the Religion of Israel*, Baltimore, 1942; *The Archæology of Palestine*, London, 1949; *The Early Alphabetic Inscriptions from Sinai and their decipherment*, B.A.S.O.R., No. 110 (Apr., 1948).

BAQIR, T. 'The Origin of the Alphabet,' *Sumer*, 1945.

BAUER, H. 'Der Ursprung des Alphabets,' *Der Alte Orient*, Leipzig, 1937.

BEA, A. 'Die Entstehung des Alphabets,' *Miscellanea Giovanni Mercati*, Vatican City, 1946.

BODMER, F. *The Loom of Language*, London and New York, 1944.

BORK, F. *Das Ukirutische, die unbekannte Sprache von Ras Schamra*, Leipzig, 1938.

BURROWS, M. *What Mean These Stones?* New Haven, 1941.

COHEN, M. *L'Écriture*, Paris, 1953; *La grande Invention de l'écriture*, Paris, 1958.

CONTENAU, G. *Manuel d'Archéologie orientale*, IV, Paris, 1947.

COWLEY, A. E. in *J. Egyptian Archæology*, 1916.

CROSS, F. M. 'The Evolution of the Proto-Canaanite Alphabet,' *B.A.S.O.R.*, No. 134 (Apr. 1954).

CROSS, F. M. and FREEDMAN, D. N. *Early Hebrew Orthography*, New Haven, Conn., 1952.

CURTIUS, E. *Schrift und Buchmetaphorik*, etc., Halle, 1942.

DENMAN, F. *The Shaping of our Alphabet*, New York, 1955.

DIRINGER, D. *L'Alfabeto nella storia della civiltà*, Florence, 1937; *The Alphabet*, London and New York, 1948; *The Hand-produced Book*, London and New York, 1953;—and FREEMAN, H., *Alphabet Exhibition*, London, 1953; 'Inscriptions' in *Lachish IV*, London and Oxford, 1956; *The Story of the Aleph-Beth*, London, 1958; New York, 1960; *Writing*, London and New York, 1962, and so on.

DHORME, E. 'Déchiffrement des Inscriptions pseudo-hiéroglyphiques de Byblos,' *Syria*, 1946-8, Paris, 1948.

DRIVER, G. R. *Semitic Writing from Pictograph to Alphabet* ('The Schweich Lectures,' 1944), London and Oxford, 1948, and subsequent edition.

DUNAND, M. *Byblia Grammata*, Beirut, 1945.

DUSSAUD, R. 'L'Origine de l'alphabet et son évolution première d'après les découvertes de Byblos,' *Syria*, 1946-8, Paris, 1948.

FÉVRIER, J. G. *Histoire de l'Écriture*, Paris, 1948, and subsequent edition.

FLIGHT, J. W. 'The Present State of Studies in the History of Writing in the Near East,' *The Haverford Symposium*, Cambridge, Mass., 1938.

FOSSEY, CH. *Notice sur les caractères étrangers anciens et modernes*, etc., 2nd ed., Paris, 1948.

FRIEDRICH, J. *Phönizisch-punische Grammatik*, Rome, 1951.

FRONZAROLI, P. *La fonetica ugaritica*, Rome, 1955.

GARDINER, A. H. in '*J. Egyptian Archæology*, 1916; *Legacy of Egypt*, Oxford, 1942.

GASTER, T. H. 'The Archaic Inscriptions,' in *Lachish II*, London (and Oxford), 1940.

GELB, I. J. *A Study of Writing*, London and Chicago, 1952, and subsequent edition.

GINSBERG, H. L. *The Ugaritic Texts* (in Hebrew), Jerusalem, 1936.

GORDON, C. H. *Ugaritic Grammar*, Rome, 1940.

GRAY, J. *The Krt Text in the Literature of Ras Shamra*, London, 1955.

GRAY, L. H. *Foundations of Language*, 2nd ed., New York, 1950.

GRIFFITH, C. L. T. *The Story of Letters and Numbers*, London, 1939.

GRIMME, H. *Altsinaitische Forschungen*, Paderborn, 1937.

HARRIS, Z. S. *Development of the Canaanite Dialects*, New Haven, 1939; *Methods in Structural Linguistics*, Chicago, 1951.

HOGBEN, L. *From Cave Painting to Comic Strip*, London and New York, 1949.

JENSEN, H. *Geschichte der Schrift*, Hanover, 1925; *Die Schrift in der Vergangenheit und Gegenwart*, Glückstadt and Hamburg 1935; rev. ed., Berlin (East), 1958.

KAPELRUD, A. S. *Baal in the Ras Shamra Texts*, Copenhagen, 1952.

Lachish, II, London, 1940; *Lachish, IV*, London, 1956.

DE LANGE, R. *Les Textes de Ras Shamra-Ugarit*, 2 vol., Louvain, 1945.

LEIBOVITCH, J. *Les Inscriptions protosinaïtiques*, Le Caire, 1934.

LIPS, J. E. *The Origin of Things*, London, 1949.

MAISLER (now Mazar), B. 'Zur Urgeschichte des phönizisch-hebräischen Alphabets,' *Journal of the Palestine Oriental Society*, 1938.

McMURTRIE, D. C. *The Book: The Story of Printing and Bookmaking*, 3rd ed., New York, 1943.

MENDELSOHN, I., *Religions of the Ancient Near East; Sumero-Akkadian Religious Texts and Ugaritic Epics*, New York, 1955.

MOORHOUSE, A. C. *Writing and Alphabet*, London, 1946; *The Triumph of the Alphabet*, New York, 1953.

MORAN, H. A. *The Alphabet and the Ancient Calendar*, Palo Alto, Calif., 1953.

OBERMANN, J. *The Archaic Inscriptions from Lachish*, New Haven, 1938.

OGG, O. *The 26 Letters*, New York and London, 1949.

OTTO, W. *Handbuch der Archäologie*, I, Munich, 1939.

PEI, M. A. *The World's Chief Languages*, London, 1949;— and GAYNOR, F., *A Dictionary of Linguistics*, New York, 1954.

POPE, M. H., *El in the Ugaritic Texts*, Leiden, 1955.

RELANO, E. and A. *Historia grafica de la escritura*, Madrid, 1949.

SATTLER, P. and v. SELLE, G. *Bibliographie zur Geschichte der Schrift*, etc., Linz, 1935.

SCHAEFFER, C. F. A. *The Cuneiform Texts of Ras Shamra-Ugarit*, London and Oxford, 1939; *Ugaritica*, Paris, 1939.

SCHLAUCH, M. *The Gift of Tongues*, London, 1943.

SCHMITT, A. *Die Erfindung der Schrift*, Erlangen, 1938.

SETHE, K. *Vom Bild zum Buchstaben. Die Entstehung der Schrift*, Leipzig, 1939.

SPRENGLING, M. *The Alphabet. Its Rise and Development from the Sinai Inscriptions*, Chicago, 1931.

THOMPSON, T. *The ABC of Our Alphabet*, London and New York, 1942.

TIBÓN, G. *Prehistoria del alfabeto*, Mexico D. F., 1956.

TSCHICHOLD, J. *Geschichte der Schrift in Bildern*, Basel, 1946.

WEIDMÜLLER, W. 'Phoinikische Buchstaben-ägyptische Bildzeichen', *Börsenblatt für den Deutschen Buchhandel*, 1960, Nos. 39 and 46.

WEILL, R. *La Phénicie et l'Asie Occidentale*, Paris, 1939.

YEIVIN, S. *The History of the Hebrew Script* (in Hebrew), I, Jerusalem, 1938.

CHAPTER 13

South Semitic Alphabets

ANCIENT SOUTH ARABIA

THE South Semitic group of alphabets, generally speaking, remained confined within Arabia, where the following pre-Islamic scripts developed: Minæan, Sabæan, Ḥimyaritic, Qatabanic, and Ḥaḍramautic, in South Arabia; and Thamudene, Dedanite, Liḥyanite, and Ṣafaitic, in North Arabia. The Sabæan script spread into the African continent, becoming the progenitor of the Ethiopic alphabet and so of the modern Amharic, Tigré, Tigriña, and other alphabets, the only South Semitic off-shoots still in use.

However, the importance of such inscriptions can be gauged when we consider that practically all we know of early South Arabian history is based upon them. They concern the territory facing on the Indian Ocean and the Red Sea, known from the Biblical Table of Nations (*Gen.*, x) as Sheba' and Hazarmaveth (Ḥaḍramaut). The name Yemen (*al-Yaman* 'right hand, southern') is also ancient.

These inscriptions are our main source for the study of the once flourishing king-doms for which we had no authority other than vague references in classical writers. They are the only important remains of the empires of the Minæans, Sabæans, Qatabanians, and Ḥaḍramautis, whose splendour has been immortalized by the biblical account of Solomon and the Queen of Sheba. These kingdoms were in later times in contact with the entire ancient world, from Rome to India, and beyond; in fact, objects of Egyptian, Mesopotamian, Greek, Indian and Roman manufacture have been found in various sites of South Arabia, and of South Arabian manufacture on the Aegean island of Delos.

'The Empty Quarter, probably the world's largest stretch of sheer and utter desert without oasis and without relief, acts as the centre of a ring, about which are set the Arabian kingdoms, like jewels of different hue and lustre' (Carleton S. Coon, in *Papers of the Peabody Museum*, Vol. XX, 1943, p. 187). In this land so hostile, both physically and politically, to the intruder—present-day Yemen would never allow regular excavations—no such excavations have yet been made. The explorations of intrepid investigators such as Bertram Thomas, H. St. J. Philby, Miss Caton Thompson, Miss Freya Stark, and the Master of Belhaven (Robert Anthony Carmichael Hamilton) have provided much valuable material, but they are not sufficient.

SOUTH SEMITIC ALPHABETS

The South Semitic inscriptions (Figs. 13.1–3), discovered in considerable numbers during the nineteenth and twentieth centuries, present various problems. The two main ones, still awaiting solution, are the date of the inscriptions and the origin of the script. While the earliest dated inscription is connected with Cambyses' invasion of Egypt in 525 B.C., the earliest non-dated inscriptions belong probably to the eighth century B.C., although some scholars, for instance Glaser and Hommel, dated them in the last centuries of the second millennium B.C.

Professor N. Glueck discovered, in 1938, at Tell el-Kheleifeh (the ancient Ezion-Geber), situated on the north coast of the Gulf of 'Aqabah, a large broken jar, on which were incised, after baking, two letters in the early South Semitic script. 'The broken jar was found on the floor of a room in level III, which may be dated approximately in the eighth century B.C. These letters then become the first letters of the South Arabic alphabet which have been discovered in a stratified excavation. . . . The origin of the jar is a matter of speculation. It is not impossible that the Midianites used the South Arabic script, and there must have been active trade between Ezion-Geber and South Arabia' (Glueck). However, if Professor Glueck's dating is right, we must allow some two to three centuries, at least, for the development and spread of the South Semitic alphabet.

Thus, there can hardly be any doubt that the South Semitic alphabet was employed about the end of the second millennium B.C.; so that the extreme dates, which place the earliest South Semitic inscriptions either (1) in the thirteenth century B.C., or even an earlier period, or else (2) 'at the very earliest' in the eighth or even the seventh century B.C., can be discarded. One of the main reasons of the difficulty in dating the South Semitic inscriptions is the fact that while the North Semitic alphabet presents cursive forms as far back as the Aḥiram inscription, the South Semitic writing is either a purely monumental, graceful, symmetrical, very elegant script (the South Arabian), or it consists of irregular, short rock-*graffiti* (the North Arabian). Neither of these types is easily datable on epigraphical grounds.

The date of the establishment of the South Arabian kingdoms cannot yet be determined with any accuracy. It may be assumed, however, that after a certain non-datable prehistoric period, southern Arabia became an important centre of civilization in the last centuries of the second millennium B.C. During the first millennium B.C. it was a highly civilized agricultural region, a land of international commercial relations, producing gold and the frankincense so valued by ancient religion. It served also as the principal route by which goods from India were transhipped and carried overland to the ports of the eastern Mediterranean. In the Roman period the region was known as *Arabia Felix*. By the time of the establishment of Islām, southern Arabia had lost its importance to northern Arabia. The later development wrecked the older civilization, and relegated these fertile lands to the backwoods of history.

Until recently the Minæan kingdom, with its capital at Ma'in (north-west of the modern Sanaʿa, in Yemen), was considered the oldest. The Qatabanian kingdom, with its capital at Tamnaʿ or Timnaʿ (which according to some scholars was situated in the district of Baihan), lying to the south-east of Yemen, was roughly contemporary, while the Sabæan kingdom, with its capital at Marib, lying between the Minæan and Qatabanian kingdoms, attained its importance after the decay of the Minæan empire. Glaser, in 1889, suggested dating the beginnings of the Minæan kingdom in the second, or even the third, millennium B.C. He was criticised by Halévy, Müller, Mordtmann, and others, and defended by Winckler, Hommel, and other scholars. Hommel placed the Minæan kingdom between 1300 or 1200 B.C. and 700 B.C.; according to his opinion, the latest Minæan inscriptions could not be later than the earliest Sabæan. Other scholars proposed a kind of middle way. For instance, according to Tkatsch, the Minæan kingdom was contemporaneous with the Sabæan, beginning 'at the very earliest' in the eighth century B.C. and lasting down to the second century B.C. In Mordtmann's opinion, epigraphically the Minæan inscriptions are later than the earliest Sabæan texts and older than the Sabæan inscriptions of the later period. Albright, after his expedition to the Ḥaḍramaut in 1950, dates Qatabân from c. 400 to c. 50 B.C. (destruction of Timnaʿ).

The Canadian authority on South Semitic epigraphy, Professor F. V. Winnett, re-examined the chronological problem of the Minæans in an excellent article ('The Place of the Minæans in the History of pre-Islamic Arabia') in the *Bulletin of the American Schools of Oriental Research*, No. 73, February, 1939. According to him, some of the inscriptions discovered by Pères Jaussen and Savignac at al-ʿUla (*see* below), and by them regarded as Liḥyanite, are really Minæan, while others 'betray a strange mixture of the Liḥyanite and Minæan characters,' and may be regarded as 'Liḥyanite texts exhibiting Minæan influence.' On this and other evidence, such as the bilingual Minæo-Greek inscription found on the island of Delos and dated by the French oriental epigraphist Clermont-Ganneau to the latter half of the second century B.C., Winnett arrives at the following conclusions:

The theory which would place the beginning of the Minæan kingdom around 1200 B.C. or even earlier should be rejected. Its beginnings should not be dated beyond 500 B.C. The Minæan kingdom was flourishing in the Hellenistic period. Its collapse occurred somewhere between 24 B.C. and A.D. 50 and the collapse of its power in the north of the peninsula, where it was succeeded by Nabatæan control, probably occurred earlier. Albright, however, dates the end of the Minæan state much earlier, somewhere between 125 and 75 B.C. (*B.A.S.O.R.*, No. 119, October 1950).

During the second half of the first millennium B.C., the Sabæans established themselves as the principal people of southern Arabia; the term 'Sabæan' is, therefore, often applied to the whole South Arabian civilization. Ḥaḍramaut, the most easterly of the South Arabian kingdoms, was a very important trade depot, but very little is known of its political history. At the end of the second century B.C., the Ḥimyarites, a Sabæan noble family, succeeded in founding a new kingdom centred in Raidan (the title 'lords of Raidan' appears about 115 B.C.). The term 'Ḥimyarites' was later applied to the whole people, and even, erroneously, to the whole South Arabian civilization.

The South Semitic inscriptions can be distinguished into two groups: (1) the South Arabian inscriptions, and (2) the North Arabian inscriptions.

SOUTH ARABIAN INSCRIPTIONS

The South Arabian inscriptions (Figs. 13.1–3), of which about 2,500—some of very considerable length—have already been published (mainly in the *Corpus Inscriptionum Semiticarum*, Pars IV. *Inscriptiones Himyariticas et Sabæas continens*, which, in its three volumes, published in 1889–1932, contains over 1,000 Sabæan inscriptions), are generally divided into five groups: Minæan (Fig. 13.2c), Sabaæn (Fig. 13.2a, b), Himyaritic (Fig. 13.2d), Qatabanic and Ḥaḍramautic. A sixth South Arabian dialect, the Awsanic, is of minor significance for our purpose.

The writing used in these inscriptions—many of them are very well preserved—is a graceful, symmetrical, very elegant script of twenty-nine letters: it is known as the South Arabian or Sabæan alphabet (Fig. 13.1, cols. II and III).

Most of the inscriptions read from right to left, but some are written *boustrophedon* (alternate lines from right to left and left to right). The alphabet has been deciphered. The texts offer us knowledge of the earliest dialects of Arabic, which (in distinction from (1) Hebrew, Phœnician and Aramaic, belonging to the north-western group, and (2) Babylonian and Assyrian, belonging to the north-eastern group), together with the later Ethiopic of Abyssinia, constitute the southern group of the Semitic languages.

NORTH ARABIAN INSCRIPTIONS

There are other epigraphical remains couched in ancient Arabic; these are the North Arabian inscriptions, which were found in north-western Arabia, Syria and Trans-jordan, and constitute the second group of the South Semitic inscriptions. They are mostly very irregular, cursive, short rock-graffiti; and were incised by ancient nomad populations which did not play a great part in history.

The North Arabian inscriptions (Figs. 13.1 and 3) can be separated into three groups:

(1) Thamudene or Thamudic (Figs. 13.1, cols. IV and V, and 13.3); nearly 2,000 inscriptions are extant; the upper dates are uncertain, some scholars suggesting as early as the middle of the first millennium B.C.; the most recent specimens belong to the fourth century A.D. Thamudic inscriptions have been found all over north-western Arabia, and they are generally of a religious character.

The great authority on the subject, Professor F. V. Winnett, classifies the Tham-udic inscriptions into five groups; attributing (a) to the fifth century B.C.; (b) to the

Hellenistic period; (c) to the first two centuries A.D.; (d) to the Roman period (c. third century A.D.); and (e) to about the fourth century A.D.

(2) The Dedanite inscriptions (Dedan, the present oasis al-'Ula, an important and ancient trade depot in the north of the Hejaz, was for some time an independent state) belonging partly to the middle of the first millennium B.C.—the oldest of them, being attributed by Professor Winnett to about the sixth century B.C., and by Professor Albright to the seventh century B.C., 'i.e., to about the same time as the oldest South Arabian inscriptions now known'—and the Lihyanian or Lihyanite inscriptions (numbering about 400 and written in a script which can be regarded as neo-Dedanite), belonging probably to the fifth-second centuries B.C., have been found mainly in the district of the oasis of al-'Ula (see Fig. 13.1, col. III).

The Lihyanite inscriptions can be divided into two groups; one belonging to the fifth century B.C. (according to Winnett) or to the fifth-third centuries B.C. (Albright); and the other belonging, according to Winnett, to the first half of the fourth century B.C., or, more probably, to the third-second centuries B.C. (Albright).

(3) The Safaitic or Safahitic inscriptions (Fig. 13.1, col. V), which have been found in a still greater number than the Thamudene inscriptions, come mainly from the volcanic rocks in the district of es-Safa, to the south-east of Damascus. They belong to the first two centuries A.D.

ORIGIN OF SOUTH SEMITIC ALPHABETS

The origin of the South Semitic alphabets is still an open problem.

Apart from unlikely theories (such as that of the French scholar R. Dussaud and other experts), which connect the South Semitic scripts with the Greek alphabet, there are the following main theories:

(1) According to some scholars, the Sabæan alphabet is the parent of all the other South Semitic scripts, and on the other hand, is an offshoot of the North Semitic alphabet. The first part of this theory is almost generally accepted, though the German scholar H. Grimme not only regarded the Thamudene alphabet as the earliest North Arabian script, but also as the prototype of the Sabæan and the other South Arabian alphabets. Grimme had no followers in this part of his theory. At the same time, Grimme considered the Thamudene a direct offshoot of the Proto-Sinaitic script (see further on). As to the connection between the South and the North Semitic alphabets, it is noteworthy that only the following Sabæan letters resemble North Semitic characters having the same phonetic value: g, teth, l, n, 'ayin, sh, t, and, in a lesser degree, d and q. On the other hand, difference in external shape does not necessarily exclude a direct relationship.

(2) Some scholars hold that all the South Semitic alphabets derived from one original South Semitic alphabet. This 'Proto-South Semitic' alphabet and the original North Semitic alphabet, or 'Proto-North Semitic,' would derive from a common source, a 'Proto-Semitic' alphabet. This theory was propounded by the

German scholars Weber, Prätorius, Lidzbarski, Jensen, by the English scholar A. Evans, and by others.

(3) Maurice Dunand suggests that the South Semitic branch was connected with the pseudo-hieroglyphic system of Byblos (*see* pp. 113 ff. and 152); in the Sabæan alphabet, he finds eighteen signs corresponding exactly to pseudo-hieroglyphic symbols, and three more presenting a certain resemblance to other Byblos characters. However, Dunand thinks that only the graphic aspect of the Byblos-system was adapted by the Sabæans, and not its phonetic side; furthermore, he believes that direct relations between Byblos and the Sabæans may have existed about the nineteenth century B.C., and that as a result of these, the Sabæans may have created their script.

(4) Sethe, Nielsen, Grimme, and other followers of the Sinaitic theory (*see* p. 148 ff.) regarded the Palaeo-Sinaitic script as the Proto-Semitic alphabet, *i.e.*, as the ancestor of both the North Semitic and the South Semitic alphabets. According to Albright, the early North Arabian and the early South Arabian scripts go back to a common older source of South Semitic type, but in several cases the North Arabian characters are considerably closer to the presumptive Palaeo-Semitic prototypes than is true of the Minæo-Sabæan forms.

According to Professor Albright, 'In view of what we know about the course of evolution followed by the Proto-Sinaitic alphabet in Canaan back to before 1500 B.C. .., it is impossible to suppose that the Proto-Arabic script diverged from the Canaanite branch after that date. We thus have a full millennium of still-unknown monumental history to recover before the emergence of the Arabian branch *c.* 700 B.C.' I agree with him except for the first half of the first sentence.

The graphic connection between the Proto-Sinaitic script and the South Semitic alphabets seems more likely than between the former and the North Semitic alphabet, but it has to be borne in mind that—as the decipherment of the Proto-Sinaitic script has not yet been satisfactorily accomplished—a graphic connection alone is not sufficient to establish an undisputed relationship. There is the possibility that the Proto-Sinaitic script was the link between the Early Canaanite script and the South Semitic alphabetic group. If we accept the theory that the Early Canaanite script was the (direct or indirect) ancestor of the South Semitic alphabets, we may the more easily understand how the five extra letters (or some of them), which we find in the Ugaritic alphabet, but not in the North Semitic alphabet, have been transmitted to the South Arabian scripts. (South Semitic languages have preserved some of the Semitic sounds lost in the North Semitic languages.)

This does not mean, however, that I hold the opinion that the South Semitic alphabets are a direct offshoot of the Proto-Sinaitic script. According to my view, there is no doubt that the South Semitic alphabets originated some centuries later than the North Semitic script, of which the highly civilized southern Semitic travellers had certainly some knowledge. They were thus impelled to produce a script, and the choice between the alphabetic script and the complicated scripts of Egypt and Mesopotamia was obvious. Having decided to invent an alphabet based probably on the North Semitic writing, they may have borrowed some signs from other sources such as those connected with the early Sinaitic attempt or the so-called 'wasms' (*wusum*), the ancient cattle-marks employed by Bedouins (*see* p. 8). Thus the original South Semitic alphabet may have originated as a deliberately formed type.

However, it is difficult to see a direct relationship between the North and the South Semitic alphabets, though it may be the only instance of alphabetic writing not descended from the North Semitic. At the same time, we have to agree with G. R. Driver, 'that these two alphabets are independent inventions is improbable; for it is difficult to believe that the two branches of the same race can have almost simultaneously invented alphabets and devised closely similar symbols without some degree of contact with or influence on one another.' What exactly this 'degree of contact' was, cannot as yet be determined. There is also the possibility, though hardly a probability, that the two alphabetic prototypes (the North and the South Semitic) were results of two parallel, interdependent, rather than independent attempts at creation of alphabetic writing.

The South Arabic numerals and their origin present various problems which cannot be examined in the present book.

ETHIOPIC SCRIPT

THE PEOPLE

The Ethiopians, numbering between 10 and 12 million people, can be distinguished into three great ethnic groups: (1) Semitized Cushitic peoples (Tigré, Tigriña, Amhara); (2) Cushitic peoples (Beja, Agaw, Galla, Somalis, Sidama), who have remained relatively free from the influx of outside elements; (3) Nilotic negroid peoples, such as the Kunama, Baria, Beni Shangul, and others. Here we are mainly concerned with group (1).

ORIGIN OF THE SCRIPT

The origin of the Ethiopic alphabet has also been disputed. The Greek alphabet (Tychsen, Wahl, Paulus, Gesenius, Klaproth, and others), the Indian scripts (William Jones and R. Lepsius), the Syriac (Kopp) or Coptic (De Sacy, and partly also Tychsen) or the Samaritan alphabet (Job Ludolf and Silvestre), or even the runes, have been proposed as its source. Wellsted (1834), Rœdiger (1837) and Bird (1844) have rightly suggested a connection with the Sabæan alphabet, although Bird thought also that there were some Coptic influences.

Nowadays, it is generally accepted that South Arabian colonies established in Abyssinia in the second half of the first millennium B.C. introduced into that territory the South Semitic speech and script. In fact, a fairly large number of South Semitic inscriptions (Figs. 13.3*b*, *c*) have been discovered on many sites in northern Ethiopia and southern Eritrea, *i.e.*, the Tigré province, identical with what was once the Aksumite Empire.

At the beginning, Sabæan was the literary language and script of Ethiopia. It seems that in the first half of the fourth century A.D., in the period when the strong king-dom of Aksum flourished, the Sabæan speech and script were replaced by the early Ethiopic language and writing. The Ethiopic language existed much earlier, and vocalized Ethiopic script may have been used already in the first and second century A.D. What the epigraphic documents from Aksum, referred to below, show is the introduction of vocalization and the fact that the Sabæan language and script con-tinued to be used for ornamental and often archaizing purposes. In fact, Sabæan speech and alphabet were still employed for such purposes on Aksumite territory up to the seventh and eighth centuries A.D.

Inscriptions (Figs. 13.3, *b*, *c*) belonging to the first half of the fourth century A.D. have been found, couched in (1) Ethiopic language strongly intermixed with South Arabic, and in the South Semitic alphabet. (In Professor Ullendorff's opinion, it is not quite correct to say that the Ethiopic language was still strongly intermixed with South Arabian, but what had happened was merely the archaizing addition, quite senselessly, of the mimation to each word regardless of its meaning. Noeldeke had already pointed out that there is no intermixture here of Ethiopic and South Arabian, but simply what he termed *'graphischer Unfug'*); (2) in Ethiopic speech and South Semitic alphabet; (3) in Ethiopic speech and Ethiopic non-vocalized alphabet; and (4) in Ethiopic speech and Ethiopic vocalized script.

The problem is still open as to whether the early Ethiopic alphabet was a gradual transformation of the South Semitic script or was the deliberate work of an individual. Both these opinions have been suggested. It is, however, more probable that while the script as a whole is a gradual development of the South Semitic alphabet, the introduction of the vocalization was effected by a single person and was probably influenced by the Greek alphabet. According to Ullendorff, however, there is rather more evidence in favour of a gradual development of vocalization than for ascribing it to the deliberate invention of an individual. The Ethiopic numerals were borrowed from the Greeks. In regard to the external form of the early Ethiopic letters, Meroitic influences have been noticed.

DEVELOPMENT OF ETHIOPIC WRITING

The Ethiopic script consists of twenty-six letters (Fig. 13.4). Of the twenty-eight Sabæan letters, four have been abandoned and the letters *pait* and *pa* have been added.

The letters became more and more rounded. The direction of writing, originally from right to left, became, probably under Greek influence, from left to right. Originally, a vertical dash was used to separate the words, later two dots were employed.

The names of the letters are in great part different from the names of the letters in the Hebrew, Syriac and Greek alphabets. Indeed, according to Ullendorff, it can be proved beyond doubt that the names of the Ethiopic letters, quite unknown to indigenous scholars, were in fact invented in Europe in the sixteenth century. The order of the letters differs completely (Fig. 13.4).

An interesting peculiarity of the Ethiopic alphabet is its vocalization. The vowel following each consonant is expressed by adding small appendages to the right or left of the basic character, at the top or at the bottom, by shortening or lengthening one of its main strokes, and by other differentiations. There are thus seven forms of each letter, corresponding to the consonants, followed by a short *a* or *e*, or a long *a, e, u, i, o*. In Ullendorff's opinion, however, 'despite different views held in the past it can now be satisfactorily proved that quantity had no place in the Ethiopic vowel order. All the vowels differ in quality only, the first order being *ä* and the sixth *ə* (corresponding to Hebrew *sh'wa*), i.e., *ä, u, i, a, e, ə, o*, without distinction of length.' Four consonants (*q, kh, k, g*) have five additional forms when they are 'incorporated' by a *w* and a vowel. The basic form is not the pure consonant (column marked *e* in Fig. 13.4), but a consonant followed by a short *a* (column marked *a*).

After the conversion of northern Ethiopia to Christianity (in the fourth century), there came into being a literature which for obvious reasons was essentially Christian, particularly in view of the intensification of Christian propaganda by many Syrian monks, who introduced Greek and Syriac influences. The Ge'ez literature which thus developed consists largely of translations of ecclesiastical works from Greek and (after Arabic replaced Greek and Coptic in Egypt) particularly from the Christian-Arabic literature which then flourished in Egypt.

The Ethiopic script was extremely conservative, particularly from the thirteenth century onwards, although there was a certain external evolution in some details, especially in the *ductus*. From the calligraphical point of view, the Ethiopic uncial script, which arose about the middle of the seventeenth century, is interesting.

The Ethiopic script is the writing of the Ge'ez language (*lesana ge'ez*), which as a spoken language has been long dead, but to this day has been preserved as the language of the Ethiopian Church and of Ethiopic literature. At the beginning of this millennium, and particularly after the 'reconstitution' of the 'Solomonic dynasty' in the thirteenth century, Amharic (related to Ge'ez) became the main speech of Ethiopia and the official language of the court (*lesana Negush*, 'the language of the King'). In the north its place was taken by two other related languages, Tigré and Tigrai or Tigriña, this being nearer the ancient Ge'ez than is Amharic. The Ethiopic script has been adapted to all three tongues, Amharic (at least from the fifteenth century), Tigré and Tigriña, as well as to practically all the many Ethiopian languages, Semitic as well as Cushitic.

BIBLIOGRAPHY

Corpus Iscriptionum Semiticarum (*CIS*). Pars IV: *Inscriptiones himyariticas atque sabæas continens*, Paris, 1889 onwards. Pars V: *Inscriptiones saracenicas continens*, Tomus I, Fasc. I: *Inscriptiones Safaiticae* (n. 1–5380), Paris, 1950 (appeared 1951). RYCKMANS, G. *Répertoire d'Épigraphie Sémitique*, Paris, 1900 onwards.

HALÉVY, J. 'Études sabéennes,' *Journal asiatique*, 1873–5.

MÜLLER, D. H. *Epigraphische Denkmäler aus Arabien*, Vienna, 1889.

LITTMANN, E. *Zur Entzifferung der Ṣafa-Inschriften*, Leipsic, 1901; *Bibliotheca Abessinica*, 4 vols., Leyden and Princeton, 1904–11; 'Zur Entzifferung der thamudenischen Inschriften,' *Mitteilungen der Vorderasiatischen Gesellschaft*, 1904; *Thamud und Ṣafa*, Leipsic, 1940; *Safaitic Inscriptions*, Leyden, 1943.

HOMMEL, F. *Exploration in Arabia* (Hilprecht, *Explorations in Bible Lands*), Edinburgh, 1903.

CHAÎNE, M. *Grammaire éthiopienne*, Beyrouth, 1907 (new edition, 1938).

DUSSAUD, R. *Les Arabes en Syrie avant l'Islam*, Paris, 1907; *Syria*, X (1929).

PP. JAUSSEN and SAVIGNAC, *Mission Archéologique en Arabie*, 2 vols., Paris, 1909, 1914.

GROHMANN, A. 'Über den Ursprung und die Entwicklung der äthiopischen Schrift,' *Archiv für Schriftkunde*, 1915.

RHODOKANAKIS, N. 'Altsabäische Texte,' *Sitzungsberichte der Wiener Akademie der Wissenschaften*, 1927 and 1932.

NIELSEN, D. (in collaboration with HOMMEL, F., RHODOKANAKIS, N. and others), *Handbuch der altarabischen Altertumskunde*, Copenhagen, 1927.

GUIDI, I. *Summarium grammaticae veteris linguae arabicae meridionalis*, Cairo, 1930.

CERULLI, E. *Studi Etiopici*, vol. I-IV, Rome, 1936–1951; *Storia della letteratura etiopica*, Rome, 1956.

GRIMME, H. 'Die südsemitsche Schrift. Ihr Wesen und ihre Entwicklung,' *Buch und Schrift*, 1930; article in *Orientalische Literatur Zeitung*, 1938.

CONTI ROSSINI, K. *Chrestomathia arabica meridionalis epigraphica*, Rome, 1931; *Studi Etiopici*, Rome, 1944.

RATHJENS, C. and VON WISSMANN, H. *Vorislamische Altertümer*, Hamburg, 1932.

VAN DER MEULEN, D. and VON WISSMANN, H. *Ḥaḍramaut*, Leyden, 1932.

RYCKMANS, G. 'Où en est la publication des inscriptions sud-sémitiques?' *Actes du XVIIIe Congr. Intern. des Oriental.*, 1931, Leyden, 1932; *Les noms propres sud-sémitiques*, 3 vols., Louvain, 1934; 'Rites and croyanes,' etc., *Acad. d. Inscript., Comptes Rendus*, Paris, 1942; 'Inscriptions safaïtiques au British Museum et au Musée de Damas,' *Muséon*, LXIV (1951).

MONTGOMERY, J. A. *Arabia and the Bible*, Philadelphia, 1934; 'The Present State of Arabian Studies,' *The Haverford Symposium*, New Haven, 1938.

MITTWOCH, E. 'Aus der Frühzeit der Sabäistik,' *Orientalia*, 1935.

STARK, F. *The Southern Gates of Arabia*, London, 1936; New York, 1945; 'Some Pre-Islamic Inscriptions,' etc., *J. Roy. Asiat. Soc.*, 1939.

COHEN, M. *Traité de la langue amharique (Abyssinie)*, Paris, 1936; *Nouvelles études d'éthiopien méridional*, Paris, 1939; *Essai comparatif sur le vocabulaire et la phonétique du Chamito-Sémitique*, Paris, 1947.

ZANUTTO, S. *Bibliografia etiopica*, 2nd ed., Rome, 1936.

WINNET, F. V. *A Study of the Lihyanite and Thamudic Inscriptions*, Toronto, 1937; *Safaitic Inscriptions from Jordan*, Oxford, 1958.

THOMAS, B. *The Arabs*, London, 1937.

HITTI, PH. K. *History of the Arabs*, London, 1937.

DIRINGER, D. 'Le origini della scrittura etiopica,' *Atti del III Congresso di Studi Coloniali*, Florence, 1937.

MONNERET DE VILLARD, U. *Aksum*, Rome, 1938.

MORENO, M. M. *Grammatica della lingua galla*, Milan, 1939.

BEESTON, A. F. L. *On the Inscriptions Discovered by Mr. Philby* (H. St. J. B. Philby, *Sheba's Daughters*,

Appendix), London, 1939; 'Phonology of the Epigraphic South Arabian Unvoiced Sibilants,' *Trans. of the Philol. Soc.*, 1951.

LESLAU, W. *Documents Tigrigna*, Paris, 1941; 'Short Grammar of Tigré,' *J. Amer. Orient. Soc.*, 1945 and 1948; 'The Influence of Cushitic on the Semitic Languages of Ethiopia,' *Word*, I, New York, 1945; *Bibliography of the Semitic Languages of Ethiopia*, New York, 1946.

HOEFNER, M. *Altsüdarabische Grammatik*, Leipsic, 1943; 'Das Südarabische der Inschriften und der lebenden Mundarten,' *Handb. d. Oriental.*, III, 2–3, Leiden, 1954.

NAMI, KH. Y. *Record and Description of the Old Semitic Inscriptions from Southern Arabia*, Cairo, 1943.

CATON THOMPSON, G. *The Tombs and Moon Temple of Hureidha (Hadramaut): Epigraphy* by G. Ryckmans, Oxford, 1944.

PHILBY, H. ST. J. B. and TRITTON, A. S. 'Najran Inscriptions,' *J. Roy. Asiat. Soc.*, 1944; 'Three New Inscriptions from Hadramaut,' the same journal, 1945.

ULLENDORFF, E. *Exploration and Study of Abyssinia*, Asmara, 1945; 'Catalogue of Ethiopic MSS. in the Bodleian Library,' Oxford, 1951; 'The Obelisk of Matara,' *J. Roy. Asiat. Soc.*, 1951; 'Studies in Ethiopic Syllabary,' *Africa*, 1951; *The Semitic Languages of Ethiopia*, London, 1955; *The Ethiopians*, London, 1960.

JAMME, A. *Classification déscriptive générale des inscriptions sud-arabes* (Suppl. of *Rev. de l'Inst. des Bell. Lettres Arab.*), Tunis, 1948; *Inscriptions on the Sabaean Bronze-horse of the Dumbarton Oak Collection*, Cambridge, Mass., 1954.

ALBRIGHT, W. F. 'The Chronology of Ancient South Arabia in the Light of the First Campaign of Excav. in Qataban,' *Bull. of the Amer. Schools of Orient. Res.*, No. 119 (Oct. 1950).

VAN DEN BRANDEN, A. *Les inscriptions thamoudéennes*, Louvain, 1950; *Les texts thamoudéennes de Philby*, Louvain, 1956.

KLINGENHEBEN, A. 'Die Laryngalen im Amharischen,' *Zeitschr. der Deutschen Morgenl. Gesellschaft*, 1950.

POLOTSKY, H. J. *Notes on Gurage Grammar*, Jerusalem, 1951.

AŠECOLY, A. Z. *Recueil de Textes Falachas*, Paris, 1951.

HONEYMAN, A. M. 'The Letter-order of the Semitic Alphabets in Africa and the Near East,' *Africa*, 1952.

WISSMANN, H. and HÖFNER, M. *Zur historischen Geographie des vorislamischen Süderabien*, Wiesbaden, 1953.

HUNTINGFORD, G. W. B. *The Galla of Ethiopia*, London, 1955.

PIRENNE, J. *Paléographie des inscriptions sud-arabes*, Brussels, 1956.

RYCKMANS, J. *La persécution des chrétiens himyarites au sixième siècle*, Istanbul, 1956.

DORESSE, J. *Au pays de la Reide de Saba. L'Ethiopie antique et moderne*, Paris, 1956.

VAN BEEK, G. W. *South Arabian History and Archaeology*, in *The Bible and the Ancient Near East* (ed. by G. E. Wright), London, 1961.

CHAPTER 14

Canaanite Branch

CANAANITES

THE term 'Canaan' (Hebr. *K⁽e⁾na⁽ʿ⁾an*; hierogl. *K'-n'-n'*; cuneif. *Ki-na-akh-khi* or *Ki-na-akh-na*; Greek and Latin *Chanaan*) appears as the ancient name of Palestine. Its etymology is unknown, the common explanation as 'Lowland' (from the Hebr. root *kn⁽ʿ⁾*, 'to be low') has now been abandoned by serious scholars, as the name seems to be of non-Semitic origin. (*See* Walter Baumgartner, 'Was wir heute von der hebräischen Sprache und ihrer Geschichte wissen', in *Anthropos*, xxxv–xxxvi, 1940–1, p. 611). In the Biblical Table of Nations (Gen., x), Canaan, the eponymous ancestor of the Canaanites, is not regarded as a 'Semite,' but as a 'Hamite'. However, the Biblical review of peoples known to the Hebrews was clearly planned on lines that were neither primarily ethnological nor primary linguistic, but, to use a modern term, political. Thus, the descendants of Ham include hostile peoples, amongst them certain non-Aramæan peoples of Palestine (the Canaanites, the Hittites and the Philistines). On the other hand, the expression 'the language of Canaan' of Isaiah, xix, 18, indicates obviously the Hebrew tongue. On the whole, the term 'Canaanites' was somewhat loosely employed. *See* now W. F. Albright, 'The Role of the Canaanites in the History of Civilization,' in *The Bible and the Ancient Near East* (ed. by G. E. Wright), London, 1961.

The ethnic problem of the Canaanites is still far from being solved. Some scholars regard them as the pre-Semitic aborigines of Palestine, others as the Semitic pre-Israelitic inhabitants of that country. However, broadly speaking, modern archæology and philology consider the Canaanites to be the main group of the 'Second Semitic immigration' which invaded Palestine and Syria at the beginning of the third millennium B.C. and were, during the second millennium, partly extinguished and partly assimilated to the peoples of the 'Third Semitic immigration,' such as the Hebrews and the Aramæans. According to Professor W. F. Albright, the word 'Canaanite' is historically, geographically, and culturally synonymous with 'Phœnician,' although he himself, for convenience, employs 'Canaanite' to designate the north-west Semitic people and culture of western Syria and Palestine before the twelfth century B.C., and the term 'Phœnician' to indicate the same people and culture after this date. However, in its conventional sense, 'Canaanite' includes Phoenician, Early Hebrew and allied linguistic groups (Ammonites, Moabites, Edomites, and so on) as well as the Semitic pre-Hebrew, and in a certain way, pre-Phœnician or Early Canaanite dialects of Palestine and Syria. More comprehensive still is the term North Semitic (north-west Semitic would be more accurate, though more cumbersome), which would include both the Canaanite and the Aramaic branches. Finally, referring to an earlier stage—i.e., including both North Semitic and South Semitic—the term Proto-Semitic is also sometimes used.

From the modern philological point of view, 'Canaanite' is one of the two main branches of the north-west Semitic group of languages, the other being the Aramaic branch. The 'Canaanite' group includes Hebrew, Phœnician—the Phœnicians, and even the Carthaginians, regarded themselves as *Chanan*, down to the fifth century A.D.—and some secondary branches such as Moabite and Ammonite. (*See* Z. S. Harris, 'Development of the Canaanite Dialects,' *American Oriental Series*, Vol. 16, 1939). Although this use of the word 'Canaanite' may not be exact, for the lack of a more suitable term I am employing it here in its conventional sense.

For the very same reason I feel unable to accept Professor Moscati's theory—so brilliantly suggested in *I predecessori d'Israele*, Rome, 1956; *The Face of the Ancient Orient*, London, 1960, and so on. We have to agree that 'The customary division into two areas, Syria and Palestine, to which Lebanon and Phœnicia may be added, is far from satisfactory from the historian's viewpoint, since it conveys both too little and too much.' So also, at least in part, I would agree that ' "Canaanites" is a collective term which includes a number of individual elements; and so in the last analysis it is defined rather by the negative "other than Aramæan." It includes the Amorites, the Moabites, the Edomites, the Ammonites, even the Hebrews.' On the other hand, I would not agree that 'the only applicable term is that of Syria, taken in the broad sense, including the entire area bounded by Egypt and Mesopotamia, the Arabian desert and the Mediterranean Sea.' Also, 'just as we choose the term "Syria" to cover the entire area, so we may use the term "Syrians" to cover its inhabitants.' The terms 'Syria,' 'Syrians,' 'Syriac' have already too many connotations, and to add now the term 'Syria' and 'Syrians' with the meaning suggested by Sabatino Moscati would further confuse the matter, the more so as (*see* also pp. 196 and 217) the terms 'Syria'—'Syrians' are actually synonymous with the terms 'Aram'—'Aramæans'.

The 'Canaanite' main branch of alphabets may be subdivided into two following branches: (1) Early Hebrew, with its three secondary branches, the Moabite, the Edomite, and the Ammonite, and its two offshoots, the Samaritan and the script of the Jewish coins; and (2) Phœnician, which can be distinguished into (*a*) Early Phœnician, (*b*) Phœnician proper, and (*c*) 'colonial' Phœnician, out of which the Punic and neo-Punic varieties, and probably also the Libyan and Iberian scripts developed: *see* Fig. 14.1.

EARLY HEBREW ALPHABET (Figs. 14.1–13)

The alphabet used by the Hebrews in the first half of the first millennium B.C., presents certain peculiar characteristics which induce us to regard it as a particular branch. The term 'Early Hebrew' is employed in distinction from the 'Square Hebrew' alphabet, which was the parent of the modern Hebrew script. Early Hebrew is the writing used by Israel from *c.* 1000 B.C. onwards, roughly in the pre-exilic period, that is, until the sixth century B.C., although some inscriptions may belong to the fifth or the fourth century B.C.

INSCRIPTIONS

The epigraphical remains of ancient Israel are very scarce. No *stelæ* of victory like those of the Egyptian or Mesopotamian monarchs have been preserved, no public documents on a 'pillar of stone,' such as those of the Greeks or the Romans have reached us. David, Solomon and the other great kings of Israel are known to us only from the Biblical record.

This paucity of early Hebrew inscriptions has been accounted for in various ways. The following are the most acceptable theories:

(1) The ancient Hebrews possessed none of that genius for 'imperial conquest,' for administration on a large scale or for civic order, which inspired the great and numerous monumental inscriptions of the ancient world.

(2) Another opinion suggests that there were inscriptions in early Hebrew Palestine, but that these have not been allowed to survive, because, from the standpoint of later Judaism, the religion and the general outlook of the pre-exilic Hebrews was essentially unorthodox.

(3) The majority of the inscriptions were destroyed in the numerous invasions and occupations of Palestine by hostile armies.

(4) Until recent times, excavations in Palestine were not conducted in accordance with rigid scientific methods, and many small inscriptions may have been lost for ever.

(5) The vast majority of the early documents, and particularly all the literary works, were written upon papyrus, imported from Egypt, or on parchment; in the soil of Palestine, however (except in the desert caves), no papyrus or parchment could be expected to endure to our time.

In short, we may suppose that there were many early Hebrew inscriptions, but that the vast majority of them were destroyed through the agency of men (whether enemies or not), by the action of time and climate, and by other factors, known or unknown.

Nevertheless, as Professor Albright pointed out, the long silence of Early Hebrew epigraphy has now been broken at least in part, and we can already list several hundreds of inscriptions. Their value as specimens of language and writing is great, so also is their importance for the historian. But this importance is more incidental than primary; the history recorded is, with one or two exceptions, not the history of great events or of striking figures (as some scholars suggest), but the history of everyday life. These little monuments do not palpitate with the life, feeling and thought which render the writings of the great prophets so poignant, but they supply details which are of the utmost value in supplementing those works.

A recently deciphered fragmentary inscription, found in 1938 at Lachish and dated to the late twelfth or eleventh century B.C., may, if the present author's decipherment is correct, be regarded as the *incunabula* of the Early Hebrew writing. Only part of the inscription is preserved; the three or four signs may be read *la'ûth* (or *ba'al*: according to Professor Yadin).

I have already mentioned (p. 158) the most ancient document extant of Early Hebrew writing, the so-called Gezer Calendar (Fig. 14.3*e*), belonging probably to the age of Saul or David (*c.* 1000 B.C.). It is a small soft-stone tablet, discovered in 1908 at Gezer (southern Palestine), on which is inscribed a sort of agricultural calendar beginning in October, or rather a list of eight months with the agricultural operation for each. According to some scholars it was a schoolboy's exercise tablet. The majority of the letters used in the Gezer Calendar are still nearly identical with those of the earliest North Semitic inscriptions, although some signs have already assumed the distinctive Early Hebrew character. Thus, for example, the letters *kaph, mem, nun, pe* are marked by the tendency to bend their main stems to the left.

Towards the ninth to eighth century B.C., the transformation becomes almost complete, at least in the northern kingdom, as we see from the *ostraca* (documents written in ink on potsherds after the vases were broken), numbering about eighty, which have been found in Samaria (Fig. 14.3 *b, c*). Most of these *ostraca* were evidently invoices handed in with tributes of oil and wine paid in kind to the king's official within the city. In them we have the form *yn* (or *yen*), 'wine,' instead of the Biblical *yyn* (*yayyin*), and *sht*, 'year,' instead of the Biblical *shnt* or *shnh* (*shenath* or *shanah*). On epigraphical grounds the writing could be ascribed to the ninth or eighth century B.C., but on archæological grounds they are now commonly assigned to the early eighth century B.C.

While the Samarian *ostraca* provide us with examples of the script and dialect of Israel, certain other inscriptions illustrate those of Judæa, the most important being the Siloam inscription (Fig. 14.4 *c*), attributed to about 700 B.C. and discovered in 1880 in the wall of an aqueduct.

The famous 'Lachish letters' (Figs. 14.7–8), eighteen in number, were discovered in 1935 at Tell ed-Duweir (in southern Palestine), the ancient Lachish, by the Wellcome-Marston Archæological Expedition. Three other *ostraca* were discovered in Lachish in 1938. What we have now is all that has survived of a large collection of correspondence and other documents. As the burnt debris, in which the *ostraca* were found, dates from the destruction of the city by Nebuchadrezzar's army at the close of Zedekiah's reign, the documents were probably written about the beginning of

o

587 B.C. Some of the *ostraca* (Figs. 14.7–8) are almost as clear as on the day they were written, nearly 2,550 years ago.

On various sites in southern Palestine many hundreds of jar-handles have been found which bear impressions of factory stamps (Fig. 14.5). Some of these are royal trade-marks, others reproduce the names of private pottery works, while others are *Yehûd* stamps, 'Jerusalem' stamps, and so forth. A considerable number, about a hundred and fifty, of inscribed stone seals have also been discovered in Palestine (Figs. 14.4*a, b*). Another important group of short inscriptions is that of the inscribed weights and measures (Figs. 14.5 and 8*b*).

THE SCRIPT

Like current Hebrew, the Early Hebrew alphabet contained twenty-two letters. Their names probably corresponded with the current names: *'aleph, beth, gimel, daleth, he, waw, zayin, heth, teth, yod, kaph, lamed, mem, nun, samekh, 'ayin, pe, sade, qoph, resh, shin, taw*. The value of each letter was that of the first letter of its name (b, g, d, etc.), but the exact phonetic value of letters such as *'ayin, sade*, and *shin* has been lost.

The main characteristics of the Early Hebrew alphabet, when compared with Phœnician writing, are: the letters, especially the *zayin* and the *sade*, are more squat, wider and shorter, also more accurate. The main stems of the letters *beth, kaph, lamed, mem, nun* and *pe* are curved or rounded at the bottom. In the *heth*, the vertical strokes go beyond the horizontal ones. In the *he*, the upper horizontal stroke goes beyond the vertical, and there are sometimes four horizontal strokes instead of three (strangely enough, a similar feature appears in the Etruscan alphabet). In the *mem* and *nun* the short vertical strokes are often not joined to the main stem. *Zayin* and *sade* curve back at the end of the lower horizontal stroke. There are often some beautiful ligatures; they are generally of two letters, though there is an interesting instance of a ligature of three letters. The current hand, however (*see* particularly Fig. 14.8*a* showing the script of the more important 'Lachish Letters'), does not always conform to these general characteristics.

SAMARITAN ALPHABET AND SCRIPT ON JEWISH COINS

The Samaritan alphabet (Figs. 14.10–12) is the only descendant of the Early Hebrew script which is still in use (among the Samaritans, the remainder of an ancient sect but numbering today only a few hundred people). The Samaritan, a beautiful, neat and symmetrical script, is used only for liturgical purposes.

The writing on Jewish coins (Fig. 14.13) from the Macabæan age to Bar-Kochba's revolt (135 B.C.–A.D. 132–135), is another direct derivative of the early Hebrew alphabet. It is commonly believed that the script of these coins was artificially revived some centuries after the Early Hebrew alphabet had fallen into disuse, but one can hardly believe that an obsolete script would have been chosen for objects such as coins which are in general use. It is more probable that the Early Hebrew alphabet continued to be used among certain sections of the population for some centuries after the Aramaic language and script had become the official means of communication.

SCRIPTS OF MOABITES, AMMONITES, AND EDOMITES
(Figs. 14.13–14)

We must say a few words about the three eastern sub-divisions of the Canaanite branch of which some documents are extant. All the three scripts were closely related to the Early Hebrew alphabet.

Of the Moabite alphabet there are two seals extant and the famous victory-*stele* (Fig. 14.14), discovered in 1868 at Dibon, some twenty-five miles east of the Dead Sea, and now in the Louvre. The monument, known as the Moabite Stone or Mesha' *stele*, is a self-glorification of Mesha', King of Moab, 849–830 B.C. (2 *Kings*, iii, 4), and belongs to the middle of the ninth century B.C. Until the discovery of the Aḥiram epitaph (*see* p. 158), it was regarded as the earliest inscription in alphabetic writing.

Only three seals are extant in Ammonite script (Fig. 14.13*a* centre), which does not differ much from the Early Hebrew alphabet.

The able American excavator and scholar Nelson Glueck, in his first campaign at Tell el-Kheleifeh (situated on the north coast of the Gulf of 'Aqabah)—identified by him with the ancient site of both Ezion-geber and Elath—discovered in the spring, 1938, an inscription incised after firing on a jug, 'in what are perhaps specifically Edomite characters' (Glueck). There are six letters, of which one is damaged and another uncertain. The jug was found in a room, attributed to the eighth-seventh centuries B.C.

Still more interesting was the find of twelve stamped jar handles with seal-impressions made apparently with the same small seal. No one inscription is clear, but a composite inscription reads (according to Professor Glueck) *l Qws'nl* in the upper line, and *'bd hmlk*, in the lower, that is '(belonging) to *Qws'nl*, the servant of the king.' The proper name of this high royal official is a theophorus name beginning with the element *Qws*, probably *Qôs* or *Quas*, the name of the chief Edomite deity. As Professor Albright points out, the forms of some letters of the seal impressions 'are strikingly like those in the six-letter graffito' on the aforementioned jug. The impressions seem to belong to the seventh century B.C.

There is no doubt that this script was a sub-division of the Canaanite main branch, and probably of the Early Hebrew branch, and it seems to have been the writing employed by the ancient Edomites.

PHŒNICIAN ALPHABET (Figs. 14.1 and 15–25)

At the outset, it may be said that the term 'Phœnician' is not altogether accurately applied to the predecessors of the later 'Phœnicians.' Whoever the Phœnicians were, they never called themselves by that name; and the Greek term *Phoínikes* can hardly refer either to the geographical area or to the period in which the Alphabet is thought to have been invented, or to the people, meaning the whole ethnic or linguistic group, who in the late second millennium and the early first millennium B.C. inhabited the territory to which the Greeks applied the term *Phoinikia*. Thus, we limit the term 'Phœnician' to the script of the Phœnician inscriptions.

The importance of the Phœnician script for the history of writing cannot be over-estimated. We have mentioned (p. 158; Figs. 12.7–8, 11–12) the earliest Phœnician inscriptions, when dealing with the origin of the North Semitic alphabet. With the exception of the Karatepe inscriptions, there is a great lacuna between those very early inscriptions and the datable monuments belonging to the Persian period (Fig. 14.16a). Less than a dozen inscriptions, mostly short, have been found in Phœnicia proper.

On the other hand, while the Early Hebrew inscriptions were almost exclusively discovered in Palestine, Phœnician inscriptions have been found not only in Phœnicia, but also, and particularly, in the whole of the Phœnician colonial empire, in the island of Cyprus (Fig. 14.18b), in Greece (Fig. 14.21b), in northern Africa (Fig. 14.18c), in Malta, Sicily, Sardinia (Figs. 14.18d, 19–20), Marseilles and Spain. Extremely important Phœnician-Hittite bilingual and other Phœnician inscriptions (Figs. 15.17 and 5.7) of the eighth century B.C. were discovered in 1945, and studied from 1947 onwards, at Ayricatapesi (Karatepe), in eastern Cilicia—a mound situated far up in the foot-hills of the Taurus Mountains where the Jeyhan River (Turkish 'Ceyhan,' the classical Pyramus) forces its way into the plain of Adana. In 1945, a village school teacher, Sayin Bey Ekrem Kusha, informed Professor H. Th. Bossert of the Istanbul University of the existence of the inscriptions. Bossert and his colleagues superficially examined them on the following day, but only in 1947 were Bossert and his Turkish colleagues able to excavate the site. It appears that we have here a single bilingual text—twice repeated—in Phœnician and Hittite. The most complete of the Phœnician inscriptions fills some eighty lines in four columns and is thus the longest Phœnician document in existence.

We can, thus, distinguish three main sub-divisions of the Phœnician branch (Fig. 14.1):

(1) the Phœnician script proper, used in the inscriptions already mentioned, found in Phœnicia itself and covering a period of over a millennium, up to the second or even first century B.C.;

(2) the Phœnician colonial branch, of which at least three varieties can be distin-guished:

(a) the Cypro-Phœnician script, from c. the tenth century B.C. to, perhaps, the second century B.C.; the earliest inscription published by A. M. Honeyman, in *Iraq*, 1939, VI/2, pp. 106–8, is attributed by Professor Albright to about 900 B.C. or the first half of the ninth century B.C. (Fig. 14.18b);

(b) the Sardinian sub-division: the Nora stone and two fragmentary inscriptions belong probably to the early ninth century B.C. (Figs. 14.19 and 20a);

(c) the Carthaginian sub-branch, which subsequently became a main branch of the Phœnician script (see following);

(3) the Carthaginian or Punic alphabet, with its secondary branch, the more cursive script termed neo-Punic, in two types, monumental and cursive, constitutes a story in itself. Figures 14.22a and 23 show some specimens of the different varieties. The last Punic inscriptions belong to the third century A.D. It is thus apparent that the Punic script was employed for some five centuries longer than the Phœnician.

The development of the Phœnician alphabet in all its sub-divisions, including Punic and neo-Punic, and in all its forms, was, like that of the Early Hebrew and early Aramaic alphabets, purely external: the number and the phonetic value of the letters remained always the same. The direction of the lines, always horizontal, was constantly from right to left. The main distinctive characteristics of the Phœnician scripts was that the letters became constantly longer and thinner while, as already mentioned, the Early Hebrew letters became increasingly thicker and shorter. Several problems —such as the method used in the separation of words—cannot be dealt with in the present treatise.

BIBLIOGRAPHY

Corpus Inscriptionum Semiticarum, Vol. I, Paris, 1885 onwards; Répertoire d'Épigraphie Sémitique, Paris, 1900 onwards.

LIDZBARSKI, M. Handbuch der nordsemitischen Epigraphik, 2 vols. (Vol. I, Text; Vol. II, Plates), Weimar, 1898; Kanaanäische Inschriften, Giessen, 1907; Ephemeris für semitische Epigraphik, 3 vols., Giessen, 1900–15.

CLERMONT-GANNEAU, CH. Recueil d'archéologie orientale, 8 vols., Paris, 1888–1924.

COOKE, G. A. A Text-book of North-Semitic Inscriptions, Oxford, 1903.

BERGER, PH. La Tunisie ancienne et moderne, Paris, 1906.

DUSSAUD, R. Les Monum. palest. et jud. au Mus. d. Louvre, Paris, 1912.

DHORME, P. 'La langue de Canaan,' Revue Biblique, 1913 and 1914; Langues et écritures sémitiques, Paris, 1930.

GSELL, S. Histoire ancienne de l'Afrique du Nord, 4 vols., Paris, 1913–20.

BAUER, H. and LEANDER, P. Historische Grammatik der hebräischen Sprache des Alten Testaments, Halle, 1918–22.

BERGSTRÄSSER, G. Hebräische Grammatik (29th ed. of W. Gesenius' Hebräische Grammatik), 2 vols., Leipsic, 1918 and 1929.

CHABOT, J. B. 'Punica,' Journ. Asiat., 1918.

GRESSMAN, H. Altorientalische Texte zum Alten Testament, 2nd ed., Berlin, 1926.

CONTENAU, G. La civilisation phénicienne, Paris, 1926; 2nd ed., 1939.

DIRINGER, D. Le iscrizioni antico-ebraiche palestinesi, Florence, 1934; The Story of the Aleph Beth, London, 1958 (new ed., New York, 1960) [bibliography].

GRAY, L. H. Introd. to Sem. Comp. Linguistics, New York, 1934.

ALBRIGHT, W. F. Archæology of Palestine and the Bible, 3rd ed., New York, 1935; 'The Rôle of the Canaanites in the History of Civilization,' Studies in the History of Culture, Menasha, Wisconsin, 1942; 'The Old Testament and the Canaanite Language and Literature,' Catholic Biblical Quarterly, 1945.

HARRIS, Z. S. A Grammar of the Phœnician Language, New Haven (Conn.), 1936; Development of the Canaanite Dialects, New Haven, 1939.

YEIVIN, S. *The History of the Jewish Script* (in Hebrew), Part I, Jerusalem, 1938.

FLIGHT, J. W. 'History of Writing in the Near East,' *The Haverford Symposium*, New Haven (Conn.), 1938.

TORCZYNER, H. *The Lachish Letters, Lachish I (Tell Ed-Duweir)*, (The Wellcome Archæological Research Expedition to the Near East), Oxford University Press, London–New York–Toronto, 1938. (*See* also D. Diringer, in *Lachish III* and *Lachish IV*.)

BAUMGARTNER, W. 'Was wir heute von der hebräischen Sprache und ihrer Geschichte wissen,' *Anthropos*, 1940–1.

LAPEYRE, G. G. and PELLEGRIN, A. *Carthage punique (814–146 avant J.-C.)*, Paris, 1942.

DRIVER, G. R. 'Seals from Amman and Petra,' *The Quarterly of the Departm. of Antiq. in Palestine*, 1944.

FRIEDRICH, J. 'Phönizisch-punische Grammatik,' *Analecta Orientalia*, 32, Rome, 1951.

CROSS, F. M. and FREEDMAN, D. N. *Early Hebrew Orthography*, etc., Baltimore, Md., 1952.

BERTHIER, A. *Le sanctuaire punique d'El-Hofra à Constantine*, Paris, 1955.

ROWLEY, H. H. (ed.), *The Old Testament and Modern Study*, Oxford, 1957.

PRITCHARD, J. B. *Hebrew Inscriptions and Stamps from Gibeon*, Philadelphia, Pa., 1959.

WRIGHT, G. E. (ed.) *The Bible and the Ancient Near East*, London, 1961.

AHARONI, Y. *Excavations at Ramat Raḥel*, Rome, 1962.

PROBABLE OFFSHOOTS OF PHŒNICIAN ALPHABET

It is quite probable that the following groups are connected with the Punic or neo-Punic scripts, at least, in part. We therefore consider it fitting to deal with them in this chapter.

LIBYAN SCRIPTS (Figs. 14.15, 23 e–g)

The ancient Libyans, the progenitors of the Berbers, the present indigenous population of northern Africa, employed a particular writing termed early Libyan or Numidian. About five hundred inscriptions (found mainly in eastern Algeria, and particularly in the province of Constantine, and in Tunis), belonging mostly to the Roman period, are extant. Some of these inscriptions are bilingual, Libyan-Punic, Libyan - neo-Punic, and Libyan-Latin (Fig. 14.23 *f*). This script was the prototype of the Tamachek, called by the natives *Tifinagh* ('characters'), still used by the Tuareg, a Berber tribe.

The Libyan inscriptions are either cut in stone, or engraved or painted on rocks. The direction of the writing is generally from right to left; sometimes, however, vertical, downwards. The alphabet (Fig. 14.15) consists of consonants only, and it contains also special signs (not reproduced in the figure) for the double consonants, such as *gt*, *lt*, *mt*, *ft*, *nk*.

The origin of this script (or scripts) is still uncertain. Various suggestions have been advanced, some considering it as an offshoot of the South Arabian or North Arabian alphabets, or of a pre-alphabetic Aegean script, or else of the early Greek alphabet, or of the Phœnician or neo-Punic alphabets, or even of Egyptian hieroglyphics. The correct solution of the problem is probably this: the early Libyans borrowed the idea of writing from the Carthaginians, but they did not adopt the whole Punic or neo-Punic alphabet: they took over some signs, the direction of writing from right to left and the consonantal method of writing. At the same time they adopted also some local signs—some Berber tribes, the Dag R'ali and Kel R'ela, for instance, still employ ancient geometrical property marks—and modified some of the borrowed Punic letters, so that the external form of the Libyan signs became quite different from that of the Punic or neo-Punic alphabets.

BIBLIOGRAPHY

FAIDHERBE, L. L. C. *Collection complète des inscriptions numidiques (libyques)*, etc., Paris, 1870.

LITTMANN, E. 'L'origine de l'alphabet libyen,' *Journal Asiatique*, 1904.

CHABOT, J.-B. 'Inscriptions punico-libyques,' *Journal Asiatique*, 1918; 'Les inscriptions libyques de Dougga,' *Journal Asiatique*, 1921; *Recueil des Inscriptions libyques*, Paris, 1940–1 (1947).

BEGUINOT, F. A series of articles in *L'Africa Italiana*, 1927; *Annali del R. Inst. Orient. di Napoli*, 1929 and 1935; *La Riv. d'Oriente*, 1935, etc.

MEINHOF, C. *Die libyschen Inschriften*, Leipsic, 1931.

ZYHLHARZ, E. 'Die Sprache Numidiens,' *Zeitschrift für Eingeborne Sprachen*, 1931–2.

REYGASSE, M. *Contrib. à l'étude d. grav. rup.* etc., Algiers, 1932.

MARCY, G. *Les inscriptions libyques bilingues de l'Afrique du Nord*, Paris, 1936; *Hesperis*, 1937; *Rev. Afric.*, 1937.

On the Libyan inscriptions of the Canary Islands, *see* RÆSSLER, O. 'Libyca,' *Wiener Zeitschrift für die Kunde des Morgenlandes*, 1942.

IBERIAN SCRIPTS (Figs. 14.15, 24–25)

About a hundred and fifty inscriptions have been found in Spain, written in the *Iberian* scripts. There were two distinct systems of writing: (*a*) the script of *Hispania Citerior*, that is, the *Iberian* script in the narrow sense of the word, and (*b*) the *Turdetan* or *Andalusian* alphabet, that is, the script of ancient Tartessus (by some scholars regarded as the Biblical Tarshish) and the southern Iberian peninsula. The former is the more important; the latter is referred to by Strabo (64–63 B.C.–A.D. 21 at least), 3.I.6.

The inscriptions are engraved on stone monuments (Fig. 14.24*b*) or on lead, bronze or silver, or painted on pottery (Fig. 14.24*c*) or on walls. Iberian coins bearing inscriptions have also been found.

The longest inscription (regarded by some scholars as a forgery) is on lead and was discovered at La Serreta, nearly two miles from Alcoy, south of Valencia. The text engraved on both sides of the tablet contains three hundred and forty-two letters in fourteen lines. Another long inscription is that of Castellon de la Plana with a hundred and fifty-five signs, while the third longest engraved inscription, on bronze, comes from Luzaga. An interesting group of forty inscriptions on pottery (Fig. 14.24*c*), discovered in the years 1933 to 1936 at San Miguel de Liria, was published in 1942 by the Diputación Provincial de Valencia.[1] One of them (Fig. 14.24*c*) contains as many as a hundred and fifty-seven signs. This inscription has been attributed to the last third of the fifth century B.C. Other inscriptions may belong to the fourth or third centuries, but the majority belong to the later centuries and the most recent may be attributed to the age of the Roman Empire.

The direction of writing is generally from right to left; sometimes, however, vertically downwards.

Figure 14.24*a* shows the Iberian alphabet as deciphered by Professor Manuel Gómez Moreno, with a few additions by Pío Beltrán Vilagrasa. If this decipherment, which has not yet found general agreement, be right, the following would be the main characteristics of the Iberian script: (1) The whole system consisted of thirty letters, namely twenty-five consonants and five vowels. (2) There was no distinction between *b* and *p*, *g* and *k*, and *d* and *t*. (3) There were no signs for *f*, *h*, *v*; on the other hand there were special signs for double *n* and double *r*. (4) The script was partly alphabetic and partly syllabic, having five different forms for each of the letters *b-p*, *g-k*, *d-t*, according to the vowel-sound following it. The latter suggestion is hardly acceptable.

The origins of the Iberian scripts are still uncertain. Some scholars hold that the two scripts are varieties of the same system, others (more rightly, I think) believe that they are quite different. The Turdetan script is regarded by some scholars as purely consonantal and as a simple variant of the early Libyan script. The Iberian script is regarded by some scholars as a derivative of the Phœnician or Punic alphabets, by others (Taylor, for instance) as a descendant of the early Greek alphabet. Sir Arthur Evans suggested a connection with the Cretan scripts, while other scholars (including Wilke, and Dejador y Frauca) regarded the Iberian script as a prehistoric indigenous creation connected with the geometrical signs employed in prehistoric Spain (*see* p. 5 and Fig. Introd. 2.2).

It seems that we have to deal with a very complicated problem. In my opinion, the origins of both Iberian scripts can be compared with that of the early Libyan writing, that is, while borrowing the idea of writing and some of the letters used by the Phœnicians or Carthaginians, the ancient populations of Spain also made use of the geometrical signs current in prehistoric Spain (p. 5) but, in addition, used arbitrary symbols and possibly characters derived from other scripts.

The whole problem is also in some measure connected with the ethnic problem of ancient Spain. It is a fact that the origin of the Iberians is still uncertain. Various theories have been put forward. We will mention the more important. It should be noted: (1) The old opinion connecting the Iberians of Spain with the ancient Caucasian Iberians is now out of date. (2) Another theory connects the Iberians with the Libyans, and some scholars hold that the names of the Iberians and the Berbers spring from the same source, the latter being a Libyan duplication of the element *ber* (Ber-

---

[1] I wish to thank Dr. T. M. Batista i Roca for indicating to me the recent bibliography and for lending me certain books which I had not been able to find.

ber), the former consisting of the same element preceded by the Libyan article *i-*
(*i-Ber*). (3) Some scholars (this is essentially W. von Humboldt's opinion, suggested
in 1821) consider that the present Basques, who inhabit the region of the Pyrenees in
north-western Spain, are the descendants of the ancient Iberians who are supposed
to have inhabited the Iberian peninsula since the Stone Age. This opinion is at present
held mainly by certain Spanish scholars. Other investigators connect the Basques
with the ancient Ligurians and regard the ancient Iberian language as an offshoot of
the early Libyan speech, *see* under (2). A correct solution of the linguistic problem
would certainly help in solving the question of the origins of the Iberian scripts and
vice versa.

BIBLIOGRAPHY

ZOBEL DE ZAGRONIZ, J. in *Zeitschr. der Deutschen Morgenl. Gesellschaft*, 1863.

HÜBNER, E. *Monumenta linguæ ibericae*, Berlin, 1893.

WILKE, G. *Südwesteuropäische Megalithkultur und ihre Beziehung zum Orient*, Würzburg, 1912.

SCHULTEN, A. *Numantia*, I–IV, Munich, 1914–29; *Zeitschr. der Deutschen Morgenl. Gesellschaft*, 1924.

VICEDO, R. 'Historia de Alcoy y su región,' *El Archivo de Alcoy*, 1920.

GÓMEZ-MORENO, M. *De epigrafía ibérica. El plomo de Alcoy*, Madrid, 1922; *Sobre los iberos y su lengua*,
    Madrid, 1925; 'Las inscripciones ibéricas,' *Homenaje a Menéndez Pidal*, III, 1925; 'Notas sobre
    numismática hispana,' *Homenaje a Mélida*, 1934; *Las lenguas hispánicas*, Valladolid, 1942; 'La
    escritura ibérica,' *Boletín de la Real Academia de la Historia*, 1943; *La escritura bastulo-turdetana
    (primitiva hispanica)*, Madrid, 1962.

SCHUCHARDT, H. 'Die iberische Inschrift von Alcoy,' *Sitzungsb. d. Preuss. Akad. d. Wissensch.*, 1922.

VIVES, A. *La moneda hispánica*, Madrid, 1924; new ed., 1926.

CEJADOR Y FRAUCA, J. *Alfabeto e inscripciones ibéricas*, Barcelona, 1926 (also in French, *Alphabet et
    inscriptions ibériques*, 1929).

MEINHOF, C., in *Zeitschrift der Deutschen Morgenl. Gesellschaft*, 1927, 1930, etc.

FERRANDIS TORRES, J. *La moneda hispánica*, Barcelona, 1929.

HILL, G. F. *Notes on the Ancient Coinage of Hispania Citerior*, New York, 1931.

ZYHLHARZ, E. in *Zeitschr. der Deutschen Morgenl. Gesellschaft*, 1934.

VILAGRASA, P. B. *Sobre un interesante vaso escrito de San Miguel de Liria*, Diputación Provincial de
    Valencia, 1942.

CARO BAROJA, J. *Observaciones sobre la hipótesis del vascoiberismo*, Madrid, 1942–3; 'La Geografía
    linguistica,' etc., *Bol. de la Real Acad. Esp.*, 1947.

LEJEUNE, M. *Celtiberica*, Salamanca, 1955.

CHAPTER 15

Aramaic Branch

THE ARAMÆANS

The Aramæans, a main branch of the 'Third Semitic migration,' are mentioned in Biblical sources and in cuneiform inscriptions. The Biblical *Aram* applies to an ethnical group and also to the territory occupied by this group. In the 'Table of the Nations' (Gen., x), Aram, the 'ancestor' of the Aramæans, is described as a son of Shem, while Gen., xxii, 21, makes him a grandson of Nahor, Abraham's brother. Jacob is termed 'a wandering Aramæan,' his mother and his wives are also represented as Aramæans.

Apart from an obscure term *A-ra-am* in an Akkadian inscription of the second half of the third millennium B.C., the earliest cuneiform sources which mention the Aramæans are the Amarna Tablets (of the fifteenth and fourteenth centuries B.C.), which refer to them as *Akhlame* or *Akhlamu* ('members of the federation'?), who have been regarded as identical with the *Akhlame Armaya* mentioned in sources belonging to the end of the twelfth century B.C., while in the Assyrian sources they are called *Arumu* or *Aramu* (pl. *Arimi*). The etymological connection with the *Eremboi* and *Arimoi* of the Homeric poems, which until about forty years ago was held as possible, is now considered to be improbable.

'Syria' and 'Syrians' were the Greek terms for 'Aram' and 'Aramæans.' In the rabbinic literature, where the term 'Aramæan' is equivalent to 'heathen,' because the heathen neighbours of the Jews spoke Aramaic, the Jews preferred to use the Greek term 'Syriac' to designate their Aramaic speech. The terms 'Syria' and 'Syrians' are usually explained as abbreviations of 'Assyria' and 'Assyrians'—Herodotus (VII, 63) regarded the term 'Assyrians' as the barbarian form for the Greek spelling 'Syrians' —but the suggestion of the German scholar Winckler to regard the term 'Syria' as a derivation from *Suri* of the cuneiform inscriptions, the Babylonian designation for 'the west,' including the regions inhabited by the Aramæans, seems to be more acceptable.

On the other hand, according to Thureau-Dangin, the reading *ri* (in *Su-ri*) is mistaken for *-bir* (*Shu-bar*, Subartu). More recently, Forrer suggested a derivation from '*sur*, Taurus,' which in his opinion seems to be denoted by an ox-head in Hittite hieroglyphic writing. Finally, Tkatsch holds that 'Syria' may be a local form (not connected with the name of Assyria) of uncertain etymological origin.

The original home of the Aramæans is unknown. In the Amarna Tablets, mentioned above, they are described as invading wandering hordes. It is generally held that they moved from north-eastern Arabia into Syria on one side and into Mesopotamia on the other. When, towards the close of the thirteenth century B.C., the Hittites and the Mitanni ceased to control the land, minor Aramæan states made their appearance in north-western and south-western Mesopotamia.

The period of the ultimate settlement of the great Aramæan wave of migration which flowed into northern Syria in the twelfth and eleventh centuries B.C. witnessed a great revolution in the distribution of political power. The reign of Rameses III (1198–1167 B.C.) marks the beginning of the decline of Egyptian power. Assyria declined slowly after Tiglath-pileser I (1113–1074 B.C.). The Hittite empire, in the north, and the Minoan power in the west, had come to an end. The Aramæan tribes took the maximum advantage of this period of unparalleled political and social disintegration. By force of arms and numbers they established a chain of petty kingdoms in the most favourable lands of northern and southern Mesopotamia and in western Syria. Thanks to the effective domestication of the Arabian camel, about the end of the twelfth century B.C., which increased the caravan trade enormously, rich trade-depots were established, the best known being Palmyra.

ARAMÆAN STATES

By far the most important of these small states was Damascus (*Aram Dammesheq* or simply, *Aram*), followed by *Aram Naharaim* and *Sam'al* (Zenjirli, in northern Syria); Aleppo and Carchemish (also in northern Syria) were other important Aramæan centres. The end of the eleventh century B.C. and the first half of the tenth century mark the climax of Aramæan political power. However, Semitic Syria never had a political unity of its own. In time of danger, loose federal unions of fortified towns were organized. Not one was sufficiently strong to assert its complete supremacy over the rest. The little states could never combine for long, and they were always ready to fight one against the other, while Assyria was just as prompt to intervene. From the reign of the Assyrian king Tukulti-Ninurta II (889–884 B.C.), a slow process of Assyrian recovery and the establishment of an imperial system of conquest are to be observed. In the course of the almost yearly campaigns which can be traced, with some interruptions, for more than a century, the Aramæan states, one after the other, succumbed to the Assyrian empire. Damascus stood out for a few decades, but fell at last in 732 B.C. and never again appeared as an independent power.

SPREAD OF ARAMAIC SPEECH

However, the loss of political independence does not mean the end of Aramaic history. On the contrary, the political decay of the states marks the beginning of Aramæan cultural and economic supremacy in western Asia. Indeed, the policy of transplanting masses of Aramæans as of other conquered populations, bore remarkable fruit. Deportation in those days did not necessarily mean captivity; it was merely a political measure to break up military alliances. There is ample evidence of the considerable extent to which the Aramaic language and alphabet became commonly employed in Assyria from the end of the eighth century B.C. onwards.

At the end of the seventh century B.C., all Syria and a great part of Mesopotamia became thoroughly Aramaized. Aramaic was then the *lingua franca* of the day. Under the Persian Achæmenidae it became one of the official languages of the Empire and the principal speech of traders from Egypt and Asia Minor to India. The vitality of the language was such that it was used for more than a thousand years after the political decay of the Aramæans. The various languages and dialects which descended from it flourished for many centuries more. In some isolated villages (for instance, in three villages some thirty miles north of Damascus; one of these villages is still Christian) Aramaic dialects are still spoken, though now it is fast losing ground. Each village has its own pecularities of speech. The unifying force of Arabic and Islām is the main reason for the extinction of Aramaic. The importance of Aramaic in the religious field is paramount. For more than a thousand years it was the vernacular of Israel and became a second holy tongue, taking the place next to Hebrew in the religious and literary life of the Jewish people. It was the vernacular of Jesus Christ and the Apostles, and probably the original language of the Gospels. The majority of the religious works of the various oriental Churches are written in dialects descended from Aramaic and in scripts descended from the Aramaic alphabet.

ARAMAIC ALPHABET (Fig. 15.1)

The Aramaic scripts are a main branch of the North Semitic alphabet (chapter 12), the Canaanite branch (chapter 14) being the other main branch. According to Professor W. F. Albright, the acknowledged authority on the subject, 'it seems probable that the use of the North-west Semitic alphabet to write Aramaic does not ascend beyond the tenth century B.C.' The earliest Aramaic written document extant is a short inscription discovered in Gozan or Tell Halaf, which was published in 1940, but the first inscribed monument of importance is the inscription (Fig. 15.2*d*), bearing the name of a king of Damascus. Professor Albright attributes it to about 850 B.C. An ivory tablet, discovered in 1928, by F. Thureau-Dangin and A. Barrois, in Arslan Tash, in the Serug Valley (Eastern Cappadocia), seems to be dedicated to the king Hazael, belonging to the ninth century B.C. The next oldest inscription of significance (Fig. 15.2*b*) is the *stele* of Zakir, king of Hamath and Lu'ash, attributed by Albright to about 775 B.C. It was discovered in 1904, by the French Consul H. Pognon, in Afis, to the south-west of Aleppo. Fragments of a most important *stele* were discovered in 1930 in Sujin, to the south-east of Aleppo. On the whole, the earliest Aramaic inscriptions (Fig. 15.2), very few in number, belong to the ninth, eighth and seventh centuries B.C. A royal Canaanite-Aramaic inscription (from

Zenjirli) of Kilamuwa, of the last third of the ninth century B.C. is shown on Fig.
15.2a. A well-preserved inscribed gold sheath, also from Zenjirli, of the same Kilamuwa, was published in Berlin in 1943 and re-edited in *B.A.S.O.R.*, No. 119
(October, 1950).

Several hundred documents mainly of smaller dimensions represent the succeeding centuries. Numerous Aramaic papyri and *ostraca* come from Egypt, amongst them
the famous Elephantine papyri (Figs. 15.3–4), which give us information of a religious
and economic nature concerning a Jewish military colony in Egypt. The earliest
Aramaic papyrus found in Egypt seems to belong to 515 B.C. Amongst the most
important Aramaic inscriptions, the following may be mentioned: Greek-Aramaic
and Lydian-Aramaic bilingual inscriptions; the *stele* from Nerab, attributed to the
sixth century B.C.; the inscription from Taima, in North Arabia, belonging to the
fifth century; the *ostraca* recently found at Tell el-Kheleifeh (*see* pp. 174 and 189) by
N. Glueck, and attributed to the sixth-fourth centuries B.C. (*see* the articles by N.
Glueck, W. F. Albright and C. C. Torrey, in the *B.A.S.O.R.*, No. 80 onwards,
1940–1), and the inscription found at Taxila, in north-west India, formerly attributed
to the fourth and now to the third century B.C.

In the second half of the first millennium B.C. Aramaic became by far the most
important and widespread script of the whole Near East, and the official character of
the western provinces of the Persian empire, its diplomatic script.

On the whole, two main periods can be distinguished in the development of the
Aramaic script: (1) the early period, from the ninth to the seventh century B.C.; (2)
the Aramaic 'golden age,' when Aramaic became the *lingua franca* and the official
language of the Near East, and the Aramaic script was the official hand of the Persian
empire (generally known as 'Reichs-Aramäisch). In the opinion of some scholars
(for instance, Rosenthal), a kind of transition script may be seen in an Aramaic letter
written on six *ostraca* (found in the 1903–13 excavations of ancient Aššur), belonging
to the middle of the seventh century B.C.: the heads of the letters *b*, *d* and *r* are already
open, but the *sh* still preserves the old form (W): *see* Fig. 15.5a. According to Dr.
Rosenthal, the Aramaic script of the Achæmenian empire (which in the opinion of
some scholars originated not in the west but in the eastern portion of the empire),
down to about the second century B.C. was throughout uniform, whether it was
engraved on stone or written on papyrus or parchment; this uniformity being due
to the fact that Aramaic was the official language of some regions where it had never
been a spoken tongue. Professor Albright distinguishes four classes in the early
Aramaic cursive script: (1) the writing of the seventh century B.C.; (2) and (3) the
scripts of the first and the second half of the sixth century B.C.; (4) the script of
the early fifth century B.C. (Fig. 15.5a).

Interesting Aramaic documents found in Egypt were the subject of a paper read
by Professor G. R. Driver at the International Meeting of the Society for Old Testament Studies held in Cardiff from the 9th to the 13th September, 1946; *see* now G. R.
Driver. The documents are written on leather, and thirteen of them are more or less

well preserved. Their discovery was announced in 1933. During the war they were bought by the Bodleian Library at Oxford. These documents, which are dated by Professor Driver *c.* 411–408 B.C., are according to him almost all Persian official documents; their language and script closely resemble those of the Aramaic papyri found in Egypt. Professor Driver also announced the discovery of seven well-preserved Aramaic papyri from a subterranean gallery about two hundred miles to the south of Cairo.

Two peculiar facts must be noted. First, the Aramaic language (*see* above) and script had no great importance at the time of the existence of the Aramaic states. It was long after the Aramæans had lost their independence that their speech and writing became the *lingua franca* of the Near East. Second, only a very few Aramaic inscriptions have been found in the Aramaic native country. There are no known Aramaic inscriptions from Syria after the sixth century B.C. A very few inscriptions have been found in Palestine, but they are short. By far the most important Aramaic inscriptions are those found in Assyria, Persia, Cappadocia, Lycia, Lydia, Cilicia (Fig. 15.3*b*), North Arabia and especially in Egypt; others have been found in Greece, Afghanistan, India and other countries.

In 1958, on the ancient site of Kandahar (Alexandria Arachotum), there was discovered an inscription belonging to the tenth year after the consecration of Aśoka as king [*i.e.,* 259/258 B.C.]; in this he promulgated his religious and governmental principles, especially the prohibition of meat eating. The inscription is bilingual, in Greek and Aramaic, and is the easternmost Aramaic and one of the easternmost Greek inscriptions so far known (*see,* for instance, Gallavotti, 'The Greek version of the Kandahar Bilingual Inscription of Asoka,' *East and West*, N.S. 10, pp. 185 ff., 1959). *See* also pp. 266 and 363.

From its inception, the Aramaic alphabet, in a sense, had to fight a duel with the cuneiform system of writing. It was a long struggle—it lasted until the commencement of the Christian era—between the complicated theocratic system of writing accessible only to certain priviliged classes and the simple 'democratic' system accessible to everybody.

Development (Figs. 15.1–5)

The Aramaic script gradually assumed a distinctive character which is marked by the following main tendencies: (1) the opening of the tops and the sides of a few letters (the *beth*, the *daleth* and *resh*, the *'ayin*) is a prominent feature; (2) the endeavour to reduce the number of separate strokes, in the *ḥeth* and *ṭeth*, for instance, is also noticeable; (3) angles become rounded and ligatures develop. These tendencies were pronounced during the Persian period. By the fifth century B.C. the transformation is complete, as we can gather from the inscription at Taima, in northern Arabia, and especially from the cursive Aramaic writing on papyrus used in Egypt between 500 and 200 B.C.

'Dog-Aramaic'

Some extant Aramaic written documents are in Aramaic script, but couched in a kind of 'Dog-Aramaic,' that is Aramaic mixed with a foreign language or strongly influenced by a foreign form of speech; *see* also under *Nabatæan Script, Persian Script,* and so forth.

An inscription found in 1923, by E. E. Herzfeld, in Naqsh-i-Rustam, and published in 1938, was at first regarded as Aramaic and later as Persian in Aramaic script. Indeed, some words seem to be in Aramaic, while others have not yet been explained.

Armazi-Aramaic (Fig. 15.6)

Two interesting inscriptions were discovered in 1940 at Armazi, twenty-two kilo-metres from Tiflis, in excavations under the direction of the Georgian archæologist I. Javakhishvili. They were reported briefly in the same year at the session of the Scientific Council of the Marr Institute of Languages, History and Material Culture, Tiflis, and on the following 1st March at the first conference of the Academy of Sciences of the Georgian SSR (*Sark'-art'-velos SSR Mecnierebat'a Akademia*), Tiflis.

One of the two inscriptions is bilingual, in Greek and Aramaic. The Greek text, containing ten lines, was published in 1941 by S. Qaukhchishvili and A. Shanidze; *see* Fig. 15.6b. The Aramaic text (Fig. 15.6) was published by Professor George Tsereteli, in the *Bull. of the Marr Institute*, Vol. XIII, 1942, 'A Bilingual Inscription from Armazi near Mcheta (Mtskhet'a), in Georgia'. It contains eleven lines in a new variety of the Aramaic script, which Tsereteli suggests calling Armazi Aramaic. It is couched in a 'barbaric' ungrammatical language, with irregularities similar to those of the Aramaic words in the Sasanian inscriptions. Tsereteli dates the inscription to the first or second century A.D. (It is interesting to compare the Armazi-Aramaic script with Nabatæan–neo-Sinaitic writing: *see* Fig. 15.22.)

An excellent summary of this article, with many useful observations and additions, is given by Professor (now Sir) H. W. Bailey, in 'Caucasica,' *J. Roy. Asiatic Soc.*, 1943 (Parts 1 and 2), pp. 1–3. According to Professor Bailey, the inscription represents the stage when the originally completely Aramaic text was admitting Persian words, a process which increased with time, 'just as we find in Buddhist Sogdian texts a larger proportion of Aramaic heterograms than we find in the Manichæan, till in Christian texts they are altogether absent.' *See* also M. N. Tod in *J. Hellenic Studies*, 1942.

Professor Tsereteli, in his above-mentioned article, also quotes three lines of the other Aramaic inscription: *see* also Fig. 15.6a.

I am indebted to Professor Bailey for his kind help and to my friend Dr. J. Teicher for having drawn my attention to some of the above-mentioned articles.

OFFSHOOTS OF ARAMAIC ALPHABET

It seems as though an agreement had been reached between the Phœnician alphabets and their offshoots on the one hand, and the Aramaic branch on the other. All the alphabetic scripts west of Syria seem to have been derived, directly or indirectly, from the former, whereas the hundreds of alphabetic writings of the east have sprung apparently from the offshoots of the Aramaic alphabet.

'The differentiation between local Aramaic scripts began soon after the collapse of the Persian Empire brought about the end of the domination of the official Aramaic language and script' (Albright). It is not, however, until the end of the second century B.C. and during the first century B.C., that the various offshoots of the Aramaic script assume distinctive features.

The direct and indirect descendants of the Aramaic alphabet can be divided into two main groups: (1) The scripts employed for Semitic languages, and (2) those adapted to non-Semitic tongues. With regard to the Semitic offshoots, six separate centres of development may be discerned: (1) Hebrew, (2) Nabatæan-Sinaitic-Arabic, (3) Palmyrene, (4) Syriac-Nestorian, (5) Mandæan and (6) Manichæan. These alphabets became the links between the Aramaic alphabet and the numerous scripts used for the non-Semitic languages of central, southern and south-eastern Asia. These can be divided into various groups which will be dealt with in the following chapter.

CLASSICAL HEBREW ALPHABET (Figs. 15.5b, 7–10)

Origin

It is generally believed, in accordance with Jewish tradition, that the Early Hebrew alphabet—*see* preceding chapter—was superseded by the Aramaic alphabet during the Babylonian exile, and the Aramaic script therefore became the parent of the 'square Hebrew' and so of the modern Hebrew alphabet. This opinion is only partly right; the *ketabh meruba'* or 'square script,' or 'Assyrian' writing, although based mainly on the Aramaic alphabet, seems to have been strongly influenced by the early Hebrew alphabet.

A sepulchral inscription (Fig. 15.10a) from 'Araq el-Emir (Wadi es-Sir, to the south-east from es-Salt, Transjordan) can be considered as written in a transition script from the Early Hebrew character to the Square Hebrew. This inscription has been variously attributed to dates between the late sixth century B.C. and 176 B.C.

At any rate, a distinctive Palestinian Jewish variety of script can be traced from the third century B.C. (Fig. 15.10 b). According to Professor Albright, it became standardized just before the Christian era. It is from this script that the modern Hebrew alphabet letter-shapes eventually, though gradually, developed.

Inscriptions and Manuscripts

Square Hebrew inscriptions (Fig. 15.10) have been found on Palestinian ossuaries of the Maccabæan period and later, on some tomb-monuments in various countries, in catacombs near Rome and Venosa, and in ancient synagogues in Palestine and other countries. *See* now, for instance, F. M. Cross, Jr., 'The Development of the

Jewish Scripts,' in *The Bible and the Ancient Near East* (ed. by G. E. Wright), London, 1961. The Biblical manuscripts belong to a much later date, with the exception of some fragments written on papyrus, the earliest being the famous 'Nash-papyrus.' This important document, which had been attributed by S. A. Cook to the second and by F. C. Burkitt to the first century A.D., is dated by W. F. Albright to the Maccabæan age, between 165 and 37 B.C. ('A Biblical Fragment from the Maccabæan Age: The Nash Papyrus,' *J. Bibl. Liter.*, 1937.) The Nash papyrus (Fig. 15.11*a*) is now at Cambridge University Library; *see* below.

Many thousands of fragments of Hebrew 'Babylonian' and other Biblical MSS. were discovered in the famous Cairo *Genizah*, and these partly belong to the seventh and eighth centuries A.D. One of the earliest Hebrew manuscripts of which the date is known is that of the Later Prophets, dated A.D. 916, now preserved at Leningrad. The 'Cairo Codex' of Prophets is dated in the ninth century; the earliest Hebrew manuscript preserved in England is a British Museum MS. (Or. 4445), undated, but belonging to the ninth century A.D. The majority of Hebrew manuscripts are of the twelfth to sixteenth centuries.

The Dead Sea Scrolls

The phenomenal discovery of these scrolls has become a focus of world interest. Since the whole subject is full of explosive theological implications, it is not surprising that long before the contents of the Scrolls became available for specialist study, certain scholars and pseudo-scholars not only propounded theories, more or less plausible, but took up definite standpoints, so that, for good or ill, they became involved in the defence of particular positions.

The importance of these documents cannot be over-estimated. We have acquired a new wealth of data for the study of Hebrew epigraphy and palæography; philology, lexicography, grammar and syntax; liturgy and history; Bible and theology; New Testament, and so on. For the present purpose, controversies concerning the sect of the Scrolls or the theological implications of the texts do not much matter. What concerns us here is the chronological problem; but the essential chronological controversy—whether the documents are to be dated mainly to the second-first century B.C. or to the first-second century A.D.—is not of particular gravity.

The fact is that quite unexpectedly we have now thousands of old Square Hebrew literary and cursive documents. Some are written in beautiful book-hands; others in current styles. The Muraba'at and other finds, particularly those at Masada, which furnish personal documents belonging to the legendary Bar Kochba (A.D. 132–135), give us valuable chronological help and confirm the MS.-dating obtained on palæographical grounds.

The tens of thousands of fragmentary MSS. composing what are loosely termed 'Dead Sea Scrolls,' may be divided into four main groups:

(1) The 'Dead Sea Scrolls' proper (Figs. 15.7–8, 11–12) found, from the late

spring months of 1947 onwards, in eleven caves high up the steep rock in the Wady Qumran (some seven miles south of Jericho, along the track to 'Ain Feshkha, over one mile west of the Dead Sea, and about 1,000 yards north-west of Khirbet Qumran). The eleven caves are known as 1Q, 2Q, 3Q, 4Q, and so on. From 1Q, eleven MSS. and several fragments, on leather, came into the hands of scholars (Figs. 15.11–12). This material has, in whole or in part, been published. So also have the fragments from 2Q, 3Q and 6Q, the Copper Scroll (of paramount importance) from 3Q, and the fragments from 5Q. Of particular interest is the material from 6Q, more than 90 per cent being papyrus.

Tens of thousands of fragments have come to light from 4Q, which was discovered in 1952. After four years' work, 382 MSS. (about one quarter being Biblical) have been identified. A fragmentary copy of *Samuel* (4Q *Sam. b*), is regarded as the earliest extant MS. of Qumran, and thus as the earliest MS. so far known in the Hebrew square script. It probably belongs to the late third century B.C. A fragmentary copy of *Exodus* (4Q *Ex. f*) may even be earlier, but it is written in a hitherto unknown cursive style. A copy, also very fragmentary, of *Jeremiah* (4Q *Jer. a*) is probably slightly later than 4Q *Sam. b.* Not all the finds of 11Q have been published: their importance seems to rival those of 1Q and 4Q. They contain a magnificent scroll of *Psalms*, a copy of *Leviticus* in Early Hebrew character, an Aramaic *Targum* of *Job*, and so on.

(2) Documents found in 1952 in the prehistoric caves of Wady Muraba'at (which were used as a refuge during the Bar Kochba War) include Hebrew literary texts on papyrus and parchment—fragments of books of the Bible (unlike those from Qumran, they are identical with the Massoretic text); a complete phylactery; a Greek marriage contract (?) dated to A.D. 124, and other miscellaneous documents, particularly some original documents concerning the Second Jewish or Bar Kochba War (A.D. 132–135). One document refers to 'Year 1 of the deliverance of Israel by Simon son of Kosebah [that is, Bar Kochba], Prince of Israel.' There are two letters from Simeon ben Kosebah, a letter from the administrators of the village of Beth Mashkho, and other cursive documents (Fig. 15.13c).

(3) A number of Bar Kochba letters (in Hebrew, Nabatæan, Aramaic, and Greek) discovered under thrilling conditions in 1960 and the following years—particularly at Masada by Israeli archæologists under the leadership of Professor Yigael Yadin. This discovery is a contribution of paramount importance to the study of the Bar Kochba War. Also several Biblical and other scrolls were discovered.

(4) Several manuscripts found in 1952 and 1953 (in the latter year by a Belgian expedition under the leadership of Professor R. De Langhe) in an underground chamber among the ruins of a Byzantine monastery, known as Khirbet al-Mird— two and a half miles north-east of the ancient Christian monastery Mar Saba, not far from Bethlehem. The documents, belonging to the fifth-ninth centuries A.D. consist of Greek and Arabic papyri, and of Christian Palestinian Aramaic documents, including fragmentary MSS. from the Old and New Testaments.

BIBLIOGRAPHY

NUMEROUS authors, in more than 2,000 books and articles, have taken part in the 'Battle of the Scrolls.' This active interest shows little sign of abating. An eminent book-reviewer quotes a maxim which should be recommended to all who read about the Scrolls—perhaps to scholars most of all. 'The first of the virtues of God which we ought to imitate is patience, by which we are able to bear with the foolishness of unbelievers.' The following is a small selection of comprehensive, recent works on the subject (in alphabetical order of the authors):

ALLEGRO, J. M. *The Dead Sea Scrolls*, Penguin Books, Harmondsworth (Middx.), 1956 (bibliography); *The Treasure of the Copper Scroll*, etc., New York–London, 1960.

BURROWS, M. *The Dead Sea Scrolls*, London, 1956; *More Light on the Dead Sea Scrolls*, London, 1958 (bibliography).

CROSS, F. M. *The Ancient Library of Qumran*, etc., New York, 1958; *The Development of the Jewish Scripts* (already referred to), London, 1961.

DIRINGER, D. 'The Battle of the Scrolls', in *Caravan. Jewish Quarterly Omnibus*, New York and London, 1962.

(Various authors), *Discoveries in the Judaean Desert*, vol. I, Oxford, 1955.

DRIVER, G. R. *The Hebrew Scrolls*, etc., Oxford, 1951.

DUPONT-SOMMER, A. *Aperçus préliminaires sur les manuscrits de la Mer Morte*, Paris, 1950; *Nouveaux aperçus* etc., Paris, 1953.

FRITSCH, C. T. *The Qumrân Community*, etc., New York, 1956.

GASTER, T. H. *The Dead Sea Scriptures in English Translation*, New York, 1956.

HABERMANN, S. M. *'Edah we'eduth. Megillôth Qedumôth*, etc., Jerusalem, 1952.

KAHLE, P. *Die hebräischen Handschriften aus der Höhle*, Stuttgart, 1951.

MARTIN, M. *The Scribal Character of the Dead Sea Scrolls*, 2 vols., Louvain, 1958 (bibliography).

DEL MEDICO, H. E. *Le Mythe des Esséniens*, Paris, 1958; *The Riddle of the Scrolls*, London, 1958.

MILIK, J. T. *10 anni di scoperte nel deserto di Giuda*, Rome, 1957 (also translated into several languages).

ORLINSKY, H. M. 'The Textual Criticism of the Old Testament,' in *The Bible and the Ancient East* (ed. by G. E. Wright), London, 1961.

RABIN, C. *The Zadokite Documents*, Oxford, 1954; *Qumrân Studies*, Oxford, 1957.

ROWLEY, H. H. *The Zadokite Fragments and the Dead Sea Scrolls*, Oxford, 1952 (bibliography).

SCHONFIELD, J. J. *Secrets of the Dead Sea Scrolls*, London, 1956.

SCHUBART, W. *Die Gemeinde vom Toten Meer*, Munich and Bâle, 1958.

Scripta Hierosolymitana, Vol. IV, Oxford, 1958.

SUKENIK, E. L. *The Dead Sea Scrolls*, etc., Jerusalem, 1955.

VERMÈS, G. *Les manuscrits du désert de Juda*, Tournai and Paris, 1953.

VINCENT, A. *Les manuscrits hébreux du désert de Juda*, Paris, 1955.

YADIN, Y. *The Message of the Scrolls*, London, 1957; *Masada* (particularly ch. 13, 'The scrolls', and ch. 14, 'The synagogue and its scrolls'), London, 1966.

ZEITLIN, S. *The Dead Sea Scrolls*, etc., Philadelphia, 1956.

Varieties of Hebrew Alphabet

In the evolution of the modern Hebrew alphabet four fundamental types of writing can be traced (Fig. 15.9).

(*a*) the square script which developed into the neat, well-proportioned printing type of modern Hebrew: *see* below.

(*b*) the mediæval formal styles;

(*c*) the rabbinic, employed mainly by the mediæval Jewish savants, and also known as Rashi-writing; and

(d) the cursive script, which gave rise to many local varieties in the Levant, Morocco, Spain, Italy, and other countries, of which the Polish-German form became the current Hebrew cursive script.

This division must be a very old one, for it already appears in fragments of the seventh and eighth centuries A.D.

The local Hebrew scripts were strongly influenced by the non-Jewish script and art of their regions. As a result, there appear, for instance, the elegant forms of the Italian-Hebrew scripts, and the Hispano-Moresque influence on the Spanish-Hebrew writings. Hebrew oriental scripts have a particular style of their own.

Specimens of Hebrew scripts from Babylon, Egypt, Spain, Italy, and other countries, are reproduced on Figs. 15.10 g, 14–19.

MODERN HEBREW ALPHABET

The modern Hebrew script (Fig. 15.9)—in which copies of the Holy Scriptures in Hebrew are printed, and the scrolls of the Law are inscribed—is essentially the ancient 'Square Hebrew' script, which must, as mentioned, be distinguished from the Early Hebrew writing.

The Hebrew alphabet consists of the ancient twenty-two Semitic letters, which are all consonants. The script is read from right to left. The letters are bold and well proportioned, although there exist certain, but superficial, resemblances between *b* and *k*, *g* and *n*, *w* and *z*, *ḥ* and *h* or *t*, and so forth. The letters *k*, *m*, *n*, *p* and *ṣ* have two forms; one, when initial or medial; the other, when final.

The Hebrew letters are also used as numerical signs; the first nine, representing the units (1–9); the next nine, the tens (10–90); and the last four, the numbers 100, 200, 300 and 400.

Vowel Marks

The Hebrew alphabet, as already mentioned, is purely consonantal, although four of the letters (*aleph*, *he*, *waw* and *yod*) are also employed to represent long vowels. Professor Chomsky points out that these four letters, which were originally employed consistently as consonants, but gradually began to lose their weak consonantal value in some instances, and became silent, eventually were utilized as the so-called long vowels. These letters have sometimes been called *vowel-letters*, or with more reason *vocalic consonants*, also *matres lectionis*.

The absence of vowel-letters was not strongly felt, because Hebrew, like other Semitic languages, is essentially consonantal, and, unlike the Indo-European languages, the vowels serve principally to denote the terminations of inflection in nouns and the moods of verbs, or other grammatical variations.

However, as Hebrew speech passed out of daily use, and familiarity with biblical Hebrew steadily dwindled, it became necessary to introduce some form of vocalic distinction in order to read and explain the Holy Scripture correctly. On the other hand, no change in spelling nor addition of letters was permitted; 'the omission or the addition of one letter might mean the destruction of the whole world,' says the Talmud.

Until about a century ago, only the Tiberias vocalization system was known. Since then, some other systems have come to light, and it is thought that they are the records of different schools, and preserve variations in pronunciation in different countries or localities.

The three main vowel-systems now extant are the 'Babylonian,' the 'Palestinian' and the 'Tiberiadic.' The Babylonian is a 'superlinear' system of both vocalization and accentuation; its main characteristic feature is the representation of vowel-sounds by small vowel-letters, ' for long a, ' for short a, w for u, and y for i; double y for long e, and double w for long o. These small letters and some other graphic signs were placed above the consonants, leaving the textual orthography unchanged. The Babylonian system is preserved in a number of Biblical manuscripts and fragments mainly discovered in ancient synagogues at Chufutkale, Karasubazar and Theodosia, in the Crimea.

The 'Palestinian' system was also 'superlinear,' but its basic element was the dot. The varying position, as well as the change in the arrangement and in the number of the dots, determined the value of the vowel-sound. The Palestinian vowel-system is preserved only in some fragmentary manuscripts discovered, since the end of the last century, in the Cairo *Genizah*.

The Tiberiadic' system is partly 'superlinear,' but mainly 'sublinear.' It consists of dots and little dashes, and also denotes semivowels. It is a highly developed system and far more precise and comprehensive than the others. The Tiberiadic notation marks regularly the word-tone and secondary stresses, and so forth; *see* Fig. 15.20a. It finally gained general acceptance, whereas the others fell into gradual disuse and oblivion. As its main element is the dot, the 'Tiberiadic' or Tiberian 'punctuation' was probably considered to be too insignificant to infringe the prohibition of change in traditional orthography.

Other Diacritical Marks

Of the other diacritical marks, special mention must be made of the use of a dot in the consonants b, g, d, k, p and t, to harden their sounds; and of a point above the letter sh (respectively to the right or to the left), to differentiate the sound s from sh.

Origin of Punctuation Marks and their Employment

The origin of the Hebrew 'punctuation' systems is still a matter of discussion among scholars. While, according to some scholars (*see* Professor Blake's article, 'Vowel Symbols in Alphabets,' *J. Amer. Orient. Soc.*, 1940), the 'Hebrew systems are all based on the Nestorian dot system and therefore later than A.D. 750'—according to others (V. Chomsky, 'The History of our Vowel-system in Hebrew', *The Jewish Quarterly*

Review, 1941), 'the process of establishing the Hebrew vowel-systems was gradual and of long duration'; it 'had been going on for centuries,' and 'had gone through several stages in its evolution,' but 'mutual influence and borrowing in this regard, in the case of Hebrew and Syriac, must not be discounted.' This latter view is probably correct. According to Professor Chomsky, the origin of the Hebrew punctuation systems 'may be traced even as far back as the period of Ezra and the Great Synagogue,' although 'the Tiberian system was probably not definitely fixed until about, sometimes, the latter part of the eighth century C.E.'

Punctuation marks must not be employed in the synagogue scrolls, but they have always been used in the printing of the Bible. Otherwise they are omitted in modern printing—except in poems and in literature for children (Fig. 15.20*b*) and, sometimes, in private correspondence.

Yiddish and Judezmo

The Hebrew script has been adapted to some other languages, such as Arabic, Turkish (as employed by the Karaite Jews in the Crimea), and so forth, but particularly to German and Spanish. It has, thus, been adopted for Judæo-German or Yiddish, and Judæo-Spanish or Judezmo.

Yiddish probably originated in the Middle Ages in the Rhineland; it is based on early mediæval German and Hebrew, but it also contains words from early Romance languages (French and Italian), and later absorbed words from the languages of the countries in which it was spoken, such as Polish, Russian, English, etc. Yiddish is nowadays the language of East European Jewry and of its many emigrants to other parts of Europe and overseas; in the U.S.A. and in Latin America there are about five million Yiddish speakers. There is a rich literature in Yiddish.

Yiddish employs the modern Hebrew alphabet: it is written from right to left. The letters *aleph*, *waw*, *yod* and *'ayin* are employed as vowels, respectively as *a* or *o*; *u*; *i* (*y*); and *e*; double *yod* represents the diphthongs *ei* or *ai*, whereas the diphthong *oi* is represented by the combination *waw-yod*: *see* Fig. 15.20*c*.

Judezmo or Judæo-Spanish, called also Ladino, contains many Hebrew words, but is principally based on Old Spanish or Castilian, as spoken in the fifteenth century in Spain, before the Jews were expelled from that country in 1492. Judezmo has also absorbed many words from Arabic, Turkish, and other languages. There is a comparatively rich literature in this language, which is still spoken by the descendants of the Spanish Jews scattered in some Mediterranean countries.

Judezmo employs the Hebrew alphabet, and reads from right to left.

THE NABATÆANS AND THEIR SCRIPT

The Nabatæans (Gr. *Nabataioi*, Lat. *Nabateni*, perhaps the *Nebayoth* of the Bible), a nomadic tribe speaking Arabic, living between northern Arabia, Transjordan and Sinai, constituted in the last two centuries B.C. and the first two centuries A.D. an important kingdom with a capital at Sela' (Lat. Petra). Even before these dates a Nabatæan tribe was known which in 312–311 B.C. was powerful enough to gain the victory against Antigonus, one of the successors of Alexander the Great, who attempted to subdue them. 'Their rise was simultaneous with and in a way parallel to that of the Jews under the Maccabees' (Burkitt). Nabatæan coins have revealed an almost unbroken succession of kings, from Obedas I (90 B.C.) to Malichus III (A.D. 106). For a short period, their influence extended from the Euphrates to the Red Sea and to the centre of Arabia (at Hejra, great numbers of Nabatæan tombs and inscriptions have come to light); in 85 B.C. the Nabatæans occupied Damascus.

The kingdom of Petra lost its independence in A.D. 106 and became the 'Arabian Province' of the Roman Empire, with Bosra (on the south of the Jebel Druse), as the capital. The term 'Nabatæan' survived for some years the fall of the kingdom; the name 'Annalus the Nabatæan' appears on an inscription of A.D. 140.

According to some scholars, the Nabatæans were originally pure Aramæans, who in the course of their migrations mingled with the Arab population; this opinion is based on the fact that while the oldest Nabatæan inscriptions contain no Arabisms, from the beginning of the first century A.D. Arab influence makes itself clearly felt. However, nowadays it is generally believed that the Nabatæans were Arabs who used Aramaic as their written language, Arabic being their speech of daily life.

Nabatæan culture was essentially Arabic, but the language of the inscriptions is Aramaic with some Arabic influences. There is extant a number of important Nabatæan inscriptions and coins. Some Nabatæan inscriptions have been discovered in Egypt; some in Palestine; three have been found in Italy; a Græco-Nabatæan bilingual inscription has come to light in the Aegean island of Cos.

The Nabatæan alphabet (Fig. 15.21, col. 2) can be traced from the late second century B.C., but distinctive Nabatæan inscriptions (Fig. 15.22) hardly begin until after the middle of the first century B.C. The script became standardized about the beginning of the Christian era.

NEO-SINAITIC ALPHABET

After the Nabatæan kingdom came to an end, Nabatæan inscriptions followed suit. The Nabatæan alphabet gave way to a more cursive alphabet (Fig. 15.21, col. 3) known as *Sinaitic* or neo-Sinaitic (to distinguish it from the early Sinaitic script which has already been dealt with). It is the script of many short rock-inscriptions found in the Sinaitic peninsula (Fig. 15.22), particularly in the Wadi Mukattab ('Valley of the Writings'), not far from the mining village of Abu Zeneima, lying about 75 miles from Suez. These inscriptions consist mainly of names and votive scribblings of the local Arab population.

'The linguistic and historical importance of the Sinaitic inscriptions is not very considerable: unlike the inscriptions on Nabatæan monuments they are not the work of professional calligraphists and practised masons, but of members of the caravans which traded between South Arabia (and India) and the Mediterranean. . . . The in-scriptions may be said to represent the type of cursive writing used by the Nabatæans' (B. Moritz).

This script developed out of the Nabatæan alphabet, probably in the first century A.D., although the extant inscriptions presumably belong to the second and third centuries, and some may even belong to the fourth century. The neo-Sinaitic alpha-bet is the probable link between the Nabatæan and the Arabic scripts. The evolution of the form of the letters of the Nabatæan-Sinaitic-Arabic branch has been the most rapid amongst all the branches of alphabetic scripts. All the letters have completely changed their form in the course of a few centuries (*see* Fig. 15.21).

ARABIC ALPHABET

Lidzbarski adduced as one of the reasons of the great changes in the Nabatæan-Sinaitic-Arabic branch, the geographic situation, whereas Rosenthal considers as its main reason the fact that the users of these scripts were not Aramæans. However, neither of these explanations is sufficient, the geographic situation of the users of other varieties being not very dissimilar, and on the other hand not all the users of other scripts of Aramic origin were Aramæans.

In my opinion, there must have been various concomitant reasons.

Arabic Language and Script (Speech and Writing follow Religion)

The Arabic alphabet is, after the Latin, the most generally used in the world today. The Arab conquests of the seventh and eighth centuries, the consequent expansion of the religion of Mohammed and the diffusion of his holy book made Arabic one of the chief languages of the universe. It is spoken, in some form or another, through-out the vast territories which lie between India and the Atlantic Ocean. It was formerly spoken in Spain, in the Balearic Islands and in Sicily, and is still spoken in Malta.

Mohammed's holy book, the Qur'ân (commonly written 'Koran' or 'Coran'), contains his religious teachings, and is considered by the Moslems to be a direct revelation from Allâh through the angel Gabriel to Mohammed. It consists of 114 sûrahs of different length. The entire revelation was delivered over a period of twenty years down to the prophet's death in A.D. 632. Some sûrahs were delivered at Mecca between A.D. 610 and 622, and others at Medina after the *Hijra* (or emigration of the prophet to that city), which took place in April A.D. 622, and which marks the beginning of the Moslem era.

The Qur'ân was for the first time put down coherently in writing a year after Mohammed's death by his devout follower, secretary and friend, Zayd ibn Thâbit, at the command of the first Caliph Abû Bakr; the collation of the work was accom-plished under the third Caliph 'Uthmân (644–656). The Qur'ân is held in great esteem and veneration by the Moslems, and endless pains are taken in the preparation of copies of the text. According to tradition, seven years in paradise are assured to any Muslim who makes a copy of the Qur'ân.

The *ṣalats* ('devotions,' 'set prayers') in Arabic language, which are a daily ritual to be strictly observed by all faithful (*Sûrah*, II. 239), contributed to the diffusion of Arabic in the Muslim world.

Arabic script spread even farther than Arabic speech. Becoming in turn the script of the Persian and, especially, of the Ottoman empire, it spread in the course of time to the Balkan peninsula, to what is now southern, or rather south-eastern Russia, to western, central and south-eastern Asia, and to a great part of Africa. The Arabic alphabet has thus been adapted not only to Arabic, which is a Semitic speech, but also to languages belonging to various linguistic groups: Indo-European or Indo-Aryan, such as Slavonic (in Bosnia), Spanish (the Arabic script employed for Spanish is called *aljamiah*), Persian, Hindustani (Fig. 15.0), Turkish; Hebrew; and various African languages, such as Berber, Swahili (Fig. 15.0), Sudanese, and so forth. On the other hand, there are rare instances of Arabic being written in non-Arabic scripts, for instance, in *garshuni*, or *karshuni*, which is the Syriac script adapted to Arabic, and Roman character, the script of the Maltese. Arabic script has driven out of use various scripts derived from the Syriac alphabet, as also the Coptic and the Persian. It has expelled the Greek alphabet from Anatolia, Syria and Egypt, the Latin from northern Africa, and the Cyrillic from Bosnia.

Many Arabic dialects developed with time, even in Arabia itself, and diverged one from the other, but the written language has invariably conformed to that type which is generally termed classical Arabic. The latter has an enormously rich vocabulary and a great variety of grammatical forms. The alphabet, in spite of its puzzling appearance to the novice, is comparatively easy to learn, and should not deter the earnest student from learning to read and write Arabic.

Origin of Arabic Alphabet (Fig. 15.21)

The history of the Arabic script is relatively short, and nothing is known of written Arabic literature prior to the compilation of the Qur'ân. It is generally held that the specific Arabic alphabet originated about the end of the fourth or during the fifth century A.D. However, a Nabatæan inscription found at en-Nemarah, to the south-east of Damascus, and dated A.D. 328 is couched in Arabic speech and already reveals certain characteristics of the Arabic script, but the earliest Arabic inscriptions extant are a trilingual Greek-Syriac-Arabic, of A.D. 512, found in 1879 at Zabad near Aleppo (Fig. 15.23a), and a Greek-Arabic bilingual discovered about 1860 in the vicinity of Damascus.

A learned correspondent of mine—Dr. S. Mahdi Hassan, of Bombay—in his article *The Arabic Writing as related to Devanagari: A Comparative Study of some of their Characters*, has suggested that 'the ancient Arabs were a poor people who could only afford bones as a writing material.' They had no script of their own 'and wrote Arabic in capital Hebrew characters.' Modern 'Arabic evolved as a space-saving script from

Proto-Devanagari for writing upon bones.' His proofs of evidence are based on 'comparative calligraphy.' Not many scholars will agree with this view.

While it is generally admitted that the Arabic alphabet descended from the Nabatæan, it is still uncertain how, when and where it originated. An Arabic tradition attributes the invention of the script to a member of Mohammed's family, but there is no doubt that it was in use long before the rise of Islām. The American scholar A. Jeffery even points out that 'if the dating of the Arabic graffiti on the Temple of Ramm (Iram, in the vicinity of 'Aqabah, to the north-east of the Red Sea.—D.D.) could be assured, we should have evidence of the use of the Arabic alphabet in North Arabia as early as A.D. 300.'

The majority of modern scholars agree with an earlier Arabic tradition which places the invention of the Arabic script at al-Hira, in Mesopotamia, whereas according to some modern Arab scholars it originated in Hejaz, and according to others, the two main branches of the Arabic script, Naskhi and Kufic, developed simultaneously from the Nabatæan alphabet, the former in the northern Hejaz, whence it passed to Mecca and Medina, and the latter in Mesopotamia, at Kufa and Basra.

Early Development of Arabic Alphabet

The early history of the Arabic character is also obscure. According to the Arabic writer Nadim, or Abulfaraj Mohammed ibn Ishaq ibn abi Ya'qub un-Nadim, of Baghdad, who lived in the latter half of the tenth century A.D., the early branches of the Arabic script developed in the following cities and in the following order: (1) Mecca, (2) Medina, (3) Basra, and (4) Kufa. There is, however, no doubt that while in these important cities, as in some others, such as Damascus, there existed famous schools in which local scripts developed, the order given by Nadim was influenced by Islamic orthodoxy.

From early times, the varieties of the script were not only geographical; there were also some variants according to the style of writing. Indeed, according to Nadim, the early Mecca-Medina branch had three varieties, and the Kufa-Basra branch had six. Nadim distinguishes also three varieties of the somewhat later Isfahani branch, one of which, the qairamuz, became the prototype of the Persian. Of these various early styles mentioned by Nadim, only two have been identified, the ma'il, a sloping delicate hand, and the mashq, an elongated or 'spread-out writing with undue spacing between the letters, which was common in early Cufic Codices' (Jeffery).

Development of Arabic Script: Kufic and Naskhi (Fig. 15.21, cols. 4–10)

On the whole, it may be said that in the early Mohammedan period there were two main types of Arabic writing, the Kufic or Cufic—so termed from the town Kufa, in Mesopotamia, the seat of a famous Moslem school—and the Naskhi. Kufic, which developed towards the end of the seventh century A.D. in the two old centres of Kufa and Basra, was a beautiful, monumental script. It was employed mainly for writing on stone and on metal, and especially in painted or carved inscriptions on the walls of the mosques, and on coins (Figs. 15.23*b*, *d*; 24*a–c*).

There are, however, many beautiful Qur'ân manuscripts extant which were executed on broad parchment rolls, and written in the heavy lapidary Kufic style. It was a large, bold, but stylized hand; its letters are generally thick, squat and upright, and rather angular. With the high development of Arabic calligraphy, Kufic became more and more consistent in the height, thickness and form of the letters, and became an exceptionally æsthetic script. For its ornamental use in Western art, *see* Erdmann. Kufic gave rise to a number of varieties, mostly mediæval, in northern (known as Maghribi, or 'western,' Fig. 15.21, col. 8) and central Africa, Spain, northern Arabia and southern Mesopotamia (Figs. 15.21, col. 9; 23*b*). One variety is known as Qarmathian—being mainly employed in Qarmathian manuscripts—and is regarded by some scholars as 'a particular kind of Naskhi.' Kufic has been discontinued except for formal purposes, where cursive writing cannot be employed.

Nadim gave three main characteristics of the Mecca-Medina or Naskhi type: its *alif* bends to the right; the upright strokes of its letters are long; and it is a somewhat slanting script. On the whole, Naskhi is a round and extremely cursive hand. In early times (Fig. 15.21, col. 4) it was mainly employed on papyrus. In course of time it became the parent of a number of different styles of writing used at the courts of various sultans, and elsewhere, and developed into the modern Arabic script (Fig. 15.21, col. 10). Of its innumerable varieties, the most important are: the elegant *ta'liq* (and its approximately seventy secondary forms) (Fig. 15.24*i*) used in Persia; the *ryq'a* (Fig. 15.24*h*), which was the script most commonly used in the Ottoman Empire; the *diwani* (Fig. 15.24*e*), or 'ministerial' script, which was used for the Turkish official documents; the *thuluth* or *thülth* or *sülüs* (Fig. 15.24*g*), employed more for ornamental than practical purposes; the *syakat* (Fig. 15.24*l*), used mainly by the Janissaries. *See* also Figs. 15.25–29.

MODERN ARABIC ALPHABET (Fig. 15.21, col. 10)

Arabic, like other Semitic scripts, is written from right to left. The alphabet consists of twenty-eight letters, the twenty-two of the ancient Semitic alphabet, and six new consonants placed at the end of the alphabet in its 'numerical order,' *i.e.*, according to their numerical value. Grammatically and graphically, however, the Arabic alphabet is arranged differently, according to the external form of the signs and the likeness of sounds.

The Arabs tried to distinguish in writing the finer shades of South Semitic sounds, and such distinction required no less than the aforementioned six additional letters: (*a*) tha, the weak glottal *dhal*, and the emphatic *za* were lisping modifications of ta, *dal*, and the hard glottal *ta*; (*b*) the hard glottal *dad* was the modification of the glottal *sad*; (*c*) the guttural *kha* (pronounced like the Scotch *ch*) and the *ghain* (a kind of soft *g*) were harder forms of *ha* and 'ayin.

The ordinary sequence of the letters in the Arabic alphabet, called the grammatical order of the letters, is generally employed in the modern grammars and vocabularies. The following is its order: *alif* ('), *ba* (*b*), *ta* (*t*), *tha* (*th*), *jim* (*ǧ*), *ḥa* (*ḥ*), *kha* (*kh*), *dal* (*d*), *ḍhal* (*ḍh*), *ra* (*r*), *za*(*z*), *sin* (*s*), *shin* (*sh*), *ṣad*(*ṣ*), *ḍad* (*ḍ*), *ta* (*ṭ*), *ẓa* (*ẓ*), *'ayin* ('), *ghain* (*gh*), *fa* (*f*), *qaf* (*q*), *kaf* (*k*), *lam* (*l*), *mim* (*m*), *nun* (*n*), *ha* (*h*), *waw* (*w*), *ya* (*y*). The letters *ṭa*, *kha*, *ḍhal*, *ḍad*, *ẓa* and *ghain* are the specific additions of the Arabic alphabet.

All the letters represent consonants, though three of them (*alif*, *waw* and *ya*) are also used as vowels. To the twenty-eight letters may be added the *hamza* ('), or glottal stop; it is a click produced by a quick compression of the upper part of the throat.

The majority of the letters have different forms in accordance with their position in a word, whether at the beginning, middle or end, and whether they stand alone or joined to others. When single or at the end of a word, the letters, for the most part, terminate in a bold swish; when joined to the following letter this swish is replaced by a small upward curve. On the whole, with the exception of six letters, which can only be joined to preceding, not to following letters, the initial and medial forms are much abbreviated, whereas the final form consists of the initial form and a 'flourish.' However, the essential part of the letters remains unchanged.

Another of the difficulties a beginner meets in the Arabic script is that in manuscripts and elegantly printed books, many of the letters are interwoven with one another, and form beautiful, but not always easily readable ligatures of two or three letters.

Diacritical Points (and Vocalization)

In the vocalized Arabic texts the consonants are provided with a vowel sign (*see* below), or with a sign (called *sukun*), indicating the absence of a vowel. The vowel marks are three in number, and are written above or below the consonant which precedes the vowel. They are used also as terminations of inflection in nouns and the moods of verbs. These signs represent the vowel-sounds corresponding to those of the letters *alif*, *waw* and *ya*, that is the 'weak letters'; and when combined with them, they form the long vowels. Rules for the cases in which these vowel marks retain their original sounds (*a*, *i* and *u*), and for those in which they are modified into *é*, *e*, *i*, *o* or *æ*, do not exist, because the various dialects of the spoken Arabic differ from one another in these points; and besides, owing to the emphasis with which the consonants are uttered, the vowels are in general somewhat indistinctly pronounced.

A peculiar characteristic of the Arabic alphabet is the great number of diacritical points; they are employed either to distinguish certain consonants or to represent vowel-sounds. Their origin is uncertain; some scholars believe that the diacritical marks of the consonants may, at least in a few cases, go back to the Nabatæan script, but there is no evidence for this theory. As to the system of the points and other marks used as vowels, it is commonly admitted that this has been borrowed from the Syriac script.

The earliest Arabic manuscripts extant are purely consonantal, they are also without marks for division of groups of words and for division of single words (breabing up at the end of a line and the beginning of the next; in later manuscripts such breaking of words was avoided). The consonants *alif*, *waw* and *ya* were used to represent the long *a*, *u*, and *i*. In the course of time, subsidiary and inadequate vowel-representation was introduced, consisting in diacritical marks. In some older manuscripts or fragments, little dashes are employed instead of dots. There are also some old Qur'ân manuscripts, in which a very simple diacritical system is used; the vowels are expressed by dots, usually red, one above the consonant for the sounds *a* or *e*, one below, for *i-y*, and one in the middle, or on the line, for *u-o*.

On the other hand, owing to the degeneration of the cursive script, many letters became similar. In order to avoid ambiguities, it became necessary to distinguish some consonants by diacritical points, the *ba*, *ta* and *tha*, the *jim* and the two variatio nsof *kha*, the *dal* and *dhal*, the *ra* and *za*, the *şin* and *shin*, the *şad* and *dad*, the *ţa* and *za*, the *'ayin* and *ghain*.

It is generally admitted that the diacritical points were introduced in Basra in the early eighth century A.D.; the Arabic traditions attribute this innovation either to Yakhya bin Ya'mar or to Naşr bin 'Aşim.

Adaptation of the Arabic Character to Other Languages

The Arabic script, as already mentioned, has been adopted for many forms of speech, belonging to various linguistic families (Figs. 15.28–33); in Europe, particularly for Slavonic (in Bosnia) and for Spanish (*aljamiah*); in Africa, for Berber, Hausa, Swahili, Malagasy, etc.; and especially in Asia, for Persian, Turkish, Hindustani, Pushtu or Afghan, Malay; and for many other languages of the three continents of the Old World.

When the Arabic script was adapted to the requirements of other languages, sometimes letters changed their pronunciation—for instance, the Arabic *ḍ* is pronounced in Persian as *z* and the Arabic *k* as *g* in Turkish—and sometimes new letters were created by employing diacritical marks: in Turkish, *g* and *ñ*; in Persian, Putshu and Urdu, *p*, *ch*, *zh*, and *g*; in Urdu and Pushtu, cerebral *t*, *d* and *r*; in Pushtu only *ts*, *g*, *ṇ*, and *ksh*; in Malay, *ch*, *ng*, *p*, *g*, *ny*, and so forth (*see* also pp. 436 and 439 f.).

For Turkish *see* also pp. 429 and 439 f.; for Urdu *see* p. 284 f.; for Malay *see* pp. 331f.

Pushtu, known also as Pashto, Pakhsto, Pakkhto, etc., is the vernacular of eastern Afghanistan; it is also spoken in Baluchistan. It is an eastern Iranian language. The official language of Afghanistan is Persian, which is also spoken in the western portion of the country—the Persian-speaking Afghans are known as Parsiwans—whereas in northern Afghanistan Turkish is widely spoken.

The following four offshoots of the Aramaic branch are almost extinct: Fig. 15.34.

PALMYRENE ALPHABET

Palmyra, the Semitic Tadmôr, an ancient city in an oasis of the Syrian desert, on the trade route between Syria and Mesopotamia, enjoyed an era of great prosperity in the first and second centuries A.D.

According to Professor Burkitt, 'There is no probability that the Tadmôr (or rather Tamar) mentioned in I Kings ix, 18 was anywhere even in the neighbourhood of Palmyra. It is clearly somewhere south of Judæa.' 'Palmyra is first heard of in 42 B.C., and there is nothing in the existing remains to suggest a much earlier date for the city, though of course semi-nomad Arabs may have had their settlements round the natural wells from time immemorial.' This statement is now superseded by J. Starcky's information that Tadmôr is already referred to in a Cappadocian cunei-form tablet of the early second millennium B.C. and that 'four Palmyrenians' are mentioned in two cuneiform letters from Mari of the eighteenth century B.C. At any rate, Professor Burkitt rightly pointed out that when the Seleucid empire was perishing, the Arabs who lived in the fertile oasis of Palmyra found that the carrying trade between east and west was a very profitable concern. 'So for nearly three hundred years Palmyra grew and prospered. Then came half a century of glory, followed by utter collapse.'

For a short period Palmyra exerted influence as far south-west as Egypt and as far north-west as western Asia Minor, and stood up against the mighty Rome herself. Palmyra was situated between the Roman Empire and the Parthians. In A.D. 226 the Parthian empire came to an end, and its place was taken by the Sasanians. Palmyra took the maximum advantage of the military and political crisis of the third century A.D. Between 265 and 267, its chief, Odenathus or Odainath occupied Syria and Egypt, and became virtually the emperor of the Roman East. His wife, Septimia bath Zabbai or Zenobia was still more famous. Shortly afterwards, however, in 272, Palmyra surrendered to the Romans. After a revolt, Palmyra was destroyed, and, although later it rose from its ruins, 'it never recovered its political or commercial prosperity' (Burkitt).

Palmyrene was originally the cursive script of the Aramaic-writing population of Seleucid Syria in the second and the early first century B.C. It is an elegant and ornamental script in two forms, monumental and cursive (Fig. 15.34, col. 2). J.-B. Chabot distinguished three varieties of the Palmyrene alphabet, the ornamental character, the 'vulgar' hand, and the cursive script, resembling the Syriac writing. J. Cantineau, however, pointed out that the suggested 'vulgar' variety is nothing but a mixture of the other two varieties, as written by uneducated people. On the other hand, Cantineau distinguished two sub-varieties of the ornamental or monumental class: (1) the *écriture arrondie*, commonly employed in the first century A.D., which slowly developed into (2) the *écriture brisée*, employed in the late second century, and until the end of Palmyra.

According to Cantineau, the Palmyrene monumental and cursive scripts originated and were employed contemporaneously, but in Professor Albright's opinion the prototype of the Palmyrene cursive character branched off from the Aramaic script between 250 and 100 B.C., whereas the Palmyrene monumental script developed from the cursive during the first century B.C. The early changes in the Palmyrene scripts consisted primarily in calligraphical details and rather faulty ligatures.

Palmyrene inscriptions have been discovered in Palmyra, Dura-Europos, Palestine, Egypt and in other parts of north Africa, on the site of the ancient Tomi (old Constantza) on the Black Sea, in Hungary, in Italy, and even in England. The Latin-Palmyrene (Fig. 15.35a) bilingual inscription, discovered at South Shields, in the neighbouring Roman camp, is now in the Free Library of South Shields. Its Latin text, runs: D[is] m[anibus] Regina liberta et conjuge (sic!) Barates Palmyrenus natione Cattuallauna an[nis] XXX. Figure 15.35c shows another Palmyrene inscription. The earliest Palmyrene inscription, belonging to the year 44 B.C., was discussed at the XXIst. Intern. Congress of Orientalists (Paris, 1948)—Fig. 15.35b (See now J. Starcky, Palmyre, p. 20). Another early inscription, belonging to the year 33 B.C., was previously discovered at Dura-Europos. The latest inscription, written in the Palmyrene cursive script, is dated A.D. 274, that is only two years after the Roman conquest of the city. The most important Palmyrene epigraphic monument is a Greek-Palmyrene bilingual inscription, dated A.D. 137, and containing the famous 'Palmyrene Tariff,' or law of taxes. With its 162 lines in Palmyrene, it is the second longest North Semitic text. It was discovered in 1881 by Prince S. A. Lazarev. Figure 15.35d represents a Palmyrene inscription from the Fitzwilliam Museum, Cambridge.

SYRIAC SCRIPTS

Syrians

The terms 'Aramæans' and 'Syrians,' 'Aram' and 'Syria,' as already mentioned, are synonymous. The Hebrew *Aram* is rendered in the LXX by 'Syria.' However, the term 'Syriac' conventionally denotes the ancient Semitic language and literature of the 'Syriac Christians,' but the latter term is not synonymous with 'Christian inhabitants of Syria'; it roughly denotes those Christians who employed the Syriac descendant of Aramaic, or were part of the Syriac Church under influence of Syriac thought and Hellenistic culture.

Their Scripts (Fig. 15.34, cols. 3–8)

The early Syriac alphabet (Fig. 15.34, col. 3) was the last important descendant of the Aramaic branch.

The French scholar J. Cantineau considered the Syriac alphabet to be related to the cursive Palmyrene, suggesting that it was influenced by the latter on account of the commercial activities of the Palmyrenians. Rosenthal, however, is probably right in suggesting that the resemblance between the Palmyrene cursive and the Syriac scripts should be explained by their origin from a common source, and by mutual influences. Already Lidzbarski pointed out that the Syriac *Estrangela* did not derive from the cursive Palmyrene, but both were parallel developments.

However, the early Syriac script was an offshoot of a cursive Aramaic writing, perhaps of the Palmyrene cursive in its early stage. The earliest Syriac inscriptions extant belong to the first half of the first century A.D. and to the second half of the second century. Very few inscriptions, however, are earlier than the seventh century A.D. (Fig. 15.36*a*).

The earliest datable Syriac written document is the sepulchral inscription of Ma'nu found near Serrin, and belonging to A.D. 73. Another inscription is dated 513 Seleucid era, that is A.D. 201–202. A contract of sale, written on parchment, and dated from A.D. 243, comes from Dura-Europos: it is the earliest extant document not inscribed on stone, couched in Edessene Syriac and written in Estrangela character (it was published in 1935, by Professor C. C. Torrey).

The earliest dated Syriac MS., of A.D. 411, is 'probably the earliest *dated* codex in any language that is still extant' (Hatch).

The principal development of the Syriac scripts was encouraged by the Syriac Church, especially between the fourth and seventh centuries.

Syriac

Syriac was then the language and script of the extensive Syriac literature, which is a Christian literature in a very special sense, all original documents dealing exclusively with Christian subjects. It is important not to overlook the fact that the city of Antioch of Syria was one of the most important centres of early Christianity; it was there that 'the disciples were called Christians first'; and it remained a great centre of Christian doctrine through the centuries 'till Moslem conquest swept it within the new orbit of Islam.' The influence of Antioch on the Orontes extended to the north-west over Cilicia and Cappadocia in Asia Minor; to the east, through Syria proper, into regions beyond the Roman frontiers: north Mesopotamia, Persia, Armenia and even Georgia. Antioch, however, although the chief town of Syria, was a centre of Greek culture.

Edessa, in north-western Mesopotamia was the first centre of Christianity in the Syriac-speaking world, and it became its principal *focus*. In fact, it was the only centre of early Christian life where the language of the Christian community was other than Greek. Here, the native Aramaic or Syriac dialect had already been used for some time as a literary language even before Christianity acquired power in the country. Edessa (called in Syriac Ur-hai, now Urfa) was then the capital of Osrhoëne (a Greek name, derived from Ur-hai), a small kingdom east of the Euphrates. In A.D. 216, this kingdom lost its independence to the Roman Empire. Christianity was preached in Edessa already in the second century, and the city became the Christian metropolis of East Syria. From Edessa the Christian faith spread to Persia. The Aramæan Christians of the neighbouring countries, even those who lived in Persia, adopted the Edessan Syriac as the language of the Church, of literature, and of cultivated intercourse. At the same time, this dialect was the medium of commerce in the valley of the Euphrates and was used far and wide as a *lingua franca*. It became, thus, the most important of the Syriac dialects, and, after Greek, the most important language in the eastern Roman Empire.

In the third century, the city was the stronghold of Syrian national Christianity; here the scriptures were translated into Aramaic or 'Syriac,' which 'now took its place, beside Greek, in Christian literature; here, and at Nisibis (about 120 miles almost due east from Edessa) not far away, were schools of theology, the influence of which in later times extended far through the Christian world' (Wright). The most important Syriac literary monument is the *Peshito* or *Peshitta* ('pure, simple'), a standardized but faithful Syriac version of the Bible which was composed about A.D. 200.

As Wright, the great authority on Syriac, pointed out, 'with the seventh century begins the slow decay of the native literature of the Syrians, which was promoted partly by the frightful sufferings of the people during the great war with the Persians in its first quarter, and partly by the Arab conquest of Persia.'

When Syriac became extinct in Edessa and its neighbourhood is not known with certainty. From the seventh century onwards, Arabic everywhere put a speedy end to it, though Syriac has remained in use for liturgical purposes, and until recently it was still spoken in a few villages near Damascus and in the Lebanon by some 'Assyrians' (*see* below).

However, some Syrians were able to come to terms with the invaders, and for five centuries were a recognized institution within the territory of Islām. But the Mongolian invasions of the thirteenth and fourteenth centuries 'fell with crushing force on the Nestorians.' About 1400, 'Those who escaped capture by Timur fled to the mountains of Kurdistan, and the community that had played so large a part in Mesopotamian history for a thousand years was thus shattered.'

Christian Palestinian or Palestinian Syriac

The Palestinian Christian community was remarkable for several reasons. According to some scholars, this Church consisted originally of Jews and Samaritans whom the Roman emperors of the fifth and sixth centuries, and particularly Justinian, compelled to become Christians. According to Schulthess, this community originated in the sixth century, formed for themselves a literature 'out of their peasant Palestinian Syriac dialect,' but M. Black rightly points out that for several centuries previous to the establishment of the Palestinian Melkite Church (*see* below), there existed already a Palestinian Aramaic literature among the Jews and a literary activity among the Samaritans. Thus, Palestinian Aramaic or Syriac already enjoyed the position of a literary language.

Q

However, the terms 'Christian Palestinian' or 'Palestinian Syriac' denote the Christian literature written not in 'classical' or Edessene Syriac, but in the vernacular dialect of Palestine, that is the indigenous language of Palestine in the time of Jesus Christ. The written documents consist almost exclusively of liturgical manuscripts, all of them being translations from Greek originals. There are a couple or so of sepulchral inscriptions. The manuscripts, preserved mainly in palimpsests (that is manuscripts which have been effaced and used for fresh writings), show that the literature was never extensive. The earliest manuscripts seem to belong to the ninth century A.D., while the dialect was, at least since A.D. 700, replaced by Arabic as the speech of daily life, remaining for some centuries more the liturgical language. Furthermore, as F. Schulthess pointed out, the manuscripts belonging to the eleventh-thirteenth centuries show that even the clergy did not have a sufficient knowledge of the language.

Only two places are known where the Palestinian Syrians were settled, 'Abud, a large village to the north-west of Jerusalem, and somewhere in Egypt. The fragments of the Palestinian Syriac manuscripts come from the libraries of Sinai monks.

The Palestinian Syriac community was the only one Aramaic-speaking Christian group who remained "Melkite" (*see* below), while all the other communities were either Nestorian, Monophysite or Maronite.

SYRIAC ALPHABET (Fig. 15.34, cols. 3–8)

The Syriac alphabet consists (like the Aramaic) of the twenty-two old Semitic letters, all of them having consonantal values. The order of the letters in the alphabet is the same as in Hebrew, but the names of some of them are slightly different: *alaph* for *aleph*, *gamal* for *gimel*, *dalath* or *daladh* for *daleth*, *lamadh* for *lamedh*, *mim* for *mem*; the names of the letters *samek* and *'ayin* have changed into *semkath* and *'e*. The pronunciation of the names of some of these letters was modified in the later West Syrian or Jacobite alphabet: *olaph*, *gomal*, *dolath* or *doladh*, *lomad*; also the names of other letters were changed: *yodh* in *yudh*, *nun* in *non*, *tsadhe* or *ṣadhe* (the emphatic *ṣ*) in *ṣodhe*, *resh* in *rish*.

The letters *b, g, d, k, p, t* had a twofold pronunciation: one being hard (corresponding to the English *b, g, d, k, p, t*); the other, soft, aspirated or sibilated (*v, gh, dh* or *th* as in 'the,' *kh* as the Scotch *ch*, *ph*, and *th* as in 'thank').

As in the Arabic alphabet, the majority of the Syriac letters have different forms in accordance with their position in a word, whether at the beginning, middle or end, and whether they stand alone or joined to others, on right or on left, or on both sides, right and left. Eight letters (', *d, h, w, z, ṣ, r* and *t*) have only two forms, the unconnected, and the connected on right.

Vocalization

As in other Semitic languages, the consonants ', *w* and *y* were originally employed to express vowel sounds. The ' expressed every final long *a* (pronounced as long *o* by the

Jacobites) and *e*, and sometimes the long *e* within the word. (The long *e* was in certain cases pronounced as long *i* by the Jacobites). The *w* denoted any long or short *u* or *o*. The *γ* expressed any long *i*, and sometimes a long *e* in the middle of a word. The letters *w* and *γ* denote the diphthongs *au, ai, iu* and *eu* (with long *i* or *e*). In the transcription of Greek words, the *a* was denoted by '; the *i* in the middle of a word was often expressed by *γ*; the *o* was often omitted, etc.; on the whole, the transcription of the vowels in Greek words fluctuated.

The insufficiency of such a fluctuating representation of vowel sounds in the transcription of Greek words (especially for theological purposes), on the one hand, and, at a later period, the fact that in the seventh century A.D. Arabic replaced Syriac as the language of daily life, were the main reasons for the introduction of fixed forms of vocalic distinction. At first, diacritical points were used. The single point above or below a letter was employed to mark the stronger or the weaker pronunciation respectively; farther, a second or third point was often added to distinguish more exactly between verbal forms in particular.

On the whole, three main vowel-systems developed: (1) The earliest, but less complete, was the Nestorian system; it consisted partly of a combination of the consonants *w* and *γ* and the dot placed above it or below it, and partly of one or two dots placed above or, mainly, below the consonant to be vocalized. (2) The Jacobite system of vocalization, created about A.D. 700 was more complete. It consisted of small Greek letters placed above or below the line. (3) The late *Serta* or West Syrian system, consisting of a combination of the diacritical vowel marks and the small Greek letters.

Punctuation
The system of punctuation consisted mainly of two, three or four dots, differently grouped.

Direction of Writing
Like other Semitic alphabetic scripts, the Syriac scripts read horizontally, from right to left. There are, however, some written documents, in which the letters are on their sides, showing that though read horizontally, the lines were written downwards. Vertical direction in the Nestorian script from at least the eighth to the fourteenth century, was already noticed in 1890, by D. Chwolson, but this practice was probably much older. Indications of it may be seen in an inscription from about A.D. 500, discovered in 1862 in Dehes, and in the famous trilingual inscription from Zabad (*see* p. 211). It also seems to appear in early Syriac inscriptions and in cursive Palmyrene inscriptions.

Some derivative scripts were even read downwards.

VARIETIES OF SYRIAC SCRIPTS

Estrangela and its Descendants
The most important variety of the Syriac scripts is *Estrangelo* or *Estrangela*. The term derived perhaps from *satar angelo*, the 'evangelical' writing, or else from the Greek

strongyle, the 'round (script).' Estrangela was employed almost exclusively until about the middle of the first millennium. Two styles of writing can be distinguished: (1) a very beautiful current hand, known as *majusculæ*, which appears in the early manuscripts—the earliest belonging to the fourth and fifth centuries A.D.; and (2) the lapidary style, which is known from some early inscriptions of Edessa (Fig. 15.36*a*).

After the Council of Ephesus (A.D. 431) and the schism in the Church (*see* below), the Syriac language and script split into two branches. Of these, the western, termed *Serta* or *Serto*, 'linear' (Fig. 15.36*b*), is the less important. This developed later into two varieties, the 'Jacobite' and the 'Melkite.' A particular characteristic of the western branch is its vocalization which, as mentioned, consists of small Greek letters added above or below the Syriac letters.

The eastern Syriac branch, called Nestorian, had greater importance in the history of writing.

Figures 15.36*d* and 37–41 represent some of the more famous Syriac manuscripts.

'ALPHABET FOLLOWS RELIGION'

(*See* also under *Arabic Script* and the next chapter.)

The splitting up of the Syriac alphabet into the various secondary branches was a direct result of the religious and political situation of eastern Christianity.

Eastern Christendom is riddled with sects, 'heresies' and schisms, but nearly all spring from the two great 'heresies' of the fifth century, Nestorianism, condemned by the Council of Ephesus, in 431, and its extreme opposite, Monophysism, condemned by the Council of Chalcedon, in 451.

Nestorians

Nestorius was not the founder of the 'Nestorian' Church. The term 'Nestorians' is a 'nickname' given to this Christian community, which had been in existence long before Nestorius was born. Nestorius was a Greek, born and reared in the Byzantine Empire, educated at Antioch, and in A.D. 428 created Patriarch of Constantinople. The eastern Church was called 'Nestorian,' because Nestorius himself supposedly held the same Christological beliefs as the Christian refugees to Persia who were condemned as 'heretics' and banished from the Roman Empire.

However, the Nestorian Church asserted that it was possible to distinguish the two persons as well as the two natures in Christ, as opposed to the western Christian doctrine of the Incarnation. After the secession of the Nestorian Church from the Imperial Orthodox Church of Byzantium, the Nestorian faith became the official religion of the then flourishing Persian Church.

The tension between the opposing parties became so great that it shook the very foundations of the Church throughout the Christian world; it widened the breach between East and West and ultimately caused the decline of Christianity in the East.

'The coincidence of the opening of the trade routes into Further Asia with the ascendancy of the Nestorian Church offered a ready outlet for missionary effort. The Nestorians eagerly seized this opportunity. Marco Polo tells us that in his times the trade routes from Baghdad to Peking were lined with Nestorian chapels. In 1265, there were twenty-five Asiatic provinces, with seventy bishoprics.'

The extremely active Nestorian missionaries carried their teachings, their language and their script into the Kurdistan highlands, into southern India (where in some parts Syriac is still employed as the liturgical language of a few Christian groups), into Turkestan (where they influenced the Sogdians: *see* the next chapter); amongst the Turki and Mongol tribes of central Asia, and into China, where a Nestorian mission arrived in 635, as attested by the Nestorian-Chinese inscription of 781, preserved in the great historic city of Hsi-an-fu, former capital of the Middle Kingdom.

This important monument is ten feet high by three and a third feet in width and a little under a foot thick, and weighs two tons. The inscription consists of nearly 1,900 Chinese characters and about seventy Syriac words, besides many Syriac names in rows on the narrow sides of the monument with the corresponding Chinese characters. The inscription was excavated in A.D. 1623, in the district of Chou-Chih. *See* particularly P. V. Saeki, *The Nestorian Documents and Relics in China*, Tokyo (The Academy of Oriental Culture. Tokyo Institute), 1937. According to the author of that book, the immigration of great Nestorian families into the Chinese territory took place as early as A.D. 578. *See* also A. C. Moule, *Christians in China before the year 1550*, London, 1930.

One can gather some idea of the extent of Nestorian influence in China from the Imperial Edict promulgated in 845.

Gradually all the activities of the Nestorian missions ceased and nothing remained to tell the tale except the numerous sepulchral and other inscriptions and written documents in various parts of central Asia and in south-western India.

'Mongolian invasions and Mohammedan tyranny have, of course, long since swept away all traces of many' of the Nestorian monuments and written documents.

'It was in 1885 that some Russian explorers first came into contact with two Nestorian cemeteries of the thirteenth and fourteenth centuries in the Russian province of Semiryechensk in South Siberia, or Russian Turkestan, near the towns of Pishpek and Tokmak. So far as I can ascertain, more than six hundred and thirty gravestones bearing Syriac inscriptions have since that year been either photographed or brought into the important museums of Europe, chiefly into Russia' (A. Mingana, 'The Early Spread of Christianity in Central Asia and the Far East,' etc., *Bull. of the John Rylands Library*, 1925 and 1930).

'Assyrians'

The 'Assyrians,' who were in the news some years ago because of their persecution by the Moslems, and who live in Kurdistan and in the district of Mosul under a religious head, known as the 'catholicos,' are the only exponents of this once flourishing faith. In the course of centuries, groups of 'Assyrians' gravitated from northern

Mesopotamia to the highlands of Kurdistan, where they developed a semi-autonomy, owing allegiance only to their *maliks*. In the latter half of the sixteenth century, the Assyrians of the district of Mosul separated from those of Kurdistan, and formed the *Mar Elia* ('Lord Elias') or Church of the Plains (in opposition to the *Mar Shimun*, 'Lord Simon,' or Church of the Mountains); *c.* 1700, they became subservient to the Catholic Church, and later became known as the 'Chaldæan Uniate Church,' that is to say, a Church acknowledging the sovereignty of the Pope, whilst at the same time adhering to its own rituals. The estimated number of 'Chaldæans' is about 100,000, of whom about 85,000 are in Iraq. The downfall of the remnants of the 'Assyrians' commenced during the first world war and culminated in mass slaughter by the Iraq Army in 1933.

'Confined at last to their mountain fastnesses, the little remnant continue steadfast in the faith. Trial, suffering, abundant opportunity to prosper through apostasy has left them unshaken' (Bishop J. G. Murray).

Jacobites

In the first half of the fifth century, a new direction was given to the Christological controversy by the teaching of Eutyches, which led eventually to *Monophysitism*, that is the doctrine (extreme opposite to that of the Nestorians), holding that Christ had but one (*mónos*) composite *nature* (*physis*). About the middle of the fifth century, James from Tella (55 miles east of Edessa), known as Jacob Baradæus (al-Barada'i, meaning the man wearing a horse-cloth), became Bishop of Edessa. He reorganized the Monophysite Church, ordaining priests and consecrating bishops. It is after him that the term 'Jacobites'—first found in a synodal decree of Nicæa, A.D. 781—was given by hostile Greeks to the Syrian monophysists, whose official designation is 'Syrian Orthodox.' They are also known as West Syrians ('East Syrians' being another term for 'Nestorians').

The condemnation of the Monophysite 'heresy' was even a greater and more disastrous event than that of the Nestorian 'heresy.' The Churches of Egypt (*see* under Copts), Syria, and Abyssinia were Monophysite. The Roman Empire could get rid of the Nestorians, but it was not so easy to get rid of the Monophysites. The excommunication and persecution of the Monophysites, aimed at the consolidation and the unification of the complex races of the East and their remoulding into a united empire, only resulted in strengthening the feeling of violent antagonism to the Empire and its rulers. The predominant feeling of the Syrian and Egyptian Christians (both the Nestorians and Monophysites) at the Arab invasion appears to have been a sense of relief that they were now able to practise their religion unhindered by the persecution of the Roman emperors. It is quite obvious that such feeling largely facilitated the rapid and easy victory of Islām in Syria and Egypt. However, in the Middle Ages there were 150 Jacobite archbishops and bishops; about the middle of last century the total number of the Jacobites dwindled to about 100,000.

Melkites

After the Council of Ephesus, nearly the whole of the eastern part of the Antioch patriarchate remained Nestorian; after the Council of Chalcedon, the 'orthodox' bishop lost nearly all his sheep. The small community which carried on, in union with Constantinople and, until the great schism, with Rome, adhered to the doctrine supported by the authority of the emperor and thus accepted the decrees of Ephesus and Chalcedon. To this community the Jacobites gave the nickname 'Melkite' or 'Malkite' (Syriac *malka*, Arabic *malik*, Hebrew *melek* = 'king'), meaning 'the king's men,' 'royalists' or 'imperialists': the Semitic word for 'king,' like the Greek *basileús*, also denotes the 'emperor.'

The Melkites mainly used Greek, although there was also a Melkite liturgy in the aforementioned Palestinian Syriac. However, as the Melkite Patriarchate became more and more dependent on Constantinople, it began to use the Byzantine rite.

DEVELOPMENT OF NESTORIAN, JACOBITE AND MELKITE SCRIPTS

The political separation between the East Syrians (Nestorians) and West Syrians (Jacobites and Melkites) and the exclusiveness and mutual hatred of the various communities, produced divergences between the liturgies and traditions of the various schools. The local dialects had also some influence over the pronunciation of the liturgical tongue. However, the changes in the derivative scripts are not great; the phonetic values of the letters remain the same, and their shapes change only in some minor details, that is in the style of writing (Fig. 15.34, cols. 5–8).

Strangely enough the Jacobite style (Figs. 15.34, col. 7; 36c) is further removed from the Estrangela than the Nestorian, and is also less graceful than the latter (Figs. 15.34, col. 6; 36b). The main differences between the various scripts consist in the vocalization, which has already been dealt with. On the whole, the Nestorian system is more complicated, but more accurate. Nestorian manuscripts, particularly those of later origin, are often fully vocalised, and the method of distinguishing consonants by means of diacritical points is largely employed. In other manuscripts this system is used only in very careful writing.

Already J. P. N. Land, in 1862, distinguished three main varieties in the styles of writing of the Syriac manuscripts:

(1) The aforementioned majusculae, known as *Estrangela* (Fig. 15.34, col. 4).

(2) The minusculae, developed out of the majusculae in the sixth century, and used mainly after 700; it corresponds with the *Serta* or *Serto* of the Jacobites (Fig. 15.34, col. 5).

(3) A variety of the minusculae, strongly influenced by the majusculae, was also used by the Jacobites; it is termed by Land semi-minusculae (Fig. 15.34, col. 7).

After the middle of the ninth century the changes in the Jacobite manuscripts are very slight, and the dating of the manuscripts on pure palæographical grounds becomes very difficult.

The Melkite script—more properly called Christian Palestinian or Palestinian Syriac (Fig. 15.34, col. 8)—has some characteristics which are not found in other Syriac scripts.

Two varieties can be distinguished: (1) a kind of Uncial Melkite, of the lapidary, inscriptional type. Nöldeke called it 'stiff and angular' or 'thick and coarse.' Schulthess termed it 'coarse, angular, and lapidary.' The ligatures are more frequent than in other Syriac scripts. A new letter (the 23rd) was added, having the shape of an inverted *pe*, and thus known as *P inversum*, with the numerical value of 90; it was employed to denote the Greek explosive *p*. (2) The late Palestinian Syriac MSS., belonging to the eleventh-fourteenth centuries, are written in a more cursive style; it is a square-formed, rather ugly type of writing and not easy to read. Of all the Syriac varieties, it is farthest removed from the original Estrangela.

The origin of the peculiar ductus of the Palestinian Syriac character has been hotly disputed. Land saw in it an imitation of the Greek uncial script; Duval, who regarded the Syriac script as a direct descendant of the Palmyrene, considered the Melkite *ductus* as a 'vestige' of the earliest Syriac character, and saw in it a special resemblance to Palmyrene letters. Kokovtsov suggested the influence of the square Hebrew character of the fourth-fifth century A.D. Schulthess suggested influences from the use of the script for liturgical purposes, and/or influences from the uncial style of writing of the Greek lectionaries used as models. The last suggestion seems to be the most probable.

Neo-Syrian Character

About 1840 the American Protestant missionaries, headed by J. Perkins, reduced to writing the east Syrian or neo-Aramaic dialect still spoken in and around Urmia or Urumiyah (now Rezaieh) on Lake Urmia, near Tabriz, in the Persian Azerbaijan province. They adopted the old Nestorian character. In Urmia they founded the first printing press. In 1886 they were followed by the Assyrian Mission of the Archbishop of Canterbury, headed by A. J. Maclean. See A. J. Maclean, *Grammar of the Dialects of Vernacular Syriac*, etc. Cambridge, 1895; *A Dictionary of the Dialects of Vernacular Syriac*, etc., Oxford, 1901.

Two Catholic missions, of the Lazarists and the Dominicans, reduced to writing respectively the dialects spoken in the Plain of Salamas and in the Plain of Mosul; *see* J. Rhétoré, *Grammaire de la Langue Soureth*, etc., Mosul, 1912.

Still more recently, a periodical paper in 'Assyrian' was published in Tiflis.

GARSHUNI

When Arabic became the speech of daily life, it was sometimes written in Syriac script; the term for it is *karshuni* or rather *garshuni*, but its meaning is uncertain.

The system of transliteration was not constant. In the manuscript of the *Liturgy of the Nile* (Brit. Mus., Or. 4951), 'Karshuni is employed in several of the headings, but chiefly, though not exclusively, in the rubrical directions' (Black). It may be noted as follows: *tha* is expressed by pointed *t*; *kha* by *k* with two points above it; *dal* by *d* and *dhal* by pointed *d*; *ra* by *r* with two points instead of one, *za* by *teth* marked by two points, ' by *'E*, sometimes pointed, *ghain* by *g* marked by two points. Long *a* is usually represented by *aleph*, the short *y* and *w* are sometimes denoted by *y* or *w* respectively, written within the word alongside the consonants. According to M. Black, this system of transliteration is not always strictly adhered to.

On the whole, 'The letters lacking in the Syriac alphabet were supplied by pointing those already in existence, but in doing this more attention was paid to the sound than the shape of the Arabic letter.' 'Vowels are placed sometimes in the Syriac and sometimes in the Arabic way' (C. Brockelmann).

GREEK IN SYRIAC SCRIPT

In the aforementioned *Liturgy of the Nile*, Greek is also employed, transcribed into the Melkite cursive character. As M. Black points out, 'The Greek presents a strange appearance in its foreign dress.' Margoliouth already noted the 'barbarous nature of the Syriac transcriptions,' but Black points out that 'some kind of a system has been followed in transcribing the Greek. However, there is a great confusion in the transcription of the vowels, and an uncertainty in the transcriptions of *b-p*, *s*, *t*, *kh*, *p* ', and so forth.

MANDÆAN ALPHABET (Fig. 15.34, col. 9)

The Mandæans (the indigenous term is Mendai; the Moslems call them Sabi'un, Sabba or Subba; other terms are Nazaræans or Nasurai, Galileans or Christians of St. John), are a gnostic pagan-Jewish-Christian sect. They are probably of Syriac origin, but they have lived in Babylonia since ancient times. According to Theodore bar Koni's (eighth century A.D.) and an-Nadim's (tenth century) statements, the Mandæans derived from older sects, including that of the Baptist Dositæans. In F. C. Burkitt's opinion, the sect arose in southern Mesopotamia about the fifth century A.D. under Dositæan, Marcionite and Manichæan influences. However, it is now more or less agreed that the Mandæan system originated in Mesopotamia in the latter part of the first half of the first millennium A.D., and that the Mandæan religious writings were completed before the seventh century. The Mandæan speech, now purposely archaic and highly symbolic, is an eastern Aramaic dialect very closely related to Babylonian Aramaic, but is influenced by the neighbouring Persian and Arabic languages and dialects. Its orthography is late in type (not earlier than A.D. 500) and there is a confusion of laryngals even in the earliest inscriptions.

Nowadays, the Mandæans are almost extinct; according to the 1932 census, they numbered then 4,805. Only a few villages remain in the marshes near the junction of the Tigris and the Euphrates.

Very few inscriptions have survived. Some are on lead and some (magic texts) inside earthen bowls, of the seventh and eighth centuries A.D. According to Albright, the oldest Mandæan inscriptions can hardly antedate the sixth century; thus, a lead amulet dated by Lidzbarski to *c.* 400 A.D., would probably belong to 'a date a century or more later.' There are many Mandæan manuscripts (consisting of magical, astrological, ritual and liturgical writings) in the British Museum, in Oxford, Paris, Berlin and in the Vatican, belonging mainly to the seventeenth, eighteenth and nineteenth centuries A.D., the oldest in Europe being of the sixteenth century A.D.

The chief work is the post-Islamic *Book of Adam* (also called *Ginzâ,* 'treasure,' or *Sidra rabba,* the 'Great Book'), a mass of extravagant ravings. The priesthood is hereditary, and until recent times the priests alone had access to the ancient secret codices containing the interesting Mandæan prayers. Mandæan is the most corrupt of all Aramaic dialects and its script (Fig. 15.34, col. 8) also differs very much from the other members of the Aramaic branch.

The Mandæans look upon their alphabet as magic and sacred. Lady Drower (formerly Miss E. S. Stevens), an authority on the subject, says that 'the marsh people go to the Mandæan priests for charms written either in Arabic or Mandaic. The latter, being in an unknown language and script, are thought very potent. . . . Large sums of money are paid for such writings.' The Mandæans call their alphabet *abaga*; the verb *abaga* means also 'he read a spell.' Writing is patronized by the planet Nbu. Lady Drower points out that according to the Mandæans, each letter represents a power of life and light, and that the first and last letters, in the form of a small circle, are the same and represent perfection of light and life. 'Letters of the alphabet, inscribed on twenty-four scraps of silver or gold, are placed under the pillow of a person who desires heavenly guidance in some matter of difficulty.'

The origin of this alphabet is uncertain. Two of the greatest authorities on North Semitic epigraphy, Nöldeke and Lidzbarski, pointed out the likeness of the Mandæan and Nabatæan scripts, but according to Rosenthal, the main resemblance lies in the letter *aleph,* and it might have depended not on a direct connection between the two scripts but on their parallel development from the Aramaic alphabet.

In my opinion, the Mandæan script might have descended from a cursive Aramaic script similar to that which was the parent of the Nabatæan, but influenced by the Syriac script. The Mandæan vocalization is interesting; *e.g.,* the consonants *alef, waw* and *yod,* abbreviated, became vowels and are added as appendages to the consonants. The Mandæan alphabet has thus become in practice a syllabary similar to the Ethiopic script.

MANICHÆAN ALPHABET (Fig. 15.34, col. 10)

Mani, known in the Christian literature as Manes or Manichæus (born about A.D. 215 in Babylonia, of Persian parentage, and probably crucified about 273), founded in 247 the religion known as Manichæan, which for a millennium (from the third to the thirteenth century A.D.) was one of the most widely disseminated throughout the world. At the end of the third and during the fourth century it spread through western Asia, southern Europe, northern Africa (St. Augustine was for nine years a follower of Manichæism), Gaul and Spain, but by the seventh century it was already practically extinct in these regions. Manichæism is essentially gnostic and developed a magnificent cosmogony and philosophy of history. Typologically it belongs to the highest religions of mankind.

On the other hand, it was carried into eastern Turkestan during the fourth century and into China at the end of the sixth century, and greatly enlarged its influence in the latter country during the seventh and eighth centuries. When the kings of the Turkish Uighurs (see the next chapter) adopted the Manichæan faith in 762, it became the official religion of that powerful empire. Even after the Uighur empire came to an end in 840, Manichæism continued to hold its own in the successor states until about the thirteenth century. In some parts of China it continued to have adherents, but later it completely disappeared. Generally speaking, the Uighur empire was the only territory where Manichæism had been favoured and not persecuted. Before the middle of the present millennium it had been utterly exterminated through the repressive measures of Christians, Mohammedans and Chinese alike.

Mani and his followers employed a clear, legible and very beautiful script known as the Manichæan alphabet (Fig. 15.34, col. 10). A few inscriptions of magic texts on earthenware bowls are extant, but much more important are the Manichæan manuscripts—of which many fragments have been found in ancient convents in eastern Turkestan—and which are beautifully written on excellent paper in various coloured inks and are ornamented with surprisingly beautiful miniatures. These manuscripts are in different languages, especially in a number of Iranian dialects and in early Turki.

The origin of the Manichæan script is uncertain. It was considered by the adversaries of Manichæism to have been a secret script invented by Mani himself. This was obviously incorrect. It seems to have descended from a regional cursive variety of the Aramaic scripts, similar to the Palmyrene cursive and the parent script of the Estrangela, but it should be remembered that Mani was a great artist and undoubtedly contributed greatly to the standardization of the Manichæan alphabet. P. Kokovtsov, in 1909, and J. A. Montgomery, in 1913, recognized the relationship between the Palmyrene cursive and the Manichæan script.

BIBLIOGRAPHY

WRIGHT, W. *Facsimiles of Manuscripts and Inscriptions*, London, 1875–83; *A Short History of Syriac Literature*, London, 1894.

NÖLDEKE, TH. *Mandäische Grammatik*, etc., Halle, 1875; *Kurzgefasste syrische Grammatik*, 2nd ed., Leipsic, 1898; *Beiträge sur semitischen Sprachwissenschaft*, and *Neue Beiträge*, etc., Strasbourg, 1904 and 1910.

CHWOLSON, D. A. (Khvolson), *Corpus Inscriptionum Hebraicarum*, etc., St. Petersburg, 1882; *Syrisch-nestorianische Grabinschriften*, etc., St. Petersburg, 1897.

EUTING, J. *Nabatäische Inschriften aus Arabien*, Berlin, 1885; *Sinaitische Inschriften*, Berlin, 1891.

NEUBAUER, A. *Facsimiles of Hebrew Manuscripts in the Bodleian Library*, Oxford, 1886.

Corpus Inscriptionum Semiticarum, Part 2, *Inscriptiones Aramaicas Continens*, Paris, 1888 onwards.

MÜLLER, D. H. 'Palmyrenica aus dem Britischen Museum,' *Vienna Oriental Journal*, 1892 and 1894.

COOK, S. A. *Glossary of the Aramaic Inscriptions*, Cambridge, 1898; 'A Pre-Masoretic Biblical Papyrus,' *Proceedings of Biblical Archæology*, 1903.

BROCKELMANN, C. *Geschichte der arabischen Literatur*, 5 vols., Weimar, etc., 1898–1942; *Syrische Grammatik*, 4th ed., Berlin, 1925; *Lexicon Syriacum*, 2nd ed., Halle, 1928; *Geschichte der islamischen Völker und Sprachen*, Munich and Berlin, 1939.

POGNON, H. *Inscriptions mandaïtes des coupes de Khouabir*, Paris, 1898–9.

MARGOLIOUTH, G. *Descriptive List of Syriac and Karshunic MSS.*, etc., London, 1899.

BURKITT, F. C. in *The Journal of Theological Studies*, 1901 and 1923; *The Religion of the Manichees*, Cambridge, 1925; *Petra and Palmyra* (*The Schweich Lectures*, The British Academy), London, 1926.

LITTMANN, E. *Semitic Inscriptions*, New York, 1905; 'Nabatäisch-griechische Bilinguen,' *Florilegium Melchior de Vogué*, Paris, 1909; *Semitic Inscriptions*, Leyden, 1914; *Syriac Inscriptions*, Princeton, N.J., 1934.

PORTER, H. and TORREY, C. C. in *Amer. J. Semit. Langu.*, 1906.

JAUSSEN, A. and SAVIGNAC, R. *Mission archéologique en Arabie*, I, Paris, 1909; II, Paris, 1914.

SCHIFFER, S. *Die Aramäer*, Leipsic, 1911.

SACHAU, E. *Aramäische Papyrus und Ostraka*, etc., Leipsic, 1911.

DELAPORTE, L. *Épigraphes araméens*, Paris, 1912.

MONTGOMERY, J. A. *Aramaic Incantation Texts*, Philadelphia, 1913.

MORITZ, B. *Syrische Inschriften*, Leipsic, 1913; 'Arabic Writing,' *The Encyl. of Islam*, Leyden and London, 1913, pp. 381–3 (bibliography).

KAHLE, P. 'Masoreten des Ostens' and 'Masoreten des Westens,' *Beiträge zur Wissenschaft vom Alten und Neuen Testament*, 1913, 1927 and 1930; 'Die hebräischen Bibelhandschriften aus Babylon,' *Zeitschrift für die Alttestamentliche Wissenschaft*, 1928; *The Cairo Genizah* (*The Schweich Lectures*, The British Academy), London, 1947.

TISSERANT, E. *Specimina codicum orientalium*, Bonn, 1914.

TORREY, C. C. in *J. Amer. Orient. Soc.*, 1915.

BARNETT, L. D. and COWLEY, A. E. in *J. Roy. Asiatic Soc.*, 1915.

LIDZBARSKI, M. 'Die Herkunft der manichäischen Schrift,' *Sitzungsb. d. Preuss. Akad. d. Wissensch.*, 1916; *Mandäische Liturgien*, Leipsic, 1920; *Altaramäische Urkunden aus Assur*, Leipsic, 1921; *Ginza, der Schatz oder das grosse Buch der Mandäer*, Göttingen–Leipsic, 1925.

KRÆLING, E. G. H. *Aram and Israel*, etc., New York, 1918; 'The Origin and the Antiquity of the Mandæans,' *Amer. Orient. Soc.*, 1929.

ALFARIC, P. *Les écritures manichéennes*, 2 vols., Paris, 1918–9.

KLEIN, S. *Jüdisch-palästinisches Corpus Inscriptionum*, Vienna, 1920.

BAUMSTARK, A. *Geschichte der syrischen Literatur*, Bonn, 1922.

BHABOT, J.-B. *Choix d'inscriptions de Palmyre*, etc., Paris, 1922; *Littérature syriaque*, Paris, 1934.

COWLEY, A. E. *Aramaic Papyri of the Fifth Century B.C.*, Oxford, 1923.

LE COQ, A. *Die manichäischen Miniaturen*, Berlin, 1923.

BANG, W. 'Manichäische Laien-Beichtspiegel,' *Le Muséon*, 1923.

BERNHEIMER, C. *Paleografia ebraica*, Leghorn, 1924.

LAGRANGE, M.-J. 'L'origin de la version syro-palestinienne des Évangiles,' *Revue Biblique*, 1925.

BAUER, H. and LEANDER, P. *Grammatik des Biblisch-Aramäischen*, Halle, 1926.

BAUER, TH. *Die Ostkananäer*, Leipsic, 1926.

INGHOLT, H. *Studier over Palmyrensk Skulptur*, Copenhagen, 1928.

TIXERONT, J. *Histoire des dogmes dans l'antiquité chrétienne*, Paris, 1928.

WAGENAAR, C. G. *De joodsche Kolonie van Jeb-Syene*, Groningen, 1928.

ROWLEY, H. H. *The Aramaic of the Old Testament*, London, 1929.

FORRER, E. 'Aramu,' *Reallex. für Assyriologie*, 1929.

CANTINEAU, J. *Le nabatéen*, 2 vols., Paris, 1930–2; *Grammaire du palmyrénien épigraphique*, Cairo, 1935; *Inventaire des inscriptions de Palmyre*, Paris, 1939.

JACKSON, A. V. W. *Researches in Manichæism*, etc., New York, 1932.

GINSBERG, H. L. 'Aramaic Dialect Problems,' *Amer. J. Semitic Languages*, 1933–4.

EL-HAWARY, H. M. 'The Most Ancient Islamic Monument Known Dated A.H.31 (A.D.652),' *Journal Asiatique*, 1930.

COMBE, E., SAUVAGET, J. and WIET, G. *Répertoire chronologique d'épigraphie arabe*, Cairo, 1931 onwards.

PALLIS, S. A. *Essay on Mandaic Bibliography*, London–Copenhagen, 1933.

SCHLIER, H. 'Zur Mandäerfrage,' *Theologische Rundschau*, 1933.

GROHMANN, A. *Arabic Papyri in the Egyptian Library*, 3 vols., Cairo, 1934, 1936 and 1938 (in preparation, *Einfüehrung und Chrestomathie zur arabischen Papyruskunde*, Vol. XII of the Monographs of the Archiv Orientální, Prague).

MESSINA, G. *L'aramaico antico*, Rome, 1934.

DROWER, E. S. 'Mandæan Writings,' *Iraq*, London, 1934; *The Mandæans of Iraq and Iran*, Oxford, 1934; 'A Mandæan Phylactery,' *Iraq*, 1938; *The Canonical Prayerbook of the Mandæans*.

POLOTSKY, H. J. *Abriss des manichäischen Systems*; and *Manichäische Homilien*, Stuttgart, 1934.

NYBERG, H. S. 'Forschungen über den Manichäismus,' *Zeitschrift für die Neutestamentliche Wissenschaft*, 1935.

SUKENIK, E. L. *The Ancient Synagogue of el-Hammeh*, Jerusalem, 1935.

YAHYA NAMI, KH. 'The Origin of the Arabic Script and Its Historical Development' (in Arabic), *Bull. Fac. of Arts, University of Egypt*, 1935.

THOMAS, J. *Le movement baptiste en Palestine et Syrie*, Gembloux (Belgium), 1935.

ROSENTHAL, F. *Die Sprache der palmyrenischen Inschriften und ihre Stellung innerhalb des Aramäischen*, Leipsic, 1936; *Die aramaistische Forschung seit Th. Nöldeke's Veröffentlichungen*, Leyden, 1939.

ALBRIGHT, W. F. Various articles in *Amer. J. Semitic Languages*, 1936; *J. Biblical Literature*, 1937; *Bull. Amer. Schools of Oriental Research*, etc.

ALT, A. *Völker und Staaten Syriens im früehen Altertum*, Leipsic, 1936.

GORDON, C. H. 'Aramaic and Mandaic Magical Bowls,' *Arch. Orient.*, 1937.

HANSEN, O. *Die mittelpers. Papyri der Papyrussamml. d. Staatl. Museen zu Berlin*, Berlin, 1938.

ALLBERRY, C. R. C. and IBSCHER, H. *Manichæan Manuscripts*, etc., Stuttgart, 1938.

ABBOT, N. *The Rise of the North Arabic Script and its Kur'anic Development*, Chicago, 1939; *Studies in Arabic Literary Papyri*, Chicago, 1957.

BLACK, M. *Rituale Melchitarum*, Stuttgart, 1938.

ARBERRY, A. J. *Specimens of Arabic and Persian Palæography*, London, 1939.

ROSTOVTZEFF, M. I., BROWN, F. E. and WELLES, C. B. *The Excavations at Dura-Europos*, New Haven, 1939.

SEYRIG, H. 'Les tessères palmyréniennes,' etc., *Memorial Lagrange*, 1940.

KHÜNEL, E. *Islamische Schriftkunst*, Berlin-Leipsic, 1942.

MINORSKY, V. 'Some Early Documents in Persian,' *J. Roy. Asiatic Soc.*, 1942.

CHRISTENSEN, A. *L'Iran sous les Sassanides*, Paris, 1944.

HATCH, W. H. P. *An Album of Dated Syriac Manuscripts*, Boston, 1946.

'The Newly Discovered Jerusalem Scrolls,' *Bibl. Archaeol.*, Sept. 1948; *Bull. Amer. Schools of Oriental Research*, Oct. and Dec., 1948.

ERDMANN, K. *Arabische Schriftzeichen als Ornamente in der abendländischen Kunst des Mittelalters*, Wiesbaden, 1954.

RICE, F. A. (ed.), *Classical Arabic; the Writing System*, Washington (U.S. Foreign Service Institute), 1954.

FEKETE, L. *Die Siyāḳat-Schrift der türkischen Finanzverwaltung*, Budapest, 1955.

CANTERA BURGOS, F. *Las inscripciones hebraicas de España*, Madrid, 1956.

STARCKY, J. 'Inscriptions archaïques de Palmyre', *Studi Orientalistici in Onore di Giorgio Levi della Vida*, II, Rome, 1956.

DRIVER, G. R. *Aramaic Documents of the Fifth Century B.C.*, Abbr. and rev. ed., London–Oxford, 1957.

VAJDA, G. (ed.) *Album de paléographie arabe*, Paris, 1958.

WALLENSTEIN, M. 'A dated Tenth-Century Hebrew Parchment Fragment from the Cairo Genizah in the Gaster Collection in the John Rylands Library,' *John Rylands Libr. Bull.* (Manchester), 1958.

GUBOGIN, M. *Paleografia şi diplomatica turco-osmană*, Bucarest, 1958.

Peshiṭta Institute, Leiden University, *List of Old Testament Peshiṭta Manuscripts*, Leiden, 1961.

SPERBER, A. *A Historical Grammar of Biblical Hebrew*, Leiden, 1962.

MALAGASY SCRIPTS—PROBLEMS AWAITING SOLUTION

I am very grateful to the Rt. Rev. Dr. Ronald O'Ferrall, Bishop of Madagascar, for the following information. My thanks are also due to the late Canon Dr. H. Danby, Regius Professor of Hebrew at the University of Oxford, for having me introduced to Bishop O'Ferrall.

Extract from Bishop O'Ferrall's letter, dated 3.4.1940:

In Madagascar, the earliest form of writing the Malagasy language (Malayo-Polynesian) was in Arabic character, similar though not quite identical with the modern Arabic characters. This is supposed to have been introduced by Arab traders (from Mecca?) between the fifteenth and seventeenth centuries. The writings extant are concerned with religion (extracts of the Koran and explanations), divination, and tribal history. One day I noticed one of my old clergymen use this script and he wrote vertically, from top to bottom, beginning at the left top corner of the pages. I have wondered whether this custom might in any way date the arrival of the Arabs—date still quite uncertain—or give any idea of where they came from. The actual Malagasy tribe proper, the Hova, are straight-haired, and are supposed to have come from the direction of S.E. of Madagascar. The language is certainly Malayo-Polynesian, and it has spread all over the island, and there are hardly any remains of Bantu words except perhaps in place names. This points to the arrival of the Malay type having been very early.

Now, did these Malayan Malagasy perhaps bring in the writing at a very early date—i.e., before the Arabs came? If so, it is strange there are no inscriptions surviving, though as wood is the medium, they might have all perished.

I myself think it is unlikely that the writing came before the Arabs, but that the arrival of the Arabs may be much earlier than generally supposed.

The Latin script introduced by missionaries early in the nineteenth century soon drove out the Arabic script, and it is now only used in a few out-of-the way villages, though the books are still used by diviners.

The problem mentioned by the Bishop of Madagascar is much more complicated than would appear to a layman. Malagasy, the native language of Madagascar, is, as we know, quite different from all the other African languages; it belongs to one of the most widespread linguistic families in the world, Malayo-Polynesian. We don't know when this form of speech was introduced into Madagascar, nor whether there was any direct relationship between the Malagasy-speaking population and the other groups of the family. What we do know, or rather we think we know, is that the natives of Madagascar, the only one of the main branches of that linguistic family, had no script before the invasion of the Arabs. Have we now to revise our opinion? It is perhaps not generally known that various Malayo-Polynesian peoples employed *vertical* systems of writing.

On the other hand, it is quite possible that the vertical direction of writing was introduced under Chinese influence, either by early Arab traders or by Malayo-Polynesian immigrants; in any case, at a very early period. Finally, there is also the possibility of some influence, probably an indirect one (through south-western India?), of the very active Nestorian missionaries. Whatever the result of research on this question, some important points of the history of that region will have to be revised.

PART-ADAPTATIONS FROM THE ARABIC

Mention has been made of the various languages for which the Arabic script has been adopted and the languages to which it has been adapted (p. 215). There are, however, some instances in which scripts may be considered as in part adaptations, the shapes of their letters being arbitrary inventions and not imitations of the signs of the prototype. I should include the following three scripts in this category:

YEZIDI CRYPTIC SCRIPT (Figs. 15.42a–c)

The sect of Yezidis constitute a community of about 25,000 people, concentrated mainly in the Balad Sinjar and Shaikh 'Adi districts of northern Iraq; some Yezidis live in Syria (at Aleppo), Turkey (Mardin and Diarbekr) and in the Caucasus (Tiflis, and in Azerbaijan). Their origin is uncertain; they seem to be mainly of Kurdish race. They speak Kurmanji, a Kurdish dialect, but also Arabic. They are called also 'devil-worshippers' because of their religion, which is said to be based on the propitiation of the Evil Principle, termed *Melek Taus*, the 'Peacock King'; their religion is on the whole a strange mixture of paganism, Islām, Christianity, Judaism, Zoroastrianism, and other creeds. It is easy to understand why they employ a cryptic script, if one considers the fact that they live amongst the Moslems whom they hate and by whom they are hated. It is written in the Yezidi holy books: 'If any Yezidi hears a Moslem in prayer he should kill the Moslem or commit suicide,' while one of the most scornful expressions of the Moslem neighbours is *Ya ibn Yezidi!* 'O thou, son of Yezid!'

For the Yezidis, *see* Henry Field and J. B. Glubb, *The Yezidis, Sulubba, and other*

Tribes of Iraq and Adjacent Regions, General Series in Anthropology, Number 10, Menasha, Wisconsin, U.S.A., 1943: *see* also the bibliography mentioned there on p. 17.

Curiously enough, the Field-Glubb monograph does not mention the two main holy books of the Yezidis, and their cryptic script. The two books are *Kitab al-Jalweh* (*c.* A.D. 1162–3), the 'Book of the Revelation,' a kind of New Testament attributed to the secretary of Shaikh 'Adi, the founder of the community of the Yezidis, and *Miskhaf Resh*, known also as *Maṣḥaf-i räsh*, or *Miskhefa Resh* (*c.* A.D. 1342–3), the 'Black Book,' a kind of Old Testament, attributed to Khasan al-Bashi. There are also poems attributed to Shaikh 'Adi, stories about Shaikh 'Adi and Yezidi notabilities, genealogies and proclamations. An edition of these 'literary monuments' is written in a hitherto unknown script. It is interesting to note that custom forbids the ordinary Yezidi man the use of writing, since according to *Maṣḥaf XXXI*, God alone has written the Creation.

The *al-Jalweh* consists of loose pages, made of fine gazelle-skin parchment; the pages are roughly shaped in the form of a crescent moon, the sun, the earth, two rivers, a man's head with two ears or horns, and so forth. The pages are not numbered, but at the bottom of each page is written the word with which the next page begins. Each page contains sixteen lines of writing. Since 1911, when these books were published in *Anthropos*, VI, pp. 1–39, various scholars have dealt with this matter. Professor Mingana (*J. Roy. Asiatic Soc.*, 1916, pp. 507–12, and 1921, pp. 117–9) considered the books to be forgeries of the last century. His opinion has been accepted by various scholars, such as Roger Lescot (*see* his excellent manual 'Enquête sur les Yezidis de Syrie et du Djebel Sindjar,' *Memoires de l'Institut Français de Damas*, V. Beyrouth, 1938). Others hold that the doubt of authenticity is unwarranted (*see*, for instance, Giuseppe Furlani, *Religione dei Yezidi*, 1930, and *Rivista degli Studi Orientali*, 1932, pp. 97–132, and so forth).

However, there is no doubt that the curious, probably cryptic, script of the Yezidis exists or existed. Figure 15.42a shows its alphabet, and Figs. 15.42b–c reproduce two specimens. The script is based partly on the Persian-Arabic writing, and partly on the Latin alphabet, but the majority of signs do not resemble either Arabic or Roman letters. The date of origin of this script is uncertain.

According to Professor Furlani, not only was the Persian-Arabic alphabet the prototype of the new script, but the texts must have been written first in the Persian-Arabic alphabet, and then transcribed in the new cryptic script. This is quite possible; the phonetic values of all the letters of the new script are identical with those of the Persian-Arabic letters. On the other hand, the shapes of the signs of the new character are quite different, with the exception of a few letters, such as ', h, and w. The great majority of the letters seem to be arbitrary inventions, based mainly on geometric elements, such as straight strokes, little squares, triangles and circles, angles, and so forth, and some are similar to those Latin letters which have geometric forms (l, V, T, L, etc.), but the phonetic values are quite different.

BALTI ALPHABET (Fig. 15.42e)

There are some manuscripts extant, which are couched in the Bhotia of Baltistan, or Balti, a Tibetan dialect spoken by about 150,000 people, in the province of Baltistan, formerly an independent state, and now part of the ex-State of Kashmir. These manuscripts are written in a script which according to Sir George A. Grierson (*Linguistic Survey of India*, III-i, pp. 33 sq.), was perhaps invented at the time of the conversion of the Baltis to Islām, about A.D. 1400.

Three kinds of signs can be noted:

(1) Some signs have the shape of Latin capital letters, but the phonetic values are not the same; in some cases there is a likeness (K representing *g*, P representing *b*, and R representing *l*), in other cases, there is no similarity at all (a reversed B, that is ᗺ, represents an *r*, an E represents an *n*). I think that we may conclude that the inventor of the Balti scripts knew the Latin alphabet, and with this purpose avoided giving to its sign the same phonetic value.

(2) Some signs (*k*, *kh*, *ts*, *ng*, *th*, etc.) have purely geometric forms, such as combinations of little squares and straight strokes.

(3) A few signs represent various sounds which are distinguished by the addition of diacritical marks; for instance, the sign *b* with a point below it, represents a *p*, with a point to its left, represents a *t*; an *s* with a point to its left, represents the sound *sh*, and so forth.

(4) The vocalization is rather peculiar; it is not unlike the Indian and Ethiopian systems. There are six vowels marks: short *a*, long *a*; *e*, *i*, *o* and *u*. With the exception of the long *a*, indicated by a kind of capital *s* (S) above the consonant with which it is connected, all the other vowels are represented by signs marked at the bottom left hand of the connected letter: short *a* by a dash (−), *e* by an oblique stroke, *i* by a hook, *o* by a kind of comma, and *u* by a curl. The final consonant (that is a consonant which is not followed by a vowel) is marked by a point on its top.

On the whole it may be said that the inventor of this script knew various scripts and made ample use of his knowledge. For the Latin alphabet, *see* point (1). The direction of writing of the Balti script—from right to left—and the diacritical points, seem to indicate that the inventor was mainly influenced by the Arabic script. The vocalization may indicate Indian influence. The signs, however, are arbitrary inventions.

Nowadays, the educated Baltis employ mainly the Persian-Arabic alphabet, which is most unsatisfactory and misleading. For the Balti form of speech *see* A. F. C. Read, *Balti Grammar*, London, 1934, which, however, does not mention the script examined above.

SOMALI ALPHABET (Fig. 15.42d)

This script, called locally *al-kitabah al-ʿusmaniyyah*, 'the Osmanya script,' from the name of the inventor, has been created recently for the Somali language by ʿIsman

Yusuf, son of the Sultan Yusuf 'Ali, and brother of 'Ali Yusuf, the last sultan of Olbia. 'Isman Yusuf belonged to the tribe of Bal Yaqub and the sub-tribe of 'Isman Mahmud (Italian Somalia).

Previously an attempt was made by Shaikh Awes of the Confraternity Qadiriyyah (who died in 1909) to adapt the Arabic alphabet to Somali, but without success.

'Isman Yusuf had a good knowledge of Arabic, a fairly good knowledge of Italian, and probably also of the Ethiopic script, and he made the maximum use of the various elements found in the three systems of writing.

The new alphabet consists of twenty-two consonants, arranged according to the order of the Arabic alphabet, with the addition of the five vowels *i, u, o, a, e* (as pronounced in Italian). Long vowels are treated in two ways: (1) by the addition of an *aleph* to the *a* to express the long *a*; of a *w* to the *u* to represent a long *u*, and to the *o* to represent a long *o*; of a *y* to an *i* and to an *e* to represent respectively a long *i* or a long *e*. (2) The long vowels *e* and *o* can also be represented by the signs *ee* and *oo*.

The origin of the Somalian alphabet (Fig. 15.42*d*) can be analysed as follows:

(1) The general idea of the alphabet, with distinct signs for the consonants and vowels, came from the Italian script; also the direction of writing, from left to right, was adopted from Italian.

(2) The order of the letters and the way of representing the long vowels, are based on the Arabic alphabet.

(3) The general *ductus* of the script is reminiscent of the Ethiopic script.

(4) The signs are generally arbitrary inventions; there are, however, some which are like Latin letters, either capitals or minuscule, either in print or handwriting (*H, h, b, f*), or Arabic letters or else Ethiopic signs, but the phonetic values do not agree.

Linguistic Report 1961

In 1960, the new Somalian Government appointed a technical committee of nine Somalis to examine various suggestions for an alphabet to be adopted for the Somalian language and its dialects. The committee examined eighteen suggested scripts (eleven 'Somali', four Arabic, and three Latin), and on May 15th 1961, a report was presented to the Somalian Prime Minister (Dr. Abdulrashid Ali Shaarmarkeh). After several months' work, two alphabets were selected: a 'Somali' and a Latin alphabet. The latter covers all the Somalian sounds. There are the following consonants: *b, t, j, ch, kh, d, r, s, sh, dh, c, g, f, q, k, l, m, n, w, h, y, ny, jy*; the following ten vowels: five short—*a, i, u, e, o*; and five long—*aa, ii, uu, ee, oo*, and two special signs: **/** and **∧**.

CHAPTER 16

Non-Sematic Offshoots of Aramaic Branch

'ALPHABET FOLLOWS RELIGION'

It has been said in reference to the Arabic alphabet that 'the alphabet follows religion'. This was also true of various other alphabets of Aramaic origin, some varieties of which became the sacred scripts of the five great faiths of Asia—Zoroastrianism, Judaism, Christianity (also including Nestorian as well as Armenian and Georgian Christianity), Buddhism and Islām. We may add Manichæism (*see* the preceding chapter). The importance of the Aramaic offshoots is even greater from the linguistic point of view; indeed, besides the various peoples of Semitic speech who employed alphabets of Aramaic origin (*see* preceding chapter) many peoples speaking other languages, such as Indo-Iranian, Turki and Mongolian, have adopted and adapted to their speech, alphabets derived from the offshoots of the Aramaic branch.

KHAROSHTHI SCRIPT AND THE PROBLEM OF INDIAN WRITINGS

The question of the origin of the Indian scripts is one of the most fascinating problems in the history of writing. Many Indian scripts and offshoots of Indian writing exist today, used for tongues belonging to various linguistic groups. A great number of inscriptions have been found in India, engraved on rocks or stone monuments, on copper, bronze or iron, on precious metals, or painted or engraved on pottery.

All these scripts seem to have descended from two prototypes, the *Kharoshthi* and the *Brahmī* (that is, *lipi*, 'script'). The latter may be regarded as the national Indo-Aryan system of writing and the true parent of the great majority of the Indian scripts, while the influence of the *Kharoshthi* script on other Indian writings seems to have been negligible. On the other hand, while the origin of the Kharoshthi seems to be evident, the origin of the Brahmī is still uncertain and hotly discussed. We shall deal with the latter in the next chapter; here we must mention the Kharoshthi, which is called also Bactrian (from the ancient district Bactria), Indo-Bactrian, Aryan, Bactro-Pali, north-western Indian, Kabulian (so termed by Faulmann), Kharotṣī and so forth.

However, the term Kharoṣṭī or Kharoshthi is now commonly used. In *Fa-yuan-shu-lin*, a Chinese Buddhistic work of A.D. 668, this ancient term was already in use. It has been variously explained: (1) as connected with Kharoshtha (*kharoshtha*, ass-lip'), the supposed creator of this script; (2) as used to indicate the barbaric peoples, Turks and Tibetans, on the north-western boundaries of India; (3) as connected with the Sanskrit name of Kashgar; (4) as the Indian corruption of *kharaosta* or *kharaposta* (the Indo-Aryan *khara* meaning 'ass,' and the Iranic *posta*, 'skin'), the 'ass-skin,' implying that this script had been employed for writing on ass-skins. (5) The most probable theory seems to be that an Aramaic word like *kharottha* (from *harat*, 'to engrave'—*see* also Greek *kharássō-kharáttō-kharádzō*, and *kharaktēr*, 'character') became, through popular etymology, the Sanskrit word *kharoshtha*.

Coins and Inscriptions

Kharoshthi has been known for a long time, as many Indo-Greek and Indo-Scythian coins between 175 B.C. and the first century A.D. were written in this script; but its greater importance was realized after the discovery, in 1836, of a Kharoshthi inscription incised on a rock in the vicinity of Shahbazgarhi (on the Indo-Afghan border) giving a version of Aśoka's (*see* next chapter) edicts, belonging probably to 251 B.C.

Other Documents

Later, many other Indo-Aryan documents in the Kharoshthi script were found. For instance, in the twenties of this century, Sir Aurel Stein discovered in Niya and Loulan, Eastern Turkestan, many interesting Kharoshthi documents written in Indian ink on wood, skin and paper, belonging mainly to the third century A.D. An important Kharoshthi Buddhist manuscript, apparently of the second century A.D. had previously been found in Eastern Turkestan. The most recent Kharoshthi inscriptions seem to belong to the fourth–fifth centuries A.D.

The dating is, however, not always easy; only about forty inscriptions are dated. An additional chronological difficulty is that the dated inscriptions, although indicating years, months and days, do not specify the era. The majority of the inscriptions were discovered in ancient Gandhara, now eastern Afghanistan and the northern Punjab.

The Script

Kharoshthi is not a monumental, but a popular cursive, commerical and calligraphic script. The direction of writing is from right to left (Fig. 16.2), although there are some few inscriptions and of more recent date written from left to right. The numeral signs are characteristic (Fig. 16.1, bottom line).

It is now commonly accepted that the Kharoshthi script (Fig. 16.1) has descended from the Aramaic alphabet; this theory is based on two important facts, the likeness of many signs having similar phonetic value, and the direction of writing. The connections of the Aramæans with India have been proved by the Aramaic inscription on the stone found at Taxila on the Hydaspes of the third century B.C. (*see* p. 199). The Kharoshthi script, however, must have originated in the fifth century B.C., in north-western India, at that time under Persian rule, which was the best medium for the spread of the Aramaic speech and script.

It may be assumed that the Brahmī had some influence on the origin or evolution of the Kharoshthi, especially (1) in regard to the vocalization of the script, the vowels being indicated by small circles, dashes, modifications of strokes, and so forth (Fig. 16.1), which transform the script into a rather cumbersome syllabic writing; (2) the addition of signs for sounds (such as *bh, gh, dh*) which do not exist in Aramaic; and (3) the direction of writing in the later stage of Kharoshthi.

BIBLIOGRAPHY

BÜHLER, G. *Indische Paläographie*, Strasbourg, 1896 (published in English in 1904 by J. F. Fleet, as an Appendix of *Indian Antiquary*).

SENART, E. *MS.* 'Dutreuil de Rhins,' *J. Asiatique*, 1898; 'L'inscription du vase de Wardak,' the same journal, 1914.

LÉVI, S. in *Bull. de l'École Franç. d'Extrême-Orient*, 1902, 1904, etc.

RAPSON, E. J. in *J. Roy. Asiatic Soc.*, 1904; *Specimens of Kharoshthi Inscriptions*, London, 1905.

BOYER, A. M. 'Inscriptions de Takht-i-Bahi,' etc., *J. Asiatique*, 1904, 1911, and so forth.

KONOW, S. 'Indoskythische Beiträge,' *Sitzungsb. d. Preuss. Akad. der Wissensch.*, 1916; in *Deutsche Literatur-Zeitung*, 1924; *Corpus Inscriptionum Indicarum*, Vol. II, Part I, *Kharoshthi Inscriptions*, 1929.

Kharoshthi Inscriptions Discovered by Sir Aurel Stein in Chinese Turkestan, etc., *1901, 1906–7, 1913–4*, edited by A. M. Boyer, E. J. Rapson, E. Senart and P. S. Noble, 3 vols., Oxford, 1920, 1927 and 1929.

BURROW, T. *The Language of the Kharoshthi Documents from Chinese Turkestan*, Cambridge, 1937; *A Translation of the Kharoshthi Documents from Chinese Turkestan*, London, 1940.

PERSIAN OR IRANIAN SCRIPTS

GENERAL SKETCH

When the Seleucid empire fell to pieces, the Greek dominion of its eastern portion ceased for ever, and a North Iranian dynasty became the overlords of these lands. Arsaces (*c.* 248 B.C.) was the founder of the new dynasty, whom we know as Parthian; the indigenous name is unknown, the Persians called this population *Parthava*. They seem to have spoken a North Iranian dialect akin to Sogdian (*see* below), and lived in the mountainous country south-east of the Caspian Sea. Mithridates I (*c.* 170–138 B.C.), occupying Media and Babylonia, became the real founder of the strong Parthian empire, which fought long wars with the Romans. The latter never had dominion over the Parthians; the defeat of Crassus in 53 B.C. marks the end of the period when Europeans were rulers of Mesopotamia, until the First World War.

About the year A.D. 220, the Parthian rule itself, that is the Arsacid dynasty, came to an end, 'but their successors were not the Romans but the Sassanians, a still more definitely Persian and Oriental dynasty, which lasted till the coming of Islam. . . . The new monarchy was strongly Persian, representing a revival of the Persian nationality and the Zoroastrian religion, and the new King of Kings began to dream of restoring the dominion of Darius and Xerxes over Syria and Asia Minor' (Burkitt).

PAHLAVI (Figs. 16.3–5)

Cuneiform was the Persian writing of the Achæmenid Empire (*see* part 1, chapter 11), during which the Aramaic speech spread more and more. It was employed even in official documents and coins; so also under the Arsacid dynasty (248 B.C.–A.D. 220).

Whether or not the Persians of the Achæmenid period employed the Aramaic script for writing Iranian or Persian for the purposes of daily life, there is at present no evidence to determine, but subsequently the Aramaic writing was so employed, and from it the Pahlavi alphabet is derived.

The Iranian language spoken, in its various dialects, in the aforementioned Arsacid period and during the Sassanian dynasty (A.D. 226–651) is called middle Persian to distinguish it from the early Persian of the Achæmenid period and the neo-Persian of the Islamic period. Middle Persian (or middle Iranian) is also called Pahlavi or Pehlevi.

ARAMAIC 'IDEOGRAMS'

Pahlavi was formerly supposed to be a mixed form of speech and 'one of the most enigmatical languages known to have existed' (M. Haug, 1870). Nowadays it is known that the foreign elements found in the Pahlavi inscriptions and other written documents are merely 'ideograms,' which prove to be obsolete Aramaic words. They were written in evolved ligatures of Aramaic letters, and read not in Aramaic, that is the original language, but in Pahlavi. ('Bread' was written *lakhman*, but read *nān*; 'meat' written *bastra* but read *gusht*; 'man' written *regleman* and read *mard*; 'wife' written *neshaman*, read *zan*, etc.) There are similar instances in English abbreviated Latin 'ideograms' (such as *d.*, £, &, *e.g.*, No., *i.e.*, etc.) being read not in Latin, but in English ('pence,' 'pound,' 'and,' 'for example,' 'number,' 'that is,' 'and so forth'). Sir Ellis Minns reminds me of the 'ideogram' *viz.* commonly employed in English: 'In reading aloud usually rendered by "namely".' (A. H. Murray and others, *A New English Dictionary*, Oxford, 1928). The term is an abbreviation of Latin *videlicet* (stem of *videre*, 'to see,' + *licet*, 'it is = 'that is to say,' permissible') 'namely,' 'to wit'; the *z* represents the ordinary mediæval Latin symbol of contraction for *et* or —*et* (Murray). However, the Aramaic 'ideograms' are very numerous in Pahlavi documents; all pronomina, conjunctions, as well as many nouns (such as 'day,' 'month'), and verbs are expressed by 'ideograms,' to which Pahlavi flexional terminations are simply tied on.

A typical example is *shah-an-shah* ('king of kings,' 'great king,' 'emperor'), which regularly occurs in the titles of the Sasanian kings, and is written with the Aramaic ideogram *mlk'n mlk'* (*malkan malka*).

'The Parsis possess, apparently from old times, an almost complete list of these "ideograms," that is the *Frahang i Pahlavik*, or Pahlavi-Pazand Glossary, a systematic dictionary, in which for every ideogram Iranian pronunciation is given.' There are, however, many errors due to the ignorance of the copyists.

PAHLAVI ALPHABETS (Figs. 16.3–5)

At the end of the third or during the second century B.C., the Persians created for their own language the alphabet termed Pahlavi or Pehlevi. This term, derived from *Parthava* of the inscriptions of Darius (Greek *Parthyaioi*, Latin *Parthi*), means simple 'Parthian,' and indicates that both the speech and the script developed in Parthian times. Other linguistic, graphical and historical evidence points the same way. The earliest specimens—Fig. 16.3*c*—(from Avromân, in Kurdistan) belong to the first century B.C.

It is far from clear how the Pahlavi system of writing developed. It cannot have been the creation of an individual, because in that case the system would have been more consistently worked out, and the almost contemporary appearance of two or more varieties would be inexplicable. It may, therefore, be assumed that the Pahlavi scripts were a natural development from local cursive Aramaic scripts.

We can distinguish at least three varieties of the Pahlavi alphabets (Figs. 16.3*a*, *b*):

(1) The north-western Pahlavi (that is the script of the Parthians), termed also Pahlavik or Arsacid, mainly on coins and gems of the Arsacid dynasty (Fig. 16.3, col. 3).

(2) The south-western Pahlavi (the script of the Persians, strictly speaking), termed also Parsik or Sassanian, in two forms, monumental and cursive (Fig. 16.3, col. 5). There are also various monumental inscriptions; while the Arsacid dynasty was considered to be foreign, the Sassanids rated themselves as a national dynasty and, following the tradition of the great Achæmenid kings, they immortalized their deeds in rock sculptures and inscriptions.

(3) The eastern Pahlavi, of which only a cursive form is known (Fig. 16.5*a*).

The Script

In the adaptation of the twenty-two Semitic letters to the Iranian language, the following modifications were introduced: *aleph* was adopted as *a*; *w* as *v*; *y* as consonant *y* or vowel *i*; *g* was given two forms, one for *g*, and the other for *gh* (*γ*); both the letters *l* and *r* could denote either the *l* or the *r*; *p* represented either the *p* or the *f*; the *samekh* was adopted for the sound *s*, and the *shin* for the sound *sh*. The *sade* (emphatic *s*) was adopted for the sound *ch*. The letters *he*, *teth* and '*ayin* appear only in Semitic words. The *g* used as *gh* was distinguished from the original form by the addition of the so-called aspiration-stroke. This alphabet was, obviously, not sufficient to express all the Iranian consonants; therefore, some letters were used also for related sounds, the *p* for *w;* the *t* also for *d, dh,* and sometimes for *th* (in some instances a modification of the *samekh* was used as *th*); the *ch* was employed also as *j* (*zh*), but sometimes the letter *sh* was used for the same sound. The *ḥet* was adopted for the sound *h* or *χ* (*kh*).

Final consonants were followed by a *w* (in good manuscripts only after *b, p, t, ch, k, w* and *g*). In the inscriptions, a peculiar sign, read by some scholars as a long *e,* is used as closing vowel. Long vowels in the middle of the words were denoted by *aleph* or *yod* (with two 'sublinear' points) or *w,* but the *yod* and the *waw* could denote also the short *i* or *u,* respectively, whereas the sound *a* was marked almost only before *aleph.* Out of the compounds *v + p,* and *v + b,* two special Avesta letters were formed to distinguish the aspirant *w* from the sound *v.*

Through a steady modification of sounds, while the script remained practically unchanged, the Pahlavi writing became more historical than phonetic.

THE AVESTA

The most famous of the Persian indigenous scripts is the Pazand or Avesta alphabet, the script of the sacred Persian literature. It is a most cursive script of fifty signs (Figs. 16.3*a, b*). Its origin is uncertain. In my opinion, unlike the Pahlavi scripts, it is an artificial creation, in which the inventor used both Pahlavik and Parsik elements, and his knowledge of the Greek alphabet.

The Iranian or Persian or Zoroastrian sacred literature is called *Avesta*; this term comes from the Middle Persian or Pahlavi form *avistak,* which some scholars prefer to read *apastak*; the Pazand form is *avasta,* and the Sanskrit term, *avista. Avistavak* or *Avistavani* denotes 'Avesta-speech.' The origin of the word is uncertain; F. C. Andreas, the German authority on the subject, suggested a derivation from *upasta,* meaning 'foundation,' 'foundation-text.' *Zand* denotes the traditional explanation of the Avesta texts handed down by the traditional schools, which served as the foundation of the Pahlavi translation reduced to writing. The term 'Zendavesta,' still popularly used (applying the term 'Zend' to the language in which the sacred writing Avesta was composed) is a misnomer.

The Avesta literature was composed in a dialect now called 'Avestic' or simply 'Avesta.' According to the Parsis, 'nothing which was not written in this dialect can claim to be considered as part of the sacred literature.' On the other hand, there is no other document extant, whether inscription or profane literature, written in 'Avestic.' The original home of this dialect is unknown. The Avesta literature is a complex collection of writings, containing the liturgies, the 'law,' solemn invocations, prayers, etc., and is still used amongst Parsis as 'Bible' and 'Prayer-book,' in India (where there are about 100,000 Parsis) and in Persia (about 15,000 Parsis).

The manuscripts of the Avesta fall, therefore, into two classes, the Indian (the oldest dating from the thirteenth and early fourteenth centuries A.D.), and the Persian MSS. (which do not go further back than the seventeenth century, but surpass their Indian contemporaries in point of correctness and carefulness of execution). The Iranian or Persian style of writing is 'a very vigorous cursive and oblique' hand, whereas the Indian style is 'rather straight and pointed' (D. Mackichan).

BIBLIOGRAPHY

THOMAE, E. 'Sassanian Inscriptions,' *J. Roy. Asiatic Soc.*, 1868.

STOLZE, F. (and Nöldeke, T.), *Persepolis: die Achämenidischen und Sassanidischen Denkmäler und Inschriften*, 2 vols., Berlin, 1882.

JACKSON, A. V. W. *The Avestan Alphabet and Its Transcription*, Stuttgart, 1890; *Avesta Reader*, Stuttgart, 1893.

GEIGER, W. and KUHN, E. (ed.). *Grundriss der iranischen Philologie*, 2 vols., Strasbourg, 1895–1904.

ANDREAS, F. C. 'Die Entstehung des Awestaalphabetes und sein ursprünglicher Lautwert,' *Verhandlungen des XIII. Internationalen Orient.-Kongr.*, 1904; the same and Wackernagel, in *Nachrichten der Gött. Gesellsch. der Wissensch.*, 1909, 1911 and 1913.

REICHELT, H. *Avestisches Elementarbuch*, Heidelberg, 1909; *Avesta Reader*, Strasbourg, 1911.

MINNS, E. H. 'Parchments of the Parthian Period from Avroman in Kurdistan,' Appendix, *J. Hellenic Studies*, 1915.

COWLEY, A. E. The Pahlavi Document from Avroman, *J. Roy. Asiatic Soc.*, 1919.

SYKES, P. M. *History of Persia*, London, 1921.

GARDTHAUSEN, V. in *Zeitschr. des Deutsch. Vereins für Buchwesen und Schrifttum*, 1921.

NYBERG, H. S. 'The Pahlavi Documents from Avromân,' *Le Monde Oriental*, 1923; *Hilfsbuch des Pehlevi*, 2 vols., Uppsala, 1928 and 1931.

HERZFELD, E. E. *Paikuli, Monument and Inscription of the Early History of the Sassanian Empire*, Berlin, 1924.

GELDNER, K. F. *Die Zoroastrische Religion*, Tübingen, 1926.

JUNKER, H. F. J. 'Das Awestaalphabet und der Ursprung der armenischen und georgischen Schrift,' *Caucasica*, 1925–7; 'The Origin of the Avestan Alphabet, *Dr. Modi Memorial Volume*, Bombay, 1930.

SALEMANN, G. and BOGDANOV, L. *A Middle-Persian Grammar*, Bombay, 1930.

SCHÄDER, H. H. 'Iranische Beiträge,' *Schriften der Königsberger Gelehrten Gesellschaft*, 1930.

BAILEY, H. W. *Zoroastrian Problems in the Ninth-century Books*, Oxford, 1943.

ARBERRY, A. J. (ed.) *The Legacy of Persia*, Oxford, 1953.

SOGDIAN ALPHABET (Figs. 16.6–7)

The Sogdians were an ancient population who inhabited the northernmost satrapy of the Persian Empire, which in Avestic was called *Sughda*, in early Iranian *Sughuda*, in Greek *Sogdianē*, in Latin *Sogdiana*. It was situated on the upper reaches of Oxos and Iaxartes (Syr Darya and Amu Darya), corresponding roughly to Samarkand and Bukhara, now Uzbekistân in the U.S.S.R. In Hellenistic times it was united with Bactria.

After Alexander's conquest of the Persian Empire, some groups of the Sogdians emigrated as far as northern India or Mongolia.

In the first seven or eight centuries of the Christian era, the Chinese province of Sin-Kiang or Eastern Turkestan, now almost wholly a sandy waste, was 'a land of smiling cities with rich sanctuaries and monasteries stocked with magnificent libraries.' This ancient melting-pot of peoples of quite different forms of speech (Iranian, Indian, Tibetan, Chinese, Turki, etc.), of script, and religion (Manichæan, Nestorian, Buddhist, etc.) is now inhabited by a sparse population mainly of Turkish tongue and Muslim religion.

Until the beginning of the twentieth century the Sogdian language was unknown.

The epoch-making discoveries of British-Indian, German, Russian, Japanese, French and other expeditions, have yielded extremely important results, published by the discoverers themselves:

A. Stein, *Ancient Khotan*, London, 1907; *Serindia*, 3 vols., London, 1921; *Innermost Asia*, 4 vols., Oxford, 1928.

A. Grünwedel, *Alt-Kutscha*, Berlin, 1920; *Recherches archéologiques en Asie Centrale*, Paris, 1931.

A. von Le Coq, *Auf Hellas Spuren in Ost-Turkestan*, Leipsic, 1926, and others.

The Sogdian speech and script (Figs. 16.6–7) were widely used in Central Asia for many centuries, and particularly in the second half of the first millennium A.D., as proved by the trilingual (Turki, Sogdian and Chinese) inscription of the ninth century found in the vicinity of Qara Balgasun, on the Orkhon, the then capital of the vast Uighur Empire, 25 miles north of Qara Korum, at the foot of the Khangai mountains.

This important monument seems to mark the northern limit of the diffusion of ancient Sogdian, while its southern limit seems to be marked by a stone inscription, consisting of six lines, discovered at Ladakh, on the Tibetan frontier.

Sogdian was actually for a long time the *lingua franca* of Central Asia.

As the result of the Mongolian and Arabian conquests, Sogdian slowly died out, although 'a poor descendant' of it is still to be found in the valley of Yaghnāb.

Many fragments of Sogdian manuscripts (Fig. 16.6c) were found in Eastern Turkestan at Turfan; others were discovered at Ch'ien- or Ts'ien-fo-tung, the 'Caves of the Thousand Buddhas,' in Tun-huang, Kansu, north-west China. The manuscripts extant are now in London (British Museum and India Office Library), Paris (Bibliothèque Nationale), Leningrad (Academy of Science) and Berlin (Academy of Science). In recent times, other important finds in Sogdian were made by Russian scholars.

The decipherment of Sogdian is due to the labours of various scholars, especially the Germans F. C. Andreas and F. W. Müller, and the French R. Gauthiot. The manuscripts are mainly of a religious nature, Christian, Manichæan or Buddhist. The earliest manuscripts extant (those found at Ts'ien-fo-tung) belong to the fourth century A.D., but the great majority of the other texts belong to the ninth and perhaps tenth century A.D.

The Sogdian script (Fig. 16.7), of which there were a few varieties, was, like the Semitic alphabets, purely consonantal. The vowels *a, i* and *u* were often left unmarked, but sometimes they were expressed by the use of the consonants *aleph, γ* and *w*: *aleph* could express the long or short *a*; *γ*, the long or short *i*, or the long *e*; *w*, the long or short *u*, or the long *o*. Sometimes, however, two *aleph* were employed, or the combination *aleph-γ* or *aleph-w*.

The Sogdian script also contained some Aramaic ideograms, but not as many as the Pahlavi scripts; *see* above.

The Sogdian alphabet descended from a local cursive variety of Aramaic script connected with the Palmyrene alphabet, perhaps from early Pahlavik; later, it was influenced by the Nestorians; indeed, many Sogdian manuscripts, written in Syriac script have been found there dealing with Nestorian Christianity.

BIBLIOGRAPHY

GAUTHIOT, R. 'De l'alphabet sogdien,' *J. Asiatique*, 1911.

Essai de grammaire sogdien, I. by R. Gauthiot, Paris, 1914–23; II. by E. Benveniste. Paris, 1929

VON LE COQ, A. in *Mitteilungen des Seminars für Orientalische Sprachen*, Berlin, 1919.

GAUTHIOT, R. and PELLIOT, P. *Le Sûtra des Causes et des Effets*, etc., Paris, 1920.

REICHELT, A. *Die soghdischen Handschriftenreste des Britischen Museums*, 2 vols., Heidelberg, 1928 and 1931.

BENVENISTE, E. 'Notes on Manuscript Remains in Sogdian,' in A. Stein's *Innermost Asia*, Oxford, 1928; 'Notes sogdiennes,' *J. Roy. Asiatic Soc.*, 1933; *Journal Asiatique*, 1933 and 1936; *Bull. School of Oriental Studies*, 1938; *Mission Pelliot en Asie Centrale*, Vol. III, *Textes sogdiens*, Paris, 1940.

HANSEN, O. in *J. Société Finno-Ougrienne*, Helsingfors, 1930; New Christian Texts, *Abh. D. Akademie d. Wiss. u. Litt.*, 1954.

HENNING, W. B. in *Orientalia*, 1939; 'The Sogdian Texts of Paris,' *Bull. School of Oriental Studies*, 1946.

GRÖNBECH, K. *Monumenta Linguarum Asiae Maioris*. Vol. III. *Codices Sogdiani. Manuscripts de la Bibliothèque Nationale (Mission Pelliot), reproduits en fac-similé*. Introduction by E. Benveniste, Copenhagen, 1940.

KÖK TURKI RUNES

The southern part of central Siberia, north-western Mongolia and north-eastern Turkestan have yielded many inscriptions belonging to the seventh and eighth centuries A.D., and some later fragments of manuscripts written in a script variously known as Orkhon-script (the first inscriptions having been found near the river Orkhon, to the south of Lake Baikal), or Siberian, or Early Turki, Kök Turki or pre-Islamic Turki.

There are two forms of this script, the monumental, of which a few varieties are known (Fig. 16.8*a*), and the cursive form (Fig. 16.6*b*). The monumental inscriptions are written in a runic character, termed Kök Turki runes, which Professor Sir Ellis H. Minns compared with the Germanic runic script (Fig. 16.8*b*), not for any phonetic connection, but because the forms assumed are similar, being conditioned by carving on sticks: indeed, actual objects have been found.

The Kök Turki script was deciphered by the Danish scholar Wilhelm Thomsen. The language of the inscriptions is Early Turki, the oldest form known of the Turkish tongue, which differs very widely from the Ottoman Turkish. Although the earliest inscriptions extant belong to the seventh–eighth centuries, the script must already have been in use in the sixth century.

The script was written either horizontally, from right to left, or in vertical lines, under Chinese influence (?), and consists of thirty-eight letters. Many consonants vary in form according to the intended vowel-sound, for instance, *k* has five forms —for (1) *ka*, (2) *ky*, (3) *ko* or *ku*, (4) *kä*, *ke*, *ki*, (5) *kö* or *kü*—other consonants have only two forms or even one (Fig. 16.8a). It is thus a mixed syllabic-alphabetic system.

Its origin is uncertain. It may have derived either from a local variety of the Pahlavik script or else from the Sogdian alphabet in its early stage.

BIBLIOGRAPHY

RADLOV, V. V. *Die alttürkischen Inschriften der Mongolei*, St. Petersburg, 1894–9.

BANG, W. and MARQUART, J. *Osttürkische Dialektstudien*, Göttingen, 1914.

THOMSEN, V. 'Turcica,' *Mem. de la Soc. Finno-Ougrienne*, 1916 (with bibliography);' Alttürkische Inschriften aus der Mongolei,' *Zeitschr. der Deutsch. Morgenl. Gesellsch.*, 1934.

BANG, W. *Vom Köktürkischen zum Osmanischen*, etc., 3 parts, Berlin, 1917, 1919 and 1921.

BANG, W. and VON GABAIN, A. 'Türkische Turfantexte', etc., *Preuss. Akad. der Wissensch.*, 1929–34.

GRÖNBECH, K. *Der türkische Sprachbau*, I, Copenhagen, 1936.

EMRE, A. C. *Sur l'origine de l'alphabet vieux-turc, dit alphabet runique de Sibérie*, Istanbul, 1938.

VON GABAIN, A. *Alttürkische Grammatik*, Leipsic, 1941.

BROCKELMANN, C. in *Zeitschr. der Deutsch. Morgenl. Gesellsch.*, 1942.

FORRER, L. in *Anthropos*, 1942–5.

RÆSÆNEN, M. *Beiträge zu den türkischen Runeninschriften*, Helsinki, 1952.

MALOV, S. E. *Monuments of the Old Written Language of Mongolia and Kirghisia* (in Russian), Leningrad, 1959.

EARLY HUNGARIAN SCRIPT (Fig. 16.8c)

The script of some mediæval (sixteenth century; the earliest document belonging to A.D. 1501) inscriptions from Transylvania and southern Hungary is termed Szekler or early Hungarian; it seems to have descended from the Kök Turki script, but this is still an open question. Some scholars consider it a cryptic script of the Szeklers.

The isolated group of Hungarians settled in Transylvania, and called Szeklers or Szekels, numbering about 450,000, are generally considered the purest descendants of the Magyars or Hungarians, who at the end of the ninth century A.D. invaded the country now known as Hungary. Some scholars, however, consider the Szeklers as a Finno-Ugrian people, akin to the Hungarians. Others explain the word *szekely* as 'frontier guards,' and hold that the Szeklers were transplanted to Transylvania in order to form a permanent guard for the frontier.

BIBLIOGRAPHY

NAGY, G. 'A székely irás eredete, *Ethnographia*, 1895.

SEBESTYÉN, J. *Rovás és Rovásirás*, Budapest, 1909; *A magyar rovásirás hiteles emlékei*, Budapest, 1915.

BABINGER, F. and MÜLLER, K. 'Ein schriftgeschichtliches Rätsel,' *Keleti Szemle*, Budapest, 1913–4.

MUNKÁCSI, B. 'Zum Problem der Székler Runenschrift', the same journal.

NEMETH, J. 'Die Inschriften des Schatzes von Nagy-Sz.-Miklós,' *Bibliotheca Orientalis Hungarica*, II, Budapest, 1932.

FÀBRI, C. L. 'The Ancient Hungarian Script and the Brâhmî-character,' *Indian Culture*, Calcutta, 1934.

UIGHUR ALPHABET (Fig. 16.7, 11*a*)

The Uighurs, originally Toquz Oghuz, the 'Nine Oghuz,' were a strong people of Turki speech. They lived in Mongolia and were Shamanists. About the middle of the eighth century A.D., they invaded eastern Turkestan, where they accepted the religion of Buddha. Later, however, their kings embraced Manichæism (*see* p. 229), while a part of the population were converted to Nestorianism. Finally, they became Moslems.

The vast Uighur empire of Mongolia, which had its capital at Qara Balgasun of today, did not last long; it was destroyed about the middle of the ninth century. From the cultural angle it was less important than the later Uighur kingdom of eastern Turkestan, which was politically weaker. The Uighurs ruled Kashgaria in the tenth–twelfth centuries, when they subdued the whole land, but intermixed with the local population of Iranian origin. The assimilation was so complete that they may conveniently be called Iranized Turks; the region became a true 'country of the Turks' = 'Turkestan.' After the conquest by Temujin (Chinggiz Khan) the Uighurs retained a semi-autonomy for some time.

The influence of the Uighurs on the neighbouring countries is best illustrated by the use at the beginning of the thirteenth century of the Uighur alphabet as the script of the Mongolian Empire.

The Uighur alphabet (Fig. 16.7) is an offshoot of the Sogdian script. The adaptation of this consonantal alphabet to the Turki form of speech, rich in vowels, was not without difficulties. Generally, the vowels *a*, *i* and *u* were left unmarked. At a later stage, it became the custom to use the letter *aleph* for *a* or *æ*, and often a double *aleph* for an initial *a*; *γ* for *i* and *ï*, *e* not being distinguished; *w* for *u*, *o*, *ü* or *ö*, *wγ* being often used for *ü* or *ö* when in the first syllable. In foreign words, many Sogdian spellings were adopted.

The Uighur script was written and read vertically.

BIBLIOGRAPHY

VON LE COQ, A. 'Ein manichäisches–uigurisches Fragment aus Idiqut Schahri,' *Sitzungsb. der Preuss. Akademie der Wissensch.*, Berlin, 1908; 'Ein christliches und ein manichäisches Manuscriptfragment in türkischer Sprache aus Turfan,' the same journal, 1909; *Türkische Manichäica aus Chotscho*, I, II, and III, Berlin, 1912, 1919, and 1922; *Kurze Einführung in die uigurische Schriftkunde*, Berlin, 1919.

MÜLLER, F. W. K. *Uigurica*, I–III, Berlin, 1908, 1911 and 1922; IV, edited by A. von Gabain, Berlin 1931; 'Ein uigurisches-lamaistisches Zauberritual,' etc., *Sitzungsb. der Preuss. Akad.*, etc., 1928.

BANG, W. 'Zur Kritik und Erklärung der Berliner uigurischen Turfanfragmente,' *Sitzungsb. der Preuss. Akad.*, etc., 1915; *Studien zur vergleichenden Grammatik der Türk-Sprachen*, 3 parts, Berlin, 1916; W. Bang and A. von Gabain, *Analytischer Text zu den fünf ersten Stücken der türkischen Turfantexte*, Berlin, 1931.

RADLOV, V. V. *Uigurische Sprachdenkmäler*, Leningrad, 1928.

MONGOLIAN SCRIPTS

The Mongols had no importance before the early thirteenth century A.D., but then Temujin (Chinggiz Khan) united Mongolia; and in a few years its dominion extended from Korea to southern Russia. The Mongolian language belongs to the Altaic linguistic family. Mongolian dialects are now spoken by tribes occupying the territories from the Great Wall of China to the River Amur, and across the Gobi Desert as far as the Altai mountains. The three principal dialects, Khalkha, Kalmuck (Kalmyk) and Buriat, do not differ much. Literary Mongolian is that form of the Khalkha dialect which has been reduced to writing by the lamas Sa-skya Paṇḍita, hPhags-pa and Čhos-kyi hod zer, in the thirteenth and fourteenth centuries.

The Mongols used the Uighur as their official language and script until 1272, when the script *Pa-sse-pa* or *'p'ags-pa*, an adaptation of the Tibetan writing, was adopted for the Mongolian speech (see pp. 279 f.). This was replaced about 1310 by the *Galica* or *Kalika* (from *ka-lekka*, the '*ka*-script,' the 'script' of the system '*ka*'), which was based mainly on the Uighur alphabet, partly influenced by the Tibetan script, using the experience of the *Pa-sse-pa* system.

During the fourteenth century, the Galica alphabet (in which the Mongolian translations of the Buddhist Sanskrit and Tibetan works were written) developed and became the Mongolian national alphabet.

Dr. Rörich has re-examined the whole problem of the origin of the Mongol alphabet. It would appear that Tibetan and Mongol historical tradition ascribes the creation of the Mongol alphabet to two Sa-skya lamas—the Sa-skya Paṇḍita Kundgah rgyal-utshan (1182–1251) and Čhos-kyi hod-zer (thirteenth or first half of the fourteenth century). The Mongol ruling classes had adopted the Uighur script in the early days of the Mongol Empire after the conquest of the Naïman tribal lands in 1204. The Sa-skya Paṇḍita is said by some Tibetan chronicles (and also in some Mongolian works) to have created a new Mongolian script between 1247 and 1251, but the evidence suggests that he only reformed the Uighur script (currently used in Mongol chancellaries), the main objects apparently being to adapt the script to the requirements of Mongol speech and to facilitate the translation of Tibetan Buddhist texts into Mongolian. The Sa-skya Paṇḍita was succeeded as court-priest of the Mongolian emperors by his nephew hPhags-pa bLa-ma bLo-gros rgyal-utshan (1235/39–80), the famous preceptor of emperor Khubilai. HPhags-pa invented the Mongolian 'square' script or *dürbelǰin üsüg*, which (long dead in Mongolia and China) is still studied in the Tibetan province of Amdo. Also Chos-kyi ḥod-zer is regarded in some Tibetan and Mongolian chronicles as co-inventor of the Mongolian alphabet ('inventor of the first Mongolian script,' 'inventor of a script of ninety-eight signs, based on the invention by the Sa-skya Paṇḍita'; he used the new script in his translation of the Buddhist scriptures). Other Tibetan and also Chinese sources make no mention of Chos-kyi ḥod-zer's invention or reform of a new script. Therefore, modern scholars assume that he did not really invent a new script, but simply availed himself of the existing Uighur script, instead of the official Mongolian alphabet, or *Hor-yig*, created by the ḥPhags-pa bLa-ma. However, he was an outstanding author and translator.

The Mongolian script (Figs. 16.9*a*, 10 and 11*b*) is written vertically downwards, probably under Chinese influence, but, unlike Chinese, the columns follow each other from left to right. As a system of writing it is imperfect, *g* and *k*, *d* and *t*, *o* and *u*, *γ* and *j*, and others are written alike; as a result, many words of widely different meaning are written alike, as, for instance, *urtu* ('long') and *ordu* ('palace').

MANCHU SCRIPT

The Manchu population, speaking a southern Tungus tongue, allied to the Tungus division of the Altaic linguistic group, had no historical importance before the seventeenth century. Nurhachu, who when he became emperor in 1616, assumed the name Ahkai Fulingga (in Chinese, *T'ien Ming*, 'Appointed by Heaven'), may be considered the creator of the Manchu script and literature. This consists mainly of translations from, or imitations of, Chinese works.

Originally the script was a mere adaptation of the Mongolian alphabet to the Manchu tongue. In 1632, some diacritical marks were added. In 1748, the Manchu script was revised by the Manchu emperor of China, Ch'ien-lung, who, according to tradition chose one form of the thirty-two existing variants (Fig. 16.9*a*). Manchu is written, like Mongolian, in vertical columns running from left to right (Fig. 16.9*b*).

KALMUCK ALPHABET (Fig. 16.11*c*)

The Kalmucks, a branch of the Mongols, are nomads who inhabit a vast region of Mongolia, in the eastern part of the T'ien Shan range, on the western border of the Gobi Desert, spreading east into Kansu and westwards to the Kalmuck Steppes. They also settled on the banks of the Volga.

The Kalmucks adapted the Mongolian alphabet to their speech in 1648, under the lama Zaya Paṇḍita. The Kalmuck alphabet (Fig. 16.9*a* and particularly Fig. 16.11*c*) is more precise than the Mongolian.

BURIAT ALPHABET

The Buriat dialect belonging to the Mongolian group, is spoken by about 300,000 people in the provinces of Irkutsk and Transbaikalia (Siberia).

The Buriat national script of this oriental branch of the Mongolian linguistic group, is the last descendant of the Mongolian alphabet.

The Russian alphabet has also been adapted to the Buriat tongue.

BIBLIOGRAPHY

LAUFER, B. 'Skizze der mongolischen Literatur,' *Keleti Szemle*, Budapest, 1907; 'Skizze der manjurischen Literatur,' *Keleti Szemle*, Budapest, 1908; 'Jurci and Mongol Numerals,' *Kærœsi Csoma Archivum*, Budapest, 1925; *A Summary of Mongolian Literature*, Leningrad, 1927 (in Russian).

RAMSTEDT, G. J. 'Mongolische Briefe,' etc., *'Sitzungsb. der Preuss. Akad. d. Wissensch.*, 1909; *Kalmükkische Sprachproben*, etc., Helsingfors, 1909; 'Ein Fragment mongolischer Quadratschrift, *'J. Soc. Finno-Ougrienne*, 1912.

GILES, H. A. *China and the Manchus*, Cambridge, 1912.

POPPE, N. N. 'Beiträge zur Kenntnis der altmongolischen Schriftsprache,' *Asia Major*, I, Leipsic, 1924.

HÄNISCH, E. 'Beiträge zur mongolischen Schrift- und Volkssprache', *Mitteilungen des Seminars für Orientalische Sprachen*, Berlin, 1925.

PELLIOT, O. Les systèmes d'écriture en usage chez les ancient Mongols, *Asia Major*, II, Leipsic, 1925.

WHYMANT, A. N. T. *A Mongolian Grammar*, etc. London, 1926.

LESSING, F. *Mongolen*, etc., Berlin, 1935.

LATTIMORE, O. *The Mongols of Manchuria*, 2nd ed., London, 1935.

BERNARD, H., S. J., *La Découverte de Néstoriens Mongols aux Ordos et l'histoire ancienne du Christianisme en Extrême-Orient*, Tientsin, 1935.

HEISSIG, W. and BLEICHSTEINER, R. *Wörterbuch der heutigen mongolischen Sprache*, etc., Vienna and Peking, 1941.

RÖRICH, G. N. 'Kun-mkhyen Čhos-kyi hod-zer and the Origin of the Mongol Alphabet,' *J. Roy. Asiatic Soc. of Bengal Letters*, 1945.

HOPE, E. R. *Karlgren's Glottal Stop Initial in Ancient Chinese, with particular reference to the hPhags-pa script*, Ottawa, 1953.

POPPE, N. N. *The Mongolian Monuments in Hp'ags-pa Script* (2nd ed., transl. and edit. by J. R. Krüger), Wiesbaden, 1957.

N.B. The whole problem of the Altaic linguistic family has been re-examined by Prof. Nicholas Poppe in *Vergleichende Grammatik der altaischen Sprachen*, I, Wiesbaden, 1960.

PROBABLE OFFSHOOTS OF ARAMAIC BRANCH

ARMENIAN SCRIPTS

A script for the Armenian language, philologically a most important and independent member of the Indo-European family, was not introduced until the spread of Christianity in Armenia and after the Armenian Church became independent or autocephalic in 369. In fact, in or about A.D. 406-7 St. Mesrop or Masht'otz (the 'saint'), in collaboration with St. Sahak and a Greek from Samosata called Rufanos, was the creator of this script so excellently suited to the Armenian speech. The fifth century was also the Golden Age of Armenian literature. A famous school of translators (*thargmanitchk'* or *surb thargmanitchk'*, 'holy translators'), founded by St. Sahak, produced versions of the Bible from Syriac and Greek and of the masterpieces of Greece and Rome. The early Armenian codices extant generally belong to the twelfth century A.D., although—as Professor Bailey kindly informs me—there are a few earlier ones; for instance, the facsimile of a Gospel MS. of A.D. 887 was published at Moscow in 1899, and E. Mader published the facsimile of a manuscript of 989.

Armenian

Armenian—the language which Lord Byron considered 'a rich language which would amply repay anyone the trouble of learning it'—can now be divided into (1) early or classical Armenian, termed *Grabar* (from grel, 'to write'), the 'written language,' which is still used as the learned and liturgical language; and (2) the 'vulgar' speech, the modern Armenian employed since about the middle of the present millennium. The latter, termed *Ashksarhabar* or *Ashksarhik* (from *ashksarh*, 'world'), is the language of the modern Armenian literature and of the newspapers. It has two main dialects, the eastern Armenian, which is nearer to the *Grabar* and is spoken principally in the mother country, and the western dialect spoken elsewhere. Eastern Armenian is the more correct. The differences are chiefly grammatical and in the pronunciation of the consonants *b-p*, *g-k*, and *d-t*. The Armenian scripts are used both for classic Armenian and for the vulgar forms of speech.

Armenian Alphabet

The Armenian alphabet originally contained thirty-six letters. Later, two more signs were added. There are two types, capitals and minusculæ. The letters have changed their outward semblance very slightly. Figure 16.12 shows the Armenian alphabet, while Figs. 16.13–16 reproduce some important Armenian manuscripts.

Origin of Armenian Writing

According to Armenian tradition there was a previous unsuccessful attempt by the Syriac bishop Daniel to adapt the Greek alphabet to the Armenian speech.

Among the various theories regarding the script on which St. Mesrop based his creation, the following are the more important: (1) A suggestion that the Armenian alphabet is based on the Greek; (2) that a cursive Aramaic-Persian, Pahlavi, alphabet was the foundation with some Greek influence; (3) while the most recent theory advanced by the German scholar Junker suggests that both the Armenian and the Georgian alphabets are based on the Pahlavik script (*see* p. 307) with the addition of some letters of the Avesta alphabet. Greek influence, however, was felt in the creation of vowels, the direction of writing, and the upright and regular position of the

S

characters, not in the form of particular signs. The only criticism of the latter theory is that not sufficient account has been taken of the inventive power of the creator.

According to local tradition, St. Mesrop invented the consonants, the *catholicos* (St.) Sahak, supreme head of the Armenian Church, added the vowels, and King Vramshapukh supported them by ensuring that the version of the Bible in the new script became sanctified. The script was the chief means of crystallizing Armenian speech, which was an important factor in upholding the existence and the unity of the Armenian Church and nation.

BIBLIOGRAPHY

LAUER, M. and CARRIÈRE, A. *Grammaire arménienne*, Paris, 1883.

HÜBSCHMANN, H. *Armenische Grammatik*, Leipsic, 1897.

KARST, J. *Historische Grammatik des Kilikisch—Armenischen*, Strasbourg, 1901.

LIDÈN, E. *Armenische Studien*, Gœteborg, 1906.

ASLAN, K. *Etudes historiques sur le peuple Arménien*, Paris, 1909.

MARQUART, J. 'Über das armenische Alphabet,' etc. *Handés Amsorya*, 1911.

ORMANIAN, M. *The Church of Armenia*, London, 1912.

MEILLET, A. *Altarmenisches Elementarbuch*, Heidelberg, 1913.

LALAIAN, Y. *Catalogue of Armenian MSS. of Vassbourajan*, Tiflis, 1915.

MADER, E. *L'évangile arménien*, Paris, 1920.

PETERSSON, H., *Arische und armenische Studien*, Lund, 1920.

GARDTHAUSEN, V. *Zeitschr. des Deutsch. Vereins für Buchwesen und Schrifttum*, 1921.

JUNKER, H. F. J. 'Das Awestaalphabet und der Ursprung der armenischen und georgischen Schrift,' *Caucasica*, 1925-7.

ZELLER, H. 'Armenisch,' *Grundr. d. Indo-Germ. Sprach- u. Altertumskunde*, Berlin, 1927.

ABEGHIAN, M. *Theory of the Armenian Language* (in Armenian), Eriwan, 1931; *Neuarmenische Grammatik*, Berlin and Leipsic, 1936.

PISANI, V. 'Contributi armeni' (with bibliography), *Giornale della Società Asiatica Italiana*, 1934.

MEILLET, A., MARIÉS, P. and BENVENISTE, M. *Esquisse d'une grammaire comparée de l'Arménien classique*, 2nd ed., Paris, 1936.

DER NERSESSIAN, S. *Manuscrits arméniens illustrés des XIIe, XIIIe, et XIVe siècles*, Paris, 1937.

TREVER, K. V. *Sketches on the History of Old Armenia from the Second to the Fourth Century of our Era* (in Russian), Moscow, 1953.

GEORGIAN ALPHABETS (Figs. 16.7–25)

Georgian (the term is probably a corruption of *Gurjian*).

Georgia, the ancient Colchis or Iberia, a part of southern Caucasia, has been inhabited from about the seventh century B.C. by Georgians (the indigenous term is K'art'li or K'art'velni), numbering about two millions. A south-western Caucasian language known locally as *K'art'uli'ena* is spoken; there are various dialects, the principal of which are Kartlian, Mingrelian with Laz, and Svanian. The connection of the Caucasian group of languages—which are of the agglutinative type, and are also called Alarodian or Japhetic—is still uncertain. While some scholars (Friedrich,

Müller, Lepsius and Schuchardt) regarded them as 'isolated,' others found connections with the 'Turanian' linguistic group (De Morgan and Max Müller), with the Semitic languages (Trombetti) or with Sumerian (Ts'ereteli).

In course of time, Georgian has acquired many foreign elements, such as Armenian, Iranian, Turki and Russian. According to Dr. O. N. Kazara, who is of Laz extraction, the physical type throughout Caucasia is remarkably uniform, representing—with some variations towards dolichocephaly along the litoral of the Black Sea coast—a marked brachycephalic or round-headed type.

GEORGIAN SCRIPTS

The earliest Georgian inscriptions extant go back to the fifth century A.D. (Fig. 16.18) and the earliest manuscripts to the eighth century A.D.

The 'golden age' of Georgia was the twelfth and early thirteenth centuries under the kings David II and George III, and the Queen Tamara, and lasted for almost a century until the defeat of George IV by the Mongols in 1223. Figures 16.19–25 reproduce several Georgian MSS., which give us a summary of the development of Georgian writing.

The Georgians formerly employed two scripts (Fig. 16.17): (1) *Khutsuri* (*khutsi*, 'priest'), the 'ecclesiastical writing,' an angular character, of thirty-eight letters, in two forms (capitals, *Aso-mt'avruli* and minusculæ, *Nuskha*); and (2) *Mkhedruli* (*mkhedari*, 'knight, warrior'), the script of the 'warriors,' the 'military, lay' writing, in one form only, of forty letters (seven of them are obsolete, namely, long *e* and *o*, another variant of *e*, *ie*, *v*, *ph*, and an emphatic *h*).

Mkhedruli is the script commonly employed at present in printing; a cursive form, which is slightly modified and contains frequent ligatures, is the Georgian hand-writing of today.

Professor Bailey informs me that Dzanašia (*History of Georgia*, 1946, p. 94) has a plate illustrating the development of Georgian script from 'ecclesiastical' to 'civil' forms.

Origin

The origin of the Georgian writing and the connection between its two main varieties are still uncertain.

Traditionally it is considered a creation of St. Mesrop, parallel to that of the Armenian writing. According to Allen, 'the Georgian alphabet is a perfect instrument for rendering the wealth of varied sounds in the language; the letters give each different sound with accuracy and clearness, and no other alphabet, including the Armenian, compares with it in efficiency.' Allen, therefore, concludes that 'it would seem that the alphabet had a long and slow evolution to its present state of perfection, rather than it was invented whole by a foreigner.' In conclusion, 'the Georgian script is, like the Georgian language, ancient and original, and in its perfection to the use for which it is required, it bears the stamp of a venerable individuality.'

According to a local tradition the Mkhedruli was invented about A.D. 300 by P'arnavaz, the first Georgian king, and it was more than a century older than the Khutsuri. According to another tradition, the latter was as many as nine centuries older than the former. Marr, a leading Russian linguist, while accepting the common opinion that the Khutsuri was a Georgian Christian creation, considers the Mkhedruli a development of a pre-Christian Georgian script, which was modified in later times, under the influence of the Khutsuri, and continued in use by the military and lay circles. It also influenced the development of the Nuskha Khutsuri. The German scholar Junker holds that both Mkhedruli and Khutsuri are based, like the Armenian alphbaet, on Aramaic-Pahlavi scripts, the former being connected with older and simpler forms. He also suggests Greek influences.

Junker's opinion is the most probable. It may be possible that both the varieties were parallel derivations, Mkhedruli being the more recent cursive form, perhaps introduced only at the beginning of the present millennium. A local tradition attributes the origin of the Khutsuri to the creator of the Armenian alphabet, which is quite possible. In fact, the Khutsuri seems to be somehow connected with the Armenian alphabet, although nowadays only some letters of the two scripts look alike.

Sir Ellis H. Minns rightly points out that the Georgian script must be derived from Aramaic or Syriac as it has in their right places letters corresponding to *waw*, *ṣade* and *qoph*. Armenian possesses these, but out of order.

BIBLIOGRAPHY

WARDROP, O. *Catalogue of Georgian MSS.*, London, British Museum, 1913.

BORK, F. *Beiträge zur kaukasischen Sprachwissenschaft*, I, Königsberg, 1907; *Das georgische Volk*, Leipsic, 1915.

MARR, N. Y. *Contributions to the Study of the Present Georgian Language* (in Russian), Petrograd, 1922; *Grammar of the Early Georgian Literary Language* (in Russian), Leningrad, 1925; *Help for Learning the Present Georgian Language*, Leningrad, 1926.

BROSSET, M. P. *Histoire de la Géorgie*, re-edition, Paris, 1923.

JUNKER, H. F. J. (*see above*), in *Caucasica*, 1925–7.

JAVACHVILI, J. A. *Georgian Palæography* (in Georgian), Tiflis, 1926.

DIRR, A. *Einführung in das Studium der kaukasischen Sprachen*, Leipsic, 1927; *Theoretische–praktische Grammatik der modernen georgischen (grusinischen) Sprache*, etc., Vienna and Leipsic, *s.a.*

MECKELEIN, R. *Georgisch-deutsches Wörterbuch*, Berlin, 1928.

MARR, N. Y. and BRIÈRE, M. *La Langue géorgienne*, Paris, 1931.

BLAKE, R. P. 'Catalogue of the Georgian MSS. in the Cambridge University Library,' *The Harvard Theological Review*, 1932.

ALLEN, W. E. D. *A History of the Georgian People*, London, 1932; 'The Present State of Caucasian Studies,' *Georgica*, London, 1935.

GUGUSHVILI, A. 'The Georgian Alphabet,' *Georgica*, 1935.

PERADZE, G. 'Georgian Manuscripts in England,' *Georgica*, 1935; 'Über die georgischen Handschriften in Östrereich,' *Wien. Zeitschr. für die Kunde des Morgenl.*, 1940.

van Ginneken, J. *Contribution à la grammaire comparée des Langues du Caucase*, Amsterdam, 1938.

Nyberg, H. S., 'Quelques inscriptions antiques découvertes récemment en Géorgie,' *Eranos*, 1946.

Tschekneli, K. *Einführung in die georgische Sprache*, 2 vols, Zurich, 1958.

Tsereteli, G. *The Most Ancient Georgian Inscriptions from Palestine* (in Georgian, with summary in Russian and English), Tiflis, 1960.

Various books and articles published by Trubetskoy and Dumézil.

ALBAN OR ALVAN ALPHABET (Fig. 16.26)

According to Armenian traditions, St. Mesrop created yet another alphabet, for the Albans or Alvans. According to the Armenians the territory in question (that is the classical kingdom of Albania), is called Aghvanir in their language; it is also known as Shirvan.

This people, of uncertain ethnic origin, lived in the Caucasus, now the Soviet Republic of Azerbaijan; they were quite important anciently, especially during the wars between Rome and Mithridates of Pontus. They developed a rich literature between the fifth and eleventh centuries A.D., but at the end of that period they disappeared as an ethnic entity. According to some scholars, Caucasian Albanian still survives in the Udi language, spoken in the villages of Vartashen and Nish in the district of Nukha to the north of the river Kur or Kura.

Many ancient and modern savants dare to connect the Albanians of the Balkans with the Caucasian Albanians.

No original Alban documents are extant; until recently it seemed as though twenty-one Alban letters (Fig. 16.26a) were reproduced in an Armenian manuscript of the sixteenth century. (*See* Karamianz, 'Einundzwanzig Buchstaben eines verlorenen Alphabets,' in *Zeitschr. der Deutsch Morgenl. Gesellsch.*,' XL, 1886, pp. 315 ff.). Professor A. Shanidze, however, shows that Karamianz's is merely queerly written Armenian. On the other hand, Shanidze thinks that a potsherd from Old Ganja may contain an Albanian inscription; *see* 'The Newly Discovered Alphabet of the Caucasian Albanians and its Significance for Science', *Bull. of the Marr Institute of Languages, History etc.*, published by the Academy of Sciences of the Georgian Soviet Republic, Tiflis, Vol. IV, 1938 (in Russian with summaries in Georgian and French). However, Professor H. W. Bailey points out ('Caucasica, *J. Roy. Asiatic Soc.*, 1943, p. 4), that 'the published photograph is not clear enough to permit of comparison.'

Professor Bailey mentions also I. Abuladze's article, 'On the Discovery of the Alphabet of the Caucasian Albanians,' which appeared in the same Bulletin of the Marr Institute. Abuladze publishes 'the lost alphabet which he found in an Armenian manuscript of the fifteenth century A.D., containing a miscellaneous collection of the Greek, Syriac, Latin, Georgian, Coptic, Arabic and Albanian alphabets.' 'Under each letter of the Albanian alphabet its name was written in Armenian script.'

This manuscript is now at Etchmiadzin (No. 7117). The Albanian alphabet seems to consist of fifty-two letters, of which twenty-nine are regarded as indigenous, twelve as borrowed from the Armenian alphabet, eight from Khutsuri, and three from Greek.

Sir Ellis H. Minns informed me that the MS. in question 'has tables of Greek, Syriac, Latin, Georgian, Albanian, Coptic alphabets, and Indian and Arabic cyphers with Armenian transcriptions. There are mistakes, but the alphabets are genuine. Therefore, the Albanian with fifty-two letters is possibly genuine': see Fig. 16.26b. (I owe the photograph of this illustration to the kindness of Professor Bailey.)

On the Caucasian Albanians see also G. Dumèzil, 'Une chrétienté disparue—les Albanais du Caucase,' Mélanges Asiatiques, I, 1940–1, and Journal Asiatique, 1940.

CHAPTER 17

Indian Branch

(Figs. 17.1–29)

IN dealing with the Kharoshthi script (pp. 301ff.), the general problem of Indian scripts was mentioned; all of them, except the Kharoshthi, are considered to be descendants of the Brahmī, which will be examined in the present chapter.

ORIGIN OF INDIAN WRITING

The problems connected with the origin and development of the numerous Indian scripts are so vast and complicated that it is impossible to deal with them in detail.

The early history of Indian writing, like the early history of India, is still imperfectly known. Until recently most historians were disposed to date the beginning of Indian writing in the early centuries of the first millennium B.C., and no serious scholar dated the origin in India earlier than the influx of the first tribes speaking Aryan dialects, which probably took place in the latter half of the second millennium B.C.

However, the recent discovery of the relics of the Indus Valley civilization (part 1, chapter 4), much older than the first Aryan settlements in India, came upon the world as a surprise, and it gave rise to numerous problems including the relationship of the Indus Valley culture to the early Indo-Aryan civilization. Much is being written on this subject, though little of it is of scientific value. For instance, the attempts of Fr. H. Heras, S.J., to equate the most up-to-date South Indian linguistic forms with the undeciphered seals belonging to the third millennium B.C. might put the unwary on the wrong track. Not a single link exists to cover the long gap between the Indus Valley script and the Indian writing, though the possibility of connection between the two scripts cannot be rejected categorically. A satisfactory answer to this problem will be obtained should strata bearing early Indian settlements be discovered, when their relationship to the Indus Valley civilization would be proved. It is useless to discuss the whole problem until sites in the land of origin of the Rig Veda hymns have been sufficiently explored, excavated and studied. The whole history of India prior to the middle of the seventh century B.C. is, indeed, still the province of archæology.

Indian scholars who patriotically regard the Brahmī as the descendant of an indigenous prehistoric script, may be reminded of the following facts:

(1) The existence in the same country of two or more successive scripts does not prove that one depends on the other; for instance, the early Greek alphabet employed in Crete did not descend from the early Cretan or Minoan scripts, nor the Arabic alphabet from the ancient South Semitic alphabet.

(2) Even if similarities could be proved between the shapes of the Indus Valley characters and those of the Brahmī letters, evidence would still be lacking that the latter descended directly from the former, unless the likeness of the signs belonging to the two systems corresponds with identity in their phonetic values. In this connection, the Minoan script as well as the Cypriote syllabary contained many signs resembling early Greek letters, but one was not derived from the other.

(3) I have already made clear (p. 216), that the main importance in the origin of an alphabet is not the invention of signs, but the establishment of an alphabetic system of writing; this applies for instance (p. 189) to the origin of the Meroitic scripts. The Indus Valley writing was presumably a transitional system or a mixed syllabic-ideographic script, whilst the Brahmī script was a semi-alphabet. As far as we know, no syllabic-ideographic script became alphabetic without the influence of another alphabetic script, and this was more important historically than the material origin of the single signs. No serious scholar has ever tried to show how the Indus Valley ideographic script could have developed into the Brahmī semi-alphabetic writing.

(4) The extensive Vedic literature gives no indication whatever of the existence of writing in early Aryan India. As Professor Rhys Davids rightly pointed out, it is one of those rare cases when negative evidence, where some mention would be reasonably expected, is good evidence. Many passages show that recording by writing was not practised while there is pretty constant reference to the texts as existing, but 'existing only in the memory of those who learnt them by heart.' For instance, the Indian priests were exceedingly keen to keep the knowledge of the mantras, the charms or verses, on which the magic of the sacrifice depended, in their own hands. 'The ears of a Sudra who listens, intentionally, when the Veda is being recited are to be filled with molten lead. His tongue is to be cut out if he recite it. His body is to be split in twain if he preserve it in his memory.' The priestly view was that the Deity had bestowed the exclusive right of teaching upon the hereditary priests, who each claimed to be great diviners. Writing is never mentioned. Among the ancient Indian divinities there was no god of 'writing,' but there was Sarasvati, the goddess of knowledge, learning and eloquence.

(5) Only the Buddhist literature gives clear references to writing in ancient times. A Buddhist tract of the Suttantas (or the conversational discourses of the Buddha) called *Sila-sutta*, attributed to the middle of the fifth century B.C., mentions a game for children—*akkharika* ('lettering'). In the Buddhist canonical scriptures *lekha* ('writing') is praised (Vinaya, IV, 7), and the career of *lekhaka* ('writer') is considered a very good one: 'he will dwell at ease and in comfort' (Vin. I, 77; IV, 28); many other words, such as *phalaka* (wood tablet for teaching to write), *lekham chindati* ('scratches a

writing'), and so forth, also presuppose the use of writing for public and private affairs.

We may thus assume that in the fifth century B.C., and probably also in the sixth century B.C., knowledge of writing was widespread, known to adults and children of both sexes. The Lalita Vistara, a life of the Buddha, relates that the Buddha studied writing in his childhood (that is, in the first half of the sixth century B.C.). Dr. L. D. Barnett reminded me that Panini (*see* below) in his grammar, III, ii, 21, which may be of the fifth century B.C., mentions *lipi* ('writing'), which is in origin a Persian word (information from Professor Bailey).

(6) Although no Indo-Aryan inscription can be attributed to a period earlier than the third or fourth century B.C., on epigraphic grounds alone it is supposed that the Brahmī script existed at least in the sixth century B.C. Professor Rhys Davids and other scholars considered at one time that the oldest inscription was the dedication of the relics from the Buddha's funeral pyre in the Sakiya Tope at Piprava, believed to date from about 450 B.C., but more recent criticism has thrown doubt upon that theory. At present, the oldest extant inscription seems to be the Sohgaura copper plate from the Gorakhpur district (Fig. 17.3*a*), belonging probably to the second half of the fourth century B.C.

A coin found at the village of Eran in the Saugor district of Madhya Pradesh, with an inscription from right to left (Fig. 17.3*b*), belongs to much the same period. The legend reads *Rano Dhamapalasa*, '(coin) of King Dharmapala.' A few other short inscriptions, two seals of Nadaya (Namdaya) and Agapalasa (Amgapalassa), a few Persian *sigloi* in Brahmī script, and perhaps the inscription of Mahasthan (Fig. 17.3*c*), may be attributed to the same period. More important are the Aśoka inscriptions (*see* below), belonging to the middle of the third century B.C.

(7) According to great authorities on the subject, such as Sir George Dunbar, J. Kennedy, Professor Rhys Davids, V. E. Smith, and others, the period 800–600 B.C. in India shows a remarkable advance in industrial life; a host of trades have been developed, from jewellers, usurers and weavers to sellers of dried fish, professional acrobats, astrologers and barbers; astronomy had made considerable progress. This period coincided with the development of maritime commerce. 'Sea-going merchants, availing themselves of the monsoons, were in the habit, at the beginning of the seventh (and perhaps at the end of the eighth) century B.C., of trading from ports on the south-west coast of India . . . to Babylon, then a great mercantile emporium'; 'it is highly probable that there was such trade much before that time.' It is generally agreed that the development of commerce favoured the diffusion of a knowledge of writing.

I do not think that much can be concluded for the subject we are here treating, from the fact of the ancient trade relations between India, including Dravidian India, with the western Semitic world in the times of Solomon (tenth century B.C.), as suggested by the presence in early Hebrew and other Semitic languages, of some Indo-Aryan and Dravidian loan-words, such as *kinnor*, 'guitar' (from Indian *kinnari*?), *'almuggim* (*'algummim*), 'sandals,' *qophim,* '*monkeys,*' *tukkiyim,* 'peafowls,' *sappir,* 'sapphire,' and a few other words. (*See* J. Kennedy, 'The Early Commerce of Babylon with India,' *J. Roy. Asiatic Soc.,*' 1898, pp. 241 ff.; H. G. Rawlinson, *Intercourse between India and the Western World,* Cambridge University Press, 1916; 2nd. ed., 1926; W. Baumgartner, 'Was wir heute von der hebräischen Sprache und ihrer Geschichte wissen', *Anthropos,* 1940–1, p. 612, n. 104, with copious bibliography.)

(8) Very little is known about the early Aryan history of India. The fantastic theories such as that of Mr. Tilak who attributed the earliest hymns of the Vedic literature to about 7000 B.C., or that of Mr. Shankar Balakrishna Dikshit who attributed certain Brahmanas to 3800 B.C., cannot be taken seriously. A learned Indian correspondent of mine—V. S. Bendrey of Lele's Bungalow, Gokhale Road, Poona—has expressed the view that the nature of my reference to Tilak 'is apparently due to some misunderstanding. What Mr. Tilak attempted to calculate was the culture of the Aryan race as reached in India, and not the culture which Aryans possessed in India.'

The immigration of Aryan tribes into India is now attributed to the second half of the second millennium B.C., and the entire Vedic literature—the sacred scriptures of the ancient Indians—is assigned to the same period continuing into the early part of the first millennium B.C., but they do not contribute much to the historical knowledge of ancient India.

Somewhere in the seventh century B.C.—no data exist for accurate chronology— we find ourselves upon somewhat firmer ground. The whole of India was becoming organized. Besides progress in commerce, it was a remarkable age in many ways. The ruler of the Magadha kingdom, Bimbisara, of the Sisunaga dynasty (middle of the seventh or the sixth century B.C.), made the first serious attempt to unify a great tract of India into a single political state with a central government, and this certainly favoured the diffusion of writing.

(9) In the sixth century B.C., northern India witnessed a remarkable religious revolution which profoundly influenced the course of Indian history. It was, in some respects, a popular reaction against the cumbersome rituals and bloody sacrifices which in those days constituted the essence for the 'exclusive' priestly classes of the Vedic religion. Two great sons of India largely brought about this mighty transformation. They were Vardhamana Mahavira, the Jina ('Conqueror of passions,' the 'leader of the school of thought'), the founder of Jainism (apart from Parswa, who ranks in the succession of the Jainas as the predecessor of Mahavira), and Gautama Sakyamuni Buddha (the 'Enlightened One'), the founder of Buddhism. Both lived in the sixth century B.C., and were anxious to make their spiritual teachings accessible to the common people and refused to confine them to Sanskrit, the language of the small privileged class. The new teachings of the Buddha especially, with their popular appeal, have long been recognized as the potent cause of the development of the languages of the people; Buddhist monks and nuns carried far and wide the gospel of the Enlightened One. There is no doubt that while the knowledge of writing may

have favoured the diffusion of Jainism and Buddhism, these two religions, and especially the latter, contributed much to the diffusion of the knowledge of writing.

(10) On the whole, many different lines of evidence suggest a date between the eighth and the sixth century B.C. for the introduction of writing into 'Aryan' India, thus confirming the conclusion that the Brahmī script was much later than the Indus Valley writing, and that the knowledge of writing flourished from the seventh–sixth century B.C. onwards.

THEORIES CONCERNING ORIGIN OF BRAHMI SCRIPT

The theories concerning the origin of the Brahmī script can be divided into two main groups: the first ascribes the Brahmī script to India, and the second regards it as borrowed from a foreign source.

(1) Many scholars, for instance, Edward Thomas, thought that the Brahmī script was a Dravidian invention, while General Cunningham, Dowson, and others believed that the Indian priests had developed it from picture writing. Since the discovery of the Indus Valley civilization, this latter theory has been connected with the Indus Valley script (*see* part 1, chapter 4).

Many Indian scholars follow this opinion, which, however, cannot be upheld for the reasons already explained.

(2) The other theories can be subdivided into two groups: (*a*) James Prinsep, Raoul de Rochette, Otfried Müller, Émile Senart, Goblet d'Alviella, and others believed that the Brahmī script derived from the Greek alphabet. Hellenic influence on the invention of the Brahmī script has been also suggested by Joseph Halévy, Wilson and others. I do not think that this theory is satisfactory: (1) the Indians came in direct contact with Greek civilization (probably in the period of Darius the Great, 522–486 B.C.) only after they had long been in contact with other peoples using alphabetic writings, and the invention of the Brahmī script seems to be at least one or two centuries older than the earliest Indo-Greek cultural relations; (2) the main improvement of the Greek alphabet on the Semitic was the introduction of vowels, while the chief weakness of the Indian scripts is their unsatisfactory solution of vocalization.

(*b*) Most historians of writing consider the Brahmī to be a derivation of a Semitic alphabet. This theory, already suggested in 1806 by Jones, in 1811 by von Seetzen, in 1821 by Kopp, in 1834 by Lepsius, was extended in 1856 by Weber and at the end of the last century by Bühler.

Within this general theory, four secondary ones have been propounded:

(1) The derivation of the Brahmī from the Phœnician alphabet suggested by eminent scholars such as Benfey, Weber, Bühler, Jensen, and others, who tried to prove that about one-third of the Phœnician letters were identical with the earliest forms of the corresponding Brahmī signs; that another third were somewhat similar, and the remainder can be more or less harmonized. The chief objection to this

opinion is that there was no direct communication, at the requisite date, between India and the eastern shores of the Mediterranean, and it seems probable that the Phœnicians had no influence whatever on the origins of the scripts of countries lying to the east of them.

(2) According to Professor Deecke, Canon Taylor and, more recently, the late Professor Sethe, the Brahmī script descended from the South Semitic alphabet. This view is also unacceptable; although it is quite probable that there was direct communication between India and southern Arabia, cultural influences of the latter on the former do not appear to have taken place as early as the eighth–seventh century B.C., to which period we may attribute the origin of the Brahmī; besides, the resemblance between the South Semitic letters and the Brahmī characters is slight.

(3) Still less probable is the derivation of the Brahmī alphabet from the cuneiform script propounded by Professor Rhys Davis, who suggested 'that the only hypothesis harmonizing these discoveries is that the Indian letters were derived, neither from the alphabet of the northern nor from that of the southern Semites, but from that source from which these, in their turn, had been derived—from the pre-Semitic form of writing used in the Euphrates Valley.' This great authority on Buddhist literature is practically alone in his theory, which is unsubstantiated by any important evidence in its favour.

(4) All historical and cultural evidence is best co-ordinated by the theory which considers the early Aramaic alphabet to be the prototype of the Brahmī script. The acknowledged resemblance of the Brahmī signs to the Phœnician letters also applies to the early Aramaic letters, while in my opinion there can be no doubt that of all the Semites, the Aramæan traders were the first who came in direct communication with the Indo-Aryan merchants.

We need not assume that the Brahmī is a simple derivative of the Aramaic alphabet. It was probably mainly the *idea* of alphabetic writing which was accepted, although the shapes of many Brahmī signs show also Semitic influence and the original direction of the Brahmī character, from right to left, was also of Semitic origin. It is generally admitted that the earliest known form of the Brahmī is a script framed by Brahmans for writing Sanskrit, and it may be assumed that they were the inventors of this essentially national alphabet, regardless of the problem concerning the original source of the idea. The fully developed Brahmī system, an outcome of the remarkable philological and phonological precision wherein the early Indians surpassed all ancient peoples, provided the various Indian languages with an exact reflex of their pronunciation.

It is an open question, and quite unimportant, whether the Aramæans or the Indian merchants, who may have learned it in Babylon or elsewhere, introduced it into India.

Some scholars hold that, as the Indian writing is in appearance a syllabary, it could not have been derived from an alphabet; alphabetic script being obviously more advanced than syllabic. These scholars seem to have forgotten that the Semitic alphabet did not contain vowels, and whilst the Semites could, if necessary, dispense with vowel-signs, the Indo-European languages could not do so. The Greeks solved the problem of vocalization satisfactorily; but the Indians were less successful. It may be that the inventor of the Brahmī, who probably had no knowledge of the Greek alphabet, did not grasp the essence of the alphabetic system of writing. It is quite possible that the Semitic script appeared to him as semi-syllabic, as it could seem to any speaker of an Indo-Aryan language. Indeed, the Hebrew even now writes *k-t-b* to indicate any word having a meaning connected with 'writing,' although the word would never be read *ktb*, but *kᵃtᵃb* ('he wrote'), *kᵒtᵉb* ('he is writing'), *ᵉktᵒb* ('I shall write'), and so forth, according to the sense of the sentence; whereas in an Indo-Aryan tongue, a word written with mere consonants would have many meanings or no meaning at all (*e.g.*, in English *c-t* could mean 'cat,' 'cut,' 'cot,' 'city,' 'cute,' 'act,' 'acute,' or no meaning at all).

The fact that the sound *a* is inherent in all the consonants of the Indian scripts unless otherwise indicated, is perhaps due to the influence of the Aramaic language, in which the final *aleph* predominated.

As to the date of the origin of the Brahmī script, nothing is certain; the eighth or seventh centuries B.C. seem to be the most probable.

Over seventy-three years ago, R. N. Cust, the then Hon. Secretary of the Royal Asiatic Society, published an article in the journal of that Society ('On the Origin of the Indian Alphabet,' *J. Roy. Asiatic Soc.*, N.S., XVI, 1884, pp. 325–9). Since then, many new discoveries have been made, and the problem has been discussed in many hundreds of books and articles, and yet, concerning the origin of the Brahmī script, I even now fairly well agree with the first two of his conclusions:

'I. The Indian Alphabet is in no respect an independent invention of the People of India, who, however, elaborated to a marvellous extent a loan, which they had received from others.

'II. The *idea* of representing Vowel and Consonant Sounds by symbols of a pure alphabetic character was derived from Western Asia beyond any reasonable doubt.' The Indian characters, however, are semi-alphabetic and not pure alphabetic).

INDIAN INSCRIPTIONS

Unquestionably the most copious and important source for the study of the Indian scripts is the epigraphic, and the present knowledge of many periods of the long-forgotten past is also derived mainly from the patient study of the numerous Indian inscriptions during the last hundred years. The great majority of these inscriptions belong to three classes: (1) commemorative, (2) dedicatory, and (3) donative. The first two classes are mostly incised on stone, and they comprise a vast variety of records, from the mere signature of a pilgrim's name to an elaborate panegyrical Sanskrit poem. On the other hand, the donative inscriptions relating to religious endowments or secular donations are mostly engraved on plates of copper, whilst many

Indian inscriptions are recorded on iron, gold, silver, brass, bronze, clay, earthenware, bricks, crystals, or even palm leaves and birch bark. The earliest known Indian work in ivory is an inscription at Sanchi dating from the first half of the second century B.C. The languages used in the inscriptions are as varied as the materials on which they were written, Sanskrit, Pali, Sinhalese, Tamil, Bengali, Oriya, Nepali, Telugu, Malayalam, and others.

Southern India is particularly rich in inscriptions of all kinds, some of which attain extraordinary length. Many thousands of these inscriptions belong to a relatively recent date. Until recently, with the exception of the Aśoka inscriptions and the brief dedications of the Bhattiprolu caskets (Bhattiprolu lies south-east of Guntur in the Kistna river delta), no important document was attributed to the pre-Christian era, and relatively few inscriptions were regarded as earlier than the seventh century A.D.

However, in 1916–7, a Brahmī inscription of the first century B.C. was noticed in the Buddhist cave at Guntapelle in the Kistna district; the year 1923–4 brought to light a Brahmī inscription of about the second century A.D. at Allur(u), also in the Kistna district (19 miles north north-east of Nellore); and, finally, in 1941, members of the Bombay Kannada Research Institute discovered a Prakrit pillar inscription in Brahmī characters of the second century B.C. at Wadgaon or Vadgaon-Madhavapur near Belgaum (north-east of Goa), which is the earliest Brahmanical Prakrit document known to exist in the Bombay Karnatak (Kanara): *see* also p. 267.

The carliest extant manuscripts on palm-leaves seem to belong to the fourth century A.D. (for instance, some fragments from Kashgar, in the Godfrey Collection), and to the sixth century (the Horiuzji MS.); the majority, however, belong to the ninth and the following centuries. The oldest manuscript found in the south is dated A.D. 1428, according to Burnell.

DEVELOPMENT OF INDIAN SCRIPTS
EARLY PERIOD (UP TO FOURTH CENTURY A.D.)

The intricate development of the numerous ancient and modern Indian scripts presents many problems. The *Lalita Vistara* mentions sixty-four alphabets known at the time of the Buddha. We do not know whether this number is correct; it may be exaggerated, or late conditions may have been anticipated. The framework of the *Lalita Vistara* is perhaps 2,000 years old, but the extant Sanskrit and Tibetan versions cannot be older than the seventh century A.D., and passages, like those concerning writing, are considered to be interpolations of the ninth or tenth century A.D.

However, some of the scripts can be identified: the *Brahmi* or *Bambhi*, the *Kharoshthi* or *Kharotthi*, the *Yavananaliya* or *Yavananiya*, which is obviously the Greek script, the *Dravidi* or *Damili*, the Tamil prototype (?) script, and so forth; others are probably only varieties of the main types. At any rate, there is no doubt that even in early times, there were many Indian scripts. A very ancient slab in Jain temple No. 1

at Deogarh bears specimens of eighteen scripts and eighteen forms of speech (*bhasha*). (Deogarh, with famous Jain and Rajput ruins, lies in the Jhansi district of the Betva, 16 miles south south-west of Lalitpur.)

The traditional name of the ancestor of the Indian scripts, the *Brahmī* (*sc. lipi*) appears in the third or fourth century A.D., about a thousand years after its invention. At that time, its creation was attributed to Brahma himself, as its true origin had already been forgotten.

James Prinsep (b. 1799, d. 1840), the unfortunately short-lived Boden Professor of Sanskrit in the University of Oxford, laid the basis for the decipherment of the Brahmī script. Within the short period of five years, 1834–9, he established the foundation of modern knowledge of the ancient Indian scripts; 'he was one of the most talented and useful men that England has given to India,' was rightly said of him by another great English Indianist, Edward Thomas. Masson, Lassen, Norris, Cunningham and other scholars, mostly English, also contributed to our knowledge of these earliest scripts.

MAIN TYPES OF EARLY INDIAN OR BRAHMI SCRIPTS

Bühler, the greatest authority on the history of Indian writing, distinguished eight main types of the early Indian scripts:

(1) *Script Written from Right to Left*

It is the script already mentioned of the brief legend of five syllables, Dhamapalasa, of the Eran coin (Fig. 17.3*b*), written from right to left, of the fourth or third century B.C. Till recently, the evidence of the Eran coin could not be regarded as conclusive concerning the direction of writing of the original Brahmī. Many scholars assumed it to be due to a fault in the matrix from which the coin had been cast. Curiously enough, these scholars still adhere to their view and have overlooked the fact that in 1929 a new discovery was made. In that year Anu Ghose, a geologist from Calcutta, found at Yerragudi, Kurnool district in north Madras province, near the river Kistna, important Aśoka (*see* below) inscriptions, which were published in 1933 by Ray Bahadur Daya Ram Sahni in the *Annual Report of the Archæological Survey of India*, 1928–9, pp. 161–7. The best preserved inscription is a version of Aśoka's Minor Edict. The most important feature of this document is that eight of the twenty-three lines, namely lines 2, 4, 6, 9, 11, 13, 14, 23, are incised from right to left, or—if we eliminate from consideration lines 8 and 14—more than half of the inscription appears to be written in *boustrophedon*, or alternating lines. As Mr. Sahni points out, this inscription leaves no doubt that the *boustrophedon* style was known in the time of Aśoka. There is, thus, sufficient evidence of the existence of an earlier Brahmī script written from right to left, followed—as in the development of the early Greek script —by a transitional system of writing in *boustrophedon* style.

(2) *Early Maurya Type, Third Century B.C.*

Soon after Alexander the Great's death, Chandragupta, known to the Greeks as Sandrokottos, overthrew the Magadha kingdom, and founded the Maurya dynasty. His grandson was Aśoka ('sorrowlessness, joy')-vardhana ('increasing'), with the royal titles Devanampiya ('dear to gods') Piyadasi ('of gracious mien'), by which he is described in his edicts. He is the famous Aśoka, who has been compared with the emperors Constantine and Marcus Aurelius, King Alfred, Charlemagne, the Indian emperor Akbar, and other great historical personalities. He is considered by some Indian scholars as one of India's greatest prophets.

Pre-eminent among Indian monuments are Aśoka's famous inscriptions (Fig. 17.3 *d-e*), over thirty-five in number, some of them in many versions, incised upon rocks, boulders, cave-walls and pillars, which supply the only reliable records for the history of his reign—which lasted from 269/268 B.C. to about 237 B.C.; they fully expound both his principles of government and his system of practical ethics, and supply many interesting autobiographical details. The majority of the inscriptions have a special character, no other sovereign having engraved ethical exhortations or precepts on the rocks. These inscriptions appear throughout India, extending from the Himalayas to Mysore, and from the Bay of Bengal to the Arabian Sea. *See* also p. 305.

The inscriptions Aśoka left (*see* particularly *Corpus Inscriptionum Indicarum*, New Edition, I, *Inscriptions of Aśoka*, 1925, edited by E. Hultzsch) are milestones in the history of the Indian languages and scripts. These monuments have been classified in eight or nine groups in chronological order, from 257 to about 235 B.C.; six groups are edicts and two or three are dedications and brief commemorative records. The inscriptions were intended to appeal to all, learned and unlearned alike, and were placed in suitable positions on high roads or at places of pilgrimage, and were written not in Sanskrit (*samskrita*, the 'cultivated, literary' language), but in ancient local dialects or Prakrits (*prakrita*, 'natural, uncultivated'), out of which have arisen most of the modern languages of northern India. The Aśoka inscriptions were obviously intended to be understood by the public, and their existence presupposed a widely diffused knowledge of the art of writing.

Two recensions of the so-called Fourteen Rock Edicts, inscribed on rocks at places near the north-western frontier of India, were written in the Kharoshthi script (*see* preceding chapter); all the other inscriptions (Fig. 17.3) extant are written in one or other variety of the early Maurya type of the Brahmi (Fig. 17.1). Recently, a bilingual Aśoki rock-inscription (written in Greek and Aramaic) has been discovered at Kandahār, southern Afghanistan.

The local Brahmī varieties can be divided into a northern (Fig. 17.3*d*) and a southern group, the most southerly being the Siddapura inscriptions (Siddapura lies 47 miles north north-east of Chitaldroog in Mysore province). Figure 17.3*e* reproduces one of the South Indian Aśoka inscriptions published by Professor Turner ('The Gavimath and Palkigundu Inscriptions of Aśoka', *Hyderabad Archæological Series*, No. 10, 1932).

Though the Aśoka script is still imperfect, it is, in comparison with the few earlier inscriptions, which were roughly and rudely written, without long vowels or combinations of consonants, a great improvement; the long vowels are marked and there are various combinations of consonants. However, the short vowel *a* was inherent in every consonant unless the latter was associated with another vowel-sound.

(3) *Early Kalinga Type—the 'Dravidi' Script*

Kalinga is an ancient region on the east coast of southern India, lying between the Mahanadi in the north, the Godavari river in the south, the eastern Ghats and the sea (roughly corresponding to northern Madras and southern Orissa). When Aśoka ascended the throne, Kalinga was an important independent kingdom, but Aśoka conquered it in 262 B.C. This event brings into the picture non-Aryan India south of the Vindhyas, which had hitherto been a *terra incognita*. Soon after Aśoka's death Kalinga regained its freedom from Magadha, its power had greatly increased, and about 150 B.C. Kharavela, king of Kalinga, claimed to have made two successful invasions, advancing the second time as far north as the Ganges. This story is related in the 'Elephant Cave' inscription.

The 'Elephant Cave' inscription, attributed to about 150 B.C., represents *the early Kalinga type* of the Brahmī character.

The inscriptions on the reliquary vessels from a Buddhist *stupa* at Bhattiprolu in Kistna district of Madras province (p. 264), represent a still earlier variety, called by Bühler *Dravidi*, and attributed by him to about 200 B.C. The type, on the whole, seems to agree with the southern form of the Aśoka inscriptions, but it contains, according to Bühler, certain more archaic features, amongst them the following: (1) three signs, that is *dh*, *d* and *bh*, are in the position of a script running from right to left; (2) three signs, those for the sounds *c*, *j* and *sh*, are more archaic than the forms of the Eran coin (belonging to the fourth or third century B.C.) or the Aśoka inscriptions (third century B.C.); (3) two signs (*l* and cerebral *l*) resemble early Semitic forms; (4) one new sign, *gh*, was derived from an early form of *g*. All these peculiar features induced Bühler to conclude that whatever the age of these inscriptions, the 'Dravidi' alphabet was separated from the main stock of the Brahmī character by the fifth century B.C. at the latest.

'This is undoubtedly the reason why so many archaic forms are noticed in the few inscriptions so far known in the Dravidi script. The development of forms after separation could not be so fast in Dravidi as in the regular Brahmi . . .' (Dr. N. P. Chakravarti). Over fifty short inscriptions, engraved on rocks at natural rock-shelters in South India, especially in the districts of Mathurai (Madura) and Tirunelveli (Tinnevelly), are written in this script. Some are attributed to the third century B.C. (the Mamandur inscription), others to about 200 B.C. (the Bhattiprolu inscriptions) or to the first century (the Hathibada and Ghosundi inscriptions), but Dr. R. E. M. (now Sir Mortimer) Wheeler's dating (*Ancient India*, 1946) of the eighteen graffiti found in the 1945 excavation at Arikamedu, near Pondicherry, on the tropical Coromandel

T

coast, in the first or second centuries A.D., is the only one based on safe archæological ground.

(4) *Early Western Deccan or Andhra Script*

Amongst the powers mentioned as under the empire of Aśoka were the Andhras (or Telugus, as they are now called), then apparently living along the east coast around their capital at Dhanakataka, south of the Kalingas. The dynasty of the Satavahanas were not Andhras originally: they did not settle in Telingana or Andhra (in central Deccan) until late. They became, however, powerful in the deltas of the Godavari and Kistna rivers, and became a South Indian, Dravidian, dynasty. After Aśoka's death, the Andhras asserted complete independence and gradually expanded north-westwards, occupying all the Deccan from sea to sea. This must have been about the middle of the second century B.C. From their secondary capital, Patitthana (Pratish-thana, Paithan), in the north-west of their kingdom, they often waged war on the Aryan kingdoms in Avanti and Gujarat. Later, they extended their power north-wards, and in 27 B.C. they overthrew the Brahman Kanvas and occupied Magadha.

It is evident that the Andhras, centred then in the western Deccan, had already attained a civilization comparable with that of the Aryan settlements. By A.D. 200, they spread across India to Nasik (south-east of Damas) and gradually pushed their way northwards. About A.D. 236, after an existence of over four and a half centuries, the Andhra dynasty came to an end, almost at the same time as the dynasty of the Kushanas in the north. These two events occurred during one of the most obscure periods of Indian history.

The 'early western Deccan' or 'Andhra' script was employed from the first half of the second century B.C., till the first century A.D. Its most important document is a large inscription of the Andhra queen Naganika in the Nanaghat cave (Nanaghat Pass, Poona district, Bombay), which cannot be later than 150 B.C. Other important inscriptions written in this script were discovered in the caves of Nasik, Pitalkhora and Ajanta.

(5) *Late Maurya Type*

It is an unfortunate coincidence that, in Indian history, in the five odd centuries following Aśoka's death, the main parts into which India can be divided are shrouded in mist. From time to time, a name of a ruler, or of a kingdom illumines the dark-ness.

It seems that Aśoka's pacifist policy produced political disintegration and foreign domination of the northern and north-western provinces. However, Aśoka is known to have been followed by four successors; the last of the imperial Mauryas, Brihadratha, was assassinated by his general Pushyamitra, about 184 B.C.

Few inscriptions are extant of this period; consequently the development of writing cannot be followed with accuracy.

The type of writing in this period, the end of the third century B.C. and early second century, is termed by Bühler *Late Maurya*. This script was used both in the north-east (Bihar) and in the north-west. Græco-Indian coins show that the use of the 'late Maurya' character continued till the middle of the second century B.C.

(6) *Sunga Type*

Pushyamitra, apparently a Brahman, was the founder of the Sunga dynasty, which lasted till about 72 B.C., and was overthrown by the Brahman Kanva. The period of the Sungas and the Kanvas—the latter dynasty lasting forty-five years—was the age of Sanskrit revival in Hindustan. Parallel with the employment of the Prakrits, that is the vernaculars, Sanskrit, which was originally a refined form of the language of the 'Madhyadesa' (the Indian homeland), developed into an artificial, literary language. Sanskrit represents the language of the Brahman civilization, while the Prakrits, particularly the form known as Pali, became the language of Buddhist and Jain literature.

Sanskrit evidently owed its development to the efforts of early grammarians, the most important of whom was Panini, who lived in the fifth or fourth century B.C. Pantanjali, another important grammarian, is generally believed to have been a contemporary of the founder of the Sunga dynasty; he probably contributed much to the revival of Sanskrit. Indeed, traces of this influence are already apparent in the second century B.C.

According to some scholars, the first Sanskrit inscription dates from 33 B.C. (on a Brahman sacrificial post at Isapur), while others maintain that the earliest inscription in good literary Sanskrit is that of Rudradaman I, at Girnar in Kathiawar (Girnar is a hill just east of Junagadh in south central India), attributed to the middle of the second century A.D. However, in spite of the efforts of grammarians, it is clear from epigraphical evidence that Sanskrit was not in common use before the second century A.D. At that period, Sanskrit began to supersede Prakrit in north-western India, but it was only from the time of the great king Samudragupta (A.D. 340–75) that Sanskrit became almost the only inscriptional language of northern India.

The development of the *Sunga type* of the Brahmī script took place in the schools of the Brahman priests, and was connected with the revival of literary activity under the Sunga dynasty. The script is represented by the inscription of Dhanabhuti *Vacchiputa*, 'son of a princess of Vatsa (Kausambi)' on the *torana* of the Bharhut *stupa* (or sepulchral monument), near Satna, in Vindhya, Pradesh state, the Pabhosa (probably the ancient kingdom of Kausambi) cave inscriptions, and the oldest dedications from Mathura (Muttra), on the upper Jumna (30 miles north-west of Agra). (Pabhosa lies 5 miles west north-west of Kosam; Kosam, 28 miles west south-west of Allahabad, on the northern bank of the Jumna River, is identical with the famous ancient capital Kausambi of the Hindu kingdom, founded in the first or second century B.C. by Kuru). Bühler sees in the Sunga character close connections with the late Maurya type on the one hand and with the early Kalinga character (*see* above) on the other.

(7) *Prototypes of North Indian Sub-division*

Out of the Brahmī scripts mentioned under (2), (5) and (6), there developed in the last century B.C. and the first centuries A.D., various scripts which became the *prototypes of the North Indian sub-division* (Fig. 17.1).

Dr. Bühler mentioned the following two main groups:

(*a*) Closely connected with the latest form of the Sunga type is the script of the northern Kshatrapas, as shown in the inscriptions of Rajuvala (Ranjubula) and of his son Sodasa (late first century B.C.) and in some votive inscriptions from Mathura.

(*b*) More important in the development of Indian writing were the inscriptions of the Kushana kings Kanishka, Huviska and Vasudeva.

Kanishka overthrew the Sakas in the eastern and southern Punjab, and founded the Vikrama dynasty. Nothing within historic times is more uncertain than the chronology of the Kushanas and the founding of the Vikrama era. Scholars differ by over three hundred years in estimating the latter date, ranging from the middle of the first century B.C. to A.D. 278. The most probable dates seem to be either 58 B.C. or A.D. 78: Kanishka was probably the founder of the well-known Saka era, which began in A.D. 78 (*see* below). The dynasty of the Kushanas came to an end about A.D. 225, only eleven years before the fall of the great southern dynasty of the Andhras (*see* above); chaotic darkness had by then enveloped India.

Over seventy inscriptions are extant with the names of the above-mentioned Kushana kings. Some of them are Buddhist, but the majority are attributed to the Jains. In spite of some local variations in the single letters, the Kushana script possesses a very characteristic appearance. Some letters as, for instance the advanced forms of the medial vowels *a*, *u*, and *e*, show forms leading up to the Gupta character (*see* below). The board strokes of the signs and their thick tops indicate that the Kushana letters imitate a literary script written with ink.

The characters of Fig. 17.1, sect. 1, were used respectively in the first century B.C., in the second century A.D. and the fourth century A.D.

For Kanishka *see* Girshman, *J. Asiatique*, 1943–5.

(8) *Prototypes of South Indian Scripts*

The types mentioned under (3) and (4) became the *prototypes of the South Indian scripts*. The following six main varieties of the South Indian sub-division of scripts were, according to Bühler, developed between the second and fourth century A.D.:

(*a*) The character used by the Kshaharata dynasty of Malwa and Gujarat from the time of Rudradaman I, first half of the second century A.D.; (*b*) the archaistic or retrograde type of the western Deccan, the Konkan, and of some Amaravati inscriptions, from the time of the Kshatrapa Nahapana, beginning from the second century A.D.; (*c*) the slightly later character in use by some Andhra kings in the same district, seen in Nasik inscription No. 20, and other documents; (*d*) the ornamental variety of the same district with more fully developed southern peculiarities, represented in the

Kuda and Junnar inscriptions, end of the second century A.D.; (e) the highly ornamental variety of the eastern Deccan from Jagayyapeta, in the Kistna district, Madras, and some Amaravati inscriptions, of the third century A.D., developed from the preceding variety; and (f) the script of the Prakrit inscriptions of the Pallava king Sivaskandavarman from Kanchi, the modern Conjeeveram, near Madras, in the Tamil district, of the fourth century A.D. It is a highly cursive hand, but it shows a certain relationship to group (e).

The writing of the western Deccan and the Konkan, as seen in the caves at Nasik, Junnar, Karli, Kanheri, Kuda, and so forth, shows the three varieties mentioned above under (b), (c) and (d). All were employed more or less promiscuously in the second century A.D. The oldest dated inscriptions of the Kshaharata dynasty are dated from the years 41 to 45 (A.D. 119 to 123) of the Saka dynasty, the principal era of southern India, beginning in A.D. 78. These inscriptions are in a clumsy script, which seems to be a direct development of the early Andhra character mentioned under (4). Other inscriptions, such as those from Nasik of the Satavahana kings, who overthrew the Kshaharata dynasty soon after 125 A.D., are written in a very neat script, in a *ductus* resembling, according to Bühler, the northern script of Sodasa (first century B.C. or A.D.; *see* p. 270).

The inscriptions of Amaravati are very important: Amaravati or Amravati, on the south bank of the Kistna river, in the Guntur district of Madras province, was one of the chief centres of the Buddhist kingdom of Vengi, where the most important Buddhist remains of southern India were discovered. The inscriptions of Amaravati *stupa* show that the western Deccan and Konkan scripts were also used on the eastern coast of South India.

FURTHER DEVELOPMENT OF INDIAN SCRIPTS

During the next century, three main branches of Indian scripts are distinguishable: the northern, the southern, and the further-Indian branch; a few other types were of mixed or uncertain origin; *see* the following sections.

NORTH INDIAN SCRIPTS
(FOURTH–FOURTEENTH CENTURIES A.D.)

The mediæval and modern Indian characters arose from the early scripts, particularly from the prototypes mentioned under (7) and their cursive varieties. Dr. Bühler points out that the ancient MSS. and various peculiarities of the letters such as the formation of wedges at the ends of the verticals clearly prove that they were always written with a pen or a brush and ink. Granting the probability of these writing materials, I should not insist on the word 'always.' In the course of time, the letters were equalized in height and breadth as far as possible.

Bühler distinguished seven main types in the development of the North Indian scripts during the millennium from the middle of the fourth century A.D.

NORTH INDIAN MONUMENTAL TYPE KNOWN AS GUPTA (Fig. 17.1)

This character was employed in the fourth–sixth centuries A.D.

Little is known about the origin of the Gupta family, and it is not even certain whether Gupta was a title or a name. At the beginning of the fourth century the Guptas rose to power. Chandragupta I, who was the first independent sovereign, probably reigned from A.D. 319–20 to about 336. He established the Gupta era. For a century and a half the Guptas unified a very large portion of India. The mighty empire lost its power at the end of the sixth century A.D., but the Gupta state lingered on for another 200 years.

The period of the imperial Guptas has often been regarded as the 'Periclean age' of classical India and as the golden epoch of Hindu history and literature. Long-lived and versatile sovereigns reigned, who brought about a re-unification of northern India and ushered in an era of internal security and material prosperity accompanied by a tremendous development in religion, literature, art and science.

Meanwhile, a long and bitter strife took place between the Brahmans and Buddhists; in the end Brahmanism triumphed. Inscriptional Prakrit then became rare, and from the fifth century A.D. it almost disappeared in northern India. Sanskrit, which was especially associated with Brahmanism, was what Latin is to the Roman Catholic Church; it became the literary language and the *lingua franca* of religion. Later, Sanskrit was also used by Buddhists and Jainists and like Latin in mediæval Europe, it became the language of learning throughout India. The predominance of Sanskrit in the cultural, scientific and magical sphere remained unchallenged until the Islamic invasion brought a new literary language into prominence.

As a result of these political and cultural conditions, the Gupta script (Fig. 17.1), employed in the fourth and fifth centuries A.D. spread over the vast territories of the Gupta empire and became the ancestor of the great majority of the Indian scripts.

Dr. Hœrnle, basing himself on the letter *ma*, recognized two main varieties in the monumental Gupta character, a southern and a northern; the latter having two sub-varieties (the text letter being *sha*), an eastern and a western. According to Dr. Bühler, the main varieties of the Gupta character were the western and the eastern.

Modern Indian scholars partly disagree with this sub-division of the Gupta character. R. D. Banerji recognized four varieties, namely: the eastern, the western, the southern and the central Asian; the first two of them mainly appearing in the inscriptions of the early Gupta emperors. According to S. N. Chakravarti, the expression 'eastern variety of the Gupta alphabet' is misleading; he shows that the eastern variety was in existence before the Gupta period. However, 'the eastern variety gradually came to be displaced by the western one, in comparatively early times'; 'this displacement was completed before A.D. 588' (Chakravarti).

CENTRAL ASIAN GUPTA SUB-VARIETIES

The western variety of the Gupta character spread into the territory now called East- or Chinese Turkestan, and two important Gupta subvarieties developed there: (*a*) the type known as Central Asian Slanting Gupta, which probably already existed in the fourth century A.D., and (*b*) the Central Asian Cursive Gupta, fully developed in the sixth or seventh century A.D.

CENTRAL ASIAN SLANTING GUPTA (Fig. 17.5)

In 1890, the first manuscripts written in this script and in a new language were found, and were published in 1893 by Dr. Hœrnle. Later, many other documents were discovered. Their decipherment, facilitated by some bilingual manuscripts (one of the two languages, that is Sanskrit, being known), was soon accomplished, thanks to the labours of Hœrnle, Leumann, Sieg, Siegling, and other scholars.

Agnean and Kuchean (commonly but wrongly known as *Tokharian*)

The decipherment of the new documents revealed that in the latter part of the first millennium A.D., the population living between the river Tarim and the mountains T'ien-shan, including the territories of Turfan, Qarashahr and Kucha, spoke a language belonging to the *centum* group of the Indo-European family of languages. The new language, however, presents several features not paralleled in the other Indo-European languages, and its relationship with the other groups has not yet been sufficiently cleared up. Some scholars suggest affinities with Thracian-Phrygian-Armenian, others with Italo-Celtic, and others with Hittite. Other theories suggest that the new language may hold an intermediate position between Italo-Celtic, Slavonic and Armenian, or between Balto-Slavonic and Greek, or else between Armenian and Thraco-Phrygian.

The language of the documents extant is not uniform; two dialects can be distinguished. It was assumed, at first, that the new language was the language of ancient Tokharistan, the country situated between Sogdiana at the Iron Gates, and Bamiyan; its capital was Balkh. The population was called by the Greeks Tokharoi, Thaguroi; by the Romans Tochar; or Thogarii (in Sanskrit, Tukhara; in Tibetan, Thod-kar or Tho-gar; in Khotanese, Ttaugara; in Uigurian, Twghry; in Armenian, T'ukhri-k', the country being called Tokharastan). Modern scholars therefore called the language *Tokharian*, and they distinguished the two dialects by calling them 'Tokharian Dialect A,' and 'Tokharian Dialect B.' It was, however, soon discovered that 'Dialect B' was the language of the ancient kingdom of Kucha or Kuci (in Sanskrit, Kauceya; in Uigurian, *Küsän tili*, 'language of Kuci'; the indigenous term is unknown). There is, thus, a general agreement to call 'Dialect B' *Kuchean*.

As to 'Tokharian Dialect A,' Professor Bailey pointed out that the term Tokharian is not correct, as Toghara or Tokhara was the indigenous term of a people whose original language is now unknown, but it is known that they had no linguistic affinities with Indo-European. He, therefore, suggests calling 'Dialect A' *Agnean*, from the ancient kingdom of Agni, later known as Qarashahr (the indigenous name was Arsi). Some scholars call this language Qarashahrian, but this term reflects a later period. Many scholars, however, still employ the terms Tokharian, Dialect A, and Dialect B.

Agnean and Kuchean Characters (Fig. 17.11*a*)

The numerous documents extant were discovered by British (Sir Aurel Stein), Russian (Klementz and Berezowski), French (R. Pelliot), German (A. Grünwedel and A. von Le Coq) and Japanese (K. Otani) scholars, and are now in collections in London, Oxford, Paris, Calcutta, Leningrad, Berlin, Peking and Tokyo. They were found in the eastern part of the Tarim basin (eastern Turkestan), and in Tun-huang (north-west China). They belong to the second half of the first millennium A.D.

The writing is, as already mentioned, a variant of the western type of the Gupta character, called by Dr. Hœrnle, Central Asian Slanting (Fig. 17.5). The script is thus based on the Indian Gupta system. As in Indian, the basic consonants of the Central Asian Slanting have generally the inherent *a*, but, unlike the Indian, there are special signs (*Fremdzeichen* in German, *doublettes* in French) which have an inherent *ä*. The Indian Gupta signs for which there were no sounds in the indigenous languages were eliminated, while some new signs were invented to represent the peculiar indigenous sounds. On the whole, about twelve signs were added. The new script had, thus, symbols to represent the following vocalic and consonantal sound: long and short *a*, *i* and *u*; the vowels *ä*, *o* and *e*; the diphthongs *e* and *o* in Agnean, and *ai* and *au* in Kuchean; the semi-vowels *y* and *w*; four forms of *s*; three forms of *n* and three liquids (*r*, *l* and *ly*), and the occlusives *p*, *t*, *k*, *c*, and *ts*; there were no surds.

As already mentioned, two varieties may be distinguished, the Agnean and the Kuchean; the latter script being more cursive than the former. The texts preserved are largely religious works, but in Kuchean also business documents and medical MSS. are extant.

BIBLIOGRAPHY

HŒRNLE, A. F. R. 'The Weber MSS. Another Collection of Ancient Manuscripts from Central Asia, *J. Roy. Asiat. Soc., Bengal Branch*, 1893.

SEIG, E. and SIEGLING, W. 'Tocharisch die Sprache der Indoskythen,' *Sitzungsb. der Preuss. Akad. der Wissench.*, Berlin, 1908; *Tocharische Sprachreste*, Berlin and Leipsic, 1921.

LÉVI, S. 'Étude des documents tokhariens', etc., *Journal Asiatique*, 1911.

LIDÉN, E. *Studien zur tocharischen Sprachgeschichte*, I, Gœteborg, 1916.

LÜDERS, H. 'Zur Geschichte und Geographie Ostturkestans', and 'Weitere Beiträge zur Geschichte', etc. *Sitzungsb. der Preuss. Akad.*, etc., 1922 and 1930.

REUTER, J. N. 'Bemerkungen über die neuen Lautzeichen im Tocharischen', *Studia Orientalia*, Helsingfors, 1925; ' "Tocharisch" und "Kutschanisch" ', *J. Soc. Finno-Ougrienne*, Helsingfors, 1934.

SCHULZE, W. 'Zum Tocharischen,' *Ungarische Jahrbücher*, Budapest, 1927.

PocHuA, P. 'Tocharica,' *Archiv Orientální*, Prague, 1930; *Tocharische Etymologien, Zeitschr. der Deutsch. Morgenl. Gesellschaft.*, 1939.

SIEG, E., SIEGLING, W. and SCHULZE, W. *Tocharische Grammatik*, Göttingen, 1931.

MEILLET, A. *Fragments de textes koutchéens* (with S. Lévi's introduction *Le 'tokharien'*), Paris, 1933.

SCHWENTNER, E. *Tocharisch*, Berlin-Leipsic, 1935.

SIEG, E. *Und dennoch 'Tocharisch,'* Berlin, 1937.

BAILEY, H. W. 'Ttaugara,' *Bull. of the School of Oriental and African Studies*, 1937.

HENNING, W. B. 'Argi and the "Tokharians",' the same Journal, 1938.

PEDERSEN, H. *Tocharisch vom Gesichtspunkt der indoeuropäischen Sprachvergleichung*, Copenhagen, 1941; *Zur tocharischen Sprachgeschichte*, Copenhagen, 1944.

VAN WINDEKENS, A. J. *Lexique étymologique des dialects tokhariens*, Louvain, 1941; *Morphologie comparée du tokharien*, Louvain, 1944.

CENTRAL ASIAN CURSIVE GUPTA (Fig. 17.6)

Until 1897, when the first manuscripts couched in 'Khotanese' were published by A. F. R. Hœrnle, nothing was known of the existence of this language. It is the language of many manuscripts discovered in Chinese or eastern Turkestan, and now in London (British Museum and India Office Libr.), Paris (Bibliothéque Nationale) and Berlin (Prussian Academy). This language was spoken in the ancient kingdom of Khotan, called in Sanskrit Gaustana and in Tibetan Khu-then; the indigenous terms for the kingdom were Hvatana- (later Hvamna-), Hvatanai (later Hvamnai), adject. nom. sing., etc. The greater part of the extant Khotanese manuscripts was found at Ch'ien or Ts'ien-fo-tung (the 'Caves of the Thousand Buddhas') in Tun-huang, Kansu, north-west China.

Khotanese

The term 'Khotanese' is not generally accepted. The German scholar E. Leumann called the new language North Aryan, and regarded it as an autonomous branch of the Indo-European languages. French scholars call it East Iranian: it was indeed the easternmost middle Iranian form of speech, but the term 'East Iranian' would include also Sogdian. S. Holstein called it Tokharian; his theory was accepted by some scholars, amongst them, at first, S. Konow, but this opinion is now abandoned. According to the German scholar Lüders, the name Khotani, which has been propounded by Konow, is too narrow, because the Saka rulers of western India spoke practically the same language; Lüders therefore suggested the name Saka. Indeed, the ancient Persians called all Skythians 'Saka,' while in Konow's view there is no doubt that this language was a Skythian form of speech. On the other hand, the term 'Saka' or 'Sacæ' is too wide, because there was probably more than one Saka dialect. The most accurate term would therefore be that devised by Konow, 'Khotani Saka,' but for brevity we can use the term Khotanese, employed by the British authority on the subject, Professor H. W. (now Sir Harold) Bailey.

The material contained in Khotanese manuscripts is of great variety; there are official and business documents, translations of Indian tales, religious poems, medical texts, and documents of other matters.

Khotanese Script (Fig. 17.7)

There are some indications to show that Khotanese began to be used in writing in the second century A.D., but the manuscripts extant are considerably later, ninth or tenth centuries, the earliest belonging probably to the eighth or at most seventh century A.D. 'It is evident that the Brahmi alphabet was adapted to the language long before our oldest manuscripts were written; and this adaptation was based on the pronunciation of Sanskrit and Prakrit then in vogue in Khotan.'

The adaptation of the Gupta script to Khotanese probably took place in the eastern oases of Chinese Turkestan. The pronunciation of the Khotanese consonants was, however, somewhat different from the Indian. The letters *y*, *l*, *v*, *s* and *h* were also used as 'hiatus-consonants.' Double consonants were simplified when connected with another consonant; on the other hand, new compounds were invented, such as *tch*, *js*, *ts*, *ys*. The Khotanese character seems to have comprised the following vowel-sounds: long and short *a*, *i* and *u*; *ä*, *e*, perhaps *rh* (*ri*), *o*, *ai*, *ei*, *au*, and some apparent diphthongs beginning with *u*.

On the whole, the *ductus* of the Central Asian Cursive Gupta is similar to that of the Kharoshthi script (*see* the preceding chapter), and it is therefore not impossible that the latter may have had some influence on its development. According to Dr. Hœrnle, the Khotanese script was strongly influenced by a Semitic alphabet. 'Modern archæological discoveries have shown abundantly that Semitic influences were at work very early in eastern Turkestan.' Some of the MSS. extant contain the cursive Gupta alphabet, syllabary and numerals, and one manuscript contains 1,108 lines of writing.

BIBLIOGRAPHY

HŒRNLE, A. F. R. 'Three Further Collections of Ancient Manuscripts from Central Asia,' *J. Roy. Asiat. Soc., Bengal Branch*, 1897.

STEIN, M. A. *Ancient Khotan*, Vol. II, London, 1907; *Serindia*, Vol. IV, London, 1921; *Innermost Asia*, London, 1928.

LEUMANN, E. *Zur nordarischen Sprache und Literatur*, Strassburg, 1912; *Das nordarische (sakische) Lehrgedicht des Buddhismus* (edited by M. Leumann), Leipsic, 1933–6.

THOMAS, F. W, and KONOW, S. *Two Medieval Documents from Tun–Huang*, Oslo, 1929.

KONOW, S. *Saka Studies*, Oslo, 1932; 'Ein neuer Saka-Dialect,' *Sitzungsb. der Preuss. Akademie der Wissenschaft*, Berlin, 1935; *Khotansakische Grammatik*, etc., Leipsic, 1941.

LEUMANN, M. *Sakische Handschriftproben*, Zurich, 1934.

BAILEY, H. W. 'Iranian Studies V, Hvatanica, Indo-Turcica,' *Bull. School of Oriental and African Studies*, 1935, 1937 and 1938; *Khotanese Texts*, I, Cambridge, 1945.

GRÖNBECH, K. *Monumenta Linguarum Asiae Maioris*, II. *Codices Khotanenses*, etc. Introduction by H. W. Bailey, Copenhagen, 1938.

CHINESE IN CURSIVE GUPTA CHARACTER

Extremely interesting is the adaptation of Central Asian cursive Gupta to Chinese. *See* F. W. Thomas, 'A Buddhist Chinese Text in Brahmi Script,' *Zeitschrift der Deutschen Morgenländischen Gesellschaft*,' 91 (1937), pp. 1–48; the manuscript, described in *Serindia*, p. 1,450, as bearing '93 lines Cursive Gupta, in Khotanese', appears to contain a Chinese and not a Khotanese text. The script 'is of a cursive type, predominant in Saka-Khotani documents' (F. W. Thomas), and belongs to the eighth–ninth centuries A.D.

WESTERN BRANCH OF EASTERN GUPTA

The western branch of the eastern Gupta variety appears in two forms, a cursive round-hand, and the angular, monumental type of the imperial Gupta inscriptions. The literary script of the Bower MSS. is connected with the former variety.

The famous Bower MSS. were acquired by Lieutenant Bower in 1889 in the course of his journey through Kucha (eastern Turkestan). They are written in Sanskrit on birch-bark in a Gupta character attributed to the fifth century A.D. They consist of a miscellaneous collection of medical treatises, proverbial sayings, and the like. They were edited by Dr Hœrnle. Other manuscripts of similar type, from the Central Asian collections called after Godfrey, Macartney and Weber, were edited by Hœrnle in the closing years of the last century.

BIBLIOGRAPHY

Hœrnle, A. F. R. 'The Bower Manuscripts,' *Archæological Survey of India*, Calcutta, 1893–1912.

TIBETAN SCRIPTS AND THEIR OFFSHOOTS

Tibetan is the language of Tibet and the adjoining districts of India; it is spoken by about six million people. It is a member of the Tibeto-Himalayan branch, which belongs to the Tibeto-Burman sub-family and the Tibeto-Chinese family of languages. The Indian term Bhotia has been accepted by modern philology to designate the group of languages, of which Tibetan is a member; other Bhotian dialects are spoken in Bhutan, Sikkim, Nepal, Ladakh and Baltistan. The word Tibetan is also employed to designate the *lingua franca* of Tibet, that is, the dialect spoken in central Tibet, in the provinces of Ü and Tsang.

The connection of Tibet with India was old and intimate. It borrowed from India the Buddhist religion together with the sacred scriptures. Intimate acquaintance with Buddhism must have been acquired by the Tibetans through their invasion and conquest of Chinese Turkestan. They found there numerous monasteries and libraries in existence. The Tibetans themselves soon took kindly to writing and had an aptitude for literature. The earliest extant Tibetan literature belongs to the seventh century A.D. It consists mainly of translations of Sanskrit books, and these translations not only transformed Tibetan speech into a literary language, but in many cases preserved works which had been lost in their original form.

It is generally accepted that the Tibetan script (Fig. 17.1, sect. 2) was invented in A.D. 639 by Thon-mi-Sam-bhota, minister of the great king Srong-btsan-Sgam-po, who established the capital at Lha-sa and founded the state of Tibet. The Tibetan character is, however, not an invention, but a revision of an older script, already in use in Tibet at an earlier period. It is, at any rate, closely modelled in form and arrangement upon the Gupta character, but with additional signs for representing certain sounds existing in Tibetan and not in Indian languages and with omission of the Indian soft aspirates, which were not required. It is uncertain whether its proto-type was the Eastern Turkestanic Gupta or the Gupta which was the ancestor of the Nagari character.

The following theory seems to be right: A. H. Francke, followed by Dr. Hœrnle, suggested that the usually held view of the Tibetan tradition on the subject of the introduction of the Tibetan alphabet should be corrected. 'The Tibetan script agrees with the Khotanese script in making the vocalic radical *a* to function as a consonantal radical, and this fact shows quite clearly that the Tibetan script was introduced from Khotan' (Hœrnle). 'The consonantal use of a vocalic radical is quite foreign to the Indo-Aryan language and script' (Hœrnle).

In short, according to Dr. Hœrnle, the Tibetan alphabet can be called Indian only in the sense that its direct source, the Khotanese alphabet, is ultimately an Indian alphabet. 'The curious fact that the Tibetan alphabet makes the *a*-radical to close its series of consonantal radicals (*gsal byed*) is instructive from the point of view above explained. In the Indian alphabetic system, the vocalic radicals for *a*, *i*, *u*, *e* occupy a place in advance of, and separate from, the consonantal radicals' (Hœrnle).

Tibetan in its original square form, and also in the derivative current hands of elegant appearance has served the Tibetan speech down to the present time. There is no doubt that the spelling originally represented the actual pronunciation (in the western and north-eastern dialects, the characteristic combinations of initial consonants are still generally preserved), but the above mentioned *lingua franca* of Tibet has undergone extensive changes, including the introduction of some new sounds and the loss of some consonants, so that the writing is nowadays very far from being a true representation of speech. The Tibetan character has been adopted also for other Bhotian dialects.

The Tibetan script can be distinguished into two main varieties:

(1) the literary character, called *dbu-chan* (pron. *u-chän*, the component *db* being dropped in most dialects), that is, 'head-possessing,' which is the ecclesiastic script *par excellence* and is used for printing (Fig. 17.8); it has a few varieties, the most important being the seal-script.

(2) The cursive scripts, used for everyday purposes, called *dbu-med* (pron. *u-med*), that is, 'headless' (Fig. 17.8), which is the secular script; its main variety is the *'khyug-yig*, the 'current hand.' The main difference between dbu-chan and dbu-med consists, as the names indicate, in the characteristic top-line of the Deva-nagari character being a part of the dbu-chan signs and absent in those of the dbu-med. *'khyug-yig* is an extremely abbreviated script. In compound words, the suffixes of the first syllable and the prefixes of the second are omitted. J. Bacot's 'L'Écriture cursive tibétaine,' *J. Asiatique*, 1912, contains a list of seven hundred contractions of words usually employed in the current hand. Mention may be made of the various peculiar ornamental and ritual scripts employed for inscriptions and decorative purposes, titles of books, sacred formulæ, etc.

There is also a kind of cypher, a secret script used for official correspondence, called *rin-spuns*, from the name of its inventor Rin-c'(hhen-) spuns (-pa), who lived in the fourteenth century A.D.

In comparison with the Deva-nagari character, the Tibetan script is very much simplified, although they agree in their main features. The dbu-chan, which is the more important, has the vowel *a* inherent in every consonant and not separately indicated, while other vowels when they follow a consonant are marked by small signs placed either above the consonant (in the instances of *e*, *i* and *o*) or at its foot (in the case of *u*). The *y* when it is inserted, as in *kya*, *pya*, and so forth, and the *r* and *l* when they are parts of consonantal compounds are also similarly indicated. The end of each syllable is marked by a dot placed at the right-hand side of the upper end of the closing letter. As to the consonants, the most important feature of the dbu-chan is that the cerebrals (or cacuminals) in borrowed words are written by reversed dentals, while in spoken Tibetan cerebrals are found only as contractions of certain compound consonants.

See J. Bacot, *Grammaire du Tibetain littéraire*, Paris, 1946.

For modern Tibetan *see* the series of three books (to be continued with further books on the *Alphabet*, *Verbs* and *Grammar Notes*) published by B. Gould and H. R. Richardson: (1) *The Tibetan Word Book*, with an informative introduction by Sir Aurel Stein; (2) *Tibetan Sentences*; (3) *Tibetan Syllables*; Oxford University Press, 1943.

There were two main offshoots of the Tibetan character:

Passepa Character

A famous Grand Lama of Sa-skya (Bashbah or 'p'ags-pa['honourable'] bLo-gros-rgyal-mthsan—in Chinese, P'a-k'o-si-pa, known as P'a-sse-p'a or 'Phags-pa; 1234–79, invited to China by Qubilay Khan) played a great part in the conversion to Buddhism of the Mongolian imperial court, and adapted the Tibetan square script to the Chinese and Mongolian languages, replacing the Uighur alphabet (*see* preceding chapter). Under Chinese influence, this script, commonly called Passepa, was written in vertical columns, downwards, although unlike Chinese, the columns read from left to right. This character, officially adopted in 1272, was only sparsely used owing to the convenience of the Uighur script, and did not last long, but it lingered on at the imperial Chancery under the Yüan dynasty, particularly in the official seals.

Lepcha Character

The writing (Fig. 17.9) employed by the Rong, the aboriginal population of Sikkim, a native state in the eastern Himalayas, is also of Tibetan origin.

The Rong are called also Lepchas—this term being a Nepalese nickname—or Rong-pa, 'dwellers in the valleys,' or Mom-pa, 'dwellers in the low country.' They number about 25,000; their speech is a non-pronominalized Himalayan language, belonging to the Tibeto-Burmese sub-family; they are probably of Mongolian race. Because of their promiscuous sexual relations and innate addiction to drink, their disappearance as a distinct race is said to be only a matter of time. What civilization and literature the Lepchas possess, they owe entirely to the Tibetan form of Buddhism generally known as Lamaism, which is believed to have been introduced into Sikkim about the middle of the seventeenth century by Lha-b-Tsun Chhen-po, a Tibetan title meaning 'the Great Reverend God,' the patron-saint of Sikkim.

(For the Lepchas *see* John Morris, *Living with Lepchas. A Book about the Sikkim Himalayas*, London, 1938).

The Lepcha character (Fig. 17.9) seems to have been invented or revised by the Sikkim raja Chakdor Namgye, Phyag-rdor rnam-gyal (b. 1686). Peculiar features of this character are the vowel-signs and the final marks of eight consonants (*k, ng, t, n, p, m, r, l*), which consist of dashes, dots and small circles, and are placed above or before the preceding letter.

ADAPTATION OF THE TIBETAN CHARACTER TO OTHER LANGUAGES

Nam Language

The Tibetan character was also adapted to other languages. Two of these survived in a few fragmentary Central Asian manuscripts, and their existence was unknown until quite recently. They were discovered by Professor F. W. Thomas and made known in the *J. Roy. Asiatic Soc.* (1926, pp. 312–3: 'A New Central Asian Language,' and pp. 505–6; 'Two Languages from Central Asia,' 1928, pp. 630–4: 'The Nam Language'; and 1929, pp. 193–216: 'The Nam Language').

One of the two new languages, according to Professor Thomas, was a dialect akin to Lepcha; the script used was the Tibetan character. The other new language, called by F. W. Thomas the Nam language, a monosyllabic form of speech, 'as old as Tibetan and in structure more primitive, is likely to have been closely related to that of the Tibeto-Burman people known to the Chinese by a name which has been

transliterated ... as *Jo-K'iang*, *Ti-k'iang* ..., and *Dža-K'iong* ..., a people who
... occupied from remote times the whole stretch of country immediately south of
the mountains ... from the Nan-shan to the longitude of Khotan, and who may be
shown to have furnished an element in the population of Southern Turkestan'
(Thomas).

The script used was Tibetan, 'of a squarish kind,' with some few peculiarities
characteristic of the early period: 'the hand is rather coarse, and the letters fairly large
and wide-spaced' (Thomas).

Chinese in Tibetan Writing

Chinese offers some interesting instances of the difficulties of adaptation of a script to
other languages. It seems that it was quite frequently written in Tibetan script. F. W.
Thomas and G. L. M. Clauson (partly in collaboration with S. Miyamoto) published:
(1) 'A Chinese Buddhist Text in Tibetan Writing,' *J. Roy. Asiatic Soc.*, 1926, pp. 508–
26, consisting of two fragments of thick yellowish paper, partly couched in Chinese
language and 'in an elegant, rather cursive, Tibetan script,' of the eighth–tenth
centuries A.D.; (2) 'A Second Chinese Buddhist Text in Tibetan Characters' (in the
same journal, 1927, pp. 281–306), written in a script being 'a rather formal copybook
Dbucan,; (3) 'A Chinese Mahayana Catechism in Tibetan and Chinese Characters'
(the same Journal, 1929, pp. 37–76), 'an extensive and well-written MS.', consisting
of 486 lines 'of good, rather calligraphic, cursive Tibetan writing,' probably in more
than one hand, perhaps of the eighth–ninth centuries A.D.

SIDDHAMATRKA CHARACTER

Out of the western branch of the eastern Gupta character, the Siddhamatrka character developed during the sixth century A.D. It was an angular script; the vertical
strokes ended with wedges or 'nailheads'; this script was therefore termed 'nail-
headed.' Bühler called it 'acute-angled alphabet' or Siddhamatrka. A peculiar feature
of this character is that the letters slope from right to left. Two main types are
known: the monumental, preserved in inscriptions, such as the Bodh-Gaya inscription from Mahanaman (A.D. 588–9) and the Prasasti from Lakhamandal, end of the
sixth century A.D.; and the cursive hand, preserved in some manuscripts on palm-
leaves, such as those from Horiuzji, probably belonging to the same century.

Little is known about its development; the documents extant are very scarce, it
was the period of the invasion of the Huns and of the devastating menace to Hindu
civilization.

There is a blank in the history of northern India until the accession, in 606, of
Harsha-vardhana, who succeeded in uniting for a short time a great portion of
northern India, when Pulikesin II, the greatest of the Chalukya kings conquered
much of southern India.

However, during the seventh century, the Siddhamatrka character continued to develop. A variety, characterized by a more marked twist of the lower ends of the strokes, was termed by Prinsep, Fleet, and other scholars, 'the Kutila variety of the Magadha alphabet of the seventh century.' Kielhorn, Bühler, and others, consider this term erroneous. At any rate, these so-called Kutila inscriptions of North India from the seventh century onwards (Fig. 17.1, sect. 2) already represent the ancient form of the Nagari character.

DEVA-NAGARI SCRIPT

The most important Indian script, the Nagari or Deva-nagari (Fig. 17.1, sect. 4) developed from a variety of the Gupta character through the Siddhamatrka. The original meaning of the term Nagari is uncertain. According to some scholars it occurs first, as the name of a script, in the Lalita Vistara (*see* p. 264), *Naga-lipi*, or 'writing of the Nagas'; according to Dr. L. D. Barnett, however, there is no connection between Naga-lipi and Deva-nagari. Another local explanation is 'writing of the Nagara' or the Gujarat Brahmans. Nowadays, Nagari is usually referred to as *Nagara*, and explained as 'writing used in cities' or 'town-script.'

The earliest Nagari inscriptions belong to the seventh and eighth centuries A.D. Signatures are found on inscriptions belonging to the first half of the seventh century, whilst the earliest extant documents written throughout in Nagari belong to the middle and the end of the eighth century A.D.

The Nagari letters were long-drawn and tailed, and had long horizontal strokes on the top, the latter feature being most characteristic of this script. These straight topped strokes, known as *matra*, replaced the wedges of the vertical strokes of the Siddhamatrka character; there are, indeed, documents with a mixture of wedges and straight strokes, or with wedges which are so broad that they produce the same effect as the long straight top-strokes.

The Nagari script developed slowly in the first two or three centuries of its existence. However, by the eleventh century it was mature and was already predominant in many districts of northern India (Fig. 17.10a). Many palm-leaf manuscripts, dating from the tenth, eleventh and the following centuries, discovered in Gujarat, Rajputana and the northern Deccan, are also written in this script.

Nandi-nagari

The South Indian form of Nagari is nowadays known as *Nandi-nagari*, which is an obscure term. Its archaic variety already appears in the eighth century A.D. (perhaps even earlier), and is fully developed by the beginning of the eleventh century. It differs from the northern variety mainly 'by the want of the small tails slanting to the right from the ends of the verticals and in general by stiffer forms' (Bühler). Its later developments are represented in inscriptions of the thirteenth–sixteenth centuries of the Kanarese country, and in the modern Nandi-nagari still used for manuscripts. *See* also below, under 'Modi character.'

Deva-nagari Character (Figs. 17.1, sect. 4, and 13*a*)

The Nagari character is known nowadays as the *Deva-nagari*, from Sanskrit *deva*, 'heavenly,' *i.e.*, the 'Nagari of the gods' or Brahman, the 'divine' or royal Nagari. It is one of the most perfect systems of writing apart from its main weakness of the short *a* inherent in each consonant unless otherwise indicated, which is not always pronounced and is often omitted in transliteration; the Deva-nagari character is therefore a semi-syllabary. The system was obviously evolved by the learned grammarians of the Sanskrit language. The Deva-nagari script consists of forty-eight signs, of which fourteen are vowels and diphthongs, and thirty-four basic consonants known as *aksharas*.

The basic forms of the vowels are only employed as 'initial' vowels, at the commencement of words or syllables; when used after a consonant they take, except the *a*, new, 'non-initial' forms, which are generally abbreviations. The basic consonants are divided into seven groups (*vargas*); six of them, the gutturals, palatals, cacuminals, dentals, labials and semi-vowels consist of five basic consonants, whilst the seventh group consists of three sibilants and one aspirate. I have used the term 'basic consonant' or *akshara*, to indicate the consonant when followed by the short *a*. When a word contains two or more syllables, the last of which contains a consonant, the inherent *a* in this last syllable is not pronounced; moreover, in reading prose, not poetry, custom demands that in the unaccented syllables of a word the inherent *a* should only be very slightly pronounced or not at all; this unaccented and unpronounced *a* is sometimes represented in western transliteration by an apostrophe.

'The practice of writing *o* and *au* with the radical *a* is quite modern, dating no further back than the early eighteenth century. It arose from the gradual blending of the characters for the vowels *a* and *au* from the tenth century onwards. The Nagari practice does not extend to the *i* and *e* vowels, which had no tendency to blend, and therefore retained their ancient special vocalic radicals' (Hœrnle).

The Deva-nagari type has no pure consonants, that is consonants written by themselves. In order to represent them, whenever possible compounds of two or three consonants are used. These are formed in various ways, some are quite irregular; or else an oblique stroke, called in Sanskrit *virama*, is placed below the consonant in question. When a nasal consonant precedes another consonant, the quiescent nasal *m* or *n* may, as a *compendium scripturae*, be denoted by the *anusvara*, namely a dot placed over the letter it follows in sound. A variety of the *anusvara*, called *anunasika*, consisting of a dot in a half circle, is used to give a nasal tone to any syllable over which it may be placed.

The Deva-nagari character, of which there are two main varieties, the eastern and the western, is used for Sanskrit, a purely literary language, which was never employed in daily life; indeed after a long course of literary treatment and grammatical refinement Sanskrit remained practically standardized during the last two millennia or so. In consequence, the Deva-nagari has remained essentially unaltered for many

U

centuries, being obviously easier to write correctly and consistently in a language not habitually used than in a living, especially a primitive, tongue.

However, the importance of the Deva-nagari is paramount: it is the script of the educated classes, and the common means of communication between learned men throughout India. Its history is mainly connected with that of Sanskrit, which for many centuries was the exclusive literary language of northern India. Serious competition with Sanskrit arose when, shortly after A.D. 1000, the successful raids of Sultan Mahmud culminated in the Moslem conquest of the Punjab, followed by the final conquest, towards the end of the twelfth century, which extinguished the Hindu political power in northern India, and thus brought the neo-Persian script and language into use. Roughly about this time, the Indian vernaculars began to develop into literary languages; these will be mentioned further on.

Figure 17.10*b* shows the evolution of the northern and southern Deva-nagari and Tamil *aksharas a* and *ka* from the early Brahmī type of *c.* 250 B.C. till the present day.

The Deva-nagari script is still the main literary vehicle of various Indian languages and dialects, amongst them those of the western Hindi group. This covers the country between Sirhind in the Punjab and Allahabad in the former United Provinces, between the Himalaya range in the north and the river Narbada in the south; in other words, the Madhyadesa or 'Midland' of ancient Sanskrit geographers, the holy land of Brahmanism, the centre of Hindu civilization. Western Hindi is spoken nowadays by about 50 million people.

One of its various dialects, Hindustani, which is primarily the language of the northern Doab, was carried over the whole of India by the Moslems, while the literary Hindustani (in its two forms, Urdu and Hindi), used by Moslems and Hindus, has become the modern literary language of India. Early in the seventeenth century it was already known in England that Hindustani was the *lingua franca* of India. Hindustani can be written in various scripts; it is mainly a matter of religion; Moslems employ the Persian-Arabic alphabet with a few additional signs for sounds peculiar to Indian languages not found in Persian (Figs. 15.21 and 33*a*); most Hindus use the Deva-nagari character for literary purposes and the current hands Kaithi and Mahajani for daily life; *see* below. Figures 17.16*a* and 20*b* are specimens in Hindi.

Simple Hindustani can be, and often is, written in both the Persian-Arabic and Devanagari scripts.

There are, however, two forms of Hindustani which cannot be written in both the Persian alphabet and the Deva-nagari character. *Urdu* is that form of Hindustani which makes a free use of Persian and Arabic words in its vocabulary. The term derives perhaps from *urdu-e-mu'alla*, or royal military bazaar outside the Delhi palace; *zaban-i-urdu*, 'language of the camp.'

Urdu is used chiefly by Moslems and by Hindus influenced by Persian culture, and is written in a variety of the Persian-Arabic alphabet. Hindi is the development of Hindustani which has continued to be free from Persianization and owes more to Sanskrit instead; it is used only by Hindus who have been educated on a Hindu system, and is usually printed in Deva-nagari character, its current hands being Kaithi, Mahajani and similar scripts, which will be dealt with below. The Indian scholar V. S. Bendrey has drawn my attention to the fact that while Urdu came into being after A.D. 1600, 'Hindi has much older literature still extant.' 'The Pakistan Education Advisory Board accepted the suggestion that Arabic script should replace Persian for the national language, Urdu' (*The Times*, 7/2/1949). *See* also p. 276 f.

ŚARADA SCRIPT

This script (Figs. 17.10c, 13b and 22) is described by Bühler as descendant of the western type of the Gupta character. It originated in the eighth century A.D. and is still employed for Kashmiri, a language which is spoken by over 2 million people in the valley of Kashmir and the contiguous valleys to its south and east. Kashmiri can be divided into the Kashmiri of the Moslems and that of the Hindus; the former, who are in the majority but are mainly uneducated, and those Hindus, who have Moslem education, both employ a variety of the Persian-Arabic alphabet; while the other Hindus, who are the educated minority, generally use the Śarada script, which is also taught in Hindu schools. Much of the Kashmiri literature is written in Sanskrit and in the Deva-nagari character. The Śarada script appeared in Kashmir and in north-eastern Punjab, and the earliest known inscriptions are dated A.D. 804.

This script corresponds letter for letter with the Deva-nagari, although their shapes differ greatly. A general feature of the Śarada is the stiffness and thickness of the strokes, which, according to Bühler, give the signs 'an uncouth appearance and a certain resemblance to those of the Kushana period.' In the later development, owing to the use of long top-strokes, the heads of several letters are closed. Each Śarada letter is given a separate name, for instance *adau a* for *a*, *khoni khö* for *kha*, *kol vethi ksha* for *ksha*, and so forth. In V. S. Bendrey's opinion, it is doubtful whether this 'practice indicates the names of letters'. He writes that, as in the west the pronunciation of 'a' may be indicated as in 'table,' 'so we have on this side a practice to teach the alphabet by pointing out the sound in a common word or syllable. . . . In fact the names we give to the alphabet is in the nature of "Ka-kar," "A-kar," etc.'

PROTO-BENGALI CHARACTER

The proto-Bengali was a peculiar cursive script with circular or semi-circular signs, hooks or hollow triangles attached to the left of the tops of the vertical strokes. 'The triangle itself is a modification of the top-stroke with a semi-circle below,' and this form is connected with the common form of 'the thick top-strokes, rounded off at both ends.'

The proto-Bengali character developed according to Bühler out of the Nagari as used in eastern India in the late eleventh century A.D.

A different opinion about the origin of this script has been expressed in the excellent monograph of S. N. Chakravarti, 'Development of the Bengali Alphabet from the Fifth Century A.D. to the End of the Muhammadan Rule' (*J. Roy. Asiatic Soc. of Bengal*, Vol. IV, 1938, pp. 351–91). According to Chakravarti, in the seventh century A.D. out of the eastern variety of the lapidary North Indian character two branches developed, an eastern and a western, the latter becoming the Siddhamatrka character while the former, represented by the Faridpur grant of Samacharadeva, progressed in the direction of the proto-Bengali character, developed independently during the seventh–ninth centuries, became influenced in the tenth century by the Nagari, and at the end of the same century became the proto-Bengali script.

The earliest proto-Bengali inscription is the Bangarh grant of Mahipala I (*c.* A.D. 975–1026). The earliest proto-Bengali manuscripts belong to the eleventh–twelfth centuries A.D.

EARLY NEPALI OR NEWARI CHARACTER

The early Nepali or Newari character was strictly connected with the proto-Bengali.

Newari (another form of the word 'Nepali'), a non-pronominalized Himalayan language, belonging to the Tibeto-Himalayan branch, was the state language of Nepal until 1769 when the Gurkhas overthrew the Newar dynasty. Newari has a considerable literature consisting of commentaries on, or translations of, Sanskrit Buddhist works, dictionaries, grammars, dramatic works, and so forth. The oldest work of historical nature was written in the fourteenth century. Some ancient documents belong to the twelfth–fifteenth centuries A.D.

A peculiar feature of the Newari script, named 'the hooked alphabet' by Bühler, are little hooks attached to the letters, which according to this authority and Bendall, prove the influence of the Bengali script. The Cambridge MS. No. 1691, of A.D. 1179, seems to be the oldest extant document written in this script.

'ARROW-HEAD' TYPE

Another ancient script of similar origin is represented in a few later Bengali and Nepali inscriptions written in an 'arrow-head' type. Some scholars, such as Bendall, identified it as the *Bhaishuki lipi*, mentioned by the Arabian scholar Biruni (973–1048). This character seems to have been confined to eastern India and to have been an offshoot of a local variety of the eastern Brahmī script.

B. H. Hodgson, Sarat Chandra Das and other scholars mention other, mostly ornamental, scripts of eastern India, used also in Nepal and Tibet, but little is known about their origin and development.

MODERN NORTH INDIAN SCRIPTS

The many scripts employed nowadays in northern India have descended from the characters already mentioned, but their exact 'genealogical tree' and their inter-relations have not as yet been established. We must take into consideration that these modern scripts are essentially current hands, used for daily purposes, and for the majority of them we only know the last stage, that is, the forms employed in recent times.

Bengali Character (Figs. 17.2, sect. 1; 12a–b; 17a; 19a)

Bengali is a language of the eastern group of the Indo-Aryan languages, and is spoken by over 50 million people in the province of Bengal. It is divided into several dialects, but literary Bengali is employed all over the country in books and news-papers, and when speaking formally, Bengali literature goes back as far as the fifteenth century A.D. and earlier.

The Bengali script is a development of the proto-Bengali type (pp. 285f.). In the fifteenth and sixteenth centuries the Bengali character appears fully developed. In-deed, during the seventeenth and eighteenth centuries there appear no changes at all. In the nineteenth century the forms of the letters became stereotyped by the intro-duction of the printing press. The order and the number of the letters are the same as in the Deva-nagari character.

A variety of the Bengali character is used to represent modern Assamese; the Oriya, Maithili and Early Manipuri characters seem also to be somewhat connected with the Bengali script: *see* below.

Oriya Script (Figs. 17.2, sect. 1, and 12c–f)

Oriya or Odri is a sister language to Bengali; it is spoken by about 10 million people in Orissa (the ancient Odra-desa), Bihar, Bengal, the eastern districts of the former Central Provinces and northern Madras province.

A peculiar script is employed for the Oriya speech. The Oriyas probably devel-oped their written character from the same source as the preceding script, under the influence of their South Indian neighbours, the Telugus and the Tamils. However, the peculiar shapes of the Oriya letters are due to technical reasons.

The talipot palm leaves, which are long and narrow, were the only writing material in ancient Odra, as in other parts of the sea-coast provinces of southern India. The local scribes employing an iron stylus to scratch the letters were com-pelled to avoid straight lines, and particularly the characteristic horizontal *matra* of the Deva-nagari and of similar scripts. Indeed, any scratch in the direction of the longi-tudinal fibre, running in the palm leaves from the stalk to the point, would split the palm leaf, which is excessively fragile. Thus, this gave rise to the rounded shapes of the Oriya letters. Moreover, in order to make the signs plainer, ink is rubbed over the surface of the leaf and it fills up the scratches that form the letters.

The curves, which take the place of the horizontal top-lines of the Deva-nagari, form the greater part of the single signs and are the same in nearly all letters, while the central part of the letter, by which one is distinguished from another, has been so reduced inside that it is difficult to see, and therefore at first glance the majority of the letters appear to look alike.

The Oriya writing (Figs. 17.2, sect. 1 and 12, *c–f*) can be distinguished nowadays into three main varieties:

(1) One called Brahmani, used mainly in palm-leaf manuscripts; it owes its name to the Brahmans of Orissa, who are generally the writers of the *sastras* or religious works.

(2) Another, called Karani, having originated among the Karans, is now generally used in writing out documents.

(3) In parts of Ganjam (the ancient Utkala), on the eastern coast of India, to the south of Orissa, the Oriya characters have become more rounded than in Orissa proper, owing to the greater influence of the Telugu script, used by the neighbouring people.

Maithili Character

Bihari is another sister language to Bengali; it is spoken by over 37 million people in Bihar, Chota Nagpur, in the valleys of the rivers Ganges and Jumna. Originally it was confined to the districts of the Gangetic plain, but in mediæval and modern ages it spread southwards. It has three main dialects, Maithili, Magahi and Bhojpuri, which are closely connected with one another. Maithili or Tirhutia is the dialect of ancient Mithila or Tirhut; it is spoken nowadays by about ten and a half million people in Tirhut, Champaran, eastern Monghyr, Bhagalpur and western Purnea. The Maithili literature goes back to the fifteenth century.

No less than three different characters are employed by the Tirhutians:

(1) the Deva-nagari, used only by the few highly educated people, particularly by those who are under the influence of the liberal literary circles of Benares;

(2) the Tirhuti variety of the Kaithi character (*see* below), which is the current hand; and

(3) the so-called Maithili character (Fig. 17.14*a*), used by Tirhut Brahmans, and not by persons of other castes. The Maithili character resembles the Bengali script, but is much more difficult to read, at least at first sight.

Early Manipuri Character

This script (Fig. 17.14*b*), probably a descendant of the Bengali character, was adapted about A.D. 1700 in the reign of Charairongba to Manipuri or Methei, a Kuki-chin speech, which belongs to the Tibeto-Burman group of languages. This early Manipuri script is now very rarely used.

Manipuri is spoken nowadays by about 400,000 people in the valley of Manipur. The Manipurs are mentioned from A.D. 777 onwards and have a fairly high culture; the most important manuscripts are *Takhelgnamba* and *Samsokgnamba*.

Assamese Character (Fig. 17.17b)

This is also a variety of the Bengali script, and is employed for Assamese, a language belonging to the most eastern group of Indo-Aryan; the language is spoken by over two million inhabitants of the Assam valley. Assamese literature is quite important, especially on historical subjects. Certain adjustments had to be made to equate the Assamese sounds with the Bengali letters. The main difference between the Assamese and the Bengali characters is that the former has special signs to represent the sounds *w* and *r*.

Kaithi Character

Kaithi or Kayathi (Fig. 17.14c–d) is really the script employed by the Kayaths or Kayasthas, or the writing caste of northern India. It is the character most generally used, with many local variations, all over northern India, from the Gujarat coast to the river Kosi. Its exact origin is uncertain. Although it is commonly described as a corruption of the Nagari character, it is certainly not its descendant, but rather a collateral development. Both probably derived from an ancient common source, and developed *pari passu*; one, the Deva-nagari, developing as a literary script, the other as a running hand for everyday purposes. The main difference between the Kaithi and the Deva-nagari characters is that, in the former, the horizontal and perpendicular strokes are omitted where possible, so that, with a few exceptions, the single signs can be written neatly with one stroke.

Besides, the Kaithi is not as complete as the Deva-nagari. It generally uses the long *i* and *u* for both the long and the short forms of *i* and *u*, and it makes no distinction between *s* and *sh*, using the latter form for both *s* and *sh*. It is unusual for semi-literate people to separate single words (such was generally the case in earlier times), but only to mark full periods by stops in handwriting, contrary to the practice for print and formal use. When written on ruled paper, the signs are put below the lines, and not on them as in European scripts.

As mentioned, Kaithi varies locally. In the two extreme countries, Gujarat, to the east, and Bihar, to the west, it has attained the position of a national script, but nowadays the two scripts, Bihari and Gujarati (if the latter is at all connected with the Kaithi) are essentially different.

Gujarati Script (Figs. 17.1, sect. 5; 14e–g; 20c)

Gujarati, a member of the 'Inner sub-branch' of the Indo-Aryan languages, is spoken by some 12 million people in the province of Gujarat, in the state of Baroda and other neighbouring provinces.

Three varieties of writing are used for Gujarati:

(1) the Deva-nagari, which until quite recently was employed exclusively for books, and nowadays is rarely used except by the Nagara Brahmans—who claim to have given the script its name—and some few other tribes;

(2) the Gujarati character, which is nowadays the official script, employed for printing and general purposes; and

(3) the Vaniai (from *vanio*, 'shopkeeper') or Sarafi (from *saraf*, 'banker'), or else Bodia (*bodi*, 'clipped' or 'shorn'), a variety of the Gujarati character, used by merchants and bankers; its main distinction is the omission of all vowels except when initial, and it is therefore very difficult to read, but the shapes of the letters of the two scripts are often identical.

The Gujarati character is essentially the literary, refined form of the script, now represented in its cursive form by the Kaithi type; the order and the phonetic values of the Gujarati letters are, on the whole, similar to those of the Deva-nagari character, although their shapes are different.

Bihari Character (Fig. 17.18)

Although the Deva-nagari is used occasionally for writing books, Kaithi is, as mentioned, the official character of Bihar. Three local varieties of the Bihari Kaithi can be distinguished:

(1) the Tirhuti, for the Tirhutians, which is considered the most elegant.

(2) The Bhojpuri which is a Bihari dialect spoken by about twenty two million people in the eastern districts of the former United Provinces and the adjoining country; its script is said to be the most legible Kaithi variety.

(3) The Magahi script, which is employed for Magahi, another Bihari dialect, spoken by about seven million people of ancient Magadha, the country around Patna and Gaya. The Magahi type had been adopted by the Bengal Government for official Bihari publications; books are printed in it in Patna, and the character has become more or less standardized. On the other hand, the Bengali and Oriya characters are also employed to write eastern Magahi.

Eastern Hindi Varieties

Eastern Hindi, a main branch of the Indo-Aryan languages, is spoken by about 27 million people in Uttar Pradesh, Windhya Pradesh, Madhya Pradesh and the surrounding districts. Ardha-magadhi, an ancient dialect of eastern Hindi, was the sacred language of the Jains; but there were many other dialects making up the sum of eastern Hindi, and more than half of Hindi literature has been written in this language.

Apart from the Persian-Arabic alphabet, which is used occasionally, and the Deva-nagari character, which is employed for writing books, some local Kaithi varieties (Fig. 17.14*d*) are used in daily life for all its three eastern Hindi dialects, Awadhi, Bagheli and Chhattisgarhi.

Mahajani Character (Fig. 17.21*b–c*)

Rajasthani, spoken mainly in the United States of Rajasthan, is a very important member of the central group of the Indo-Aryan languages and is allied to Gujarati (*see* above). It has over twenty dialects, the most important being Marwari, which has a considerable literature, and may be heard in many parts of India.

The United State of Rajasthan was inaugurated—in its capital Jaipur—on 30th March, 1949. It comprises fourteen states with a combined population of 12 millions and an area of 121,000 square miles (almost as large as Italy), thus becoming the largest single unit in the Indian Union.

Marwari and all the other Rajasthani dialects use the Deva-nagari character as their literary script, whilst the Marwari hand is used for everyday needs and has been carried all over India in the course of trade. One of the most important peculiarities of the Marwari script is that it has distinct characters for the sounds *dh* and *rh*.

This Marwari hand is generally known as the Mahajani character or the script of the merchants and bankers (*mahajans*), a great part of whom are Marwaris. It is nowadays the current hand of upper India.

As to its origin, the Mahajani is a corrupt type of the Deva-nagari character. Many forms are peculiar, there is great carelessness in the spelling, and it is a kind of short-hand, the vowels being quite commonly omitted. It is often illegible except to the writer. According to Dr. Bühler and Sir George A. Grierson, this illegibility gave rise to numerous stories about misreadings, one of the most popular being that of the Marwari merchant who went to Delhi; his agent wrote home: *Babu Ajmer gayo, bari bahi bhej-dije*, 'the Babu has gone to Ajmer, send the big ledger,' but the letter was read *Babu aj margayo, bari bahu bhej dije*, 'the Babu died to-day, send the chief wife' (apparently to perform his obsequies).

The Indian scholar V. S. Bendrey has drawn my attention to the fact that it is not the omission of vowels which is always responsible for the trouble over the meaning '(as vowels are not omitted, nor have they been omitted in the example quoted)', but it is the 'non-separation of words from each other.' The 'mess' is due to the reconstruction of the group of letters by the reader. Instead of joining *mar* to the preceding *aj*, he joined it to the following *gayo*: thus, the meaning of the sentence was disastrously altered. The defect in the 'kayasth' hands is that the writing is continuous and words are not written separately. 'The same "mess" is experienced in the case of Modi and other Kayasthi scripts. The writer is not prevented from writing the words separately, but as the script is used often for the day-to-day business, not much care is taken for accuracy.'

There are many local varieties of the Mahajani character; one of them is the script employed for writing Malvi, a dialect of Rajasthani, spoken by over four and a half million people in Malwa (central India and the adjoining districts).

Modi Character (Figs. 17.15*a* and 21*a*)

According to Bühler, the Balbodh ('instruction of children') or Deva-nagari of the

Maratha districts, is a survival of the southern Nagari (*see* p. 282). According to Burnell, this character was introduced into southern India by the Maratha conquest of Tanjore in the latter part of the seventeenth century A.D., and was chiefly employed in Tanjore, where it is still used among the descendants of the Deccan Brahmans. V. S. Bendrey writes: 'Dr. Burnell is correct when he says that Modi was introduced in the Deccan through Tanjore at the beginning of the seventeenth century. When he makes this remark he, as is done by all other historians, distinguishes Deccan from Maharashtra. His Deccan commences from Karnatak and not from Narmada, which is always taken as a boundary line between upper or northern India and lower or southern India. Unfortunately there is no attempt to follow uniform demarcation of provinces as these boundary lines changed with the political changes.'

Burnell's theory regarding the introduction of the Balbodh has been proved inconsistent: as a matter of fact, the earliest Balbodh documents extant belong to the thirteenth century A.D. (personal information from Mr. A. Master).

The Modi or 'twisted' character is considered to be the running hand of the Balbodh. It seems to be related to the Mahajani and like it is used for private correspondence and for commercial purposes. *See* also what has been said about the Mahajani script.

It is, however, also used in government offices, and the London School of Oriental Studies has many documents in this character. It is employed for Marathi, the southern language of the Indo-Aryan group, spoken by about 20 million people in the northern regions of the western Deccan. Marathi (Fig. 17.16*b*) has about forty dialects or sub-dialects. Deva-nagari is its literary and now also its main administrative script.

The Modi character is said to have been invented by Balaji Avaji, secretary to Sivaji, who lived from 1627 to 1680, but its origin is certainly much earlier, as there is a document extant, dated 1429 Saka era, corresponding to A.D. 1507 (information from Mr. Master). V. S. Bendrey writes: 'Balaji Awaji is credited with introducing a peculiar mode (which is considered to be the best and still continues in practice) of writing Modi. There was no attempt to modify the system but only in shape. It is more pleasing and distinct. We have old Marathi records in Modi in contemporary works from the eleventh century.'

Konkani, one of the most important Marathi forms of speech used by over two million people in the Konkan, in the former Portuguese colony of Goa, and the neighbouring territories, is now rarely written in the Deva-nagari, much more often in the Kannad (*see* below), and mainly in the Roman alphabet adapted by the Portuguese priests, who introduced some additions and other modifications. In V. S. Bendrey's opinion, however, Konkani is a language or dialect current as a second language—the population being bilingual—amongst the population inhabiting the bordering territories of Marathi-speaking people, Kannad-speaking people, and of Goa. 'Naturally they transliterate Konkani in the script they use for their regional languages.'

MODERN NORTH-WESTERN SCRIPTS

The Śarada character, already mentioned, is employed for Kashmiri. There are three other main varieties of scripts used in north-western India: the Takri, the Landa and the Gurmukhi (Fig. 17.22). According to Grierson, the Śarada, the Takri and the Landa are sister-scripts, that is characters descended from a common source, whilst Bühler, who did not mention the Landa character, considered the Takri or Takkari, as he termed it, to be a descendant of the Śarada.

Takri Character and its Varieties

The term Takri or Thakari, according to Sir George A. Grierson, is derived from the name of the Takkas, a powerful tribe who ruled the country round the famous Sakala, the modern Sialkot.

Like the Mahajani and unlike the Śarada, the Takri (Fig. 17.22) is a rude script built on the same lines as the Deva-nagari, but adapted to the needs of lower-class traders: its representation of the vowels is most imperfect, medial short vowels often being omitted and medial long vowels are frequently used in their initial forms.

The Takri, in its many varieties, is used over the lower ranges of the Himalayas north of the Punjab.

The languages, for which the Takri varieties are mainly employed, are nowadays termed Pahari, 'of or belonging to the mountains.' According to the definition of Grierson, these Indo-Aryan languages, spoken by over two and a half million people in *Sapa dalaksha*, that is the lower ranges of the Himalayas from Nepal in the east to Bhadrawal in the west, can be classified into three groups: eastern, central and western Pahari.

While the eastern and central Pahari use almost exclusively the Deva-nagari, the western Pahari dialects, which are politically centred on Simla, employ the various Takri scripts. Varieties of Takri are also employed for a Punjabi and a Kashmiri dialect. The following are the main varieties of the Takri, the first two having become official scripts.

Dogri Character

This writing is employed for Dogra or Dogri, a dialect of Punjabi (*see* below), spoken by over one and a half million people in the Jammu state and its neighbourhood. About 1880 the Takri was adopted as the official character of Jammu state for all purposes except printing. As such it was much improved, at least in theory. It has all the signs found in the Deva-nagari character, except those for sounds not used in the local speech, but in practice the vowel-signs are not employed in a consistent manner. For instance, *e* and *i*, or *o* and *u* are frequently interchanged, the initial forms of the vowels are often used for internal long vowels, and sometimes vowels are omitted altogether. Double letters are never written.

Chameali Character

In the adjoining state of Chamba, a similar variety of the Takri was also improved and adopted as the official script under British influence in the first decade of this century. This character is termed Chameali or Chamiali or Chambiali, and is employed for Chameali, a western Pahari dialect of the Chamba group spoken by 65,000 people in the Chamba state. This script is also used for the other dialects of the same group, Gadi (15,000 people), Churahi (30,000) and Pangnali (4,000).

The Chameali is the best revised Takri variety; it has a complete series of vowels, and is as legible and correct as the Deva-nagari. Types have been cast and books have been printed in it, including some portions of the Bible. As there are no types for the Dogri character used in the neighbouring Jammu state, the types of the allied Chameali are also employed for books printed in Dogri.

Mandeali Character

This is another variety of the Takri. The most peculiar feature of this script is the sign *yo* which represents the sound *va*, and sometimes also an initial long *o*. This script is employed for Mandeali and Suketi, both belonging to the Mandi group, which is the most occidental of the western Pahari dialects. Mandeali is spoken by about 150,000 people in Mandi state, and Suketi by about 55,000 people in Suket state.

Sirmauri Character

The Takri variety known as the Sirmauri character is employed for Sirmauri, a western Pahari dialect spoken by about 125,000 people in Sirmur or Sirmaur state (Punjab), also in Ambala and Jubbal. The Sirmauri script is partly influenced by the Deva-nagari character.

Jaunsari Character

The Jaunsari script is allied to the Sirmauri. It is employed for Jaunsari, another western Pahari dialect spoken by about 50,000 people in Jaunsar-Bawar, who also use the Deva-nagari character.

Kochi Character

The Kochi writing is also a variety of the Takri character. Like the preceding two scripts, it has also struck out on independent lines, and suffers from the same imperfections; initial vowels often represent non-initial long vowels. The initial *y* is frequently dropped; often no distinction is made between short and long vowels, both forms being represented either by the short form (in the instances of *u* and *a*) or by the long form (in the case of *i*). The Kochi script is used for Kochi, a Kiuthali sub-dialect of western Pahari, spoken by 52,000 people in Bashahr, the most extensive of the Simla Hill states.

Kului Character

The Kului is another allied script. It is employed for Kului, a western Pahari dialect of the Kulu group, spoken in the Kulu Valley (Punjab) by about 55,000 people. There are two varieties of this script.

Kashtawari Character

The Kashtawari writing, another Takri variety, is considered by Grierson to be a connecting link between the Takri and the Śarada characters. It is used for Kashtawari, which is a dialect of Kashmiri (see p. 285), but is much influenced by the Pahari and Lahnda languages, spoken by its southern and south-eastern neighbours. Kashtawari is spoken in the valley of Kashtawar, lying to the south-east of the valley of Kashmir.

Landa Scripts (Fig. 17.22)

The Landa, or 'clipped' character, is current all over Punjab and Sind as a national alphabet for Punjabi, although it is used mainly by shopkeepers.

Punjabi belongs to the central group of Indo-Aryan languages, and is spoken by about 18 million people in the central Punjab. It was also spoken by the British Sikh soldiers. As Sir George A. Grierson pointed out, Punjabi 'is the one which is most free from borrowed words, whether Persian or Sanskrit.'

The Landa character is also used for two other groups of the north-western Indo-Aryan languages. These are:

(1) Lahnda—meaning '(sun-) setting,' or 'west,' which has nothing to do with Landa—or western Punjabi, spoken by over 7 million people; and

(2) Sindhi, spoken by three and a half million people in Sind, on both banks of the lower Indus, the terms Sind and Indus being etymologically identical.

The Landa, like the Takri and the Mahajani characters, is difficult to read, and varies locally. It is closely allied to the Takri, both in development and present form and, thus, has most of its disadvantages, being imperfectly supplied with vowel-signs. The Landa character frequently omits the representation of the vowels; it has no signs for internal vowels and only two or three symbols for initial forms. The consonants are also represented in an inconsistent and obscure manner.

Multani Character (Figs. 17.1 sect. 5; 21d)

Several varieties of the Landa character may be mentioned; different localities and various classes of people favour distinct styles. Among them is the Multani character, employed for Multani, the most important of the twenty-two Lahnda dialects, which is spoken by nearly three million people.

Sindhi Varieties

George Stack, in his Sindhi Grammar, published over a century ago, mentioned a dozen varieties of the Landa character used for Sindhi: Khudawadi, Shikarpuri, Sakkar, Thattai (Luhanas, Bhatias), Larai, Wangai, Rajai, Khwajas, Maimons (Thatta,

Hyderabad), Sewhani Bhabhiras, Achiki Punjabi. Stack pointed out that none of these scripts, with the exception of the Khwajas, has more than four signs for the ten vowel-sounds, simple and compound; and even these few were mainly used for initial forms. On the other hand, these scripts possessed six consonantal signs for sounds (a kind of *tr*, *dr*, and so forth), for which there are no equivalents either in Indian or European languages.

The most important is the Khudawadi character, used at Hyderabad and known by most educated merchants throughout the country. The Shikarpuri and Sakkar varieties differ very little from the Khudawadi script.

Sindhi Character (Figs. 17.1 sect. 5; 21*e*)

The Landa script, called in Sindhi *baniya* or *waniko* (the 'mercantile' script), became almost an official character in 1868. This script is also used in schools and for printing books in Sind.

It must, however, be remembered that the majority of Sindhi speakers—numbering over 3 millions, in Sind and neighbouring districts—who are Moslems, generally employ the Urdu or Persian-Arabic alphabet with additional letters for the sounds peculiar to the local speech. The Deva-nagari and the Gurmukhi (*see* below) character are also used. The majority of Lahnda speakers are also Moslems, who thus usually employ the Urdu or Persian-Arabic alphabet.

For the Limbū character see Fig. 17.20*a*.

Gurmukhi Script (Figs. 17.1 sect. 5; 15*b*; 22)

Tradition ascribes the invention of the Gurmukhi character to Angad (1538–52), the second Sikh Guru; the term Gur-mukhi means that the script proceeded from the mouth of the Guru. It is said that Angad found that Sikh hymns written in Landa character were liable to be misread, and therefore he improved it to record the sacred scriptures of the Sikhs. The Gurmukhi is commonly, but incorrectly, considered to be the Punjabi writing, and sometimes it is even wrongly applied to Punjabi speech.

Actually, the Gurmukhi script is not peculiar to Punjabi, but is the character of the Sikh Scriptures, which are written in various dialects. The Gurmukhi character has spread widely, and being the vehicle of Sikh religious literature, it became an essential element for the consolidation of the Sikh religion. Its importance was augmented when, towards the end of the Mogul dynasty in India, in the eighteenth century, the Sikhs rose to be a great military power, and when at the beginning of the nineteenth century they established political authority over the Punjab and Kashmir.

The Gurmukhi script seems to be a polished form of the Landa character with the addition of some signs borrowed from the Deva-nagari. A peculiar feature of the Gurmukhi is that the order of the vowels is different from that in the Deva-nagari script, and that the vowels are followed by the signs *sa* and *ha*, which thus precede the other consonants, whilst in the Deva-nagari the two signs follow the other consonants. Instead of the three sibilants of the Deva-nagari, the Gurmukhi has only one sibilant, *sa*, which is sufficient for the purposes of Punjabi; in borrowed words, a dot is placed under *sa* to represent the sound *sha*. There are ten vowel-signs: three short ones (*a, i, u*), five long ones (*a, i, u, e, o*), and two diphthongs (*ai* and *au*). When the vowels are initial (the *a*, as in Deva-nagari, cannot be non-initial), special signs are added (*aira* for *a, ai* and *au*; *iri* for *i* and *e*; *uru* for *u* and *o*). All the vowels and consonants have definite names, *a-kanna, i-siara, sassa, haha*, and so forth. The inherent *a* of the final consonant is not pronounced.

SOUTH INDIAN SCRIPTS

DRAVIDIAN LANGUAGES

India may be divided into two parts, India proper (known also as Hindustan), or North India, the classical Aryavarta ('the abode of the Aryas') or Uttarapatha ('the path of the north, the northern road'), and peninsular or South India, the classical Dakshinapatha ('the path of the south, the southern road'), out of which was formed the modern Deccan. The classic dividing line—which is neither exact nor complete— between the two parts is either the sacred river Narbada or the Vindhya range. On palæographic considerations, we must fix the border line on the west as running north of Kathiawar, and that on the east, as running south of Bengal.

South India was occupied in the historic period by a group of peoples known as 'Dravidian,' a term devised by the bishop Dr. Robert Caldwell from *Dravida*, or *Dramida* (in Pali *Damila*), the Sanskrit form of Tamil, which is the most important member of this linguistic family.

The main features of the primitive Dravidian race seem to have been: short stature, almost black complexion, head long, nose very broad. However, anthropological identification being very doubtful, 'Dravidian' is nowadays essentially a linguistic term. Bishop Caldwell distinguished twelve Dravidian dialects, six cultivated (Tamil, Telugu, Kanarese, Malayalam, Tulu, and Kudagu or Coorg), and six uncultivated. Many other dialects and sub-dialects exist, but the main languages are four:

(1) Tamil, which possesses the ealiest Dravidian literature and is spoken nowadays by over 18 million people in southern India and in Ceylon;

(2) Telugu, spoken by the largest number of people, over 22 million, in the central and eastern part of South India;

(3) Malayalam, closely akin to Tamil, but more influenced by Sanskrit, spoken by over 5 millions; and

(4) Kanarese, more akin to Telugu than to Tamil, spoken by over 8 million people.

It may be roughly said that the north-eastern portion of South India—stretching roughly north from Madras to the borders of Orissa and far inland into the Deccan

—is the Teluguland, or Telingana; the north-western portion, including Mysore and Kanara, is Kanarese; the south-eastern portion is the Tamil country, comprising the great plain of the Carnatic, from Madras to Cape Comorin, South Travancore, and northern Ceylon; whilst the south-western part of South India—principally the country on the western side of the Ghats, from Mangalore to Trivandrum—is Malayalam. The total number of speakers of all the Dravidian dialects and sub-dialects is over 80 millions. The group of the Dravidian languages is nowadays usually considered to be an isolated family, that is with no affinities whatever to any other form of speech, although recently the theory of its affiliation with Finno-Ugrian has been revived.

The Indo-Aryan languages spoken in South India are Marathi in the Deccan, Saurashtri in Madras, and Hindustani, which is spoken by the Moslem population of the Deccan and in some other parts of the country. The Indo-Aryan languages have also greatly influenced the main Dravidian forms of speech, but their influence was just enough to enrich and not sufficient to extirpate the Dravidian languages. On the whole it may be said that the Dravidians accepted the culture and religion of the Indo-Aryans—whilst Dravidian elements were also consciously or unconsciously borrowed by the Aryans—but linguistically they did not lose their individuality.

The earliest history of the Dravidian languages is obscure. There are apparently no records extant in any of the Dravidian dialects belonging to the pre-Christian era. The Aśoka inscriptions so far discovered and all the other documents in Brahmī characters, some of which were brought to light in 1912, as far south as the ancient Pandya country (*see* below), are all in Prakrit. There are also some early Sanskrit records, but no Dravidian certainly datable. *See*, however, pp. 267 f. and 301 f.

DEVELOPMENT OF SOUTH INDIAN CHARACTERS

The South Indian characters were generally used since the middle of the fourth century A.D. throughout the country and some of them still survive in the modern characters of the Dravidian languages.

These characters (for their origins, see pp. 270 f.) can be divided, according to Bühler, into the following varieties:

WESTERN VARIETY

The western variety was the ruling script between *c.* A.D. 400 and 900 in Kathiawar, Gujarat, the western portion of the Maratha districts, partly in Hyderabad and in Konkan. Northern scripts were used simultaneously and their influence on this script is evident. The shapes of the signs seem to indicate that this character was ordinarily written with ink.

CENTRAL INDIAN SCRIPT (Fig. 17.23*a*)

The 'Central Indian' script was very similar, but later it developed into the slightly different 'box-headed' character, so termed because the heads of the letters resembled small boxes or squares which were either hollow or filled with ink. This character (Fig. 17.23*a*) was employed in northern Hyderabad, the former Central Provinces, in Bundelkhand, and occasionally also farther south in the Bombay state and in Mysore, and perhaps even in Further India (*see* Chapter 7).

KANNAḌA OR KANARESE AND TELUGU CHARACTERS
(Figs. 17.2 sect. 2; 19*b*; 23*b*; 24; 25*a*)

The Kannaḍa, generally known as Kanarese, and Telugu characters are the most important scripts of southern India, from every point of view. They developed in the southern parts of Bombay and of Hyderabad, in Mysore and in the north-eastern portion of the Madras state. The earliest form of these scripts appears in inscriptions attributed to the fifth century A.D. (Fig. 17.23*b*): while the earliest Kanarese literary text preserved, the *Kavirajamarga*, dates from the later part of the ninth century (*c.* A.D. 877), the earliest Kanarese inscription yet found, at Halmidi, is dated *c.* A.D. 450. 'This state of affairs is quite opposite of that which prevails in Tamil, where a copious body of literary texts, excellently preserved, antedates the earliest inscriptions by several centuries' (Burrow). (*See*, however, pp. 301 f.)

Burnell distinguished the following varieties: (*a*) the Vengi alphabet, from about the fourth century A.D.; (*b*) the western Chalukya character, from about A.D. 500 until the temporary fall of the dynasty; (*c*) the eastern Chalukya, from 622 onwards; and (*d*) the transitional, from A.D. 1000 to A.D. 1300.

Burnell's theory is partly obsolete; it is preferable to accept the following classification by Dr. Bühler:

(*a*) The archaic variety, the inscriptions of the Kadamba kingdom, fifth and sixth centuries A.D., and the early Chalukya inscriptions, A.D. 578–660. At present, the cliff inscription of Chalukya Vallabhesvara (Pulikesin I), dated Saka 465 and corresponding to A.D. 543, discovered in 1941 at Badami, by the Bombay Kannada Research Institute, is the earliest example extant of the use of the Saka era in documents and the only inscription of the famous king Pulikesin I.

(*b*) The intermediate script, from *c.* A.D. 650 to A.D. 950, subdivided into the western and the eastern varieties. The cursive signs are a feature common to all the later inscriptions of the western Chalukyas, with a marked slope towards the right, while the eastern variety is remarkably square and upright, and the lettes are broader and shorter.

(*c*) The third variety, corresponding to Burnell's 'transitional,' is not properly termed by Bühler (after Fleet) 'old Kanarese.' It belongs to the flourishing period of early Dravidian literature. This character appears first in the west, in inscriptions of the second half of the tenth century, and a little later in the east, in Vengi inscriptions of the eleventh century.

Figures 17.23*b*, 24 and 25*a* show specimens of the ancient and modern Kanarese and Telugu scripts.

LATER KALINGA SCRIPT

The later Kalinga script—for the early Kalinga inscriptions, *see* p. 267—is the writing of inscriptions of the seventh–twelfth centuries discovered on the north-eastern coast of the Madras state. In earlier documents, the script is strongly mixed with northern forms and with Central Indian forms, while in later times the mixture of the characters is even greater, some letters being developments of the older signs, and the majority of the characters being southern Deva-nagari forms. This mixture is explained by the fact that the Dravidian population of that territory, lying not far from districts where Deva-nagari, Central Indian, Karanese-Telugu and Grantha (*see* below) characters were used, knew all those scripts.

GRANTHA CHARACTER

The term 'Grantha,' which already appears in the fourteenth century A.D., indicates that this character was used for writing books. It is distinguished into the following varieties.

Early Grantha

The early Grantha is the script of the ancient Sanskrit inscriptions of the eastern coast of Madras, south of Pulicat, of the early South Indian kingdoms of the Pallavas of Kanchi, now Conjeeveram, south-west of the city of Madras (fifth–ninth centuries), of the Cholas (ninth–fourteenth centuries) and the Pandyas—*see* below.

The Pandyas, mentioned in the fourth century B.C., constituted an independent kingdom in the time of Aśoka, but the earliest indigenous documents extant belong to the beginning of the tenth century A.D.; the Pandya historical dynasty can be traced from the twelfth till the middle of the sixteenth century A.D. That of the Pandyas was the most southerly kingdom: it extended from coast to coast (comprising the greater part of the Madura and Tinnevelly districts, and of southern Travancore), to the north there was the Chola kingdom, lying on the east coast, from near the mouth of the Krishna to the south of Tondi.

The most archaic forms of the early Grantha character are found in India on the copper plates and other inscriptions of the Pallava kings of the fifth and sixth centuries. This script in general agrees with the early Kanarese-Telugu character, and was used till about the middle of the seventh century A.D.

During the earlier period of Pallava rule, however, their documents seem to have been restricted to copper-plate grants. It is only at the beginning of the seventh century that, as far as we now know, the first Pallava stone inscriptions make their appearance. The style of the copper-plate is obviously more cursive and less ornamental and conservative than the style of the monumental stone inscriptions. It is due to a lucky coincidence that examples of the early Grantha lithic style seem to be preserved in the early inscriptions of Further India (Fig. 17.24c).

Middle Grantha

The middle Grantha character appears first on Kuram copper-plates belonging to the third quarter of the seventh century A.D. It is a current hand, used contemporaneously with a more archaic monumental script, represented in an inscription—running from right to left—of Narasimha II, of the end of the seventh century.

Transitional Grantha

The 'transitional' Grantha (so termed by Bühler) or 'Chola or middle Grantha' (Burnell) seems to have originated towards the end of the eighth or in the ninth century A.D.

Modern Grantha (Fig. 17.2, sect. 2)

The modern Grantha alphabet dates from about A.D. 1300. The oldest modern Grantha MSS. extant belong to the end of the sixteenth century. There are at present two Grantha varieties: the Brahmanic or 'square' hand, used chiefly in Tanjore, and the 'round' or Jain hand, used by the Jains still remaining near Arcot and Madras; the latter has preserved the original characteristics of the early Grantha far better.

Tulu-Malayalam Character (Fig. 17.26a)

The Tulu-Malayalam character is a variety of the Grantha, and like it was originally used only for writing Sanskrit. According to Burnell, it was formed in the eighth or ninth century A.D. There were two varieties: (a) the neater one of the Tulu country, which has preserved its form up to the present; and (b) a very irregular sprawling hand, extant in MSS. from Malabar, where it was termed Arya-eluttu. The latter has, since the seventeenth century, supplanted the Vatteluttu character (see below) for writing Malayalam. This modern Malayalam writing is, however, according to Burnell, a mixed script, being influenced by the old Vatteluttu and by the Tamil character. The Malayalam script has some local varieties: the most important is the Travancore hand, which is more angular than the others.

TAMIL CHARACTER (Figs. 17.2, sect. 2; 26b)

The origin of this script is still uncertain. According to Bühler, it derived from a Brahmī alphabet of the fourth or fifth century A.D., which in course of time was strongly influenced by the Grantha, used in the same districts for writing Sanskrit. But according to Burnell, it was a Brahmanic adaptation of the Grantha to Tamil speech, replacing the old Vatteluttu, from which the Tamil character retained the last four signs, the Grantha not possessing equivalents. Thus in his view, the Tamil character represents the later Brahmanic Tamil culture as opposed to the older civilizations of the Jains of Tanjore and Madura, and of the Buddhists of Tanjore.

The relationship between the ancient 'Dravidi' script (p. 267) and the Tamil character is still uncertain; so also is the exact nature of the language of the 'Dravidi' inscriptions, 'but they appear to be in Early Tamil (as distinguished from the Tamil found in the early Tamil literature, as well as modern Tamil), with a sprinkling of Prakrit' (R. E. M. Wheeler, *Ancient India*, 1946).

In the fifteenth century, the modern Tamil script was already fully formed, although there was a certain graphic development of the single signs in the nineteenth century owing to the increased use of writing and to the introduction of printing.

VATTELUTTU CHARACTER (Figs. 17.2, sect. 2; 26c–d)

This script offers many problems. The term means 'round hand' in modern Malayalam; it may either indicate a distinction from Koleluttu, or 'sceptre hand' (*see* below) or from the common Tamil writing, or alternatively it may be a simple description of the script, as practically all the letters are circular. The script is an ideal current hand. All its letters, with perhaps one exception, are made with a single stroke from left to right, and are mostly inclined towards the left.

According to Burnell, the Vatteluttu is the original Tamil character, and it may also be termed the Pandyan writing, 'as its use extended over the whole of that kingdom at its best period' and it 'was once used in all that part of the peninsula south of Tanjore and also in southern Malabar and Travancore where it still exists though in exceedingly limited use, and in a more modern form.' Burnell also held that all the early Tamil works were written in this script, and that from the eleventh century A.D., after the conquest of the Cholas, it was gradually supplanted by the Tamil character; it disappeared from that country by the fifteenth century. In Malabar it remained in general use among the Hindus up to the end of the seventeenth century, and it was used even later, in the *Koleluttu* form, by Hindu sovereigns for writing their grants. The Mappilas of the neighbourhood of Tellicherry and on the islands, used this character until modern times, when it was superseded by a modified Arabic alphabet.

As to the origin of the Vatteluttu, Burnell traced it, possibly through the Pahlavi (*see* the preceding chapter), to a Semitic source, considering both the southern Aśoka character and the Vatteluttu as 'independent adaptations of some foreign character, the first to a Sanskritic, the last to a Dravidian language.' This opinion has been accepted by various scholars, including Reinhold Host in his article on the Tamils in the *Encyclopaedia Britannica*, but is now out of date.

There is much ingenuity in this theory, and Burnell was certainly the greatest authority on South Indian palæography, but there is little evidence to corroborate it. The number of the inscriptions extant is very small, and the dates appear to be relatively late. The earliest Vatteluttu documents extant are two grants in favour of the Jews (Fig. 17.26*d*) and of the Syrians in Travancore. Burnell attributed them to the eighth century A.D., while Bühler, probably more correctly, thought they may belong to the tenth or eleventh century.

Unless new evidence becomes available, Bühler's opinion seems preferable, that the Vatteluttu should be considered to be an ancient cursive variety of the Tamil character. Bühler suggested it may have been in use by the seventh century A.D., but was modified in course of time by the further development of the Tamil and the Grantha characters.

SINHALESE CHARACTER
(Figs. 17.2, sect. 3; 27, 28, 29 *a-b*)

ISLAND OF CEYLON

The island of Ceylon, also known as Lanka, is the Taprobane of the Greeks and Romans, and Tambapanni of Pali literature. After the Sinhalese settlement (*see* below) it was styled in Sanskrit Sinhala-dvipa, and in Pali Sihala-dipa, a term which ultimately passed into Arabic as Serendib or was known simply as Sinhala or Sihala. The form Sinhale survives as the name of a region, while Sinhala, through the medium of Arabic and Portuguese, became Ceylon. The term Sinhalese is used particularly to indicate the Indo-Aryan population of the island, and their speech. About a third of the population speak Tamil. The Tamil term for the island is Ilam. Ceylon had in 1959 an estimated population of 9,625,000.

Although there are still some who maintain that Sinhalese is essentially a Dravidian language, it is generally admitted by serious scholars that it is an Indo-Aryan vernacular, but during its development it was strongly influenced by Dravidian, and its vocabulary contains a great number of Tamil loan words. (*See* C. E. Godakumbura, 'The Dravidian Element in Sinhalese,' *Bull. School of Oriental and African Studies*, 1946, pp. 837–41).

The history of Ceylon begins with the first Aryan immigration which probably took place in the fifth century B.C. As to the original home of these first immigrants, and, consequently, of the origin of Sinhalese, opinion is divided. Dr. L. D. Barnett was most likely right in assuming that the tradition of two different streams of immigration, one from eastern India, Orissa and southern Bengal, and the other from the western, Gujarat, were interwoven in the local story of Vijaya, the leader of the first immigration. However, from the earliest times an intense mixture of blood and forms of speech took place between the Aryan immigrants on one side, and the later Aryan immigrants with the aborigines and the inhabitants of southern India on the other. The next greatest event in Sinhalese history was the conversion to Buddhism which took place in the second half of the third century B.C. The Pitakas, called also Tripitaka, or teachings of the Buddha, which were being handed down orally, were committed to writing probably at the end of the first century B.C., and the commentaries on these were composed in Sinhalese and perhaps committed to writing at the same time.

The influence of Buddhism and of its sacred language, Pali, on the population of Ceylon, on its language and its history, as also on the civilization of the whole of Further India (*see* below) was paramount. The term Pali means actually the 'text,' the text *par excellence*, that is the text of the Buddhist scriptures, but it indicates also the language in which the sacred scriptures of Buddhism are recorded, and the script in which these are written.

DEVELOPMENT OF SINHALESE LANGUAGE AND SCRIPT

Four main periods can be distinguished in the history of the Sinhalese language and script, which can be traced, with few interruptions, from the third or second century B.C. down to the present day.

Pali-Prakrit Sinhalese

This language and the Brahmī character of the earliest inscriptions found in Ceylon may be dated from the third century B.C. to about the fourth century A.D. Both the language and the script may have been imported by the first Aryan immigrants, but there is no evidence that the latter was much used before Aśoka's time, and the language was later influenced by Pali, the sacred language of the dominant religion.

No written document dating before the establishment of Buddhism in the island, is extant. The earliest inscriptions are engraved either in caves or on rocks; the former are found all over Ceylon, and their epigraphic style is nearly always the same; some inscriptions contain only three words ('the cave of . . .'), others contain also the title of the donor and of his father and a dedication to the priesthood. The rock inscriptions contain a greater variety of words and grammatical forms; they are generally found near tanks, and relate the dedication of the tank to a temple. The earliest inscription known seems to be that found, in three copies, at Naval Niravi Malei, 'the Hill of the Jambu Well,' about 8 miles north-east of Vilankulam, in the northern region. It belongs probably to the third quarter of the third century B.C., and it is thus almost contemporary with the Aśoka inscriptions. No less than fourteen inscriptions found on the same hill, and about seventy other inscriptions belong partly to the end of the third century B.C. and partly to the second or to the first half of the first century B.C.

They were found in various districts of the northern, north-western, north-central and eastern regions, and even in the extreme south-east of Ceylon (at Bowata).

This early writing, on the whole, resembles that of the Aśoka northern inscriptions. As in Aśoka, there are no duplicated consonants and no compound letters, while there appears the cerebral *l*, which until about thirty five years ago was supposed to be a very rare letter in the northern pre-Gupta inscriptions. It is now known that it formed part of the Brahmī character from the very beginning. (*See* H. Lüders, 'The Lingual *la* in the Northern Brahmi Script,' *J. Roy. Asiatic Soc.*, 1911; and also his article in *Antídoron presented to Wackernagel*, 1924: information by Professor H. W. Bailey, who also informs me that the cerebral *la* occurs quite often in the Aśoka inscriptions.)

On the other hand, unlike the Aśoka northern inscriptions, there appear the aspirated consonants, the letter *j* (represented later by the Indian form for the aspirated *jh*), and long vowels appear occasionally in the earliest inscriptions, but not in those of the first century B.C. The long initial *i* replaces the form of the short *i*; there appear special forms of *m* (in the shape of a deep cup with a central horizontal cross-bar) and of *s* (the trifid form). At the end of the first century B.C. the local development of the script seems to have been already complete.

Proto-Sinhalese

The so-called Proto-Sinhalese period may be dated from the fourth or fifth century A.D. to about the eighth century. There are few inscriptions extant belonging to this period, and only some of them have been published. That of Tonigala, belonging probably to the fourth century A.D., seems to be the earliest inscription of this period. Its writing does not differ very much from that of the former period. On the other hand, the inscriptions of the next period are so radically different, linguistically and graphically, that the difference looks nearly like a break. A reasonable explanation may be that in the course of the first millennium of the national existence, the daily life speech gradually developed stylistically, phraseologically and grammatically, whilst a new type of writing, derived from the Grantha (*see* pp. 300 ff.), which came into use for the purposes of daily life, was also later employed for official inscriptions.

Mediæval Sinhalese

The inscription of Gärandigala, attributed to the first half of the eighth century A.D., may be regarded as the oldest extant mediæval Sinhalese inscription. The inscriptions of the ninth and tenth centuries are very numerous, and some of them are very extensive. The epigraphs of the eleventh century are rare, perhaps because a flourishing literary activity began in the ninth century. The mediæval Sinhalese script, which—as mentioned—is based on the Grantha character, developed into the modern Sinhalese character.

Modern Sinhalese

It is difficult to trace an exact boundary line between the mediæval and the modern period. Generally the thirteenth century is considered to be the border line; it was then that the famous grammar *Sidat-sangarava* or *Sidatsangara* was composed, which has the same importance for Sinhalese as Panini's grammar has for Sanskrit (*see* p. 269). The Sinhalese literary language was thus brought to a standard where for all practical purposes it has remained to the present day. The inscriptions of this period, the latest belonging to the nineteenth century, show a slight development.

The modern Sinhalese character (Figs. 17.2, sect. 3; 27, 28, 29*a–b*) contains fifty-four letters, of which eighteen are vowels and thirty-six consonants or 'dead letters.' It is more perfect than the ancient script, containing only thirty-three signs (twelve vowels and twenty-one consonants), or the Deva-nagari character, from which the other twenty-one letters were borrowed to express Sinhalese sounds called impure.

There are, indeed, nowadays, two forms of Sinhalese, the pure form, called Elu, which is often used, for instance, in writing poetry and for which the letters of the ancient script are sufficient, and Sinhala, which is mixed with foreign words. Actually, the two terms Elu and Sinhala are etymologically identical, 'Elu' being a simple development of the words 'Sinhala'—'Sihala'—'Hela'—'Helu.' The full Sinhalese character is sometimes called Misra, or 'mixed,' as it can be used both for writing Elu and for foreign words assimilated to Sinhalese.

The Tamil speaking population of Ceylon employ the Tamil script.

BIBLIOGRAPHY

MUELLER, E. *Ancient Inscriptions of Ceylon*, 2 vols., London, 1883.

Epigraphia Zeylanica (edit. by Don Martino de Zilva Wickremasingh), Vol. I, 1904–12; Vol. II, 1912–28; Vol. III, Part I (edit. by S. Paranavitana), 1928; Parts II–VI, 1929–33; Vol. IV, Part I, 1934 (University of Oxford Press).

PARKER, H. *Ancient Ceylon*, 1909.

CODRINGTON, H. W. *A Short History of Ceylon*, London, 1926.

DE SILVA, W. A. *Catalogue of the Palm Leaf Manuscripts in the Library of the Colombo Museum*, Colombo, 1938.

MENDIS, G. C. *The Early History of Ceylon*, 3rd. ed., Calcutta, 1938.

GEIGER, W. *A Grammar of the Sinhalese Language*, Colombo, 1938.

MALDIVIAN SCRIPTS

General Sketch (Fig. 17.29*c*)

The coral archipelago known as the Maldive Islands—the indigenous term being Divehi Rajje, 'the (Maldive) Island Kingdom'—lies in the Indian Ocean to the south-west of India. The most northerly atoll is some 350 miles from the Indian continent, whereas Male, the capital, lies 400 miles south-west of the nearest port of Ceylon. Of the nearly 2,000 islands, only 217 are inhabited, by *c.* 93,000 people. There was a close kinship between the original Maldive and the Sinhalese languages, but gradually, in the course of many centuries, the continuous contact and intercourse with South Indian peoples and the influx of Arabs and other aliens, brought many modifications particularly in the speech of the population of the northern atolls, whereas the southern islands have been less affected by foreign influences. Arabic linguistic influence is notable particularly in the Maldivian vocabulary, in the vowel changes, and in the adoption of the dento-labial *f* for the labial *p*. Buddhism was for many centuries the ruling religion of the Maldivians. Their conversion to Islām—prepared by the centuries-old trade and commerce with the Arabs—took place in the mid-twelfth century.

Evela Akuru

The earliest form of Maldivian writing yet discovered is the Evela Akuru, or 'ancient letters.' Only a few early copper-plate grants (*lomafanu*), issued by Maldive rulers, in this script are still extant. The most interesting is that granted by Sultana Rehendi (Khadijah), daughter of Sultan 'Umar Vira Jalal-ud-din in the sixteenth year of her reign, A.H. 758 (A.D. 1356). The character, running from left to right, has close affinities with that of Sinhalese stone inscriptions of the tenth to the twelfth centuries A.D., and is probably dependent on it, or else on the Grantha character, the ancestor of the Sinhalese mediæval script.

Dives Akuru (Fig. 17.29c)

The Evela Akuru gradually developed into the Dives Akuru (or Devehi Hakura), 'the (Maldive) Island letters,' also read from left to right. There are few manuscripts (mainly *fatkolu* or royal grants on parchment or paper, and government orders) extant in this writing, but there are many inscriptions on walls and gravestones; more than thirty gravestones and other slab records are preserved at Male. Until recently, very little was known about this script, *i.e.*, the 'Memoir' of the naval lieutenants Young and Christopher, published in the *Transactions of the Geographical Society of Bombay*, 1836–8, and the partial alphabet (eighteen signs) communicated by Christopher to Dr. Wilson, and published in the *J. Roy. Asiatic Society*, 1841, pp. 42–76, and reproduced by Sir Albert Gray in the same journal, 1878. Nowadays, however, this script is sufficiently known.

There were two varieties of the Dives Akuru: (1) the monumental, lapidary script, in which each *akshara* or letter was written separately; and (2) the current hand, in which two *aksharas* were united, usually by carrying the Maldive forms of the Sinhalese *elapilla* or *ispilla* signs round the head of its consonant to unite it with the next letter. The Dives Akuru probably contained, originally, like other Indian characters, a more complete set of signs, but in the course of time, under the influence of Arabic, there was no need for the aspirated letters or the palatal and cerebral sibilants, and these signs were discarded.

In the seventeenth and eighteenth centuries the Dives Akuru gradually gave way more and more to the Tana character, although in the southern atolls it was still used until the last century.

Gabuli Tana (Fig. 17.29c)

The population of the Maldive Islands employ nowadays two different characters: (1) the Arabic alphabet, used for the Arabic speech, but also, though very rarely, for Maldivian, which can be written wholly in the Persian-Arabic alphabet, with dots here and there to represent particular Maldivian sounds; (2) the Tana or Gabuli Tana character, which, since the eighteenth century has supplanted the Dives Akuru.

The Gabuli Tana is a curious script, being formed from a combination of Arabic and Maldivian numerals with the admixture of a few needed Persian-Arabic letters. On the whole, the character consists of twenty-six letters, of which the last eight are modified Persian-Arabic additions, used only when absolutely necessary to give Persian-Arabic pronunciation to Arabic or Persian words written in Maldivian character. The first section of the Tana consists of the Arabic numerals 1 to 9— representing the sounds *h, rh(th), n, r, b,* the cerebral *l, k,* the *a*-consonantal sign, and the *v(w)*. The second section, namely the letters *m, f(ph), dh, t, l, g, n(g), s, ḍ,* are drawn from the Maldivian numerals 1 to 9, several of which resemble Sinhalese and Indian numerical symbols. The direction of writing is, as in Semitic scripts, from right to left. Besides, the single letters, as in Semitic scripts (unlike the earlier Maldivian and all the Indian and Sinhalese characters, where the sound *a* is inherent in the single consonants), are pure consonants; the vocalization is provided by superscript or subscript or by diacritical marks. We can conclude from these peculiar features that the Gabuli Tana was invented either by the Arabs, who did not bother to master the Dives Akuru, or by the natives, in order to make it easy for the Arabs to learn Maldivian.

There are several varieties of the Gabuli Tana, such as the semi-secret and semi-apparent scripts, consisting in transposition of the values of the single letters. We may mention the Harha Tana (*h* in Harha corresponding to *rh* of Tana), in which the consecutive letters are interchanged (*h-rh, n-r,* etc.), and the De-fa(t) Tana, in which the mutation is effected between the halves of the Gabuli Tana.

SYRO-MALABARIC ALPHABET

I may mention here the curious alphabet still used by some Christian communities, the so-called Christians of St. Thomas, who live in Malabar, south-west India; the country is mainly inhabited by people of the Dravidian stock speaking Malayalam. The Syrian Christians no doubt owed their origin to Nestorian missionaries who came from Persia, and lived as a close caste, under their own kings. The Malabar liturgy remained essentially a form of Nestorian rite. Pahlavi inscriptions, as old as the seventh or eighth century A.D. are shown at Kottayam in Travancore, and on Mt. St. Thomas, near Madras. One of the inscriptions has a line also in Syriac, in Estrangela characters, perhaps of the tenth century A.D.

There are now five crosses which testify to the existence of this ancient Christian community. The first cross was discovered in 1547 on St. Thomas' Mt.; it was found by the Portuguese while repairing an old hermitage; it is now preserved on the

Mount in the Church of the Madonna. This stone-slab was 'identified' as the one which the Apostle St. Thomas is said to 'have embraced while on the point of death; its miraculous virtues speedily obtained great fame' (Mingana). Two other crosses are preserved in the Valiya Palli or 'Great Church' at Kottayam. A replica of the first cross was discovered in 1921 in Katamarram, North Travancore, by T. K. Joseph; and the fifth cross was found in 1924 at Mattuchira.

The earliest reliable witness for the existence of an organized Syrian Church in South India is that of the Alexandrian merchant who afterwards became a monk, and whom we know as Cosmas Indicopleustes; he lived in the first half of the sixth century A.D. On the other hand, the earliest dated Syriac manuscript from South India (Vatican MS. No. XVII) according to Professor Wright belongs to 1510, being thus almost 1,000 years later.

Dr. Mingana, however, attributes the earliest extant Syriac manuscript from South India (*Cod. Syr. Vatic.* No. XXII) to A.D. 1301, and a manuscript in Paris to A.D. 1504.

The Christian Catholic inquisition, established by the Portuguese at Goa in 1560, accounts for the destruction of all earlier books and liturgies, which were opposed in any way whatsoever to the doctrine of the Church of Rome. The Synod of Diamper, in the south of Cochin, held in 1599, united the Malabarese Christians to Rome, but in 1653 many returned to their 'heretical' rites. In 1665—some years earlier the Dutch gained supremacy—a great part of the Malabarese acknowledged as their head the Jacobite metropolitan of Jerusalem.

This Christian community is also known as 'Nazarani' or Nazaræans, 'Syriani' or Syrians, etc. As to its alleged foundation by the Apostle St. Thomas—a legend still accepted by such a scholar as Professor J. N. Farquhar—it is suffcient to quote the words of T. K. Joseph, a scholar who is himself a St. Thomas Christian of South India. 'The more I study it, the more I am confirmed in my belief that St. Thomas, the Apostle, never went to South India.'

The script of the special liturgy employed by the Christians of St. Thomas was perhaps descended from the Nestorian alphabet, but nine special Malayalam signs were added to represent Dravidian sounds, which could not be expressed by Syriac letters. On the other hand, Dr. Burnell, the great authority on South Indian palæography, suggested that 'A few tombstones and similar relics in Travancore show that the Syriac-Malayalam alphabet is of recent introduction, and that the Syrians originally used only the Vatteluttu character.' He, however, admits that 'Buchanan mentions bells with inscriptions in Syriac and Malayalam.' Wright seems to accept Burnell's opinion about the recent origin of this curious character. This theory is possible, but hardly probable; indeed, we know that 'the alphabet follows religion' (*see* pp. 210ff., 222f., 237ff., etc.), especially in connection with religious literature, and I would hardly admit that a religious community having accepted the local script and used it for many centuries, at a later stage goes back to the old script. It is, however, possible that the Syro-Malabarese script was created after the 'Christians of St. Thomas' became Jacobites.

BIBLIOGRAPHY

LAND, J. P. N. 'Südindisches Kârshun,' *Zeitschr. der Deutsch. Morgenl. Gesellsch.*, 1868.
BURNELL, A. C. *On Some Pahlavi Inscriptions in S. India*, Mangalore, 1873.
RAE MILNE, G. *The Syrian Church in India*, Edinburgh and London, 1892.
WRIGHT, W. *A Catalogue of the Syriac Manuscripts*, I, Cambridge, 1901.
MEDLYCOTT, A. E. *India and the Apostle Thomas*, London, 1905.
JOSEPH, T. K. in *Indian Antiquary*, 1923; and *Young Men of India*, 1926.
DANIEL, K. N. in *Indian Antiquary*, 1924.
MINGANA, A. 'The Early Spread of Christianity in India,' *Bull. John Rylands Library*, 1926.
FARQUHAR, J. N. 'The Apostle Thomas,' etc., the same journal, 1926 and 1927.

SAURASHTRAN SCRIPT

Until 1943, very little was known in Europe of the character employed for the Saurashtri language. This form of speech was listed in the *Linguistic Survey of India*, Vol. IX, Part II (1908), pp. 447–8, as 'Patanuli, also called Saurashtri (or the language of Surat) and Khatri,' 'the language of the silkweavers of the Deccan and Madras.' The language is described there as 'ordinary Gujarati with . . . a slight addition of local words to its vocabulary.'

The Saurashtrans, called by the Tamils Patnulkarens, or 'silk-weavers,' numbered, in 1931, 104,000 people, and were resident in the Tamil country, mainly in Madura and Madras. The great majority of them are bilingual, Tamil being their subsidiary language, while some are trilingual, knowing also Telugu. According to Mr. Randle, the Saurashtri language is, through and through, an Indo-Aryan language; it appears to belong to the Gujarati-Rajasthani linguistic type, but it should not be regarded as a dialect of Gujarati, as its inflections are not those of Gujarati and its basic vocabulary is predominantly Marathi; besides, it has been strongly influenced by Dravidian. However, Mr. A. Master of the London School of Oriental and African Studies, does not think (according to the personal information he gave me) that Saurastri belongs to the Gujarati-Rajasthani group, but should be regarded as an independent Indo-Aryan language.

H. N. Randle, former Librarian of the India Office Library, has brought to the knowledge of European scholars not only the existence of this language, but also the employment for it of a peculiar script: *See* H. N. Randle, 'An Indo-Aryan Language of South India: Saurastra-bhasa,' *Bull. School of Oriental and African Studies, University of London*, XI, Part I (1943), pp. 104–21; and Part II (1944), pp. 310–27; idem, 'The Saurashtrans of South India,' *J. Roy. Asiatic Soc.*, 1944, pp. 151–64. Mr. Randle bases his researches concerning this matter on two little books, written in the Saurashtran script, by T. H. Rama Rou, *First Catechism of Saurashtra Grammar*, Madras, 1905; and *Saurastra-bodhini*, 1906; the script, in the usual order of the Indian characters, and the lists of the complex combinations of all the vowels with all the consonants, published in the latter, have enabled Mr. Randle to read both these books.

Both Mr. Randle and Mr. Master suggest that there may be a connection between the modern Saurashtrans and the ancient community of silk-weavers whose activity is recorded in the famous inscription discovered in Mandasor (western Malwa), and dated in the years 493 and 529 of Malava era, corresponding to A.D. 437–8 and 473 (*see* J. F. Fleet, *Corpus Inscriptionum Indicarum*, Vol. III, 'Inscriptions of the Early Gupta Kings and their Successors,' Part I, No. 18). I do not think that the modern Saurash-tran script, which since 1880 is also used in print, is directly connected with the Mandasor inscription. The origin of the Saurashtran character is still an open problem. In my opinion, it is a more or less recent invention, being employed for an isolated language, completely surrounded by languages belonging to a totally different linguistic family. According to Mr. Master, the script may have descended from a very ancient writing, which was probably employed in the Indo-Aryan country of origin of the Saurashtrans, but in the course of its development it became influenced by the scripts of the Indo-Aryan countries, through which the Saurashtrans passed in their migration before reaching their new homeland. My doubt as to this theory arises from this: the script appears as a uniform system, based on sound foundations, and not as an outcome of long development.

TEXT OF SPECIMENS OF MODERN INDIAN SCRIPTS

Figures 17.16 and 17 show specimens of modern Indian scripts. They are a rough version of the following letter.

'Dear Dr. Diringer,

I am pleased to oblige with this short note, to be published in your book on the Alphabet, as a specimen of ... writing, and hope it will be sufficient for your purpose.

Yours truly,

... ,

BIBLIOGRAPHY ON THE INDIAN SCRIPTS

The immense debt which the foregoing chapter owes particularly to Dr. G. Bühler's *Indian Palæography* and Sir George A. Grierson's *Linguistic Survey of India*, is I hope, too obvious from the text to need further emphasis. Without access to the *Linguistic Survey of India*, that unrivalled guide to the hundreds of Indian forms of speech and writing, and without consulting Bühler's '*Indische Paläographie*' (*Grund-riss der Indo-Arischen Philologie und Altertumskunde*, I, ii, 1896; edited in English in 1904 by J. F. Fleet, as an appendix of the *Indian Antiquary*), a book of imaginative scholarship, the greater part of this chapter could never have been even attempted. The *Linguistic Survey of India* was published in the years 1904–28, in eleven volumes, some of them consisting of two or three large parts. Bühler's book, however, partly out of date, is still essential for the study of the origin and the early development of the Indian characters. The Indian inscriptions are collected in the *Corpus Inscriptionum Indicarum*. Readers who wish to go more deeply into the subject will find a copious bibliography in the three aforementioned works, as also in the specialized journals, annuals, transactions of learned societies, and so forth.

The publications bearing upon the various Indian scripts have been so numerous that it is impossible to provide a complete bibliography, even when the first-class authorities only are referred to, while a too short selection must be arbitrary and invidious.

However, some publications have already been quoted, and some more, mostly recent books, are cited here:

The Indian Antiquary, Bombay, 1872 onwards.

Corpus Inscriptionum Indicarum, Calcutta (and Oxford), 1877 onwards.

BURNELL, A. C. *Elements of South-Indian Palæography*, 2nd ed., London, 1878.

FLEET, J. F. *Pali, Sanskrit and Old Canarese Inscriptions*, etc., London, 1878; 'Epigraphy,' in *The Imperial Gazetteer of India*, Vol. II, Chapter I, new edition, Oxford, 1908.

FERGUSSON, J. and BURGESS, J. *The Cave Temples of India*, London, 1880.

GRIERSON, G. *A Handbook to the Kayathi Character*, Calcutta, 1881.

BURGESS, J. *Tamil and Sanskrit Inscriptions*, etc., Madras, 1886.

Epigraphia Indica, Calcutta, 1892 onwards.

CLAIR TISDALL, W. S. *Simplified Grammar of Gujarātī Language*, London, 1892.

DUTT, R. C. *History of Civilization in Ancient India*, London, 1893.

FRANKE, R. O. *Pali und Sanskrit*, etc., Strasbourg, 1902.

KITTEL, F. *A Grammar of the Kannada Language*, Mangalore, 1903.

HŒRNLE, A. F. and STARK, H. A. *A History of India*, 2nd ed., Cuttack, 1904.

Epigraphia Indo-Moslemica, Calcutta, 1908 onwards.

LUEDERS, H. 'A List of Brahmi Inscriptions from the Earliest Times to about A.D. 400' (*Epigraphia Indica*, Append.), Calcutta, 1910.

KRISHNASWAMI AIYANGAR, S. *Ancient India*, Madras, 1911; *The Beginnings of South Indian History*, Madras, 1918.

BARNETT, L. D. *Antiquities of India*, London, 1913.

ANDERSON, J. D. *Peoples of India*, Cambridge, 1913.

RAPSON, E. J. *Ancient India*, Cambridge, 1914; and others, *The Cambridge History of India*, Cambridge 1922 onwards.

SMITH, V. A. *The Early History of India*, 3rd ed., Oxford, 1914; *The Oxford History of India*, Oxford, 1919 (2nd ed., 1923).

JOUVEAU-DUBREUIL, G. *Pallava Antiquities*, I, London, 1916; II, Pondicherry, 1918; *Ancient History of the Deccan*, Pondicherry, 1920.

KRISHNA SASTRI, H. *South Indian Inscriptions*, Madras, 1917.

MARSHALL, J. *A Guide to Sanchi*, Calcutta, 1918.

LAUFER, B. 'Origin of Tibetan Writing,' *J. Amer. Orient. Soc.*, 1918.

PANDIT GAURISHANKAR HIRACHAND OJHA, R. B. *The Palæography of India*, 2nd ed., Ajmer, 1919.

CODRINGTON, K. DE B. *Ancient India*, etc., London, 1926.

PANCHANANA, M. *Prehistoric India*, etc., Calcutta, 1927.

VENIMAHDAVA, B. *Old Brahmi Inscriptions*, etc., Calcutta, 1929.

SEWELL, R. *The Historical Inscriptions of Southern India*, etc., Madras, 1932.

WAUCHOPE, R. S. *Buddhist Cave Temples of India*, Calcutta, 1933.

NILAKANTA SASTRI, K. A. *The Colas*, Madras, 1935.

ALLAN, J. *Catalogue of the Coins of Ancient India*, British Museum, London, 1936.

RAWLINSON, H. G. *India, a Short Cultural History*, etc. Edited by C. G. Seligman, London, 1937.

GANGULY, D. C. *The Eastern Calukyas*, Benares, 1937.

LÉVI, S. *L'Inde civilisatrice: aperçu historique*, Paris, 1938.

CUMMING, J. *Revealing India's Past*, etc., London, 1939.

SHAMA SASTRY, R. *South Indian Inscriptions*, Madras, 1939 onwards.

SACHCHIDANANDA, BHATTACHARYA, *Select Aśokan Epigraphs*, Calcutta, 1941 (2nd rev. ed., 1960).

KAKATI, B. *Assamese, its Formation and Development*, Assam, 1941.

NARASIMHIA, A. N. *A Grammar of the Oldest Kanarese Inscriptions, Studies in Dravidian Philology*, I, University of Mysore, 1941.

KRISHNAMACHARLU, C. R. *List of Inscriptions Copied by the Office of the Superintendent for Epigraphy*, Madras, 1941.

SANKALIYA, D. H. *The Archæology of Gujarat*, etc., Bombay, 1941.

JONES, D. *The Problem of a National Script for India*, Lucknow and Hertford, 1942.

Progress of Indic Studies, 1917–42, by various authors, Poona, 1942.

LAMBERT, H. M. *Marathi Language Course*, Oxford University Press, 1943.

(BARODA STATE) *Important Inscriptions from the Baroda State*, I, Baroda, 1943.

BENDREY, V. S. *A Study of Muslim Inscriptions*, Bombay, 1944.

MEILE, P. *Introduction au Tamoul*, Paris, 1945.

BLOCH, J. *Structure grammaticale des langues dravidiennes*, Paris, 1946; *Les inscriptions d'Asoka*, Paris, 1950.

MUGALI, R. S. *The Heritage of Karnataka*, etc., Bangalore, 1946.

GAI, G. S. *Historical Grammar of Old Kannada*, etc., Poona, 1946.

Ancient India, Delhi (Calcutta), 1946 onwards.

RENOU, L. *Anthologie sanskrite*, Paris, 1947; *La Grammaire de Panini*, Paris, 1948.

MEHENDALE, M. A. *Historical Grammar of Inscriptional Prakrits*, Poona, 1948.

MAJUMDAR, R. C., RAYCHAUDHURI, H. C. and DATTA, K. *An Advanced History of India*, 2nd. ed., London, 1948.

Proceedings of the Committee for Finalizing the Report of the Hindustani Shorthand and of the Hindi Typewriter Standardization Committee, New Delhi, 1951.

ARYAN, K. C. *Rēkha, a Book on Art and Anatomy of Indian Languages and Symbols*, Delhi, 1952.

LAMBERT, H. M. *Introduction to the Devanagari Script*, London and Oxford, 1953.

MIRASHI, V. V. *Inscriptions of the Kalachuri-Chedi Era*, Potacamund, 1955.

PARANAVITANA, S. *Sigiri Graffiti, being Sinhalese Verses of the Eighth, Ninth and Tenth Centuries*, London and New York, 1956.

PANDEY, R. B. *Indian Palæography*, 2nd rev. ed., Varabasi, 1957.

NIKAM, N. A. and McKEON, R. *The Edicts of Asoka*, Chicago, 1959.

PUGLIESE CARRATELLI, G. *Gli editti di Asoka*, Florence, 1963 (bibliogr.).

MEISEZAHL, R. O. *Alttibetische Handschriften der Völkerkundlichen Sammlungen der Stadt Mannheim im Reiss-Museum*, Copenhagen, 1961.

Further-Indian Branch

GENERAL SKETCH

THE first difficulty I encountered in writing this Section was to find a suitable heading. Until recently, the scripts here discussed were considered as descendants of the so-called Pali script (Figs. 17.27, 28; Fig. 18.8). In my Italian book on the Alphabet I too treated them as such under the heading 'the scripts of the Pali branch.'

It is well known that the cultural expansion of India into Ceylon, Burma, Cambodia, Laos, Thailand, Vietnam, Malaya, Indonesia, was due to a large extent to Buddhism. The scripts of the Buddhist monks became the vehicle of their culture and their outward organization. The Austro-Asiatic peoples of south-eastern Asia fell into line with the spiritual attitude of India when they adopted and gradually assimilated Buddhism. A unique empire was built up: an empire based not on political and military unity, but on the common cultural and spiritual life of politically more or less independent peoples. The culture of Buddhist India has been one of the great civilizing and humanizing factors evolved by man. In other words, Buddhist scripts played in south-eastern Asia a part similar to that of Roman Christian Latin scripts in western and central Europe in the Middle Ages, and it must be stressed that Pali-Buddhism, that is so say, the particular form of Buddhism based on the sacred Pali books brought over from Ceylon in the eleventh-twelfth century A.D., was only a reinforcement of earlier forms of Buddhism. Because of this we now know that the majority of the various scripts with which we shall have to deal in this section do not derive from the Sinhalese script of the Pali Books.

The movement which carried Indian colonization and culture into the Indonesian world in the first millennium A.D. inaugurated a new route, which was to branch out in further directions. This movement was neither sudden nor violent. According to Chinese sources, the ancient Indian trade with south-eastern Asia, including the Malay Archipelago, ante-dated by some centuries the Christian era. With merchants, warriors and magicians, came Hindu priests who taught a new ritual in Sanskrit, while for their daily speech the newcomers adopted the indigenous tongue, enriching it with their own vernaculars and their literary language. In the first half of the first millennium A.D., various new kingdoms arose, ruled by Hindu dynasties.

Epigraphical evidence has proved that the earliest Hindu colonists in historical times—who settled in Champa and the Malay Archipelago—came from the country of the Pallavas of Kanchi (*see* p. 271), that Coromandel coast whose ships have continued to visit the Malacca coast until the present day. It was no doubt through the Brahmans of South India in the first place that Indian civilization was carried to Champa, Cambodia and Java. The South Indians brought their own early Grantha alphabet and used Sanskrit for their inscriptions. Indeed, the South Indian style of writing agrees exactly with the script of the earliest inscriptions discovered in southern Vietnam, Cambodia, Borneo and Java. The prevalence of the worship of Shiva, as appears from these inscriptions, and the exclusive use of the Saka era (which was emphatically the era of South India) also point to the South Indian origin of the colonists. In consequence, the general heading 'Pali scripts' seems inappropriate, and I have preferred to introduce a cultural geographical classification.

FURTHER INDIA

An intermingling of races, languages and scripts has been going on, group upon group, for centuries in the whole of the Peninsula. The numerous indigenous tribes, classified under the three great linguistic families, the Tibeto-Chinese, the Austro-Asiatic and the Malayo-Polynesian fought, and overran each other, and influenced each other linguistically and racially, while the importation of Buddhist religion and Indian culture, including South Indian scripts, implied a preponderance of Indian ideas in the culture of the upper classes. The influence of Buddhism has been so deeply rooted in the region that whereas in India, its place of origin, it ultimately expired through absorption by Hinduism and Moslem destruction, Further India has preserved its Buddhist religion until the present day. Buddhism and Buddhist literature and culture advanced hand in hand. The scripts and the scriptures were the vehicles by which the religion and the culture were spread.

The common term 'Indo-Chinese languages' is not correct, as it would comprise an endless series of different forms of speech belonging to the three linguistic families mentioned above. It is, however, often applied to the Sino-Thai sub-family of languages, which are all spoken by Mongolian races and have some characteristics in common, the most important being isolation and monosyllabism (*see* pp. 63 f.).

THE CHAMS (Figs. 18.1–3)

The most ancient Hindu settlement in Further India, as far as we can deduce from the epigraphical evidence, seems to lie in the south of modern Vietnam (formerly Annam) between 'Cochinchina' and the mountain range which terminates near Cape Varella (13°N.). This Hindu colony was perhaps the nucleus of the shadowy kingdom of Champa, which modern studies have rescued from the realm of legendary traditions. It is now known that from the early centuries of the Christian era there really existed a kingdom of that name. It was founded by princely adventurers from India

Y

in the year A.D. 192 (according to Chinese sources), and extended rapidly towards the north up to the frontier of Tongking. The indigenous population of that kingdom—who inhabited the eastern coasts from pre-historic times down to the fifteenth century A.D.—spoke a Malayo-Polynesian language.

In the twelfth century A.D., Champa yielded to the rising power of the Khmers or Cambodians, becoming temporarily their vassal. Towards the end of the fifteenth century, Champa ceased to exist as an independent state. The Vietnamese of Tongking, who apparently are of Shan origin, but nowadays speak a language mixed with Mon-Khmer and Chinese elements, and who from early times had adopted the Chinese character, freed themselves politically from China in the tenth century A.D. and gradually extended their possessions towards the south. Nowadays, the Chams are reduced to two isolated main groups, one in southern Vietnam, the other chiefly in Cambodia.

The earliest epigraphical document of Champa and of the whole of Further India, is the rock-inscription of Vo-Canh, which belongs perhaps to the second or third century A.D. It is in Sanskrit, but the script is obviously of South Indian origin. Of all the early inscriptions, this is the only Buddhist document. It was in the ninth century only that Buddhism made its definite appearance, and its importance was steadily growing at least up to the thirteenth century. The Champa inscriptions are often bilingual, partly in Sanskrit and partly in Cham, but written throughout in the Cham character, which did not completely lose its similarity with the South Indian writing. About the eighth century, the Champa script was fully developed, while at the same time the Cham language definitely supplanted Sanskrit.

The script of the 'box-head' type (see p. 299 and Fig. 18.23a), is identical with that of the inscriptions of Bhadravarman (see below), couched in Sanskrit, and on palæographical evidence attributed to the middle of the fourth century A.D., or, with more probability, to the middle of the sixth century A.D.

The earliest extant inscription couched in Cham language is the rock-inscription of Dong-yen-chau, province of Quang-nam (Vietnam). Professor G. Coedès points out that it is also the earliest text extant couched in a Malayo-Polynesian dialect.

Before the discovery, in 1935, of the Dong-yen-chau inscription, the earliest Cham documents were attributed to the beginning of the ninth century A.D. See G. Coedès, 'La plus ancienne inscription en langue cham,' A Volume of Eastern and Indian Studies, presented to Professor F. W. Thomas, C.I.E., Bombay, 1939.

The Cham inscriptions are written from left to right, but nowadays, under Moslem influence, the impagination of some Cham books begins with the 'last' page. The Cham character has discarded the Indian cerebral consonants; on the other hand, new vowel signs have been created for the rich Cham vocalization, and some consonants have been added for Cham peculiar sounds. Nowadays, the Cham character possesses seven long and seven short vowels, nine diphthongs; five guttural consonants, six palatals, six dentals, six labials, four semi-vowels, two sibilants and one aspirate (Figs. 18.1–2); see also p. 318.

THE KHMERS

Khmer is the indigenous term for Cambodia.

Cambodia is the Europeanized form of the Sanskrit term Kambuja, which is said to have derived from Kambu, the legendary founder of the nation. The Arabs use the indigenous name, Khmer. The Khmer language forms with the Mon (*see* below) a group which has been called the Mon-Khmer group or sub-family, and is a branch of the Austro-Asiatic family of languages. The area occupied in the remote past by this family was very extensive. Languages with the Austro-Asiatic common substratum are still spoken in Assam (Khasi), in Cambodia, Burma, Thailand and Vietnam (Mon and Khmer), on the Malay Peninsula (Senoi), and over the whole of Central India (Kolarian or Munda).

About the middle of the first millennium A.D. or perhaps earlier, immigrants from southern India began to exert a powerful influence over the coastal region, into which they introduced Brahmanism and Sanskrit. This 'Hinduizing' process became more marked during the sixth century, when the Khmers as an organized people rose into prominence, obtained their political independence, and took the place of the ancient state called in the Chinese sources Fu-nan. The Khmer kingdom was at its zenith from the ninth century to *c.* 1200. In the first half of the tenth century, the Khmers conquered the valley of Menam from the Mons; in the twelfth, they subdued the Chams. A little afterwards, the advance of the Khmers towards the north brought them into contact with another race, which was in a short time to drive them back on the Mekong and later to seize the hegemony of the western Peninsula. This was the race of the Thai or Shans (*see* below), the ancestors of the modern Thai or Siamese. In 1350, the Thai made a bid for the sovereignty of the whole region and transferred their capital to a more central position. From this time, the Khmer empire ceased to hold any sway over the country now called Thailand, and in 1430 was given the *coup de grâce*, when the empire itself was invaded by the Thai, its capital, Angkor (-Thom), sacked, and thousands of prisoners carried off to slavery.

The earliest inscriptions found in Khmer country are in Sanskrit and are undated. Three of them, those connected with the king Bhadravarman, belong probably to the middle of the sixth century (*see* above). Thirty years ago Professor Coedès deciphered two earlier documents which are attributed, the one to the first half of the fifth century A.D., the other to the early sixth century. The earliest dated inscription belongs to the year 526 of the Saka era (corresponding to A.D. 604); the Saka era was used throughout in Cambodia epigraphy. The first mention of Buddhists occurs in an inscription of A.D. 664. From the end of the seventh century, there begins a long succession of inscriptions in both Sanskrit and Khmer. The earliest inscription written in Khmer language belongs to A.D. 629.

All the early Cambodian inscriptions are in a script closely connected with the early Grantha character, except the inscriptions of Yasovarman (A.D. 889–910), which are digraphic, in Grantha script and in a kind of North Indian script from Bengal.

Cambodian inscriptions are generally in a symmetrical and elegant style, rarely found in Indian epigraphy.

DEVELOPMENT OF CHAM-KHMER CHARACTERS (Figs 18.1–3)

According to the French scholars Aymonier and Cabaton, there were originally two varieties of the Cham and Khmer scripts: (1) the lapidary script, preserved in various inscriptions, and (2) the current hand, of which some traces can be seen in a few inscriptions, and which was the ancestor of nearly all the following scripts used nowadays (Fig. 18.3):

(*a*) In Vietnam and Cambodia: (i) Akhar Srah or Thrah or 'straight letters,' the current hand of the Chams; it corresponds to (ii) Aksar Chrieng used by the Khmers. The Akhar Srah can be subdivided into two varieties, the round hand employed in Vietnam, and the angular hand used in Cambodia (Figs. 18.3*a–b*).

(*b*) In Cambodia two other scripts are used: (iii) Akhar Tapuk, the 'script of the books,' employed by the Chams; it corresponds to (iv) Aksar Mul used by the Khmers. The script is slightly more artificial than the current hand. (v) Akhar Garmin, 'spiders' feet,' is another Cham writing, used in Cambodia.

(*c*) In the Cham manuscripts of Vietnam, and on the amulets and seals of the same population, three other varieties can be distinguished:

(vi) Akhar Rik, 'sacred, hieratic writing,' This script seems to be the only one descended from the early lapidary script. The letters have peculiar shapes; they are also bigger and more complicated than those of the other scripts (Fig. 18.3*c*).

(vii) Akhar Atuo'l, the 'suspended character' or seal-writing: it resembles modern monograms (Fig. 18.3*d*).

(viii) Akhar Yok, the 'mystic script'; its main peculiarity is that its symbols are regarded (like the European alphabets and unlike the other Indo-Chinese scripts) as pure consonants, that is, not containing the inherent *a*, while the vowels are added in their full form (Fig. 18.3*e*).

CHAKMA CHARACTER (Figs. 18.4–5, 6*a*)

It may be worth mentioning that the Khmer character has been adopted for Chakma, a south-eastern dialect of Bengali (*see* p. 287), spoken by about 20,000 people in the Chittagong Hill Tracts, Bengal. According to Sir George A. Grierson, the Chakma dialect 'has undergone so much transformation that it is almost worthy of the dignity of being classed as separate language.'

The Chakma character is particularly cursive. Another peculiarity of this script is that the vowel inherent in each consonant is not a short *a*, as in other Indian scripts, but a long *a*.

BURMA

The republic of Burma, which has an area of over 260,000 square miles, and a population (1952) of 19 millions, is a melting pot of numerous peoples belonging to different races and linguistic groups. Its languages and dialects, which are said to number about a hundred, are classified under the three important families, the Tibeto-Chinese, including Burmese, the Austro-Asiatic, including the Mon-Khmer languages, and the Malayo-Polynesian.

Burma is one of the richest countries of Indo-China in epigraphic material. The three principal centres are Pagan, Pegu and Prome. The earliest documents have been found in Prome; two of them are written in Pali and contain passages from the Buddhist canon; the others are very short and are written in Pyu (*see* below).

About 40 years ago Charles Duroiselle discovered at Pagan many Buddhist terra-cotta votive tablets inscribed in Sanskrit, Pali, Pyu, Mon and Burmese. Some of the Sanskrit tablets are in Nagari character of the eleventh century A.D.

THE MONS (Fig. 17.2, sect. 5)

Burmese true history begins about A.D. 1000. When the ancestors of the modern Burmans came to the Irrawaddy basin, they found the people whom they call Talaings well established in southern Burma, that is in the delta lands and along the coasts. The Talaings are generally known by their indigenous term Mon.

The Mons were the earliest civilized race of Burma. Their language belongs to the Mon-Khmer group (*see* above). In early times, their power extended from Prome in the north to Ligor and Johore in the south.

The Khmers were pushed further east and, as has been said, became the progenitors of the Cambodians, while the Mons remained behind. In A.D. 573, the latter founded Hanthawady or Pegu, and many centuries later they came to be known to the early merchant adventurers as Peguans. Suddhammapura or Thaton (in the Karen states, Burma), then a seaport, had been for many centuries their chief town. While the Burmans, then in the north, were at war with the Shans (*see* below) and the Chinese, the Mons were busy with trade and amassing riches; tales of the magnificence of Pegu attracted more and more merchant adventurers. Nowadays, the Mons are racially indistinguishable from the Burmans, but their language is still spoken by some 225,000 people, principally in Amherst and Thaton (Karen state); they use also the Burmese characters.

The Mons claim to have been visited by Buddhist missionaries as far back as the time of Aśoka (middle of the third century B.C.; *see* pp. 266 f.). In the first millennium A.D., Thaton was an important seat of Buddhist culture; there were many learned men, well versed in the Tripitaka and also in Vedic literature. Unfortunately, there are no extant written documents of this first and most important period of Mon history. The earliest Mon inscriptions belong to the late eleventh and the early twelfth centuries A.D. During this second period of their history, which began in the middle of the eleventh century, the Mons were annexed by the Burmese kingdom of Pagan, but in the thirteenth century they freed themselves and founded the so-called 'mediæval' kingdom, which was centred in the fifteenth and sixteenth centuries at Pegu. In 1540 the Mons definitely lost their political independence to the Burmans. The majority of the Mon inscriptions belong to the Mon 'mediæval' kingdom.

The decipherment of the ancient Mon inscriptions is mainly the work of Professor C. O. Blagden; the two stone pillars, known as the Myazedi inscriptions, found near the Myazedi pagoda (Myinkaba, Pagan), and belonging to the beginning of the twelfth century A.D., are the 'Rosetta stones' of the Mon and Pyu (*see* below) languages. The better preserved pillar, discovered in 1886-7, contains the same document in four languages, one on each face, Pali, Burmese, Mon and Pyu.

It is now generally accepted that the Mons borrowed their script from South India. Indeed, the shapes of the letters of the early Mon character are nearly identical with those of the early inscriptions of Champa and Java, and are probably connected with the Grantha alphabet of the Pallavas of Kanchi, in the east of South India. In adapting the South Indian character to their speech, the Mons discarded some of the Indian letters, as they had no use for them; some others were used only in words of Indian origin. At the same time, the Mons added two signs, both labial letters; one, a new invention, for a *b* deprived of sonority, somewhat between *b* and *p*, the other, a modification of the Indian combination of *mb* (Fig. 17.2, sect 5).

As the French scholar Duroiselle rightly points out, in the early stage the Mon letters, though already showing a tendency to become circles, or parts of circles, were still very distinctive and included some complex and beautiful forms, while in the 'mediæval' period the tendency was towards less dinstictiveness, certain of the letters and combinations of letters having become very similar to one another. The early Mon character was not only the ancestor of the modern Mon script, but also of the Burmese and some Shan characters.

THE PYU (Fig. 17.2, sect. 5)

Very little is known about the Pyu; even their true name is still unknown, the term Pyu having been chosen only for convenience. However, the Pyu spoke a Tibeto-Burmese language, which disappeared over 600 years ago. They were forerunners of the Tibeto-Burmese group of immigrants into the lower Irrawaddy valley many centuries before the invasion of the Burmans. It may be assumed that the Pyu received their civilization from South India about the middle of the first millennium A.D.

Until Professor C. O. Blagden's decipherment of the Myazedi inscriptions (mentioned above), the very existence of the Pyu speech was a puzzle. The Pyu epigraphical material is very scanty; the documents, apart from the Myazedi inscriptions, are very short and mostly either illegible or still practically unintelligible. Even nowadays only about a hundred Pyu words are known.

The important excavations of the French scholar Ch. Duroiselle on the site of Hmawza (Prome) in 1926–7, resulted in the discovery of a gilt silver Buddhist *stupa* of the sixth–seventh centuries A.D. with a mixed Pali-Pyu inscription and a manuscript of twenty gold leaves in Pyu characters of the sixth century containing extracts from the Pali canon. In the following year, 1927–8, a gold-plate inscription in similar characters was found, as also a bronze Buddha image with Sanskrit inscriptions in Gupta character, and a Buddha stone statue with a bilingual Sanskrit-Pyu inscription in late Gupta character of the seventh–eighth centuries A.D.

Professor Blagden's decipherment was facilitated by the occurrence of proper names and foreign loanwords, and by the resemblance of the shapes of many symbols to those of South Indian letters. On the other hand, Blagden himself points out (1) that some of the Pyu letters resemble one another so closely that it is difficult to distinguish between them, and (2) that the conjunct letters offer special difficulties of identification. The Pyu character is not connected with the Mon script or its offshoots; it seems to have derived from another South Indian variety, namely from the Kadamba script of Vanavasi in northern Kanara, to the west of South India. On the other hand, the aforementioned discovery in Prome of early inscriptions in Gupta character would seem to point to still other influences.

THE BURMANS (Figs. 17.2, sect. 5; 27–28; Figs. 18.6*b*, 7*a*, 9*a*)

Burmese, now spoken by nearly ten million people, is a monosyllabic tongue, belonging to the Tibeto-Burmese sub-family of the Tibeto-Chinese family of languages. There are two, three or four tones (*see*, however, p. 64) in Burmese, and these affect all the vowels.

Anawrat'a or Anuruddha, who became king of Pagan about A.D. 1010, made Burma a kingdom and confirmed it in Buddhism. He invaded the Delta and reduced a number of states, amongst them the Mons of Thaton and the Pyu of Prome, to vassalage.

The Burmans, having subdued the Mons, assimilated their culture and adopted their script. The script of the Buddhist monks of Thaton became therefore the main vehicle of the Mon-Burmese culture, based originally on an overflow from South India. In the eleventh and twelfth centuries A.D., the importation of Pali Buddhism from Ceylon was a reinforcement of Buddhist religion and culture.

It may be assumed that the Burmans adapted to their speech not only the Mon script, but also the script used for the Sinhalese Pali Buddhist canon. Indeed, the Burmese character contains only the Pali letters. There were thus two varieties of the ancient Burmese script: (1) The lapidary form, Kyok-cha or Kiusa, the 'script (on) stone,' made up of straight strokes meeting at right angles; this was employed for monumental inscriptions. (2) The more important 'square' Pali script, a capricious, highly calligraphic character, which was generally employed for writing the religious Buddhist books. This script is not easily readable. The letters were painted with a broad brush (generally in dark brown lacquer, and sometimes on a plate of gilded metal), and were correspondingly very thick. All the vertical lines of the letters were enormously exaggerated in width, whilst the horizontal strokes were reduced to appendages and the central spaces were nearly eliminated. The corners of the letters had already a tendency to be rounded.

A variety of the lapidary script, through a series of gradual and slow changes, developed into the Cha-lonh or 'round script', which is the Burmese current hand and print-character. The tendency to round off the more or less angular and square letters into soft curves became more and more marked. The peculiar form of the present letters, which are made up almost wholly of circles or parts of circles in various combinations, is due mainly to the writing material used in Burma, the palm leaves on which the symbols were traced with a stylus. Apart from the round shapes of the single symbols, the main difference between the early Burmese script and the modern character lies in the subscript letters h and m.

The modern Burmese alphabet consists of forty-two letters, of which thirty-two are consonants and ten vowels. As in the Indian scripts, every consonant when not combined with any other letter has the sound of the vowel a inherent in it. The vowels are written in their full form when they form distinct words or are part of a compound word. When combined with consonants, they are represented by the abbreviated form. The consonants are: four gutturals (ka, kha, ga, nga), five palatals (ca, cha, ja, jha, nya), five cerebrals (ta, tha, da, dha, na), used only in words of Pali origin, five dentals (ta, tha, da, dha, na), five labials (pa, pha, ba, ma), four liquids (ya, ra, and two forms of la), the semi-vowel wa, the sibilant sa, and the aspirate ha. The vowels are the long and short forms of a, i, u, e, and aw. See also Figs. 17.27–28.

The oldest extant Burmese MS. is attributed to the fifth century A.D. It consists of twenty gold leaves encased in a gold cover, and contains a Buddhist text in Pali. It was discovered in 1922. Burmese religious literature is strongly influenced by the Buddhist literature of India. But, besides, there are also some chronicles and an epic Yama Yekkan which corresponds to the Indian Ramayana. The most independent branch is the popular literature, consisting of fairy tales, love stories, witticisms and riddles.

BIBLIOGRAPHY

The first Corpus of Burmese inscriptions was published by Taw Sein Ko, in six volumes, 1892–1913. Still more important is the collection published in Epigraphia Birmanica, Rangoon, 1919 onwards; especially the articles by Professor Blagden.
DUROISELLE, CH. A List of Inscriptions found in Burma, Rangoon, 1921.

PE MAUNG TIN, and LUCE, G. *Inscriptions of Burma* (University of Burma. Oriental Series Publications), Oxford, 1933, and London, 1939.

Journal of the Burma Research Society, Rangoon, 1911 onwards.

QUIGLY, E. P. *Libraries, Manuscripts and Books of Burma*, 1956.

The Karens

The Karens are the third most numerous race in Burma, but they are not indigenous and it is not known whence and when they immigrated. It is, however, generally believed that they came from the east, and not from the west, like the other peoples of Burma. They number over one and-a-half million, and are sub-divided into three main groups, speaking dialects of one and the same language, which belongs to the Sino-Thai sub-family. All the dialects are tonic (*see* p. 64) and are believed to have the same five tones.

The Karen character is a modern adaptation of the Burmese script to the Karen tongue. It was invented by the missionary Rev. T. Wade in 1832. A somewhat similar, although unsuccessful, attempt had been made some decades earlier by Catholic missionaries. Further, according to T. De Lacouperie, it is not unlikely that in former times the Karens had an original character based on the Cham script, but there are no extant written documents of earlier times.

Taungthu and Yao

The Burmese characters are also employed for Taungthu, which is spoken by nearly 200,000 people in the south-western part of the Shan States, and south into the Thaton district of Burma.

Also the Yao use a variety of the Burmese character. For the Yao tribe *see* p. 104.

THAILAND (FORMERLY SIAM)

THE SHANS

(Figs. 17.2, sect. 5; 27–28; Figs. 18.6*e*, 7*b*, 9*b*)

The Shans are a numerous and widely spread race. They inhabit a strip of territory extending from China in the north to Burma in the south, from Assam and Khamti in the west to Thailand (Siam) in the east. Shan is a Burmese term, the indigenous name being Thai. The names Siam and Assam seem to be merely corruptions of Shan. The Shan dialects belong to the Thai group of the Thai-Siamese sub-family of the Tibeto-Chinese family of languages.

The early history of the Shans is largely shrouded in mystery. They seem to have first appeared in the last centuries B.C., when they were settled in central and southern China. They form even nowadays a great percentage of the total population of four of the southern provinces of China, Yün-nan, Kwei-chow, Kwang-si and Kwang-tung, and there are traces as far as Canton, and perhaps even across the sea to the island of Hainan. The ancient indigenous name seems to have been Ai-Lao or Lao, that is 'man,' 'person.' The name Lao is still applied to the Shans of upper Thailand and, needless to say, to 'Laos.' Formerly split up under a number of independent kinglets, the Lao were united about A.D. 650 under a ruler named Hsi Nu Lo in a kingdom called by the Chinese Nan Chao or 'the country of the southern lord.' About 764, the capital was shifted to Tali-fu. During the ninth century, the Tali-fu kingdom came very near to overthrowing the Chinese dynasty, but in 1234 it was destroyed by the Mongols.

In the meantime, for many centuries, under the pressure of the Chinese, and later of the Mongol wars of conquest in China, the Thai gradually moved south-eastwards down the valley of Mekong, and south and south-westwards into the 'Shan States' and down the Salween valley. In the early eleventh century they were the most powerful race in central Indo-China. In the west the Ahoms, a Shan tribe—Ahom seems to be a variant pronunciation of Assam, this term being, apparently, as already mentioned, a corruption of 'Shan'—invaded Assam in 1228, and became its master in 1540. Another Shan tribe occupied the country to which they gave the name Khamti. The Shans also overran northern Burma and furnished kings for Burma for about a couple of centuries. The thirteenth century witnessed a general advance of the Thai or Shan race, facilitated by the fall of Pagan dynasty which followed the Chinese invasion.

After the conquest of northern Burma, the Shans passed onwards into the basin of the Menam where they very soon came into conflict with the Khmers. The most important events occurred about 1275 when the Shans founded the kingdom of Sukhotai, the ancestor of modern Thailand, and about 1350, when they established themselves in the great delta of the Menam; at this time they founded Ayudhya, the capital of Thailand proper, and formed thus a wedge of Thai-speaking people between the Mon-Khmers of Tenasserim and Cambodia. The Khmer kings, pushed to the east, had to abandon their capital Angkor, after 1430 (see p. 317). This event marks the disappearance of pure Hinduism. The whole country now professes the Theravada (a composite Buddhist religion), which the Thai influence introduced at the end of the thirteenth century and to which the triumph of Thailand assured an uncontested hegemony.

Many external, geographical, ethnical and linguistic influences from varying sources were brought to bear upon the different Shan tribes, and sharp divisions began to be formed particularly between the more civilized southern Shans, or Siamese, and the more primitive, northern Shans, so that today the various Thai tribes present widely divergent characteristics. The different communities are also geographically separated by hill and dale. The river Salween, with its mountainous bank, has formed a serious barrier even to transmission of writing. This splitting up accounts, at least in part, for the difference in the written character. Even of greater importance was the influence of the various peoples with whom the Shans came in contact in their new homelands; the Khmers played a great part in moulding the Shans who settled in what is now Thailand proper, whilst the chief influence in the north of Thailand was exercised by the Mons and the Burmans. The 'Shan States'—there are over fifty of them—include a great number of peoples who are absolutely distinct from the Shans. The mixture of races is bewildering, the area being regarded as a museum of hybrid languages. Notwithstanding, the difference between the various forms of speech in the Shan group is one of dialect, not of language.

The early spread of Buddhism and the reduction of the various dialects to written form had unquestionably a certain unifying and conserving influence. Indeed, an educated Shan born anywhere within the region (measuring 600 miles each way, from Assam to N. Vietnam and from the sources of the Irrawaddy to Thailand), will find himself able to carry on a conversation in Shan with any member of the different Shan tribes.

The Thai have many different scripts; of these Siamese is nowadays the chief, but it is not the earliest. The Lao writing is the earliest, and the Lao people are linguistically and racially the most pure Shan tribe.

LAO CHARACTER

The Lao speakers in the state of Laos number (1954) one and a half million; but the language is nowadays also widely spoken in northern Thailand and in the former Amherst district of Burma.

According to local tradition, it was in the 1,000th year of the Buddha, corresponding roughly to the middle of the first millennium A.D., that King Ruang, who was a Lao, introduced the Thai alphabet. The precise date is obviously legendary and it is certainly too early. According to other Lao traditions, Buddhism was introduced from Burma in the Burmese Pali form; these traditions would give us a date which is too late.

The modern Lao script and those of some other northern Thai tribes show that they have derived from the Mon character. It is known that the Lao came into contact with the Mons before they met the Burmans and before the Khmers subdued the Mons. Consequently, the Lao must have adapted the Mon character to their language before the early tenth century A.D., that is before the Khmer conquest of the valley of Menam. Indeed, a Lao palm-leaf manuscript of the thirteenth century A.D. shows that the script was then already fully developed and had been in use for a few centuries.

The early Lao writing is known as Fak Kham, the 'tamarind-pod' character.

The present Lao script is essentially the same as that of the thirteenth century, although it has been influenced by the Burmese character and its Shan offshoots, in use among the kinsmen of the Lao and their neighbours of similar speech in the former British Shan States.

The Lao character has sixty-two letters: twenty-seven simple consonants, six 'combined' consonants, and twenty-nine vowels and diphthongs; in addition, there are two accents which are necessary because Lao has 'tones' like the Chinese. Of the twenty-seven simple consonants, eight are classified as 'middle,' thirteen as 'low' and six as 'high'; the 'high' consonants are pronounced with a tone climbing from low to high, similar to the tone used by us in a question. The shape of eight consonants is slightly modified when they close a syllable or a word.

The twenty-nine vowels and diphthongs consist of the following: short *a, i, u* (two letters), *e* and open *e, o* and open *o, ö, wa* (two letters), *ya, ai, ei, ao* and *am*; long *a, i, u* (two letters), *e* and open *e, o* and open *o, ö, wa* (three letters) and *ya*.

Some varieties can be distinguished; they are employed for the following dialects:

Thai Lao or Eastern Laotian, spoken in eastern Thailand and Laos; Thai Lu, spoken by about 500,000 people in western Indo-China, eastern Burma and southern Yün-nan; the Thai Ya (in south-western China) and the Thai Yüan or Western Laotians (in the region around Chieng-mai, northern Thailand), employ the Yüan-Laotian variety.

The Lao characters have also been adopted for Na-khi, spoken in the mountain valleys of the Mekong and Yang-tze rivers, southern China. For the Na-khi tribe *see* pp. 102 f.

BIBLIOGRAPHY

Alphabet et orthographe Lao, Lao Nhay, Ventiane, 1943–4.
REINHORN, M. *Dictionnaire Laotien-Français*, 4 vols., Paris, 1956.

LÜ AND HKÜN CHARACTERS (Fig. 18.6*c*)

The trans-Salween Shan tribes of the Shan State of Kentung, just north of the frontier of Thailand, vaunt themselves distinct from all the other Thai peoples, but the dialects they speak, that is Lü and Hkün, do not noticeably differ from other Shan forms of speech. They are intermediate between Siamese and Shan.

They have scripts of their own (Fig. 18.6*c*), which—although presenting nowadays an exasperating form—are closely connected with the Lao character and have apparently descended from it.

AHOM CHARACTER (Fig. 17.2, sect. 5; Fig. 18.6*d*)

Ahom, a Shan dialect, has been dead for some centuries; it lingered on, however, as a kind of sacred language, and is still believed to be known by about a hundred people in the Sibsagar district of Assam. The population of Assam, which was conquered by the Burmese in the eighteenth century and became British in 1824, has become completely Hinduized.

The Ahom character is apparently the nearest to the ancient prototype. It consists of forty-one letters, of which eighteen are vowels and twenty-three are consonants. The vowel inherent in every consonant is the long *a*. The Ahom character does not contain the letters *y* and *w*.

THAILAND

The kingdom of Thailand, formerly known as Siam, is the only independent Thai state in existence. Thai is mainly spoken in southern and central, and increasingly in northern Thailand, as also in Vietnam, Laos, Cambodia, the former Amherst and Mergui districts of Burma, and especially in south-eastern China. Thai possesses, like some Chinese dialects, five or six tones (*see* p. 64); it has no prefixes whatever.

The great majority of the inhabitants of Thailand are the Thai, doubtless the most civilized and advanced Shan people.

The Thai call their country Thaï or Muang-Thaï ['the Kingdom of the Free'] or 'Prades Thai.' Thailand has an area of slightly under 198,000 square miles and a population (census of 1956) of 23 millions, *i.e.*, only 115 per square mile. Bangkok, the capital, has about one and a quarter million inhabitants.

The Thai have a high civilization. They are mainly Buddhists, and so *Niti* (the literature of tradition, translations of Indian Buddhistic lore) forms a main part of the literature. There is an important legal literature, especially the five old Codes of Thai law. But the greatest accomplishment of Thai literature are love-lyrics. In the twentieth century, under the auspices of well-educated kings, literature has risen to great heights.

Thai art is, as is to be expected, mainly Buddhist, and excels in architecture and carved sculpture, in music, theatre and dance; magnificent 'wats' (pagodas) are to be found all over the country, but especially in Bangkok and the old capital Ayudhya (some thirty miles to the north, on the Menam river). The Thai, together with the akin Shan tribes, form about half of the population; the Lao form another third; there are also numerous Chinese. About 30,000 Karens live in the west, as far south as the 13°; in the southernmost district of Patani there are some Malayans who are Muslim.

Origin of Thai Script

The origin of the Thai script is still not quite clear. The earliest known inscription, discovered at Sukhotai or Sukhodaya, and now in the National Library of Bangkok, is a curious and unique document. It is a stumpy stone obelisk containing exactly 1,500 words; it bears the date of 1214 Śaka era, corresponding to A.D. 1292–3 (the Śaka era, beginning A.D. 78, was the dominant era of ancient South India) and it tells that its author, King Ram Khamheng, was *writing* the Thai language for the first time. If Ram Khamheng did actually invent the Thai script, he probably based it on the Khmer character. C. B. Bradley has recently invalidated both the generally accepted theory which considered the Thai character as being of Sinhalese Pali origin, and the rival theory which derived it from the Burmese script, on the grounds that Thai writing contains all the letters of the Grantha character which are not found in Pali or Burmese, and that the single letters of the Sukhotai inscription have no internal resemblance to the signs of the Sinhalese Pali texts or of the Burmese script, although the Thai letters, being four-square, give externally an impression similar to that of the Pali script. Indeed, there is no doubt that the Buddhist monks had greatly influenced the spread of the knowledge of writing amongst the Thai and that the Buddhist Thai monks knew and also used the Pali language and script.

The script of the Sukhotai inscription 'is singularly bold, erect, four-square, with gently rounded corners, beautifully aligned and singularly clear' (C. B. Bradley). In it, all the letters, consonants and vowels alike, are written on the same line, but shortly afterwards a change was introduced, and many of the vowels were written either above or below the consonants.

Development

There are no written documents extant of the two centuries following the Sukhotai period, but there is no doubt that the modern Thai writing is a descendant of the Sukhotai script. On the whole, it may be said that the later development of the script does not present great changes; the changes of the single signs were due mainly to the writing materials used in Thailand. Figure 18.6e reproduces a specimen of the important Patimokkha manuscript (Fig. 17.2, sect. 5 shows the character used in that manuscript).

Until quite recent times, the monasteries were the only important seats of learning and the only Thai institution which preserved written documents. Sacred works were written on corypha (*Corypha gebanga*) palm leaves, their edges being gilded or painted with vermilion, and the leaves threaded on strings and folded like a fan. More important copies of the religious books were engraved on ivory tablets. Generally speaking, the material used was an indication of the social standing of the person for whom the written document was intended: the king's letters were engraved on sheets of gold when they were sent to princes, or on paper, either black or white, when written to lesser people. However, the peculiar shapes of the modern Thai letters are due mainly to the employment of the corypha palm leaves as the chief material of writing.

Modern Thai Alphabet

The modern Thai alphabet (Fig. 17.2, sect. 5) consists of forty-four consonants, in each of which the vowel *a* is inherent, and of thirty vowels, each consisting not of an individual letter, but of a mark written above, below, before or after the consonant with which it is pronounced. The letters *a* and *u* are not regarded as vowels but as consonants, and they are used as such in support of the vowel signs. The main reason for the great number of the vowel marks lies not in the vowels themselves, but in the tones, five or six in number (*see* p. 64).

The difficulties in reading Thai are increased by the existence of a host of accents and by the absence of punctuation. The words are not separated from each other and the stream of letters flows on uninterruptedly until the idea changes. Juxtaposition is the only means of indicating syntactical relations between words. An important result of the use of the printing press, since the early nineteenth century, was the introduction into printing of spacing between the words. The typewriter, introduced in 1891, has also had an influence on the development of the shapes of the single letters.

BIBLIOGRAPHY

For the inscriptions discovered in Thailand *see* G. Coedès, *Recueil des Insciptions du Siam*. Part I (dealing with the inscriptions in Pali and Thai of the Sukhodaya kingdom of the fifteenth-sixteenth centuries A.D.), Bangkok, 1924, and Part II (Pali and Mon inscriptions of the Dvaravati kingdom, seventh-eighth centuries A.D.; Sanskrit and Khmer inscriptions of the Śrī Vijaya kingdom, eighth-twelfth centuries; and Pali and Mon inscriptions of the kingdom of Haripunjaya, twelfth-thirteenth centuries A.D.), Bangkok, 1929.

THAI CHARACTER ADAPTED TO MIAO

The Thai character has been adopted for some non-Thai languages, such as Miao spoken by a small tribe on the borders of Chiengmai and Nan, northern Thailand: it was adapted only about 35 years ago by C. K. Trung of the American Bible Society. For the Miao tribes *see* p. 104

Shan proper, that is what was known as 'British Shan' or '*cis*-Salveen Shan,' is spoken all over the Shan States, both the former British and the Chinese. It has a northern, a southern, and a Chinese Shan dialect. All the three dialects contain as many as ten tones (*see* p. 64).

It is possible that the Shans once used a script borrowed from the Khmers, of which there are some traces in rock-inscriptions of the thirteenth century.

Nowadays, the Shans use at least two varieties of writing, one for 'the British Shan' dialects, the other one for the 'Chinese Shan' dialect. Both varieties, however, are descended from the Burmese character. The Shan scripts do not contain the consonants *g*, *gh*, *j*, *jh*, *d*, *dh*, *b* and *bh*, and the long vowel *e*. The *a* is considered to be a consonant and is used only for carrying vowels when initial. The vowel inherent in every consonant, when this is not connected with another letter, is usually the short *a*. A consonant standing alone is distinguished by a special mark. There is generally a particular letter for the long *i*, but sometimes this vowel is represented by the short *i* which represents also the long and short *e*'s.

For the Taungthu tribe and the Yaos *see* p. 323.

KHAMTI CHARACTER (Figs. 18.10*a–c*)

Khamti or Kamti is spoken nowadays in eastern Assam and in the Chinese district Khamti Long; however, the place of origin of the Khamti-speaking population seems to have been upper Burma. Unlike their Ahom neighbours, the Khamti have retained their Shan speech. This contains only three or four tones (*see* p. 64). The Khamti are the most cultured northern Thai tribe.

The Khamti script is a variety of the Shan character. It contains thirty-three signs (sixteen vowels and seventeen consonants); the character is, thus, not so complete as was the old Ahom script, although it does contain the letters *y* and *w*. All the consonants missing in the Shan characters are also wanting in the Khamti script. As to the vowels, not only the long *e* is wanting, as in Shan, but also the long *a*.

There are two main varieties of Khamti script, the current hand, its principal peculiarity being the black dot inside the letters (Fig. 18.00), and the printed script, without that black dot (Fig. 18.00). There are also some local varieties, such as those for the dialect of Tairong (Fig. 18.00).

AITONIA CHARACTER (Fig. 18.10*a*)

Another variety of the Shan scripts is used for Aiton or Aitonia or 'Shan Doan,' 'Doan' meaning in Assamese 'foreign tongue'; it is a dialect spoken in Sibsagar, Assam.

THAI MAO OR THAI KHE'

Well up to the north of the 'British Shan' States there are the Thai Mao or Thai Khe', who use a written character which is quite different from those of the other Shan tribes. Its origin and its affinities are still uncertain.

CHAN LAO OF TONGKING

These tribes had a writing of their own, composed of about thirty-six letters, quite different from other Lao and Shan scripts. According to some scholars, it was apparently derived from the Thai, as shown, for instance, by the characteristic forms of *m* and *n*, the numerous vocalic diacritical marks and the large number of letters.

'CHINESE SHANS'

The Pai-i or 'Chinese Shans,' called also Yünnanese Shans, numbering about 3 million people, in the south-west of China, have two characters according to their geographical location. The tribes living in the vicinity of Burma have adapted the

Burmese script to their language. The others, that is those living more to the north, as far as they can write, use the Chinese character, but they had previously an altogether different script, the Yünnanese Shan script, of which, according to Professor De Lacouperie, some specimens are still extant.

The Shui-kia ('Water People') or Pu-shui, which is the indigenous term, a Shan tribe of south-west Kwei-chow, employed a character which according to De Lacouperie consisted of adaptations and contracted forms of ancient Chinese symbols mixed with non-Chinese pictorial signs.

INDONESIA

Throughout all the Malay Archipelago, the natives speak languages of a single general stock known as Malayo-Polynesian, one of the most widespread linguistic families in the world. Its hundreds of branches extend all the way from eastern Madagascar, off the coast of south-eastern Africa, through the East Indies and the Philippines to Formosa in the north and to New Zealand in the south, up through the Malay Peninsula to the borders of Burma and Thailand, and across the Pacific to Hawaii and Easter Island. (In that vast oceanic area, only Australia, New Guinea and a few interior districts of the Melanesian islands have languages not belonging to the Malayo-Polynesian family.) All these languages are closely related. Moreover, nowadays the entire language problem in the Indies is simplified by the fact that there is a kind of 'basic' Malay, known as 'bazaar' or 'pidgin' Malay, a minimum language, strongly coloured by the influence of foreign languages (Indian, Chinese, Arabic, Persian, Portuguese, English and Dutch). This *lingua franca* (*bahasa Indonésia*, 'Indonesian Language') is spoken in all except the interior districts of the larger islands.

Over 90 per cent of the Indonesian natives are illiterate. Nowadays, educated natives use for their languages mostly either the Arabic or the Roman alphabets. Apart from these two alphabets, some of the native peoples of the archipelago, among them several quite primitive tribes, still employ ancient scripts, all derived, indirectly, from Indian writing, a survival of the period when Indian civilization was spread over the islands. The most advanced people use paper, some of it made locally from the inner bark of certain trees and glazed with rice gruel, but the bulk of native writing was and still is done by scratching signs on the shiny surface of bamboo strips or palm leaves, which are then strung together into books.

The ancient scripts are still used in parts of Sumatra and Celebes, in Bali and a few others of the Nusu Tenggara (or Lesser Sunda) islands, and even to some extent in interior Java. Two of the most primitive Philippine tribes, the pagan tribes of Mindoro and Palawan, have also their ancient indigenous scripts. There is, however, only one language and its script which have a true history; that is Javanese, the oldest phase of which is known as Old Javanese or Kawi or Kavi. Of the earlier phases of Batak (Sumatra) and Bugis (Celebes), there are also documentary records available

z

(Fig. 18.16, 7–8), but these are far less important than those of the Old Javanese language (Figs. 18.11*a*; 16, 1–6).

It is now accepted by the most authoritative scholars that all these ancient scripts descended from Indian characters. E. E. W. G. Schräder, who suggests that the Malayo-Polynesian culture was based on the Semitic civilization and not on the Indian, is practically alone.

Borneo

The enormous bulk of Borneo, the third greatest island in the world, being 4,000 miles long and 1,000 miles wide, with a surface of 290,000 square miles and only two and three-quarter million inhabitants, presents an open problem as regards the existence of an ancient indigenous script. There can be no doubt that writing was once known to the indigenous inhabitants of some parts of Borneo; as a matter of fact, the inscriptions discovered in that island are the earliest written documents hitherto found in the Malay Archipelago. However, these inscriptions are in pure Sanskrit and are, like a few other written documents found in Borneo, of Indian origin and not produced by the native Dayaks. Another inscription, on the bottom of a vase, which was bought in northern Borneo, is considered to be written in the Mangyan character of Mindoro. There is, consequently, no proof of any connection between the people who made use of writing in ancient Borneo and the present Dayaks.

Malaya

There is likewise no evidence that there existed any indigenous script in the Malay Peninsula, although there, too, early Sanskrit inscriptions have been discovered, and Malaya played an important part in the ancient trade between India and the Far East.

ANCIENT JAVA

It is a remarkable fact that whereas the splendid architectural monuments of ancient Java are found in the central part of the island, the earliest written documents have been discovered in western Java. They consist of four rock-inscriptions (a fifth, found at Mocara Jianten, is as yet undeciphered), all found in the province of the present city of Batavia. These inscriptions (Fig. 17.24*c*) are undated, but on palæographical grounds they are attributed to the fourth or fifth centuries A.D. They bear ample testimony to the high degree of civilization of western Java at that period. The inscriptions eulogize a ruler of the name of Purnavarman; they are all composed in Sanskrit verse and prove that the ancient western-Javanese civilization was of Indian origin.

Apparently towards the end of the sixth century A.D., western Java fell into decay and central Java rose into prominence. In the eighth century A.D. two centres of power were emerging in the Malay Archipelago, one in southern Sumatra and the other in central Java. Intermittent wars punctuated the early period of Indonesian national history. The constant struggle for the control of the archipelago was marked by a long series of wars between the Sumatran and Javanese dynasties, and was finally decided in favour of the Javanese. About the middle of the eighth century, central Java passed into the hands of the Śri Vijaya rulers of Sumatra, but about 863 the Sumatran period of Javanese history came to an end, and the hegemony of Java passed again to central Java.

A thousand years ago a great empire flourished in the East Indies with its centre in Java. The period from about A.D. 850–900 to 1400 marked the height of native civilization, when all the islands and part of the mainland of Asia were gradually brought together in a centralized empire known as Modjopahit or Majapahit. From the capital in eastern Java, it exercised during the fourteenth and most of the fifteenth century supreme dominion over most of the archipelago as far north as Luzon in the Philippines and as far east as the coastland of New Guinea. It was during this period that Hindu-Javanese civilization spread most widely over the entire area, and one of the relics of this influence, in the form of offshoots of ancient Indian scripts, is found in the north, in the scripts of some native Philippine tribes.

At the very height of its power, the Majapahit empire was suddenly threatened by a new force which entered the Indies from the west. Islām, brought from India—that is, from the same country which was the source of the earliest civilization of the Malay Archipelago—to Malaya and Sumatra in the twelfth and thirteenth centuries, spread inevitably over the vassal states of Majapahit in Sumatra and western Java, which one after another broke away. During the fifteenth century, the last strongholds of the Majapahit empire in eastern Java were destroyed by the Moslem conquest.

Thus ended the greatest era of Indonesian early native history. The waves of Islām at length engulfed Java; there was no means of keeping it out. 'Java has now been a Mohammedan country for nearly five hundred years. It would doubtless have been so far earlier if it had not been so well off the track' (Ponder). Moreover, it would have been nowadays a desert, if 'the Mongol conquerors who ravaged half Asia had chanced upon it' (Ponder).

Two places have remained unaffected by the Moslem conquest; the small island of Bali, off the eastern shore of Java, which continued to be the only one where the Indian culture survived until the present day; and the isolated district of the Badoejs, who live in a remote corner of Banten or Bantam, in the extreme north-western end of Java: an utterly primitive tribe, of a few hundred souls, who have managed to resist all attempts at 'conversion' and 'civilization' (Ponder).

OLD JAVANESE OR KAVI CHARACTER (Fig. 17.2, sect. 5; Figs. 18.11a, 12–13)

Origin

The Dinaya inscription is the earliest extant written document in the Old Javanese or Kawi or Kavi character (Kavi is an abbreviation of *Basa Kavi*, 'the language of poetry'). It was found at Dinaya, situated to the east of central Java, and is dated in the Śaka year 682, that is A.D. 760. The inscription was first mentioned in 1904 by Dr. Brandes, who since 1887 had suggested that the Kavi script was introduced in the eighth century A.D. into Java, by immigrants from Gujarat. But Professor Krom stated in his Hindu-Javanese history (published in 1926) that the supposed similarity between the Kavi script and the Girnar character disappears on closer investigation. According to Krom, the Kavi character was not a new borrowing, but a local and later development of the South Indian script in use in Java since the fifth century A.D. It is now generally accepted that the early colonists who brought the Indo-Aryan civilization (including the script) to Java, must have come from southern India, and most probably from the Coromandel coast. A Javanese tradition, quoted in the *Aji Saka*, attributes the introduction of writing into Java to a Brahman called Tritresta, who is a half-mythical person.

Until recently, there has been no agreement among scholars regarding the term to be applied to the peculiar script of the early Sanskrit inscriptions of Indonesia. Professor Kern adopted the term 'Vengi character,' but Professor Vogel proved that it is advisable to discard it, and he substituted the name 'Pallava character.' Dr. Burnell used the term 'Eastern Chera.' Neither of these terms is appropriate.

As has been already mentioned (*see* p. 300), Dr. Bühler applied the term 'Grantha' to the character used by the Pallava rulers of Kanchi in southern India in writing Sanskrit. The script employed in the aforementioned Purnavarman inscriptions of Java is almost identical with, but slightly later than, that of the Sanskrit inscriptions found at Kutai in eastern Borneo (*see* above), and similar to the script employed in early Champa (*see* p. 316).

It is now accepted by the most authoritative scholars that this early Javanese script originated from the early Grantha, although the extant written documents of the lithic early Grantha found in southern India, the place of its origin, belong to a later period than the early inscriptions found in Borneo, Java and Champa. It is thus in the distant lands of Indonesia and of the coasts of Further India that we find the prototypes of the lithic Grantha character.

Kavi Inscriptions (Figs. 17.2, sect. 5; Figs. 18.12–13)

The Dinaya inscription, although written in Kavi script, is still couched in Sanskrit, but later inscriptions are mostly in Kavi character and the Kavi or Old Javanese language. The oldest Kavi record, which is also the oldest Buddhist inscription of Java, is written, however, in the Deva-nagari script of northern India of the eighth–eleventh centuries; it is the Kalasan inscription (it was found in the Kalasan temple in Central Java) of the Sailendra dynasty of Śri Vijaya, belonging apparently to *c.* A.D. 778. A slightly later inscription, found at Pareng in Central Java, and dated 785 Śaka era (A.D. 863), is partly in Sanskrit verse and partly in Kavi prose, but written in Kavi character. Most important is the Kavi inscription known as the 'Minto stone,' having been sent as a present by Sir Stamford Raffles, the founder of Singapore, who was then the British governor of Java, to the Lord Minto in Scotland; this inscription was found in Java-Pasuruhan. It is dated 876 Śaka era (that is, A.D. 954), and contains an inscription of King Vava, the last ruler of Central Java. The opening couplet of the monument is in Sanskrit.

After the shifting of the political centre from central to eastern Java, which took place in the tenth century A.D., the Kavi or Old Javanese literature began to flourish. An inscription of King Er-langga (or Airlangga), one of the most enlightened rulers of ancient Java, under whose reign there was vigorous activity in the domain of arts and literature, has been found at Penang-Gungen (Surabaya); it is dated 963 Śaka era (A.D. 1041), and is inscribed on both sides in Kavi character; it is, however, wholly bilingual, being couched on one side in the Kavi language, and on the other side in pure Sanskrit.

The epigraphic records of early Java continue in almost unbroken series down to the end of the Indo-Javanese period. The last Kavi inscription on copper-plate is of 1473, the last stone inscription is dated 1408 Śaka era, corresponding to A.D. 1486. The Kavi inscriptions are much more numerous (about two hundred of the longer ones) than those in Sanskrit; the number of the latter, however, is much smaller than that of similar records discovered in Champa and Cambodia. There is also a great number of Javanese manuscripts, some of which are based on originals of the end of the tenth century A.D.

Modern Javanese Character (Fig. 17.2, sect. 5; Figs. 18.11*b–c*)

After the fall of Majapahit in about A.D. 1478 (the traditional date), Kavi was gradually replaced by 'Middle Javanese,' although it continued to be a literary language long after it had become archaic. Middle Javanese persisted up to *c.* 1628, when it made room for the New Javanese, but the former is still represented by the dialects of Banyumas, North Cheribon, North Krawang and North Bantam. Modern Javanese gradually breaks up into several sub-divisions, such as Krama Inggil, a form of speech used in addressing gods and the aristocracy, the Basa Kedatan, a kind of court-language, Ngoko, the language of the commoner, and Madya or Madhya, a sort of compromise dialect between Krama and Ngoko. All the dialects of Middle Javanese and New Javanese have been greatly influenced by the penetration of Islamic culture. With a few exceptions, no literary work of subsequent date can stand comparison with the works of the classical period of the Kavi or Indo-Javanese literature. Notwithstanding the sub-division into Old (or Kavi), the Middle and New Javanese, there was no break of historical continuity in the development of the language. The same may be said of the history of the Javanese writing. Nowadays, the Roman character is largely employed for the necessities of modern life.

The Javanese script, however, is still used for the Javanese, Sundanese, Madurese and Balinese languages, and also to some extent in Borneo. Javanese is spoken by about 35 million people, mainly in central and eastern Java, but is known all over the island. Sundanese is perhaps the most ancient vernacular language of the country; it is spoken nowadays by about nine million people, mainly in the mountainous districts of western Java, but seems to have been formerly, down to the period preceding the Moslem conquest, the general language of western Java. Madurese is spoken by about four and a half million people in Madura and north-eastern Java. Balinese is spoken by about 1,250,000 people on the island of Bali and on the south-eastern coast of Java.

The Javanese character (Fig. 18.11a) consists of twenty consonants or *aksara*, including *y* and *w*, and five vowels. As in nearly all the Indian scripts and their off-shoots, the vowel-sound is inherent in the consonant unless contradicted by a particular sign. Beside these basic letters, called *Aksara Jawa* or 'Javanese letters,' there are twenty auxiliary signs called *Aksara Pasang'an* or 'corresponding, similar' letters, which have the same phonetic value, but are used only in connection with and immediately after the main consonantal signs, for the purpose of suppressing their inherent vowel-sounds. Three of the Pasang'an signs are always placed after the *aksara*, the others below them. The inherent vowel is generally *a*, but in some dialects it is *o*.

The vowels, termed *Sandang'an* or 'clothing, dress' are written in their full form when they are used alone, or in their abbreviated form when combined with consonants. In the latter instance, each of them has a particular name; in some instances they are placed above the consonant; in other cases, below it; or else the consonant is placed in the middle of the vowel-sign. The sign termed *papet*, which is considered as a vowel and is pronounced as *le* in French, is placed above the consonant with which it is connected.

There are two other signs which are also considered as vowels, that is *ng'a lalet*, pronounced like *le*, and *pacherak*, pronounced like *re* in Sanskrit. I may mention, finally, that there are many other peculiar signs, of which the most important is the *pangkun*, placed after a consonant, which serves as a mark of elision destroying the final vowel-sound.

The order of the letters in the Javanese character is different from that of the Indian scripts, though it appears that the Indian arrangement was not unknown to the Javanese peoples.

Javanese is written from left to right. Every *aksara* is written separately, and no space is left between the words. One or two short diagonal lines, in poetry, or, commonly, a comma, are the only marks in ordinary writing which indicate stops. In Java, the natives usually write with Indian ink upon paper manufactured by themselves, and sometimes on European or Chinese paper. In Bali, some natives still use an iron style and cut the symbols on a prepared palm leaf, in the same manner as in some parts of India. This practice is still partially continued in some parts of the more eastern portion of Java, and was no doubt at a former period general throughout the island.

SUMATRA

Sumatra is the westernmost and third largest island of the East Indies; it is the largest, after Borneo, of Indonesia. Chinese records tell us that a Hinduized kingdom existed in south-eastern Sumatra in the fifth century A.D. This maritime kingdom has been identified, since 1918, by Professor Coedès, Dean of the French School of the Far East, with the ancient mighty empire of Śri Vijaya, the San-fot-si of the Chinese. In the late eighth and the early ninth centuries A.D., the Buddhist kingdom Śri Vijaya embraced not only the greater part of Sumatra, but also the Malay Peninsula, Central Java and numerous islands of the archipelago; there is even a tradition that Cambodia was also overrun. This kingdom was a stronghold of Mahayana Buddhism since the seventh century A.D. In the ninth and eleventh centuries, Śri Vijaya had monasteries in Bengal and South India. In the thirteenth century it seems to have declined, and in 1377 it was conquered by the Javanese. Śri Vijaya left memorials in some important inscriptions of the last quarter of the seventh, and of the eighth century A.D., found in Sumatra, on the island of Bangka, in Ligor and in Central Java.

Explorers and scholars alike have, therefore, been surprised to learn that Sumatra is extremely poor in antiquities, and it is also curious that this island which, generally speaking, experienced the same civilizing influences as Java, should nevertheless have remained backward in development. The indigenous literature as well as much of the old civilization has fallen into decay. Here and there, however, the population possesses a fairly high degree of civilization. Hindu-Javanese, Chinese, Arabs, Indians and others have long been settlers round the coast, and the resulting mixture of blood and other factors have produced there a much higher civilization than that in the interior. Indeed, many of the indigenous tribes of the interior are still in a comparatively low state of development.

The slight density of population, about 18 per square mile (as compared with the extremely high density of over 820 per square mile in Java), which is due mainly to the unhealthiness of the country, must certainly have played a considerable part in the backwardness of Sumatra. Lying across the equator, the island is obviously tropical. The whole of eastern Sumatra forms vast almost impenetrable jungle marshes, with the concomitants of malaria, dysentery, beriberi, hook-worm and endemic cholera. About 115,000 square miles out of the total of 163,000 square miles of the island are covered by tropical forests. The rest of Sumatra consists mainly of a high mountain chain running down its western flank like a backbone. Sumatra's population has therefore never been large, although the elimination of the old inter-tribal quarrels, improved health conditions, and immigration of native farmers from other Indonesian islands (especially from Java, whence in 1939 about 150,000 people emigrated to Sumatra), increased its population from 3,168,000 in 1900 to about eight and a half millions at the outbreak of the war with Japan, and reached almost ten millions in 1945.

Many languages—there are fourteen main Malaysian dialects, some with many sub-dialects—and a number of scripts are used by the different peoples of the island. The

Achinese or Achehnese numbering 800,000, who live in north-western Sumatra, and the coastal Malays, numbering nowadays nearly three and a half millions, who occupy the entire eastern coast and nearly half of the southern coast, are the most advanced of the Sumatran races. Both these peoples are Moslems, and they adopted the Arabic alphabet; the Malay press, however, uses the Roman alphabet. The Menangkabaus or Minangkabaus, who live in the central-western part of the island, and number something more than two millions, formed at one time a powerful kingdom covering the greater part of central Sumatra. According to R. O. Winstedt, the great authority on the Malayan languages, the Minangkabaus are the highland inheritors of Śri Vijaya, and their ruling family claimed to be descended from the Sailendra dynasty which had ruled Śri Vijaya. Formerly, the Minangkabaus used the Javanese character; nowadays, they employ the Arabic script.

SUMATRAN NATIVE CHARACTERS (Fig. 18.16, 7–9)

The other principal native peoples, namely the Bataks, the Redjangs and the Lampongs, possess scripts of their own. All these characters directly or indirectly originated from the Kavi or Old Javanese character.

Batak (Figs. 18.14–15; 16,9)

The Bataks, of whom there are more than one million, are a peculiar and interesting race. They were cannibals not so very long ago, and although that cruel custom and slavery have disappeared, many of their old habits are still followed. For the most part, they are pagans; some have recently been converted to Christianity, whilst Islām has never gained a foothold among them. They occupy the greater part of the former residency of Tapanoeli, and are centred in the mountainous region around the great lake Toba, which was regarded as sacred by the Bataks, and many foreigners who dared to penetrate so far had to pay for their courage by death and were possibly eaten. A large part of the northern and the western coasts is also inhabited by the Bataks. They are divided into several groups, differing considerably in language and customs, the most important of the tribes being that of the Tobas, who live on the southern shore of Lake Toba.

The art of writing has been known among the Bataks from a date beyond the reach of tradition. Their character is peculiar; and also their mode of writing, for they begin at the bottom of the page at the left-hand side, and place letter above letter in a vertical column till they reach the top, when they return to the bottom; the columns follow each other from left to right. This peculiarity gives a strange appearance to the writing.

According to Professor De Lacouperie, the reason for their having adopted the present curious method of writing is explained by the material they use to write upon. It consists of long strips of bamboo welded by beating one to the other, then folded together, accordion-like, between wooden covers, and bound together with a string of woven rushes. Originally, the writing was from left to right in horizontal lines, one following the other, as in modern European writing, from top to bottom. The completed document, when bound up, was held for purposes of reading at an angle of ninety degrees, so that the original successive horizontal lines from left to right and from top to bottom, appeared as vertical columns consisting of letters written one above the other from the bottom to the top; the columns consequently followed each other from left to right. (*See* also below, what is said on the question of the direction of writing in the Philippine scripts.) Instead of bamboo strips, sometimes long strips of thin bark of trees are used. The ancient books of the Bataks are written in brilliant ink on paper made of bark.

Lampong and Redjang Characters

In Redjang-Lampong, in south-western Sumatra, there are the Redjangs, a rather truculent people. Hindu-Javanese antiquities are scattered in that region. Lampong is spoken in the southern end of the island, and this language is related both to some Javanese dialects and to the Batak form of speech. The Lampongs were largely under Hindu-Javanese influence, and have still retained a certain degree of civilization of Hindu-Javanese origin. The Redjang and Lampong tribes number about half a million people. Both races use indigenous scripts, indirectly descended from the Kavi character. The Lampong and Redjang scripts are closely related. As a rule, they are scratched on bamboo, tree bark, or certain forms of leaves.

Both these characters are more complete than the indigenous scripts of Celebes (*see* below); they not only possess a mark for the elision of the inherent vowel, but also another mark to signify an *a* following the inherent vowel, and two other marks for the nasals *n* and *ng*; there is even a distinct sign for the aspirate following a vowel.

CELEBES

This third-greatest island of Indonesia, measuring about 72,600 square miles (an area much larger than that of Java), has only about 5 million inhabitants. Celebes is remarkable for its extraordinary shape which has been compared to a spider or a starfish with one arm gone. Until comparatively recent years, a great part of the island had not been explored; and even today much of it is known in but little detail. The natives speak numerous languages and dialects, the isolation of the mountain districts having very greatly contributed to this. They are usually divided into six groups. The part best known to Europeans is Macassar, situated nearly at the southernmost extremity of the western side; it was here that the first European settlement of the island was established.

The larger part of the southern peninsula—which is the most fertile portion of the island—is occupied by tribes speaking the two principal languages of the island, called by Europeans Macassar and Bugis, and by the natives Mengkasa or Mengkasara and Wugi or Ugi. The Macassarese and the Buginese, who together number perhaps 2,600,000 people, making up more than half the entire population, are the most important and the most advanced peoples of the island and have been the dominant natives long before the arrival of the Europeans.

The Buginese (Orang Bugis) call themselves 'To Wugiq' (people of Wugiq) and their language is *basa To Wugiq*.

Macassarese is spoken nowadays in all the districts from Balu Kumba to Segere. Bugis is much more general beyond and over the whole tract extending from Boni to Luwu. The Buginese are the great maritime and commercial people of the archipelago. They have spread from their homeland in the south-western peninsula to settle coastal regions in other parts of the island and in parts of Borneo.

In Mandhar and its vicinity, the Mandhar language is spoken. The centre of Celebes is inhabited by the Turajas or Harafuras, whose form of speech is the most pure native language of the island. The north-eastern peninsula is occupied by the Manadu, Gunuhg Telu, Tontemboan and Bulu.

CELEBES SCRIPTS (Fig. 18.16, 10)

It is not known whether the Turajas and the tribes of the north-eastern peninsula are at all, or ever were, acquainted with the art of writing. Macassarese and Buginese (partly also Mandharese), which may be regarded as dialects of one and the same language, use characters which are varieties of one and the same script. Each people considers its own writings as the most ancient character and as the prototype of the others. It seems that the Buginese are right; their character is apparently the ancestor of the others.

Origin

Although the origin of these scripts and their early developments cannot be determined in detail, there is no doubt that they derived from the Kavi character, probably through the medium of the Batak script. The intercourse of the peoples of Celebes with the natives of Java seems to have been ancient and frequent. The date of the invention of the Celebes scripts is also uncertain. No inscription has been discovered in Celebes and no other ancient written documents are extant.

Buginese Character

The Buginese or Bugis character is the most complete of the three varieties. It consists of twenty-three letters, of which eighteen are simple and the remainder compound, being combinations of the consonants *chh*, *mp*, *nk*, *nr*, and *nch*. It possesses the full form of *a*, but lacks the full form for the vowels *e-i*, and *o-u*. There are, however, diacritical marks for the vowels *e*, *i*, *o* and *u*, as also for the termination *ong*. The vowel *a* is inherent in every consonant, but there is no mark to annul that sound and to cause the word or the syllable to end in a pure consonant. This lack of a mark of elision is fortunately not very important because in Bugis no consonant, nasals excepted, can follow another without the intervention of a vowel. The form of the single letters is peculiar; the character as a whole resembles that of the Bataks.

Beside the Bugis alphabet now in use, there is another obsolete local alphabet which is still to be found in some manuscripts.

CONCLUSION

Summing up the history of writing of Indonesia, we may say that the great majority of the Malaysians, with the exception of the Javanese, through Islām lost their ancient scripts and took to the Arabic alphabet. The Dutch in turn have taught them the use of the Latin alphabet in the schools, so that the latter is becoming more and more used for ordinary purposes.

BIBLIOGRAPHY

Exhaustive bibliographies on Further-Indian scripts will be found in H. Cordier, *Bibliotheca Indosinica*. Dictionnaire bibliographique des ouvrages relatifs à la peninsule indochinoise. Publications de l'École Française d'Extrême Orient, 5 vols., Paris, 1912–32 (Vol. I, Burma, Assam, Siam and Laos; II, Malay Peninsula; III–IV, Indo-China; V, compiled by Mme. A.-M. Roland-Cabaton, Index).

PAVIE, A. *Mission Pavie*, etc., *Études diverses*, 3 vols., Paris, 1898–1904.

TUN NYEIN, *Inscriptions of Pagan, Pinya and Ava*, Rangoon, 1899.

AYMONIER, E. *Le Cambodge*, 3 vols., Paris, 1900–4; *Histoire de l'Ancien Cambodge*, Strasbourg, 1920.

BRADLEY, C. B. 'The Proximate Source of the Siamese Alphabet,' *J. Siam Soc.*, 1913; 'Some Features of the Siamese Speech and Writing', *J. Amer. Orient. Soc.*, 1924.

MASPERO, G. *Le Royaume du Champa*, Hanoi, 1914 and 1928; *Grammaire de la langue Khmère* (Cambodgien), Paris, 1915; *L'Indochine*, etc., Paris and Brussels, 1929–30.

FINOT, L. *Notes d'épigraphie indochinoise*, Hanoi, 1916; *Inscriptions d'Angkor*, Hanoi, 1925; 'Recherches sur la littérature laotienne,' *Bull. de l'École Française d'Extrême Orient*, Hanoi, 1917.

COEDÈS, G. 'Le Royaume de Çrivijaya,' *Bull. de l'École Française d'Extrême Orient*, Hanoi, 1918; 'Inscriptions' (in *Listes générales des inscriptions et des monuments*), Hanoi, 1923; 'Documents sur l'histoire politique et religieuse du Laos Occidental,' Bangkok, 1925 (*Bull. de l'École Française d'Extrême Orient*, XXV); *Bibliographie de l'Indo-Chine Française 1913–26*, Hanoi, 1929; *1927–29*, Hanoi, 1932; *Inscriptions du Cambodge*, Hanoi, 1937 onwards.

DUROISELLE, CH. 'Mon Inscriptions,' *Epigraphia Birmanica*, 3 vols., 1920–8.

CROSLIER, E. *Recherches sur les Cambodgiens*, Paris, 1921.

HARVEY, G. E. *History of Burma*, London, 1925.

SCHRÄDER, E. E. W. G. *Der Ursprung der ältesten Elementen des Austronesischen Alphabets*, Medan, 1927.

MAJUMDAR, R. C. *Champa*, Lahore, 1927; *Kambuja-Desa or An Ancient Hindu Colony in Cambodia*, Madras, 1944; *Inscriptions of Kambuja*, Calcutta, 1957.

SCHRAMM, A. 'Kurze Einführung in die Schrift der Toba-Batak,' *Archiv für Schreib- und Buchwesen*, I, 1927.

CHATTERJI, B. R. *Indian Cultural Influences in Cambodia*, Calcutta, 1928.

HALLIDAY, R. 'Les Inscriptions Mon du Siam,' *Bull. de l'École etc.*, 1930.

KROM, N. J. *Hindoe-Javaansche Geschiedenis*, 2nd ed., The Hague, 1931.

CHHABRA, B. CH. 'Expansion of Indo-Aryan Culture during Pallava Rule as evidenced by Inscriptions,' *J. Roy. Asiatic Soc., Bengal.*, 1935.

Inscriptions of Burma (*University of Rangoon. Oriental Studies Publications*), London, 1933 and 1939.

GANGOLY, O. C. 'Some illustrated Manuscripts of Kamma-Vaca from Siam,' *Ostasiatische Zeitschrift*, 1937.

Atlas van Tropisch Nederland, Batavia, 1938 (Map 9b).

HOSPITALIER, J. J. *Grammaire laotienne, Paris*, 1939.

MARCHAL, H. *Musée Louis Finot, Hanoi. La Collection Khmère*, Hanoi, 1939.

NILAKANTA SASTRI, K. A. 'Sri Vijaya,' *Bull. de l'École etc.*, 1940.

McFARLAND, G. B. *Thai-English Dictionary*, Bangkok, 1941; photo-lithographic reproduction of the same, California and Oxford, 1944.

GHOSHAL, U. N. 'Progress of Greater Indian Research during the last twenty-five years (1917-1942),' *Progress of Indic Studies, 1917-42*, Poona, 1942.

SCHAEFER, R. 'Further Analysis of the Pyu Inscriptions,' *Harvard J. Asiatic Studies*, 1943.

CROSBY, J. *Siam*, London, 1945.

HAAS, M. R. *Thai System of Writing*, rev. ed., New York, 1956.

PHILIPPINE ISLANDS

GENERAL SKETCH

The Philippine Islands were discovered by the Portuguese navigator Fernão de Magalhães (*Span.* Fernando Magallanes; *Engl.* Ferdinand Magellan) on March 16th, 1521, and called by him 'Islas de St. Lazaro.' In 1543, the name was changed into 'Islas Filipinas' in honour of the heir apparent of the Crown of Spain, Felipe, the future king Philip II. The Spaniards occupied the islands progressively from 1565 to 1600, but before 1763 their possession was hardly peaceful. In 1898, the Philippines were ceded by Spain to the U.S.A. for $20 million. In 1935, self-government was granted to the Commonwealth of the Philippines, and on July 4th, 1946, the independent republic of the Philippines came into existence.

The Philippines have an area of *c.* 115,600 square miles and consist of 7,083 islands and islets; but only 462 have an area of one square mile or more. There are twelve islands of importance: Luzon, Mindanao, Samar, Negros, Palwan or Palawan, Panay, Mindoro, Leyte, Cebu, Bohol, Basilan and Masbate; the first eight have an area of over 103,000 square miles; Luzon (with 40,420 square miles) and Mindanao (with 36,537 square miles) are larger than all the rest of the islands.

The population (1955) numbers about 22 million and is increasing rapidly; Manila, the traditional capital of the Philippines, has over 1,200,000 inhabitants.

The Negritos are the aborigines of the islands; they number now only about 30,000. They are of very small stature, have very dark skin and black curled hair; their civilization is rather primitive. It is probable that they are the remnant of an earlier larger group; there are other remnants on the Andamanes and on the Malayan peninsula. Akin to them are some Indo-Australian tribes: the Australian aborigines, the Wedda on Ceylon, the Munda- and Kola-people in north-eastern India, the Senoi in Further India and the Kubu in the primitive forests of southern Sumatra. In the Philippines, Negritos are found on the islands of Zambales, Pampanga, Luzon, Bisayas and Mindanao. There are about 700,000 Muslim Malays, called Moros or Moros Filipinos; they have a strong spirit of independence and gave considerable trouble to all governments who tried to control them. Islām was introduced in the islands before 1300. The Moros live on Sulu, western Palawan and western Mindanao. About 250,000 speak Sulu, about 5,000 Molbeg and 160,000 Magindanaw. Buddhism—and with it Kawi script—was introduced from Java during the old Javanese empire (c. 850/900–c. 1400). There are now some 50,000 Buddhist Filipinos. The Igorots, Bontoks, Kakanai, Nabaloi, Ifugas, Kalinga, Tinggians, Apayo and Ilonget, who live in the mountainous regions of northern Luzon, and some groups on Mindoro, and the Negritos, are pagan; they number about 650,000. Besides them, there are about 200,000 Chinese, some Japanese, Spaniards, and Americans. There was extensive intermarriage between the various groups.

The great bulk of the inhabitants of the Philipines are Christian Malays, who constitute about 93 per cent of the whole population, so that one is entitled to regard the Filipinos as the only Christian nation of Asia; about 17 million are Roman Catholics, half a million Protestants and 2 million are members of the Filipino Independent Church or Aglipayan.

There are as many as eighty-seven different languages and dialects in the Philippine islands, but the bulk of the indigenous population speak languages belonging to the Malayo-Polynesian linguistic family. The principal languages are Tagálog (the official national language), Iloko or Ilocano and Visáyan. Tagálog is in most general use and is the common language in Manila; it is now a compulsory subject in all the elementary schools. As secondary languages English and Spanish are used. The Spanish language of the Filipinos was known as 'español de cocina' ('Kitchen-Spanish').

Between 50 and 60 per cent of the Filipinos can read and write at least one language, and this percentage is on the increase.

In point of number, the three most important groups of the Filipinos, that is the Christian population of the Philippines, are:

(1) the Bisayans or Visayans, numbering c. 6 million, who constitute the bulk of the inhabitants of the islands in the central part of the archipelago, and of the northern and eastern coasts of Mindanao. They were perhaps the most civilized people in the archipelago when discovered by the Spaniards, by whom they were called 'Pintados,' because they used to paint their bodies;

(2) the Tagalogs or Tagals, numbering about 3 million people, who are the principal inhabitants of central Luzon, including Manila, and of a great part of Mindanao; they are nowadays the most advanced and energetic people among the Filipinos; they live in the most thickly populated district of the archipelago and they

have a practical superiority over the other sections of population, and their language—which is the most euphonious, the most homogeneous and the most developed of all the Filipino tongues—is understood by every native of average education throughout the islands;

(3) the Iloko or Ilocanos, numbering about one and a quarter million, most of them living in the western part of northern Luzon.

The other important vernaculars spoken by the Filipinos are: (1) Pangasinan, spoken by about 600,000 people living mostly in the province of Pangasinan, which borders on the Gulf of Lingayen (north Luzon); (2) Pampangan, spoken by over half a million people, mostly in the province of Pampanga, which borders the north shore of the Manila Bay; and (3) Bikol or Bicol, spoken by over a million people, living mostly in Albay, Camarines Norte and Camarines Sur, Luzon.

Special mention must be made of the islands of Palawan and Mindoro, because in them alone in the entire archipelago there has been a survival of the ancient alphabets. Palawan lies across a narrow strait from northern Borneo. It is long and narrow, and its total area is 4,725 square miles. Its population has increased tremendously in the last 70 years; it can be divided into four communal groups: (1) Christians, mainly Kuyonon and Tagalog, who inhabit the coastal towns; (2) Moslems or 'Moros,' who inhabit the southern part of the island; (3) a small number of 'Negritos,' who inhabit a portion of the northern part; and (4) Tagbánuwás, mostly pagans—although some have been converted to Islām—who inhabit most of the remaining interior of the island; to the north-east of the Tagbánuwás, there are two sub-tribes, Tangdulánen and Silangánen; also to the north-east there is the tribe of the Batáks; and to the south-west, there are the tribes of the Paláwans and of the Ke'neis—all these being pagan. The Tagbánuwá tribe only is literate.

Mindoro, lying south of Luzon, measures 110 miles north-west to south-east, and 56 miles north-east to south-west, having an area of 3,794 square miles. There are about 50,000 Christians who live mostly on the coast; the mountainous interior is inhabited by nine pagan tribes (with three sub-tribes), numbering about 20,000. Formerly they were known as Mangyans (Manguianes, Mangyanes), but Professor Conklin (of Columbia University) rejects this term as unscientific and a source of confusion. He observed Iráya, Alángan, Nauhán, Pulá, Batangán (sub-tribe Tagaídan), Bángon (Boribí), and Gubatnón (Ratagnán); the two most interesting tribes are the Hanunóo (numbering about 8,000) and the Buíd (about 3,500)—they alone have a script.

Apart from the two principal islands, Luzon and Mindanao, Mindoro has the largest number of pagans. The terms 'Mangyan' is actually a common name meaning 'forest man' and was applied generally to the various native tribes of the archipelago. According to their traditions, they lived formerly on the island of Tablas and were forcibly deported by the Spaniards to Mindoro. Their traditions tell also that before the Spanish conquest they had a much higher culture, and wrote their communications on banana leaves.

The Tagbánuwás (on Palawan) as well as the Hanunóo and the Buíd (on Mindoro) belong to the Malayo-Polynesian linguistic family. 'They are a happy, kind and gentle people, going to great lengths to avoid trouble; the easiest way to achieve this aim is obviously to slip away into the mountains.'

ANCIENT CHARACTERS (Figs. 18.16, 11–30; 17–18)

When Magellan 'discovered' the Philippine Islands in 1521, the main native peoples of those islands possessed scripts of their own. In a little more than a century of Spanish conquest and early colonial 'development,' which was roughly coëval with the Spanish inquisition, all the main native scripts were superseded by the Latin alphabet, and the reading and writing of the ancient characters became for the natives a lost art. We do not know whether the Spanish ecclesiastical authorities did the same in the Philippines an they did in Central America with the Maya books (*see* p. 87), and it is quite possible that the Philippine peoples were more fortunate, their scripts being non-pictographic and without apparent connection with 'the salvation of souls.' On the other hand, all the writing material used was perishable and the written documents, unless specially preserved, vanished within a few years, so that a deliberate wholesale destruction of books was unnecessary, and the undisguised contempt of the Spanish priests and the other authorities was probably sufficient to destroy in the more cultured natives any predilection for the indigenous art of writing. Not a single inscription, either on stone or pottery, or any other ancient document of indigenous origin, has been found in the Philippines.

However, as in the case of the Maya script, though here in an even greater degree, all we know about the ancient Philippine writing is based on the notes of the Spanish catholic priests, and curiously enough, just as there was apparently no 'bishop Landa' (*see* p. 89) to destroy Philippine native manuscripts, so there was no similar personality who, like Landa, would have taken a real interest in the history and the customs of the Filipinos.

Indeed, the Spanish record of the Philippine scripts is rather casual. The extinct forms for the most part, with the exception of the Tagalog characters, are represented by very few specimens, and even some of these may be suspect. In the early years of Spanish domination, indeed, some catholic priests used the native writing for printing religious books for the natives, but even of these only a few copies have been preserved, the best known being the *Belarmino* or 'Ilocano Short Catechism,' published in Manila in 1631, and republished in 1895 by P. Francisco Lopez (Fig. 18.17c)

Spanish sources mention the following ancient characters of the Philippine natives (Fig. 18.16, 11–30): for the Tagalog language, four varieties; for Bisayan two varieties; for Ilocano, two; for Pangasinan, one; and one for Pampangan. Dr. Pardo de Tavera—who, in 1884, was the first to carry out serious research on this matter— pointed out that the difference between these various ancient characters was not fundamental. The main general difference consisted in the shapes of the letter *ga*, while the form of the *ha* was the most constant. The Iloco character lacked the letters *wa* and *ha*, because Ilocano does not possess these sounds. The Pangasinan had the letters *a*, *ta* and *ha* different from the Tagalog forms. The Pampangan lacked the letters *ya*, *wa* and *ha*; the first two seem to have been forgotten, because the corresponding sounds exist in Pampangan, while the *ha* does not exist in this language which, like Malay, is without aspirates. All the ancient Philippine characters possessed three vowels: one for *a*, one for *e* and *i*, and one for *o* and *u*, the sounds *e-i* and *o-u* being easily confused in the Philippine languages. The number of the consonants varied between eleven and fourteen, mainly according to the phonetic needs of each language.

The question of the direction of writing has been hotly discussed; some scholars believe that it was horizontal, others think that it was vertical from above downwards, and others again hold that the script was vertical, but from below upwards. Some scholars think that originally the direction was vertical, when the writing material consisted of palm leaves and bamboos, but with the general adoption of paper, the writing became horizontal. Others believe that the direction was originally from right to left, as in Arabic, but that after the arrival of the Spaniards, it was changed to 'from left to right.' The explanation given by Dr. Fletcher Gardner seems to solve the problem; that is, the ordinary method of writing on the bamboo was to scratch with a sharp instrument holding in the other hand the bamboo, which might have been either split or round, and pointing it directly away from the body; the writing started at the end of the bamboo closest to the writer and continued the line away from himself; the second and succeeding lines were added in a similar way, the columns following in order from left to right (*see* also p. 338).

TAGALOG CHARACTER

The Tagalog character (Fig. 18.16, 11–14) was probably the most important of all the ancient scripts of the Philippines. It consisted of fourteen consonants, each having the inherent *a*, and three vowels. Apart from the vowel *a*, there were two vowel marks, placed either above the consonant (for *e* or *i*) or under it (for *o* or *u*). The Tagalog *ba* is the same as in the Batak character; the *pa* and the *na* nearly the same as in the Buginese character; the Tagalog *ba*, *la* and *ta* resemble the Buginese *ha*, *ga* and *nga*; the Tagalog *ha* resembles the Batak *a*.

Like the Buginese script, the Tagalog character apparently did not possess any mark for the elision of the inherent vowel *a*, but while in Buginese it did not matter, it was otherwise in Tagalog; the latter contained many syllables or words with final consonants. Thus, according to the Spanish sources, the Tagalog character was very deficient, or in other words, 'it was a writing as easy to write as it was difficult to understand' (Fr. Gaspar de S. Agustin). For instance, the two letters *la* with a dot over each could be read *lele, lili, lilim, lilip, lilis, lilic, lilig, linin*, etc. In the *Belarmino* (*see* p. 345, and Fig. 18.19c), Ave Maria is transliterated *a-be ma-di-a*. P. Francisco Lopez, however, introduced an innovation, a small cross appended to a character annuls the inherent vowel, thus permitting a word or a syllable to end in a consonant.

Because of this deficiency, a modern scholar (Costantino Lendoyro, *The Tagalog Language*, 1909) suggested that the ancient Tagalog character was not a real alphabet and was never used for practical purposes; he also writes 'had it ever acquired any appreciable hold on the native mind, it could never have been so easily eradicated and superseded by the Spanish one.' This suggestion is too far reaching; I do not think it is acceptable.

Nowadays, the Tagals use the Roman alphabet, introduced by the Spaniards, with the addition of the cerebral nasal *ng* for a sound peculiar to Tagalog.

TAGBÁNUWÁ AND MINDORO CHARACTERS

In the late nineteenth century, European scholars were surprised to hear that the ancient Philippine scripts were not completely out of use; in 1886, the French scholar A. Marche mentioned the existence of the Tagbánuwá character; in 1890, the Spaniard P. A. Paternó published a Mindoro alphabet; the whole Mindoro material available at the time was examined and published in 1895 by A. B. Meyer, A. Schadenberg and W. Foy (*Die Mangianenschrift von Mindoro*). Since Spain ceded the Philippine Islands to the U.S.A. (in 1898), many hundreds of pieces of inscribed bamboos have been collected in the islands of Mindoro and Palawan, and they are now preserved in American collections. The great majority of the written 'documents' are from Mindoro, but some are in the Tagbánuwá character; for instance, about twenty-five inscribed cylinders deposited at the Library of the University of Michigan. The subject was dealt with by Dr. Fletcher Gardner in 'Philippine Indic Studies,' *Indic Bulletin* No. 1, Series of 1943, The Witte Memorial Museum, San Antonio, Texas, 1943 (with an extensive bibliography). In 1939, Dr. Gardner succeeded in obtaining from all over the southern half of Mindoro various specimens of 'Mangyan' writing, some of which are written on bamboo, and others on ordinary paper.

Notwithstanding, until 1947 'no accurate description of writing techniques or comparison of Mindoro and Palawan scripts had yet been made.' Moreover, 'the areas where these scripts are used today were still undefined, the extent of their use, state of preservation as a culture trait, and the linguistic groups involved still largely unknown.' (Harold C. Conklin, 'Preliminary Report on Field Work on the Islands of Mindoro and Palawan, Philippines,' *American Anthropologist*, 1949; *see* also *idem* in *Pacific Discovery*, 1949.)

Dr. Conklin, who, in 1947, carried on field work on Mindoro (for six months) and on Palawan (for about three months) collected nearly 500 specimens of writing in the native scripts (most of them being now preserved in the Philippine National Museum, at Manila). Almost all the specimens are in the form of bamboo inscriptions; they contain songs, prayers, and 'a peculiar type of love-talk known as *pahágot*.' On the

A a

other hand, 'Hanunóo inscriptions are never of magical import, nor are they on mythological or historical topics. Written messages (love letters, requests, etc.,) are occasionally sent by means of inscribed bamboos, but by far the most common use of this script is for recording *ambáhan* and *urúkai* chants. Both of these types consist largely of metaphorical love songs.' Also, the Tagbánuwá inscriptions apparently have no religious or magical connections or uses. Curiously enough, however, even 'documents typed or printed in English, Tagalog, or Spanish concerned with legal transactions, marriages, and the like are still frequently signed in Tagbánuwá characters.'

On Mindoro, lime containers, tobacco containers, bamboo boxes, musical instruments, weapons, and even house-beams can be inscribed with various chants. Love letters are meticulously inscribed on embellished bamboo-sticks, while common letters of request, notification of ceremonials, and so on, are written on any piece of bamboo. All the inscriptions are on perishable material: 'there are no rock inscriptions and the ever-present tropical weevils make the preservation of bamboo records for more than one generation impossible,' 'and continuous recopying is necessary in order to preserve the ancient signs and poetry.' On Palawan, on the other hand, the ancient writing is rarely used and is preserved only as a tradition or relic of former times.

Varieties of Scripts

The Tagbánuwá character (Fig. 18.16, 21) does not seem to have varieties; Dr. Gardner pointed out that it 'varies only slightly in writings from various hands collected over a period of 35 years,' whilst the Mindoro character has several forms for many characters and at least two quite distinct varieties, the 'Buhil' (Fig. 18.16, 27–30) and the 'Mangyan proper' (Fig. 18.16, 22–26). The latter, according to Gardner, can be divided into a few sub-varieties, the most important being those of Bulalacao and Mansalay. However, all the types agree fairly closely, although the 'Buhil' character seems to be more elaborate than the others. Dr. Gardner pointed out that the style of the 'Buhil' script is quadrate, that of the Hanunóo is angular, and that of the Tagbánuwá is rounded.

Also Dr. Conklin writes that a recent development in certain Tagbánuwá areas has been the shift from the angular letter-form to the cursive. This shift is without doubt due to the change of writing-material and tools. 'Paper and pencil replaced the knife and bamboo. In the north several reforms were attempted in the old script and in general the pre-Christian practice of inscribing letters and songs on long strips of bamboo has now come almost to a stop.'

Vowel-signs

The vowel-signs or *korlits*, which in the old scripts had the form of dots or commas, are dashes (-) in the Mindoro scripts, and a kind of **V** turned sidewards (>) in the Tagbánuwá, The Mindoro dashes or commas may be either vertical or horizontal or slanting. The *korlits* are always placed above or to the left of the consonant when they indicate *e* or *i*, and below or to the right, when *o* or *u*.

Punctuation

Dr. Gardner distinguished three types of punctuation in the contemporary Philippine scripts: (1) A small cross, like a plus mark, indicates frequently the beginning of a written document. This mark is separated from the text in order to distinguish it from the letter *ka*. (2) A vertical line is used in the Mindoro characters to separate words. (3) Also in the Mindoro characters alone, two vertical lines separate sentences. These rules, however, are not followed consistently. The end of the writing has no mark at all.

Peculiar Postal Service

According to the majority of scholars, there are not many Mindoro natives who can read or write; it is therefore astonishing to hear of the interesting postal service which exists in southern Mindoro: 'A bamboo letter is fastened in a cleft stick and placed by the trailside. The first passer-by, who is going in the direction of the addressee, carries it as far as his plans allow and leaves it again by the trail, to be carried on by some other person. Perhaps half a dozen volunteers may assist in conveying the letter to its designation' (Fletcher Gardner). Would such a postal service be possible if really only few people could write? I do not think so.

Dr. Conklin's research has confirmed that notwithstanding the absence of schools and of formal instruction, in a jungle area, parts of which have not yet been explored by any outsider, literacy amongst the Hanunóos is relatively high, 'in some communities, literacy among adults in their own script is as high as 60 per cent. . . .'

Direction of Writing

The direction of writing in the Tagbánuwá and Mindoro scripts has been a matter of much controversy. According to Professor Kröber (*Peoples of the Philippines*, 1928, p. 216), the natives on Mindoro write horizontally from left to right, while the Tagbánuwás write in vertical columns from top to bottom, the columns following in order from right to left. Other scholars stated that the Tagbánuwás write from below upwards, beginning at the left-hand side, and adding additional columns to the right. According to Dr. Fletcher Gardner, there is no difference in the direction of writing between the Tagbánuwá and the Mindoro scripts, and there has never been any difference in the direction of writing of the Philippine writings. 'All ideas of this kind have arisen from misinterpretation or misquotation of the earliest writers on the subject.'

The problem has been re-examined by Dr. Conklin. He emphasizes the differences between the Palawan and the Mindoro methods. In the Buíd-Hanunóo area (south Mindoro), which consists largely of trackless, mountainous terrain, there are no roads, churches, or foreign settlements of any importance (hence, the Latin alphabet is there unknown); writing is there never done with pen or pencil on paper, but rather with a knife either on bamboo or wood. The direction of writing is always away from the body (*i.e.*, upwards) in columns proceeding to the right (*i.e.*, from left to right). In certain Tagbánuwá areas, on the other hand, roads, schools and churches have been known for over half a century with the result that many Tagbánuwás have studied English and Tagalog, and use both the old native script and the Latin alphabet. The direction of writing was originally the same as on Mindoro, but—owing to the study of English or Spanish and to the introduction of lined paper—this rule is no longer rigidly observed.

Dr. Conklin has drawn our attention to an interesting peculiarity of the Hanunóo script—apparently unknown on Palawan: left-handed people write in a completely inverted manner, in a 'mirror script,' holding the knife in the left hand and reversing both the axis of the characters and the direction in which the columns progress, but because of its syllabic nature, the script can be read almost as rapidly as that used by those who are right-handed.

ORIGIN OF PHILIPPINE SCRIPTS

I frankly admit that this problem has been made more complicated than it actually is. The Spanish writers of the late seventeenth and the early eighteenth centuries had already connected the origin of the Philippine scripts with those of the Malayau Archipelago. The great German scholar Humboldt and other contemporary scholars proved that connection.

A new suggestion, however, was made in 1852 by an authority on the Malay languages, the Englishman Crawfurd (in *Grammar and Dictionary of the Malay Language*). According to him, 'The Malays . . . have at present no native alphabet; and the Tagala alphabet is peculiar and bears little resemblance to any native written character of the nations of the western part of the Archipelago.' Crawfurd's opinion was, in brief, that 'the Tagala alphabet . . . has all the appearance of an original and local invention; and, at all events, there is assuredly no evidence to show that it has been derived from a foreign source.' This opinion, rightly, was not shared by any other scholar. The connection between the Philippine characters and the native Malay scripts was generally accepted; *see*, for instance, Meyer, Schadenburg and Foy, *Die Mangianenschrift von Mindoro*, and Constantino Lendoyro, *The Tagalog Language*.

There is a still further suggestion, one by an authority on Philippine scripts, Dr. Fletcher Gardner. In his opinion, the Philippine scripts do not depend on the characters of the Malay Archipelago, but were devised in very ancient times by Indian priests, who based their invention on the Kharoshthi and various Brahmi characters. These priests were familiar with some or all of the ancient systems of writing, and it may be presumed that they picked their letters from those which were common in the various ancient Indian characters, including the Kharoshthi alphabet. It was very easy, because 'They had at most 17 letters to consider out of the 40 or more to be found in each of the Aśoka series.'

The curious theory of Dr. Gardner, which to him 'seems to be well supported by the fact that in the three living Philippine Indic languages the letter forms are all simple and capable of rapid writing,' is a good example to show how slippery can be the ground of the history of the alphabet if one does not keep to the safe track. The plain facts are: (1) There is no indication whatever that in the times of Aśoka (third century B.C.) the Indians were in direct contact with the Philippine Islands. (2) No complete Philippine system, ancient or modern, can be considered as directly dependent on any ancient Indian script. (3) Comparisons are possible of single letters of the different Philippine scripts, ancient and modern, not only with single letters of the different Brahmī and Kharoshthi writings (as Dr. Gardner tries to prove), but also with single letters of different types of the Aramaic or the mediæval Latin alphabets; and the direct connection of the Philippine scripts with the Indian characters is as improbable as it is with the Aramaic alphabets or their offshoots, or with any offshoot of the Latin alphabet. (4) There is no indication whatever that the origin of the Philippine scripts can be antedated to the occupation of the archipelago by the Majapahit empire of Java (*see* p. 333). (5) In short, I believe that the Philippine scripts descended either directly or indirectly from the Kavi or Old Javanese character. It is possible that the Buginese were the mediators; indeed, many peculiar characteristics of the Buginese character appear also in the Philippine scripts, for instance in the Tagalog character, as proved particularly by Lendoyro, in his book, already mentioned, on the Tagalog language.

BIBLIOGRAPHY: *see* pp. 345, 347, 349 f.

KOREAN CHARACTER (Fig. 18.19)

Reference to the Korean script should not be omitted. Hence, perhaps, it is not in its correct context, but it would be equally difficult to fit it in elsewhere.

The Korean language is quite different from the Chinese. Chinese is monosyllabic (*see* pp. 64 ff.). Korean, on the contrary, is polysyllabic and agglutinative (*see* p. 124). By far the greater number of roots are either verbal stems or noun stems. Some scholars connect it with Japanese and with the Ural-Altaic languages, others with the Dravidian languages of India. However, the Koreans have been under Chinese cultural and political influence for many centuries, and, therefore, it is natural that they should have adopted Chinese writing. Local tradition attributes the introduction of the Chinese characters into Korea to Wan-shin (third century A.D.). For many centuries, all Korean writing was confined to the intricate system of the Chinese analytic script (*see* part 1, chapter 6). It is also not surprising that the Korean language, too, has been largely influenced by Chinese. Many Chinese words have been borrowed, especially those which are employed in literary essays by the higher classes. The pronunciation, however, is entirely different from that nowadays heard in China, and the Korean characters of Chinese origin differ from those employed in China.

ÜN-MUN OR ÖN-MUN

A totally different character is in use among the common Koreans who are literate. It is called Ün-mun or Ön-mun, *i.e.*, 'vulgar.' Whereas the Japanese greatly reduced some of the difficulties of the Chinese characters by the invention of syllabaries (*see* pp. 125 f.), the Koreans achieved a far higher stage by inventing (?) a script which is practically an alphabet, and is easy to learn and apply. Curiously enough, the higher social classes still prefer to use the characters of Chinese origin, but employ the Korean letters (similarly to the use in Japan of the *kana*-syllabaries, *see* p. 125 f.) mainly to indicate terminations, though sometimes also the pronunciation, when it is ambiguous, *i.e.*, when the word can be read either in Chinese or in Korean. It seems that mental culture in Korea has never had a national character, formed as it nearly always was along Chinese lines.

Thus, until recently all the official writing and the books of instruction were not in Korean, but in Chinese. Pure Korean literature was regarded with contempt, and was reserved for women and the illiterate. A Korean scholar of old, proud of his mastery of the very difficult Chinese characters, made it a point to appear ignorant of Korean script.

However, the Christian missionaries, who were the first to realize that Ön-mun was better adapted to their use than the cumbersome Chinese characters, and more easily taught to the illiterate people, published many of their books in it, including the New Testament, grammars and dictionaries. In 1895, the official *Gazette*, which hitherto had been printed only in Chinese characters, adopted a combination of the Ön-mun and Chinese, and for some time before the Japanese occupation (in 1910) all public edicts were in the Ön-mun as well as in the Chinese characters. More recently, the desire for a pure Chinese education practically vanished, and Ön-mun has received much attention, especially after education was completely re-organized. Nowadays, it is generally used in schools.

Vowels and Consonants (Fig. 18.19)

Ön-mun consists of twenty-five letters, of which eleven are vowels and fourteen consonants. Each consonant and each vowel has its own symbol. The letters are written in syllables arranged, under Chinese influence, in vertical columns, written from top to bottom; the columns consequently follow each other from right to left (as in Chinese). Of the fourteen consonants, eight letters seem to be the basic consonants, and each one of them has its name. They are *k* (*kiök*), *n* (*iün* or *niün*), *t* (*tjigüt*), *l-r* (*iül* or *riül* or *niül*), *m* (*miom*), *p* (*piop*), *s* (*siot* or *shiot*), *ng* (*ihäng*), the last being a nasal sound only used at the close of a syllable. All these consonants are used both before and after the vowels. Also the letter *ch* (pronounced as in '*church*') has its name (*chaat*), but, like the letter *h* and the four remaining consonants, it is used only before the vowels. These remaining consonants, *kh, th, ph* and *chh*, are strongly aspirated sounds, and are represented by the signs *k, t, p* and *ch*, modified by the addition of a horizontal dash. Also *ch* is only a variation of *s*. Previously, there was also a special sign, in the shape of a small triangle (△) for a sound like a palatal *n* or a weak nasalized *y*, but it disappeared long ago.

The eleven vowels are usually placed under the name of *i* between *s* and *ng*. They are *a, ya, ö, yö, o, yo, u, yu, i-ü, i* and short *a*; the letters *ya, yö, yo* and *yu* are merely modifications (by the addition of a dash or stroke) of the letters *a, ö, o* and *u*. Besides, by the addition of the stroke of the letter *i* to the other vowel signs, the diphthongs *ai, öi, yöi, oa*, and others, are obtained. These are considered as special vowels and are sometimes pronounced as single vowels. The vowels have two forms, the full form and the abbreviated one, the former being used when the vowel is initial. The whole alphabet is reducible to ten basic consonants and six vowels.

IS THE KOREAN ALPHABET PERFECT?

The Korean alphabet is the only native alphabet of the Far East. Some scholars regard it as the most perfect phonetic system 'that has been called upon to stand the test of time and of actual use.' 'Only one of its vowels is used for more than one sound, and these are so closely allied that they hardly form an exception.' 'Of its consonants, only one is used to represent two sounds, and these are the sounds of *l* and *r*,' which, as in many other languages, are interchangeable; moreover, their pronunciation in Korean varies according to dialects. (*See* H. B. Hulbert, *A Comparative Grammar of the Korean Language and the Dravidian Dialects of India*, Seoul (Korea), 1906.) The opinion that the Korean alphabet is phonetically perfect is exaggerated, for it has more sounds than written characters. There are no separate signs for the sounds *g, b, d, j*, although these sounds exist in Korean, and are represented by the letters *k, p, t* and *ch*. These voiceless sounds vary with half-voiced *g, b, d, dj* and voiced *g, b, d, j*. Euphonic considerations alone determine whether the letter shall be pronounced as a surd or as a sonant. Thus the word *an-ta*, 'to know,' is pronounced *anda*; *an-pank* is read *ambang*, *to-ra po-ta* sounds like *tora boda*, *ka-ke* like *kage*, *an-cha* like *anja*. (*See* the excellent manual written by G. J. Ramstedt, *A Korean Grammar* (*Memoires de la Société Finno-Ougrienne*, LXXXII), Helsinki, 1939. However, the Korean alphabet is quite sufficient for reading correctly.

ORIGIN OF KOREAN ALPHABET

The origin of this interesting script is a moot question. According to local tradition, accepted by some scholars (*see* P. Andreas Eckardt, O.S.B., 'Der Ursprung der koreanischen Schrift,' *Mitteilungen der deutschen Gesellschaft für Natur- und Völker-kunde Ostasiens,*' XXII/C, Tokyo, 1928), a great scholar Syöl Chong, A.D. 690, made the first attempt at an indigenous script. He invented a syllabary, called *Nitok*, of thirty-six signs, based on the Chinese characters and perhaps also influenced by Indian scripts. It was probably the same script which is mentioned in Japanese tradition as the 'divine script' (*see* p. 123), but had no influence on the invention of the Japanese syllabaries, *kata-kana* and *hira-gana*. Further, according to Eckardt, in course of time the number of Nitok syllables was gradually increased, and in 1375 the script called *Hongmu*-alphabet was formed, also based mainly on Chinese phonetic signs.

With the overthrowing of the Mongolian dynasty in China and the establishing in Korea, in 1392, of a new dynasty, various reforms, based mainly on Chinese culture, were introduced in Korea. Confucianism was established as the state religion, replacing Buddhism; there followed a violent reaction against the latter and the triumph of the former. The Korean king Ta-jong (1401–19) first conceived and carried out the idea of movable copper types. (Movable type was used in China A.D. 1041–9: information from Sir Ellis Minns.) In 1403 (47 years before the first printing from movable types was known in Europe), within a few months several hundred thousand types were cast. This invention increased still more the difficulties of using the cumbersome Chinese characters.

It is, thus, not surprising that the new king Set-jong (1419–51) sent missions to Nanking and Pyolmun to seek advice about the possibility of introducing a simplified script. These missions having failed, the king—with the assistance of some of the *literati* of the court—invented the new script. It happened probably in 1446; other dates, such as 1443, or 'the beginning of the fifteenth century,' and so forth, have also been suggested. Some scholars, instead, hold that Ön-mun was invented, in 1446, by a Buddhist priest named (like the inventor of the Nitok syllabary, already referred to) Syöl Chong; this opinion may have been caused by confusion with the generally accepted theory, although I do not exclude the possibility that the Korean alphabet was a Buddhist creation, and that it was, at a later time, attributed to the Korean king. In the years 1777–81, the Korean alphabet was revised.

According to some scholars, the Deva-nagari character was the *model* of the Ön-mun, but only six Korean letters, eventually, can be considered as having some similarity with Deva-nagari signs. Besides, the two systems are, on the whole, quite different. A connection with the Latin alphabet, though chronologically quite possible and though suggested by some scholars, must also be excluded.

The most general theory is that the origin of the Ön-mun is connected with the ancient diffusion of Buddhism in Korea, and with the great influence there of the Buddhistic, especially Tibetan literature. It is, therefore, suggested that the Tibetan system of writing was the prototype of the Korean alphabet. This theory has been accepted by Taylor and other scholars, such as G. J. Ramstedt. If this theory is right, it would be reasonable to attribute the invention of this script to Buddhists, and we could more easily understand why Ön-mun until recently was looked upon with contempt by the Korean higher social classes.

Another theory has been suggested by P. Andreas Eckardt; according to him, the Korean alphabet consists of very simple elements, such as small circles, strokes, angles, and has been invented as a whole on the basis of the shapes of Korean windows and doors. (This theory is rather unlikely.) Other scholars, for instance Jensen, also believe that Ön-mun was an independent invention, that is to say, it was not connected with any other script.

The problem is still open. In my opinion, the Korean letters are mainly arbitrary inventions, although as a whole the alphabet is not an independent creation but the ideal adaptation of idea–diffusion (*see* pp. 30, 58, etc.) to the Korean tongue. There is no doubt that at the beginning of the fifteenth century A.D. various scripts, including, obviously, the Tibetan writing, were known in the Chinese and Korean Buddhist monasteries, and gave king Set-jong the idea of the creation of an alphabetic script. If this be true, the problem of the invention of the single letters would be of secondary importance.

A few other points should be considered: (1) More attention should be paid to the achievement of king Set-jong (*see* what has been said about the inventors of other alphabetic scripts, St. Mešrop, St. Cyril, Wulfila, Bashbah, and so forth), who used his own method of working upon pre-existing bases, either by borrowing or differentiation or by arbitrary invention of the written characters. (2) The invention of the Korean alphabet occurred at a relatively recent date, that is at a time when the idea of alphabetic writing was far from being a novelty. (3) The Chinese characters then employed in Korea did not at all suit the Korean language.

See also, 'Système de transcription de l'alphabet coréen,' *J. Asiatique*, 1933; G. M. McCune and E. O. Reischauer, 'Romanization of the Korean Language.' *Trans. Roy. Asiatic Soc., Korea*, 1940.

CHAPTER 19

The Greek Alphabet and its Offshoots

THE GREEKS

THE importance of the Greeks in the history of alphabetic writing is paramount. All the alphabets in use in Europe today stand in direct or indirect relation to the ancient Greek. Although the Greeks did not invent the alphabet, they improved it to such a degree that for 3,000 years it has furnished a most convenient vehicle of expression for the thoughts of, and communication between, men of all races, creeds and tongues.

The Island of Crete, as already mentioned (p. 40), was the only part of Europe which had a civilization to compare with the contemporary civilizations of Egypt and Mesopotamia. Its scripts 'Pictographic Class A,' 'Pictographic Class B,' and 'Linear A' were dealt with in chapter 3 (pp. 41 ff.), whereas the recently deciphered syllabic 'Linear B' is treated in chapter 10 'Syllabic Systems of Writing' (pp. 116 ff.). This chapter also deals with the 'Linear B' tablets discovered on the Greek mainland (mainly at Pylos and Mycenae).

In the second half of the second millennium B.C. a new ethnic element that we know now as Greek, emerged into the light of history, and in the subsequent centuries nurtured one of the greatest civilizations ever produced; this became the foundation of our western art, philosophy and science.

Nothing is known about the cradle-land of the composite Greek people. It is generally accepted that they came from the north and arrived in waves, sweeping down upon the older pre-Hellenic civilization that had flourished in Crete, on the Ægean islands and on the Greek mainland (part 1, chapter 3). Greek tradition tells of two main waves of invading Greeks. The first wave, generally described by the name 'Achæan,' came in the fourteenth and thirteenth centuries B.C. as the movement of bands who arrived in successive relays, and gradually established themselves in many parts of Greece. Leading authorities now agree—on the basis of the Hittite *Aḫḫiyawā* texts—that the Achæans were active in western Asia Major in the thirteenth century B.C.; and it is agreed that '*Aḫḫiyawā*' was a land inhabited by Achæans of the Mycenæan age. In the last decades of the thirteenth century we find the Akaiwasha or Akaivosh (?)—by some scholars identified with the 'Achæans'—attacking Egypt. By 1200 B.C. Greek tribes were the ruling people in Crete and in the chief principalities of the Peloponnesus and they were responsible for the sacking of Troy (1183 B.C.?).

The recent decipherment of Minoan 'Linear B' (*see* pp. 117 ff.) has induced the decipherers to suggest that by about 1400 B.C. either the economic centre of gravity of the Ægean 'had already shifted to the Mainland, requiring the use of Greek as the language of commerce; or a Greek aristocracy, despite stylistic indications of Minoan continuity, was established at Knossus in L.M. II.' (*J. Hellenic Studies*, 1953, p. 84.)

The thirteenth and the twelfth centuries are called the 'heroic age,' this being the period of the action of the heroic poetry. In the main the coming of the 'Achæans' seems to have been a relatively peaceful infiltration. Mycenæ, which supplanted Knossos as the chief focus of Ægean culture, did not destroy the Minoan culture, although it completely overshadowed it.

The second great wave of invading Greeks, known as the 'Dorian' invasion, brought to Greece a 'dark age,' such as that which came to Europe at the fall of the Roman Empire in the west. The 'Dorian' invasion coincided with the end of the Bronze Age and of the Mycenæan civilization—dated about the end of the twelfth century B.C.—and with the beginning of the Iron Age.

The tribal movements caused by the 'Dorian' invasions came to rest about 1100 B.C., but the period of disturbance and obscurity endured for some time. It was the Ionians of the coastal cities of Asia Minor who first kindled the torch of Hellenic civilization.

Out of the troubled darkness, which shrouded the transition from the Bronze Age and the Mycenæan civilization to the Iron Age and the early Greek primitive geometric art of the tenth and ninth centuries B.C., there came the wonderful achievement of the invention of the Greek alphabet.

EARLY GREEK THOUGHT ON SOUNDS AND ALPHABET

The Greek pre-Socratian philosophers were perhaps the first to ponder about the nature of sounds and letters, about vowels and consonants (even the mutes), about syllables and words; but very little of their writings has come down to us.

Frank and Koller reconstructed the Pythagorean ideas from the writings of the peripatetic philosopher Adrastos of Aphrodisias in Caria (second century A.D.) and think that theories about language and music as a unity were formed already among the early Pythagoreans, roughly according to the following scheme:

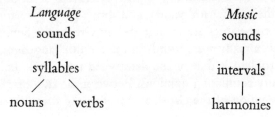

Language	Music
sounds	sounds
|	|
syllables	intervals
/ \\	|
nouns verbs	harmonies

Kratylos, disciple of Herakleitos of Ephesos and Plato's teacher, seems already to distinguish between sounds (*stoicheîa*) and letters (*grámmata*) and the names of letters (*e.g.*, *alpha*), between vowels (*phonêenta*) and consonants (*aphôna*) and mutes (*aphthonga*), although it seems that he often inadvertently omits to distinguish sharply between sounds and letters. He has a kind of onomatopœic theory, attributing to each sound an idea, as *e.g.*, to R 'motion,' to I 'subtleness,' to PH, PS, S and Z 'blowing,' to D and T 'binding' and 'rest.'

See Plato, *Cratylus*, 393 C–E; 423 E–427 C; *Hippias maior*, 285 D; *Theaitetus*, 201 D–206 A; *Sophistes*, 253 A–C; *Philebus*, 17 A–18 E; L. Lersch, *Die Sprachphilosophie der Alten* (Bonn, 1838–41); H. Diels, *Elementum*, 1899; R. H. Robins, *Ancient and Medieval Grammatical Theory in Europe*, London, 1951; E. Frank, *Plato und die sogenannten Pythagoreer*, Appendix II; H. Koller, 'Stoicheion,' *Glotta*, 34 (1955), pp. 161–89.

ORIGIN OF THE GREEK ALPHABET

Greek and Roman traditions attributed the invention of the Greek alphabet (and also of the alphabet in general) or the introduction of certain letters, to various mythical personages such as Palamedes, Prometheus, Orpheus, Musaios, Linos, Epicharmos, Cecrops, Simonides, and especially to Cadmos, son of Agenor, king of Tyre. Cadmos is credited with the introduction of writing into Greece (as indicated by the terms *Kadméia grámmata, etc.—see* further on), though according to one tradition, he introduced only sixteen letters (in 1313 B.C., as computed by Eratosthenes). Palamedes during the Trojan war (about 1183 B.C.) added the letters *th*, *x*, *ph* and *kh*, and Simonides the letters *z*, long *e*, *ps*, and long *o*. The letters of the Greek alphabet were called *Kadméia grámmata* (Herodotus, V, 59) or else *Kádmou týpoi* or *Kádmou grámmata*. Herodotus (V, 58) also calls the letters *Phoinikéia grámmata*. The same phrase occurs in an inscription of Teos dated about 475 B.C. (Dittenberger, *Sylloge Inscriptionum Græcarum*, 38, 37; information by Dr. M. N. Tod).

Indeed, Greek tradition, with very few exceptions, takes the view that the Greeks learned the art of writing from the Phœnicians, and the opinion now commonly held by all serious scholars is in agreement with that tradition. The main facts, ignored by any theory that would deny the Phœnician or, rather, North Semitic origin of the Greek alphabet are: (1) the shapes of nearly all the early Greek letters and the early Etruscan letters (the Etruscan alphabet being a derivation from the Greek) clearly recall their Semitic origin; (2) the order of the Greek letters corresponds, with a few understandable exceptions, to the order of the Semitic letters (the order of the Greek letters is also evident from their numerical value); and above all (3) the names of the letters: whereas the Greek letter-names are meaningless in Greek, the Semitic names of the letters are, as we have already seen, words in the Semitic languages.

A very difficult problem is that of the date when the Greek alphabet came into being. There are many conflicting opinions. Between the two extreme views—that which assigns the invention of the Greek alphabet to the fifteenth century B.C., and that which places it in the seventh or eighth century B.C.—each century has its own advocates. Indeed, even as low a date as 554 B.C. was suggested by an eminent eighteenth-century English scholar (Robert Wood, c. 1717–71). Until recently, the date usually preferred was the ninth century: nowadays either the latter or an earlier date, such as about 1000 B.C., if not a little earlier (Professor Ullman suggests not later than c. 1100 B.C.), is commonly accepted.

Dr. L. H. Jeffery, in her magnificent work on *The Local Scripts of Archaic Greece* (Oxford, 1961), advanced the theory that the Greek alphabet may have had its birth in Al Mina (perhaps the ancient Posideion), a Greek colony on the north Syrian coast; that the date of birth 'was somewhere about the middle of the eighth century;' that some 'illiterate' trading Greeks 'learnt the twenty-two letter alphabet from the local Φοίνικες' with no conscious desire to improve the set of letters by deliberate removals, alterations, and additions. I disagree with her method and conclusions. No Semitist will be able to agree, for instance, that the Semitic 'āleph, hē and 'ayin resembled the Greek sounds *a*, *e* and *o*.

The best evidence for the earlier origin of the Greek alphabet is provided by (1) the earliest Greek inscriptions, those found on Thera and at Athens belonging to the first half of the eighth or even to the late ninth century B.C. (Figs. 19.1, 2); (2) the Etruscan alphabet (*see* next chapter), which, as mentioned above, was descended from the Greek and was probably already in existence in the eighth or even perhaps in the late ninth century. On the whole, all the evidence points to the conclusion that the alphabet was probably taken over by the Greeks from north-west Semitic sources about 1000 B.C.

Like the Semitic alphabetic scripts, the earliest Greek script was written from right to left (Fig. 19.2), a style which was later superseded by the *boustrophedon* direction of writing (Fig. 19.3), that is, as already explained, alternately from right to left and from left to right, as the ox draws the plough. In both styles, the writing sometimes began from the bottom and went upwards. There are, however, extant some early inscriptions written from left to right (Figs. 19.3c, 4). After 500 B.C. Greek writing invariably proceeded from left to right and from top to bottom.

CHANGES INTRODUCED IN THE GREEK ALPHABET
(Fig. 19.5)

The letters *b*, *g*, *d*, *z*, *k*, *l*, *m*, *n*, *p*, *r*, *t*, which expressed sounds common to the Semitic and Greek languages, were taken over without change. Other Semitic letters were adopted for slightly different Greek sounds: the letter *waw* was adopted to express the Greek *digamma*, the *teth*, which represents the hard Semitic *t*, was adopted for the Greek *th*, the *qoph*, which expresses the Semitic emphatic *k*, was adopted as *koppa*, differentiated from *kappa*. By the fifth century B.C. *koppa* had disappeared from the eastern alphabets, because the language did not require it, but it lingered on in the west, and survived as the numeral 90. Interestingly enough, the use of the letter *koppa*—the *san* (*see* further on) is a parallel case—lingered on in the name of the 'Koppa-branded' horse (*Koppatías*, in Aristophanes, 424–422 B.C.; *Koppaphóros*, in Lukianos of Samosata, *c.* 150 A.D.). It was also used on the coins of Corinth (perhaps as abbreviation for 'Korinthos') as late as the fourth century B.C.

The most remarkable adaptations made by the Greeks were: (1) the introduction of vowel-representation (the Semitic alphabet being entirely consonantal), or rather the allocation of certain of the twenty-two Semitic consonants to Greek vowel-sounds; (2) the different arrangement of the hissing or sibilant sounds (of which the Semitic alphabet had a great variety); (3) the addition of certain letters for the representation of sounds not expressed by any of the Semitic letters, such as *ph, ps, kh* and *x*.

VARIETIES OF EARLY GREEK ALPHABET

The different ways in which these adaptations were carried out permit us to distinguish the two main branches of the early Greek alphabet, the eastern and the western (Fig. 19.5), which again sub-divide, each into secondary branches. But within this general grouping there were many local peculiarities. In practice many little states had each its own variant and it was long before anything like uniformity was introduced.

The eastern alphabets—of which the most important was the Ionic—included the alphabets of Asia Minor and the adjacent islands, of the Cyclades and Attica, of Megara, Corinth, Sicyon and Argos, and of the Ionian colonies of Magna Græcia. The early alphabets of the Dorian islands of Thera, Melos and Crete constituted a secondary branch of the eastern alphabets.

The western family included the Chalcidian alphabet (of Eubœa), the alphabets of Bœotia, Phocis, Locri, Thessaly, of the Peloponnesus except its north-eastern part, and those of the non-Ionian colonies of Magna Græcia.

We do not know whether the two main branches were independent or interdependent, that is, whether the Greek alphabet was first constructed in one place (most likely) or in several. Some scholars consider the Ionic alphabet as the earliest, others hold that the western forms were earlier than the eastern. It is more probable, but far from certain, that the early alphabet of isle of Thera was the prototype of all the Greek alphabets. Dr. Jeffery's most recent theory (1961)—see p. 359—that the Greek alphabet was a mere adaptation of the Phoenician alphabet to the Greek language, introduced by Greek merchants in the Greek colony of Al Mina (north Syria), will not find many followers.

GREEK VOWELS

In all Greek alphabets the Semitic consonants *'āleph, hē, waw, yodh* and *'ayin* were adopted to represent vowels.

'*Ăleph*, a smooth breathing in the Semitic alphabet, was consistently used as *alpha* in the Greek alphabets for the sound *a*. A parallel case was the Semitic consonant *yodh*, which came to represent consistently the vowel-sound *i* (the consonant *y* having disappeared from Greek in prehistoric times).

Hē became the Greek *epsilon*; it was used as short or long *e* in those alphabets (belonging mainly to the western family) in which the Semitic *heth*, a guttural, rough breathing sound *h*, was adopted to denote the rough breathing, *spiritus asper*—also in the Athenian jar of the National Museum at Athens, No. 1002, attributed to the late seventh century B.C.—while in the other Greek alphabets it came to represent the short *e*, and *heth* the long *e*.

A secondary form of *waw* became the *digamma* (a consonantal *u*, akin to English *w*); this sound was given up in some dialects (in Ionic for instance), in which, therefore, the letter not being needed was discarded; it survived in certain dialects till it was gradually discontinued in classical times, the sign surviving as the numeral 6. Interestingly enough, on the Elis coins the *digamma* lingered on at least until the period of Philip II (359–36 B.C.)—*see*, for instance, K. Regling, *Die antike Münze als Kunstwerk*, Berlin, 1924, Nos. 179 (*c.* 500 B.C.), 324 (*c.* 480 B.C.), 460–4 (*c.* 440 B.C.), 668 ff. (*c.* 400 B.C.), and 791 (*c.* 350 B.C.). Another form of the Semitic *waw* was taken into use as the vowel *upsilon* and placed at the end of the Greek alphabet, following *tau*.

The Semitic guttural consonant *'ayin* was taken over, as the Greek *omikron*, to represent the vowel *o*; in some alphabets, however, particularly of the eastern family, it represented only the short vowel, while another sign, *omega*, probably created from the same *omikron*, came to represent the long open *o*, and was placed at the very end of the Greek alphabet.

GREEK SIBILANTS

The Greek voiced sibilant, *z*, was expressed, as already mentioned, by the Semitic *zayin*. The Semitic *samekh*, which still existed in the Theran and the Etruscan alphabets, was retained, as *xei* with the value of *x*, in the eastern Ionic alphabet, while the name *samekh*, which became (perhaps by metathesis from an Aramaic form, otherwise unknown, *simkha*) *sigma*, was transferred to the letter derived from the Semitic *shin*. The Greek sound *s* was represented in the various Greek alphabets by symbols derived from two Semitic letters, that is either by signs descended from the *ṣade* (*san*) or by the prototype of the classical *sigma* derived from the Semitic *shin-sin*. *Ṣade* and *samech* do not both appear together in any Greek alphabet, but they do appear in the Etruscan. The letter *ṣade* (*san*) is found mainly in Crete, Thera and Melos, in Phocis, in the Peloponnesus and its colonies. For the letter 'san' *see* the very interesting passages in Pindar, fr. 79 (ed. by Sir John Sandys, London, 1915), supplemented by *Oxyrhynchos Papyrus* 604 (fr. I, II/3); Herodotus, I, 139; Alexis, in

Athenaius, 467 *a*. Like the letter *koppa*, the use of the letter *san* lingered on as signifying a brand for a horse: *Samphóras* in Aristophanes (424/422 B.C.).

ADDITIONAL CONSONANTAL SIGNS

The addition of the new consonantal signs is likewise remarkable, inasmuch as the signs were not the same in the various Greek alphabets or had a different phonetic value. This addition is another proof that the original Greek alphabet, *i.e.*, the Greek prototype, contained all the Semitic letters, otherwise the letters which were later rejected would have been used instead of the additional symbols. The letter *phi*, employed to express the unvoiced labial aspirate *ph*, was the earliest in general use; it was placed after the *upsilon*. The unvoiced velar aspirate *kh* was expressed by the symbol × or +, which followed the *phi* in the order of the letters of the Greek alphabet, but in the western group it was used to express the *x*-sound. The letter *psi*, employed to denote the combination *ps*, became later standardized for this purpose and constituted the last letter but one, of the Greek alphabet; this symbol, however, was used in the western alphabets to denote the sound *kh*.

Beside these general additions, some local alphabets had their own additional letters; for instance, the alphabets of Halicarnassus, Ephesus, Teos and Thrace had a T-like sign to express the double *s*; so also—a most remarkable fact—in the Athenian jar No. 1002 of the National Museum at Athens, already referred to (in that early period, the *tau* had still the form of the Semitic *taw* and not yet the shape of the classical *t*). Later writers seem not to have known about this symbol (T = ss) and confuse it with the τ. Thus, Lucian of Samosata in Commagene (*c.* 125–*c.* 180), or perhaps Pseudo-Lucian, in his writing on *The Consonants at Law—Sigma* vs. *Tau— in the Court of the Seven Vowels*, attacks the πρὸς τὸ πονηρότατον τουτὶ Ταῦ ('this out-and-out rascal Tau') for its kidnapping of the letter *sigma*.

As to the origin of the additional consonantal signs, there are two main theories; according to some scholars they were borrowed from other scripts, for instance, the Cypriote syllabary or the South Semitic scripts; according to other scholars, they are differentiations from other letters, the *ph* being formed from *ṭeth–theta* or from *qoph–koppa*; the *kh* from *kaph–kappa* or from *ṭeth–theta*, and the *ps* from *ph* or from *waw–upsilon*. It is, however, more probable that they were artificial creations.

CLASSICAL GREEK ALPHABET

Gradually, the Greek local alphabets approximated more and more to one another. In 403 B.C. the Ionic alphabet of Miletus was officially adopted at Athens, and later also in the other states; for instance, about 370 B.C. in Bœotia. Generally speaking, by the middle of the fourth century B.C. all the local alphabets had disappeared in favour of the Ionic, which thus became the common, classical Greek alphabet of twenty-four letters.

The Ionians, having felt the need of distinguishing short and long *e*, and having lost the sound *h*, used the sign H for long *e*, and the halves of it (⊢ and ⊣, which through the forms ⊢ and ⊣ became ' and ') for the rough and smooth breathings, which in time lost any distinction in pronunciation. However, by adopting this system of rough and smooth breathing (*spiritus asper* and *spiritus lenis*) for the vowel sounds, or, in other words, by aspirating them or leaving them unaspirated, the Greek alphabet helped to preserve flexibility in the Greek speech. The three accents, acute, grave and circumflex, which were rarely employed in ancient times, were apparently invented about the middle of the third century B.C. by Aristophanes of Byzantium in order to assist students, especially foreigners, in the correct pronunciation of Greek. These accents marked, it is important to remember, musical tone or pitch, not stress.

DEVELOPMENT OF GREEK WRITING
(Figs. 19.5–6, 11)

The subsequent development of the Greek characters consists essentially in the transformation of the writing to make it more expeditious. While the classical alphabet was always retained as the monumental script and for the capital letters in manuscript, being still employed for the capitals in the modern printed Greek alphabet, more cursive forms, all of them being developments from the classical alphabet, were employed in writing on parchment, papyrus, wax and other soft writing material.

Thus from the classical alphabet there sprang the Greek uncial script, the cursive script, and the minuscule, consciously adapted as a book-hand about A.D. 800, after which uncial quickly went out of use for books. The cursive scripts developed into the modern Greek minuscule. The capitals of modern Greek handwriting are partly borrowed from the Latin handwriting.

GREEK INSCRIPTIONS AND MANUSCRIPTS (Figs. 19.7–10, 12–27)

So many inscriptions have been discovered all over, and beyond (*see*, for instance, p. 266) the Hellenic world, that they can scarcely be counted: annals, codes of law, decrees, lists of citizens, accounts of moneys expended and received by temples, votive offerings, sepulchral inscriptions, lettering on vases, on coins, and so forth. They are of paramount importance for history in all its branches, and they form the subject of a special field of study, Greek epigraphy. Greek manuscripts, ancient and mediæval, numbering many thousands, form one of the main bases of modern civilization: Greek palæography deals with their study and deciphering.

B b

CONCLUSION

The Greek alphabet occupies a unique place in the history of writing. It transformed the consonantal Semitic script into a modern alphabet, and gave it symmetry and art. Through its direct and indirect descendants, the Etruscan and Latin alphabets (*see* the following chapters) on the one hand, and the Cyrillic alphabet (*see* below) on the other, it has become the progenitor of all the European alphabets. In the course of its long history it produced some other offshoots, which will be dealt with in this chapter.

BIBLIOGRAPHY

The many tens of thousands of Greek inscriptions are collected in *Corpus Inscriptionum Græcarum*, Berlin, 4 vols., 1825–77, and in its successor, *Inscriptiones Græcae*, Berlin, 14 vols., sub-divided into many parts, arranged geographically. Early inscriptions (prior to 403 B.C.) are collected in H. Röhl, *Imagines inscriptionum Græcarum Antiquissimarum*, etc., 3rd ed., Berlin, 1907.

Convenient selections are: Ch. Michel, *Recueil d'inscriptions grecques*, Brussels, 1900 (two supplements were issued in 1912 and 1927); Hicks and Hill, *Greek Historical Inscriptions*, 2nd ed., Oxford, 1901: this book has been superseded by M. N. Tod, *A Selection of Greek Historical Inscriptions*, vol. I, Oxford, 1933 (2nd ed., 1946), vol. II, 1948; *see* also W. Dittenberger, *Sylloge Inscriptionum Græcarum*, 4 vols., 3rd ed., Leipsic, 1915–24.

Photographic facsimiles: O. Kern, *Inscriptiones Græcæ*, Bonn, 1913, W. Wattenbach, *Scripturæ Græcæ specimina in usum scholarum*, 4th ed., Berlin, 1936.

ROBERTS, E. S. *Introduction to Greek Epigraphy*, Vol. 1, Cambridge 1887; Vol. II, with E. A. Gardner, *The Inscriptions of Attica*, Cambridge, 1905.

KIRCHHOFF, A. *Studien zur Geschichte des griechischen Alphabets*, 4th ed., Gütersloh, 1887.

KENYON, F. G. and BELL, H. I. *Greek Papyri in the British Museum*, London, 1893 ff.

KENYON, F. G. *The Palaeography of Greek Papyri*, Oxford, 1899.

GRENFELL, P. P., HUNT, A. S., BELL, H. I. and others, *The Oxyrhynchos Papyri*, London, 1898 ff.

WILCKEN, U. *Griechische Ostraka aus Ägypten und Nubien*, Leipsic-Berlin, 1899.

WESSELY, L. *Studien zur Paläographie und Papyruskunde*, Leipsic, 1902 ff.

THOMPSON, E. M. *Handbook of Greek and Latin Palæography*, 3rd ed., London, 1906; *An Introduction to Greek and Latin Palaeography*, Oxford, 1912.

VOGEL, M. and GARDTHAUSEN, V. *Die griechischen Schreiber des Mittelalters und der Renaissance*, Leipsic, 1909.

GARDTHAUSEN, V. *Ursprung und Entwicklung der griechisch-lateinischen Schrift*, Heidelberg, 1909; 'Die römischen Zahlzeichen,' *Germanisch-romanische Monatsschrift*, 1 (1909); *Griechische Paläographie*, 2nd ed., Leipsic, 1911–3.

SCHUBART, W. *Papyri Graecae Berolinenses*, Bonn, 1911; *Einführung in die Papyruskunde*, Berlin, 1918; *Das Buch bei den Griechen und Rämern*, 2nd ed., Berlin and Leipsic, 1921; 'Griechische Paläographie', in Iwan von Müller-W. Otto, *Handbuch der Altertumswissenschaft*, Vol. 1, Munich, 1925; *Zeitstil und Gattungsstil in der griechischen Schrift*, Berlin-Leipsic, 1938; *Die Papyri als Zeugen antiker Kultur*, Berlin, 1938.

MITTEIS L. and WILCKEN, U. *Grundzüge und Chrestomathie der Papyruskunde*, Berlin-Leipsic, 1912. (Photographic reprint, 4 parts, Darmstadt, 1957–8.)

CHADWICK, H. M. *The Heroic Age*, Cambridge, 1912.

LEAF, W. *Troy*, London, 1912; *Homer and History*, London, 1915.

MILNE, J. G. *Theban Ostraca*, III, *Greek Texts*, Oxford, 1913.

TOD, M. N. 'The Progress of Greek Epigraphy', *J. Hellenic Studies*, 1914, 1928, 1931, 1933, 1935, 1937, etc.

LARFELD, W. 'Griechische Epigraphik,' in Iwan von Müller's *Handbuch der klassischen Altertumswissenschaft*, 3rd ed., Vol. 1, Munich, 1914.

WHIBLEY (ed.), *A Companion to Greek Studies*, Cambridge University Press, 3rd. ed., 1916: 'Books and Writing' by M. R. James (pp. 606–10); 'Epigraphy,' by E. S. Roberts and E. A. Gardner (pp. 687–705); *Palaeography*, by E. H. Minns (pp. 705–19).

VIERECK, P. *Ostraka aus Brüssel und Berlin*, Berlin-Leipsic, 1922; *Griechische und griechisch-demotische Ostraka aus der Universitäts- und Landesbibliothek zu Strassburg in Elsass*, Berlin, 1923.

WALLACE, W. 'Index of Greek Ligatures and Contractions,' *J. Hellenic Studies*, 1923.

HILLER VON GÄRTRINGEN, F. 'Griechische Epigraphik,' in Gercke-Norden, *Einleitung in die Altertumswissenschaft*, vol. I, Berlin, 1924.

SCHISSEL VON FLESCHENBERG, O. *Kataloge griechischer Handschriften*, Graz, 1924.

BURY, J. B. 'The Alphabet', in *Cambridge Ancient History*, vol. IV (pp. 469–71), Cambridge, 1926.

SCHOLDERER, V. *Greek Printing Types*, London, 1927.

PREISENDANZ, K. *Papyri graecae magicae*, Leipsic-Berlin, 1928 ff; *Papyrusfunde und Papyrusforschung*, Leipsic, 1933.

CALDERINI, A. *Papiri milanesi*, Milan, 1928; *Manuale di papirologia antica greca e moderna*, Milan, 1938 (with bibliography).

DE' CAVALIERI, P. F. and LIETZMANN, J. *Specimina codicum graecorum Vaticanorum*, 2nd. ed., Bonn, 1929.

TAIT, J. G. *Greek Ostraca in the Bodleian Library at Oxford and various other Collections*, London, 1930.

DÖLGER, F. *Facsimiles byzantinischer Kaiserurkunden*, Munich, 1931.

EDGAR, C. C., BOAK, A. E. R., WINTER, J. G. and others, *Michigan Papyri*, Ann Arbor, 1931 ff.

HUNT, A. S., EDGAR, C. C. *Select Papyri*, London, 1932 ff.

WINTER, J. G. *Life and Letters in the Papyri*, Ann Arbor, 1933.

AMUNDSEN, L. *Ostraca Osloensia*, Oslo, 1933; *Greek Ostraca in the University of Michigan Collection*, Ann Arbor, 1935.

LAKE, K. and S. *Monumenta Palaeographica Vetera. Dated Greek Minuscule Manuscripts to the Year 1200*, Boston (Mass.), 1934–40.

LEWIS, N. *L'industrie du papyrus dans l'Egypte gréco-romaine*, Paris, 1934.

MILNE, H. J. M. *Greek Shorthand Manuals*, London 1934.

SIGALAS, A. Ἱστορία τῆς Ἑλληνικῆς Γραφῆς, Thessaloniki, 1934.

Les ostraca de la Collection Charl.-Edw. Wilbour au Musée de Brooklyn, New York, 1935.

WILCKEN, U. *Urkunden der Ptolemäerzeit*, Berlin-Leipsic, 1937 ff.

'Fifty years of Papyrology,' *Actes de Vᵉ Congrès International de Papyrologie*, Bruxelles, 1938, pp. 1–11.

ADLER, E. N., TAIT, J. G. and HEICHELHEIM, F. M. *The Adler Papyri*, Oxford, 1939.

REHM, A. 'Die Zeit der Entdeckung des Alphabets durch die Griechen', in OTTO, W. *Handbuch der Archäologie*, 1, Munich, 1939.

VAN GRONINGEN, B. A. *Short Manual of Greek Palæography*, Leyden, 1940.

PEREMANS, W. and VERGOTE, J. *Papyrologisch Handboek*, Louvain, 1942.

DAVID, M. and VAN GRONINGEN, B. A. *Papyrological Primer*, Leyden, 1946.

DAVID, M., VAN GRONINGEN, B. A. and KIESSLING, E. *Berichtigungsliste der griechischen Papyrusurkunden aus Ägypten*, 2 parts, Leiden, 1956 and 1958.

MIKHAILOV, G. *Inscriptiones Graecae in Bulgaria repertae*, Sofia, 1956.

KLAFFENBACH, G. *Griechische Epigraphik*, Göttingen, 1957; *Varia Epigraphica*, Berlin, 1958.

TCHERIKOVER, V. A. *Corpus papyrorum Judaicarum*, Vol. I, Cambridge, Mass., & Oxford, 1957; Vol. II (ed. by A. Fuks), *ib.*, 1960.

Mythological Papyri, 2 parts, Toronto, 1957.

PAAP, A. H. R. E. *Nomina Sacra in the Greek Papyri*, Leiden, 1959.

BOAK, A. E. R. and YOUTIC, H. C. (ed.), *Archive of Aurelius Isidorus*, Ann Arbor, 1960.

STARR, C. G. *The Origins of Greek Civilization*, 1100–650 B.C., New York, 1961.

JEFFERY, L. H. *The Local Scripts of Archaic Greece*, Oxford, 1961.

BLEGEN, C. W., GUTHRIE, W. K. C., STUBBINGS, F. H. and COOK, J. M. in *Cambridge Ancient History*, Vols. I & II, rev. ed., Cambridge, 1961 ff.

DIRINGER, D. 'Greek Scripts', *Studium Generale*, Heidelberg, 1967.

PFOHL, *Griechische Inschriften*, Munich, 1965; *Greek Poems on Stones*, Leiden, 1967; *Monument und Epigramm*, Nurenberg, 1964; Griechische Inschriften als Zeugnisse des privaten und öffentlichen Lebens, Munich, 1966.

ASIANIC ALPHABETS
(Figs. 19.28–29)

In passing to the examination of the direct offshoots of the Greek alphabet, I propose in the first place to deal briefly with a group of interesting alphabets which in one way or another are connected with Greek writing, although their origin is still to some extent uncertain. The term Asianic, applied to this group, is purely geographical, and comprises a number of alphabets mainly employed by the non-Hellenic peoples of western Asia Minor in the last centuries of the first half, and the first centuries of the second half of the first millennium B.C. The following scripts belong to this group:

LYCIAN ALPHABET

The Lycians were an ancient people mentioned, as *Luku* or *Ruku*, in Egyptian monuments of the thirteenth century B.C. The indigenous term was *Trmmli, Trkhmli*, in Greek *Termilai* or *Tremilai* (Herodotus I, 173): according to Greek tradition they migrated from the island of Crete. However that may be, they were a non-Indo-European people, whose speech belonged perhaps to the family of the South Caucasian languages. They inhabited the south-western part of Asia Minor.

About 150 inscriptions (Figs. 19.28–29) dating from the fifth and fourth centuries B.C. and some coins belonging to the same period are extant. The chief inscription, on a pillar discovered at Xanthos, is still undeciphered. The other inscriptions, including a few short Græco-Lycian bilingual documents, are of a funerary nature. The Lycian alphabet (Fig. 19.28) is certainly of Greek origin; but some other influences may be admitted (Fig. 19.29c).

PHRYGIAN ALPHABET

The Phrygians, who in the eighth century B.C. had the strongest kingdom of Asia Minor, situated to the west of the river Halys were, according to Herodotus and Strabo, of Thracian origin. What we know about the Phrygian language—and it is very little—supports this Greek tradition.

Not many Phrygian inscriptions, and those very short, have been discovered. Some of them belonging to the seventh–sixth centuries B.C. are written in an earlier dialect and in an indigenous alphabet of Greek origin (Fig. 19.28). Recently, eighth-century (B.C.) inscriptions have come to light.

The neo-Phrygian inscriptions of the Roman period are written in Greek script.

PAMPHYLIAN ALPHABET

Pamphylia, situated on the low-lying coast of Asia Minor, between Lycia and Cilicia, was inhabited by a mixture of peoples who pushed their way in from outside.

The Pamphylians employed an alphabet (Fig. 19.28) of Greek origin; only one long inscription and some coins are extant. At a later period the Pamphylians used a mixed Greek-Aramaic script.

LYDIAN ALPHABET

The state of Lydia, occupying the west coast of Asia Minor, between Mysia in the north and Caria in the south, was the strongest in Asia Minor after the fall of the Phrygian kingdom, particularly during the seventh and sixth centuries B.C. Crœsus, the last and most renowned Lydian king, fell into the hands of Cyrus, king of Persia, in 546 B.C.

The Lydians had an ancient civilization. Whence they may have come cannot as yet be determined. Many modern scholars have found affinities between the Lydians and the Etruscans, but perhaps the only affinity between the Lydian and the Etruscan languages is the fact that both are more or less still undeciphered. It seems, however, that Lydian was a non-Indo-European speech, although it had some grammatical affinities with the Indo-European languages.

According to Albright, it may be regarded (like Lycian) as a younger cognate of the 'Asianic' family, to which also Armenian belongs (for Armenian see, however, p. 250).

Over fifty Lydian inscriptions have been discovered; thirty-six of them have been found in the course of the American excavations of 1910-3 at Sardes (the indigenous term was Sfart), the ancient capital of Lydia. The datable inscriptions belong to the fourth century B.C., but others may belong to the fifth century or perhaps earlier. According to Strabo (xiv, 4, 17), Lydian was spoken for some centuries more. The inscriptions are mostly funerary. What is known of Lydian is based on a long Lydio-Aramaic bilingual inscription belonging to the middle of the fifth century or to the beginning or the middle of the fourth century B.C. Another Lydio-Aramaic inscription was discovered in 1911 in Falaka (Kaystros Valley). There are also two short Lydio-Greek bilingual inscriptions.

The Lydian alphabet (Fig. 19.28) contained twenty-six letters. It was an offshoot of the Greek, but there were additional symbols, partly of uncertain (probably local) origin, for Lydian sounds—some are still uncertain—which did not exist in Greek. It is interesting to find in the Lydian alphabet as the sign for *f* a letter shaped like the modern numeral 8, which appears also in the Etruscan alphabet. Lydian was written usually from right to left.

CARIAN SCRIPT

The historical Caria was situated on the west coast of Asia Minor to the south of Lydia and to the east of Lycia, but the Carians were believed by the ancients to have occupied at one time many of the Aegean islands and even the mainland of Greece itself.

Very little is known about their ethnic and linguistic affinities, but it seems that the Greek tradition was right in regarding them as immigrants from the Aegean islands. Their language was certainly a non-Indo-European speech; it seems to have had some affinities with Lycian. On the other hand, it is probable that they were a mixed people; they were also called, or at least a part of them, Leleges, and a section of them called Cauni had a particular dialect.

There are about eighty short Carian inscriptions extant—the earliest belonging to the middle of the seventh century B.C., and consisting in great part of names of Carian mercenaries, scratched upon Egyptian monuments on the banks of the Upper Nile. There are also three Egyptian-Carian bilingual inscriptions. The Carian script (Fig. 19.28) seems to have been based on the Greek alphabet, but some of its signs were apparently syllabic and borrowed from the Cretan and Cypriote scripts (Fig. 19.29); it contained also other elements of unknown, probably local, origin.

CONCLUSION

Summarizing this short section on the Asianic scripts, we deduce that the first three alphabets (Lycian, Phrygian and Pamphylian) were directly dependent on the Greek, while the two last were only in part linked—the Lydian more so and the Carian less— with the Greek alphabet. The marvellous adaptations to the various languages point to initiative and ingenuity. We do not know whether there were other Asianic scripts. Some scholars mention a Mysian, a Cilician and a Cappadocian alphabet, but no sufficient evidence is available. Some inscriptions extant are written in mixed scripts, others in scripts not yet deciphered.

BIBLIOGRAPHY

SAYCE, A. H. 'The Carian Language and Inscriptions,' *Trans. Soc. Bibl. Archaeol.*, 1885; 'The languages of Asia Minor,' *Anatolian Studies presented to Sir W. M. Ramsay*,' 1923; 'The Decipherment of the Lydian Language, *Amer. J. Philol.*, 1925; 'The New Neo-Phrygian Texts,' *J. Hellenic Studies*, 1926.
KRETSCHMER, P. *Einleit. in die Gesch. der griechischen Sprache*, Göttingen, 1896.
BURESCH, K. *Aus Lydien*, Leipsic, 1898.

KALINKA, E. *Tituli Lyciae lingua lycia conscripti. Tituli Asiæ Minoris*, Vol. I, Vienna, 1901.

KLUGE, T. *Die Lykier: ihre Geschichte und ihre Inschriften*, Leipsic, 1910.

FRASER, J. 'Phrygian Studies, I. Language,' *Trans. Camb. Philol. Soc.*, 1913; 'The Lydian Language,' *Anatolian Studies etc.*, 1923.

SUNDWALL, J. 'Zu den karischen Inschriften,' etc., *Klio*, 1915.

Lydian Inscriptions ('Sardis,' Vol. VI), Part I (by E. Littmann) and Part II (by W. H. Buckler), Leyden, 1916 and 1924.

DANIELSSON, O. A. *Zu den lydischen Inschriften*, Uppsala, 1918.

ARKWRIGHT, W. 'Lycian Epitaphs,' *Anatolian Studies*, etc., 1923.

BACHOFEN, J. *Das lykische Volk*, etc., Fribourg, 1924.

AUTRAN, C. 'Les Langues de l'Asie Antérieure ancienne,' *Les Langues du Monde*, 1924.

STURTEVANT, E. H. 'Remarks on the Lydian Inscriptions,' *Language*, 1925.

BORK, F. *Skizze des Lykischen*, Königsberg-Leipsic, 1926; 'Die Schrift der Karier,' *Archiv für Schreib- und Buchwesen*, 1930.

CALDER, W. M. and others, *Monumenta Asiæ Minoris antique*, Manchester, 1928.

SOMMER, F. and KAHLE, P. in *Kleinasiatische Forschungen*, 1930.

FRIEDRICH, J. *Kleinasiatische Sprachdenkmäler*, Berlin 1932.

GŒTZE, A. *Kleinasien* (Otto, W. *Handbuch der Altertumswissenschaft*), Munich, 1933.

BRANDENSTEIN, W. 'Karische Sprache,' and 'Kleinasiatische Ursprachen,' in Pauly-Wissowa, *Real-Encyclopädie*, Suppl. VI, 1935.

MENTZ, A. 'Zu den lydischen Inschriften,' *Glotta*, 1942.

BITTEL, K. *Kleinasiatische Studien*, Istanbul, 1942.

VETTER, E. *Zu den lydischen Inschriften*, Vienna, 1959.

HEUBECK, A. *Lydiaka. Untersuchungen zu Schrift*, etc. *der Lyder*, Erlangen, 1959.

HOUWINK TEN CATE, PH. H. J. *The Luwian Population Groups of Lycia and Cilicia Aspera during the Hellenistic Period*, Leiden, 1961.

COPTIC ALPHABET
(Figs. 19.30–36)

There was one other non-European descendant of the Greek alphabet, and that the only one in Africa, the Coptic script. The term 'Copt' (from Arabic *qopt, qubt, qibt*, a corruption from Greek *Aigyptios-gyptios*) is employed nowadays to indicate the indigenous population of Egypt, which, after the Arabic conquest of that country, in A.D. 641, maintained their Christian monophysite faith, the 'Coptic' religion, and continued to use the 'Coptic' speech (that is the last stage of the Egyptian language) as their spoken and written language until the thirteenth century A.D. (although it was still employed, but very rarely, until the seventeenth century), and later as the liturgical language of the Coptic Church, when Arabic had been adopted as the speech of everyday life. Spoken Coptic, called now *Zēnīyah*, has survived in Christian villages of Upper Egypt; the existence of a living Coptic speech was unknown until the Czech scholar W. Vycichl described it in 1936 (as being spoken in the village Zēnīyah).

The earliest Coptic documents and inscriptions may be attributed to the fourth, perhaps even to the third century A.D., but the earliest manuscripts which can be definitely dated belong to the fifth century A.D. There were five main Coptic dialects the more important of them being the Saʿidic or Sahidic dialect of southern or Upper Egypt, around the old Egyptian capital Thebes (now Luxor); and the Bohairic dialect of Lower Egypt; this latter (since Alexandria was the seat of the Coptic Patriarch) became the Coptic liturgical language, and ultimately drove out the other dialects. Fayyûmic (spoken in the Fayyûm), Akhmîmic (spoken in Akhmîm, Upper Egypt), and Assiûtic (spoken in Assiût, also Upper Egypt) or Subakhmîmic, were the other main dialects; there was also a number of mixed dialects.

Coptic was essentially the non-cultivated speech of Egypt, for the Egyptian 'aristocracy' was thoroughly Hellenized.

The early Egyptian Christians came from the lower classes and it was only after the fourth century that Christianity became more firmly established, and civilization passed gradually into the hands of the Christian Egyptians; even then pagan culture did not disappear, until towards the end of the fifth century. As Coptic was mainly the speech of rural districts, it was more easily able to survive the Arab conquest.

Coptic has a large admixture of Greek elements, especially in all that belongs to Christian doctrine, life and worship.

The Coptic alphabet (Fig. 19.30) consisted of thirty-two letters, twenty-five borrowed from the Greek uncial script, and seven taken over from a more cursive variety of the demotic script (*see* part 1, chapter 2) to express sounds which did not exist in Greek. Needless to say, the development of the Coptic script was independent of the Greek.

BIBLIOGRAPHY

HYVERNAT, H. *Album de paléographie copte*, Paris and Rome, 1888; *Check List of Coptic MSS. in the Pierpont Morgan Library*, New York, 1919.

CRUM, W. E. *Coptic Ostraca*, London, 1902; *Catalogue of the Coptic MSS. in the John Rylands Library*, Manchester, 1909; *New Coptic Manuscripts*, etc., Manchester, 1920; *Short Texts from Coptic Ostraca and Papyri*, London, 1921; *A Coptic Dictionary*, Oxford, 1939.

MALLON, A. *Grammaire copte*, Beyrouth, 1907.

BUDGE, E. A. W. *Miscellaneous Coptic Texts in the Dialect of Upper Egypt*, London, 1915.

SPIEGELBERG, W. *Koptisches Handwörterbuch*, Heidelberg, 1921.

DÉVAND, E. *Études d'étymologie copte*, Fribourg, 1923.

WHITE, H. G. E. *New Coptic Texts*, etc., New York, 1926.

TILL, W. *Achmîmisch-koptische Grammatik*, Leipsic, 1928; *Koptische Dialekt-grammatik*, etc., Munich, 1931; 'Koptische Briefe,' *Wiener Zeitschr. für die Kunde des Morgenl.*, 1940, etc.

VAN LANTSCHOOT, A. *Recueil des Colophons des manuscrits chrétiens d'Egypte*. Tome I. *Les Colophons coptes des manuscrits sahidiques*, Louvain, 1929; Tome II. *Les Colophons monolingues des manuscrits bohairiques*.

SIMON, J. 'Repertoire des bibliothèques publiques et priv. conten. des mss. coptes,' *Le Muséon*, 1931.

MURRAY, M. A. and PILCHER, D. *A Coptic Reading Book for Beginners*, London, 1933.

CHAÎNE, M. *Eléments de grammaire dialectale Copte*, Paris, 1933; *Les dialectes coptes Assioutiques*, Paris, 1934.

STEGEMANN, V. 'Koptische Zaubertexte,' *Sitzungsb. der Heidelb. Akad.*, 1934.

GEHMAN, H. S. 'The Garrett Sahidic Manuscript of St. Luke,' *J. Amer. Orient. Soc.*, 1935.

HEUSER, G. *Die Kopten*, Heidelberg, 1938.

WORRELL, W. H. *Coptic Texts in the University of Michigan Collections*, Ann Arbor, 1942; *A Short Account of the Copts*, Ann Arbor, 1945.

KAMMERER, W. 'A Coptic Bibliography,' *Traditio*, New York, 1944.

HOUGHTON, H. P. *The Coptic Verb. Bohairic dialect*, 2nd rev. edition, Leyden, 1959.

Nubian Character

The ancient Nubians, occupying the territory south of Egypt, adopted the Coptic script, but in adapting it to their own language they were compelled to borrow from the cursive Meroitic writing (*see* pp. 140 f.) three signs for sounds which could not be expressed by Coptic letters. The extant fragments of Christian Nubian manuscripts belong to the tenth–eleventh century A.D.; some are in the British Museum, others in Berlin.

Recently new discoveries of MSS. have been made.

BIBLIOGRAPHY

SCHMIDT and SCHÄFER, 'Die ersten Bruchstücke christlicher Litteratur in altnubischer Sprache,' *Sitzungsb. der Preuss. Akad. der Wissensch.*, Berlin, 1906; 'Die altnubischen christlichen Handschriften der K. Bibliothek zu Berlin,' the same journal, 1907.

BUDGE, A. E. W. *Texts relating to S. Mena of Egypt*, etc., London, 1909.

GRIFFITH, F. LL. *The Nubian Texts of the Christian Period*, Berlin, 1913; *Christian Documents from Nubia*, London, 1928.

ZYHLARZ, E. *Grundzüge der nubischen Grammatik im christlichen Frühmittelalter*, Leipsic, 1928; 'Neue Sprachdenkmäler des Altnubischen,' *Studies presented to F. Ll. Griffith*, London, 1932.

STEINDORFF, G. 'Nubien, die Nubier,' etc., *Studies presented* etc., London, 1932.

MONNERET DE VILLARD, U. *Storia della Nubia cristiana*, Rome, 1938.

MESSAPIAN ALPHABET
(Figs. 19.37; 20.5)

Apart from the Etruscan (*see* next chapter), the Messapic or Messapian was the earliest European offshoot of the Greek alphabet.

The Messapii (*Messapioi* in Herodotus, vii, 170) were an ancient tribe who inhabited in pre-Roman times the south Italian region corresponding roughly to the present Apulia, that is the 'heel' of Italy. According to tradition, confirmed by the names of places and tribes and other sources, they immigrated from the opposite shore of the Adriatic Sea, that is from the Illyrian coast. They seem, indeed, to have belonged to the Illyrian linguistic family and to have been related to the Piceni and the Veneti (*see* pp. 390 f.).

About 200 Messapic inscriptions have come to light. They are mainly fragmentary or very short. A few only contain more than one line; the longest of them, discovered at Brindisi, contains fifteen lines, and belongs to the third century B.C. The majority of the inscriptions belong to the second century B.C., but a few may be dated in the first century B.C., while some are earlier than the fourth century B.C., and one is even attributed by some scholars to the eighth century B.C. The inscriptions fall into two groups; the southern group consists of pure Messapian documents found in the modern provinces of Lecce, Taranto and Brindisi. Less homogeneous and not purely Messapian is the northern group, consisting of inscriptions discovered in the territory to the north as far as Lucera in the province of Foggia and attributed to mixed Messapian-Apulian tribes.

While there is no doubt that the Messapian alphabet (Fig. 20.5) was of Greek origin, there is some disagreement regarding the Greek variety from which it descended. According to some scholars, it was borrowed from the Tarentine alphabet (Tarentum, the modern Taranto, was perhaps the earliest Greek colony in Magna Græcia), belonging to the Ionic branch of the eastern Greek groups, as is shown by the shape of the letters *kh* and *ps* (which are amongst the main criteria for the classification of the Greek alphabets). According to other scholars, however, the Messapian alphabet was connected with that of Locri; and Rhys Carpenter suggests (*Amer. J. Archæol.*, 1945, pp. 455–6) that the Epizephyrian Locri, an important Greek colony in Messapian territory, and Syracuse, the great ancient Corinthian colony in Sicily, which transmitted its alphabet to other neighbouring Greek colonies, both derived their alphabets from the Ozolian Locrians. These in their turn had probably borrowed their script from 'that nearby centre of enlightenment, Delphi.'

The solution of the problem is not easy, especially since the exact phonetic value of some Messapian letters is still uncertain.

BIBLIOGRAPHY

MAGIULLI and DUCA DI CASTROMEDIANO, *Le iscrizioni messapiche raccolte*, Lecce, 1871.
DROOP, I. P. in *Ann. Brit. Schools of Athens*, 1905-6.
RIBEZZO, F. *La lingua degli antichi Messapii*, Naples, 1907; 'Corpus Inscriptionum Messapicarum,' *Rivista Indo-greco-italica*, VI, 1922 onwards.
KRETSCHMER, P. in *Glotta*, 30 (1943), pp. 161 ff.

GOTHIC ALPHABET
(Fig. 19.38)

(This is quite different from the 'Gothic script,' a variety of the Latin alphabet; *see* further on.)

The Goths, or rather Visigoths, or Western Goths, were a Germanic people who played an important part in the European history of the fourth and fifth centuries A.D. In the fourth century A.D. they lived in what is now Bulgaria. They were the first Germanic people to be converted to Christianity.

The Gothic bishop Wulfila (or Ulfilas), who lived in the fourth century and died in 381 or 383, translated the Bible into Gothic, 'with the exception of the Books of Kings which he omitted, because they are a mere narrative of military exploits and the Gothic tribes were especially fond of war.' Of Wulfila's translation some fragments are extant in manuscripts of the fifth and sixth centuries, the most important being the *Codex Argenteus* (Fig. 19.38*b*, *c*), preserved at Uppsala in Sweden (187 pages, written in silver and gold on purple-red parchment). They preserve what is by several centuries the oldest specimen of Germanic speech. However, this early Gothic civilization with its distinctive language and script had not the slightest influence on the subsequent Germanic culture.

Wulfila employed an alphabet—generally known as Gothic, or Mœso-Gothic—invented by himself, which consisted of twenty-seven letters (Fig. 19.38*a*); some nineteen or twenty signs were taken over from the Greek uncial script, some five or six (modified in part) from the Latin alphabet, and two letters seem either to have been borrowed from the Runes (*see* chapter 21) or freely invented.

Although the greater part of the Gothic symbols are identical in form and phonetic value with the Greek uncial letters or with the Latin characters, there are, as stated, some which are different either in shape or in phonetic value, but it is not easy to determine their origin. It is obviously not always possible to know everything behind the achievements of great men like Wulfila.

There was also a Gothic cursive script for everyday use, as is shown by a document in the National Library of Naples and by an alphabet written on a manuscript in the Vienna National Library.

BIBLIOGRAPHY

MEYER, L. *Die gotische Sprache*, Berlin, 1869.

LUFT, W. *Studien zu den ältesten germanischen Alphabeten*, Gütersloh, 1898.

UHLENBECK, C. C. *Kurzgefasstes etymologisches Wärterbuch der gotischen Sprache*, 2nd ed., Amsterdam, 1900; *Bemerkungen zum gotischen Wörtschatz*, Halle, 1905.

MENSEL, E. H. in *Modern Philology*, 1904.

WRIGHT, J. *Grammar of the Gothic Language*, Oxford, 1910; 2nd ed., Oxford, 1955.

VON FRIESEN, O. in J. Hoops, *Reallexikon der germanischen Altertumskunde*, II, 1913–15; *Om Codex Argenteus*, Uppsala, 1928; and A. Grape, *Introduction to Codex Argenteus Upsaliensis* (A facsimile reproduction), Uppsala, 1928.

STREITBERG, W. *Die gotische Bibel* etc., 2nd ed., Heidelberg, 1919–28.

STAMM F. L. and HEYNE, M. *Ulfilas oder die uns erhaltenen Denkmäler der gotischen Sprache*, 14th ed., Paderborn, 1920.

JELLINEK, M. H. *Geschichte der gotischen Sprache*, Berlin and Leipsic, 1926.

KIECKERS, E. *Handbuch der vergleichenden gotischen Grammatik*, Munich, 1928.

HERMANN, E. in *Nachrichten der gelehrten Gesellschaft zu Göttingen*, 1930.

KRISTENSEN, H. K. *Lille vejledning i laesning af gotisk skrift*, Lund, 1956.

EARLY SLAVONIC ALPHABETS
(Figs. 19.39–40)

Much more important than the preceding alphabets were the two early Slavonic alphabets, the Cyrillic and the Glagolitic.

The name 'Old Slavonic' is applied to the literary language which was employed by the brothers St. Cyril (the ecclesiastical name of Constantine, the more learned and literary of the two brothers), b. *c.* 826, d. 869, and St. Methodius, b. *c.* 815, d. 885, and their disciples. The brothers were Greeks from Salonica, and they became the Apostles of the Southern Slavs, whom they converted to Christianity. Other terms are also used to denote the language: it is known as Old Church Slavonic or Old Bulgarian or Pannonian Slavonic, and in the indigenous documents of the ninth-tenth centuries A.D. simply as *slovenskij jezyku*, the 'Slovene' or Slavonic language, but none of these terms is exact; they indicate either too much or too little. Thus 'Old Slavonic' would include also the other languages spoken by Slavonic peoples in ancient times; 'Ecclesiastical Slavonic,' or 'Old Church Slavonic,' would not include profane literature and vulgar speech; 'Pannonian Slavonic' would be too restricted in place, and 'Old Bulgarian' would indicate not a Slavonic speech, but a Turkic language, since the early Bulgarians were a Turki tribe who at the end of the seventh century A.D. immigrated into the Slavonic country called nowadays Bulgaria. At the same time each term describes to a certain extent the language in question, which was the speech of early Slavonic peoples, living approximately near Salonica, in Macedonia, and the neighbouring regions; the language, while it provided a liturgical vehicle for the early Slavonic Church, yet belonged to the group which nowadays includes the Bulgarian language. It is now a dead language, except as still read in the churches.

The earliest dated Old Slavonic documents (Fig. 19.44) belong to the end of the tenth and to the eleventh centuries A.D. There is a funerary inscription of 993. According to Prof. M. N. Tikhomirov (*see* the article 'Origins of Christianity in Russia,' *History*, 1959), the only extant Russian document of the tenth century is an inscribed jar of *c.* 900–950, discovered in Gnezdovo, near Smolensk; it 'is written in Cyrillic characters and resembles the monuments of Bulgarian epigraphy of the same period.' All the other early documents are religious manuscripts: *see* further on.

The two alphabets, the Cyrillic and the Glagolitic, employed for the early Slavonic language, differed widely in the form of their letters and in the history of their development, and partly also in the number of the letters, but they were alike in representing adequately the many sounds of the Slavonic language and were richer than any other European alphabet.

ORIGIN OF CYRILLIC AND GLAGOLITIC ALPHABETS

The origin of the two scripts is still uncertain; there is no doubt, however, that the Cyrillic alphabet was based, as already mentioned, on the Greek uncial script of the ninth century, and that the Glagolitic alphabet was in some way connected with the Cyrillic. According to Slavonic chronicles of the ninth century, the pagan Slavs made divinations by means of scratches and notches. Then, on becoming Christians, they employed for their Slavonic tongue Greek and Latin letters, without any proper rules, although they could not write words such as *zhivot*, *zelo*, *tserkov*, and so forth. 'But then God, loving the human race, had pity on the Slavs and sent them St. Constantine, the philosopher, called Cyril, a just and true man, who made for them an alphabet of thirty-eight letters, of which some were after the Greek style, and some after the Slavonic tongue.'

The early tradition, however, in attributing to Cyril the invention of an early Slavonic writing, does not indicate whether it was the Cyrillic or the Glagolitic. The term 'Cyrillic' given to one of the two scripts, would solve at least the problem of the Cyrillic, but it cannot be excluded that the attribution of this script to Cyril was made at a later period, after the Glagolitic was discontinued, and Cyrillic became the only writing employed for the Slavonic orthodox liturgy.

Modern theories, while agreeing that the Cyrillic alphabet was based on the Greek (Figs. 19.39-40), have suggested different origins for the Glagolitic. Various scripts have been successively propounded as its prototype, among them some various eastern alphabets, for instance Hebrew, Phœnician, Samaritan, Ethiopic, Armenian or Georgian, or western scripts, such as an indigenous Albanian alphabet; and more particularly the Greek cursive hand—according to the opinions of Taylor and Jagić— or a Latin cursive—according to Wessely—or else an early Slavonic runic script. According to the most common theory, Cyril invented the Glagolitic alphabet on the basis of a Greek cursive script in use in the ninth–tenth centuries A.D., while the 'Cyrillic' alphabet was created later.

According to G. Vernadsky, 'Constantine did not invent the Glagolitic alphabet, consequently the alphabet *he* invented must have been the Cyrillic.' 'It may be argued that, while inventing the Cyrillic for general use, Constantine kept using the Glagolitic as a kind of cryptic script for confidential messages, initiating into its use only the most trustworthy of his disciples. Later, after Constantine's death, secrecy may have lifted and the Glagolitic may have been used together with the Cyrillic or, in some regions, even preferred to it.' On the whole, Vernadsky prefers to accept, 'with certain reservations and to a certain extent,' N. K. Nikolsky's theory that the 'Russian characters' mentioned in Constantine's *Life* as pre-existing to the script invented by St. Cyril, were the Glagolitic characters. On the other hand, he does not exclude the following possibility: 'It may be argued that Constantine did not accept the "Russian characters" as he found them but revised and adapted them more closely to the needs of the Slavic language.' 'Such revision and adaptation may have been called his invention. In such a case, Constantine may still be considered the inventor of the Glagolitic alphabet, which would refer the invention of the Cyrillic to Methodius' disciples.'

As to the origin of the letters, in Vernadsky's view, 'a certain similarity between the Armenian and Georgian alphabets on the one hand and the Glagolitic alphabet on the other cannot be denied.' (*See* also M. Gaster, *Ilchester Lectures on Græco-Slavonic Literature*, London, 1887); such similarity, however, is categorically denied by Professor E. H. Minns. His view is that Constantine invented both the Glagolitic and Cyrillic alphabets; he rightly points out ('Saint Cyril Really knew Hebrew,' in *Mélanges publiés en l'honneur de M. Paul Boyer*, Paris, 1925) that 'No two men setting out to reduce the multitudinous sounds of Slavonic to writing would have hit on systems so nearly identical in everything but the shapes of the letters and the numerical values'; and that 'The general impression of Glagolitic is singularly unlike any sort of cursive Greek.' After having proved that Cyril took over from the Hebrew alphabet two letters (*tsade* and *shin*) and transformed them into three Slavonic letters adopting them for both alphabets, the Cyrillic and the Glagolitic, for the sounds *ts*, *tch* and *sh*, which do not exist in Greek, and for which therefore the Greek alphabet had no letters, he decides 'to regard both alphabets as the conscious creations of the same mind.' 'Cyril first made Cyrillic, using the natural basis of uncial Greek as described above and intending his creation for the benefit of Slavs about Salonica. Afterwards when sent on a mission into a land where Greek influence was struggling with Latin he transformed the Greek letters to make them less suspect in Latin eyes.' 'At the same time one or two signs were added or omitted in accordance perhaps with the phonetics of the dialect to which Cyril was transferring his work,' Professor Minns therefore concludes: 'We can put Cyril side by side with Mesrob as having invented two alphabets quite different in form but closely allied in system. Both scholars used the same method of working upon a pre-existing basis by differentiation, borrowing and invention.' Even if one does not agree in all the details, there is no doubt that Professor Minns is right in opposing the current theories which minimized the part consciously played by individuals in the formation of new alphabets.

CYRILLIC ALPHABET

This consisted of forty-three letters (Figs. 19.39–51), which are simpler than the Glagolitic signs. There is no doubt that the Greek uncial alphabet of the ninth century A.D. is the prototype of the Cyrillic; the greater number of the letters are identical in form and in the phonetic and numerical values. But we have to bear in mind that the phonetic values of the Cyrillic letters most probably represent the phonetic values of the Greek language as pronounced in the region of Salonica in the ninth century A.D. This may be exemplified by the Greek letter *b*, which was pronounced *v*. Thus, an additional letter was required to represent the Slavonic sound *b*. The order of the Cyrillic letters is a little different and some letters have retained their numerical value only.

The richness of Slavonic sounds, however, involved the addition of many signs to represent sounds not existent in the Greek speech, for which the Greek naturally had no letters. The origins of these additional signs are in some instances apparently clear, in others uncertain. Some letters indeed, for instance the Cyrillic *b* and *zh*, were probably modifications of other Greek letters, the nasal vowel-sounds *a* and *e* (*ǫ*, *ę*) were perhaps formed from the letter *a*. Some other Cyrillic letters, 'mostly it appears subsequent developments,' as Professor Minns has rightly suggested, are simple ligatures and combinations placed either in the logical order of the alphabet (for instance *sht*, the combination of *sh* and *t*, or *ou*, formed by the ligature of *o* and *u*) or towards the end of the alphabet, where *ya*, *ye*, *yo* are combinations of a short *y* with the vowel-signs *a*, *o*, and so forth. Some Cyrillic letters, on the other hand, appear to have been arbitrary inventions.

The Cyrillic alphabet developed, with slight modifications, in course of time into the national scripts of the Slavonic peoples who accepted their religion from Byzantium, that is the Bulgarians (nearly nine and a half million), the Russians (over 120 million), the White-Russians or Byelo-Russians (over 12 million), the Serbs (nearly 19 million), and the Ukrainians (nearly 47 million). It had been also adopted, but later discontinued, for the Roumanian language (Fig. 19.43 *f*), and through the Russian script by many other peoples (*see* below), such as the Zyryans or Syryans (now called Komi), a people of north-east Russia, numbering about 230,000, and speaking a Finno-Ugrian language; the Votyaks, a related people numbering about 560,000 and living in the Vyatka region; the Mordva (also called Mordvinians or Mordvins), numerically the most important Finno-Ugrian people of Soviet Russia (numbering over 2 million), who live in the middle Volga provinces and the neighbouring districts to the south and east; the Voguls in the Ural mountains; the Chuvash, an important tribe speaking a Turkic language, with strong Finno-Ugrian influences, who live mainly in the area lying between the right bank of the Sura and the Volga; they constitute an autonomous republic in the U.S.S.R.; and the Ossetes, numbering about 370,000 people, in the central Caucasus, north of Tiflis; they speak an Iranian language and are descendants of the ancient Sarmatians and Alani; they employ also the Roman character.

On the whole, it may be said with regard to the scripts of the Slavonic peoples that (as in the case of the Arabic alphabet and of other offshoots of the Aramaic alphabet, *see* pp. 210 f., 237, etc.) the alphabets followed religion. Indeed, while the Russians, Ukrainians, Bulgarians and Serbs accepted the Cyrillic alphabet with the Greek orthodox religion, Roman Christianity brought with it the use of the Latin alphabet to the Slovenes, Croats, Czechs (about 6 million), Slovaks (about 3 million), Poles (about 30 million), Wends and Lusatians, the most interesting case being that of Serbo-Croatian, which in practice is a single speech, although it is written differently by the Orthodox Serbs and the Catholic Croats. The line of demarcation between the Eastern Church and the Western Church runs, thus, right through the Slavonic peoples; and, generally speaking, wherever the Church is Catholic, there the Roman alphabet is used (with the insignificant exception of the Croatian Glagolitic script); where the Church is orthodox, there the Cyrillic alphabet is used.

ADOPTION OF THE CYRILLIC ALPHABET FOR,
AND ITS ADAPTATION TO, NON-SLAVONIC LANGUAGES
(Figs. 19.47–51)

The adoption of the Cyrillic alphabet for, and its adaptation to, numerous non-Indo-European languages constitute a story in themselves, and cannot be dealt with extensively in the present book. Indeed, each new script offers new problems, and the space at my disposal is much too narrow. For the Cyrillic script employed for Turki or Turkish forms of speech, *see* also pp. 377 and 440.

Of particular interest is the way the Cyrillic alphabet was employed for Ossetic (probably, apart from Roumanian, the oldest non-Slavonic variety). Ossetic, an Iranian language, was first reduced to writing towards the close of the eighteenth century, when the Cyrillic Russian alphabet was employed with the addition of several letters to express sounds foreign to the Russian language. In the course of time, many Latin letters were adopted, and later the Roman character was mainly used.

The Cyrillic Ossetic alphabet consists of forty-three letters, including the following additions: the letter *æ*, to represent the short *a*; a modification of the Latin *h* to represent the *h*, and another modification of the same to express a sound similar to the Scottish *ch*; the *q* to represent a back palatal sound similar to the Semitic *qof*; a combination of the letters *d-z* and *d-s*, to represent the sounds *dz* or *ds*, and *dzh* or *dsh*, respectively. Other new letters have been created by the addition of diacritical marks inserted above the following letters *u* (*ü* = *w*), *k*, *p*, *t* (by the addition of the acute accent, the guttural endings are expressed), *c* (for the sound *c*) and *ch* (for a hard *ch*).

Here is a list of the most recent adaptations of the Russian alphabet, *i.e.*, during the last 25 years, or so.

Language or Dialect	Where spoken	Approx. No. of Speakers	No. of Letters of new Alphabet
INDO-EUROPEAN LINGUISTIC FAMILY			
Romance Languages			
1. Roumanian: Moldavian dialect	Moldavia (Bessarabia)	2,000,000	30
Iranian Languages			
2. Tajiki	Tajik S.S.R.	1,400,000	39
3. Kurdish	Armenian, Georgian, and Azerbaijan S.S.R., and in parts of Central Asia	50,000	39
4. Ossetic	Central and Southern Ossetic A.S.S.R.	370,000	43

Language or Dialect	Where spoken	Approx. No. of Speakers	No. of Letters of new Alphabet
	CAUCASIAN LINGUISTIC FAMILY		
Western Group			
5. Abkhasian	Abkhaz A.S.S.R.	70,000	58
6. Abasinian	Karachayev–Circassian Autonomous Region	20,000	73
7. Adigeh	Adigeh Autonomous Region	80,000	66
8. Kabardian–Circassian (Cherkessian)	Kabardino–Balkar A.S.S.R. and Karachayev–Circassian Autonomous Region	225,000	59
Eastern (or Checheno-Ingushian) Group			
9. Chechen	Checheno–Ingushian A.S.S.R.	420,000	49
10. Ingush	Checheno–Ingushian A.S.S.R.	100,000	46
Daghestan Group			
11. Avarian	Daghestan A.S.S.R. and Azerbaijan S.S.R.	260,000	51
12. Darghi	Daghestan A.S.S.R.	150,000	46
13. Lesghian	Daghestan A.S.S.R.	200,000	50
14. Lakh	Daghestan A.S.S.R.	60,000	55
15. Tabasaran	Daghestan A.S.S.R.	34,000	56
	FINNO–UGRIAN LINGUISTIC FAMILY		
Ugrian Group			
16. Vogul (Mansi)	Western Siberia	3,000	34
17. Ostyak (Khantian)	Western Siberia	15,000	44
Finnish Group			
18. Komi (Zyryan, Syryan)	Komi A.S.S.R.	230,000	35
19. Komi–Permian	Komi–Permian National District	150,000	35
20. Udmurt (Votyak)	Udmurt A.S.S.R.	560,000	37
21. Mari (Cheremiss)	Mari A.S.S.R.	480,000	36–37
22. Mordvine—Erzya	Mordvin A.S.S.R.	1,000,000	33
23. Mordvine—Moksha	Mordvin A.S.S.R.	1,000,000	33
Samoyed Group			
24. Nenets (Yurak)	Nenetsian, Yamalo-Nenetsian, Taimyr, and (in parts of) Khanty-Mansi National Districts	20,000	35
25. Selkup (Ostyako-Samoyed)	Nenetsian and Taimyr Nat. Districts	2,000	37

C C

Language or Dialect	Where spoken	Approx. No. of Speakers	No. of Letters of new Alphabet
TURCO-TATAR LINGUISTIC FAMILY			
Bulgaro-Chuvash Group			
26. Chuvash	Chuvash A.S.S.R.	1,450,000	37
South-Western or Turkmenian Group			
27. Turkmenian (Turkoman)	Turkmenian S.S.R.	1,000,000	38
28. Azerbaijani	Azerbaijan S.S.R.	2,820,000	33
North-Western or Kipchak Group			
29. Tatar	Tatar and Bashkir A.S.S.R.; Western Siberia; Barabinian Step; Astrakhan, Ryazan, Kyubishev, Gorki and Orenburg Districts	4,600,000	39
30. Bashkir	Bashkir A.S.S.R.	590,000	42
31. Kumyk	Daghestan A.S.S.R.	110,000	39
32. Kara-Kalpak	Kara-Kalpak A.S.S.R.	160,000	36
33. Nogai	Northern Caucasus	35,000	36
34. Kazakh	Kazakh S.S.R.	3,520,000	42
35. Kirghiz	Kirghiz S.S.R.	950,000	36
36. Altaic (Oirot)	Mountainous Altaian Autonomous District	40,000	37
37. Karachai	Karachai-Circassian Autonomous District	70,000	38
38. Balkar	Kabardino-Balkarian A.S.S.R.	40,000	36
South-Eastern or Chagatay group			
39. Uzbek	Uzbek S.S.R.	5,880,000	35
40. Uighur	Uzbek, Kazakh and Kirghiz S.S.R.	80,000	41
North-Eastern Group			
41. Yakut	Yakut A.S.S.R.	230,000	40
42. Tuva (Soyot or Uryankhai)	Tuva Autonomous District	100,000	36
43. Khakas	Khakas Autonomous District	50,000	39
MONGOLIAN LINGUISTIC FAMILY			
44. Mongolian proper	Mongolian People's Republic	3,500,000	34
45. Buryat	Buryat A.S.S.R. and neighbouring Districts	240,000	36
46. Kalmyk (Kalmuck)	Kalmyk A.S.S.R.	95,000	39

Language or Dialect	Where spoken	Approx. No. of Speakers	No. of Letters of new Alphabet
TUNGUS–MANCHURIAN LANGUAGES			
47. Tungus proper (Evenki)	Northern Siberia and Sakhalin	15,000	34
48. Lamut (Even)	Northern Siberia	8,000	33
Manchurian Group			
49. Gold (Nanai)	Chita and Irkutsk Districts (Siberia)	7,000	33
PALÆO-ASIATIC (OR PALÆO-SIBERIAN) LANGUAGES			
50. Chukcha (Luoravetian)	Chukcha or Chukotsky Peninsula (N.-E. Siberia)	11,000	35
51. Koryak (Nymylan)	Koryak National District	6,000	35
52. Nivkh (Gilyak)	Northern Sakhalin and the Lower Amur region	3,000	34
53. Siberian Eskimo (Yuit)	Chukcha National District	1,000	39
SINO–TIBETAN LINGUISTIC FAMILY			
54. Dungan	Kirghiz, Kazakh and Uzbek S.S.R.	20,000	38

See R. S. Gilyarevskiy and V. S. Grivnin, *Languages of the World according to their Scripts* (in Russian), Academy of Sciences of the U.S.S.R., Oriental Institute, Moscow, 1960.

Reform of Russian Orthography

The Slavonic alphabets are amongst the most complete systems of writing; they contain, however, too many letters, some of which have become redundant. The need for a reform of the Russian alphabet, therefore, was felt long before the Revolution, and many learned academies and scientific institutions sponsored the various changes, which were introduced under the Kerenski regime (Collection of Laws and Decrees, No. 74, of October 17th, 1918). Some letters have been dropped and replaced by others representing similar sounds; so, for instance, the letter *ye* is replaced now by *e*, the letter Ѳ by *f*, the sound *i* is expressed only by one letter. Of the two mute letters of Fig. 19.42, the first indicating that the preceding consonant is hard, and the other indicating that the preceding consonant is soft, the former is dropped at the end of words and part of compound words, but is retained in the middle of words as a sign of division.

BUKVISTA

Catholic Slavs of Dalmatia and Bosnia employed for some time the alphabet termed *Bukvitsa*; it was the Cyrillic alphabet slightly modified, with some influences of the Glagolitic script.

GLAGOLITIC ALPHABET
(Figs. 19.39–40)

'Glagolitic' (in Slavonic, *glagolitsa*, from *glagol*, 'word,' 'dixit'; a frequent term in early Slavonic documents, but of uncertain connection with the origin of the name of the script), consisted of forty letters. Externally, that is considering the shapes of the single letters, the Glagolitic alphabet is unlike any known Greek variety; the general impression recalls the aspect of the Ethiopic letters. The Glagolitic characters are singularly stylized, geometric and symmetrical with their little quadrangles, triangles and circles with appendages; there are no ligatures. From the standpoint of the phonetic value of the letters, as a system of writing, the Glagolitic is, as Professor Minns pointed out, nearly identical with the Cyrillic alphabet.

We can distinguish two main types of Glagolitic script: (1) the earlier type, termed also the Bulgarian Glagolitsa, employed until the end of the twelfth century, with more rounded letters; and (2) the more recent type, termed the Croatian Glagolitsa, a more stylized form of writing, which developed in the fourteenth century (its development was parallel to that of the Latin alphabet from the 'Roman' to the 'Gothic' form), maintaining, ever since, nearly the same form.

The Glagolitic script has a curious history, connected especially with the religious history of the Slavonic peoples of the western Balkan Peninsula. In the second half of the ninth century, it was introduced in the Moravian kingdom together with the Slavonic liturgy, but it soon disappeared, the Slavonic liturgy having been banned by the Popes. It was, however, accepted together with the Slavonic liturgy in Bulgaria and in Croatia, whence it spread along the Dalmatian coast southwards into Montenegro and westwards into Istria. While amongst the orthodox Slavonic peoples the Glagolitic script soon disappeared because of the victory of the Cyrillic, it continued to be employed amongst the Catholics of the western Balkan Peninsula together with the Slavonic liturgy, notwithstanding the opposition of the higher Catholic authorities, until it succeeded finally in obtaining the special licence of the Pope. It is still employed in the Slavonic liturgy amongst some Dalmatian and Montenegrin communities, who are the only Roman Catholics to use the Slavonic liturgy.

Glagolitic had a short flourishing period in the sixteenth and seventeenth centuries, when it was employed for translations from Latin and Italian, and even for original literary works as well as for missionary propaganda of the German protestants amongst the southern Slavonic peoples. Glagolitic printing presses existed then in Venice, Fiume, Rome, Tübingen, Siena, and other places. The earliest preserved Glagolitic secular document dates from 1309; there are various Glagolitic chronicles extant, belonging mainly to the sixteenth century.

BIBLIOGRAPHY

BELYAEV, N. *Constantin (called Cyril) and Metodius* (in Russian), Moscow, 1876.

JAGIĆ, V. *Specimina linguæ palæoslovenicæ*, St. Petersburg, 1882; *The Glagolitic Script* (in Russian), St. Petersburg, 1911.

KARINSKIJ, N. *Glagolitic Specimens* (in Russian), St. Petersburg, 1908.

BOGUSLAWSKI, E. *On the Problem of the Illyrian Script called Glagolitsa* (in Polish), Warsaw, 1909.

MILCHETIĆ, I. 'Croatian Glagolitic Bibliography,' (in Croatian), *Starine*, 1911.

LAVROV, P. A. *Survey of Cyrillic Palæography* (in Russian), Petrograd, 1915; *Specimens from Yugoslav Manuscripts in Bulgarian and Serbian Writings* (in Russian), Petrograd, 1916.

SMIRNOVSKIJ, P. *Grammar of the Old-Church-Slavonic Language* (in Russian), 15th ed., Moscow, 1914.

SHCHEPKIN, V. N. *Handbook of Russian Palæography* (in Russian), Leningrad, 1920.

TEODOROV-BALAN, A. *Cyril and Metodius* (in Bulgarian), Sofia, I, 1920; II, 1934,

LESKIEN, A. *Handbuch der altbulgarischen-altkirchenslavischen Sprache*, 6th ed., Heidelberg, 1922.

NACHTIGAL, R. *On the Origin of the Glagolitsa* (in Slovenian), Lubliana, 1923.

MEILLET, A. and VAILLANT, A. *Grammaire de la langue serbo-croate*, Paris, 1924.

NIEDERLE, L. *Slavonic Antiquities* (in Czech), Vol. III, 2, Prague, 1925.

KARINSKIJ, W. M. *Specimens of Writing of the Ancient Period of the History of the Russian Book* (in Russian), Leningrad, 1925.

CRONIA, A. *L'enigma del glagolitico*, Zara, 1925.

DURNOVO, N. 'Zur Entstehung der Vokalbezeichnungen in den slavischen Alphabeten,' *Zeitschr. für slavische Philologie*, 1926.

DUROVIĆ, D. *Development of the Slavonic Script* (in Serbian), Belgrade, 1927.

OGIENKO, I. *The Origins of the Slavonic Alphabet and Literary Language* (in Polish), Warsaw, 1927; *Slavonic Script before Constantine* (in Ukrainian), 1928.

KARSKIJ, E. F. *Slavonic Cyrillic Palæography* (in Russian), 1928.

MOHLEBERG, C. *Il messale glagolitico di Kiev*, etc., Rome, 1928.

KUL'BAKIN, S. M. *Le vieux slave*, Paris, 1929.

VAJS, J. *Handbook of Glagolitic Palæography* (in Czech), Prague, 1932.

DIELS, P. *Altkirchenslavische Grammatik*, etc., Heidelberg, 1932; *Ausgewählte Texte and Wörterbuch*, Heidelberg, 1934.

BEAULIEUX, L. *Grammaire de la langue bulgare*, Paris, 1933.

ILINSKIJ, G. *Systematic Bibliography of Cyril and Metodius* (in Bulgarian), Sofia, 1934.

WEINGART, M. *Handbook of the Old-Slavonic Language* (in Czech), Prague, 1937.

UOTILA, T. E. *Syrjänische Chrestomathie mit grammatikalischem Abriss*, etc., Helsinki, 1938.

POPRUJENKO, M. and ROMANSKIJ, *St. Cyril-Metodius Bibliography for the years 1934–1940* (in Bulgarian), Sofia, 1940.

MAZON, A. *Grammaire de la langue russe*, Paris, 1943.

VERNADSKY, G. *Ancient Russia*, New Haven, 1943.

DOBROVSKIY, J. *Glagolitica*, Prague, 1945.

CHAIEV, N. S. and CHEREPNIN, L. V. *Russian Palæography* (in Russian), Moscow, 1946.

BORSHCHAK, É. *Lectures ukrainiennes*, Paris, 1946.

VAILLANT, A. *Manuel de vieux slave*, Paris, 1948.

ENTWISTLE, W. J. and MORISON, W. A. *Russian and the Slavonic Languages*, London, 1949.

ARTCHIKOVSKY, A. V. *The Novgorod Bark Inscriptions* (in Russian), Moscow, 1953, 1958, 1960.

Soviet Academy of Sciences, *Palæographic and Linguistic Analysis of the Novgorod Bark Inscriptions*, Moscow, 1955.

International System for the Transliteration of Cyrillic Characters, Geneva, 1955.

CHEREPNIN, L. V. *Russian Palæography* (in Russian), Moscow, 1956.

DJAPARIDZE, D. *Medieval Slavic Manuscripts*, Cambridge, Mass., 1957.

BIDWELL, C. E. *Slavonic Historic Phonology*, Pittsburgh, Pa., 1959.

GILYAREVSKIY, R. S. and GRIVNIN, V. S. *Languages of the World according to their Scripts* (in Russian), Moscow, 1960.

GRIVEC, F. *Konstantine und Method*, Wiesbaden, 1960.

PARKER, F. *The Russian Alphabet Book*, Toronto, 1961.

GOSHEV, I. *Old-Bulgarian Glagolitic and Cyrillic Inscriptions of the IXth and Xth Centuries* (in Bulgarian), Sofia, 1961 (extremely important).

ISTRIN, V. A. *Origin and Development of Writing* (in Russian), Moscow, 1965, pp, 402–504, and bibliography on pp. 575–81.

LOCAL ALBANIAN ALPHABETS

The Albanians have adopted the Greek and Latin alphabets, and adapted them to their language with some modifications, the addition of diacritical marks as in *ë* for instance, and the combinations of two consonants (*ll, rr, gj, zh, nj, sh, xh,* and so forth). Since the Congress at Monastir in 1908, the Latin alphabet (with the aforementioned modifications) has been adopted officially.

In the last century, however, there existed in Albania three local alphabets:

(1) *The Elbasan script*, of fifty-three letters, employed mainly at Elbasan (central Albania) and at Berat, south of Elbasan.

(2) *The Büthakukye alphabet*, a script of thirty-two characters, said to have been invented about the middle of the last century by an Albanian called Büthakukye.

(3) *The Argyrokastron script*, consisting of twenty-two signs, employed at Argyrokastron (in Albanian, Gjinokastri), in southern Albania. A noble Albanian, called Veso Bey, belonging to the family of Alisot Pasha, gave information about this script to the Austrian consul Hahn about 1850.

All the three scripts seem to have been formed on the basis of Greek cursive writing, with various modifications, such as omissions and additions, and particularly ligatures of two or three letters, and borrowings from other scripts. It is still uncertain when and how these scripts were invented. In my opinion, they were cryptic, being in some sort national scripts of the Albanian population who needed a special means of communication in order to avoid the Turkish authorities.

These interesting Albanian scripts had only local importance.

The inhabitants of Albania number over 1,200,000, but several hundred thousand Albanians live in Yugoslavia, Greece and southern Italy.

BIBLIOGRAPHY

CRISPI, G. *Memoria sulla lingua albanese*, Palermo, 1836.

VON HAHN, F. G. in *Sitzungsb. der K. K. Akad. der Wissensch. zu Wien*, 1849; 'Bemerkungen über das albanesische Alphabet,' the same journal, 1850; *Albanesische Studien*, Vienna, 1853, and Jena, 1854.

MIKLOSICH, F. *Albanische Forschungen*, Vienna, 1870.

GEITLER, L. *Die albanesischen und slavischen Schriften*, Vienna, 1883.

PEKMEZI, G. in *Anzeiger der phil.-hist. Classe der K.K. Akad. der Wissensch.*, etc., Vienna, 1901; 'Albanische Bibliographie,' the same journal, 1909; *Grammatik der albanesischen Sprache*, Vienna, 1908.

LEGRAND, E. and GÛYS, H. *Bibliographie albanaise*, Paris-Athens, 1912.

WEIGAND, G. *Albanesische Grammatik*, Leipsic, 1913; 'Das albanische Alphabet,' etc., *Balkan-Archiv*, Leipsic, 1925.

VON THALLOCZY, L. *Illyrisch-albanische Forschungen*, 2 vols., Munich-Leipsic, 1916.

VAINA, E. *La nazione albanese*, 2nd ed., Catania, 1917.

NACHTIGAL, R. *Die Frage einer einheitlichen albanischen Schriftsprache*, Graz, 1917; 'On the Elbasan Script,' etc. (in Slovenian), *Archiv za Arbanasku Starinu*, Belgrade, 1923.

ALPHABETS OF WESTERN EUROPE

The main offshoot of the Greek alphabet was the Etruscan alphabet (*see* next chapter), which, through its descendant, the Latin script (*see* chapter 22), has become the prototype of all the modern alphabets of western Europe.

CHAPTER 20

Etruscan and Italic Alphabets

THE ETRUSCANS

THE importance of the Etruscans in the history of writing, as indeed in many other fields of civilization, cannot be overestimated. Much of the Roman civilization was of Etruscan origin, and has passed into the fabric of European civilization.

The Etruscans, an ancient people of uncertain origin and ethnic and linguistic affinities who were called by the Romans *Etrusci* (hence the name Etruscans) or, more commonly, *Tusci* (hence the modern name of Tuscany), and by the Greeks *Tyrsenoi* or *Tyrrhenoi* (hence the name Tyrrhenian Sea), were the leading power in Italy in the first half of the first millennium B.C.; an Etruscan dynasty reigned in Rome from the last decades of the seventh century to the end of the sixth century B.C.

ETRUSCAN INSCRIPTIONS

The Etruscan language has come down to us in over 10,000 inscriptions, which have been discovered in various countries and offer material for useful investigation into the cultural and commercial relations between the Etruscans and other peoples. The greater part of the Etruscan inscriptions were found in Etruria proper, which roughly corresponds to Tuscany of today, but some of them were discovered in other Italian regions (in northern Italy, in Campania, Sicily, Sardinia, and so forth), or even beyond the borders of Italy, for instance in Egypt and at Carthage.

The most remarkable is an inscription, consisting of about fifteen hundred words, written on the linen wrappings of an Egyptian mummy belonging to the Græco-Roman period, now in the Zagreb (Agram) museum. Other famous inscriptions are: the tile from S. Maria Capua Vetere (now in the Berlin Museum), belonging to the fifth century B.C., with about 300 words still preserved; the much more recent Perugia *cippus* (Fig. 20.1c) with about 120 words; the *Piombo* ('Leaden Tablet') of Magliano (now in the Archæological Museum of Florence), inscribed on both sides (Fig. 20.2a), belonging to the sixth century B.C., while another inscription on a leaden tablet in the Volterra Museum, containing about eighty words, belongs to the third century B.C. Of paramount importance for the knowledge of Etruscan mythology is the inscription (Fig. 20.2d) known as the *Templum* of Piacenza, which has the form of a calf's liver, and is covered with the names of Etruscan deities.

Recently (late September 1966) a long, though fragmentary, lead-tablet inscription has been found at the Etruscan sanctuary of Punta della Vipera, near Sta. Marinella, eight km. S.-E. of Civitavecchia.

There are many funerary inscriptions, the most important being the inscription in nine lines of the *Grotta del Tifone* at Tarquinia, the inscription of the hypogeum near the Tower of S. Manno (Perugia), consisting of twenty-eight words, and the inscription on a lid of a sarcophagus at Tarquinia, consisting of nine lines. A gold plate found at Tarquinia also contains nine lines. There are not many other long inscriptions extant, the great majority of the inscriptions consisting of a few words only. They are written on mirrors and domestic utensils, on the walls of tombs, to the left or right or above painted figures, and on statues, the most famous being the inscription on a bronze statue, called l'Arringatore ('Orator'), discovered in 1566, now in the Archæological Museum, Florence.

ETRUSCAN ALPHABET

It is a curious fact that people often forget that the history of an alphabet is altogether distinct from that of the speech which it is employed to represent. Nowadays, as in ancient times, the same script can be employed for various languages (as in the case of the Latin alphabet which is employed for English, French, German, Italian, Hungarian, Turkish, Finnish, and so forth) and the same speech can be expressed in different scripts (as for instance, the Serbo-Croatian language, which employs the Latin alphabet for 'Croatian' and the Slavonic alphabet for 'Serbian,' or the Turkish language, which was formerly written in Arabic characters and nowadays in Latin letters). This fluctuating relationship between speech and script must be pointed out to all who think that when dealing with the Etruscan alphabet we automatically try to solve the problem of the Etruscan language. As a matter of fact, while broadly speaking the latter has not yet been deciphered (although it seems that it had some affinity with the Caucasian languages), the simple reading of Etruscan inscriptions does not present great difficulties, and the knowledge of ancient Græco-Latin alphabets makes it generally an easy task.

Like the Semitic and the early Greek alphabets, Etruscan writing goes nearly always from right to left; there are, however, inscriptions in *boustrophedon*, that is, as already explained, in alternate lines from right to left and left to right.

ORIGIN OF ETRUSCAN ALPHABET

The origin of the Etruscan alphabet has been a matter of serious study, as well as of unscientific speculation. Amateurs have held the view that the Etruscan alphabet was an offshoot of a pre-Hellenic alphabet which they term Pelasgian or proto-Tyrrhenian or Cadmic (from Cadmos). Scholars generally agree that it is descended from the Greek alphabet, but while some think that it came from the east, others hold that it was derived from a type belonging to the western group (*see* p. 360) either from that of the Æolic-Chalcidian colony of Cumae (in southern Italy), or from the Doric-Corinthian branch.

The most commonly held theory of the three is that which suggests that the Etruscans borrowed their script from the Chalcidian alphabet, the Etruscan alphabet belonging thus to the western group of the Greek alphabets. This theory has been accepted by Rhys Carpenter in his article on 'The Alphabet in Italy' (*Amer. J. Archæol.*, XLIX/4, October–December, 1945). Roughly speaking, those scholars who consider the Etruscans as immigrants from the north into Italy in prehistoric times regard their alphabet as a descendant of the Chalcidian alphabet of Magna Græcia.

On the other hand, the scholars who, following Herodotus I, 94, consider the Etruscans as being of oriental origin, holding that they entered Italy by way of the sea in the first centuries of the first millennium B.C., deny the Chalcidian origin of the Etruscan alphabet. An origin in central Greece has also been suggested, and another recent theory suggests that the invention of the Etruscan alphabet, and indeed the formation of the different variants, took place 'when the Etruscans lived still in their Ægean homeland.'

In the recent studies on the Etruscan alphabet very great importance was given to the ivory tablet found at Marsiliana d'Albegna and now in the Archæological Museum of Florence. This tablet (Fig. 20.1*a*), which may have been employed for teaching purposes, contains on the top side the whole Etruscan alphabet of twenty-six letters, written from right to left. Although the tomb in which the tablet was found is now generally dated to the latter half of the seventh century B.C., in the view of the present writer the tablet itself belongs probably at least to the eighth or the beginning of the seventh century B.C. The French scholar Albert Grenier regarded this Etruscan alphabet (containing the twenty-two North Semitic letters in their exact order, but with the phonetic values of the Greek letters, plus four additional Greek letters) as a derivation from a primitive Greek alphabet employed on the Ægean islands before the subdivision into the eastern and western groups. There is, however, no Greek document extant, as we have already mentioned, which contains all the Semitic sibilants, and the *san* (or *ṣade*) and *sigma* never appear together in any particular Greek alphabet. Rhys Carpenter, who, as we have seen, holds the opinion that the Etruscan script descended from the Chalcidian alphabet, explains the discrepancies between the two by suggesting 'that Etruscan is not an alphabet of remote antiquity,' but 'is an artificial construction borrowing from more than one Greek source.' We may agree, even if with reluctance, that the Etruscans borrowed their script 'from more than one Greek source,' but we cannot allow that theirs 'is not an alphabet of remote antiquity.' I go as far as to suggest that in the Marsiliana Tablet we may have the Greek prototypal alphabet (though not so much in the shapes of the letters as in their order and in their phonetic values).

However, the probable date of the invention of the Etruscan alphabet is the late ninth or early eighth century B.C., though in Professor Rhys Carpenter's opinion its 'emergence is archaeologically verifiable around 670 B.C.'

At any rate, by the suggestion of the mixed origin of the Etruscan alphabet, it may be possible to solve many problems which cannot be solved by accepting a Chalcidian origin. Besides, the preservation of the (ṣade) san, already mentioned, the retention by the Formello and Cære alphabets (see below), but not by that at Marsiliana, of the P- form of the p, while the |same form is used for r, and of the central dot of the θ, the Phocian form of the l of the Venetic alphabet (Fig. 20.9), and other influences of the Phocian type may probably be attributed to the far-reaching influence of the Delphic oracle, Delphi having been 'a centre for diffusion of the alphabet' (Rhys Carpenter). Also, the three different methods of representing the sound f (a figure-8-like sign; the combination w-h; and a sign in the form of an arrowhead pointed upward) can be explained only by non-Chalcidian influences.

The origin of the form 8 = f has been a matter of much controversy. A similar sign seems to appear on one of the earliest Etruscan inscriptions extant, the stele of Vetulonia (Fig. 20.1b) of the seventh century B.C., and many scholars regard it as one of the evidences of the connection of Etruscan with Lydian, which latter alphabet contained a nearly identical letter with the same phonetic value. Others consider the 8-like f as a later addition to the Etruscan script, as this sign is placed right at the end of the classical Etruscan alphabet.

Some scholars hold that this Etruscan alphabet was not the oldest Etruscan writing, but that an earlier one had existed before, which they term proto-Etruscan and which they consider not only as the prototype of the early Etruscan inscriptions, but also as the parent of various other alphabets, such as the North Etruscan (Raetic, Lepontic and Venetic), the East Italic of the Piceni, and the Sicel alphabet of the Siculi (the tribe which gave the name to Sicily). However, there is no document extant of the suggested 'proto-Etruscan' alphabet.

DEVELOPMENT OF ETRUSCAN SCRIPT

The forms and order of the Etruscan letters of the Marsiliana tablet are confirmed by the slightly variant copies of the Etruscan alphabet (Fig. 20.3) on a vase found at Formello (near the site of the ancient Veii), now in the National Museum of Villa Giulia in Rome, and on a vase (containing also a partial syllabary) found in a chamber-tomb of Cervetri or Caere vetus, and now in the Etrusco-Gregoriano Museum of Rome, both vases belonging probably to the late seventh, or to the sixth century B.C.

As time went on there were reductions and other modifications in the Etruscan alphabet, which we can best follow on the many sample-alphabets (Fig. 20.3) preserved by a rare kindness of fortune at Viterbo, Leprignano, Colle (beside those already mentioned from Marsiliana, Formello and Cære), belonging to the seventh-sixth century B.C. and those from Rusellæ, Chiusi (four copies), Bomarzo and Nola (three copies) belonging to the fifth-third centuries B.C., and on a partial syllabary from Orbetello (Fig. 20.2b), of the sixth or fifth century B.C.

In the fifth century B.C. the Etruscan alphabet consisted of twenty-three letters (Fig. 20.2e), containing the digamma (F) and three signs for s of which, however, the bi-triangular s does not appear in Etruria proper, and the letters k and q soon fell into disuse.

About 400 B.C. the 'classical' Etruscan alphabet took its final form, having twenty letters, that is four vowels (a, e, i, u) and sixteen consonants (g, v-digamma, z, h, th, l, m, n, p, san, r, s, t, ph, kh, f), the letter f having the form of the figure 8, and san representing a sound akin to s. Etruscan speech knowing no distinction between the voiced and breathed sounds b and p, d and t, k and g, the letters b and d never appear in pure Etruscan inscriptions, and after the disappearance of k and q the letter C was employed for g and k.

LAST STAGE OF ETRUSCAN ALPHABET

The spelling of the late Etruscan inscriptions is not exact; there are frequent interchanges in the employment of t and th, C and kh, of the various sibilants, and so forth. The Etruscan punctuation consisted of three (or even four) points, two points or one point only. The direction of writing, which, as already mentioned, was originally from right to left, became under Latin influence from left to right, after a certain period of vacillation and boustrophedon or serpentine form.

In the later period Latin-Etruscan bilingual inscriptions appear, or Etruscan inscriptions either in Latin characters, or in Etruscan letters which gradually assumed the Latin form. Etruria, after having lost her political independence, progressively gave up her script and her language. Having been the political and cultural master of Rome, she became her servile lackey. The last datable Etruscan inscriptions belong to the early years of the Christian era, although the Etruscan language continued to be employed for some centuries, and the Etruscan pronunciation influenced the Tuscan dialect which became the modern bella lingua.

OFFSHOOTS OF THE ETRUSCAN ALPHABET

The Etruscan alphabet had thus a miserable end, but the influence of its glorious life was widespread and durable.

The most famous of all the scripts in the history of writing, the Latin or Roman alphabet, was the most important offshoot of the Etruscan. It will be dealt with in the next chapter.

ALPHABET OF THE PICENI
(Figs. 20.5–6)

The ancient Piceni, a non-Italic population, inhabited the modern central Italian regions of the Marches, particularly its southern part, and the adjoining northern portion of the Abruzzi, situated on the Adriatic coast. About ten inscriptions found in that zone are written in a language which has not been deciphered, but is considered by some scholars to be Illyrian. At a later period, the Picenti, an Italic people speaking an Oscan-Umbrian language, inhabited that same region, but none of their inscriptions has been preserved.

The alphabet (Fig. 20.5) employed by the Piceni, termed improperly 'East Italic' or 'Sabellic' or else 'proto-Sabellic' or 'Old Sabellic' or 'pre-Sabellic,' was perhaps already in existence at the end of the seventh century B.C., if the attribution of the inscription of the 'Warrior' from Capestrano (Fig. 20.6a) to the sixth century B.C., as suggested by the discoverer, Professor Moretti, is correct. Professor Rhys Carpenter considers as 'highly improbable that it is older than the fifth century B.C.,' basing his opinion not in the main on archæological criteria but on the consideration that 'all fixed dates are lacking in East Italic letters.'

The Picenian alphabet is, however, very old; the English scholar Conway and the Italian Devoto regard it as the earliest alphabet employed in the inscriptions discovered in Italy. It presents various special features, such as a great number of vowels (a, e, i, o, u, and the variants of e and u), each of them in various forms. It distinguished between the voiced and breathed sounds (b-p, d-t, k-g); it had three s-sounds, and peculiar forms for z and t; and it had no signs corresponding to the Greek letters ph, kh and ps. The h shows vertical instead of horizontal bars, there was a meander symbol like the Corinthian b, and so forth. There were, finally, peculiar v-shaped symbols as well as the same in upside-down form, with a diacritical point inside to indicate a variant of u, or with a diacritical stroke inside to indicate a variant of e or i.

Figure 20.7 represents the Novilara stele, written in Picenian, belonging to c. 550 B.C.

The origin of this peculiar alphabet still offers many uncertainties, but it is highly probable that it was descended from the Etruscan alphabet in its earliest form.

VENETIC ALPHABET
(Fig. 20.4)

The Veneti, who seem to have belonged to the same linguistic stock as the aforementioned Piceni and the Messapii, that is the Illyrian, formed in the first millennium B.C. the indigenous population of the north-western coastal region of the Adriatic Sea, which corresponded nearly to the modern Italian region of Venetia. Their territory extended in the north as far as into the modern Carinthia and Styria. They called themselves Veneti, and they gave the name to the modern city, the province and the three Venetian regions. Their chief town was Este or Ateste, where many Venetic inscriptions have been found.

The alphabet (Fig. 20.4) of the Venetic or Este inscriptions, which partly belong to the sixth century B.C., is also a very early one, the direction of writing being boustrophedon. Among the special features of this script we may mention the use of the letter o (unlike the Etruscan script), which seems, however, to have been a later addition, as it appears at the end of the sample alphabets. There is the bi-triangular *s* as in the early Etruscan alphabet; the sound *f* is represented by the combination *w-h*.

The Este inscriptions show a peculiar system of 'dotting', which has not, as yet, been explained satisfactorily. In various instances there are letters, either vowels or consonants, with diacritical dots. The acceptable theory seems to be that advanced by Professor Conway that the dots indicate accents. On the other hand, the Austrian scholar Vetter pointed out that if they were accents the vowels should be marked, whereas here, instead, in most instances the consonants are 'dotted,' and in many cases there are words with two diacritical dots. Vetter therefore suggests that the 'dotting' indicates whether the syllable is open (or normal), in which case there is no dotting, or closed (or irregular), in which case there is a dot either inside the consonant which ends the syllable or inside the vowel which opens the syllable. As such dots occasionally appear also in Etruscan, North Etruscan and Picenian inscriptions, Vetter hazards the theory that this dotting-system may have derived from the original employment of a syllabic script, and that the Etruscans used a syllabary before adopting the Phœnician-Greek alphabet. But nothing is known of the supposed existence of an Etruscan syllabic script. (*See*, however, G. Buonamici, *Studi Etruschi*, 1941).

As to the origin of the Venetic alphabet, there is fairly general agreement that it descended from the early Etruscan alphabet.

NORTH ETRUSCAN ALPHABET
(Fig. 20.4)

The North Etruscan or Alpine alphabets are used in the inscriptions discovered in the river-valleys of the Italian Alps, which were inhabited in pre-Roman times by Ligurian, Lepontic, Celtic, Raetic and Venetic tribes, the last having been already mentioned. Leaving them aside, four other groups can be distinguished:

(1) The inscriptions of Lugano, termed Lepontic, or else Ligurian-Celtic (the tribe of the Lepontii was probably of mixed Ligurian-Celtic origin, but speaking a Celtic dialect), and discovered in the region of the lakes of Orta, Maggiore, Lugano and Lecco;

(2) the inscriptions of Sondrio, found in the territory to the east of the former group, extending from Sondrio in the north to the lake Iseo in the south, and to the plateau of Asiago in the east;

(3) the inscriptions of Bolzano, near the Brenner Pass, from Matrey near Innsbruck in the north to near Trento in the south, that is roughly the territory lying between that of the previous group and that of the Veneti (*see* above);

(4) a small group of dedicatory inscriptions on fragments of split stagshorn found at Magrè (prov. of Vicenza, northern Italy), and some short inscriptions from Padua, Verona, and other neighbouring places.

The dialect in which the inscriptions of the groups (2) to (4) are written, has been called Rhætic or Rætic. It is regarded by some scholars as a kind of Etruscan, by others as an affinity of Illyric or Celtic, having many forms of Indo-European origin. However, while it seems that the Rætic tribes, that is the population inhabiting that Alpine region, were of mixed origin, they employed alphabets which were un-mistakably of Etruscan origin.

The Rætic and the other Alpine alphabets present certain features which suggest that they may be the link between the Etruscan alphabet and the runes; *see* the shapes of the letters *e, u, t*, and so forth. There are a few extremely interesting characters, for instance the letter of uncertain meaning (representing perhaps a dental fricative) shown in the last line of the Magrè alphabet in Fig. 20.4, the shapes of the *z* in the Sondrio and Este scripts, the reverse form of *m* in the Sondrio alphabet, and the form of *l* in the same script, similar to that of the Greek classical *l*; we may note also the absence of *ph* and *kh*, as well as of some other letters. All these peculiarities of the North Etruscan varieties show that these scripts were not connected directly with the Greek alphabets, either of the western group or of the eastern, because they show some particular features of the former group and others of the latter. On the whole, there is a fairly general agreement that the North Etruscan scripts were offshoots of an early Etruscan alphabet.

When these scripts ceased to be used is as yet uncertain; they were still in use in the first half of the first century A.D., that is, after the Etruscan alphabet had fallen into disuse.

ITALIC SCRIPTS
(Fig. 20.5)

The scripts of the peoples speaking Italic dialects, and thus belonging to the Indo-European family, were also offshoots of the Etruscan alphabets.

The expressions 'Italic' and 'Italia' (Italy) have a curious history. According to the Greek historian Hellanicus of Lesbos (a contemporary of Herodotus and Thucydides), reported by Dionysius, I, 35, the term *Italoi*, the Greek name of an ancient Indo-European tribe who occupied a part of the modern region of Calabria, was derived from the indigenous name *Viteliu*, 'calf-land' (the modern Italian word *vitello* means a 'calf'). This name was later applied as a geographical term to indicate the whole of modern Italy, while the expression 'Italic' is mainly used, in contrast with the term 'Latinian' (employed for the Latin and Faliscan forms of speech), to indicate the Osco-Umbrian sub-branch of the Italic branch of the Indo-European linguistic family. Another term for this sub-branch is Sabine or Safine (Safinos seems to be the indigenous term; the Greeks called them also Saphnitai or Samnitai, whence another term, Samnite). In the Social War of 91–88 B.C. the terms *Italia* and *Italica*, which up to then had only a geographical meaning, are given political significance: *denarii* issued by the 'Italian' League *c.* 90 B.C. bear the inscription *Italia*, and the town Corfinium (headquarters of the League) changes its name into *Italia* or *Italica*).

Oscan Alphabet (Figs. 20.5–6)

The Oscans (*Osca lingua* was the Roman term for their speech) or *Osci*, in Greek Oskoi or Opikoí, from *Opsci* or *Opici*, were Italic tribes who inhabited southern Italy in the second half of the first millennium B.C. The Roman terms *Osca* and *Osci* may be connected either with the indigenous word *opos* or *opsaom*, in Latin *opus*, meaning 'work,' 'to work,' or else with the Latin *ops* (gen. *opis*, plur. *opes*, *opum*), meaning 'power,' 'wealth,' or *Ops*, gen. *Opis*, 'Earth,' the Goddess of Earth, of its produce, the symbol of fertility.

About 200 Oscan inscriptions are extant (Fig. 20.6*b–c*); 150 of them have been found in Campania. They belong mainly to the third and second centuries B.C., but some inscriptions may be dated in the fifth century B.C., and others down to the Christian era. Oscan coins have been found dating from the fifth to the first century B.C. The most important inscriptions extant are: the Agnone bronze tablet, of the middle third century B.C., containing a long list of local divinities; the Abella *cippus* of the first half of the second century B.C., containing an agreement for sacred purposes between the towns of Nola and Abella; the Bantia bronze tablet, of the second half of the second century B.C., containing the local laws; an inscription from Messina and some inscriptions from Capua, belonging to the middle of the third century B.C.

The Oscan script (Fig. 20.5) was an offshoot of the Etruscan alphabet in its southern Campano-Etruscan sub-species. The direction of writing was, as in Etruscan, from right to left. It seems also that Oscan, like Etruscan, had no sign for *d*, and had to adopt a special sign for it modifying the letter *r*. On the other hand, unlike the Etruscans, the Oscans had special signs for *b* and *g* as distinguished from *p* and C, which shows that their script was partly formed under the influence of a non-Etruscan alphabet. For the peculiar forms of some letters *see* Figs. 20.5–6.

Umbrian Alphabet (Figs. 20.5, 8)

The Umbri (whence the name of the modern Italian region of Umbria), in Greek Ombroi or Ombrikoí, were, according to tradition, a people who lived in Etruria and Umbria before the Etruscan invasion. It is uncertain, however, whether they spoke the same language as the non-Etruscan population who inhabited the same territory in historical times, that is from the sixth century B.C. onwards, in which period Umbrian was an Italic speech. It is the latter meaning which has now been generally applied to the term 'Umbrian.'

The most important documents extant are the famous Eugubine or Iguvine Tables, containing parts of the liturgy of a sacred brotherhood of Iguvium, the modern Gubbio. They are seven in number, of which the tables I–IV and part of the Vth are written in Umbrian script, while the rest are written in Roman character. While the latter were in part written as late as the first century B.C., the earliest tablets belong perhaps, partly at least, to the fourth or even to the fifth century B.C. Some other Umbrian inscriptions are written in a slightly different script termed Umbro-Felsinian, Felsina being the ancient name of Bologna.

The Umbrian script is not only an offshoot of the Etruscan alphabet, but is very close to its classical form. The main features of the Umbrian writing agree with this assertion, the direction of writing is from right to left, there are no signs for *g* and *d* (the Etruscan *f* which, as already mentioned, has the form of figure 8, is employed to represent the sound *d*) and although there is a sign for *b*, its use is uncertain, and it often alternates with *p*.

Siculan Alphabet (Fig. 20.5)

The problem of the Siculi (who gave the name to Sicily) is similar to that of the Umbri (*see* above); according to tradition they once inhabited parts of central Italy and migrated into Sicily some centuries before the Greek colonization, but we do not know whether the tribes called Siculi who inhabited Sicily in historical times, and who—as far as we can judge from the scanty documents extant—spoke the Indo-European dialect termed Siculan, were the direct descendants of the ancient Siculi or Sicani. The terms Siculi and Sicani do not seem to indicate different peoples, as some ancient and modern scholars have suggested, but are adjectives of the same ethnic name.

From the linguistic point of view, however, and from that of the history of writing, the term Siculan is applied to the non-Greek documents, very few in number, which have come to light in Sicily, the two short inscriptions found at Adrano (now in the Syracuse Museum) and the fairly long inscription on an *askos* (a kind of vase) found at Centorbi, the ancient Centuripe, in the province of Enna (now in the Karlsruhe Museum). The Centuripe inscription, written *boustrophedon*, contains ninety-nine letters and may be dated in the fifth century B.C. A fourth inscription, on a *stele* discovered at Sciri between Caltagirone and Cómiso, has been published recently.

The Siculan alphabet seems to have descended from an Etruscan sub-species. The letters *kh*, *ph* and *ps* are missing as in the western Greek alphabets, but the shapes of the letters *l*, *p* and *u* show that the Siculan script has not descended directly either from the Chalcidian alphabet of Cumæ, or from other Greek varieties in use in Magna Græcia. Rhys Carpenter rejects the theory of the Etruscan derivation of the Siculan alphabet.

LATINIAN ALPHABETS

Both the Latin, or Roman, and the Faliscan alphabets have descended from the early Etruscan. The Latin writing will be dealt with at length in the next chapter. Here we shall examine briefly the Faliscan script.

Faliscan Alphabet (Figs. 20.5, 6c)

The Falisci were a tribe closely related to the Romans, and they spoke a similar language; having been for some centuries longer under Etruscan rule, they were more influenced by that people. They inhabited a small territory north of Rome centred on Falerii (the modern Civita Castellana).

Some Faliscan documents have come to light, the earliest belonging perhaps to the sixth century B.C. The most famous is an inscription in two specimens on glazed *kylikes* or *paterae* (belonging to the fourth century B.C.) which are not identical, but the two copies complete each other. The inscription round an erotic scene illustrates some phonetic and graphic differences between Faliscan and Latin. It reads *foied. vino. pipafo. ora. carefo.* which is in Latin: *hodie vinum bibam cras carebo*, that means 'today I will drink wine, tomorrow I shall be without.'

The main differences between the Faliscan alphabet and the Latin (*see* next chapter) consist in the forms of the letters *a, f, z, h, r* and *t*. Especially interesting is the form of the Faliscan *f*, an arrow pointed upwards (*see*, for instance, the first sign on the right-hand of Fig. 20.6*c*, which is also found in some Etruscan inscriptions, and according to Sir William Ramsay seems to have derived from Phrygia. Like the southern Etruscan alphabet, the Faliscan did not use the letters *k* and *c*, but only the letter C, that is —the direction of the Faliscan alphabet being from right to left—the sign Ɔ (= the Greek *gamma*), which replaced also the sign *k*.

The Capena Faliscan script was slightly different from the classical Faliscan. After the Roman conquest, in 241 B.C., the Faliscan alphabet fell into disuse.

BIBLIOGRAPHY

MÜLLER, K. O. and DEECKE, W. *Die Etrusker*, 2 vols., Stuttgart, 1877.

DENNIS, G. *Cities and Cemeteries of Etruria*, 3rd ed., London, 1882; also in Everyman's Library.

VON PLANTA, R. *Oskisch-umbrische Grammatik*, 2 vols., Strasbourg, 1892–7.

Corpus Inscriptionum Etruscarum, Leipsic, 1893 onwards.

CONWAY, R. S. *The Italic Dialects*, etc., Cambridge, 1897; *Dialectorum Italicarum exempla selecta* etc., Cambridge, 1899; 'The Ancient Alphabets of Italy', *The Cambridge Ancient History*, Vol. IV, pp. 395–403, Cambridge, 1930.

HÜLSEN, C. 'Etruria'; Thulin, C. 'Etrusca'; Körte, G. 'Etrusker'; Skutsch, F. 'Etruskische Sprache', in *Pauly-Wissowa's Real-Enzyklopädie*, VII, 1907, cols. 720 ff.

PORTRANDOLFI, G. *Gli Etruschi e la loro* lingua, Florence, 1909.

SOLARI, A. *Topografia storica dell'Etruria*, 4 vols., Pisa, 1915–20; *La vita pubblica e privata degli Etruschi*, Florence, 1928.

SETHE, K. *Von Zahlen und Zahlwörtern*, Strassburg, 1916.

PARETI, L. *Studi siciliani ed italioti*, Florence, 1920; *Le origini etrusche*, I, Florence, 1926.

Atti del Primo Convegno Nazionale di Studi Etruschi, Florence, 1926.

DUCATI, P. *Etruria antica*, 2 vols., Turin, 1927; *Storia dell'arte etrusca*, 2 vols., Florence, 1927; *Le problème étrusque*, Paris, 1928; *L'Italia antica*, Milan, 1936.

Studi Etruschi, Florence, 1927 onwards.

RANDALL MAC IVER, D. *The Etruscans*, Oxford, 1927; *Italy before the Romans*, Oxford, 1928.

TROMBETTI, A. *La lingua etrusca*, Florence, 1928.

BUCK, C. D. *A Grammar of Oscan and Umbrian*, 2nd ed., Boston, 1928.

Atti del Primo Congresso Internazionale Etrusco, Florence, 1928.

GOLDMANN, *Beiträge zur Lehre vom indogermanischen Charakter der etruskischen Sprache*, I, Heidelberg, 1929.

RIBEZZO, F. 'Roma delle origini. Sabini e Sabelli. Aree dialettali, iscrizioni, isoglossi,' *Riv. Indo-Greco-Italica*, XIV, 1930.

JOHNSTONE, M. A. *Etruria Past and Present*, London, 1930.

DEVOTO, G. *Gli antichi Italici*, Florence, 1931; *Tabulae Iguvinae*, etc., Rome, 1940; *Storia della lingua di Roma*, Rome, 1940.

BLUMENTHAL, A. v. *Die Iguvinischen Tafeln*, Stuttgart, 1931.

PARETI, L. ('Etruschi: Storia'), Devoto, G. (id.: 'Lingua'), Neppi Modona, A. (id.: 'Religione'), Ducati, P. (id.: 'Archeologia e arte'), and Cesano, S. L. (id.: 'Numismatica'), in *Enciclopedia Italiana*, XIV, 1932.

BUONAMICI, G. *Epigrafia etrusca*, Florence, 1932; *Fonti di storia etrusca*, etc., Florence, 1939.

CONWAY, R. S. WHATMOUGH, J. and JOHNSON, S. E. *The Præ-Italic Dialects of Italy*, 3 vols., London, 1933.

NOGARA, B. *Gli Etruschi e la loro civiltà*, Milan, 1934.

GIGLIOLI, G. Q. *L'arte etrusca*, Milan, 1935.

CLEMEN, C. *Die Religion der Etrusker*, Bonn, 1936.

PALLOTTINO, M. *Elementi di lingua etrusca*, Florence, 1936; *Gli Etruschi*, Rome, 1940; *Etruscologia*, Rome, 1942; 2nd. ed., 1947 (bibliography); *L'origine degli Etruschi*, Rome, 1947; *The Etruscans*, Harmondsworth, Middx., 1955

WHATMOUGH, J. *The Foundations of Roman Italy*, London, 1937; *Tusca origo Raetis*, Cambridge, Mass., 1937.

SITTIG, E. 'Germanische Spuren auf etruskichen Inschriften'. *Nogara-Festschrift*, 1937.

BRANDENSTEIN, 'Die Herkunft der Etrusker,' *Der Alte Orient*, XXXV (1937).

PISANI, V. *Il problema illirico*, Keszthely, 1937.

SLOTTY, F. 'Die etruskischen Zahlwörter,' *Arch. Orient.*, IX (1937); *Beiträge zur Etruskologie. I. Silbenpunktierung und Silbenbildung im Altetruskischen*, Heidelberg, 1952.

HRKAL, E. *Historische Grammatik der etruskischen Sprache*, Vienna, 1939.

RICHTER, G. M. A., *Handbook of the Etruscan Collection*, New York, 1940.

RENARD, M. 'La question étrusque,' in *L'Antiquité Classique*, Brussels, 1940; *Initiation à l'étruscologie*, Brussels, 1941; 2nd ed., Brussels, 1943.

VETTER, E. in *Glotta*, XXX (1943), p. 66: on the Maria-Saal inscription (forgery).

STOLTENBERG, H. L. 'Die Bedeutung der etruskischen Zahlnamen, ibid., p. 239.

ALTHEIM, F. *Der Ursprung der Etrusker*, Baden-Baden, 1950.

LOPES PEGNA, M. *Saggio di bibliografia etrusca*, Florence, 1953; *Storia del propolo etrusco*, Florence, 1959.

NEPPI MODONA, A. *A Guide to Etruscan Antiquities*, new ed., Florence, 1954.

COLI, V. *Il diritto pubblico degli Umbri e le Tavole Eugubine*, Milan, 1958.

CHAPTER 21

Runes and Oghams

(Figs. 21.1–11)

BEFORE I pass to the main offshoot of the Etruscan alphabet *i.e.*, the Roman character, which in practice has become the universal script of the modern world, I shall deal briefly with two European scripts, which do not seem to have derived either from the Latin or from the Greek letters. At least one of them appears to have originated, directly or indirectly, from a variety of the Etruscan alphabet (*see* p. 393). At any rate, whatever the source of the runes, we may assume that they were a creation and that the inventors—though working upon the basis of an existing script—succeeded in their intention to create a system best suited to their language and to their writing material.

RUNES

The Name

The old Nordic and Anglo-Saxon word *run*, the early Icelandic *runar*, and the old high-German *runa*, are connected with the old Germanic root *ru-* and the Gothic *runa*, meaning 'mystery,' 'secret,' 'secrecy,' and the old high-German *runen* and modern German *raunen*, meaning to 'whisper.' The origin of the name *runes* or 'runic,' given to the script here dealt with, is probably due to the fact that, like all primitive peoples, the ancient Germanic peoples attributed magic powers to the mysterious symbols scratched on armour, jewels, tombstones, and so forth. Indeed, early Germanic sagas and poems abound with instances of the magic power of the runes, as in the story of Sigurd the Dragon-Slayer and the story of the Icelandic hero Egill, son of Skallagrim, of the tenth century. There were even treatises on the use of the runic characters for magic. 'Othin, according to the "Ynglinga Saga," taught his magic arts by runes' (C. E. Wright).

INSCRIPTIONS AND WRITTEN DOCUMENTS

The runes were used chiefly for inscriptions; they were cut or carved on metal, stone or wood, the art of wood-cutting having been highly developed amongst the early Germanic peoples. Many runic inscriptions were executed by expert craftsmen.

The inscriptions can be divided into clearly defined conventional types; the most interesting are those, already mentioned, which were cut for magical purposes, and those appealing to heathen deities. Runes were mainly used as memorial inscriptions, but also for divination and for messages, as well as for carving the name of the artist or of the owner on weapons or ornaments; the characteristic *bracteati*, or circular pendants of thin gold, were originally imitations of Roman medallions, but about the fifth century A.D. the animal motive was introduced, the latter being either symbolic or purely ornamental. The runic calendars are another interesting class; those from Norway are known as *Primstaves*, *prim* being the equivalent of 'golden number'; those from Denmark are called *Rimstocks*, from *rim*, 'calendar,' and *stock*, 'stick.' They were a kind of perpetual calendar, and were used in some parts of Scandinavia as late as the beginning of last century. They are of various shapes, such as sword-shaped or plain staves—which vary in length from a few inches to nearly five feet—walking sticks, oval rings or tablets of wood or bone. The days of the year were represented by runic characters, feasts and certain special days of the season were represented by symbolic signs, for instance, St. Lawrence's Day, 10th August, by a gridiron, and St. Martin's day, 11th November, by a goose. The nineteen 'golden numbers,' for finding the full moon, were also inscribed in their places. These Scandinavian calendars were of pagan origin, but the earliest examples extant belong to the late Middle Ages. The English 'clog almanacks,' found in Staffordshire, resemble the later Scandinavian runic calendars, but they are not inscribed with runes.

Earliest Inscriptions

The earliest inscriptions extant (Fig. 21.2) belong, as already mentioned, to the third–fifth centuries A.D. Some scholars, however, attribute to the first century A.D. a short inscription, discovered at Trondhjem, Norway, which seems to belong to a much later period. Two short inscriptions, one from Negau, being written on a bronze helmet attributed to the second century B.C., and the other from Maria Saalerberg (Carinthia), on a horn stiletto, dated perhaps in the first century B.C., are regarded by some scholars as Rætic (*see* above), and by others as early Germanic runes; they seem to be written in a Teutonic language, and in a North Etruscan script, but not in runes (Fig. 21.5*b–c*). Some scholars regard them as forgeries.

Inscriptions found in Sweden

On the whole, *c.* 4,000 inscriptions are extant; the greater part of them, about 2,500, come from Sweden. They belong mainly (*c.* 2,000) to the eleventh and early twelfth century, whilst only about twenty-five inscriptions, including a few *bracteati*, belong to the early period (Fig. 21.2*h, i*). About half of the inscriptions discovered in Sweden were found in Upland, and about 250 in the island of Gothland. The stone-inscription from Rœk, Œstergœtland, belonging to *c.* A.D. 900, is the longest of all the runic inscriptions; it is also most interesting, being inscribed in four varieties of runic writing (Fig. 21.5*d*).

Denmark and Schleswig: the cradle of knowledge of runes

There are over fifty inscriptions extant, including some forty *bracteati*, dating between the third and sixth centuries A.D., while about 200 stone-inscriptions date mainly from the ninth to the middle eleventh century. The clasp (Fig. 21.2*c*) from Vi-mose in Fyn, south-west Denmark, attributed to the middle of the third century A.D., is considered the earliest runic inscription extant. The end-clasp of a sword-sheath (Fig. 21.2*d*) from Torsbjerg in Schleswig, attributed to *c.* A.D. 300, is another very early runic inscription. The Golden Horn (Fig. 21,2*e*) from Gallehus (northern Schleswig) of *c.* 400, found and published in 1734, but since (in 1802) stolen and melted for the sake of the gold, is also remarkable.

Norway

About sixty inscriptions, including ten *bracteati*, belong to the early period, but relatively few monuments are attributed to the later period. One of the longest inscriptions of the earlier period is that on the Tune-stone (south-east Norway) (Fig. 21.2*f*), belonging to the fifth century. The Einang stone-inscription is attributed to *c.* A.D. 400. The longest runic inscription discovered in Norway is the stone from Eggjum, *c.* A.D. 700, still presenting over 170 readable letters.

The British Isles

There are extant about fifty runic inscriptions upon raised stones, mainly stone crosses, and upon loose objects, but very few have been found in England proper. The most artistic are the celebrated Northumbrian crosses, dated about 670–680 A.D., at Bew-castle, near Brampton, Cumberland, and Ruthwell, near Dumfries in Scotland, the latter containing part of the poem on the Crucifixion by Cædmon, the herdsman poet. The inscription found at Collingham (Yorkshire) commemorates the death of King Oswiu, murdered in A.D. 650. For the Northumbrian crosses *see* W. Victor, *Die northumbrischen Runensteine*, 1895; G. B. Brown (and Q. Blyth Webster), *The Arts in Early England*, V, London 1921; R. G. Collingwood, *Cumberland and Westmorland Trans.*, XXX (1934).

Among the portable objects is the *scramasax*, or sword-knife (Fig. 21.3*b*), found in the Thames in 1857, and now in the British Museum; it is attributed by some scholars to the fifth–sixth century A.D., by others, with more probability, to about A.D. 800. The most remarkable object, however, and the best preserved, is the 'Franks Casket' (Fig. 21.3*a*); it is so named after Sir Wollaston Franks, who purchased it in 1857 and presented it to the British Museum, where it is now deposited, except for the right side, which is in the Bargello Museum at Florence. The inscriptions and illustrations of the casket, carved in whale's bone, are full of interest from palæo-graphic, literary and artistic points of view. The casket is regarded by some scholars as not later than about A.D. 650, by others as belonging to about A.D. 700. Other interesting objects with runic inscriptions are a gold finger-ring from Greymoor Hill, Kingmoor, near Carlisle, a bone comb-case from Lincoln, etc.

An important group of stone-inscriptions of Norse origin was discovered at Mæshowe (Orkney) and published by J. Farrer (*Notice of Runic Inscriptions*, etc., Edinburgh, 1862); there are about thirty stones, dated probably 1152–3. Of the runic inscriptions found in the Isle of Man and in Ireland, particular mention should be made of the stone from Kirk Michael, *c.* A.D. 1100 (Fig. 21.6*b*, *see* below), and that from Greenmount Louth, twelfth century A.D.

Other Countries

Curiously enough, Iceland, which has preserved such a rich old Germanic literature, is very poor in runic inscriptions, the earliest of them dating *c.* A.D. 1200. The runic inscription found farthest to the north-west is a stone from the island of Kingigtors-suak, Baffin's Bay, west of Greenland, in 72° 55′ north.

Only a few runic inscriptions came to light in western and southern Germany and in Austria, while single objects containing runic inscriptions have been found even in (1) the modern eastern French Department of Saône et Loire, that is the old Burgundian kingdom (the Charnay brooch, fifth century A.D., Fig. 21.2*g*); (2) in Volhynia (the spearhead from Kovel, Fig. 21.2*a*, attributed to the fourth century A.D.); (3) on the Russian Black Sea coast (the stone from Berezan', attributed to the eleventh century A.D.); (4) in Greece (the marble lion, dated *c.* 1170, found in the Piræus, Athens, and taken to Venice in 1687); and (5) in Roumania. In the last country a big golden ring was found in 1837 in the great fourth-century treasure discovered at Petrossa de jos, prov. Buzau, about 60 miles from Bucarest; the ring contains the following Gothic inscription in runic characters: *gutaniowihailag*, which has been explained as *Gutan(e) Iowi hailag*, 'sacred to Jove of the Goths' (that is, to Donar), or *Gutani owi (awi) hailag* ('Gutorum possessio sacra'), or *Gutani ingwa hailag* ('Gutorum Ingu sacrum').

Runic Manuscripts

There is no certain evidence of wide literary use of runes in early times, but some scholars hold that the runic writing was widely employed for all kinds of secular documents, such as legal provisions, contracts, genealogies, poems, etc. However, the manuscripts extant are rare and relatively late. Amongst the more important runic manuscripts are: the old Danish *Codex Runicus* written in runes, dating from the end of the thirteenth century, which is a legal manuscript; the so-called *Fasti Danici* of *c.* 1348; the *Codex Leidensis*, at Leyden, Holland; the *Codex Sangallensis* 878, at St. Gallen; the *Codex Salisburgensis* 140 (Fig. 21.5*h*) now in Vienna, etc.; there is also a runic prayer-book extant written probably for a layman who did not know Latin. The earliest MS. version of the later Old English runes now extant is MS. No.

17 in the Library of St. John's College, Oxford, dated 1110: *see* C. L. Wrenn, 'Late Old English Rune-names,' *Medium Aevum*, I, 1932.

ORIGIN OF RUNES

The Runic script, which can be considered the 'national' writing of the Teutons, especially of the North Germanic peoples, offers many difficult problems. It is still uncertain when and how the runes were invented. This problem has been hotly discussed by scholars and others. The theory of the *Urrunen* (that is, the forerunners of the runes), a supposed prehistoric German nordic alphabetic script, the parent of the runes and of all the Mediterranean alphabets alike, including the Phœnician, is based on racial and political grounds, and need not be seriously considered. We do not, however, exclude the possibility that ancient Germanic peoples, like other primitive tribes, may have occasionally employed certain symbols for magic divination, for religious purposes, and for *notae* in balloting, as Tacitus (*Germania*, ch. X) termed them, but such symbols were not a true script, and their influence on the origin of the alphabetic runes might prove, at the very most, to be purely external.

The thorny, elongated and angular shapes of the runes, which look as though they belonged to the seventh or sixth century B.C., and the direction of writing of the earlier runic inscriptions (either from right to left, or *boustrophedon*) induced the great Isaac Taylor to suggest as the prototype of the runes, the Greek alphabet as used in the sixth century B.C. in the Greek colonies of the Black Sea, and the Goths, living at that period in southern Russia, as the inventors of the runic alphabet. This theory, however, although endorsed by many other scholars, cannot be accepted because of the time-lag. Indeed, there is no evidence for the existence of the runes previous to the Christian era. For the same reason we must reject another theory, which, while accepting the view that the runic character was invented in the region of the Black Sea, suggests that it descended not directly from a Greek, but from an Asianic source (*see* Chapter 19).

Some scholars propounded the Greek cursive alphabet of the last centuries B.C. as the parent of the runes, and the Celts as the mediators, but there is no evidence for this assertion.

Others, and they are the majority, propose the Latin alphabet as the source of the runic character. Wimmer believed that the runes developed from the Latin alphabet of the end of the second century A.D. Agrell also contends strongly for a Latin origin, but he finds the counterparts of the runic alphabet in the cursive *graffiti* of Pompeii, and he regards the first century A.D. as the date of the transformation of the Latin alphabet into the runic script. According to von Friesen, a combination of Latin and Greek alphabets was the source of the runes. 'Some individual Goths—mercenaries, for instance—from the north-western coast of the Black Sea, in the course of visits to the Roman provinces. learnt Greek and Latin and the Greek and Latin forms of writing used in state edicts and in private life.... Such a Goth, or several such Goths working together, undertook to write out the Gothic language on the basis of the knowledge of Latin and Greek writing thus acquired. The result of these efforts is the runic stave' (O. von Friesen). The invention of the runes influenced by the Greek colonists of the Black Sea, is by Agrell attributed to the Goths, and is supposed to have taken place in the second or third century A.D. All these theories are unacceptable; the direction of writing of the earliest runic inscriptions, and the shapes of the letters, exclude *a priori* their origin in a late Greek or Latin alphabet, and especially in a cursive style. A few scholars, amongst them Bredsdorff, see in the Gothic alphabet the prototype of the runes, which is certainly not the case, for the very same reason.

We may with more probability accept the opinion that the runic script was derived from a North Etruscan alphabet. This theory has been propounded by many scholars, such as Weinhold, Oberziner, Bugge, Marstrander, Hammerstrœm (who also sees Gallic influences in the invention of the runes), Feist (who suggests later Celtic and Latin influences), Arntz, Buonamici, and many others. Rhys Carpenter, who also accepts this theory, rightly points out that 'the temporal chasm between the latest specimen of North Italic and the earliest specimen of runic is not too great to be spanned.'

Accepting a North Etruscan source for the runes, and not excluding some Latin influences, we can more easily understand why the runic scripts, although they have a very ancient appearance, are relatively late. The phonetic value of some letters, for instance of the letter *fe*, which would have had the value of a *w* (*digamma*) were the script of Greek origin, are also more readily explained by a North Etruscan origin, with Latin influences (*see* also p. 398).

As to the date of the invention of the runes, I agree with Rhys Carpenter that the transmission of the North Etruscan alphabet 'beyond the Italian frontier' must have taken place earlier than the time of Julius Cæsar, but need not have been earlier than the second century B.C. The Negau and Maria Saalerberg inscriptions, already referred to, may belong to the type which can be regarded as the link between the North Etruscan and the runic alphabets. For the comparison of the runes with the Kök Turki runes, *see* pp. 245 f. and Fig. 16.8*b*.

It is still an open problem whether the runes were originally employed mainly for magical purposes or as a usual means of communication. The other still unsolved question is whether the runes were originally carved on wood, in which case the straight strokes and the angular shapes could be carved with ease and so would be preferred to curves, or whether they were originally used mainly for drawing and painting on clay and metal, in which case angular shapes would be due to the script from which the runes were borrowed. In this regard, Sir Ellis Minns rightly points out the importance of the absence of horizontal strokes in the runic letters. 'Runes must have been developed for carving on round sticks. Then every letter can be very quickly made with a knife.'

THE FUTHARK (= THE FIRST SIX LETTERS)

As in the Semitic and Greek alphabets, each rune had its name (Fig. 21.1): these names are recorded in later Anglo-Saxon manuscripts, for instance, in the MS. 17 in the Library of St. John's, Oxford, as well as in an English rune-song, and, in an old Danish form, in the *Codex Leidensis*, where the names are written in runes and in Latin letters, in a late and corrupt form.

The order of the runic letters is quite different from that of the Semitic, Greek, Etruscan and Latin alphabets. We may see this from a few inscriptions, such as the Thames *scramasax*, the Charnay brooch, the Kylfver stone from Gothland, and others, as well as from some manuscripts (*see*, for instance, Figs. 21.5*k*, 6*a*).

DEVELOPMENT OF RUNIC WRITING

We can distinguish three main varieties, the last having a few sub-varieties:

EARLY OR COMMON GERMANIC OR PRIMITIVE NORSE

About 100 inscriptions extant, dating mainly from the third to eighth centuries A.D., belong to this group. The 'alphabet' or rather 'futhark' consists of twenty-four letters (Fig. 21.1). It is generally assumed that it corresponded roughly with the original *futhark* of the Goths, of which very little is now known.

In the adaptation of the symbols to the sounds of the various Germanic dialects, the phonetic values of some symbols were obviously more or less modified.

The runes were divided into three groups known as *ættir*.

The shapes of the single runes of the three *ættir* are to be seen in Fig. 21.1. The following were their phonetic values: *f, u, th* (surd), *a, r, k*, 3, *w*; / *h, n, i, γ, hw–ih, p,* R, *s*; / *t, b, e, m, l, ng, d* and *đ, o*. 3 represents a sound similar to the hard *g*; R represents the soft *s*; *đ* is the symbol for the dental *th*. These phonetic values, however, were not constant, and some of them are uncertain. The symbol representing the sound *hw* or *ih* was very rare; in the Anglo-Saxon runic writing it had the value of *eo*, or *h* or *ih*; in primitive Norse it seems to have represented either the *i* or the *e*; but originally, according to some scholars, it seems to have represented the Gothic sound *hw*.

About A.D. 600, the rune *ár* came to represent the sound *a*, while the F-like letter changed its value to nasal *a* (equivalent to French *on*) or *o*.

However, the twenty-four common-Germanic runes seem, on the whole, to have covered adequately the sounds of early Germanic forms of speech, including Primitive Old Norse.

'Old Norse' was spoken by the North Germanic or Scandinavian peoples. In the first-second centuries A.D. it began to differentiate from the other early Germanic dialects, although in the first period of its development, called Primitive Norse, which roughly lasted from A.D. 100 to 700, it still preserved the early Germanic vowels and endings. The second period, called Viking Norse (about A.D. 700–1100) is the period of vital phonetic changes and of the development of the various dialects: about A.D. 1000 the difference between western Norse (Norway and its dependencies) and eastern Norse (Sweden, Denmark, and their colonies) was already marked, while the eleventh century witnessed the development of the sub-dialects of West Norse into Norwegian and Icelandic, and of East Norse into Swedish and Danish. While the language of the first two periods is mainly preserved in runic inscriptions, the third period, called Literary Norse, A.D. 1100–1500, is, roughly speaking, outside the subject dealt with here.

Slavic Runes

According to some scholars runes were also employed for writing Slavic; others have even tried to prove the existence of a special kind of Slavic runes. This 'problem of Slavic runes' has been hotly debated. I do not think there is any certain evidence either of the employment of runes for Slavonic languages, or of the existence of Slavic runes. The problem is still *sub judice*.

ANGLO-SAXON OR ANGLIAN RUNES

Germanic forms of speech were brought to these islands during the fifth and sixth centuries A.D. by heathen invaders belonging mainly to three West Germanic tribes, the Angles, coming from what is still called Angeln, the Saxons, from the country north of the river Elbe, now called Holstein, and the Jutes, from farther south in the same region. These various tribes collectively were called by the Britons 'Saxons,' after the tribe with whom they first came in contact, or Angli or Engle. The chief changes in the development of the West Germanic or Anglo-Frisian sound-system, particularly in the Old English dialects, was the great modification caused by vowel-mutation and by other changes in the sound.

The Anglo-Saxon tribes originally made use of the runic writing. The age of the majority of the extant English runic inscriptions is uncertain; some of them certainly belong to the period when the Anglo-Saxon runic script was being superseded by an adaptation of the Roman alphabet to Old English. On the whole it may be said that the runes were employed in England for about five centuries.

The most important difference between the common Germanic and the Anglo-Saxon runic varieties is that, the former being insufficient to represent the rich-vowel system of the Old English dialects, new letters were added (new runic letters, for *a* and *o* sounds were already added in Friesland).

Later new consonantal symbols were also added (Fig. 21.1). The Anglo-Saxon runic script consisted thus of twenty-eight letters, and in the ninth century the number was increased to thirty-three (Fig. 21.5h). Also the phonetic values of the single symbols were partly different. For instance, the symbol which in the other systems has the shape of R and the value *z-s*, in the Anglo-Saxon runic writing had usually the value *x* (*ks*). This complete system has come down to us not only in inscriptions, already mentioned, but also in manuscripts (Fig. 21.5*h*) belonging to the ninth–eleventh centuries. The most important of them is a manuscript containing the poem in Old English of King Alfred's time or a little later which describes in verse each runic letter-word, in order to facilitate memorizing. Here are, as an example, the first three verses, describing the letters *f* or *feoh* (meaning 'money,' 'fee'), *u* or *ur* (meaning '*aurochs*'), and *th* or *thorn* (meaning 'thorn');

Feoh byth frofur fira gehwylcum,   Money gives comfort   to all men's moods,
sceal theah manna gehwyle miclun hyt doelan, But each who possesses should give to others,
gif he wile for drihtne   domes hleoten.   If he should have from God   a goodly fate.

Ur byth anmod   and oferhyrned,   The aurochs is bold   and horned above,
fela frecne deor,   feohteth mid hornum: A fierce animal,   he fights with horns,
mære mor-stapa: thæt is modig wuht.   That moor-dweller famous; he is a mighty animal.

Thorn byth thearle scearp   thegna gehwylcum   Thorn is most sharp   to every man,
anfengys yfyl,   ungemetun rethe   Its assault evil,   enormously harsh
manna gehwylcum   the him mid resteth.   To any man   who rests upon it.

Another MS., already referred to, the *Codex Salisburgensis* 140 (now in Vienna), belonging to the ninth or tenth century, shows on the folio 20 the Anglo-Saxon runic alphabet (Fig. 21.5*h*). The thirty-three late Anglo-Saxon runes are also reproduced in the MS. *Cotton Domitian A.* 9 (Brit. Mus.), two other relevant MSS. *Otho B.*10 and *Galba A.*2 having been destroyed by fire (fortunately, the two MSS. had already been published: *Otho B.*10 by Hickes in 1731, *Galba A.*2 in 1865; *see* C. L. Wrenn, 'Late Old English Rune-names,' *Medium Aevum*, I, 1932).

Apart from the increase in the number of symbols, the Anglo-Saxon runes differed from the other runic systems in the shapes of some letters, as can be seen in Fig. 21.1: *see*, for instance, the letters *k* and *h*. The new letters were modifications of old signs or abritrary inventions.

The Anglo-Saxon runes influenced also the adaptation of the Roman alphabet to Old English; the symbol *thorn* was employed for a long period to express the sound *th*, and the symbol *wen* was employed to represent the *w* (which was otherwise written *uu*).

NORDIC OR SCANDINAVIAN VARIETIES
(Fig. 21.4)

At the end of the Primitive Norse and during the Viking Norse period, the Nordic or Scandinavian stock of sounds reached between thirty and forty, and therefore the common-Germanic runes became inadequate to represent all the sounds. Curiously enough, the parallel linguistic development of the Scandinavian languages produced a result directly opposite to that of Old English: while, as already mentioned, the Anglo-Saxon runes were increased to twenty-eight and thirty-three letters, the Scandinavian system was reduced to sixteen. Obviously, twenty-four letters could not represent thirty or forty sounds; therefore it became the habit to represent different sounds with the same rune. Thus, for instance, the same sign was used for a voiceless consonant, and for the corresponding voiced consonant (*k* and *g*; *t* and *d*). The vowels were as ambiguous as the consonants: *a* could also represent short and long *æ* and *o*; *i* was also used for short and long *e*, *æ* and *œ*; *u* also for *w*, and short or long *o*, *œ* and *y*; *au* also for short or long *o* or *œ*; *i* for *y*; *o* was sometimes employed for *w*; *w* for *u*.

Double runes were seldom expressed as such; a single rune could stand for two, even when the latter were in separate words; sometimes, when a word ended with two runes and the following word began with the same two runes, these were written only once. The rune for *n* was often omitted before a consonant, especially after the nasal *a* (the French sound *on*); similarly, *m* was often omitted.

In conclusion, at the beginning of the Viking period, owing to confusion of spelling, which allowed one rune to represent several more or less related sounds, some of the runes began to fall into disuse: from about A.D. 800 a reduced system of sixteen runes came into use (Fig. 21.1), appearing earliest in Danish inscriptions; it appears also in the *Codex Leidensis*. This shortened system can be divided into two main varieties, the Danish (also used in south-west Sweden), and the Swedish-Norwegian. In Sweden and Norway, the shortened system appears about the end of the ninth century, and is best represented by the Œstergœthian form namely the script of the Rœk inscription, Œstergœtland, Sweden (Fig. 21.5*d*). Comparatively few monuments are cut in the Swedish-Norwegian short runic system. The main differences between the Danish and the Swedish-Norwegian varieties consist in the shapes of the letters *h*, *n*, *a*, *s*, *h*, *m*, and **R**. In Norway, there appeared in the eleventh century a peculiar mixture of the Swedish-Norwegian and the Danish varieties.

Hælsinge Runes

Another characteristic of the shortened system is the simplification of many letters, especially in the Swedish-Norwegian variety, in which the letters were gradually reduced till the writing became a kind of shorthand; they are then called Hælsinge runes (Fig. 21.5*g–h*), which according to some scholars (for instance, O. von Friesen) seem to have been invented in the region of Lake Mælar, but are found mainly on stones discovered in the region of Hælsingland, and attributed to the eleventh century.

The Manx Runes

The Manx runic system (Figs. 21.5*f*, 6*b*) is a variety of the Swedish–Norwegian short system. The script of the nearly thirty inscriptions found in the Isle of Man agrees mainly with the Œstergœthian form, and is considered by many scholars as a descendant of the Swedish short system. According to E. V. Gordon, this seems unlikely. 'The Celto-Scandinavian inhabitants of Man were of Norwegian descent, and there cannot have been many Swedes in the west. The Man inscriptions more probably preserve an early Norwegian tradition' (Gordon). It is, however, necessary not to overlook the fact that the earliest Norwegian short system resembled the Swedish one, and the Manx system of the eleventh and twelfth centuries, as represented by the Kirk Michael stone, c. 1100 (Fig. 21.5), and other monuments, seems to have been connected with this early Norwegian short system, and can therefore be considered a variety of both the Swedish and the Norwegian systems. It was only at a later stage, that is, during the eleventh–twelfth centuries, that the Norwegian short system became strongly influenced by the Danish type and produced some independent developments, so as to become differentiated from the Swedish.

The Manx system can be divided into two main sub-divisions each distinguished by the use of the fourth rune, which in some inscriptions represents the nasalized *a*, while in others it stands for *o*. A peculiar feature of the Manx runes is the absence of the sixteenth Scandinavian rune.

The Dotted Runes (*Stungnar Rûnir*)

It is not yet established where the dotted runes were invented or first used. According to some scholars it was in Norway, according to others it was in Denmark. It was, however, probably due to the influence of the Anglian runes that the Scandiavian systems began to be enlarged by the so-called pointed or dotted runes. The earliest dotted runes, appearing about the year A.D. 1000, were the symbols for *y* and *e*; the *y*, of Anglo-Saxon origin, was a *u* inside of which an *i* was marked; it seems that after this model, the symbol for *e* was constructed out of the *i*. A little later different consonantal symbols were also distinguished; out of the *k* a special letter for *g* was constructed, a dot on a runic consonantal symbol usually indicating that it was voiced. The dotted runic system spread over all the Scandinavian lands, even to the island of Kingigtorssuak, west of Greenland.

During the eleventh and twelfth centuries the employment of the dotted runes became general in Denmark, although it was not consistent—sometimes only the first and last runes were dotted. In Norway the use of the dotted runes coincided with the fusion of the short Danish and Swedish-Norwegian systems, as a result of which a complete dotted runic alphabet was produced, aiming probably at a systematic representation of the Old Norse language in order to avoid the ambiguity of the representation of more sounds by one symbol. This attempt, based probably on the Roman alphabet, could obviously not succeed owing to the increasing diffusion of the Latin script (obviously due to the spread of Christianity: once more—*Alphabet follows Religion*). Although single monuments cut in the systematic dotted system, and dated in the thirteenth and fourteenth centuries, appear in many parts of Scandinavia, it seems that it was widely employed only in Gotland. There appears a special variety of the dotted runic system.

The dotted runes were generally known all over Scandinavia and were also used for private records by cultured laymen, while circles connected with the Church employed the Roman character.

Cryptic Varieties (Fig. 21.5*i–g, l*)

There were also many cryptic varieties, some simple with dots for vowels, with transposition of letters, and so on. Then, there were various sorts of 'bind-runes,' having several characters joined together on one and the same stem; without a knowledge of the key it is impossible to decipher them. Various cryptic series are mentioned in the St. Gallen manuscript (Fig. 21.5*l*).

Some of the cryptic scripts were used for private purposes together with the short system of the Swedish-Norwegian runes.

Two peculiar runic systems must be particularly mentioned, one of them being the *kvistrûnir* or 'twig-runes' (in German, *Zweigrunen*), consisting of a vertical stem with secondary twigs or strokes branching off (Fig. 25.5*g*). For the purpose of constructing these runes, the system was divided into three groups (*ættir*): *t, b, m, l, y; / h, n, i, a, s; / f, u, th, o, r, k*. In the Rœk stone, the main stem is horizontal and the secondary strokes branch off upwards or downwards; the groups are also different, the first being *t, b, l, m, k*. The group to which the letter in question belongs is indicated on one side, while the place which it occupies in the group is indicated on the other side. The *tjaldrûnir*, 'tent-runes' or 'cross-runes,' are a simpler system; they consist of two oblique strokes in the shape of a cross, with little dashes branching off (Fig. 21.5*i*).

End of Runic Scripts

The gradual displacement of the runes by the Latin alphabet appears clearly to have coincided with the increasing influence of the Church of Rome. The victory of the Latin alphabet over the runic script corresponded with the sole dominion of the Latin church in northern, western and central Europe. Indeed, whenever a region became definitely Christianized and controlled by the Church, the custom of erecting runic inscriptions was abandoned. The runic scripts, however, lingered on, although in limited use, for a long time after the introduction of Christianity. The use of runes for charms and memorial inscriptions lasted into the sixteenth century. There is even evidence of the employment of runes in Gotland as late as the seventeenth century. According to O. von Friesen, one of the greatest authorities on the subject, 'in outlying Swedish regions like Dalarna and Hærjedalen . . . they were used for making occasional notes down to our own times.'

BIBLIOGRAPHY

BELL, W. 'On Runic Writing,' *J. Brit. Archæol. Assoc.*, 1867 onwards.

MAGNUSSON, E. 'Origin of the Runic Alphabet,' *Trans. Camb. Philol. Soc.*, 1878.

TAYLOR, I. *Greeks and Goths*, London, 1879.

STEPHENS, G. *Handbook of the Old-northern Runic Monuments*, London-Edinburgh, 1884; *The Runes. Whence Came They?*, London and Copenhagen, 1894.

SIEVERS, E. 'Runen und Runeninschriften' (in Paul's *Grundriss der germanischen Philologie*), Berlin, 1891–3.

VIËTOR, W. *Die northumbrischen Runensteine*, Marburg (Hessen), 1895.

WIMMER, L. F. A. *De Danske Runemindesmærker*, 4 vols., Copenhagen, 1895–1908; *De Danske Rune-mindesmærker*, Copenhagen, 1914; *Collectio Runologica Wimmeriana*, Copenhagen, 1915.

NECKEL, G. 'Zur Einführung in die Runenforschung,' *Germanisch-Romanische Monatsschr.*, Heidelberg, 1909.

SCHETELIG, H. *Arkeologiske Tidsbestemmelser av Ældre Norske Runeindskrifter*, Christiania, 1914.

DICKINS, B. *Runic and Heroic Poems of the old Teutonic Peoples*, Cambridge, 1915; *The Runic Inscriptions of Mæshowe*, Kirkwall, 1930.

BRATE, E. *Œstergœtlands Runinskrifter*, Stockholm, 1915.

HERMANNSSON, E. *Catalogue of Runic Literature, Forming a Part of the Icelandic Collection*, etc., Oxford University Press, 1918.

KLUGE, F. 'Runenschrift und Christentum,' *Germania*, 1919.

VON FRIESEN, O. *Rœkstenen*, etc., Stockholm, 1920, and Stockholm, 1934; *Rœkstenen i Bohuslæn och runorna*, etc., Uppsala, 1924; *Runorna*, Stockholm, 1933; *Sparlœsastenen*, etc., Stockholm, 1940.

SCHRÖDER, F. R. 'Neuere Runenforschung,' *Germanisch-Romanische Monatsschr.*, 1922.

JOHANNESSON, A. *Grammatik der urnordischen Runeninschriften*, Germanische Bibliothek, Heidelberg, 1923.

AGRELL, S. 'Der Ursprung der Runenschrift und die Magie,' *Ark. f. Nord. Filol.*, 1927; 'Zur Frage nach dem Ursprung der Runennamen' (with a summary in English), *Skrift. utg. av Vetensk.-Societ. i Lund*, 1928; *Die spätantike Alphabetmystik und die Runenreihe*, Lund, 1932.

HAMMARSTRŒM, M. 'Om runskriftens hærkomst,' *Stud. i Nordisk Filol.*, Helsingfors, 1929.

MARSTRANDER, C. J. S. 'De gotiske runeminnesmerker,' *Norsk Tidskrift for Sprogvidenskap*, Oslo, 1929.

FEIST, S. 'Zum Ursprung der germanischen Runenschrift,' *Acta Philol. Scand.*, 1929–30.

BORK, F. 'Runenstudien, *Archiv für Schreib- und Buchwesen*, 1929.

KRAUSE, W. *Beiträge zur Runenforschung*, Halle, 1932; *Was man in Runen ritzte*, Halle, 1935; *Runenin-schriften im älteren Futhark*, Halle, 1937.

ARNTZ, H. *Handbuch der Runenkunde*, Halle, 1935; *Die Runenschrift. Ihre Geschichte und ihre Denkmäler*, Halle, 1938; in Otto's *Handbuch der Archäologie*, Munich 1939; 'Upplands Runensteine,' *Germania*, 1941.

SHETELIG, H. and FALK, H. *Scandinavian Archæology*, Oxford, 1937.

Beiträge zur Runenkunde nordischen Sprachwissenschaft, Leipsic, 1938; articles dedicated to Professor G. Neckel.

ARNTZ, H. and ZEISS, H. *Gesamtausgabe der älteren Runendenkmäler*. Bearbeitet im Auftrage des Archäolog. Instit. des Deutschen Reiches, I–, Leipsic, 1939.

WESSÉN, E. *Schwedens Runeninschriften*, Stockholm, 1947.

JACOBSON, L. R. and others, *Runic Inscriptions of Denmark*, Copenhagen, 1947.

HÖFLER, O. *Der Runenstein von Rœk und die germanische Individualweihe*, Tübingen, 1952.

BENGTSSON, *Stenarna talar; anteckmingar om fornminnen i Vallentuna, Markim, Orkesta och Frœsunda*, etc., Stockholm, 1955.

MOLTKE, E. *Jon Skonvig og de andre runetegnere*, Copenhagen, 1956.

Norges innskrifter med de yngre runer, Oslo, 1956.

SCHNEIDER, K. *Die germanischen Runnennamen*, Meisenheim am Glau, 1956.

OGHAMS

The Name

The Gaelic word *'ogham'* has been alike applied to a peculiar form of cryptic speech, in which, for instance, the names of letters replaced in certain syllables the letters themselves; and to the script, with which we are concerned. Even the meaning of the word is still obscure. According to tradition the script was named after its inventor, but it is more probable that the name of the script was extended to its mythical inventor. According to Professor Rhys, the word *ogham* means 'skilled use of words.' Other scholars maintain the possibility of the connection between 'Ogham' (Old Irish *ogom*) and the Gaulish Hercules Ogmios.

L. J. D. Richardson has tried to prove (*see* 'The Word "Ogham",' in *Hermathena*, Dublin LXII, 1943, p. 12) that the word *ogham* is derived from the Greek word *agma*: he suggests that the inventors of this script intended to name it from some peculiarity which distinguished it from other scripts. And so, according to him, the script was called the 'agma'-alphabet, because it improved on the model by providing a special letter for a sound called in Greek *agma*.

OGHAMIC INSCRIPTIONS
(Figs. 21.6b, 7–11)

The use of the oghamic character was peculiar to the Celtic population of the British Isles. There are about 375 inscriptions (Fig. 21.7) extant; 316 of them have been discovered in Ireland, chiefly (261) in the southern counties (Kerry, 121; Cork, 81; Waterford, 47; and Kilkenny, 12), but some (55) have been found elsewhere in Ireland, one having come to light at the end of the last century in the north-eastern county of Antrim. Forty oghamic inscriptions have been discovered in Wales, particularly in the counties of Pembroke (15), Brecknock (8), Carmarthen (7), Cardigan (4) and Glamorgan (3); two have been found in Denbigh and one in Carnarvon. Only one inscription has come to light in Cornwall, and two in Devon. One oghamic inscription has even been found at Silchester (Hants). About ten inscriptions have been discovered on the Isle of Man and a few in Scotland (*see* below). The Welsh inscriptions are usually bilingual (Latin-Celtic) and written in oghamic and Roman characters. The Irish inscriptions, with one exception, are in ogham alone. Interesting is the runic-oghamic inscription (Fig. 21.6b) from the Isle of Man.

CELTS

The Celts did not produce a script of their own in antiquity, but they were by no

E e

means illiterate. We have to distinguish between the inhabitants of the Roman *Provincia*, the other Celts of the mainland, and the Celts in Britain.

The cultural centre of the *Provincia* was Massalia (Greek) or Massilia (Latin), today Marseille. Refugees from Phokaia had founded this city about 600 B.C., and so it had Greek civilization right from the beginning. From here and from other Greek colonies, *e.g.*, Herakles Mónoikos (Monaco), Greek civilization and especially the Greek alphabet spread through the whole of the later *Provincia*, and far beyond. When the Romans conquered the southern part of Gaul in 122 B.C. and made it their *Provincia*, they found the Greek characters in use there. The Celts of free Gaul were under the influence of the Druids, who developed a considerable moral, didactic, hymnic, epic, and even lyric poetry, but prohibited the writing down of this literature, preferring oral transmission. Unfortunately the chain of oral transmission was broken long ago—perhaps about the time of Caesar's invasion—and nothing of it has reached us; we know only that it existed. Outside the realm of Druidic literature, there are some very scanty epigraphic relics, *e.g.*, coins, medals, inscriptions on tools, swords, etc. These inscriptions are written either in Greek or Latin letters or in a mixture of both. On the whole, Celtic coins were an imitation of the Greek, and the Celtic inscriptions were apparent imitations of the Greek—at the beginning, indeed, they were pure copies made without any understanding of their meaning; later on, understanding was evident. A fine example is the inscription of the sword-smith (or owner?) Korisios on an iron blade found near the lake of Bienne (Biel) in Switzerland in 1870 (René Wyss, *Kosmos*, 52, 3, March, 1956).

When Caesar invaded Gaul in 58 B.C. he reported that he found Greek letters in use with the Helvetii (*Comm.*, I, 29, 1); he mentions that the Druids used Greek letters, which seems very doubtful; but the most interesting story he tells us is how he sent a letter to Quintus Cicero, the orator's brother, who was in dire straits in the North: Caesar wrote either in Latin and Greek letters or in Greek language and script (the two extant reports differ—Caesar, *Comm.*, V, 48, 4 and Dion Cassius, XL, 9, 3). If the letter was in Latin language and Greek characters so that it might not be deciphered by the Gauls if captured, Caesar must have forgotten that four years earlier, he found the Greek characters in use with the Helvetii; thus, it seems more plausible that he wrote in Greek language and script. The so-called 'marble statue of the Magna Mater' in Bonn, with a Celtic inscription in Greek letters, is now considered a forgery (information by Dr. Doppelfeld, Director of the Römisch-Germanisches Museum of Cologne).

The Celts in Britain, before the Roman conquest by Claudius in A.D. 43, also had no letters of their own; they used either Greek or Roman characters, which may have been brought by Roman merchants. Several coins with such inscriptions are known, *e.g.*, that of Cunobelinus (Holinsched's and Shakespeare's Cymbeline), king of the Catuvellauni at Verulamium (St. Albans); his capital and mint was at Camulodunum (Colchester), and his coins show an ear of corn with the Latin letters CVNO. After the Roman conquest the Gauls used Latin letters.

BIBLIOGRAPHY

J. Déchelette, *Manuel d'Archéologie Préhistorique Celtique et Gallo-Romaine. I. Archéologie Préhistorique.* Paris, 1909.

R. Forrer, *Keltische Numismatik der Rhein- und Donaulande,* Strassburg, 1908.

L. Lengyel, *L'Art Gaulois dans les médailles,* Montrouge-Seine, 1954.

ORIGIN OF THE OGHAMS

The origin of this peculiar script is uncertain. According to some scholars, it was imported from the east, or from Iberia. Professor Macalister, a high authority on the subject, maintaining on the whole that the ogham alphabet was invented (or, at least, used) by the druids as a secret code for private signalling—C. E. Wright agrees with this suggestion—tries to derive the additional five letters or *forfeda* from the Greek letters *kh, th, p, ph* and *x*, as found in the Chalcidian type. He thus suggests that the prototype of the oghamic alphabet is to be sought in a Chalcidian form of the Greek alphabet as used in some parts of northern Italy a few centuries B.C. Another authority, L. J. D. Richardson, suggests that the oghams were based on the phonology of that form of the Greek alphabet with which the inventors of the oghamic script were acquainted. W. Keller has emphazised that neither in the Greek alphabet nor in the runes occurs a separate group of vowels. Dr. Eisler suggested (1949) 'the obvious connection with the telegraphic signalling system of the Roman armies', which Celtic auxiliaries must have learned to practise from their overlords.

According to Professor Ifor Williams (*Trans. Hon. Soc. Cymmrodorion,* Sessions 1943 and 1944, London, 1946, pp. 152–6), the oghamic alphabet was an independent invention of a Celtic grammarian from southern Ireland, who knew either the Latin alphabet or the Greek or both, but made no attempt to make his symbols resemble either the Latin or the Greek letters. The invention took place when Old Irish knew neither diphthongs nor the sound *p*, which therefore were not included in the original alphabet of twenty letters. At a later period, when some vowels became diphthongs, and a sign for *p* became necessary, particularly for loan-words, the extra-letters, *forfeda,* were invented.

According to Professors Macalister and Ifor Williams, the division of the oghams in groups of five may have its origin in the suggested derivation of this script from a gesture-alphabet or secret code used by the druids for private signalling. Originally, the five fingers were used in relation to the nose or the leg; in writing, the strokes were used in a similar manner, in relation to the stemline on wood or stone.

However, I still maintain that the problem has not yet been solved, and hardly will be solved. In my opinion, it is one of those instances of the process, many times referred to in this book, which Professor Kroeber has termed 'idea-diffusion' or 'stimulus-diffusion'; to use Kroeber's words, a new element fills some need in a culture which has not previously possessed it. It is the idea which is accepted, but it remains for the receiving culture to develop a new expression. Obviously this process is one which will ordinarily leave a minimum of historical evidence; the specific items of cultural content, upon which historians ordinarily rely in proving connection, are likely to be few or even wholly absent. Positive proofs of such a process are, therefore, difficult to secure long after the act, or wherever the historical record is not quite so full.

If Kroeber's theory can be applied, as I think it can, to the invention of oghams, we may take it as likely, without uselessly going deeper into this matter, that the inventor or inventors of the oghams probably knew of the existence of the runic script and of the Latin alphabet. It is, therefore, *a priori* probable that one of the two or rather both of them had some influence on the origin of the oghamic script. On the whole, it seems that the oghams and the runes were in some way allied systems; this is shown, *e.g.*, in the fact that both 'share the characteristic of having full, native, semantically recognizable names for the letters' (J. A. Walker). The affinity between the two systems, and the fact that they were both employed roughly at the same time in the British Isles, have induced me to deal with the oghams immediately after the runes. But what has here been said will be enough to show that the information which would alone warrant a definite theory on the origin of the oghams is not yet forthcoming.

However, the distribution of the oghamic inscriptions and, according to Kermode, a high authority on the subject, their language and grammatical forms, point to southern Wales or southern Ireland as their place of origin, and to the fourth century A.D. as the date of their origin. Professor Rhys holds on phonetic grounds that the invention of the oghams took place in southern Wales, but the inventor belonged probably to the race of the invaders from southern Ireland.

OGHAMIC SCRIPTS
(Figs. 21.6*b*, 7–11)

The oghams were employed for writing messages and letters, generally on wooden staves, sometimes also on shields or on other hard material, and for carving on tombstones (*see* above).

The ogham alphabet (Fig. 21.8*a*) was very simple; it consisted of twenty letters, which were represented by straight or diagonal strokes varying in number, from 1 to 5, drawn or cut below, or above, or right through horizontal lines, or else, drawn or cut to the left, or right, or right through vertical lines. These horizontal or vertical lines were sometimes replaced, in stones or other squared hard material, by the arrises or edges of the object on which the letters were cut.

The oghams were divided into four groups (*aicme*), each containing five letters. The letters belonging to the first *aicme* (*b, l, f* or *v, s, n*) consisted of 1 to 5 strokes drawn below the main horizontal (or to the right of the vertical line); the second *aicme* (of the letters *h, d, t, c, q*) consisted of 1 to 5 strokes drawn above the horizontal line or to the left of the vertical line; the third *aicme* (of the letters *m, g, ng, z, r*) consisted of 1 to 5 slanting strokes right through the horizontal or perpendicular line; and the fourth *aicme*, consisting of the vowels *a, o, u, e, i*, was represented either by straight strokes intersecting the main line at right angles, or else by notches.

In some instances, special signs, *forfeda*, were used for the diphthongs *eo, oi, ui, io, æ*, placed—according to the use of either a horizontal or vertical main line—either (in the instances of *ui* and *io*) below or to the right, or else (in the case of *æ*) above or to the left, or else (*eo* and *oi*) half above and half beneath, or half to the right and half to the left of the main line. The sound *p*, which was wanting in the regular oghamic alphabet, was sometimes represented by the same sign as the diphthong *io* (Fig. 21.8*a*).

It is generally agreed that the oghams were a cryptic script. The alphabet which I have described was only the basic oghamic script. There were several secondary varieties, such as the 'wheel-oghams,' which St. Columba (521–597) seems to have known; the 'bird-oghams,' the 'tree-oghams,' the 'hill-oghams,' the 'church-oghams,' the 'colour-oghams' and so forth. The use of the oghamic scripts continued until the Middle Ages, and the fourteenth-century *Book of Ballymote* (edited by R. Atkinson, Dublin, 1887) reproduces the earliest keys for transliteration.

BIBLIOGRAPHY

RHYS, J. *Lectures on Welsh Philology*, 2nd ed., London, 1879.

MacNEILL, J. 'The Irish Ogham Inscriptions,' *Proc. Roy. Irish Acad.*, 1909; *Celtic Ireland*, London, 1921; *Archaisms in the Ogham Inscriptions*, Dublin, 1931.

MACALISTER, R. A. S. *Studies in Irish Epigraphy*, 3 vols., London, 1897–1907; *The Archæology of Ireland*, London, 1928; *Ancient Ireland*, London, 1935; *The Secret Languages of Ireland*, Cambridge, 1937; *Corpus Inscriptionum Insularum Celticarum*, I, Dublin, 1945 (bibliography).

ARNTZ, H. in *Paul und Braune's Beiträge zur Gesch. d. deutsch. Sprache und Liter.*, 1935; *Handbuch der Runenkunde*, Halle, 1935; 'Das Ogom,' in *Beiblatt zur Anglia*, 1936.

THURNEYSEN, R. 'Zum Ogom,' *Beiträge*, etc., 1937.

KELLER, W. 'Dir Entstehung des Ogom,' *Beiträge*, etc., 1938, pp. 121 ff.

VENDRYES, J. 'L'écriture ogamique et ses origines,' *Études Celtiques*, IV (1941), pp. 83–116.

PICTISH OGHAMS
(Fig. 21.11)

Two oghams found in western Scotland, one on the small island of Gigha, off the western coast, the other in Argyll, belong to the same class as the oghamic inscriptions found in Ireland and Wales. Many other oghamic inscriptions were discovered in north-eastern Scotland (three in Aberdeen, two in Kincardine, two in Sutherland, one each in some other counties), on the northern isles, as many as six of them coming from the Shetland Islands, and one of the same type from the Isle of Man (Fig. 21.6*b*). They are written in another oghamic variety, which was styled by Ferguson 'scholastic oghams,' and is now generally termed 'Pictish oghams,' these inscriptions being attributed to the ancient Picts.

The Picts

The term 'Picts,' from Latin *Picti*, 'painted,' is considered by some scholars as applied to an otherwise unknown indigenous name. The Celtic-Irish term for 'Picts' was *Cruithen, Cruithni, Cruitnech*; *Cruithentuath* being the term for the 'country of the Picts.' The Welsh term was *Prydyn, Prydain, Prythein*. Some scholars regard all these Celtic terms as connected with the Celtic words *cruth, pryd*, meaning 'shape, external appearance'; they also hold that the Roman term *Picti* might have been a translation or interpretation of the Celtic name.

The term *Prydain* was extended by the Greeks and Romans to indicate the whole of Great Britain and its population: *Pretanikè nésos, Pretanikaì nésoi, Prettanía, Pretania, Pretanoí*. The Romans, however, had another name for this Island and its population: *Brittannia* or *Britannia, Britanni*. Some scholars suggested that the terms Prettania and Britannia were etymologically identical, but, strange as it may appear to a layman, according to other authorities this theory seems to be wrong.

Very little is known about the ethnic and linguistic affinities of the Picts. They are regarded by some scholars as early Celts, by others, for instance by Sir John Rhys, Macalister and MacNeill, as the pre-Celtic aborigines of Scotland. One of the main Pictish tribes, the Caledonians, gave the Roman name to the country.

The Script

The Pictish oghams, like some Irish oghamic inscriptions, generally run upward, but, as Professor Macalister points out, the Pictish carvers began on the *right*-hand edge, and 'when the inscription crosses the top, the writing must run backward, and the side-scores must be inverted—an inconvenience that continues upon the opposite edge. Nothing more clearly proves the Pictish want of experience.' One of the main pecularities of the Pictish oghams is that some of them are marked with binding lines.

Figure 21.11*a* represents an inscription from Brandsbutt, near Inverurie, Aberdeen (Macalister, No. 5); Fig. 21.11*b* represents the ogham part of the runic inscription of Malumkun, at Kirk Michael, Isle of Man (Macalister, No. 20).

The Pictish oghams have not yet been satisfactorily translated. The Picts adopted the Irish oghams and tried to adapt them to their own language. This adaptation seems to have been faulty. According to Professor Macalister, Pictish was not only non-Celtic, but even non-Indo-European, and Pictish and Gaelic were phonetically incompatible. Pictish appear to have possessed sounds for which the Irish ogham had no provision. Therefore, in Macalister's view, additional Pictish symbols were invented to express differentiations in the pronunciation of certain letters. These additional symbols seem to have been vowels for the greater part. This suggest, according to Profedsor Macalister, that, like the Finno-Ugrian languages, Pictish possessed a large variety of vowel-sounds.

Heraldry (?)

It is noteworthy that many Pictish oghamic inscriptions and other Pictish stone monuments contain pictorial symbols, consisting of geometrical signs, representations of animals, birds, fishes, etc. Professor Macalister holds that these pictorial symbols, numbering about fifty, may represent a pictorial heraldry.

There are also a few Pictish inscriptions in a half-uncial or 'Irish' type of the Roman character.

BIBLIOGRAPHY

RHYS, J. 'The Inscriptions and Language of the Northern Picts,' *Proc. Soc. Antiq. of Scotland*, 1891–2; *Celtic Britain*, 4th ed., London, 1908.

ROMILLY ALLEN, J. *The Early Christian Monuments of Scotland*, Edinburgh, 1903.

MacNEILL, E. 'The Language of the Picts,' *Yorkshire Celtic Studies* (1938–9), 1940, pp. 3–45.

MACALISTER, R. A. S. 'The Inscriptions and Language of the Picts,' *Essays and Studies presented to Professor Eoin MacNeill*, Dublin, 1940 (with extensive bibliography).

VENDRYES, J. 'L'Ecriture ogamique et ses origines,' *Études Celtiques*, IV (1942).

Germanic Oghams (?) (Fig. 21.11c)

Two limestone tablets, discovered at Brier (Magdeburg) on the River Elbe in Saxony, are written in a script which has some similarity with the oghams, but nothing can be said about their mutual connection.

BIBLIOGRAPHY

MACALISTER, R. A. S. *Studies in Irish Epigraphy*, II, London, 1902.

CHAPTER 22

The Latin Alphabet

EARLY LATIN INSCRIPTIONS (Figs. 22.1–3)

IT is a somewhat curious fact that the Latin or Roman alphabet, which has such a great importance in the history of civilization, had a very poor beginning and a very poor history during the first five or six centuries of its existence.

The oldest record of it extant is to be found in the Præneste fibula (preserved in the Museo Pigorini, at Rome), a gold brooch (Fig. 22.1), dating probably from the seventh century B.C., rather than from the sixth or even the fifth century, as some scholars were inclined to think. The inscription runs from right to left and reads clearly: *manios: med: fhefhaked: numasioi* (that is *Manius me fecit Numerio* = 'Manius made me for Numerius'), the most interesting feature being the use of the device of combining the letters F (*digamma*) and *h* to represent the sound *f*, which was common in Latin, but was wanting in Greek; it was one of the three devices employed by the Etruscans for the sound *f* (*see* p. 389). Moreover, the presence in the Præneste fibula of the letters *d* and *o* may be another proof that the Latin alphabet was borrowed from the Etruscan in the very early stage of this latter alphabet, when these letters had not yet fallen into disuse.

Not much later than the Præneste fibula is the famous inscription from the Roman Forum (Fig. 22.2–3), belonging to the sixth century B.C., if not to the end of the seventh. It is written vertically on the four faces of a *cippus*, in *boustrophedon* style, that is, as already explained, in alternating lines from right to left and left to right. Owing to this direction of writing, and to the fragmentary condition of the *cippus*, not many words can be read with certainty. Face A in Fig. 22.2*b* reads, beginning at the bottom of the first line of the right-hand side: 1, *quoiho* :... 2, [*s*]*akros es* = 3, *ed sor*[*d*]. . .

Another inscription, known as that of Duenos (Fig. 22.1*b*), is on a vase found in Rome, near the Quirinal, and seems also to belong to the sixth century B.C., although it is dated by some scholars as late as the fourth century. The direction of writing is still from right to left.

These three are the earliest. Some Sabine inscriptions, among them one on a vase found at Tivoli, another on a plate of bronze found in the Lake of Fucino, and a few inscriptions dedicated to Juno or Juno Lucina (Figs. 22.1*c*, . . *c*), belong to the end of the fifth or to the fourth century B.C. There are also a few inscriptions belonging to the third century (Fig. 21.1 f. shows the famous inscription on the tomb of the Consul L. Cornelius Scipio, 259 B.C.) and to the second century B.C.

Only from the first century B.C. onwards do the Latin inscriptions become so numerous all over the ancient world that they cannot be counted. Of the first century B.C. mention may be made of the great inscription composed by Augustus (63 B.C.—A.D. 14) and known as the *Monumentum Ancyranum*.

ORIGIN OF THE LATIN ALPHABET

The opinion commonly held, even by some scholars, is that the Latin alphabet was derived from the Greek in the form used by the Greek colonists in Italy, and probably in the Chalcidian variety of the western group (*see* p. 360), employed at Cumæ in Campania. This theory tries to show that the Latin alphabet corresponds exactly to the Chalcidian except in regard to *g* and *p*. Recently, however, it has been proved that on the whole this theory is unlikely, and that the Etruscan alphabet was the link between the Greek and the Latin.

I have already mentioned that in the Præneste fibula the sound *f* was represented as in early Etruscan by the combination F*h*. Later, for instance in the Duenos inscription, the *h* was dropped, a development also due to Etruscan influence. Thus the Greek F (*digamma*), that is the *w*, came to represent the Latin sound *f*, but the Romans had also a *v*-sound in their language, for which they would have used the Greek F had they adopted the Greek alphabet, whereas they adapted the Greek V (*upsilon*) both for the consonant *v* and the vowel *u*.

The third letter of the Greek alphabet, *gamma* (*g*), became a Ɔ (or C) in the Etruscan alphabet with the sound *k*; it retained this sound in the Latin alphabet, but it served there for both *k* and *g* (the Etruscans had, as was noted above, no distinction between *k* and *g*), and C remained as representing *g* in the familiar abbreviations C (for Gaius), and CN (for Gnæus). On the other hand, the Greek alphabet had two other signs for the *k*-sound, the K and the Q, and we find in the South Etruscan alphabet the sign C used (as *k*) only before *e* and *i*, the K used before *a*, and the Q only before *u* (Etruscan had, as we have seen, no *o*). The Latin alphabet adopted all the three letters with their phonetic values, but in time it dropped the K (which, however, continued to be used as the initial of well-known or official words, such as *Kalendæ* or *Kæso*) and used C for the sounds of both *g* and *k*, the letter Q being retained for the sound *k* when followed by *u*. At a later stage a change attributed to Appius Claudius Censor in 312 B.C. was adopted to denote the voiced sound *g*. This was the addition of a bar to the lower end of C, thus converting it into G.

The absence in early Latin of a specific symbol for the combination *x* (*ks*), which existed in the Greek alphabets, including the Chalcidian variety, but not in the Etruscan, also indicates the derivation of the Latin alphabet from the Etruscan.

Moreover, the greater part of the Latin names of the letters, which have descended into English as into the majority of modern alphabets, were taken over from the Etruscans, for the Romans did not invent many themselves. The Semitic letter-names (*see* pp. 167 ff.), which had been taken over by the Greek (*see* p. 358), were quite different. The derivation of the letter-names from the Etruscan alphabet may also be shown by the names *ce*, *ka* and *qu* (which are explained by the aforementioned use of the three letters), and by the facts that there were in Etruscan sonant or vocalized liquids (*l, r*) and nasals (*m, n*), and that the modern names of these letters (*l, m, n, r*) are vocalized as closed syllables ('ell,' 'em,' 'en,' and so forth), whereas the names of other consonants are open syllables ('be,' 'de,' and so forth). Finally, may we assume that the term 'element' (Lat. *elementum*) refers to three letter-names 'ell,' 'em,' 'en'? And may we assume that this term, generally considered as being of uncertain etymology, is of Etruscan origin?

The creation of the Latin alphabet may be dated in the seventh century B.C.

DEVELOPMENT OF THE LATIN ALPHABET
(Figs. 22.4–5)

The original Etruscan alphabet consisted (*see* p. 388) of twenty-six letters; the Romans adopted only twenty-one of them. They rejected the three Greek aspirate letters *theta* (⊙), *phi* (Φ) and *khi* (↓), as there were no sounds in Latin to correspond to them, but they retained them to represent numbers. ⊙, ⊂, C became 100, and was later identified with the initial of *centum*; Φ, CIƆ, ω, M became 1,000, and identified with the initial of *mille*, and its half (D) became 500; ↓-↓-⊥-L became 50.

Of the three Etruscan *s*-sounds, the Romans retained the Greek *sigma*. The presence in the Latin alphabet of the letters *d* and *o*, for which the Etruscans had no use, is explained by the fact already mentioned, that the Latin alphabet was created before the Etruscans had time to reject these letters. The use of the letters C, K, Q and F has already been explained. The symbol, which represented, as in Etruscan, the aspirate, later received the shape H. I was the sign both of the vowel and consonant *i*. The X was later added to represent the sound *ks*, but it was placed at the end of the alphabet (*ultima nostrarum*, says Quintilian, i, 4.9).

The early Latin alphabet was therefore as follows: A, B, C (with the sound *k*), D, E, F, ⊏ (the Greek *zeta*), H, I, K, L, M, N, O, P, Q, P (which was the original shape of R), S, T, V, X. Roughly speaking, it was the Semitic-Greek-Etruscan alphabet; the shapes of some letters were slightly modified; the Semitic-Greek Δ became D; the Greek ≤ became S; R is but a variation of P, by the addition of a stroke below the crook; but other letters remained unchanged. At a later stage, the seventh letter, that is the Greek *zeta* (⊏) was dropped, because Latin did not require it, and the new letter G (*see* above) was placed in its position. This innovation is attributed to Spurius Carvilius, libertus of the Consul bearing the same name (after 250 B.C.).

When, after the conquest of Greece, in the first century B.C., Greek words—such as *zephyros*—were largely borrowed by the Latin language, the symbols Y and Z were adopted for the sounds *y* and *z* respectively, from the contemporary Greek alphabet (but only in order to transliterate Greek words—hence, they do not appear in normal Latin inscriptions), and were placed at the end of the alphabet. Thus the Latin script became one of twenty-three symbols; these became more regular, harmonious, well proportioned and elegant.

Although there were even in Roman times a few tentative additions of letters, such as a variant of M introduced by Verrius Flaccus of Augustus' time, and especially the introduction by the Emperor Claudius (10 B.C.–A.D. 54) of the *digamma inversum*, ⅃, for the sound *w-v* in order to distinguish it from *u*, of the reverse C (Ɔ), the *anti-sigma*, for the combination *ps*, and of the half H (Ⱶ) for an intermediate sound between *u* and *i*, on the whole it can be said that the aforementioned alphabet of twenty-three letters was constantly used, with the same order of the letters, not only in the monu-mental writing of the Roman period, but also as capital letters of the Latin alphabet during the Middle Ages and in printing until the present day.

The only permanent additions of the Middle Ages were the signs U, W and J; actually they were not additions, but differentiations from existing letters; the U (for the vowel-sound *u* to distinguish it from the consonantal *v*) and the consonantal W were easy differentiations of V, while J, the consonantal *i*, is only a slight alteration of I. In the early Middle Ages both the forms (but not the W, which appeared only in the eleventh century) were used indifferently for both the consonantal and the vowel-sound, the signs U and J being used in hands current at that time.

The subsequent history of the Latin alphabet consisted in the following essential facts: (1) the adaptation of this alphabet to various languages, and (2) the external transformation of the single letters in the 'cursive' or 'running' styles of writing.

LATIN CURSIVE SCRIPTS
(Figs. 22.5, 9–15)

The connection of the capital letters of modern writing with the ancient Semitic-Greek-Etruscan-Latin letters is evident even to a layman. The connection of the 'minuscule,' that is the 'small letters,' with the ancient Latin letters does not appear so evident, but as a matter of fact the 'majuscule' and 'minuscule' are descended from the same ancient Latin alphabet, and the different shapes of the small letters are due to a transformation of the original letters by eliminating a part of the letter (as for instance, h from H, b from B), by lengthening a part of it (for instance, q from Q, d from D), and so forth.

There were two main causes necessitating changes of form, and the history of these changes is much too long to be told in full detail in the few paragraphs which can be devoted to the subject in this book.

In ancient times the minuscule did not exist. Both the monumental writing and the cursive scripts consisted of the present-day 'capitals.' The chief considerations of monumental writing were and are today (in memorial inscriptions on tomb-stones, and so forth) permanence, beauty, including proportion, evenness, while the chief considerations of cursive or running scripts are speed and utility rather than beauty. The tool mainly used for monumental writing is, and always was, the chisel; and the material is mainly, and always was, stone. The tool usually employed today for hand-writing is the pen, and paper is the usual material for cursive writing.

In Roman times, various tools were employed; there was the primitive scratcher or marker termed stylus, employed for everyday purposes upon tablets or wax; there was the brush, as it is today, for wall-painting, and there was the pen made from reed (cut to a point and frayed to the likeness of a small brush, or cut to an edge). In all probability, since the sixth century A.D. the pen was made from quill, and became the typical mediæval tool, superseded only in recent generations by the modern metal pen (metal pens were, however, employed also in Roman times). The word 'pen' originally meant 'feather' (Lat. *penna*), and is strictly applicable to the primitive quill pen; the word was retained, however, throughout the development of the pen, so that the Latin word for 'feather' now denotes an instrument with a metal rib. The most important writing materials for cursive scripts in ancient times were papyrus and parchment, besides the tablets coated with wax.

The transformation of the Latin monumental writing into the modern script with its majuscules and minuscules is due entirely to the technical bearings of the tool, primarily the pen, and the material of writing, primarily papyrus and parchment. It was the pen, with its preference for curves, which eliminated the angular forms; it was papyrus, and still more parchment or vellum, which made these curves possible. Some details are due to the peculiarities of wax (the shapes of *d*, *g*, *f*, and probably *b* are due to wax: Sir Ellis Minns).

The use of paper, the main writing material of the present day, was unknown in Europe before the eleventh century A.D., although apparently it was invented in the second century A.D. and in the same century the Chinese carried the process of paper-making to a high degree of development. Some scholars date its invention as early as 123 B.C., others more rightly suggest A.D. 105. Paper-making was learned from the Chinese by the Koreans and the Japanese in the seventh century A.D., and by the Arabs in the eighth century. There are many Arabic manuscripts extant, belonging to the ninth century and made of pure rag (from linen and flax). By Europeans, paper was first made in the eleventh century in Spain and Italy. The earliest European extant document on paper is a deed of 1109 written in Greek and Arabic of Countess Adelasia (Adelaide), regent for her sons Simon and Roger, later the Norman King Roger II of Sicily. This document is preserved in the State Archives of Palermo (Sicily). The art of paper-making spread to France (1248), Germany (early fourteenth century), Switzerland (1380), England (1450), to the Netherlands (about the same time), to America only in 1690, although American natives had made *amatl* paper in Mexico and Central Ameirca before Columbus discovered America.

However, in the fourteenth century paper became the main literary writing material in Europe, and in the course of the next century it gradually superseded vellum.

VARIETIES OF THE LATIN ALPHABET
(Figs. 22.4–50)

Lapidary Capitals, Elegant Book-capitals, and Rustic Capitals (Figs. 22.4–8, 16–17)

We have dealt with the development of the Latin alphabet *par excellence*, that is the 'monumental' script; it derived its name from its main use for monumental inscriptions; but it was also called 'lapidary,' being chiefly employed in engraving on stone; or 'square,' because of its rectilinear formation and the mainly rectangular junctions of the strokes; or else, very frequently, 'capital' writing.

There were, in Roman times, three main varieties of this capital script: (1) the lapidary capitals, (2) the elegant book-capitals which were, naturally, slightly rounded and less stiff than the lapidary script, and (3) the rustic capitals, which were not so carefully elaborated as the lapidary script, and not so round as the book-capitals, but were quicker and easier; there were a few sub-varieties of rustic capitals, such as the Roman rustic capitals, the pictorial rustic capitals, and the book rustic capitals.

Cursive Scripts (Figs. 22.4–5, 9–15, 50)

These various styles were adapted to pen-writing, but in everyday life, with continuous modifications for greater speed, the cursive script, that is the current hand, was developed for writing with the stylus on wax-tablets, for graffiti, *i.e.*, scratching, or painting on vases, on walls, and so forth. Speed was preferred to legibility. There were several varieties of cursive, those of Pompeii and Alburnus Major (Vœrœs Patak, in Dacia), belonging to the first and second centuries A.D., being the most important. Indeed, only a few wax tablets have survived, mostly from Pompeii and Alburnus Major. In general, the ancient Roman cursive script may be divided into: (1) majuscule cursive, (2) minuscule cursive, and (3) semi-cursive minuscule.

Mixed Scripts (Figs. 22.30, 32, 50)

Between the monumental and the cursive scripts, there was a whole series of varieties which had some of the peculariarities of each group. There were: (1) lapidary mixed scripts and book semi-cursive scripts, which contained some capital letters and some cursive or semi-cursive characters; (2) the early uncial or rather semi-uncial script, of the third century A.D., which also was a mixture of capitals, cursive characters and uncials; the early semi-uncial script (the exact origin of which is uncertain) seems to have developed into the beautiful uncial script.

Uncials and Semi-Uncials (Figs. 22.5, 18–30, 50)

There is some obscurity about the meaning of the term 'uncials,' which some scholars, on the authority of St. Jerome, derived from Lat. *literae unciales,* 'inch-high letters.' The uncial script appears in official Roman documents, particularly in Africa, from the third century A.D. onwards, and was the usual book-hand for over 500 years (fourth–eighth centuries). On the whole, it was still a mixed script, the majority of the letters being capitals, some letters (*h, l, q*) being minuscule, and four letters (*a, d, e, m*) having the typical rounded shape which is the main feature of the uncial hand. It was doubtless the character best adapted for calligraphy. The semi-uncial book-hand, which was developed from the early semi-uncial script and used in the period running from the fifth to the ninth century, was a half-and-half sort of hand, easier than the uncials and more calligraphic than the cursive minuscule.

MEDIÆVAL VARIETIES OF THE LATIN ALPHABET
(Figs. 22.5, 30–38, 41, 50)

As soon as the various European countries had shaken off the political authority of the Roman empire, and the educated communities had been scattered and dissolved, a marked change took place in the development of the Latin cursive or running script. Several 'national' hands, or rather 'national' styles of the Latin cursive minuscule, assumed distinctive features, and there thus developed on the European continent and in the British Isles, the five national hands, known as Italian or Lombardic, Merovingian (in France), Visigothic (in Spain), Germanic and Insular. Each gave rise to several varieties.

Italian Semi-cursive Minusculæ (Figs. 22.32, 50)

The Italian semi-cursive minusculæ developed from the Roman cursive, was employed throughout Italy from the seventh to the ninth century, and continued to be used in Tuscany until the twelfth century. It gave way to many varieties, such as the Lombardic or Pavia minuscule, the pure cursive styles of Amalfi, Gaeta, Naples, Lucca, Florence, and so forth, the most important being the Ravenna script and the Papal curial style, the pre-Caroline book-hand in North Italy (used in the second half of the eighth century and the first half of the ninth century in Italy, France and Germany), and particularly the beautiful Beneventan minuscule in South Italy and Dalmatia; this latter lasted longer than the other varieties. Montecassino, Benevento and Salerno were amongst the most important centres of its use.

Other Continental Hands (Fig. 22.22*d.,* 31*a,* 32*c*)

The other continental hands had less importance. The Merovingian script (in France) employed in the sixth–eighth centuries, continued for some time to be used as court-hand. There were some varieties: the cursive minuscule, the semi-cursive hand and various book-hands. The Visigothic (in Spain), employed in the eighth and ninth centuries, may be distinguished into cursive and book-minuscule; it was employed also in Italy. The Germanic pre-Caroline hand was the least widespread and lasted less time (eighth–ninth centuries) than any of the other varieties.

Insular or Anglo-Irish Hands (Figs. 22.31b, 39–40, 50)

The most beautiful and the most important of all the 'national' styles was the 'Insular' or Anglo-Irish hand. It developed from the semi-uncial book-hand of the early missionaries and not from the cursive minuscule as the continental national hands did. It can be distinguished into the following varieties:

(a) Irish Hand (Figs. 22.31b, 39–40)

The Irish hand is considered by some scholars to have been introduced from Gaul by St. Patrick; already used in Ireland in the sixth century, it continued to be employed during the Middle Ages, and developed into the modern Irish script; apart from the majuscule (derived from the Roman capitals, but probably influenced by the oghamic script), used for headings, there were two varieties of this script.

(1) The semi-uncial (Fig. 22.33a), used for religious books; it had two sub-varieties, the elegant and the rustic;

(2) the minuscule or angular script, employed for documents and codices; this also had two sub-varieties, the elegant and the cursive.

The Irish system of abbreviations had a great influence on the development of the mediæval abbreviations of all the other scripts.

(b) Anglo-Saxon Hand (Figs. 22.45, 50)

In the seventh and eighth centuries the Roman uncial script was still employed in England in manuscripts and codices, but at the same time the Anglo-Saxon semi-uncial minuscule developed from the Irish script, and was employed for Latin until about 940, for English until after the Conquest (1066). The introduction of the Caroline minuscule was part of the reconstruction after the Danish wars.

In regard to the development of the Anglo-Saxon alphabet it may be noted that, apart from the transformation of the single letters, it differed mainly from the Latin alphabet in the wen, w, which was written more like a p, and there were two additional signs, representing the sounds th and dh; the thorn or th-sign disappeared only with the introduction of printing.

The Anglo-Saxon handwriting was bold and clear, and it has come down to us in copies of books and in royal and other charters, mainly written and preserved in monasteries and cathedrals. There seems to be no doubt that the reign of Alfred the Great (849–901) did much to revive the knowledge of writing; under his successors the introduction of foreign styles stimulated a new attention to literature, neglected during the Danish invasion except among a few professed scholars.

CAROLINE OR CAROLINGIAN HAND
(Figs. 22.5,50)

At the end of the eighth century, probably under Charlemagne, or perhaps earlier, the beautiful, widely spaced and rounded letters known as Caroline or Carolingian minuscule were formed in the Frankish empire as well as in northern and central Italy and in Germany, probably under the influence of the Anglo-Irish hand. It is, however, still uncertain what exact part Charlemagne (742–814) and his friend Alcuin of York (735–804), the founder of the famous school of Tours, played in the creation of the Caroline hand. However, this script became the literary hand of the Frankish empire, and during the next two centuries it became the main book-hand of western Europe. It was the official script of the Carolingian imperial government and, for a certain period, of the chancery of the Holy Roman Empire. The blending of the majuscules and the minuscules into combined service is due mainly to this script. It was employed until the twelfth century, and had a few varieties such as the Frankish, Italian and German; the most important English variety of the Caroline script was the clear Winchester School hand (Fig. 22.33*b*), partly influenced by the Anglo-Irish hand.

'BLACK LETTER' OR GOTHIC
(Figs. 22.4–5,33*c*,43–44,50)

In the course of the next centuries various book-hands, court-hands or charter-hands and other cursive scripts developed from the Caroline. At the end of the twelfth century, and still more during the next two centuries, the letters gradually assumed angular shapes—due to the pen being held so as to make a slanting stroke.

The new hand, termed 'black letter' or Gothic, or else, in reference to modern usage, German (the German term, derived from Latin, is *Fraktur*), employed in north-western Europe, including England, until the sixteenth century, is still used in Germany as the 'national' hand: indeed, Bismarck regarded it as the 'German-national' script and was hostile to German books printed in 'Latin' character. The term 'Gothic' as used for script is parallel to the term 'Gothic architecture,' etc. It was originally employed (particularly by Italian humanists) as a term of disparagement for 'Northern' (or 'barbarian') art and culture.

According to some scholars, this survival of the 'black letter' in Germany is due to the fact that it was the current style at the time of the invention of printing and was employed by Gutenberg, but Sir Ellis Minns pointed out that 'black letter' survived in protestant countries (such as Scandinavia and amongst Baltic peoples) because the humanistic hand was used by the Roman Church—this being true, it must be pointed out that it has also survived in Catholic Austria. In England it was touch and go.

ITALIC AND 'ROMAN' TYPES
(Figs. 22.4–5, 32 *f–g*, 42, 50)

In Italy both the 'black letter' and the round hand were used, but during the fifteenth century a beautiful Italian cursive minuscule, the round, neat, humanistic or renaissance hand, was introduced in Florence, and employed for literary productions, while the needs of everyday life were met by an equally beautiful (but not as clearly legible) cursive hand.

This style, based on the earlier round minuscule, which at the time was considered to be the script of the classical Roman period and called therefore *antiqua*, developed mainly into two varieties:

(1) the Venetian minuscule, nowadays known as *italics*, traditionally, though wrongly, considered an imitation of the handwriting of Petrarch, and probably the most perfect form of printed letter and the most clearly legible which has yet been invented; and

(2) the 'Roman' type of letters, perfected in North Italy, chiefly at Venice, where it was used in the printing presses about the end of the fifteenth and the beginning of the sixteenth centuries, and spread thence to Holland, England (about 1518), Germany, France and Spain.

The monumental Latin alphabet was taken over for the majuscules. This majuscule and both forms of the minuscule, the 'Roman' type and the *italics*, spread all over the world. In England they were adopted from Italy in the sixteenth century.

ADAPTATION OF THE LATIN ALPHABET TO MODERN EUROPEAN LANGUAGES

The 'national' scripts of the various European peoples are, with a few exceptions, adaptations of the Latin alphabet to Germanic, Romance, Slavonic and Finno-Ugrian languages. For the alphabets of the Slavonic peoples of orthodox faith *see* part 2, chapter 19; the modern Greek alphabet is a development of the ancient Greek influenced by the Latin alphabet.

In the history of the alphabet, it is important not to overlook the fact that the Latin language and script in ancient times had been, at first, carried by Roman legionaries and imperial officials to all parts of the vast empire, and particularly to the regions which were not Hellenized. In a few countries (Gaul, Spain and Roumania), Latin replaced the languages of the natives, and it became the ancestor of the modern Romance languages, the most important of them being Italian, Spanish (Castilian and Catalonian), Portuguese, French (and Provençal) and Roumanian, all of which adopted the Latin alphabet (for early Roumanian *see* p. 377).

Alphabet follows Religion (Map III)

At a later stage, churchmen and missionaries carried the Latin language and script still farther afield and for many more centuries. Catholic Rome was then the light of

F f

the western world, the centre whence religion and learning were disseminated to all parts of western, central and northern Europe. The emissaries of the Pope, either legates or missionaries, travelled over all Europe and carried with them the learning of their age. The abbeys were in the nature of large seminaries or colleges, where learning was carried on, and the monastic system spread Christianity and learning even to a wider extent. At the time when, for instance, neither the Saxon nor the Norman noblemen could sign their own names, but employed instead the Christian sign of the cross (still in use among illiterates) as the pledge of their good faith and witness to their consent and approval, it was in the monasteries that the lamp of learning was kept alight. Education was in certain periods almost entirely monastic, or at least conducted by teachers trained in monastic institutions. The earliest scribes, for instance, in the British Isles were either Irish or foreign monks (mainly Italian), or educated under foreign monks. But there were also important centres of learning in the Cathedral schools.

In consequence, Latin (using naturally the Latin alphabet), the language of the Roman Church, became and remained for many centuries the international tongue of the European higher intellectual world, and it is still used extensively for learned works and the theological treatises in the Roman Catholic Church—we may refer to the activity of St. Francis Xavier (1506–52), of the Order of the Jesuits (founded in 1534), and of the *Propaganda Fide* (college founded in 1622)—although it lost its dominant position in consequence of the natural development of the last three or four centuries. However, the Latin alphabet, in all its varieties, had been given ample opportunities for its adoption by the great majority of the European peoples, and its adaptation to tongues belonging to most different linguistic groups. *See* also pp. 436.

On the other hand, in more recent times the main factor expressed by the motto 'alphabet follows religion' has gradually been replaced by 'alphabet follows the flag' and 'alphabet follows trade.'

The Alphabet Today (Map IV)

The adaptation of a script to a new language is not an easy matter, especially when the new language contains sounds which do not exist in the speech from which the alphabet had been borrowed. There arises therefore the difficulty of representing the new sounds, particularly in the transliteration of foreign words. This difficulty has been solved in different ways:

(1) By representing the new sounds by existing symbols for which there is no use in the new language; for instance, the Latin letter c, which was redundant, because the letter k was accepted to represent the sound k in all circumstances, was introduced in some Slavonic languages (Polish, Czech, Croatian, and so forth) to represent the sound ts, which in Germany and central Europe is given to Latin c before e and i.

(2) Combinations of two or more letters were introduced to represent single sounds in the new languages. An interesting instance in this connection is the representation

of the sounds *sh* and *ch* (as 'church') in various languages; whereas the Cyrillic Russian alphabet has a single symbol for the combination *shch* (as in Ashchurch), Czech, another Slavonic language, would use for it the combination *šč*, Polish, again a Slavonic speech, represents it by four consonants (*szcz*), and German would need as many as seven consonants for the transliteration of this combination, that is *schtsch* (though such combination hardly occurs in German). English has some combinations of two signs for single sounds, such as *ch, sh, th, ph*.

(3) The new language, in order not to increase the number of its letters, prefers in some instances to use letters representing two or more sounds; in English, for instance, the letter *c* is used for two distinct sounds (for the sound *k* in 'cap,' 'colour,' 'cursive'; and for the sound *s* in 'cell,' 'cereal,' 'cider,'), in addition to entering into the combination *ch*, and replacing the *k* in *ck*.

(4) Some languages have preferred to add to the borrowed alphabet signs taken over from another alphabet to represent sounds which could not be expressed by the mainly adopted alphabet; for instance, the Anglo-Saxons, in adopting the Latin alphabet, added to it three new letters, one of which (for the sound *th*) was borrowed from the runic script.

(5) In other instances, new signs have been invented; the additional letters of the early Greek alphabet in adapting the Semitic alphabet to the Greek speech belong to this group.

(6) In more recent times the most common way of representing sounds which could not be represented by letters of the borrowed alphabet, has been the addition of diacritical points or other marks, inserted above or under the letter, to its right or its left or inside it; to this group belong the German vowels *ü* (*ue*), *ä* (*æ*) and *ö* (*œ*), the Spanish, Portuguese and French cedilla in *ç*, the *ñ con tilde*, in Spanish and Portuguese, the accents in Italian (*à, ì, é, ò, ù*), but particularly the great number of marks in the Latin-Slavonic scripts (Polish, Czech, Croatian, and so forth), such as *č, ć, š, ś, ž, ż, ą, ę*, and many more. In the scientific phonetic alphabets, a whole apparatus of diacritical marks is necessary to express the exact distinction of the sounds.

The Latin-Turkish alphabet, introduced into Turkey by the law passed in November, 1928, by the Grand National Assembly, and which became general throughout Turkey in 1930, contains twenty-nine letters, of which two vowels (*ö* and *ü*) and three consonants (*ç, ğ* and *ş*) are distinguished by diacritical marks, and in one instance there is a distinction in reverse, that is by eliminating the dot from *i* (*ı*) a new sound is represented. Turkish is now spoken by over 21 million people.

(7) In other cases, new letters had to be invented to represent the long vowels (for instance, in some African languages); this has been done by inserting a colon after the vowel; also reversed and upside-down letters are employed. [*See*, particularly, K. R. Lepsius's *Standard Alphabet*, of 1855, and the studies of E. Norris, Librarian of the Foreign Office, H. Sweet, Melville Bell (*Visible Speech*), and Sir William Hunter, the authority on the Indian languages, as well as the works by O. Jespersen, D. Jones and P. Passy, and others.]

ADAPTATION OF THE LATIN ALPHABET TO ENGLISH: THE
ENGLISH ALPHABET

Italian, Spanish and Portuguese are relatively simple as regards the graphic representation of their speech-sounds. The rendering of German or even Bantu in a phonetic spelling is also a more or less simple matter. In these, and some other countries, the prevailing view of the relationship between speech and writing is that writing is the proper standard of speech, 'words are pronounced as they are spelled.' Such a view is, however, erroneous; living speech hardly conforms to the written word. A perfect alphabet would, as already said, represent each sound by a single symbol, and not more than one sound by the same symbol. As it is, all alphabets omit symbols for some sounds, and all of them contain redundant letters.

The English alphabet, that is the spelling, differs so much from pronunciation that in many words it is almost an arbitrary symbolism. There are historical reasons for this condition. For one thing the influence of French orthography in the Middle Ages was disastrous. For another, during the course of centuries, the changes in English speech have become very great, and the spelling has changed much more slowly than the pronunciation. There has resulted, therefore, a lack of complete coincidence between sounds and their graphic representation. The present spelling is etymological; it is, on the whole, that of the early sixteenth century, while the speech has continued its development. Roughly speaking, it can be said that nearly all the Old English consonantal sounds have maintained their phonetic values, and so also the majority of the short vowels in closed syllables, but the long vowels and most of the short vowels in open syllables have, by insensible degrees, been totally changed.

The five conventional symbols, the traditional *a, e, i, o, u*, handed down to us from antiquity, are nowadays so inconsistently employed that they puzzle those who desire to speak English perfectly. The same vowel is pronounced very differently in different parts of the country. It is due mainly to varied methods of pronouncing the vowels, rather than to those of pronouncing the consonants, that the common Londoner finds it hard at times to understand the speech of the northener or the westerner. The actual sounds of English, however, are not very difficult to pronounce; it is their inconsistent representation by the alphabet which causes the English orthography to be considered one of the worst in existence.

The five vowel-letters are used to represent eight separate distinct vowel-sounds and twelve diphthongs; nevertheless, the great confusion is not caused by this situation, but by the fact that each vowel may assume five or more phonetic values; *a* may sound as long *a, o* or *e*, as short *a* or the diphthongs *ei* or *æ*; *e* as short *e* or *i*, long *a*, diphthong *æ* or *œ*; the final *e*, in 'table,' for instance, is practically a meaningless orthographic flourish; and so forth. The double *o* may represent a long *o, u* or *a*, or a short *u*; *ou* may sound as the diphthongs *ou* or *au*, as long *o* or *u*, as short *o, u* or *a*, etc.

Although the situation of the consonantal representation is infinitely better than that of the vowel-representation, there are nevertheless inconsistencies also in the consonantal letters. There are no single letters to represent the sounds *sh*, *th*, *ch*, and there is utter uncertainty as to the last two; on the other hand, *ph*, *q(u)* and perhaps *x* are redundant, the first for *f*, the second for *kw*, the third for *ks*; the letter *c* has already been dealt with; *wh* originated from the erroneous writing of *hw* in some early English manuscripts; and the *w* is often useless; *ng* nearly always indicates a single nasal sound, the *g* being most of the time not pronounced after the *n*. The *t(i)* is sometimes a *sh* (for instance, in 'nation'), sometimes meaningless (for instance, in 'listen'), other times an *s* or a *tch*; the *f*'s are sometimes *v*'s, the *gh* may be an *f* (in 'laugh') or is not pronounced (in 'night'); the *k* is not pronounced in *kn*. The *r*'s are in south England for the most part silent in the latter part of a syllable. In this connection reference may be made to the activity of the English S.S.S. (Simple Spelling Society), to the interesting debate in the House of Commons (11th March 1949) on the Spelling Reform Bill, to the frequent correspondence in the English national newspapers, and particularly to the activity of Sir James Pitman, M.P. and to the *I.T.A.* (= 'Initial Teaching Alphabet') Foundation; *see* Figs. 22.51–52.

On the other hand, effectual spelling reform, that is the revision of the alphabet in order that it might represent more or less the proper standard of speech, would deprive the community of a link in the history of the English speech. Indeed, both the English linguistic creative impetus and the colourful history of English international relations are reflected in the modern English speech. The once living ability of English to create fused compounds out of its Anglo-Saxon and Norman native roots and endings, has been combined with the later enrichment by the most hospitable inclusion of a host, increasing daily, of borrowed words from all sorts of languages, from all parts of the world. There is, in modern English words, a reflection of the fierce struggles with Spain and of the gentler cultural Italian influences, of the rival Dutch power and of the historical relationship with India and Africa, of the religious influence of Hebrew, and of Latin and Greek roots serving the purposes of scientific and technical advancement; words of popular etymology are mingled with conscious creations of learned words.

As a result of all this minting, English is probably the richest and the most colourful of all the modern languages. For commercial and political reasons it has spread far and wide over the globe and is spoken by great numbers of people in all parts of the world with very different pronunciations. English and its script have thus become the *lingua franca* of the World. Nowadays, to reform either the English alphabet or the English speech would mean, so to say, to discount English history.

A selection of modern type-faces is given in Figs. 22.46–49.

PROBLEM OF A STANDARD INTERNATIONAL ALPHABET
(Fig. 22.53)

We come now to another linguistic problem; until the present day the alphabet has been the only means of international communication. Its privileged position is due to a natural development lasting many centuries, and accompanied by many other elements. There have been, however, in the last two generations many attempts to aid international communication by the creation of an artificial international language; the attempts have failed. Those who tried to disseminate the study of Esperanto, Volapük, Idiom neutral, Ido, Latino sine flexione, Antido, Occidental, Novial, and others, in order to foster international amity, have been bitterly disappointed as one catastrophic war after the other has swept away the frail connections over national boundaries. An artificial language taken alone is insufficient to promote brotherhood among peoples; much more is needed than a single speech to end wars. These remarks, however, trespass upon the domain of politics.

Another problem is that of the possibility of introducing a standard alphabet for rendering English, French, Russian, German, and all the other European and non-European forms of human speech; *see The Principles of the International Phonetic Association*, University College, London, 1949.

This problem is, strictly speaking, a combination of three problems, namely:

(1) The problem, already discussed, of the reform of spelling. This reform of the English and the other European and non-European alphabets should—it is suggested—be based mainly on the Latin alphabet, accepting the consonants *b, d, f, g* (always hard as in 'go'), *h* (always aspirate as in 'hand'), *j, k, l, m, n, r* (always trilled), *s, t, v, w, y, z*, pronounced according, for instance, to the long-established English custom, while the basic vowels should be pronounced according to their values in Italian (*a* as for instance in 'father,' *e*, as for instance in 'get,' *i* as for instance in 'initial,' *u* as in 'rule' and *o* as in 'oriental').

(2) The second problem consists in establishing a uniform representation of sounds which are peculiar to some languages, such as the sounds *th* and *dh* in 'think' and 'that,' the *gh* of the Arabic *ghain*, the *ch* (as in 'church'), which is nowadays represented in Czech by *č*, in Polish by *cz*, in Hungarian by *cs* (or *ts*), in German by *tsch*, and so forth; the palatization of some consonants such as the French and Italian *gn*; the indeterminate vowel-sounds, for instance of the English terminal *e* in 'marble'; the nasal vowels in French 'un,' in English 'king,' in Polish *ą* and *ę*, and so forth; the guttural consonants of Arabic and Hebrew; the clicks of the Hottentot speech; the German *ö, ä, ü*, and many other sounds, which are, nowadays, represented differently in the various 'national' alphabets.

(3) The shape of the individual letters has to be precise, as to avoid confusion and ambiguity.

BIBLIOGRAPHY

Some 150,000 Latin inscriptions are now accessible in print. They are collected in *Corpus Inscriptionum Latinarum*, Berlin, 1862 onwards; the volumes are arranged geographically; supplements are issued as *Ephemeris Epigraphica*. A convenient selection is H. Dessau, *Inscriptiones Latinæ selectæ*, 3 vols., Berlin,

1892–1916. Excellent introductions are: R. Cagnat, *Cours d'épigraphie latine*, Paris, 1890; W. M. Lindsay, *Handbook of Latin Inscriptions, illustrating the History of the Language*, Boston and Chicago, 1897; J. C. Egbert, *Introduction to the Study of Latin Inscriptions*, 2nd ed., New York, 1908; L. Schiaparelli, *La scrittura latina nell'età romana*, Como, 1921; and J. E. Sandys, *Latin Epigraphy*, 2nd ed., Cambridge, 1927.

Palæographical Society and New Palæographical Society, *Facsimiles of Manuscripts and Inscriptions* (edited by E. A. Bond, E. Maunde Thompson, G. F. Warner, F. G. Kenyon and G. P. Gilson), two series each, London, 1873–83, 1884–94, 1903–12, 1913–30. Indices, 1901, 1914, 1932.

DE VINNE, T. L. *Historic Printing Types*, New York, 1886.

WATTENBACH, W. *Das Schriftwesen im Mittelalter*, 3rd ed., Leipsic, 1896.

MOORHOUSE, G. *Fo-no-riteng*, etc., Cambridge, Mass., 1904.

COCKERELL, S. C. and STRANGE, E. F. *Catalogue of Illuminated Manuscripts*, London, 1908.

VENDRYES, J. *Grammaire du viel-irlandais*, Paris, 1908.

THURNEYSEN, R. *Handbuch des alt-Irischen*, Heidelberg, 1909; 2nd. ed. (in English) *A Grammar of Old-Irish*, Dublin, 1946.

SAUNDERS, W. *Ancient Handwritings. Manual for Students of Palæography*, Walton on Thames, 1909.

STEFFENS, F. *Lateinische Paläographie*, 2nd ed., Trier, 1909.

MOORE, M. F. *Works Relating to English Palæography*, London, 1912.

MAUNDE THOMPSON, E. *Introduction to Greek and Latin Palæography*, Oxford, 1912; *Latin Palæography*, in Sandys' *Companion*, 1921.

LOWE, E. A. *The Beneventan Script. A History of the South Italian Minuscule*, Oxford, 1914; *Codices latini antiquiores*, Oxford, 1934 onwards (I. *The Vatican City*, II. *Great Britain and Ireland*, etc., *English Uncial*, 1960); *Scriptura Beneventana*, 2 vols., Oxford, 1929; 'The Script of Luxueil; A Title Vindicated,' *Revue Bénédictine*, 1953.

COCKERELL, S. C. *La calligraphie et l'enluminure modernes en Angleterre*, Paris, 1914.

JOHNSON, C. and JENKINSON, C. H. *English Court Hand*, A.D. 1066 to 1500, Oxford, 1915.

VAN HŒSEN, H. B. *Roman Cursive Writing*, Princeton, 1915.

JENKINSON, C. H. *Palæography and the Practical Study of Court Hand*, Cambridge, 1915; *The Later Court Hands in England*, etc., Cambridge, 1927.

JESPERSEN, O. *Growth and Structure of the English Language*, Leipsic, 1919.

MENTZ, A. *Geschichte der griechisch-römischen Schrift*, etc., Leipsic, 1920.

PROU, M. *Manuel de paléographie latine et française*, 4th ed., Paris, 1924.

JOHNSON, A. F. and MORISON, S. *The Chancery Types of Italy and France*, etc., London, 1924.

MORISON, S. 'On Script Types,' *The Fleuron*, London, 1925; *Type Designs of the Past and Present*, London, 1926; *Early Humanistic Script and the First Roman Type*, London, 1943; *The Typographic Arts: Past, Present and Future*, Edinburgh, 1944.

LARISCH, R. *Beispiele künstlerischer Schrift aus vergangenen Jahrhunderten*, Vienna, 1926.

BARFIELD, O. *History in English Words*, London, 1926.

CASTAGNE, J. *La Latinisation de l'alphabet turk dans les républiques turko-tatares de l'U.R.S.S.*, Paris, 1929.

VITTANI, G. *Nozioni elementari di paleografia e diplomatica*, Milan, 1930.

JELLINEK, M. H. *Über Aussprache des Lateinischen und deutsche Buchstabennamen*, Vienna and Leipsic, 1930.

RIPMAN, W. *English Phonetics*, New York, 1931.

IHM, M. *Palæographia Latina*, 2nd ed., Leipsic, 1931.

HEAL, A. (and Morison, S.), *The English Writing-Masters and their Copy-Books*, 1570–1800, Cambridge, 1931.

MILARES CARLO, A. *Tratado de Paleografía española*, 2nd. ed., Madrid, 1932.

JOHNSON, A. F. *Type Designs*, etc., London, 1934.

BAUGH, A. C. *A History of the English Language*, New York, 1935.

SERJEANTSON, M. S. *A History of Foreign Words in English*, New York, 1936.

BATTELLI, G. *Lezioni di Paleografia*, Vatican City, 1936.

WILCKEN, U. 'Über den Nutzen der lateinischen Papyri,' in *Atti del IV. Congresso Internazionale di Papirologia*, Milan, 1936.

Société Saint-Jean l'Évangéliste, *Le Codex VI. 34 de la Bibliothèque Capitulaire de Bénévent (XI-XII siècle)*; *Gradual de Bénévent* etc., Tournay, 1937-53.

JONES, D. *An English Pronouncing Dictionary*, 4th ed., London, 1937.

ALLEN, A. B. *Romance of the Alphabet*, New York, 1937.

CHRISTOPHER, H. G. T. *Palæography and Archives*, London, 1938.

SCHULTZ, H. C. *Gothic Script of the Middle Ages*, San Francisco, 1939.

MALLON-MARICHEL-PERRAT, *L'écriture latine*, Paris, 1939.

HAYNES, D. E. L. and HIRST, P. E. D. *Porta argentariorum*, New York, 1940.

PLANTIN, C. *An Account of Calligraphy and Printing in the Sixteenth Century* (ed. by R. Nash). Foreword by S. Morison, Cambridge, Mass., 1940.

HOLME, C. *Lettering of To-day*, New York, 1941.

CRAIGIE, W. A. *Problems of Spelling Reform*, Oxford, 1944.

MOSSÉ, F. *Manuel de l'anglais du moyen âge*, Paris, 1945.

HENNING, P. *English Alphabet*, London, 1947.

REINER, I. and H. *Alphabets*, St. Gall, 1947.

OGG, O. *26 Letters*, New York, 1948.

PARSELL, J. R. *One Alphabet*, Kansas City, 1948.

PEACEY, H. *Meaning of the Alphabet*, Culver City, 1949.

LAFITTE-HOUSSAT, J. *La réforme de l'orthographie. Est-elle possible? Est-elle souhaitable?*, Paris, 1950.

BASIMEVI M. E. (ed.) *L'adoption des caractères latins en Turquie en 1928*, Ankara, 1951.

COURTOIS C. (ed.), *Tablettes Albertini; actes privés de l'époque vandale, fin du V siècle*, Paris, 1952.

MONSON, S. C. *Representative American Phonetic Alphabets*, Ann Arbor, 1954.

ALBRIGHT, R. W. *The International Phonetic Alphabet*, Bloomington, Ind., 1958.

GORDON, A. E. *Album of dated Latin Inscriptions*, Berkeley, Calif., 1958.

CAVENAILE, R. *Corpus papyrorum Latinorum*, Wiesbaden, 1958.

HECTOR, L. C. *The Handwriting of English Documents*, London, 1958; *Palæography and Forgery*, London, 1959.

VÄÄNÄNEN, V. *Le latin vulgaire des inscriptions pompéiennes*, Berlin, 1959.

PITMAN, SIR JAMES, *The Ehrhardt Augmented (40-sound—42-character) lower-case Roman Alphabet*, London, 1959; *Learning to Read*, London, 1961.

ULLMAN, B. L. *The Origin and Development of Humanistic Script*, Rome, 1960.

SUSINI, G. *Il lapidario greco-romano di Bologna e Suppl. Bonon. ad CIL* XI, Rome, 1960.

DAICOVICĬU, C. and PROTASE, D. 'Un nouveau diplôme militarie de Dacia Porolissensis, *The Journal of Roman Studies*, 1961.

See also the books on *Lettering* written by Edward Johnston, Graily Hewitt, Edward F. Strange, and others, and the articles on *Alphabet, Inscriptions, Palæography*, etc., in *Encyclopædia Britannica* and similar works.

Conclusion

GLANCING back over the course of the development of the alphabet, which I have traced in the foregoing pages, the reader will realize how the whole of mankind has been furnished with the most convenient vehicle of expression for thought and communication. This revolutionary effect in writing was produced by the north-western Semites who in the first half of the second millennium B.C. invented the alphabet, and developed it in the second half of the same millennium.

Various peoples and tribes on every continent have developed systems of writing, many independently. A few systems have reached a high level, others have been arrested at a lower stage, some are still nascent.

Syllabism seems to have been the highest stage of writing which was reached independently by some peoples. The alphabet has been invented only once. *C'est la une invention qu'on ne peut faire deux fois* (Dunand). It is essentially the same script which we use now.

Here I should like to point out two fortunate coincidences in the development of the alphabet which influenced the whole history of the civilization of mankind.

(1) The Semites had been enabled, owing to factors of geography and culture and circumstances of time and economic structure, to invent the alphabet, but this achievement has been made easier, or even, perhaps, possible, by the fact that Semitic-Hamitic is the only group among the main linguistic families which is based on consonantal roots. Professor T. H. Gaster, however, suggests that 'the so-called consonantal "roots" are but a grammarian's abstraction; they are a device used in analysing the languages, but it must not be assumed that they ever existed in speech.'

(2) The alphabet passed from the Semites to the Greeks, and thereby came to completion, because Greek cannot do without vowels, and is moreover one of the most euphonious languages of the world. In Professor F. Rosenthal's opinion the Greeks were not conscious of the need of vowel-letters and would hardly have invented them, if they had not found themselves with the embarrassing problem of having some signs which they could not use. In his opinion, in the transmission of scripts, the procedure is to add new signs if necessary, but there is a reluctance to drop superfluous signs. 'In this case, fortunately, some of the superfluous signs were acrophonically suggestive of certain vowels. It is the immortal merit of the Greek genius to have taken advantage of offered opportunity and to have put the superfluous signs to use as vowel letters.'

435

While, however, it would be unhistorical to admit the possibility of the alphabet having been invented in another continent or in another period or for a language belonging to a different group, there seems at least a probability that it could have been completed without the intervention of the Greeks.

The alphabet has a fascinating history, lasting over 3,500 years and extending over the whole world. I have tried to trace this history in the present book. I have tried to introduce logical divisions and sub-divisions in this immense mass of material, though the space at my disposal is, obviously, too narrow to enable me to deal in detail with each problem. Some chapters (7, 17 and 18) may perhaps appear to be too long in comparison with others. They deal with matters which are commonly not taken into due consideration in general histories of writing, and are, therefore, much less known to the general reader than the other branches. I thought, therefore, it might be useful to give relatively more space to these three chapters.

The history of the alphabet, unlike any other history, does not follow up the whole development of alphabetic scripts in all their varieties, but stops at the point when the script is fully formed. The successive development of the various alphabetic characters is a matter of palæography, or 'writing' as a whole. This development consists essentially of two phases:

(1) The adaptation of the alphabetic scripts to other languages.
(2) The external development of the single letters.

ADAPTATION OF ALPHABETIC SCRIPTS TO OTHER LANGUAGES

In the last century essentially three alphabets have been adapted to other languages: the Roman or Latin alphabet, the Arabic and the Russian. As to the Latin alphabet, I have already mentioned its adaptations to various European and African languages: *see* also Figs. Conc. 1–3. It has also been adapted to many languages of Asia, Indonesia, and so forth. And in the U.S.S.R. it has been recently adapted to eight Turco-Tatar and Caucasian languages. The most important adaptation in recent times is that to the Turkish tongue (*see* p. 429). More or less successful attempts have been made to adapt the Roman character to Chinese (p. 77), Japanese (pp. 127 f.) and various Indian languages (*see*, for instance, p. 292).   Figures Conc. 4–5 represent the Chinese alphabet recently devised by the Peking government.

The Arabic alphabet has also been adapted to a great number of languages (*see* also pp. 211, 215, 233 ff.,) of Asia, Africa and Europe. In the U.S.S.R. recently it has been adapted to nine Turco-Tatar and six Caucasian languages.

The Russian alphabet has been adapted in the U.S.S.R. for numerous Finno-Ugrian, Turco-Tatar and other languages, as for Abkhasian, sometimes taking the place of earlier adaptations of Arabic or Mongolian, and even of Latin script: *see* pp. 377 ff., 440, etc.

ɔBERI ɔKAIMε SCRIPT
(Fig. Conc. 3)

Some scripts have been examined, which in one way or another seem to have been dependent on writings dealt with in the preceding chapter. It is obvious that a 'universal' alphabet like Latin must have influenced the creation of some scripts, although its main importance lies in the fact that, as already said it has been adopted for, and adapted to a great number of languages and dialects.

However, in chapter 10 a script (the Cherokee syllabary) has been examined, which originated under the influence of the Latin alphabet. Here more recent creations may be mentioned.

A new script and language are reported by R. F. G. Adams (in an article published in *African Journal*, 1947: 'ɔberi ɔkaimε: A New African Language and Script') from the Itu Division of Calabar Province, in the extreme south-eastern part of Nigeria. They are or were employed by a sect of believers in spirits of good or evil, founded about the year 1928 in the village of Ikpa, near Iyere in the Itu Division. Both the language and the script, termed ɔberi ɔkaimε—name supposed to be given by the *Seminant* or 'holy spirit' of the sect—seem to have originated about the year 1931.

In 1936 the followers of the sect founded a school in which the new language and script were employed. The leaders of the movement were prosecuted and fined for offences against the Education Code. The head of the sect declared that he received his teachings from the spirit, whereas the script 'appeared in dreams' to his assistant and was recorded the following day. The new language is different from *Ibibio*, the form of speech which is spoken in south-east Nigeria, and R. F. G. Adams has noted even the introduction of new speech-sounds.

According to Adams, the script seems to consist of thirty-two main letters, which have both small and capital forms. Diacritical marks and some special symbols are also used. Some signs represent combinations of two consonants, such as *sk, sw, ks, pt*. In Mr. Adams' view, the script bears no resemblance to any known form of writing, although in the samples of what was said to be the original spirit-writing he recognized the letters *x, h, c, z, u*, inverted *u* with two small dashes beneath it, variations of the figure 6, the symbol generally used as the 'neutral vowel,' and variations of *c* and *s*. The comma, called *apin*, is employed as in European scripts, but the full stop consists of two small parallel dashes.

The origin of this curious script is uncertain. Adams reports two current theories: (1) that the new writing is somewhat connected with the *nsibidi* script (*see* pp. 106 f.); and (2) the ɔberi ɔkaimε is a mirror writing, 'whose secret would be revealed' if one put the symbols before a mirror. Adams, however, does not accept either of these views. Neither do I. It is obvious that we have to deal with a recently created cryptic script. The symbols are probably mainly arbitrary inventions, based on the knowledge of European and perhaps also other scripts.

YÁMANA ALPHABET
(Fig. Conc. 6)

The enthusiastic activity of missionaries in reducing native languages to writing has already been referred to (pp. 132 ff.). H. W. Pointer, M.A., formerly of Godalming (Surrey), has drawn my attention to the phonetic script invented by the Rev. Thomas Bridges for the tongue spoken by the southernmost inhabitants of the earth, namely those of Tierra del Fuego.

La Tierra del Fuego ('Fireland') consists of a triangular island of 18,500 square miles and an archipelago; it forms the southernmost tip of South America from which it is separated by the Strait of Magellan. Eight thousand three hundred square miles of it belong to Argentina, the rest to Chile. The main island is surrounded by 'a collection of islands infinitely more numerous than is shown on charts and covering an area of 200 miles from north to south and 360 miles from east to west.' The whole population at the last census was 9,560–660 in the Argentine and 3,900 in the Chilean part. The native population is slowly dying out; ninety years ago there were about 7,000–9,000 natives; nowadays there are less than 150 pure-blooded Fuegian Indians and possibly a slightly larger number of half-breeds.

The Fuegians are divided into three district groups, each with its own language and customs: the Ona, who inhabit the main island; the Yámana or Yahgans, who live on the southern islands; and the Alacaloof, who live on the western islands. Bridges distinguished a fourth group, the Aush or Eastern Ona, who inhabit the south-eastern tip of the main island.

The term 'Yahgan,' devised by Bridges, is an abbreviation of Yahgashagalumoala ('the people from the Mountain Valley Channel'); but the indigenous name of the tribe seems to have been Yámana ('People').

The Yámana speech has 'lost its purity and become interlarded with Spanish terms,' but ninety years ago it was a soft, rapidly-spoken language, rich in sounds and number of words. 'Incredible though it may appear, the language of one of the poorest tribes of men, without any literature, without poetry, song, history or science, may yet through the nature of its structure and its necessities have a list of words and a style of structure surpassing that of other tribes far above them in the arts and comforts of life' (Thomas Bridges, 1886). Thomas Bridges' (1842–98) acquaintance with the Fuegians began when, as a boy of thirteen, he had gone there with his foster father, the missionary Rev. G. P. Despard. After having mastered the native language and being already conversant with its intricate grammar, Bridges began to compile a Yahgan (Yámana)–English dictionary, the monumental work that was to occupy him for nine years.

To render all the sounds of Yámana in writing, Bridges had recourse to the Ellis system of phonetics; but in adapting it he added various symbols to express sounds that this system lacked, and so devised an alphabet of his own. It consists of four types of symbols: capital and small letters, printed and cursive forms; there are as many as sixteen vowels (short and long *a*, *o*, *u*, *i*; short *e*; the diphthongs *ei*, *ai*, *oi*, *a*, *ou*, *oa* and *ae*), and twenty-five consonants: *c* as in cat; *g* as in *go*, *t*, *d*, *p*, *b*, *f*, *v*, *ch* as in *church*, *j*, *th*, *dh*, *s*, *z*, *sh*, *zh*, *l*, *ll*, *m*, *n*, *hn*, *ng*, *r*, *hr*, *ch* as in *loch*.

The Yámana–English dictionary was commenced on 24th August, 1877 and completed on 5th July, 1879; it then had 622 pages of 36–40 words to a page (about 23,000 words); but Bridges continued to work on it until in 1886 it contained 1081 pages, each averaging thirty words, thus having a total of 32,450 words. The MS. was in the hands of the Bridges' family until 1899, in which year Dr. Frederick A. Cook obtained it for purposes of publication; but for many years nothing was heard of it and it was considered lost. A few years before the first world war it reappeared and the Observatoire Royal in Brussels started printing it in agreement with the Bridges' family. But after the war broke out the MS. disappeared again; the statement in the *Yámana–English Dictionary* that the MS. was in Professor Hestermann's hands since 1909 seems to be incorrect. However, in September, 1929 the family was informed that the MS. was at Münster, in the possession of Professor Hestermann. In 1933 the Dictionary was published in 300 copies (for private circulation only) by the Missionsdruckerei St. Gabriel at Mödling in Austria, edited by Dr. Ferdinand Hestermann and Dr. Martin Gusinde. In 1939 the MS. was offered to the British Museum by Lucas Bridges (the son of Thomas) and accepted. But before it could be brought from Germany, the second world war broke out and the MS. again vanished. Immediately the war was finished, thanks to the efforts of William S. Barclay and Sir Leonard Woolley, the MS. was again recovered and was brought to the British Museum on the 9th January, 1946.

BIBLIOGRAPHY

Mission Scientifique du Cap Horn, 1882–3 (published 1888), vol. 7.

GUSINDE, M. *Die Feuerland-Indianer, I*, Mödling-St. Gabriel, 1931. (Mr. Gusinde made four expeditions through the Tierra del Fuego in 1918–24).

ESTEBAN (STEPHEN) Lucas Bridges, *Uttermost Part of the Earth*, London, 1948.

ADAPTATION OF SCRIPTS TO TURKI DIALECTS

Turkish and its various dialects are one of the best instances of dialects belonging to the same language using the most different scripts. Indeed,

(1) the *Kök-Turki alphabet* (Runes) was employed for an early Turki speech;

(2) the *Uighur alphabet* was used for the Uighur dialect;

(3) the *Arabic alphabet* was adopted for, and adapted to, Osmanli Turkish, which, as the official language of the Ottoman Empire, became the most widespread and the most literary of all the Turkish forms of speech; the Arabic character has also been adopted for: (*a*) Azerbaijani Turkish, spoken in Azerbaijan, U.S.S.R.; (*b*) Jagatai Turkish spoken by some hundred thousand Tekké Turkomans of eastern Turkestan; (*c*) Kashgar Turkish, spoken between the T'ien Shan mountains and northern Tibet;

(d) Uzbek Turkish spoken by more than 2 million nomads in Uzbekistan and Turkestan; (e) Kumuk Turkish, spoken by about 70,000 people around the north-western shores of the Caspian Sea and in the north-eastern Daghestan; (f) Nogai Turkish, spoken by nearly 200,000 people to the north-west of the Caucasus and in the Crimea; it has also been adapted (together with the Russian character) to (g) the Western Kirghiz Turkish, spoken by some hundred thousand nomads between the lower Volga and north-western Mongolia; (h) Eastern or Altai-Kirghiz Turkish or Kazakh Turkish, spoken by several hundred thousand nomads in the Altai and T'ien Shan mountains; as also (together with the Hebrew character) to (i) Karaite Turkish, spoken by the Karaite Jews mainly in the Crimea;

(4) the *Russian* or *Cyrillic character* has been adopted for (a) Gagauzi Turkish, spoken on the north-western shores of the Black Sea; (b) Chuvash Turkish, spoken by more than half a million people in the valley of the Volga; (c) Kazan Turkish, spoken by about 200,000 Tatars in Kazan, U.S.S.R. (also the Arabic alphabet is employed, but rather rarely); (d) Bashkir Turkish, spoken by nearly half a million people, west and south of the Urals; (e) Yakut Turkish, spoken by over 250,000 people along the Lena River in Siberia; as also, together with the Arabic character, for the dialects already mentioned; *see* also pp. 378 ff.;

(5) the *Armenian*; and

(6) *Greek* characters were also used by the Armenians and Greeks in Turkey, for writing Turkish;

(7) the *Hebrew character* has already been mentioned; and finally

(8) the *Roman character*, nowadays employed as the official script of Turkey.

OTHER SCRIPTS

Mention has been made of various scripts (pp. 233 ff., 310 f., 437, etc.), which can only be considered as in part adaptations of one or other alphabet to a foreign language; in all these instances the shapes of the letters of the new script do not imitate those of the alphabetic prototype, but are inventions. In some instances, the inventor of the new script is known: this is the case, for instance, with the Somali alphabet (pp. 235 f.).

In the majority of cases, not only is the inventor or inventors of the new script unknown, but also the period of invention; sometimes even the script which was used as the prototype is uncertain. Noteworthy in this connection is the Balti script (p. 235).

Interesting examples are also the cryptic script of the Yezidis (pp. 233 f.) and an Indian script, the Saurashtran, which is also of uncertain origin (pp. 310 f.).

UNKNOWN SCRIPTS AND FORGERIES
(Figs. Conc. 7–9)

Many other scripts existed, of which very little is known. Some of these have already been mentioned in connection with the problem of the origin of the alphabet, or in other chapters. Here we may add documents written in unknown scripts of uncertain origin and of doubtful period, which have been found in Mesopotamia (Figs. Conc. 7a–d), in Perú and elsewhere. Some may be spurious, others are certainly genuine; even the former have a certain interest for the history of writing.

Remarkable are the inscriptions, engraved on slates, numbering over 500, found in different localities in Spain, particularly in the province of Salamanca. The script consists mainly of signs in the shape of Roman numerals I, II, III, IIII, V, X, and some have a horizontal stroke on the top (I̅, I̅I̅, I̅I̅I̅, I̅I̅I̅I̅, V̅, X̅). Is this a cryptic system of writing consisting of numerals? Nobody knows. The script of the inscription of Perú consists mainly of signs similar to Arabic numerals 2, 3 (and its reverse form), 4, 7, 8, 9 and O. Is this inscription spurious?

Finally, examining the problem of adaptation of alphabetic scripts to other languages, important factors, like that expressed by the phrase 'the alphabet follows religion' (see pp. 210, 218, 222, 237, 409, 427 f. etc.), or that indicated by Professor Kroebers' 'idea diffusion' (see pp. 25, 30, 66, etc.) should not be overlooked.

EXTERNAL DEVELOPMENT OF LETTERS: CALLIGRAPHY

The external development of the single letters of the various alphabetic scripts is due mainly to two reasons: (1) the necessity of speed in writing, which produces the various cursive scripts, this development, however, being limited by the exigencies of legibility; and (2) technical and aesthetic reasons.

(a) The technical reasons: the materials of writing always played a great part in the external development of the single letters; for instance, the letters cut on stone or engraved on bronze generally differ in their shape from the letters written with ink on paper. (b) The study of the development of writing as dependent on æsthetic reasons is the subject of *calligraphy*. In some countries the profession of calligrapher was held in high esteem; indeed, Chinese, Arabic and Indian calligraphy have reached very high levels. In Christian manuscripts, the importance of calligraphy was perhaps slightly impaired by the development of the art of miniature.

NUMERICAL, MUSICAL, AND SCIENTIFIC NOTATION. ABBREVIATIONS AND STENOGRAPHY (SHORTHAND). SIGNALLING AND SPECIAL ALPHABETS
(Figs. Conc. 10–24)

The origin and the development of numerals (Figs. Conc. 10–11), the history of abbreviations and of shorthand are other problems connected with the alphabet, which belong rather to the history of writing in general. Also musical (Figs. Conc. 12–14) and scientific (Figs. Conc. 15–16) notation as well as the alphabetic methods of signalling (Figs. Conc. 21–23) and the special alphabets (Figs. Conc. 23–24)—such as those for the blind (Braille), the deaf and dumb, and the blind deaf and dumb, form particular departments of writing in general. Stenography or shorthand, that is to say the script which aims at the maximum speed in transmission of thought, is in a certain sense the last stage of the history of writing.

SELECTED BIBLIOGRAPHY

GINZEL, F. K. *Handbuch der mathematischen und technischen Chronologie*, 3 vols, Leipsic, 1906–14.

GARDTHAUSEN, V. 'Die römischen Zahlzeichen,' in *Germanisch-Romanische Monatsschrift*, I (1909), 401–5.

SETHE, K. 'Von Zahlen und Zahlworten bei den alten Ägyptern, etc., in *Schriften der Wissenschaftlichen Gesellschaft*, Strassburg, 25 (1916).

MENNINGER, K. *Zahlwort und Ziffer*, etc., Breslau, 1934.

TOD, M. N. 'The Greek Acrophonic Numerals,' in *The Annals of the British School at Athens*, No. 37 (Sessions 1936–7), pp. 236–58, London, 1940. [The term 'Herodianic' for the acrophonic numerals (Π for πέντε, Δ for δέκα, etc.), seems to have been introduced by Voisin in his thesis: *De Graecorum notis numeralibus*, Leipsic, 1886. . . .]

WRIGHT, G. G. N. *The Writing of Arabic Numerals*, London, 1952.

GIULIETTI, F. *Storia delle scritture veloci*, Florence, 1968.

Here our sketch must close. We have travelled across the greater part of the globe. We have passed over many old and splendid civilizations, and many recent and primitive cultures, and we have seen that between the cultured man in the ancient Near East and his brother-man in the modern West there exists one long chain of attempts, and more or less successful achievements, to obtain a common medium of communication, and consequently mutual understanding. In the years to come, when the 'civilized' world has settled down, it will be seen that each people in the past or in the present, in the West or in the East, has played an important part in promoting that true respect for all other peoples, of whatever race, creed or form of speech. True respect alone can form the foundation of a better society. In this connection the alphabet has certainly to be given its full share.

I have repeatedly tried to show that in the origins of the various scripts, in their development, and in their adaptations to other languages, something common to all mankind lies concealed behind the various phenomena. Common to all, in the main, is the part played by some individuals, such as St. Mesrop, Wulfila, Sequoya or Njoya; and everywhere we see kindred conditions in the development and adaptations of scripts, resting on a common natural foundation. May we then be permitted to say that the various systems of writing with all their diversities disclose the existence of a great common factor in man's trend of thought and man's craving for expression?

Oliver Goldsmith wrote of his prose idyll: 'There are a hundred faults in this thing. . . . A book may be amusing with numerous errors in it, or it may be dull without a single absurdity.' I hope this book will be considered neither 'amusing with numerous errors in it,' nor 'dull without a single absurdity,' although, I confess, it may contain a hundred or more faults.

The necessity of brevity and simplicity may have led to false impressions. Indeed, it may be presumptuous to attempt so brief a survey as this of such a vast field. Yet, it is to be hoped that, in some measure, the chief purposes may be served no matter what the faults may be.

GENERAL BIBLIOGRAPHY

I have attempted to skim over such a wide area—practically the whole world—and such a long period —corresponding mainly to that of the history of civilized men—that a full bibliography is impossible. The great majority of technical monographs, especially in learned journals, are therefore omitted, but works mentioned in this book will put the reader on their track.

On the subject as a whole comparatively very few people have written in English. Isaac Taylor led the way with his important work, which, although partly out of date, is still fundamental. Edward Clodd's little book is interesting and useful, but in it only certain points of the subject are taken into consideration.

In America, W. A. Mason's *History of the Art of Writing* is well illustrated, but interpretation is sometimes out of date; T. Thompson's *The ABC of our Alphabet* is very attractive. So also is Moorhouse's *Writing and the Alphabet* published in London, in 1946, and particularly the American edition, published under the title *The Triumph of the Alphabet* (New York, 1953).

Out of the very large number of publications which can be consulted for the subjects dealt with in this book, I have tried to list those which seem to me the most important (involuntary omissions will, I hope, be forgiven): they are quoted in the different chapters. I append here a list of books which, either in whole or in part, can be usefully consulted for the subject of this book as a whole. The literature dealing with allied subjects is obviously so extensive that I can do no more than select some of the more significant works which are available to the general reader.

MASSEY, W. *The Origin and Progress of Letters*, London, 1763.

DUBOIS, J. (and DUBOIS, M.), *Histoire abrégée de l'écriture et moyen simple d'enseigner et d'apprendre plus facilement la coulée*, Paris-Dijon, 1772.

ASTLE, T. *The Origin and Progress of Writing* etc., London, 1784; 2nd ed., London, 1803; another edition, London, 1876.

FRY, E. *Pantagraphia*, London, 1799.

VON KLAPROTH, H. J. *Aperçu de l'orig. des divers. Écrit. de l'ancien Monde*, Paris, 1832.

SILVESTRE, J. B. *Paléographie universelle* etc., Paris, (1839–) 1841; *Alphabet-Album*, etc., Paris, 1843; (and Sir F. Madden), *Universal Palæography*, 2 vols., London, 1850.

HUMPHREYS, H. N. *The Origin and Progr. of the Art of Writing*, London, 1853.

DE ROSNY, L. L. *Écritures figuratives*, etc., 2nd ed., Paris, 1870.

LOEW, L. *Graphische Requisiten*, etc., *bei den Juden*, 2 parts, Leipsic, 1870–1.

LENORMANT, F. *Essai sur la propagation de l'alphabet phénicien dans l'ancien monde*, Paris, 1872–3 and 1875 (posthumous); also 'Alphabet' in Daremberg and Saglio, *Dictionnarie de l'antiquité*, I (1887).

WUTTKE, H. *Geschichte der Schrift*, Leipsic, 1874–5.

FAULMANN, K. *Illustrirte Geschichte der Schrift*, Vienna-Pest-Leipsic, 1880

SAYCE, A. H. *Introduction to the Science of Languages*, 2 vols., London, 1880.

BIRT, T. *Das antike Buchwesen*, Berlin, 1882; *Die Buchrolle in der Kunst*, Leipsic, 1907.

TAYLOR, I. *The Alphabet*, etc., 2 vols., London, 1883; 2nd ed., London, 1899.

KEARY, D. F. *The Dawn of History*, new edition, London, 1888.

BERGER, PH. *Histoire de l'écriture dans l'antiquité*, Paris, 1891; 2nd ed., 1892.

MADAN, F. *Books in Manuscript*, etc., London, 1893.

GROSSE, F. *Die Anfänge der Kunst*, Fribourg-Leipsic, 1894.

HADDON, A. C. *Evolution in Art*, London, 1895; *The Races of Man*, etc. revised edition, Cambridge, 1929; *History of Anthropology*, 2nd ed., London, 1934.

PUTNAM, G. H. *Books and Their Makers during the Middle Ages*, etc., New York and London, 1896.

WARNER, G. F. *Illumin. Manuscr. in the Brit. Mus.*, London, 1899–1903.

CLODD, E. *The Story of the Alphabet*, London, 1900; New York, 1907, 1912; another edition, 1938.

WILLIAMS, H. S. *The History of the Art of Writing*, 4 vols., London-New York, 1901-08.

Archiv für Papyrusforschung (since 1901).

BLAU, L. *Studien zum althebräischen Buchwesen*, Strasbourg, 1902.

SHNIZER, YA. B. *Illustrated General History of Scripts* (in Russian), St. Petersburg, 1903.

SANDYS, J. E. *A History of Classical Scholarship*, etc., Cambridge, 1903-8.

MAIRE, A. *Materials used to write before the Invent. of Print.*, Washington, 1904.

LOTZ, W. 'Die Erfindung der Schrift,' *Velhag. und Klas. Monats.*, 1904.

SKINNER, F. N. *Story of the Letters and Figures*, Chicago, 1905.

BALLHORN, F. *Alphabete orientalischer und okzidentalischer Sprachen*, 14th ed., Leipsic, 1906 (*Grammatography*. English compilation, London, 1861).

STRANGE, E. F. *Alphabets*, London, 1907.

DAVENPORT, C. *The Book: its History and Development*, London, 1907.

STUBE, 'Grundlinien zu einer Entwickelungsgeschichte der Schrift,' *Graphologische Monatshefte*, Munich, 1907.

FROBENIUS, L. *The Childhood of Man*, Philadelphia, 1908.

SPECHT, F. *Die Schrift und ihre Entwicklung*, 3rd ed., Berlin, 1909.

MOSSO, A. *The Dawn of Mediterranean Civilization*, London, 1910.

MASPERO, G. C. C. *The Dawn of Civilization*, 5th ed., London, 1910.

MEINHOF, C. 'Zur Entstehung der Schrift,' *Aegypt. Zeitung*, 1911.

BRANDI, K. *Unsere Schrift*, etc., Göttingen, 1911.

WILSER, L. *Ursprung und Entwicklung der Buchstabenschrift*, Leipsic, 1912.

MITTEIS, L. and WILCKEN, U. *Grundzüge und Chrestomathie der Papyruskunde*, 2 vols., Leipsic, 1912.

DANZEL, TH. W. *Die Anfänge der Schrift*, Leipsic, 1912; 2nd ed., Leipsic, 1929.

RICHARDSON, E. C. *The Beginnings of Libraries*, London and Princeton, 1914; 'Alphabet and Writing,' *The Intern. Stand. Bible Encycl.*, Chicago, 1930.

WEULE, K. *Vom Kerbstock zum Alphabet*, etc., Stuttgart, 1915; 2nd. ed., *Ersatzmittel und Vorstufen der Schrift*, Stuttgart, 1921.

HERTZ, A. 'Ein Beitrag zur Entwicklung der Schrift,' *Archiv für die gesamte Psychologie*, 1917; 'Les debuts de l'écriture, *Revue Archéologique*, 1934.

CURTIUS, E. *Wort und Schrift*, etc., Berlin, 1917; *Schrift und Buchmetaphorik*, etc., Halle, 1942.

MIESES, M. *Die Gesetze der Schriftgeschichte*, Vienna and Leipsic, 1919.

TYLOR, E. B. *Primitive Culture*. A reissue, 2 vols., London, 1919; *Anthropology*, etc., new edition, 2 vols., London, 1930.

KEANE, A. H. *Man Past and Present*, revised edition (by A. Hingston Quiggin and A. C. Haddon), Cambridge, 1920.

MASON, W. A. *A History of the Art of Writing*, New York, 1920.

MENTZ, A. *Geschichte der griechisch-römischen Schrift bis zur Erfindung des Buchdrucks*, Leipsic, 1920; 'Die Urgeschichte des Alphabets', *Rheinisch. Mus. für Philologie*, 1936.

GROUSSET, R. *Histoire de l'Asie*, 2nd ed., 3 vols., Paris, 1921-2.

PARDO, M. *Storia delle scritture*, Catania, 1922.

The Cambridge Ancient History, Cambridge, 1923 onwards.

MEILLET, A. and COHEN, M. *Les langues du monde*, Paris, 1924.

DORNSEIFF, F. *Das Alphab. in Myst. und Magie*, 2nd ed. Leipsic-Berlin, 1924.

HESSEL, A. 'Von der Schrift zum Druck,' *Zeitschr. d. Deutsch. Ver. für Buchwesen und Schrifttum*, 1923

SCHNEIDER, H. *Gesammelte Aufsätze*, Leipsic, 1924.

REICHSDRUCKEREI, *Alphabete und Schriftzeichen*, etc., Berlin, 1924.

JENSEN, H. *Geschichte der Schrift*, Hanover, 1925; *Die Schrift in Vergangenheit und Gegenwart*, Glück-stadt-Hamburg, 1935; 2nd rev. ed., Berlin (East), 1958.

GORDON CHILDE, V. *The Dawn of European Civilization*, London, 1925; 1939.

OTTO, W. *Handbuch der Altertumswissenschaft*, Munich, 1926; *Handbuch der Archäologie*, Munich, 1939.

SCHMIDT, W. *Sprachfamilien und Sprachenkreise der Erde*, Heidelberg, 1926.

GRESSMANN, H. *Altorientalische Texte und Bilder zum Alten Testament*, 2 vols., Berlin and Leipsic, 1926 and 1927.

WETZIG-SEEMAN, *Handbuch der Schriftarten*, Leipsic, 1926.

WIBORG, F. B. and others, *Printing Ink: a History*, New York, 1926.

HACKH, I. W. D. 'The History of the Alphabet,' *Scientific Monthly*, 1927.

FOSSEY, CH. *Notices sur les caractères étrangers anciens et modernes redigées par un group de savants*, etc., Paris, 1927; 2nd ed., 1948 (by various authors).

KENYON, F. G. *Ancient Books and Modern Discoveries*, Chicago, 1927.

PRIES, A. *Die ältesten, alten und neuen Schriften der Völker*, etc., Leipsic, 1927.

BAUMGARTNER, A. *Über unsere Schrift*, Zurich, 1928.

VON LE COQ, A. *Buried Treasures of Chinese Turkestan*, London, 1928.

GUPPY, H. *Steepping Stones to the Art of Typography*, Manchester, 1928; 'Human Records: A Survey of their History from the Beginning,' *Bull. of the John Rylands Library*, Manchester, 1942.

DEGERING, H. *Die Schrift*, etc., Berlin, 1929; 3rd. ed., Tübingen, 1952.

FOUGÈRES, C. *Les premières civilisations*, Paris, 1929.

KÜRZ, L. and HADL, R. *Der naturlautliche Ursprung von Sprache und Schrift*, etc., Leipsic, 1930.

WODRZE, A. 'Zum Problem der Schrift,' etc., *Breslauer Dissertation*, 1930.

DUCATI, B. *La Scrittura*, Padua, 1931.

TENTOR, H. *Writing and the Origins of the Alphabet* (in Croatian), Zagreb, 1931.

PEDERSEN, H. *Linguistic Science in the Nineteenth Century*, Harvard University Press, 1931.

SPRENGLING, M. and others, *The Story of Writing*, New York, 1932.

GRAFF, W. L. *Language and Languages*, New York, 1932.

(VON OSTERMANN, G. F. and GIEGENGACK, A. E.), U.S.A. Government Printing Office, *Foreign Languages*, etc., 2nd. ed., Washington, 1935.

The Dolphin (especially *The Dolphin* No. 3), New York, 1933 onwards.

LEJEUNE, M. 'La langage et l'écriture,' in *L'évolution humaine*, Vol. III, Paris, 1934.

Typography, London, Shenval Press, 1936–9 (a magnificent quarterly, but unfortunately only the numbers 1–8 were published).

DIRINGER, D. *L'Alfabeto nella Storia della Civiltà*, Florence, 1937.

ALLEN, A. B. *The Romance of the Alphabet*, London and New York, 1937.

HOOKE, S. H. 'The Early History of Writing,' in *Antiquity*, 1937.

FRIEDRICH, J. review of D. Diringer, 'L'Alfabeto,' etc., *Zeitschr. der Deutschen Morgenl. Gesellsch.*, 1937; 'Zu einigen Schrifterfindungen der neuesten Zeit,' the same journal, 1938; *see* also below.

UPDIKE, D. B. *Printing Types, their History*, 3rd ed., Cambridge, Mass., 1937.

SCHMITT, A. *Die Erfindung der Schrift*, Erlangen, 1938; *Untersuchungen zur Geschichte der Schrift*, Leipsic, 1940.

NEWDIGATE, B. H. *The Art of the Book*, London, 1938.

JACKSON, H. *The Printing of Books*, London, 1938.

The Annual of Bookmaking, New York, 1938 onwards.

SETHE, K. *Vom Bilde zum Buchstaben*, etc., Leipsic, 1939.

PETRAU, A. *Schrift und Schriften im Leben der Völker*, etc., Berlin, 1939.

CARLETON, P. *Buried Empires*, London, 1939.

ALBRIGHT, W. F. *From the Stone Age to Christianity*, Baltimore, 1940; *Archæology and the Religion of Israel*, Baltimore, 1942.

CELADA, B. 'Cuestiones varias del Antiguo Oriente,' *Sefarad* (Madrid), I, 1941.

BURROWS, M. *What Mean These Stones?*, New Haven, 1941.

PERUZZI, E. 'Problemi grafici indo-mediterranei preindoeuropei,' *Annali della R. Scuola Normale Superiore di Pisa*, 1941; 'A propósito de las escrituras mediterráneas, *Ampurias* (Barcelona), 1942.

THOMPSON, T. *The ABC of our Alphabet*, London and New York, 1942; 1945.

McMURTRIE, D. C. *The Invention of Printing*: *A Bibliography*, Chicago, 1942; *The Book*, etc., 3rd ed., New York, 1943.

MARTIN, W. J. *The Origin of Writing*, Jerusalem, 1943.

SCHLAUCH, M. *The Gift of Tongues*, London, 1943.

BODMER, F. *The Loom of Language*, London, 1943.

TSCHICHOLD, J. *Geschichte der Schrift in Bildern*, Basel, 1946.

MOORHOUSE, A. C. *Writing and the Alphabet* etc., London, 1946; new ed. under the title *The Triumph of the Alphabet*, New York, 1953.

CONTENAU, G. *Manuel d'Archéologie Orientale*, IV, Paris, 1947.

CARLIER, A. *Histoire de l'écriture*, Cannes, 1947.

FÉVRIER, J.-G., *Histoire de l'écriture*, Paris, 1948; new ed., 1959.

DRIVER, G. R. *Semitic Writing, from Pictograph to Alphabet* (Schweich Lectures, 1944), London, 1948; 2nd. ed., London, 1954.

HOGBEN, L. *From Cave Painting to Comic Script*, London, 1949.

BOÜÜAEN, J. *Petite histoire de l'alphabet*, Brussels, 1949.

RELAÑO, E. and A. *Historia gráfica de la escritura*, Madrid, 1949.

HINGSTON QUIGGIN, A. *A Survey of Primitive Money*, London, 1949.

LANGE, W. H. *Schriftbibel. Geschichte der abendländischen Schrift von den Anfängen bis zur Gegenwart*, Frankfurt a. M., 1951.

GELB, I. J. *A Study of Writing. The Foundations of Grammatology*, Chicago, 1952; 2nd ed., 1958.

COHEN, M. *L'écriture*, Paris, 1953; *La grande invention de l'écriture et son évolution*, 3 vols., Paris, 1958.

D'ANGELO, P. *Storia della scrittura*, Rome, 1953.

KRAUS, O. *Mosche, der Erfinder der Buchstaben*, etc., Zurich, 1953.

FRIEDRICH, J. (*see* also above), *Entzifferung verschollener Schriften und Sprachen*, Berlin-Göttingen-Heidelberg, 1954 (also translated into other languages).

MILTNER, F. 'Wesen und Geburt der Schrift', *Historia Mundi*, III, Bern, 1954.

NERDINGER, E. *Buchstabenbuch; Schriftentwicklung, Formbedingungen, Schrifttechnik, Schriftsammlung*, Munich, 1954.

EULE, W. *Mit Stift und Feder*, Leipsic, 1955.

STURM, H. *Einführung in die Schriftkunde*, Munich-Pasing, 1955.

KOCHERGINA, V. A. *Short Outline of the History of Writing* (in Russian), Moscow, 1955.

RUDLAND, P. *From Scribble to Script*, London, 1955; New York, 1956.

HIGOUNET, CH. *L'écriture*, Paris, 1955.

DIAKONOV, I., ISTRIN, V. and KINJALOV, R. *Writing* (in Russian), Moscow, 1955.

KATZPRJAK, E. I. *History of Writing and of the Book* (in Russian), Moscow, 1955.

IRWIN, K. G. *The Romance of Writing, from Egyptian Hieroglyphics to modern Letters, Numbers, and Signs*, New York, 1956.

TIBÓN, G. *Nuevas investigaciones en la prehistoria del alfabeto*, Mexico, 1956.

GAINES, H. F. *Cryptanalysis, a Study of Ciphers and their Solution*, New York, 1956.

ROBINSON, R. *Phonetic Writings*; ed. by E. J. Dobson, London-Oxford, 1957.

IVANTSEV, V. P. *From Drawing to the Letter* (in Russian), Rostov on the Don, 1957.

DOBLHOFER, E. *Zeichen und Wunder*, Vienna, 1957; Engl. transl. under the title *Voices in Stone*, London and Toronto, 1961.

KULUNDŽIĆ, Z. *Book on the Book* (in Serbo-Croatian), Zagreb, 1957.

STRELCYN, S. and RUSZCZYC, B. *Script and Book* (in Polish) [Exhibition, Warsaw, 1958], Warsaw, 1957.

DURFEE, W. C. *Alphabetics as a Science*, New York, 1957.

TARDY, M. B. and WASSÉN, S. H. *Picture Writing and its Language in the Ancient World*, . . ., 1958.

GABBA, *Iscrizioni greche e latine per lo studio della Bibbia*, Torino, 1958.

FEBVRE, L. and MARTIN, H. J. *L'apparition du livre*, Paris, 1958.

DOBZHANSKY, T. *Die Entwicklung zum Menschen*, Hamburg, 1958.

MERCER, S. A. B. *The Origin of Writing and our Alphabet*, London, 1959.

MEYER, H. E. *Die Schriftentwicklung*, Zurich, 1959.

CLEATOR, P. E. *Lost Languages*, London, 1959.

GILYAREVSKIY, R. S. and GRIVNIN, V. S. *Languages of the World* (in Russian), Moscow, 1960.

OGG, O. *The 26 Letters*, 2nd. ed., 1961.

KALLIR, A. *Sign and Design*, London, 1961.

ISTRIN, V. A. *Development of Writing* (in Russian), Moscow, 1961 (excellent bibliography).

(Various Authors), *Cambridge Ancient History*, rev. ed., Vols. I–II, Cambridge, 1961.

FÖLDES-PAPP, K. *Vom Felsbild zum Alphabet*, Stuttgart, 1966.

Guides, Catalogues, Handbooks, Facsimiles, etc., published by the British Museum, and other Museums of Antiquities, Art Galleries, and similar institutions.

Index